101 945 466 0

Washi   Ideology

ONE WEEK LOAN

D1470728

Discourse Approaches to Politics, Society and Culture (DAPSAC)

The editors invite contributions that investigate political, social and cultural processes from a linguistic/discourse-analytic point of view. The aim is to publish monographs and edited volumes which combine language-based approaches with disciplines concerned essentially with human interaction – disciplines such as political science, international relations, social psychology, social anthropology, sociology, economics, and gender studies.

General Editors

Ruth Wodak and Greg Myers
University of Lancaster

Editorial address: Ruth Wodak, Bowland College, Department of Linguistics and English Language, University of Lancaster University, LANCASTER LA1 4YT, UK
r.wodak@lancaster.ac.uk and g.myers@lancaster.ac.uk

Advisory Board

Volume 23

Washing the Brain – Metaphor and Hidden Ideology
by Andrew Goatly

Washing the Brain –
Metaphor and Hidden Ideology

Andrew Goatly
Lingnan University

John Benjamins Publishing Company

Amsterdam / Philadelphia

™ The paper used in this publication meets the minimum requirements of
American National Standard for Information Sciences – Permanence of
Paper for Printed Library Materials, ANSI z39.48-1984.

Library of Congress Cataloging-in-Publication Data

Andrew Goatly

  Washing the brain – metaphor and hidden ideology / Andrew Goatly.

    p. cm. (Discourse Approaches to Politics, Society and Culture, ISSN 1569-9463 ; v. 23)

  Includes bibliographical references and indexes.

      1. Ideology. 2. Metaphor. 3. English language--Rhetoric. I. Title.

  B823.3.G58   2007

121/.68--dc22   2006052616

ISBN 978 90 272 2713 3 (Hb; alk. paper)

ISBN 978 90 272 2720 1 (Pb; alk. paper)

John Benjamins Publishing Co. · P.O. Box 36224 · 1020 ME Amsterdam · The Netherlands
John Benjamins North America · P.O. Box 27519 · Philadelphia PA 19118-0519 · USA

I dedicate this book to the memory of my father

EDGAR HAMILTON GOATLY

(1918-2000)

As a boy scout, I was verbally tested by my own father for my cycling badge, along with my friend John Hitchens. He deliberately led me to give the wrong answer to one of the questions. 'If you are cycling up a hill and finding it too difficult what would you do? Wouldn't you stand on the pedals?' I agreed, and scored one mark less than John, to whom my father had not put the second slanted part of the question.

A good man, with no selfish genes.

Typographical conventions

Single quotation marks ' ' are used for meanings and concepts.
Double quotation marks " " are used for quotations and scare quotes.
SMALL CAPS are used for metaphor themes (conceptual metaphors).
Bolding is used for metaphorical lexical items.
Italics are used for word types and, in parentheses, for (modified) example sentences of the lexis of metaphor themes taken from contemporary dictionaries of English.

Table of contents

List of tables

List of figures

Preface

I should begin with some explanatory notes on the title(s) of this book.

Ideology

What do I mean by the notoriously vague term 'ideology'? Defining this could take a whole book, so I will provisionally adopt van Dijk's definition and description in *Ideology*: "*the basis of the social representations shared by members of a group*. This means that ideologies allow people, as group members, to organise the multitude of social beliefs about what is the case, good or bad, right or wrong, *for them* and to act accordingly" (van Dijk 1998: 8). One major determinant of these social representations will be "the material and symbolic interests of the group ... power over other groups (or resistance against the domination by other groups) may have a central role and hence function as a major condition and purpose for the development of ideologies". This emphasis on power is central to my use of the term, and, for brevity's sake one might adopt Thompson's (1984) definition "meaning in the service of power".

This notion of ideology has something in common with the classical Marxist definition, which sees ideology as "false-consciousness", a misleading representation, the superstructure overlaying and distorting a material reality (Jones 2000: 234-6). I accept Gramsci's (1971) development of the Marxist concept of ideology into the theory of hegemony: instead of an overt imposition of an ideology by the ruling class, hegemony manages the mind in covert ways to construct a consensus about the social order which benefits those in power. Hegemony depends upon the naturalisation of ideology as common-sense, and thereby makes ideology latent or hidden.

However, I do not believe in the possibility of non-ideological thought. To some extent, all consciousness is false-consciousness. Ideology is not, like halitosis, just something that the other person has (Eagleton, 1991). It is, in fact, often as unnoticeable and ubiquitous as the air we breathe. After all, we are all members of a community and share the thoughts and language that make action within that community or society possible.

Though ideology is ubiquitous in thought, some ideologies or ways of understanding the world may be more useful than others. Even the same ideology may simultaneously have useful and harmful effects. It is helpful, therefore, to see ideology as simultaneously "empowering, useful and adaptive on the one hand, and disempowering, distorting and maladaptive on the other" (Balkin 1998: 126). In principle, therefore, one ought to adopt an ambivalent attitude to ideology in general and even to particular ideologies.

Some approaches to ideological analysis, such as Foucault's, have downplayed the cognitive element (O'Halloran 2005). But ideology is in your head as well as in discourse. "It arises out of cognitive mechanisms as well as out of technology and social practices" (Balkin 1998: 272). Van Dijk's definition places emphasis on both the social and cognitive aspects of ideology, and their manifestation in or construction by discourse. Since this book explores the interface between cognitive theories of metaphor and social practices it is a particularly useful definition, though my model, figure 12 in chapter 8, adds a bodily dimension.

Brain-washing and washing the brain

By one of the intricacies of word-formation and subsequent semantic drift, *washing the brain* does not mean quite the same as *brainwashing*. Though the latter may have originally stressed the removal of existing patterns of thought in order to introduce new ones, it now tends to mean the inculcation of propaganda. *Washing the brain*, by contrast, suggests the possibility of removing harmful ways of thinking. The paradox is, of course, that the metaphorical pattern that this title exploits has itself been recruited in the cause of harmful ideologies, such as ethnic cleansing and other drives towards racial or mental purity.

Why write this book?

This book draws on two traditions which have, until recently, remained pure and unadulterated by each other, but which have been the focus of my research interests over the years. It is an attempt at cross-fertilisation between cognitive linguistic (CL) accounts of metaphor, and critical discourse analysis (CDA), what has been called "Critical Metaphor Analysis" (Charteris-Black 2005: 26-29). It demonstrates the importance of metaphorical patterns in the vocabulary and grammar of English for representing and shaping ideologies and social practices. To do so it relates metaphorical patterns or "themes" to a wide range of aspects of contemporary life, including medical practice, adversarial legal systems, time and motion studies, the politics behind 9/11 and the New Right, racism, urbanisation, defence spending, commodification and privatisation, sexual exploitation, educational philosophy and practice, biological and mechanistic theories of "human nature", and our present ecological crises. It engages with the current debate over the relative importance of biology and culture, a debate partly dependent upon or reinforced by metaphorical themes, and traces the ideologies expressed by metaphorical themes back to a tradition which includes Hobbes, Newton, Hume, Adam Smith, Malthus and Darwin.

CL accounts of metaphor, beginning with *Metaphors We Live By* (Lakoff and Johnson 1980), are associated with scholars such as George Lakoff, Mark Johnson, Mark Turner, Eve Sweetser, Raymond Gibbs, Gerard Steen, Zoltan Kövecses, Gunther Radden and Antonio Barcelona. The CDA tradition comprises work by, among others, Roger Fowler, Tony Trew, Gunther Kress, Jay Lemke, Norman Fairclough, Ron Carter, Michael Toolan, Teun Van Dijk, Ruth Wodak, and Paul Chilton. (For a summary of CDA traditions see Fairclough and Wodak (1997) and for exemplification Toolan (ed.) (2002)). The aim of CDA is "to investigate critically social inequality, as it is expressed, signalled, constituted, legitimised and so on by language use" (Wodak and Meyer 2001: 2). CDA's purpose, therefore, is to investigate and uncover ideology, in so far as it is expressed and influenced by language and discourse.

More recently these two traditions have begun to come together. Hiraga (1991), Chilton (1996), Lakoff (1996), Balkin (1998), Jones (2000), Stockwell (2000), Musolff (2004) and Charteris-Black (2005), among others, have begun to seriously explore the ideological effects of metaphor. Stockwell's chapter is particularly interesting in opening up possibilities for alignment, demonstrating the similarities in Fairclough's and Lakoff's analysis of Gulf War discourse, and pointing out various commonalities between the two traditions: both are anti-objectivist, believing that discourse/metaphor construct or confer a reality or folk model rather than simply describing it; Fairclough's notion of "Members Resources" is a cognitive notion, and relies on scripts, frames and schemata, which are more or less the same as CL's Idealised Cognitive Models (ICMs); and Stockwell quotes Fairclough's recognition of the importance of choice of one metaphor rather than another as a symptom of ideology. Nevertheless he stresses that, for the most part, the CL tradition sees metaphor as a function of (universal) embodiment rather than (historical) ideology. So, although within CL Kövecses (2005) has recently emphasised the importance of culture to metaphorical patterns of vocabulary, he does not stress the centrality of ideology to culture.

An extremely important book, Balkin's *Cultural Software*, provides a theoretical basis for the intersection of CDA and CL. Balkin regards metaphor as a cognitive mechanism of ideology, which will produce ideological effects (1998: 112-3, 243-8). He stresses the need for the cognitive and psychological to be taken into account in discourse and ideological analysis (p. 186). In addition, taking up the CDA mission, he argues that

> ideological analysis does not end with a demonstration that a particular belief or symbolic form is partly or wholly false or distorted. It must ask how this falsity or distortion might create or sustain unjust social conditions or unjust relations of social power (p. 111).

The present book continues the attempt to combine the CDA tradition with the CL tradition. It addresses the agenda set by Peter Jones (2000: 243) "such CL methods, insightfully applied to the *internal* semantic resources of ideological discourse, could usefully augment and concretise the Marxist analysis of ideologies in terms of historically specific *external* relations between conceptualisations (social consciousness) and social practice (social being)". It stresses the common ground between the two approaches – that language is not some transparent medium through which we think, but that it shapes our thoughts and practices. So the conventional metaphors in the discourses of race, sex, politics, defence, economics, environment, and so on, tend to determine our ways of thinking/consciousness and acting/practice in these social spheres.

The Linguistics basis of the book

The linguistic side of the book depends upon research into the metaphorical structure of English (and to some extent Chinese) carried out as part of a research project *A Comparison of the Metaphorical Structure of the English and Chinese Lexicons*. The detailed output comprises the database at the website Metalude: <http://www.ln.edu.hk/lle/cwd/project01/web/home.html> for the original English version, and <<http://www.ln.edu.hk/lle/cwd03/lnproject_chi/home.html> for the up-dated English-Chinese version. While a great deal of work has been done on "conceptual metaphors" or "metaphor themes" in the cognitive linguistics tradition, a systematic attempt to specify the lexical details of all the important metaphor themes for English had not been fully attempted until this database was compiled (though see Deignan (1995) and the Master List of Metaphors at Berkeley <http://cogsci.berkeley.edu/lakoff/>). The database, despite its flaws and incompleteness, gives us a more secure basis for considering the ideological and cognitive effects of metaphor themes. What the database reveals is patterns of metaphors, the metaphorical cognitive system underlying the discoursal uses of conventional metaphors. These conventional metaphors are recorded in the dictionary, and Metalude compiled the patterns or system through consulting dictionaries of contemporary English, themselves based on discoursal corpora, such as the COBUILD English Dictionary and the Cambridge Dictionary of International English. Thus, although much of this book looks at the de-contextualised patterns of lexis rather than its actual discoursal instantiation, it indirectly reflects at second hand its uses in discourse.

The metaphor themes discussed in this book are, of course, selectively taken from Metalude, and perhaps paint an unduly pessimistic view of the effects of metaphor on social life. If metaphor is a form of *bricolage*, taking something which happens to be at hand to perform a task for which it was not originally designed, it may be inadequate to that present task, and though useful, also distorting (Balkin 1998). Metaphor as a mechanism of ideology is therefore ambivalent. For example, in chapter two we look at the DISEASE IS INVASION metaphor, and show how the tradition of regarding diseases as invaders who have to be killed has become dominant, but, is rather unhelpful in certain areas of medicine like auto-immune diseases. Nevertheless, it would be hard to deny that the eradication and control of disease through antibiotics, dependent upon this traditional metaphor, has had positive effects on health. In chapter eight I analyse the favourite metaphors of capitalism, metaphors of competition and war, quality as quantity, and quality as wealth. However, it would be perverse to deny that the capitalist enterprise has, in the past, unlocked human potential for invention and motivated technological advances, many examples of which are conducive to an improvement in human well-being. In both these examples, it may be that once-useful metaphors have, in a new cultural ecology, partially outlived their usefulness: growth is, for example, maladaptive for mature economies.

I could have written another book about positive metaphor themes, though I think it would have been shorter. There are a number of alternative metaphors which represent humans, not only as competitive animals, but as involved in productive and co-operative relationships: social organisations as buildings or as the human body, and relationships as music. However, I have selected the themes by way of warning. The world faces a number of pressing crises – environmental problems, economic unsustainability and exploitation, poverty, racism, disease and so on – to which neo-conservative thinking, dependent upon the metaphorical patterns themes I analyse, seems to have no answer. If this book can make a tiny contribution to raising awareness of the dangers of acting out these metaphors it may be modestly successful.

What this book attempts to do is, in fact, rather modest. It presents little empirical psychological evidence, though perhaps more sociological evidence, for the suggestions it makes about the influence of metaphorical patterns on thought and practice. All it probably succeeds in doing is to be suggestive. Of course, obtaining psychological and empirical sociological evidence for metaphoric effects on behaviour would be a very time-consuming task. One could for example follow up the claim that metaphors of sex as violence encourage rape (chapter 2) by collecting data from convicted rapists and from a control group of the male population to ascertain whether the first group was more likely to use these violent metaphors for sex. Then one would have some hard evidence of whether ways of speaking metaphorically correlate with social action or practice. In which case they perhaps (re)-produce social practices. I hope that researchers may take up this kind of challenge of providing more substantial evidence for suggestions made in the book.

What is the content of this book?

Specifically, this book attempts two things. First, in Section One, chapters 1 to 5, it suggests that the metaphorical patterns observable in the lexicon of English have widespread effects on the concepts which drive our social practices and which reinforce social patterns of inequality, injustice and environmental exploitation within our present capitalist economies. Second, in Section Two, chapters 6 to 8, I address the more theoretical question of the extent to which the metaphorical patterns to be found in the lexicon have their origins in (universal) bodily experiences, and the extent to which they are cultural and ideological constructs.

Chapter 1 introduces terminology for and background to cognitive approaches to metaphor and critical discourse analysis, and explains the nature of the database that provides the lexical evidence for this study.

Chapter 2 explores some salient metaphorical patterns with consequences for power relations, such as height, centrality, speed, fighting, violence for sex, linear and divisible space for time, colour for race, and gives evidence of their effects on architecture, medicine, race (and racing), transportation, military spending, and industrial working practices.

Chapter 3 shifts the emphasis to mechanical and commodity metaphors for humans and society (and other natural objects), in their relation to sexual, industrial, and economic practices. It considers the treatment of women as food and workers as machines, the invisible (clock) hand of the market driving capitalist economies, and the development of bioengineering. It shows commodification in the patenting of genes, the sale of body-parts, and privatisation, which reinforce structures of inequality and the equation of quality with quantifiable measures such as money.

Chapter 4 explores natural metaphors for humans, either as landscape, weather or animals, discussing the question of whether humans are literally or only metaphorically animals, and whether aggression or co-operation constitute their defining characteristics or similarities. As a snapshot of the current ideological positions at the start of the 21st century, it critiques *Gaia* theory with its principles of symbiosis, co-operation and interdependence, theories in socio-biology, right-wing theories emphasising property/trade as distinctively human, and reconstructionist theories idealistically emphasising humans' use of symbols, language and cultural institutions which distinguish them from animals. It points out the relevance to these positions of metaphors such as disease for ideas, fighting for activity, calculation for thought, and money/wealth for relationship.

Chapter 5 is concerned with the ways in which metaphorical patterns interrelate: the use of identical metaphors for different topics to merge concepts (e.g. good is high and more is high, so more is good, with its consequences for over-consumption and obesity); the use of different metaphors for the topics of emotion and education, leading to different educational practices; conflicts between the positively-evaluated metaphor themes, relationship as proximity/cohesion versus freedom as space to move, and their consequences for family life, birth rates and cold-war discourse; and complex interactions involving similarity as proximity, category as divided space, impurity as mixing, disease as invasion and its reversal, as recruited in anti-immigrant discourse.

Chapter 6 questions to what extent our thinking and ideology is determined by our bodies and the metaphors which they give rise to, and what variation we have in the metaphor themes across languages and cultures, two questions that are linked since bodily experience is assumed to be universal. Beginning with the best candidates for universality through bodily experience, that is metaphors for emotions, it explores Damasio's recent theory of their intimate relationship with bodily responses, and cites scientific and linguistic evidence to build on Kövecses' work on specific physiological responses underlying metaphor patterns. However it summarises some of the important cultural variations based on the metonymies of physical responses, showing the effect of culture and ideology on emotion metaphor. Widening the scope of the argument to metaphorical patterns in general, by examining Grady's work on primary metaphors, and comparing his data with Metalude, it reveals that a considerable number of metaphor themes lack a bodily experiential correlation as their basis, suggesting non-universality, and finds a form of reductionism in the experientialist hypothesis, a hypothesis already challenged by the idea of the body as historical and cultural as well as biological.

Chapter 7 moves from vocabulary to grammar to consider the influence that typical clauses and "grammatical metaphors" have on our thinking and ideology. It demonstrates how literal grammar imposes the rigid distinction between nouns and verbs and between things and processes, and how it structures the relationships between subjects, verbs and objects to build a Newtonian model of our experience. This model is out of step with modern scientific thinking about our physical and biological environment, and dangerous in its implications about human domination of nature – as exemplified in the environmental degradation caused by the civil engineering mega-projects described in Josephson's *Industrialised Nature*. By contrast "grammatical metaphors", which deviate from the typical clause structure, construct a worldview more sympathetic to the findings of modern physics and to ecology. But an alternative worldview is achieved even more radically by the North American language, Blackfoot. Grammatical differences in the representation of possession are also shown to have ideological consequences, as *have* languages spread throughout Europe in step with the advances in capitalism.

Chapter 8 traces the ideological tradition of Hobbes, Hume, Adam Smith, Malthus and Darwin, pointing out the ways they select, exploit and reinforce many of the metaphorical patterns already discussed and which are the basis for New Right thinking, and a resurgent socio-biology and eugenics. It simultaneously demonstrates, through selective critiques by Tawney and Weber, how the ideological tradition of Protestant capitalism broke with an earlier ideology and its metaphors. By way of summary of the contemporary dominance of neo-con ideology it critiques Lakoff's (1996) analysis of left-wing and conservative US political ideologies in his book *Moral Politics*. It concludes that these metaphor patterns are no longer ideologically neutral and universal but have undergone a process of cultural selection and reinforcement to produce and construct the dominant value system. Moreover, naïve universalist cognitive metaphor theory could be a kind of reductionism to biology, and yet theological, especially Hegelian, doctrines of incarnation proclaim that absolute embodiment, far from entailing reduction, is the realisation, fulfilment and perfection of an otherwise vacuous truth. Nevertheless we should be aware of the reductionist and misleading tendencies of metaphor itself, as well as its theories, as conveyors of partial knowledge.

Who helped with this book?

I would like to show my appreciation for help from the following: Zoltan Kövecses for his incisive and helpful comments on the first draft; Pat Gladu for her corrections and thoughts on chapter 4; Ryan Heavy Head for his insider perspectives on Blackfoot; Avijit Gupta for pointing me towards core-periphery theory; Barry Asker for introducing me to John Horgan's *The End of Science*; Peter Crisp for pushing me towards a more nuanced account of Chinese attiudes to time and the Malthus-Darwin connection; my wife Mathanee and her sister Noparat for help with the formatting; my daughter Julia for help with the Metalude examples; Ersu Ding and Wu Shixiong for furnishing and checking my Chinese examples; three anonymous reviewers who made me think more critically about my own work, suggested changes in organisation, and pointed out relevant publications which I had missed; Lingnan University Hong Kong for giving me study leave in 2003, without which this book could not have been started, let alone finished; and the Research Grants Committee of the Hong Kong SAR, for funding the research which made *Metalude* possible.

Some parts of the book build on or exploit previous publications of mine. Chapter 2's discussion of time schedules in education refers to "Corpus linguistics, systemic-functional grammar and literary meaning: A critical analysis of *Harry Potter and the Philosopher's Stone.*" *Ilha do Desterro* 46: 115-154. In chapter 3, discussing the commodification of nature, I make use of "The representation of nature on the BBC World Service." *Text* 22. 1: 1-27. A pared down version of chapter 4 appeared as "Humans, animals and metaphors." *Society and Animals* 14.1: 15-38. In chapter 5 my discussion of diverse metaphors for education summarises and draws from "Conflicting metaphors in the Hong Kong SAR educational reform proposals." *Metaphor and Symbol* 17. 4: 263-294. Chapter 7 elaborates work in my textbook *Critical Reading and Writing* chapter 10. And a short treatment of salient ideological metaphors (especially those in chapter 8) has been published as "Ideology and metaphor." *English Today* 22.3: 25-38.

I would like to acknowledge the following publishers and authors for giving permission to use texts or quotations in the text: Faber and Faber for permission to quote five lines from Louis MacNeice's 'Prayer before Birth' (epigraph to chapter 3); the Penguin Group for permission to quote from Matt Ridley's *The Origins of Virtue* (4.3); the Estate of Hamish MacGibbon for permission to quote lines from Stevie Smith (4.3.3); Oxford University Press for permission to use the Edwin Muir poem 'The Animals' (4.3.5); and Edward Marriot for permission to quote from his *Guardian* article 'Men and Porn' (5.3.1).

SECTION 1

CHAPTER 1

Introducing metaphor

"Knowing begins with the awareness of the deceptiveness of our common-sense perceptions ... most people are half-awake, half-dreaming and are unaware that most of what they hold to be true and self-evident is illusion produced by the suggestive influence of the social world in which they live." (Fromm 1983: 28)

1.1   Some terms for analysing metaphors

Before we embark upon our exploration of metaphors and their relation to ideology I need to provide some background to this study. This chapter establishes a few technical terms important for later analysis, sketches in some aspects of metaphor theory and theories of the relationship between language, thought, ideology and culture, and introduces the database from which my metaphor data is taken.

From a cognitive perspective metaphor can be briefly defined as thinking of one thing (A) as though it were another thing (B), and linguistically this will result in an item of vocabulary or larger stretch of text being applied in an unusual or new way.[1] In traditional terminology A is the Topic or Target and B is the Vehicle or Source. While both sets of terms are common in the literature, for simplicity's sake I will from now on use Target and Source. To distinguish metaphor from other figures of speech we must stipulate that metaphorical thinking of a target in terms of a source involves establishing some similarity or analogy linking A and B. This process can be called Mapping and the similarities or analogical relationships found can be called the Grounds.

An example will make this clearer. J.P. Hartley opened his novel *The Go-Between* with the following famous sentence: "The past is a foreign country; they do things differently there" (Hartley 1958). In this sentence we have these three elements of metaphor. The target is what we are actually or literally talking about, 'the past'. The source is the entity with which the target is being compared, 'a foreign country'. (Henceforth terms referring to sources will often be bolded). Third, there is the ground, the stated similarity that helps us to map features of the source onto the target, 'they do things differently there'.

---

1.   "Apply" covers various pragmatic and semantic relations such as reference, modification, predication and complementation of prepositions.

It would be misleading to assume that every time a metaphor is used the ground and target are fully specified. It is seldom true of conventional metaphors, especially those designed to fill a gap in our vocabulary and to become the accepted terms for a new thing or concept, like *hibernation*, ("when you put your computer into hibernation everything will be saved on your hard disk") or *mouse* referring to the computer attachment.

Notice that in our first example the phrases referring to target and source are noun phrases. But metaphorical sources commonly take the form of adjectives and verbs, and even adverbs and prepositions, less noticeable though the latter may be. With these parts of speech we may find that the source is not fully specified. When Matthew Arnold in the poem 'Dover Beach' refers to "the **naked** shingles of the world", we are expected to register that the usual collocate or syntactic partner of *naked* is *body*, and then explore the grounds of comparison between a naked body and a shingle beach when the tide is out. Or, with more conventional metaphors, when we talk about *spending* or *investing* time, it is not too difficult to see that time is being compared with money, the usual object collocate of *spend* and *invest*.

1.2   Inter-relations between metaphors

The terms "target" and "source" that we have defined above allow us to think more precisely about the way metaphors inter-relate. Of most importance in this book will be the relations of Diversification and Multivalency. We have cases of diversification when the same target is referred to by a range of sources, sources which belong to quite different semantic fields or conceptual schemas. In Milton's 'Paradise Lost' Book 1, for example, Satan's legions are variously compared with locusts and autumnal leaves.

> His legions, angel forms, who lay entranced
> Thick as **autumnal leaves that strew the brooks**
> **In Vallambrosa, where the Etrurian shades**
> **High overarched embower;** (*Paradise Lost* Book 1, l.301)

> Yet to their general's voice they soon obeyed
> Innumerable. As when the potent rod
> Of Amram's son in Egypt's evil day
> Waved round the coast, up called **a pitchy cloud**
> **Of locusts**...(l.337)

Diversification is found in single texts, but can also be applied to more conventional metaphors in the dictionary. Using lexicographical evidence we can examine the diverse ways in which a particular language, such as English or Chinese, structures a target like FAILURE: DIVISION (*his plans to study in Oxford came unstuck*); FALLING (*further criticism of the tottering government is unnecessary*); SHIPWRECK (*their marriage is on the rocks*); and the related SINKING (*bad weather could sink our plans for the garden party*); or GOING BACKWARDS (*after months on a diet I've been* **backsliding** *lately*). Diverse metaphors may share grounds, or may vary their grounds along with the source.

Multivalency is the opposite of diversification, because it occurs when the source remains the same, but is variously applied to different targets within its scope. For example in Macbeth:

> Lady Macbeth.   Look like the innocent flower,
> But be **the serpent** under it.
>
> (*Macbeth* Act 1. Scene 5. l. 64)
>
> Macbeth.   There **the grown serpent** lies; **the worm** that's fled
> Hath nature that in time will venom breed,
> No teeth for the present.
>
> (*Macbeth* Act 3. Scene 4. l. 28)

In Act 1 Lady Macbeth advises her husband to feign innocence while planning the murder of Duncan. The same source is used by Macbeth to refer to the dead Banquo in Act 3. For a lexicographical example, we could notice how in the dictionary of English the source LIQUID is variously or multivalently applied to CROWDS, (*the crowd flowed over London Bridge*), TRAFFIC (*there was a trickle of cars over the new flyover*), MONEY (*you'll have to dip into your savings*), EMOTION (*he poured out his feelings to his girlfriend*), and KNOWLEDGE/INFORMATION (*the main recommendations of the Butler report have been leaked in advance*).

Quite apart from the interaction of metaphors with each other, there is the widespread phenomenon of a deliberate confusion of metaphorical and literal levels. This is a frequently-used technique in advertising copy, for example "A beautiful new bathroom from Graham makes freshening up a positive pleasure. But with interest free credit as well it feels even better. Because that means you won't have to **splash out** too much." (Good Housekeeping May 1987: 155). More specifically we have cases of a lexical item being used literally at one point in the text, and at another point as a source term, a phenomenon I have elsewhere called "Literalisation of Vehicles" (Goatly 1997: 272–9). Though much used for comic effects, it can also impart a symbolic value to the literal referents. We shall wish to explore in the coming chapters cases where the patterns of metaphors in the dictionary are evidence of the symbolic value of a concrete object or action, as when, for example, tall buildings become symbolic of power, in step with the metaphors in the dictionary in which POWER (target) is conceived of in terms of HEIGHT (source).

1.3   The theory of conceptual metaphor

The first aspect of metaphor that the conceptual theorists stress is that it is everywhere. In fact many philosophers, such as John Locke, would have liked to do without metaphor, feeling that it confused thinking. However, ironically enough, the terms in which they inveigh against it are themselves loaded down with metaphors.

> But yet, if we would speak of things as they are, we must **allow** that... all the artificial and figurative application of words eloquence hath **invented**, are for nothing else but to **insinuate** wrong ideas, **move** the passions, and thereby **mislead** the judgment, and so indeed are perfect **cheat**. [*Essay concerning Human Understanding* Book 3, Chapter 10, p. 105, my bolding]

Arguably "move", "mislead" and "cheat" are being used metaphorically, "eloquence hath invented" is a case of personifying metaphor, "insinuate" depends upon a metaphor borrowed from Latin, where its literal meaning is 'work its way in, penetrate', and literally we "allow" actions rather than propositions. Hobbes, too, sees metaphor as an abuse of language, believing that words have an ordained meaning and that change to or imprecision of meaning amounts to semantic rebellion, a threat to order (Chilton 1996).

Table 1.   Lexis for the conceptual metaphor theme UNDERSTAND IS HOLD/GRASP

LEXIS	MEANING	EXAMPLE
get hold of	understand	*she finds even the easy concepts difficult to get hold of*
get a grip on/ get to grips with	understand correctly, begin to solve	*new techniques should help us get a grip on the problem*
feel	natural understanding of or ability in	*he has a feel for mathematics more than for biology*
have your finger on the pulse	know or understand everything about something	*the commodities market fluctuates really quickly so it's important to keep your finger on its pulse*
catch on	understand after initial lack of understanding	*there was a pause until the audience caught on*
have at your fingertips	have a complete understanding of something	*he's been in the job for years and has all the political factors in the company at his fingertips*
get hold of the wrong end of the stick	misunderstand	*half the class got hold of the wrong end of the stick and put the metal in the acid*
grope	try with great difficulty to think, understand or act	*the police were groping for the motive of the murder*
grasp	understand something difficult	*I managed to grasp the main points of the lecture*

Metaphor is ubiquitous (Paprotte and Dirven 1985) and we are especially reliant on it when discoursing on abstract targets. The strong claim of conceptual metaphor theory would be that abstract thought is only possible through the use of metaphor.

Though some scientists and mathematicians have held up mathematical thought as an alternative to metaphorical thought, Lakoff has demonstrated that even mathematical concepts such as Boolean logic or set theory depend on the metaphor of containers or bounded spaces, with members inside the container and non-members outside it (Lakoff 1987: chapter 20).

One of the most important insights of conceptual metaphor theory is that these concrete sources for abstract targets do not occur randomly but fall into patterns, which we might call Conceptual Metaphor Themes, or Conceptual Metaphors for short. These are conventionally referred to by the capitalised formula x IS y. For example the conceptual metaphor theme UNDERSTAND IS HOLD/GRASP gives us the set of lexical items in Table 1.

The question then arises, if metaphor is everywhere and vital to our conceptualisation of abstract ideas, where do the sources of these metaphors originate? According to Lakoff's theory, they have their source in our bodily infant experiences. Even in the womb, and when we are released from it, we acquire a schema of space or lack of space, providing the source of, for example, FREEDOM IS SPACE TO MOVE. We soon acquire the schema of containers with insides and outsides from our experience of eating and excreting, from which we draw the source for MIND IS A CONTAINER, and the notion of proximity from being picked up and separated from our carers, so that RELATIONSHIP IS PROXIMITY. We experience gravity and the sense of vertical orientation as well – MORE or POWER IS HIGH. The first most obvious changes that we notice are movements, thus CHANGE IS MOVEMENT. As we develop through the first two or three years we acquire the ability to handle objects with more and more control, initially grasping with all fingers in a palm grasp, and progressing until we can pick up small objects between our thumb and index finger; this not only provides the source for UNDERSTAND IS HOLD/GRASP, but also the motivation for CONTROL IS HANDLE. We learn to crawl towards objects that we want, and eventually to walk unaided, giving us PURPOSE IS DIRECTION and DEVELOPMENT/SUCCESS IS MOVEMENT FORWARDS.

How, then, when we begin to think abstractly, do we decide which targets to pair with which sources? To understand this we have to introduce the idea of metonymy. Unlike metaphors, metonymies are relationships between meanings based on contiguity in experience, or, linguistically, on deletion rather than substitution. We might say for example "I drank two bottles of wine" as shorthand for "I drank the contents of two bottles of wine". And this deletion depends upon the fact that bottles are containers for wine and therefore the concepts are contiguous in our experience. By contrast, by calling Tony Blair "the lapdog of Bush", I am substituting 'Blair' with 'lapdog', two concepts which have no particular association or contiguity in experience. Many of the basic links in conceptual metaphors can be traced back to metonymies such as cause and effect, or activity and place. So, for example, there is a well-established set of metaphorical vocabulary in English and other languages that conceptualises anger as heat. The origin of this is quite obviously one of cause and effect – when we become angry we do feel hot. And there are many lexical items that conceptualise activity as place, as when we talk of "filling a position", or "the office of the president" (cf. "the President's office"), where the activity is associated with the place in which it is performed. These metonymies, are, however, later developed metaphorically, so we can talk about anger "flaring up", or about being on the "verge" of doing something.

In his most important book on metaphor, *Women, Fire and Dangerous Things,* George Lakoff uses the evidence of conceptual metaphors grounded in our bodily experiences to suggest an alternative to the philosophical traditions of Objectivism and Subjectivism. We cannot accept objectivism, because, although there is a reality out there, we do not have unmediated access to it, as our thinking is inescapably mediated by the metaphors we use. Even scientific theories and models are basically metaphorical hypotheses, technically known as model-theoretic metaphors. These can only approximate to descriptions of reality, and a new model-theoretic scientific metaphor will initiate a programme of research trying to establish exactly what the grounds of the metaphorical model are, and what features of the model do not apply.

On the other hand, we have no need to accept subjectivism and complete conceptual relativism, because, after all, our infant bodily experiences, which we use as tools for thinking, are universal, and to that extent we share a common metaphorical language. Experientialism, then, steers a middle course between philosophical traditions that assume truth is something we can access independent of any description of it, and subjectivism which believes that truth is a matter of individual belief relative to circumstances (Lakoff 1987: 265–268).

Lakoff and Johnson give telling demonstrations of how features can be mapped across source domains and target domains, in other words what the grounds of such metaphors are. For example, they take the theme THINKING IS MATHEMATICAL CALCULATION, and show how correspondences can be mapped, as in Table 2 (Lakoff and Johnson 1999: 406).

Table 2. Mappings in the conceptual metaphor THINKING IS MATHEMATICAL CALCULATION

SOURCE	MAPPING	TARGET
Mathematical Calculation	→	Thinking
Numbers	→	Ideas
Equations	→	Propositions
Adding	→	Putting ideas together
Sum	→	Conclusion

However, there is an interesting question, which will recur in the course of this book, as to whether the metaphor of "mapping" is indeed a valid one. That is to say, the relatively abstract target may be quite unstructured and inchoate and the more concrete source schema gives it a structure and a order. This is unlike real maps, which, instead of structuring topographical and geographical realities, are supposed to simply reflect a pre-existing reality.[2] It may be that, in many cases, metaphorical mapping is more like the maps of Middlearth provided in Tolkein's *Lord of the Rings* in which the map constitutes or invents a reality rather than describing it. The metaphor of mapping perhaps tends to push the experiential hypothesis too far in the direction of objectivism. As Chilton remarks,

> it presupposes that the two domains are already structurally similar. Yet there are no arguments for this similarity, except the metaphorical move, the ... analogy itself. Metaphor works by projecting one relatively well-understood set of ideas onto a domain that is problematic, rather than by simply expressing a pre-existing and objective similarity (1996: 106).

1.4   Characterising conceptual metaphors and metaphor themes

The theories I have just summarised took as their starting point lexicographical evidence. And, as we have seen, conventional conceptual metaphors in the dictionary, and the poetic metaphors derived from them, do not appear singly but in groups arranged around schemas:

> Shifts in range that occur in metaphor, then, usually amount to no mere distribution of family goods but an expedition abroad. A whole set of alternative labels, a whole apparatus of organization takes over new territory. What occurs is a transfer of a schema (Goodman 1968: 73).

Here is an example of one such conceptual metaphor theme, with the lexicographical evidence to back it up (cf. Kövecses 2002).

MONEY IS BLOOD/LIQUID ⇔ QUANTITY=WATERFLOW

Movement of money is the flow or movement of liquid
cashflow (__movement of water) n. 'movement of funds' *small shops often have cashflow problems*
inflow movement of water in n. 'income' *we expect inflows of cash at the end of the month*
trickle slow thin flow n. 'small but steady income' *there has only been a trickle of funds into my account in the last few months*
outflow movement of liquid away from a place n. 'outward movement of funds' *there are strict controls on capital outflow*
run out flow out v. 'be used up' *funding for this project has run out*

---

2.   The literature on metaphor theory provides many discussions of whether we can talk of an antecedent similarity between source and target, or whether in fact the source attributes various qualities to the target. See also Goatly 1997: 121–22.

current account (strong flow of fluid in one direction __) nphr. 'checking account' I *had to transfer money into my current account*
in circulation (__blood flow) adjphr. 'being passed around' *there's too much money in circulation*

Plenty of money is plenty of liquid
flush with (v. cause liquid to flow through and clean ___) adj. 'having plenty of money' *after winning at cards he was flush with money*
juicy luscious with plenty of liquid in it (of fruit) adj. 'generous or large (of sums of money)' *lawyers usually make juicy profits out of commercial disputes*
in full (__completely occupied by liquid) adv. 'completely' *you don't have to pay in full until next month*

To make money available is to turn into liquid, and to make it unavailable is to turn into solid
liquidate (substance that is neither gas nor solid__) v. 'close down and sell off assets' *the company is bankrupt and will be liquidated*
liquidity (substance that is neither gas nor solid__) n. 'availability of funds' *the bank loan will increase our liquidity*
solvent (*dissolved) adj. 'having enough money' *my pay increase will make me more solvent*
freeze solidify because of low temperature v. 'prevent money being used' *Swiss banks are now freezing corrupt officials' bank accounts*
frozen solidified by the cold adj. 'unable to be sold or used' *the frozen assets of the last president may finally be confiscated*

To obtain or lose money is to obtain or lose blood
bleed (dry) cause to lose (all your) blood v. 'take money from in a heartless way' *the World Bank is bleeding the Third World dry*
bloodsucker animal that sucks blood from others n. 'extortioner' *money lenders in Hong Kong are real bloodsuckers*
?loan shark (___sharp-toothed fish with triangular dorsal fin) n. 'extortioner, person who lends money at high rates of interest' *never borrow from loan sharks: it's dangerous*
haemorrhage lose a large amount of blood from a blood vessel v. 'lose resources or money' *funds were haemorrhaging from the company*

– or other liquid
dip into put briefly into liquid v. 'spend some of' *to buy a car I'll have to dip into my savings*

draft amount of liquid taken from a well or drunk n. 'written order for money to be paid' *I'll send you a bank draft for $400 immediately*

overdraft (__amount of water taken from a well or drunk) n. 'amount owed to bank' *I can't pay – I already have a big overdraft*

overdrawn (v. __take water from a well) adj. 'having taken out too much money' *he's $5000 overdrawn*

drain hole for liquid to flow out of n. 'depletion, loss' *the high school fees have been a drain on my bank account*

draw take water from a well v. 'withdraw' *each week I draw $400 from my bank account*

sponge (n. mop of soft porous material) v. 'extract or obtain money' *sponging off the state is very difficult now we have a right wing government*

sponger (mop of soft porous material__) n. 'someone who lives off other people's money' *the media make all refugees look like spongers*

squeeze (v. press to remove liquid) n. 'restriction on borrowing or supply of money' *the economic squeeze reduced property prices*

squeeze press to remove liquid v. 'get money out of' *I'll try to squeeze maximum profit from the firm*

tap obtain liquid from v. 'take or get money out of' *Hong Kong will have to tap its reserves soon to increase welfare provision*

milk pump or suck out the white liquid food produced by female mammals v. 'extract money from' *now I'm rich all my relatives are trying to milk me for cash*

siphon off remove liquid through a tube using gravity v. 'take money illegally from' *he siphoned off funds from the charity for years*

soak make very wet v. 'overcharge' *the shop really soaked you for that watch*

wring remove liquid (from cloth) by twisting v. 'force money out of' *it took months to wring the payments out of him*

To provide or spend money is to provide liquid

dispenser device for giving out measures of liquid n. 'organisation that gives out funds' *the government is a main dispenser of sponsorships*

cash dispenser (__device for giving out measures of liquid) n. 'ATM machine' *most banks have a cash dispenser outside*

channel direct the flow of liquid v. 'direct funds' *more resources will be channelled to local councils*

funnel channel liquid using a pipe with a cone-shaped opening at the top v. 'concentrate financial resources' *we need to funnel capital into our sister company*

float cause to stay on the surface of a liquid v. 'finance a company' *they floated the company on the stock market*

pour cause to flow from one container to another v. 'provide a large amount of money' *the college poured funds into the research project*

pump use pressure to cause liquid to flow v. 'provide large amounts (of money)' *Japan should pump extra money into education*

ladle out distribute liquid food with a large spoon v. 'give generously' *the UK didn't exactly ladle out aid to Africa*

splash out (make water move through the air by hitting__) v. 'spend wildly' *he splashed out on a BMW*

tide over (n. flow of river or sea water__) v. 'give temporary financial help to' *I just need $200 to tide me over until next week*

pool (n. small pond) v. 'to collect (money) together' *if we pool our investments we can afford the house*

pool small pond n. 'gambling stake, investment' *how much has been bet in the Derby pool?*

infusion soaking in hot water n. 'additional funding' *the company needs an infusion of funds*

injection putting liquid into the body with a syringe n. 'provision of money' *without capital injection the company will fail*

transfusion adding blood to a person's body n. 'provision of money' *a transfusion of funds will be necessary to keep the project going*

(_ indicates that this part of the lexical item does not partake in the metaphor)

We can see quite clearly here, how a schema for liquid (blood) and its movement is mapped onto the domain of finance.

One problem for systematic research into metaphor themes is that some of the literature, such as *More than Cool Reason* (Lakoff and Turner 1989) with its list of conceptual metaphors in the index, the database Master List of Metaphors at the University of Berkeley linked to the Conceptual Metaphor Home Page (http://cogsci.berkeley.edu/lakoff/), and Barcelona (2000a) do not specify any clear criteria by which to identify important conceptual metaphors.[3] [4] The research my team and I have been pursuing over the last few years has been designed to establish in a more principled way the important conceptual metaphors or metaphor themes for English, and to compare these with Chinese metaphors. The somewhat arbitrary criteria we have used are: (1) To count as a significant conceptual metaphor the theme should be realised by at least six lexical items, taken from a dictionary of contemporary English. (2) There should be at least 200 tokens of this joint set of lexical items with the relevant metaphorical meaning in the Cobuild Bank of English/WordsOnline database (http://www.

---

3.   The result is that the formula X IS Y has become quite ambiguous in much of the literature. Some writers simply use this formula for any metaphor, while others, as did Lakoff and Johnson originally (1980) use it to represent a pattern or theme. Still others attempt to justify this typography on the basis of cognitive categories, for which there may not be any hard or lexical evidence.

4.   Though one notes with some pleasure Olaf Jakel's move towards my approach (Jakel 1995: 225).

collinswordbanks.co.uk/).[5] The website 'Metalude' (Metaphor At Lingnan University Department of English) is the result of these endeavours.[6] I used a combination of intuition, existing lexicographical evidence from the conceptual metaphor literature and dictionaries of metaphors, manual searches of dictionaries of contemporary English such as Cobuild, and the computer concordance database of *Cambridge International Dictionary of English*/CIDE+, supplemented by *The Encarta Dictionary*, data from *Collins Cobuild English Guides vol.7: Metaphor* (Deignan 1995), *A Thesaurus of Traditional English Metaphors* (Wilkinson 2002) and the BBC World Service radio. Examples were taken from the dictionaries, which use authentic corpora, though they were slightly modified to avoid copyright problems.

The lexical evidence that we have amassed supports many of the intuitions about the important conceptual metaphors from Lakoff, Johnson and researchers who have followed in their footsteps. But other quite well-accepted and much touted conceptual metaphors failed according to our criteria. TIME IS MONEY, for example, although it passes according to the second criterion due to the frequency of the collocation *spend time* in WordsOnline, fails on the first criterion: there are only three or four lexical items which collocate exclusively with money, namely *spend, cost,* and *invest.* The others posited as evidence in the literature such as *save, waste, have, give, spare, run out, budget, put aside, have left, borrow, lose* collocate with goods or commodities in general, as Lakoff and Johnson point out (1980: 7–9). So we have had to modify this equation to TIME IS MONEY/COMMODITY. Conversely, our researches reveal many new conceptual metaphors not apparent in the literature, including such ideologically significant equations as SEX IS VIOLENCE.

I would recommend consultation of Metalude, which has a map of metaphor themes as well as a database. As corroboration of the experiential hypothesis the sources of these metaphor themes can be largely classified into Space and Orientation, the (Human) Body and the Senses, Movement and Action. However, the database also includes metaphor themes which, unlike those in conceptual metaphor theory, do not concretise abstract concepts, but systematically compare one physical thing/substance with another, for example HUMAN IS FOOD, or BUILDING IS BODY.

1.5   Literal language, conventional metaphor and original metaphor

Traditional metaphor studies made a distinction between original or live metaphors and dead metaphors, the conventional ones that have become clichés and part of the lexicon of the language. Conceptual metaphor theorists object to the implications of these personifying metaphors *live* and *dead*, because they suggest that conventional

---

5.   The research was funded by the Research Grants Council of the Hong Kong SAR, project reference LC3001/99H.

6.   www.ln.edu.hk/lle/cwd/project01/web/home.html

metaphors are not exerting any powerful influence on cognition, quite the reverse of conceptual metaphor theory's claims. However, misleading though the labels may be, there is a very important distinction to be made between the original and the conventional and the literal in terms of language processing. Metaphors demand longer reading times than their non-figurative counterparts (Noveck et al. 2001). And unconventional metaphors show more right-hemisphere brain activity in fMRI brain scans (Ahrens, Liu, Lee, Gong, Fang and Hsu 2006). The relative ease with which conventional metaphors and literal language are processed suggests the possibility for considerable latent ideological effects.

When we meet an original metaphor we have to do a great deal more mental work than when we process a conventional metaphor. For example, faced with the sentence "Universities are facing financial **cuts**", we only have to disambiguate the possible meanings of "cut"; there is not much difficulty in determining the target from the several dictionary meanings of *cut*, and the grounds are more or less ignored. However, confronted with the lines in Charles Causley's poem 'Death of a Poet' "His **tractor** of blood stopped thumping/He held five **icicles** in each hand" (Causley 1973: 495) we have to establish the target to which "tractor" and "icicles" refer, i.e. the heart and the fingers, and this process will also involve working out the grounds – that a heart pulls the blood around the body in the same way as a tractor pulls machinery around a farm, that fingers and icicles are long, thin, and pointed, and the fingers of a dead man's hand are cold and stiff like icicles. If we call original metaphors "live" or "active" this is really because they are new and demand that we are active in our interpretation of them. If we call conventional metaphors "dead" or "inactive", this is because they are old and their interpretation does not demand as much conscious activity on our part. But this does not mean to say that they have less effect on our cognition. In fact, it is precisely because they are conventionalised that they may achieve the power to subconsciously affect our thinking, without our being aware of it. [7]

There is a case for saying that literal language is simply conventionalised metaphor. Quite apart from the fact that much of our conventional vocabulary for abstract targets is inescapably metaphorical, the processes of classification which we use in establishing literal categories and applying them literally depend on mapping and similarity, the very processes that metaphor relies on. It is simply the case that when we apply the word literally certain critical features that we privilege as part of the meaning match with features of the object referred to. But when we apply the word metaphorically the

---

7. This distinction between the original and the conventional is not always as clear cut as in the examples given. When William Golding says "the algebra was glue they were stuck in", although the word "glue" is apparently an original metaphor for difficulty, the word "stuck", which points us to the ground, shows that this apparent originality is little more than a re-lexicalisation of a conventional metaphor theme SUCCESSFUL ACTIVITY IS MOVEMENT FORWARD, of which "stuck" is a conventional lexical realisation. Nevertheless, I would suggest that more processing of grounds is needed to understand this superficially original metaphor than would be the case if the sentence had been "they were stuck in the algebra".

mapping or matching involves features other than the critical features necessary for literal reference.

For example, if we look at these boxes in Figure 1. and are asked to classify them into two different groups there are many possible ways of doing it.

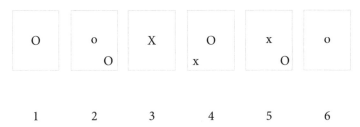

Figure 1. Alternative classifications

We could divide them into 1, 3, 6 and 2, 4, 5 on the criteria of containing one letter or two. Or into 1, 2, 6 and 3, 4, 5, because 1, 2, 6 contain only *o*'s and no *x*'s. Or into 1, 3, 4, which have an upper case letter in the centre, and 2, 5, 6 with their lower case letters, or any number of other alternatives. It simply depends upon which features we regard as critical. Once we have established the categories through selection of the critical features, application of a concept which depends on non-critical features will appear unusual and startling, in short, metaphorical. Let's assume we have established a conventional category A for 1, 3 and 6, and B for 2, 4, and 5 on the basis of containing one letter or two. I might, then, metaphorically refer to box 6 as a B, and the grounds would be that it contains the letter *o*, a feature shared with all the other examples of B. This would unsettle the conventional "literal" categories, and establish some kind of equivalence for what was originally a difference (Laclau and Mouffe 1985, Fairclough 2003: 100).

If the same "arbitrariness" is true of the classification of the world around us, then it becomes obvious that there are no given categories in nature. This was the view of Benjamin Lee Whorf, who wrote:

> It was found that the background linguistic system (in other words the grammar) of each language is not merely a reproducing instrument for voicing our ideas but rather is itself the shaper of ideas, the program and guide for the individual's mental activity, for his analysis of impressions, for his synthesis of his mental stock in trade. Formulation of ideas is not an independent process, strictly rational in the old sense, but is a part of particular grammar, and differs, from slightly to greatly, between different grammars. We dissect nature along lines laid down by our native languages. The categories and types we isolate from the world of phenomena we do not find there because they stare every observer in the face; on the contrary the world is presented in a kaleidoscopic flux of impressions which has to be organised by our minds – and this means largely by the linguistic systems in our minds. We cut nature up, organize it into concepts, and ascribe significances as we do, largely because we are parties to an agreement to organize it in this way – an agreement

that holds throughout our speech community and is codified in the patterns of our language. The agreement is, of course, an implicit and unstated one, BUT ITS TERMS ARE ABSOLUTELY OBLIGATORY; we cannot talk at all except by subscribing to the organization and classification of data which the agreement decrees.

This fact is very significant for modern science, for it means that no individual is free to describe nature with absolute impartiality but is constrained to certain modes of interpretation even when he thinks himself most free. The person most free in such respects would be a linguist familiar with very many widely different linguistic systems. As yet no linguist is in any such position. We are thus introduced to a new principle of relativity, which holds that all observers are not led by the same physical evidence to the same picture of the universe, unless their linguistic backgrounds are similar, or can in some way be calibrated (Whorf 1956: 212–14).

Schumacher puts it another way.

When we begin to think we can do so only because our mind is already full of all sorts of ideas with which to think. All through our youth and adolescence, before the conscious and critical mind begins to act as a sort of censor or guardian at the threshold, ideas seep into our mind, vast hosts and multitudes of them. These years are, one might say, our Dark Ages during which we are nothing but inheritors; it is only in later years that we can gradually learn to sort out our inheritance.

First of all there is language. Each word is an idea. If the language that seeps into us in our Dark Ages is English, our mind is thereby furnished by a set of ideas which is significantly different from the set represented by Chinese, Russian, German, or even American. Next to words there are the rules for putting them together: grammar, another bundle of ideas, the study of which has fascinated some modern philosophers to such an extent that they thought they could reduce the whole of philosophy to a study of grammar … It is very difficult to become aware of them [these ideas derived from language], as they are the instruments and not the results of our thinking … (Schumacher 1973/1999: 62)

It should immediately be pointed out that the Whorfian hypothesis is by no means accepted by all cognitive linguists or conceptual metaphor theorists, despite Lakoff's quite balanced and sympathetic treatment in *Women, Fire and Dangerous Things* (Lakoff 1987: chapter 18). But, as Cameron (2003: 22) suggests, "Cognitive linguists, in their desire to take the study of metaphor out of the realm of language, are … overoptimistic about the feasibility of separating human thought from human language use."

In this book I espouse a weak form of the Whorfian hypothesis, that is, in brief, that the particular language we speak predisposes us to think and act in certain ways. I do not adopt the strong one, which says one's language totally determines one's thought. In chapter 7 for example, I assume that the different worldview represented by Blackfoot (Niitsi'powahsin) grammar, can, though with a great deal of effort, be communicated to speakers of very different languages like English, that is, in Whorf's terms, calibration is possible. The physicists David Bohm and David Peat were already thinking along the lines of Blackfoot grammar before they encountered Blackfoot, and this suggests that, difficult though it may be, it is certainly possible to conceive the world to some extent like a Blackfoot (Niitsi'powahsin) speaker without speaking the language. But the language one speaks, especially if one is monolingual, makes it much easier to think in the commonsense categories and with the conventional metaphors which it provides. I also believe that intra-linguistically alternative metaphors within a language, for example, of education as transmission or education as growth (chapter 5), allow multiple perspectives or constructions of social practices, and the extent to which alternative metaphorical conceptualisations are available to us measures our distance from linguistic determinism. Metaphors are cognitive filters, but different metaphors filter different particles of truth.

1.6   Convention, commonsense and latent ideology

The languages we speak hand down to us ready-made categories which we regard as commonsense. They thereby unconsciously carry with them an ontology or ideology of which we may not be aware. We may think, naively, that the information conveyed by language is about the real world. But in fact "we have conscious access only to the projected world – the world as unconsciously organised by the mind: and we can talk about things only insofar as they have achieved mental representation through these processes of organisation" (Jackendoff 1983: 29).

One classic case is of kinship categories. In Thai the primary criterion for categorising siblings is by seniority, rather than by sex as it is in English. So the ontology of siblinghood is different. But this has ideological implications, too, if we define ideology as meaning in the service of power (Thompson 1984). This is because seniority in Thai culture carries rights and responsibilities quantitatively, if not qualitatively, different from seniority in the West. Traditionally Thais' elder siblings may take the role of substitute parent and can give orders and make demands of younger siblings. Along with this goes the responsibility for their welfare, for example by helping to pay for their education. Furthermore, in terms of social relations, sibling seniority has ramifications beyond the boundaries of the family. Thais use the words for elder sibling 'phîi' and younger sibling 'nɔ́ɔŋ' as terms of address, rather like 2nd person pronouns, not only with blood siblings, but also with friends and acquaintances. This means that when starting a conversation with a stranger with whom one wishes to establish a friendly relationship, and when it is not obvious from appearances which of the conversational partners is the older, at some point the question has to be asked about relative age. Otherwise polite and appropriate interpersonal discourse and behaviour are an impossibility. This example shows how commonsense ontology transmitted culturally through language may have consequences for ideology, and demonstrates how ideology influences verbal and non-verbal behaviour. It also influences perception, of course, since interlocutors would be primed by the language to look for features of relative age when initiating friendly discourse. One might put it like Yann Martel "Isn't telling about something – using words, English or Japanese – already something of an invention? Isn't looking upon this world already something of an invention?" (Martel 2002: 405).

It may be useful at this point to relate language labels and categories to the social theory of discourse as formulated by Foucault and Bourdieu. Foucault claims that discourse does not describe a pre-existing reality so much as bring a reality into being. He believed that discourse produces the objects of knowledge and that nothing that is meaningful exists outside discourse, which he defines as "a group of statements that provide a language for talking about – the way of representing the knowledge about – a particular target at a particular historical moment". Physical things and actions exist independently of discourse, but they only take on meaning and become objects of knowledge within discourse: "madness, punishment, sexuality only exist meaningfully as products of discourse" (Hall 2001: 73). Discourse creates objects of knowledge, but knowledge is linked to power since knowledge has the power to make itself true – "all knowledge once applied to the real world has real effects, and in that sense at least, 'becomes true'". Knowledge, once used to regulate the conduct of others, entails constraint, regulation and the disciplining of practices. Thus "there is no power relation without the correlative constitution of a field of knowledge, nor any knowledge that does not presuppose and constitute at the same time, power relations" (Foucault 1977: 27). This link between knowledge and power is encapsulated in the phrase "regimes of truth".

> Truth isn't outside power … Truth is a thing of this world; it is produced only by multiple forms of constraint. And it induces regular effects of power. Each society has its regime of truth, its 'general politics' of truth; that is the types of discourse it accepts and makes function as true, the mechanisms and instances which enable one to distinguish true and false statements, the means by which each is sanctioned … the status of those who are charged with saying what counts as true (Foucault 1980: 131).

Stuart Hall gives a clear example of a regime of truth in operation: if everyone in a society hears repeated in discourse and comes to believe that single parent families produce delinquent children, then legislators will try to discourage single parent families, by, for example, taking away tax allowances, and thereby produce the poverty which will make this a self-fulfilling prophecy. Thus the beliefs will become a reality, a regime of truth (Hall 2001: 76).

A similar point is made by Bourdieu (1991: 134). "How can one fail to see that a prediction may have a role not only in the author's intentions, but also in the reality of its social realisation, … as a self-fulfilling prophecy". He calls such a prediction "a performative representation capable of exerting a specifically political effect". Bourdieu is here using a term from Austin's (1962) and Searle's (1969) speech act theory. This theory states that some kinds of utterance, known as declarations or performatives, do not describe a pre-existing reality, but bring it into being by their very utterance – for example when a priest christens a child or marries a couple the act of christening or marrying is

brought about simply by the utterance of the correct words by the institutionally designated person (the priest) in the correct circumstances (at a public ceremony in church).
Bourdieu wishes to abolish Searle's (1995) distinction between brute facts which are
true independent of society, and which can be described through assertions, and institutional facts such as these church ceremonies which are self-fulfilling declarations/
performatives. Performative acts are acts of institution that cannot be sanctioned unless
they have, in some way, the whole social order behind them. Similarly linguistic form
and the information it imparts condense and symbolise the entire structure of the social relation from which they derive their existence and efficacy.

> The word or *a fortiori* the dictum, the proverb and all the stereotyped or ritual
> forms of expression are programmes of perception and different, more or less
> ritualised strategies for the symbolic struggles of everyday life, just like the great
> collective rituals of naming or nomination – or, more clearly still, the clashes be-
> tween the visions and previsions of specifically political struggles – imply a certain
> claim to symbolic authority as the socially recognised power to impose a certain
> vision of the social world, i.e. of the divisions of the social world. In the struggle to
> impose the legitimate vision, in which science itself is inevitably caught up, agents
> possess power in proportion to their symbolic capital, i.e. in proportion to the
> recognition they receive from a group (Bourdieu 1991: 106).

Conventional metaphors are not arbitrary, precisely, and paradoxically, because they
are decreed by an arbiter. That science is implicated in this process is something that
will emerge in chapter 4, where we consider different biological theories in the source
of the HUMAN IS ANIMAL metaphor.

The knowledge sanctioned or legitimised as true through discourse and through
the language one speaks usually acquires the appearance of objective commonsense.
For the influence of language upon our thought and perception of reality is most powerful when we are unaware of it, when it expresses hidden or, technically speaking,
latent ideology. We may be aware of alternative ways of conceptualising reality because
(1) we speak a second language or (2) are sufficiently alert to notice the choices made
within the language we speak. But, if not, the texts we encounter may seem the only
natural way of representing experience. This mind-set is known as *naturalisation*. It
represents "the profound realism which most often characterizes the world view of
the dominated" (Bourdieu 1991: 235). It is quite common for people to talk about
"objective", "unbiased" description, as though our language and texts can simply and
faithfully reflect a pre-existing reality. In fact we have no direct access to the world or
reality out there. Even in the act of perception we interpret rather than simply register
sensations of the world. For example, our brains invert the upside-down image on our
retina, and we often interpret the size of that image as a cue to distance rather than an
indication of the size of the object. But language is even more important than perception as a distorting medium, coming between the reality "out there" and our percep-
tions/thoughts of it.

If language and discourse constitute their own reality, then linguistic/cognitive subversion will be necessary in order to subvert the power/knowledge structures of society. Meanings and representations will need subverting in advance.

> Political subversion presupposes cognitive subversion, a conversion of the vision of the world ... Heretical subversion exploits the possibility of changing the social world by changing the representation of this world which contributes to its reality or, more precisely, by counterposing a *paradoxical pre-vision*, a utopia, a project or programme, to the ordinary vision which apprehends the social world as a natural world: the *performative* utterance, the political pre-vision, is in itself a pre-diction which aims to bring about what it utters (Bourdieu 1991: 127–8).

It is at this point that we can invoke metaphors as a means of cognitive/representational subversion. By applying language in new or unusual ways or structuring concepts differently metaphors have a potential for challenging the commonsense categories of knowledge.

Hobbes, whose ideology, formulated at the beginning of the modern capitalist period, we will be exploring later, was convinced that metaphor and literal language were matters of power and subversion. The end of metaphor he saw as "contention, sedition and contempt" – presumably of and against legitimate authority. By implication, the benefit to which perspicuous words lead must be acceptance, obedience and respect (Chilton 1996: 18).

Original metaphors perhaps have the merit of undoing ready-made linguistic and cultural categories and the ontologies and ideologies which they manifest and of suggesting new ones. However, because they are original, they are, by definition, one-off attempts to do this. Conventional metaphors, on the other hand, do not unsettle our modes of perception or action at all, since they have achieved currency as an acceptable way of constructing, conceptualising and interacting with reality. We no longer take much notice when someone says of an argument "I don't buy that", since *buy* is now a conventional metaphor with a meaning something like 'accept, agree with'. The fact that it has become current means that it may work to convey a latent ideology – that ideas and beliefs are a commodity which we choose and shop around for according to our needs or desires. This is particularly likely if it is not an isolated lexical metaphor but part of a larger metaphor theme comprising many lexical items.

The differences between original metaphors and accepted conventional ones can be seen clearly in the following example. I attempted to undermine the conventional metaphor of economic *growth*, with its positive connotations, and substitute the alternative, more original metaphor, *cancer* (Goatly 2000). The reason for this attempt was the conviction that economic expansion in already mature economies actually harms the environment and the life-support systems on which we depend, much as an expanding cancerous growth threatens the vital organs of the body. Needless to say I was not successful, and, as far as I know, this remains a one-off original metaphor. I use this example to demonstrate that there is an ideological or hegemonic struggle to get one's metaphors accepted as the conventional ones (Fairclough 2003: 45). The idea that economic growth could be as harmful as cancer is an ideological heresy within the climate of consumer capitalism we at present enjoy.

Table 3. Ideological and interpretive effects of original and conventional metaphors

LANGUAGE	INTERPRETATION	EFFECT AS METAPHOR	EFFECT AS IDEOLOGY
ORIGINAL METAPHOR	Complex: grounds and target need working out	Maximum	Minimal because fleeting
CONVENTIONAL METAPHOR	More simple: target reached through disambiguation, grounds ignored	Minimal	Considerable
LITERAL LANGUAGE	Relatively straightforward	Zero	Maximum

We can perhaps sum up the argument with the help of Table 3. The scale of metaphorical effect runs in the opposite direction from the scale of ideological effect, precisely because with literal language and conventional metaphors the ideology is latent, and therefore all the more powerful. What is powerful *qua* metaphor (active and original), thereby becomes more noticeable and debatable and therefore relatively powerless ideologically. What is relatively powerless *qua* metaphor (inactive or dead) – the literal or the conventionally metaphorical – becomes all the more powerful ideologically through its hidden workings. Lakoff calls these conventional metaphors

> both conceptual in nature and deep, in the sense that they are used largely without being noticed, that they have enormous social consequences, and that they shape the very understanding of our everyday world. It is important to contrast such deep conceptual metaphors ... with superficial [original] metaphors, which are of only marginal interest ...·(Lakoff 1995: no page number)

The division between the original metaphor, conventional metaphor and literal language is not watertight, and may, indeed, be bridged over time. What was once a self-conscious metaphor for behaviour may gradually become the accepted way of modelling social practice, become conventional, if not literal. In terms of ideology or the exercise of power within society this can be a crucial development, as for example, workers, through inculcation, accept and enact the metaphor (discourse) of an organisation as a machine.

> Inculcation is a matter of, in the current jargon, people coming to "own" discourses, to position themselves inside them, to act and think and talk and see themselves in terms of new discourses. A stage towards inculcation is rhetorical deployment: people may learn new discourses and use them for certain purposes while at the same time self-consciously keeping a distance from them. One of the mysteries of the dialectics of discourse is the process by which what begins as

self-conscious rhetorical deployment becomes "ownership" – how people become unconsciously positioned within a discourse (Fairclough 2003: 208).

The main thrust of the argument in this book is that conventional conceptual metaphors construct and reproduce ideologies, and justify or reproduce certain behaviours (Geertz 1973: 209–213, Fairclough 1989, Gibbs 1999, Mey 2006). And the project of this book is to raise awareness of these latent ideologies, and of how they may be structuring and influencing our personal, social, environmental, and political behaviour. As Murray Edelman (1971: 68) puts it:

> Metaphor, therefore, defines the pattern of perception to which people respond … Each metaphor intensifies selected perceptions and ignores others, thereby helping one to concentrate on desired consequences of favoured public policies and helping one to ignore their unwanted, unthinkable, or irrelevant premises and aftermaths. Each metaphor can be a subtle way of highlighting what one wants to believe and avoiding what one does not wish to face.

Or as Chilton (1996: 58) claims:

> Of course investigation of cognitive and linguistic structures [metaphors] would be merely academic, were it not for the strong likelihood that cognitive and linguistic patterns enter into policy decisions (to put it no more deterministically) and thus policy actions.

And Lakoff bemoans the fact that in US public discourse conservatives have developed their own moral-political metaphors in ways which liberals have not (1996: 385), possibly because the latter share with Locke and other Enlightenment thinkers a suspicion of metaphors (p.387).

1.7   Conclusion: CATEGORY IS DIVIDED AREA

As a conclusion and postscript to this first chapter, and as a metacommentary on metaphor, I wish to return to the question of categorisation raised earlier in our discussion of Bourdieu. To start with we can acknowledge that the major metaphor for categories is a divided area.[8]

This is apparent from the lexis in Metalude where **divide** means 'to distinguish as belonging to separate categories' (*how can we divide the middle class from the working class?*), to **place** is to 'categorise in a particular class or group' (*the law places road rage in the same category as wife-beating*), **separate** means 'to consider independently as belonging to different categories' (*you can't separate technology from morality*), **pigeon-hole** means 'categorize' (*he can't be pigeonholed as a jazz musician*), **bifurcate**

---

8.   Despite suggestions that CATEGORY IS CONTAINER is a better label for the theme, the lexis of *boundary, fine line, straddle, overlap* etc. makes DIVIDED AREA a better source.

'divide into two categories or spheres of action' (*the responsibility for aid was bifurcated between* UNICEF *and the Red Cross*), **subdivide** 'divide a category into smaller categories' (*we subdivide such injuries into torsion and flexion injuries*)

The results of dividing are the categories or sub-categories which are divided spaces of various kinds: **segment** 'subcategory' (*a segment of the population of the US lives in dire poverty*), **sector** 'subcategory of an economy or large group' (*the poorest sectors of the population are immigrants*), **subdivision** 'division of a category into smaller categories' (*there is a subdivision of speech sounds into vowels and consonants*), **part** 'sub-category' (*spiders are not part of the insect family*), **compartment** 'category' (*he keeps his studies and his religious beliefs in separate compartments*), **demarcation** 'separate categorisation' (*in some English departments there is little demarcation between Literature and Film*).

The last of these examples introduces the idea of a boundary, a line which separates spaces and therefore categories: **boundary, dividing line** 'distinction between two types of thing' (*the boundary between medicine and superstition is sometimes unclear*), or between the category of what is known and what is not known as in **frontier** 'limit of knowledge', (*he has extended the frontiers of particle physics*).

When categorisation is difficult then the dividing line is not clear: it may be **blurred, smudged** 'not clearly differentiated or categorised' (*the line between advertising and press reporting is becoming badly smudged/blurred*), a **grey area** 'situation difficult to categorise where the rules are uncertain' (*surrogate motherhood is a legal grey area*), or so thin it is difficult to detect – **a fine line** 'distinction that's difficult to make' (*there's a fine line between paedophilia and natural attraction to children*). Alternatively, the thing to be categorised may fall on the **borderline** 'in or between subjects' (*medicine is on the borderline of zoology and psychology*).

Category distinctions can be ignored or disappear in various ways and to various extents. The categories may **overlap** 'be partly the same' (*the areas of interest in the two organisations overlap but are not identical*). Another topic or text may fit into two categories, **straddle** 'combine two different topics' (*the study of metaphor straddles linguistics and psychology*). If one category includes another it will **colonize** 'take over another subject area' (*literary studies has been colonised by feminism*). Alternatively various categories may be subsumed into a larger more general category which covers them as in **cover-term** 'general term of classification' ('*vehicle*' *is a cover term for cars, lorries, bikes etc*), or **umbrella, blanket** 'applying generally' ('*cat*' *is also an umbrella/blanket term for tigers, lions etc*). These general classifications or inclusions are **overarching** 'including or affecting every type of area, person or thing' (*the overarching principle in all government policy is to make education a priority*). Otherwise a more general term can be seen as a large bag with several compartments – **portmanteau** 'covering a wide range of items, usually for a single purpose' (*it was kind of portmanteau bill, covering everything from fighter planes to army supplies*).

Following Benveniste, Bourdieu enjoys delving into the etymology of such categorical divisions. He identifies the power to categorise with the power of the king, by analogy with the delimitation of territory over which the king has control, using the etymology of the cognate vocabulary *regio* ('region'), *rex* ('king'), *regere fines* ('to rule straight lines or national boundaries'), *diacrisis*, ('decree'). He also connects this with language and discourse through *auctor* ('author') and *auctoritas* ('authority').

> The etymology of the word region (*regio*), as described by Emile Benveniste, leads to the source of the di-vision: a magical and thus essentially social act of *diacrisis* which introduces by *decree* a decisive discontinuity in natural continuity (between the regions of space but also between ages, sexes, etc.). *Regere fines,* the act which consists in "tracing out the limits by straight lines", in delimiting "the interior and the exterior, the realm of the sacred and the realm of the profane, the national territory and the foreign territory", is a *religious* act performed by the person invested with the highest authority, the *rex*, whose responsibility is to *regere sacra*, to fix the rules which bring into existence what they decree, to speak with authority, to pre-dict, in the sense of calling into being, by an enforceable saying, what one says, of making the future that one utters come into being. The *regio* and its frontiers (*fines*) are merely the dead trace of the act of authority which consists in circum-scribing the country, the territory (which is also called *fines*), in imposing the legitimate, known and recognised definition (another sense of *finis*) of frontiers and territory – in short the source of legitimate division of the social world. This rightful act, consisting in asserting with authority a truth which has the force of law, is an act of cognition which, being based, like all symbolic power, on recogni-tion, brings into existence what it asserts (*auctoritas*, as Benveniste again reminds us, is the capacity to produce what is granted to the *auctor*). Even when he merely states with authority what is already the case, even when he contents himself with asserting what is, the *auctor* produces a change in what is: by virtue of the fact that he states things with authority, that is, in front of and in the name of everyone, publicly and officially, he saves them from their arbitrary nature, he sanctions them, sanctifies them, consecrates them, making them worthy of existing, in con-formity with the nature of things, and thus "natural" (Bourdieu 1991: 221–2).

The point is that the authority, the arbiter, is the one with the power to make categori-sations and assign to social roles. *Kategorein* originally meant 'to accuse publicly, to be told what you are', and so "social essence is the set of those social attributes and attribu-tions produced by the act of institution as a solemn act of categorization which tends to produce what it designates" (p. 121). Though distinctions and categorisations often give the appearance of being based on objective differences, in fact, especially in the case of categorising social classes, we are dealing with continua, and different critical features used for classification will give us different categories, since these features seldom clus-ter congruently. In education, of course the continuum of marks has to be divided by the arbiter to separate the lowest pass mark from the highest failing mark (p. 120).

For Bourdieu social and political struggle is a "struggle over the power of preserv-ing or transforming the social world by preserving or transforming the categories of perception of that world" (p. 236). "Science is inevitably involved in this struggle and agents wield a power which is proportional to their symbolic capital, that is, to the recognition they receive from the group" (p. 238).

Both Lakoff and Bourdieu are looking for a middle way between Objectivism and Subjectivism. As the latter puts it this middle way is "that 'reality' which is the site of a permanent struggle to *define* 'reality'", a struggle between an objectivism which ignores how representations evoke a reality, and a subjectivism which states there is no reality apart from representation (p. 224)). One can, perhaps, propose some such framework as follows. There exists a real world, but we have no direct "real" knowledge of it, since that knowledge is produced discoursally and linguistically through conventionalised metaphors, some of which are so conventionalised we call them literal. Knowledge of the world is mediated through perception, cognition and language/discourse. However, meaning and cognition certainly is grounded in our interaction with a real world and we do experience this real world, especially through the material consequences of our actions. Although we have no direct knowledge of this world, we develop those metaphorical models and categories which are positively adaptive to our environment, both physical, and, hopefully, social, too. They are tested against experience, through feedback, and if the models and categories are more or less true they promote our physical and social survival and well-being. If these models are wrong we become sick, endangered, or fail to survive. These models, perceptual, linguistic and discoursal, are crucially dependent on the dominant metaphors or semantic categories which we absorb with our first language. And part of the purpose of this book is to raise the possibility that some of these widespread and unchallenged metaphorical themes or models are not conducive to the future survival and well-being of the human race: a lot of negative feedback is coming our way.

CHAPTER 2

Metaphors of power

"Technology recognises no self-limiting principle – in terms … of size, speed or violence" E. F. Schumacher

2.1 Introduction

In chapter 1 we saw that the lexicon of English is permeated by conventional metaphors that do not occur in isolation but belong to sets, variously known as conceptual metaphors, or metaphor themes. These metaphors are used quite unconsciously much of the time, but nevertheless structure the way we think and act. A fairly trivial example of this is the metaphor theme LESS IS LOW, which influences department stores to place goods with reduced prices in the "bargain basement". In this chapter I will take a number of important metaphor themes and show how they are associated with our social behaviour in modern capitalist societies and the power relations we observe in those societies. In other words we will be exploring how these metaphors can be realised non-linguistically (Kövecses 2002: chapter 5). We will see that most of these metaphor themes have ideological implications, in the sense that they are recruited and used by those exerting economic, scientific, political or personal power.

2.2 IMPORTANT IS BIG, POWER/CONTROL IS ABOVE, IMPORTANCE/STATUS IS HIGH

Several metaphor themes use size as a source for quality in general, and height as a multivalent source for positive qualities in particular. Four of these, which overlap to a certain extent, are IMPORTANT IS BIG, POWER/CONTROL IS ABOVE, IMPORTANCE/STATUS IS HIGH and ACHIEVEMENT/SUCCESS IS HIGH.

Big means 'important' or 'successful' when applied to things or events as in **big decision** (*whether to go to university or not is a big decision*), **big day, big time** 'state of being famous or successful', **biggie** 'something successful or of great importance' (*the movie The Quiet American could have been a biggie if it hadn't attacked US patriotism*), **make a big thing of** 'overemphasise the importance of something', **make it big** 'become famous or successful', **big league** 'most important level of a sport or activity', **have big ideas** 'optimistic ideas about future success'. And its synonyms also express importance, success or significance: **bulk large** 'be considered important', **magnitude** 'importance, status', **gigantic** 'extremely important or impressive' (*you have made gigantic improvements to your first draft*), **titanic, monumental** 'very important or outstanding'. Just as frequently large size is metaphorically applied to important or successful people: **big fish/gun/noise/shot** 'powerful or important person', **big name** 'famous or important person', **Mister Big** 'most important person in an organisation', **giant, colossus, titan** (referring literally to one of the mythical giants) both meaning 'very important and impressive in relation to an activity' (*Placido Domingo was a titan of the operatic stage*), **grand,** 'impressive and important', **great** (*history is not just the stories of great men*), and even the pejorative **fat cat.**

Upper means 'of important status' as in **upper class, upper echelons, upper crust; high** and its synonyms means 'having an important position' as in **high up, high-powered, exalted;** and 'the most important position' is **top,** as in **top job, top people, top of the pile, top dog, top level** or **summit** – 'meeting involving the most important people'. If you have reached a position of importance you can **walk tall,** and if you haven't you can always **look up to** those who have or **set your sights higher.** Things or tasks that are important are also seen as high as in **high on the list** or **top priority.**

High is also a metaphor for power and dominance, as in **high places, high handed,** and **over** or its synonyms means 'in control of' as in **lord it over, oversight, overlord, superior, on top of.** The most powerful person is the **top man/woman** or the person **at the top of the tree.**

Additionally, **height** is a source for success, meaning 'most successful period, point or stage of development' (*at the height of his career he was giving 2 concerts a week*), as also in the following compounds: **high noon** (*she produced her best-known music at the high noon of her romantic phase*), **high tide** (*the high tide of Bush's presidency was the campaign in Afghanistan*), **high-water mark** (*this was almost certainly the high-water mark of her career*). Words for the highest points of objects **peak, summit, apex, pinnacle, zenith,** mean 'most successful period or point' (*he was at the/peak/summit/apex/pinnacle/zenith of his career by the age of 35*). A person expected to be successful is a **high-flier,** and someone enjoying success or popularity is **riding high.** In some cases **the sky's the limit** 'there's nothing to prevent them achieving great success', so they may go **onward and upward** into the **stratosphere. Top** and its synonyms also convey the idea of achieving success, **top of the tree** means 'the most successful level in your profession', and if you are more successful than competitors in your field you **come out on top,** or **tower over/above** them.

The confluence of these metaphor themes make size and particularly height impressive symbols of power, success, achievement and importance. In the 1988 federal election in Canada, the successful candidate, Brian Mulroney, was judged to be taller after the election than before (Herman 1990). Moreover, this symbolism can even be translated into financial terms. A report in *Journal of Applied Psychology* (Judge and Cable 2004), which averages the result of four studies, finds that a person who is 1.8 metres tall can be expected to earn US$5,525 more per year than someone of 1.65 metres.

The symbolism of height as power is especially noticeable in the penchant for tall buildings. At least as far back as biblical times building high has been interpreted as a power statement. In the story of the tower of Babel, God interpreted it as a threat to "his" own power:

> Now the whole world had one language and a common speech. As men moved eastward they found a plain in Shinar and settled there … Then they said "Come, let us build ourselves a city, with a tower that reaches to the heavens, so that we may make a name for ourselves and not be scattered over the face of the whole earth."
>
> But the Lord came down to see the city and the tower that the men were building. The Lord said, "If as one people speaking the same language they have begun to do this, then nothing they plan to do will be impossible for them. Come, let us go down and confuse their language, so they will not understand each other."
>
> So the Lord scattered them from there over all the earth, and they stopped building the city. That is why it was called "Babel" – because there the Lord confused the language of the whole world. From there the Lord scattered them over the face of the whole earth. (*Genesis* ch. 11, verses 1–9, New International Version)

To the present day governments and corporations continue to build higher in order to express their political and economic power. Table 4 gives some indication of this continuing trend.

The first country to symbolize its power and success was the US with, among others, the Chrysler Building and Empire State Building. But Table 4 shows an increasing trend towards tall buildings in the Middle and Far East. Lack of land and density of population may contribute to the upward thrust towards the sky, as is the case with Hong Kong, but a sense of inferiority induced by colonisation and imperialism may also be a factor. Malaysia is less densely populated than parts of Europe, but it has, at the time of writing, the tallest twin towers. Many buildings in the Far East were planned during the years of the East Asian economic boom, when leaders like Mahathir Mohammed and Lee Kuan Yew were presenting their economic success as an indication of the superiority of "Asian values" over decadent Western values. (These values include, one supposes, the Chinese superstition about the luck of number 8, seen in the number of buildings with 88 floors.) Perhaps the tall buildings are a way of asserting identity in a post-colonial era, and in the teeth of the economic imperialism of the US.

Now, apparently, the countries of East Asia are vying amongst themselves for the prestige of the tallest building. Taiwanese officials were reportedly very pleased that Taipei 101 was built ahead of Shanghai's World Financial Centre, expected to be complete in 2007. This rivalry reflects politics, given the tension between China and Taiwan, which it regards as a renegade province. Others joining the skyscraper race include South Korea, beginning construction of Seoul's 580m International Business Centre in 2004, and Japan anticipating X-Seed 4000, which will be taller than Mount Fuji. Certainly many such tall buildings symbolise economic power, the vast majority housing banks or big corporations, by contrast with their religious symbolism in classical or medieval times.

Table 4. The World's Tallest Buildings
(Retrieved from http://www.infoplease.com/ipa/A0001338.html July 21st 2003)

No.	Building	Completed	Stories	Metres	Feet
1.	Taipei 101, Taipei, Taiwan	2003	106	508	1,667
2.	Petronas Tower 1, Kuala Lumpur, Malaysia	1998	88	452	1,483
3.	Petronas Tower 2, Kuala Lumpur, Malaysia	1998	88	452	1,483
4.	Sears Tower, Chicago	1974	110	442	1,450
5.	Jin Mao Building, Shanghai	1999	88	421	1,381
6.	2 International Finance Center, Hong Kong	2003	88	412	1,352
7.	Citic Plaza, Guangzhou, China	1996	80	391	1,283
8.	Shun Hing Square, Shenzhen, China	1996	69	384	1,260
9.	Empire State Building, New York	1931	102	381	1,250
10.	Central Plaza, Hong Kong	1992	78	374	1,227
11.	Bank of China Tower, Hong Kong	1989	70	369	1,209
12.	Emirates Tower One, Dubai	1999	55	355	1,165
13.	The Center, Hong Kong	1998	79	350	1,148
14.	T & C Tower, Kaohsiung, Taiwan	1997	85	348	1,140
15.	Aon Centre, Chicago	1973	80	346	1,136
16.	John Hancock Center, Chicago	1969	100	344	1,127
17.	Burj al Arab Hotel, Dubai	1999	60	321	1,053
18.	Chrysler Building, New York	1930	77	319	1,046
19.	Bank of America Plaza, Atlanta	1993	55	312	1,023
20.	Library Tower, Los Angeles	1990	75	310	1,018
21.	Telekom Malaysia HQ, Kuala Lumpur	1999	55	310	1,017
22.	Emirates Tower Two, Dubai	2000	56	309	1,014
23.	AT&T Corporate Center, Chicago	1989	60	307	1,007
24.	JP Morgan Chase Tower, Houston	1982	75	305	1,002
25.	Baiyoke Tower II, Bangkok	1997	85	304	997
26.	Two Prudential Plaza, Chicago	1990	64	303	995
27.	Kingdom Centre, Riyadh	2001	30	302	992
28.	Pyongyang Hotel, Pyongyang, N. Korea	1995	105	300	984
29.	First Canadian Place, Toronto	1975	72	298	978
30.	Wells Fargo Plaza, Houston	1983	71	296	972

If height is a metaphor for success, power, status and importance, then loss of these qualities is movement downwards. **Fall** means 'fail, be defeated and lose power' (*the Government fell after losing the support of the unions*), **fall down** and **fall down on** mean 'fail', **downfall** 'failure', **fall flat** 'fail completely', as do the synonyms **crash** and **collapse**. A terribly failure is an **abysmal** one. If you are in danger of failure or losing power you **totter,** especially if you **overreach yourself** 'fail because you are trying to achieve too much'. It follows that if you wish to reduce someone's power or bring about their failure you try to make them fall: **topple, undermine** or **cut the ground from under** them, **overthrow** them and, once they are on the ground, **come down on them like a ton of bricks.**

All the lexical items in the last sentence can be applied literally to buildings. Which brings us to the World Trade Centre. When built, at 1353 feet, these twin towers were the tallest in the world. Individually they were the tallest buildings in New York, the second tallest in the US, and, at the time of the 9/11 attacks, the 5th tallest in the world. The WTC had 110 floors and nine million square feet of office space. From the observation towers at the top it was possible to see 45 miles in every direction (http://www.greatbuildings.com/buildings/World_Trade_Center.html). There were other reasons to target these particular buildings – their symbolising the unjust world trading system that has made the poorest African countries poorer in the last 15 years, and their location in New York, the centre of the world's financial markets. But, simply because of their size and height, they made an excellent target for those wishing to assert their own power and symbolically reduce the power, success and importance of the US (Lakoff 2001). This act, this ideological statement, depends for its symbolism on the metaphor themes we have illustrated and the conceptual structure which underlies them. As an Egyptian poet put it when trying to account for 9/11 in terms of the inferiority complex and humiliation of young Arab men: "dwarves are walking the streets looking for tall buildings, for towers to pull down".

Having suffered the humiliation of 9/11, the US, quite predictably, is planning to build, on the site of the old twin towers, the Freedom Tower, the world's tallest building at 541 metres. The height of this tower is, in "imperial" measurements, 1776 ft, 1776 being the date of the US Declaration of Independence.

On a more environmental note we might consider the costs of building such large structures, and of keeping them functioning. The collapse of the Mayan civilisation in Central America – Guatemala, Honduras and Mexico – may have been precipitated by the enormous environmental costs. This civilisation appeared to have an obsession for building taller and taller pyramids. The problem was that a pyramid was made up of 16% mortar, the production of which depended on the firing of limestone. By some estimates, for every bucket of limestone produced, six buckets of wood were needed. One theory is that the Mayan civilisation collapsed because of the deforestation caused by this process. However, for the moment, the colossal waste of energy in running modern tall buildings does not seem to matter to the builders or owners, in fact, the profligacy may enhance their status. For example the Sears Tower in Chicago uses up more energy resources in a 24-hour period than the entire city of Rockford Illinois, with its 147,000 inhabitants (Rifkin 1987: 232).

2.3   IMPORTANT IS CENTRAL

When we experience objects, probably both visually and through touch, we divide them into parts, such as one side or another, or centres and peripheries. More specifically, our experience of containers is that the valuable things they contain are inside or near the centre, and the most important or vital organs of ours bodies are internal and near our core. Experience of weight may interact experientially with our visual senses so that visual centre and centre of gravity mutually define each other.

However this arises, we have a notion of centre and periphery and the idea that what is central is more important than what is on the edge. **Central** means 'most important' (*investment was central to our economic success*), **centrepiece** 'most important, interesting or attractive feature', **centre stage** 'prominence, importance', **core** 'most basic and important' and the **inner circle** 'the most powerful or important group in an organisation'. The most important element is metaphorically the centre of other objects such as the body – **heart** (*consumerism is the heart of the US economic system*), bones – **marrow**, (*let's get to the marrow of the problem*), plant – **pith, kernel** (*the pith/kernel of the argument is in the last two sentences*), arch – **keystone** (*Japan's co-operation was the keystone in the regional agreement*), cell or atom – **nucleus** (*these players will form the nucleus of a new team*). The central point is the most important thing around which others **revolve** or **pivot** (*my life in retirement revolves around butterfly collecting in summer and skiing in winter*). By contrast, the unimportant or less important elements are **peripheral, marginal,** or **fringe.** The side is also a source for relative unimportance: **sidelight** 'interesting but unimportant piece of information', **on the sidelines** 'not involved and not important', **sideline** 'to ignore as unimportant' (*I've been sidelined by the company for years,*), **sideshow** 'an activity that is less important or serious than the main one', **side issue** 'not the main problem', **sidekick** 'assistant working for someone more important', **side-effect** 'extra effect besides the main effect'.

What interests me about this pattern is that the metaphor theme can be applied to places that are not literally central. (How could a place be naturally central in any case, given the continuity of the surface of the earth?) So **centre** means 'the place which exerts the most important influence' (*Boston became a centre for genetic modification*), **hub** means 'the most important part where there is the most activity' (*the hub of the criminal operations was Chicago*) and **heartland** 'the most important area, part or sector' (*poor areas are the heartland of government support*).

The disquiet that humans felt about the views of Copernicus that the earth was not the centre of the universe, but revolved around the sun, is still prevalent in some circles. Apparently Catholic Apologetics International is offering $1,000 for the first person to prove that the earth revolves around the sun. They prefer the view that "the Earth is the centre of the universe, and the stars, sun and moon revolve around a stationary earth" (*New Scientist*, 1/6/2002: 96 (no author)).

One of the effects of this metaphor theme is that we no longer see real geographical space as equal in importance. As soon as we start talking about urban **centres** we encourage a mindset in which the countryside is less important and towns are more important. In Human Geography this has been theorised as the core-periphery model, "a model of the geography of human activity based upon the unequal distribution of power in economy, society and polity" (Lee 2000: 115). In this model the periphery is dependent upon the core, generally because of the link between the state and capital, so that there will be flows of wealth from the producers in the periphery to the ruling capitalist class in the core. The centre becomes the "locus of control over the means of production", since "unequal exchange, the concentration of economic power, technical progress and productive activity at the core, and the emanation of productive innovations from the core, help to maintain the flow of surplus value from periphery to core" (p. 116)

We saw in the case of buildings that, in order to symbolise an already perceived importance, success or power, they have been built higher and higher. We perhaps have a similar effect when countries decide that the most important cities politically and administratively, i.e. the capitals, are moved from the edge of the country to the middle of it. This has taken place in the cases of Nigeria, which moved its capital from Lagos to Abuja, Brazil, which shifted theirs from Rio de Janeiro to Brasilia, and currently Burma (Myanmar), reflecting the fact that people high up in the social hierarchy tend to be located centrally (Bourdieu 1991: 226). However, much more significant than these three rather trivial examples, the emphasis on inequality between the countryside and the town, implied by the metaphor of an urban **centre** or **hub,** may encourage population drift to the cities. At the least, the economic, political and cultural importance of towns, cities and capitals is reinforced by the application of the word **centre**.

Urbanisation represents a revolution in humans' styles of living. During the 20th century there were enormous changes in this respect. In 1900 around 14% of the world's population were living in urban areas, and there were only 12 cities that had more than one million inhabitants. In 2000, some 47% of the world's population lived in urban areas (about 2.8 billion), and the number of cities with more than 1 million people had reached 400 (Human Population: Fundamentals of Growth and Change 2001). The sheer size of urban populations can be seen in Table 5.

By 2010 the majority of the world population will be living in urban areas. By 2030, the UN estimates the proportion will reach 60%, that is 4.9 billion people. 95 percent of this huge urban increase will occur in poorer countries, as Table 6 makes clear (World Urbanization Prospects: The 1999 Revision, 2000). The urban populations of both China and India, for example, will grow by more than 340 million by 2030.

Table 5. World's ten largest agglomerations

CITY	POPULATION IN MILLIONS
Mexico City	25.6
Sao Paulo	22.1
Tokyo	19
Shanghai	17
New York	16.8
Calcutta	15.7
Mumbai	15.4
Beijing	14
Los Angeles	13.9
Jakarta	13.7

Table 6. Ten fastest-growing cities (from *An Urbanizing World: Global Report on Human Settlements* 1996 UN Centre for Human Settlements (Habitat)

Ten fastest-growing
major cities
1980-90[1]

	Annual average growth rate
Dhaka	6.2%
Lagos	5.8%
Karachi	4.7%
Jakarta	4.4%
Mumbai	4.2%
Istanbul	4.0%
Delhi	3.9%
Lima	3.9%
Manila	3.0%
Buenos Aires	2.5%

This rapid urban growth, of course, creates many problems, especially in the poor world. A huge section of urban populations live in poverty. They lack access to clean water, sanitation, and adequate housing. Many are forced to live in areas highly vulnerable to natural disasters such as flooding or landslides. Large cities in poor countries tend to develop ever-widening gaps between the rich and the poor. This can lead to political instability and a breakdown of previously existing order.[1]

Additionally, there are the social problems associated with the megalopolis. The drift into these large urban centres creates "a rapidly increasing and ever more intractable problem of 'drop-outs', of people, who, having become footloose, cannot find a place anywhere in society. Directly connected to this, it produces an appalling problem of crime, alienation, stress, social breakdown, right down to the level of the family" (Schumacher 1973/1999: 52).

But we should not romanticise the countryside, since living in the city brings counterbalancing advantages. Cities are likely to have more economic growth and employment, more opportunity for organising into unions than the dispersed populations of rural workers, chances of better education, and access to facilities such as a regular water supply, electricity and health care.[2] The importance of centres leads to more expenditure on public services, creating a vicious or virtuous circle. The logistics of transport and communications also mean that it is easier to travel from the countryside to a large town or capital, than cross country from one area in the countryside to another, as **hub** suggests, implying spokes which connect the peripheral areas with the centre. "All roads lead to Rome". Urban populations are, however, easier to monitor and control than rural ones. I doubt, for example, that the Chinese government is any less eager to control its population than the government of Singapore, but Singapore, being a city state, is much more successful in this respect.

Commodities can be more easily transported to cities too, which creates impersonal networks of trade and opportunities for consumption. In a city we consume goods and services in a market place with relationships to unknown and invisible people and places in every corner of the planet, relationships of almost unimaginable complexity, which are hidden from us when cash and commodities exchange hands and we finally consume the things we have purchased (Cronon 1991: 378–84, cited in Harvey 1996: 232).

Perhaps, then, just as important is the psychological perception that cities are places of glamour and opportunity, and this is reinforced by the two metaphor themes we have

---

1.   For example Dhaka had in 1996 the fastest growing urban population. Because opportunities for well-paid high-productivity jobs are scant the number of people defined as poor in the city grew by almost 2 million between 1980 and 2001. Only one quarter of the city's population is connected to the piped sewerage system and many have to use open latrines. Only two-thirds of the households have piped water. Not surprisingly, Dhaka has one of the highest rates of death from infectious disease of any city in Asia, and 9% of children born die before the age of five (McGee, Terry "Urbanization Takes on New Dimensions in Asia's Population Giants" *New Internationalist* October 2001).

2.   In poor countries on average, 78% of urban dwellers have access to safe water while only 64% of rural people do; 64% in cities have access to sanitation but only 20% in villages. (McGee, Terry "Urbanization Takes on New Dimensions in Asia's Population Giants" *New Internationalist* October 2001)

been considering. Not only are towns more important because they are centres and hubs, but also because they are big (See section 2. 2), in terms of size and population.

The myth of Dick Whittington is alive and well. He is a bourgeois capitalist hero, reflecting the fact that urban centres are prototypically constructed by capitalism, under which

> new networks of places arise, constituted as fixed capital embedded in the land and configurations of organised social relations, institutions, etc. on the land. New territorial divisions of labour and concentrations of people and labour power, new resource extraction activities and markets form. The geographical landscape which results is not evenly developed but strongly differentiated. "Difference" and "otherness" of space are *produced* in space through the simple logic of uneven capital investment, a proliferating geographical division of labour... (Harvey 1996: 295).

As the phrase "not evenly" suggests, the two metaphor themes that we have been considering are related, since tall buildings, investments of fixed capital, especially banks, tend to be built in urban "centres". Tall buildings become, as it were, a beacon of attraction calling the population towards them, just as the Tower of Babel was designed to prevent the people from scattering across the land. William Golding captures this well in *The Spire*, where he describes how the medieval cathedral, modelled on Salisbury, functions as the hub of a great wheel to which all roads converge. In this extract Jocelyn, the priest pursuing his vision of building a spire on top of the existing tower, surveys the countryside from its unfinished top.

> He opened his eyes and found that he was looking away from the tower and out into the world: and it had changed in nature. It had bent itself into a sort of bowl, detailed there, sweeping up and behind that into a blue rim … At the nearer ridge of the downs, there were knobs and lumps appearing, as if bushes were growing by magic. As he watched they pushed up, and became men. Behind them were more knobs which became horses, asses in foal with panniers, a whole procession of travellers with burdens. They came straight over the nearer ridge from the one so bluely outlined behind it. They were moving straight down the hill towards his eye, towards the tower, the cathedral, the city. They had not gone down by the west, circling down by Cold Harbour to make their way slanting along the deep trench that generations of hooves had cut. They were saving time, if not labour. In a flash of vision he saw how other feet would cut their track arrowstraight towards the city, understood how the tower was laying a hand on the whole landscape, altering it, dominating it, enforcing a pattern that reached wherever the tower could be seen, by sheer force of its being there. He swung round the horizon and saw how true his vision was. There were new tracks, people in parties, making their way sturdily between bushes and through heather. The countryside was shrugging itself obediently into a new shape. Presently, with this great finger [the spire] sticking up, the City would lie like the hub at the centre of a predestined wheel. New Street, New Inn, New Wharf, New Bridge; and now new roads to bring new people (Golding 1964: 105–108).

2.4   RACE IS COLOUR, GOOD IS PURE/CLEAN/WHITE

Racial classification is largely a cultural construct rather than a scientific one, and I would highly recommend Jonathan Marks' *What it Means to be 98% Chimpanzee* (2002) for the most incisive and detailed account of its construction. Before DNA analysis became possible geneticists tried to use blood groups to furnish a scientific basis for racial classification, suggesting that a pure European O blood group must have been invaded by an A race from the north and a B group from the south. However, African populations were found to belong to O, A, and B types so that blood groups could provide no basis for racial classification (Marks 2002: 63). DNA evidence also fails to support a scientific classification of race.

> The overwhelming bulk of detectable genetic variation in the human species is between the individuals within the same population. About 85% in fact. Another 9% of the detectable variation is between populations assigned to the same "race"; while interracial differences constitute only about 6% of the genetic variation in the human species" (p. 82).

Table 7. Linnaeus's Classification of the species Homo Sapiens in *System Naturae* (1798) (quoted in Marks 2002: 57, adapted by adding row 4 with information from the text)

	American	European	Asian	African
Colour	Red	White	Yellow	Black
Temperament	Irascible, impassive	Vigorous, muscular	Melancholy, stern	Sluggish, lazy
Humours	Choleric	Sanguine	Melancholy	Phlegmatic
	Yellow bile	Blood	Black bile	Phlegm
	Gallbladder	Heart	Spleen	Pituitary
Face	Thick straight black hair	Long blond hair, blue eyes	Black hair dark eyes	Black kinky hair, silky skin, short nose, thick lips, females with genital flap, elongated breasts
Personality	Stubborn, happy, free	Sensitive, very smart, creative	Strict, contemptuous, greedy	Sly, slow, careless
Covered by	Fine red lines	Tight clothing	Loose garments	Grease
Ruled by	Custom	Law	Opinion	Caprice

The explanation is that people are genetically similar and bodily similar to those who are near them geographically, because of interbreeding, and adaptation to different climates. "Skin pigment was a sunscreen for the tropics, eyelid folds were goggles for the tundra. The parts of the body that face the elements are also the parts that face the eyes of other people, which fools them into thinking that racial differences run deeper than they really do" (Pinker 2003: 143). Pure race then is a myth, and racial divisions are arbitrary, not natural and scientific (Marks 2002: 65–67). However, the imperialist enterprise felt the need to classify racially, since, if people are different, then there is an excuse to treat them differently.

Colour was a convenient mechanism for constructing the idea of different races. Linnaeus, the great botanical classifier, for example, came up with the scheme represented in Table 7. This table not only classifies by colour and facial characteristics, but correlates the four colours with the four humours of medieval and renaissance anatomy/physiology, and thereby relates the races to stereotypes of temperament and personality. Following Linnaeus, colour coding has become the main linguistic resource for preserving the illusion of race. These colour labels might seem metonymic, a person being referred to by the colour of their skin, but, whereas many Africans may have black skin, some are dark or light brown, Caucasians have pinky-grey skin, Mongolian races, including native Americans, have olive-coloured or light brown skin, and none could be literally described as red.

It seems, then that colour labels have developed into an analogical if not metaphorical system. **Colour** itself means 'racial identity' (*he felt he had been passed over for promotion because of his colour*), and we talk about racial prejudice as **colour prejudice**. Caucasians are variously and more or less pejoratively referred to as **white**, **whitey**, **lily-white**, **pinkies**, or **palefaces**. Non-Caucasians are therefore **non-whites** or **coloured**. Negroids or Afro-Caribbeans are referred to variously as **black**, **darkie**, **spade**. Native Americans become **Red Indians** or **redskins** and Chinese and other East Asians may be called **yellow**.

Caucasians have a vested interest in accepting the label **white** and Afro-Caribbeans good reason to reject the label **black**, because of the metaphor themes GOOD IS CLEAN/WHITE, and EVIL IS DARK/BLACK. Realising the first we have lexical items with positive meanings such as **white knight** 'person or organisation that rescues a company from financial difficulties', **fair** 'morally correct or just', **whiter than white** 'having a reputation for high moral standards', **lily-white** 'faultless in character', and even **white lie** 'harmless untruth', and **whitewash** 'cover up mistakes or bad behaviour'. Under the second we find mostly pejorative terms. These can either mean evil or wrong, as in **black** meaning 'bad' (*the future of the environment is very black*), or 'cruel or wicked' (*this is a blacker crime than most I've investigated*), **black and white** 'with clear distinctions between what is morally wrong and right', **black mark** 'fault or mistake that has been noted', **blackguard** 'a wicked person', **blackleg** 'someone who treacherously continues to work while other workers are on strike'; they can mean 'illegal', as in **black market**, **black economy**; or they can be associated with loss of reputation: **black sheep** 'bad person in a family who brings it into disrepute', and **blacken** 'destroy the good reputation of'. This metaphor theme also overlaps, to some extent, with EVIL IS DIRT.

The prejudice created by these associations between evil, crime and people of African race continues. For example, Peter Neufeld's programme of DNA testing to save those who have been wrongfully convicted, threw up some disturbing results.

In the US most rapes of white women are committed by white men, and of black women by black men. Only about 10% of sexual assaults are cross-racial. Yet approximately 60% of all our wrongful convictions were black men wrongfully convicted of sexually assaulting, or sexually assaulting and killing, white women (Novak 2003: 49).

As Balkin points out, the metaphor of black versus white gains much of its power from a set of interlocking oppositions or homologies: white : black :: law-abiding : criminal :: morality : immorality :: higher intelligence : lower intelligence :: knowledge : ignorance :: industry : laziness (Balkin 1998: 216). Many of these are already suggested by Linnaeus. In fact a majority of drug-users, welfare recipients and criminals are white (p.216).

To counter racial colour codes associated with the negative metaphorical lexis of EVIL IS DARK/BLACK "non-Caucasians" have promoted the alternative self-referential phrase *people of colour*. This associates Afro-Caribbeans with an altogether more positive metaphor theme EXCITEMENT IS LIGHT/COLOUR. Here **colour** means 'quality that gives interest or excitement' (*more action and conversation would add colour to your novel*) and **colourful** 'lively, interesting, amusing and exciting' (*anglers are famous for colourful stories about the fish that got away*). Words which literally mean 'lacking in colour or brightness' become negative, rather than positive as they were in GOOD IS CLEAN/WHITE, so **colourless, dull, grey, leaden, drab, pallid, monochrome** all mean 'boring, unexciting'. Perhaps people of colour, to redress the lexical bias, could begin to refer to whites as **colourless**.

The racist and imperialist enterprise is, as we have shown, predicated on strict racial divisions, an optical illusion using the metaphor of colour as a code. However, it links up in its ideological effects with a further metaphor theme GOODNESS IS PURITY, purity in the sense of being 'unmixed'. The link is provided by the fact that a white surface can be spoilt by black marks which are of a different colour. **Pure** means 'morally good' (*he has pure intentions towards you*) and **unalloyed**, literally describing an unmixed metal, means metaphorically 'not spoilt by being mixed with anything negative' (*I experienced unalloyed feelings of pleasure at the birth of my daughter*). Conversely **impure/impurity** means 'immoral/-ity, sinful/-ness' (*I begged God to take away my impurities*). If you **alloy** something you 'spoil or reduce its value' and a **mixed blessing** is an experience 'having advantages and disadvantages' (*winning the lottery turned out to be a mixed blessing*). Literally **adulterate** means 'spoil by adding something inferior' usually mixing a less valuable substance in with a food substance, but it can be applied metaphorically (*the socialist policies were adulterated with elements of fascism*). **Pollute/pollution** and **contaminate** all mean to 'have a harmful effect on morals' (*the pollution of young minds by the internet continues uncontrolled*), **defile** 'spoil the holiness of, desecrate or blaspheme against' (*the lecturer was accused of defiling the name of the prophet*), whereas **taint** means 'damage or harm someone's reputation'. Removing impurities becomes the source for two quite racist or eugenicist metaphors, **ethnic**

cleansing 'attempt by one racial group to purge a country of another racial group' and **purify** 'remove weak people from' (*Hitler wanted to purify the German population.*)

Incidentally, several of these metaphors have moral and religious meanings, and this may be related to the fact that obsessive-compulsive disorders involving cleanliness, are higher among Catholics than among the general population (Randerson 2002: 8). It is as though those who wish for high standards of morality symbolise this by a compulsion to be physically clean – "cleanliness is next to godliness". In fact, some see the desire for racial and other kinds of purity as originating in the moral sphere of divinity amongst primitive societies, with its notions of holiness and purity, as opposed to contamination and defilement, and the disgust which accompanies the latter (Pinker 2003: 273).

If, as a racist, one assumes that one race is superior to another, then, according to the logic of the GOODNESS IS PURITY analogy, physical distance between the races must be maintained, through segregation, or the banning of intimate contacts in mixed marriages. Laws against the latter continued in force in various US states until the 1950s. Nineteen states forbade black-white marriages, and some banned white marriages with Indians, Mongolians, Japanese, Chinese, and Malays (Marks 2002: 68). In the musical *Showboat* the hero avoids the charge of miscegenation by insisting that he has Negro blood in him, having just before cut his wife's hand and licked off the blood! Segregated schooling was advocated by such as Carleton Coon, who asked: "How can you put black and white children together, when the latest scientific research shows that blacks are 200,000 years of evolution behind blacks?" (quoted in Marks 2002: 77). Apartheid continued in South Africa until the 1990s.

The third way of preventing racial mixing, and adulteration of the superior race, is to have harsh immigration laws. Market capitalism, which since the collapse of the eastern bloc is supposed to have proved its superiority, would demand mobility of labour to match the mobility of capital. One can only conclude that the "distortions in the market" through defending borders against immigration may have their origin in the racist thinking that recruits the GOODNESS IS PURITY analogy.

An alternative ideology would celebrate mixing and "hybridity". In the words of Chan Kwok-bun:

> By hybridity I mean a kind of mutual entanglement of self and other, a two-way exchange that results in a fusion of belief and lifestyle so that the divide between two creatures, or two cultures, is spanned. … Hybridity is also the opposite of purity. Children know that if they mix the colour blue with the colour yellow, they will get something new – the colour green. Mixing two cultures as different as yellow and blue can result in something new, and also beautiful, as green is beautiful. In the process of becoming green, so to speak, the individual – who used to identify with yellow or blue – mixes with another culture, half forgetting himself, or herself. By the same token, that culture that has absorbed the different colour itself changes. This kind of cultural change is thus a process of remembering and of forgetting what we used to be.

> But a language of hybridity does not yet exist. We are searching for it so that
> we will not remain speechless in a world of isms: fundamentalism, essentialism,
> nationalism (Chan Kwok-bun 2003: A13).

In this quotation note, firstly, the natural recourse to metaphors of colour when discussing cultural and ethnic difference. And secondly the sense that the idea of hybridity lacks a language, whereas, by implication, and as demonstrated in this section, the
idea of purity is supported by a large number of metaphors.

2.5 DISEASE IS INVASION

One particular aspect of this schema of purity can be seen in attitudes to disease, in
the metaphor theme DISEASE IS WAR/INVASION (cf. Kövecses 2000a, TRYING TO CON-
TROL DISEASE IS WAR). This constructs disease of any kind (whether caused by bac-
teria/viruses or not) as an **attack** by **invaders** 'viruses or bacteria', or **foreign bodies**
from outside. Indeed, a recent TV series *The Body Invaders* ended with a programme
about arthritis and rheumatism! The bacteria **invade** 'enter the body', and may **strike
down** 'cause illness or death to' the victims, if they **succumb** 'become ill'. However, the
body may **defend** itself, **fight, combat** 'struggle to survive' the disease, through **resistance** 'immune response'. Medicine can attempt to **conquer** or **vanquish** 'eliminate' a
disease once and for all (though the military may keep stocks for biological warfare).

The military metaphor first came into wide use in medicine in the 1880s, when
bacteria were identified as causing disease by entering the body (Sontag 1991: 67) and
replaced a metaphor of disease as imbalance that can be traced back to Hippocrates.

> Since then military metaphors have more and more come to infuse all aspects of
> the description of the medical situation. Disease is seen as the invasion of alien
> organisms, to which the body responds by its own military operations, such as
> the mobilising of immunological 'defences', and medicine is 'aggressive' as in most
> chemotherapies (p. 95).

The extent to which this has become the commonsense way of constructing disease is
evident in this typical extract from the *New Scientist*:

Gene therapy gets the body to attack cancer

An **army** of immune cells that can **punch through the defences** of tumours has
been created by genetic engineering …

Most researchers trying to use the immune system to **beat** cancer focus on
boosting the immune response. That can have a dramatic effect. But even if the
body produces a vast **army** of immune cells against a cancer, it can still be foiled.
That's because many cancers release a slew of **protective** proteins including a vital one called transforming growth factor beta. TGF-β binds to immune cells and

tells them to stop **attacking their quarry**. It forms an invisible **fortress** around tumours. "Cancer's best **weapon** is TGF-β," says Lee.

To **breach this fortress** Lee's team added a mutated gene for a TGF-β receptor to cells from mouse bone marrow ... (Jones 2002: 10) [my bolding]

There are two areas of contemporary medical concern where this military metaphor is not particularly helpful – antibiotic resistant bacteria, and auto-immune diseases. The traditional approach, since the advent of penicillin, has been, in step with the military metaphors, to attempt to kill the invading bacteria. The problem with this approach is that bacteria multiply and mutate relatively quickly and antibiotic resistant strains develop, so eventually antibiotics decline in potency. For example *staphylococcus aureus*, a bacteria that infects wounds and causes blood poisoning in hospital patients, has become in turn resistant to penicillin and methicillin, and doctors now treat it with vancomycin. However, in 2002, the first case of resistance to vancomycin was recorded.

The new metaphor and approach for dealing with bacteria is to talk to them or, rather, prevent them talking with each other. It relies on the phenomenon of "quorum sensing". Evidently, many bacteria live in our bodies for long periods without doing us any harm, and only multiply uncontrollably when they know they are present in sufficient numbers to be successful against our immune systems. There is no point in them multiplying if they are present in such small numbers that they will be suppressed. "Quorum sensing" is their way of finding out whether there is a "quorum", i.e. that they are present in sufficient numbers to make their multiplication worthwhile. Research pioneered by Paul Williams of the University of Nottingham concentrates on developing methods of interfering with the bacteria's signalling mechanisms, so that even if they are present in sufficient numbers to get beyond the body's control, they will not know that they are, and will remain benign (Watts 2003: 30).

Auto-immune diseases occur when the lymphocytes in the body's immune system seem unable to distinguish self from non-self. They then begin to harm the body's own cells, which may lead to diseases such as rheumatoid arthritis, thyroid disease, anaemias of various types, and inflammatory bowel disease, namely, ulcerative colitis and Crohn's disease.

In relation to the latter a team of scientists from the university of Iowa has suggested a link between these bowel inflammations and the absence of certain parasites in the gut. Humans and other animals have been living with helminths, or worms, from time immemorial, and our guts have adapted to their presence. They normally reduce some aspects of our mucosal immune response. Therefore, without them we may over-produce powerful substances which cause excessive inflammation of the intestinal tract (Weinstock, Elliot, Summers & Qadir 1999).

The tendency to regard organisms from outside the body as invaders that need to be removed has led to the eradication of such worms. It may be that the consequences of their removal have been harmful, and that we should have seen this as a symbiotic relationship, not as a disease caused by invaders that need to be killed off (Elliot, Urban, Argo & Weinstock 2000). David Dunne and Anne Cooke of the University of Cambridge have shown that infestation by intestinal worms may reduce the incidence of auto-immune diseases in Africans (Ryan 2002: 232). Experiments with mice show that reintroducing helminthic worms can protect them from inflammatory bowel disease and trials of this treatment with humans are under way.

The epidemic of asthma amongst children in the industrialised towns of Europe might suggest that this too is an auto-immune disease. Some studies have found lower asthma rates in farming communities such as Bavaria, where children are raised near animals, and exposed to the pathogens they produce. This, too, suggests that isolating ourselves from other organisms and regarding them as invaders to be killed is counterproductive in treating or preventing many diseases. After all, we live in a symbiotic relationship with bacteria, especially in our gut. 90 percent of the dried weight of our faeces consists of the bodies of gut microbes. And everyone carries twenty times as many living bacteria as we do human cells. We have co-evolved with these miniscule partners with which we have reached some kind of equilibrium (Ryan 2002: 231).

These areas of research relate to a radical new conception, a new metaphor for the way the immune system works. Lymphocytes, or white blood cells, actually bind not only to foreign agents but also to many of the body's own cells, including other white blood cells. According to the traditional view this would mean that our bodies were under constant attack, in a state of perpetual civil war. But if we substitute the communication or regulation metaphor for the military one we can explain why auto-immune diseases are the exception rather than the norm.

> The entire system looks much more like a network, more like people talking to each other, than soldiers looking out for an enemy ... By interacting with one another and with the other body cells, the lymphocytes continually regulate the number of cells and their molecular profiles. Rather than merely reacting against foreign agents, the immune system serves the important function of regulating the organism's cellular and molecular repertoire (Capra n.d.).

With this new metaphor the puzzle of the self/non-self distinction can be resolved. The immune system has no need to distinguish between body cells and foreign agents, because both are regulated by the same processes. The reason that the immune system tries to eliminate infectious agents is simply because, multiplying in such large numbers, they cannot be incorporated into the regulatory network. Following the metaphor of regulation by communication, Capra sees the immune system as a cognitive, self-organizing and self-regulating network, rather than as an army ready to attack (Capra n.d.).

2.6 ACTIVITY IS MOVEMENT FORWARDS and the cult of speed

One of the most important clusters of conceptual metaphors or metaphor themes in the English language builds on ACTIVITY or PROCESS IS MOVEMENT FORWARDS, and ramifies into other equations such as DEVELOPING/SUCCEEDING IS MOVING FORWARD, INTENSE ACTIVITY IS SPEED, SUCCESS/EASE IS SPEED, and ACTIVITY/COMPETITION IS RACE. This schema is often referred to in the cognitive linguistics literature as the Event Structure metaphor.

Basically, a process or activity, whether it involves movement or not, is conceptualised as motion, and this was even the basis for Newtonian physics (See Chapter 7). **move**, then, means 'happen' (*now we have a new boss things are beginning to move faster*) and **a move** 'an action taken to achieve something' (*the cut in interest rates was a wise move*); 'to start working' is to **get moving** so that things are **in motion** 'happening or taking place'. In particular, activity/process is seen as going forwards as in **go** 'function' (*my watch isn't going*), **go on** 'happen' (*the head didn't know what was going on in the department*), **go forward** or **proceed** (*the play went forward despite the last minute changes to the cast*). More specifically the movement forward is running, as in **run** 'operate' and 'show or be performed' (*My Fair Lady is running in the theatre till May*), and **running** 'happening continuously over time' (*he also began a running feud with Saddam Hussein*); to 'become familiar with an activity' is thus to **get into your stride**, and 'a stage in a process' is a **step**. **Pursue** means 'to carry out an activity or plan'.

With a slight modification this metaphor merges into DEVELOPING/SUCCEEDING IS MOVING FORWARD (cf. Kövecses 2002). An 'improvement or successful development' is an **advance**, **progress** or a **leap**; if you 'succeed or improve' you **go places**, **go far**, **go/come a long way**, **forge ahead**; if you are 'likely to successfully complete' something you are **well on your way to** it, or **making headway** and 'to be the first to succeed at something' is to **blaze a trail**.

The intensity or rate at which an activity or process takes places is then associated with **speed/pace**: **quick**, **fast**, **rapid**, **swift**, **brisk** are such familiar metaphors that they are quite difficult to recognise as such; **rush** and **hurry** not only mean to move fast but 'do something/act quickly' (*he rushed his homework in order to watch the World Cup match*); working with extremes of intensity, energy and effort one is in **top gear** or at **full throttle** or working at **breakneck speed**, and **rush** also has the meaning of 'exhilaration'. A life style that is intense, energetic, and glamorous is thus **life in the fast lane**. To increase the rate or intensity of an activity you **accelerate** it (*the country will accelerate its privatisation programme*), **speed up**, **step/move up a gear**, **step on the gas**, **go into overdrive** or show a **spurt** 'a sudden brief increase in activity'. Activities or processes that increase their rate or intensity **pick up** or **gather pace**, and if they get out of control are **galloping** or **runaway** (*the economy was suffering from runaway/galloping inflation*). We notice, incidentally, that many such metaphors come from motoring, connecting to our later discussion of the obsession with fast cars and land speed records.

These speed metaphors for intensity or high rates of activity tend to double up as metaphors for success. In fact, etymologically, before it meant velocity, Old English *spede* meant 'success' or 'prosperity'.[3] The idea of a steady speed in the later sense arose with trains and "it was only in the machine age that people became aware of speed as a quality that could be measured, computed and adjusted. For the ancients speed was indefinable" (Gleick 1999: 51).

Developing from SUCCESS IS SPEED, we note the large number of metaphors in which activity, and especially competitive activity, is metaphorically viewed as a race. A race is, of course, one kind of competition between two or more participants in which success is measured by progress towards a destination. **Race** can mean 'competition for power or control' (*Maud and Andrew are involved in a race for promotion*), the **rat race** 'ruthless competition for success', and, because time is also seen as movement through space, it is possible to talk about the **race against time**, 'working very fast to finish before a deadline'. With less emphasis on competition we have **marathon** 'long and tiring activity', and **course**, literally 'the track along which one races' and metaphorically 'set of classes or periods of study'. One can decide to take part in competitive activities or **run** (*Gore ran in the last presidential election*), and if you **give someone a run for their money** you 'compete very strongly against someone'.

Before the (horse) race or competitive activity starts you will know who is taking part, 'all the other candidates for a job' – **the field**; who is 'the possible or probable winner of the contest' – **in the running** (*she's in the running for the leadership post*); 'the candidate or contestant most considered most likely to win' – **the favourite**; 'the contestant considered unlikely to win' – the **outsider**, or 'with no chance of winning' – **out of the running.**

'At the beginning of the race/activity' or **from the word go**, someone may **jump the gun** 'do something too soon' (*he jumped the gun by eating before everyone was served*), or be a **non-starter** 'person or idea that has no chance of success', or be **quick/slow off the mark** 'be quick/slow to act or to react to an event', while others may have a **head start** 'advantage in an activity or competition' (*good education gives your child a head start in life*).

Once racing you may **jockey for position** 'try to get into a more powerful or advantageous position than others' such as the **inside track** (*he had an inside track so his promotion is hardly surprising*), until you reach the **home stretch** 'the last part of a long or difficult activity' (*the eradication of polio is now in the home stretch*).

During the race or activity you may find it difficult to **stand the pace** 'cope with all the demanding activity', you may have **no time to draw breath** 'no opportunity to stop and think what you are doing', and so may be tempted to stop for a **breather** or **breathing space** 'period of rest or change' (*she felt she needed a breathing space between school and university*), before you get your **second wind** 'extra energy in completing a difficult task'.

Equality of speed will be a metaphor for competitive equality, so if you **keep up with** people you 'do work as well as other people', if you are **neck-a-neck** you are 'so

---

3.   This seems to reverse the normal pattern in which sources are more concrete than targets (Kövecses, personal communication)

close it's difficult to tell which will win a contest' (*the government and opposition parties are neck-a-neck in opinion polls*), and if you get behind you may be able to **close the gap on** 'reduce the difference in success rates' or **catch up with** 'reach the same standard or level as someone else' (*he's much better than me at maths, I doubt whether I can catch up with him*).

Leading in a race will indicate interim success: you may be **streets ahead** 'much better or more advanced in a field of activity' (*Singapore is streets ahead of Hong Kong in IT development*), **make the running** 'be more active than others', **set the pace** or be **the pacemaker** 'the most successful in a particular field or activity', the **front-runner** 'the person or idea that seems most likely to succeed', **streak ahead, pull ahead, get ahead** or **outdistance** 'be more successful than others' (*Airbus outdistanced Boeing in sales in 1999*).

Getting behind in the race will indicate interim failure: you may **trail** 'be less successful than' (*the government is trailing the opposition in opinion polls*), be **behind** or **lag behind**, in other words, a **laggard** 'thing which is less successful or developing more slowly than other things' (*this publishing house is a technological laggard – it still edits from hard copy not on screen*).

Winning the race is, of course, the ultimate success – as the slogan says "It's all about winning". Sometimes you do not know who will be successful until the very end and it's **down to the wire** 'until the very last moment or end of an activity/competition', where someone may overtake the leader at the last minute – **pip at the post** 'beat by a small margin' (*it was down to the wire – it looked as though Gore was going to win but Bush pipped him at the post*). Some kinds of electoral races have a **first-past-the-post** system 'election by majority of votes in one constituency'. If you lose the race or fail in the competition you are an **also ran** 'contestant that took part in a competition but did badly', and your records of successes and failures will be your **track record** (*his track record as a headmaster was excellent*).

I have gone into great detail in listing vocabulary in this nexus of metaphor themes, partly to demonstrate how important and pervasive it is, but also because it connects with many ideologies which we will be exploring in this and other chapters of the book. We will see later, for example, how constructing activity as a competitive race relates to the question of the HUMAN IS ANIMAL metaphor, through neo-Darwinians' and sociobiologists' construction of human society as inexorably competitive. For the moment, however, I simply wish to suggest that the equation of speed with success has a similar effect to the equation of power with height. It spurs humans to travel or run as fast as possible thereby creating a symbol of success and (illusory) sense of achievement.

The supreme track event in the Olympic Games is the men's 100 metres. Why? It could be the marathon, which, after all, is a formidable test of athleticism and endurance. The reason is that, because the 100 metres is run over the shortest distance, its result is supposed to tell us who is "the fastest man on earth" – and speed is the ultimate symbol of success. This desperate quest to run faster in the Olympic Games can be seen in Table 8. These relentless efforts have seen the time taken to run 100 metres fall by over 20% since the inception of the modern Olympics.

Table 8. Olympic 100 metres gold medal times

Year	Gold	Time
1896	Thomas Burke, USA	12.0
1900	Frank Jarvis, USA	11.0
1904	Archie Hahn, USA	11.0
1906	Archie Hahn, USA	11.2
1908	Reggie Walker, SAF	10.8
1912	Ralph Craig, USA	10.8
1920	Charles Paddock, USA	10.8
1924	Harold Abrahams, GBR	10.6
1928	Percy Williams, CAN	10.8
1932	Eddie Tolan, USA	10.38
1936	Jesse Owens, USA	10.3
1948	Harrison Dillard, USA	10.3
1952	Lindy Remigino, USA	10.79
1956	Bobby Morrow, USA	10.62
1960	Armin Hary, GER	10.32
1964	Bob Hayes, USA	10.06
1968	Jim Hines, USA	9.95
1972	Valeriy Borzov, URS	10.14
1976	Hasely Crawford, TRI	10.06
1980	Allan Wells, GBR	10.25
1984	Carl Lewis, USA	9.99
1988	Carl Lewis, USA	9.92
1992	Linford Christie, GBR	9.96
1996	Donovan Bailey, CAN	9.84
2000	Maurice Greene, USA	9.87
2004	Justin Gatlin	9.85

One interesting ambiguity in the word *race* is that it not only refers to competitive travel or running but also to a culturally imposed system of human classification. It is no accident that the modern Olympic Games were set up at a time of increased nationalism – the medal ceremonies and medal tables continually remind us of this link – but also at a time in which eugenic ideas were beginning to surface. The name that sticks out in this list is, for many people, Jessie Owens who won in 1936. The games, held in Berlin, were supposed to be Hitler's showcase of the superiority of the Aryan races, but the black man from the US destroyed the myth. It was, of course the hundred metres, the fastest race, which Hitler regarded as the most symbolically important.

Incidentally, one can pursue the suggestive ambiguity of *race* in the word *sport*. The less familiar meaning of the word is a "mutation", generally a plant mutation.

Given that genetic mutations are the basis for evolution, perhaps the relationship between competitive sports and eugenics is mirrored by the etymological link between the two meanings of the word.

A metaphor theme related to the idea that COMPETITIVE SUCCESS IS WINNING A RACE is IMPORTANT IS FIRST. **First, foremost, number one, primary, prior** all mean 'most important', **second, secondary** 'less important' and **third-rate** 'low in quality'. Within this framework *third world* becomes a term of condescension at best, and implies inferiority. It is hardly surprising that it has been contested with vocabulary like *the South* or *the majority world*.

Given the association of speed with engine-powered vehicles we can perhaps explain the obsession with fast cars and other vehicles. A great deal of time, enormous sums of money, and several lives have been sacrificed in competition for the World Land Speed Record (LSR). For example, the Campbell-Norris CN7 car, Bluebird, built for Donald Campbell in 1956, in an attempt to break the 400mph record, was believed to have cost over £1 million. Campbell crashed this car, miraculously surviving, but other competitors for the LSR, such as Frank Lockhart and Parry Thomas died after crashing, as did the odd spectator, though with less loss of life than with The Titanic, built by the White Star Line partly to compete with the North German Lloyd Line and the British Cunard Line for the North Atlantic speed record. Despite the costs in time, money and danger the drive to be the fastest car goes on and has risen from 143.31 mph in 1924 to 763.05 mph in 1997.

It is interesting, that, as with the Olympic Games, the World Land Speed Record has developed into a nationalistic race, in this case largely between Britain and the US, with an insignificant bit of competition from Australia, a nationalism detectable in the names of some of the vehicles involved: *Spirit of America, Aussie Invader.* In 1983, when the *Thrust 2* team set a new LSR of 633.468 mph, Richard Noble said, immediately afterwards, "For Britain, and the Hell of it" and Malcolm Campbell was knighted by King George V for breaking the record five times.[4]

Quite apart from the one-off cars specially designed for the land-speed record, manufactured sports cars have also been getting faster and faster. At present the fastest production car that can be bought and driven on the open road is the Lamborghini Diablo with a top speed of 338 km/h. One latest invention under development is the flying car, and the inventor claims that eventually "his M400 will carry four passengers, cruise at 500kms per hour, climb as high as 10,000 metres ... and travel 1400 kilometers without refuelling" (May 2003: 42).

There is evidence that this quest for speed is a male value. In an experiment boys and girls were asked to design a machine of their choice – girls tended to design flexible helpers for tasks, like an appliance for clearing snow or leaves, whereas the boys preferred powerful vehicles that did outlandish things like taking them wherever they wanted to go "the twin valve seven-booster, class 4 rocket" (Samuel 2002: 38).

---

4. Information in this section comes from the home-page of *The Splendid Whizzer Association.*

For an example of how the metaphor theme DEVELOPMENT/SUCCESS IS MOVE-MENT FORWARD is associated with car transport, consider the copy of the following ad for the Opel Vectra car.

WHEN YOU'VE MASTERED THE ART OF CONTROL PEOPLE WILL KNOW

(1) Remember all those moments when you wanted to say something, do something, but didn't?

(2) Times when you held back, because you were happier to let others take the lead. (3) And yet you know deep down that you wouldn't be who you are today, if it weren't for the decisions you'd made.

(4) Decisions that let you discover the power of individuality and the reward of independence. (5) So why should your mode of travel be so different from your mode of thought? (6) Why, indeed should you follow the pack when you could be leading it?

(7) When we designed the Opel Vectra, we set out to create a car that would sit at the very head of its class. (8) A car that gives you the power to go where you want, when you want. (9) And be capable of taking you the distance in comfort, safety and, yes, we dare say it, *style*.

(10) You know what it is to be an individual, to move while others are stationary, to take control of a situation and direct it in the way you want.

(11) When you drive the new Vectra you'll be reminded of all those moments when you pushed on with what you truly believed in. (12) And when you move others will follow, as they come to realise you have mastered the art of control.

OPEL

The copy exploits this metaphor theme so that the car comes to symbolise independence, leadership and success, as seen in the following interpretation:

QUOTE	METAPHORICAL MEANING
Times when you held back, because you were happier to let others take the lead.	Times when you were inactive and were happier for the others to do something first.
Why, indeed should you follow the pack when you could be leading it?	Why should you imitate other people's behaviour instead of initiating or modelling an activity (or obey other people instead of giving orders)?
A car that gives you the power to go where you want, when you want. And be capable of taking you the distance.	A car that gives you the power to do what you want when you want, and is capable of making you succeed.
To move while others are stationary, to take control of a situation and direct it in the way you want.	To achieve things while others are doing nothing, to take control of a situation and make what you want happen.

| When you pushed on with what you really believed in. | When you did the difficult things you really believed in. |
| And when you move others will follow. | When you do things others will imitate and obey. |

Notice, too, that the mobility given by the car symbolises independence (Sentence 4). This plugs into another metaphor theme, FREEDOM IS SPACE TO MOVE, details of which are given in chapter 5. But, as Schumacher (E.F. not Ralph or Michael!) comments, considering the environmental effects of high-energy consumption transport,

> while people with an easy-going kind of logic, believe that fast transport and instantaneous communications open up a new dimension of freedom (which they do in some rather trivial respects), they overlook that these achievements also tend to destroy freedom, by making everything extremely vulnerable and extremely insecure (1999: 68).

The logic he refers to is probably the kind of "metaphorical logic" that this book is exploring and critiquing.

The rapid urbanisation discussed under the metaphor theme of IMPORTANT IS CENTRAL is only possible if speed can be used to shrink or annihilate space and time. Before the 19th century most produce eaten in a city like Paris came from the immediately surrounding areas. It was only with the speeding up of transportation that the modern phenomenon of importing products from all corners of the globe for consumption within urban centres became possible. By this process "natural" time and space seems to shrink, increasing the ecological "footprint" of urbanisation. I enjoyed eating pink Florida grapefruit when living in Singapore, but at what cost in food miles?

Up to this point we have been seeing speed as a symbol of success, so that speed is a value in its own literal right, and the source or vehicle has been literalised. However, there is another aspect of this metaphor theme, by which the basic metaphor of activity as movement forward develops into the idea that reaching the goal, completing the activity, is more successful if it is, metaphorically, fast. Why this premium over finishing a task in a short space of time? There is nothing wrong in lingering over a poem, a cup of coffee, or sex. But once we are paid for our activities, then, as time is a commodity or money, measured by the hour, a premium is put upon completing tasks quickly. This produces a tendency to think that better is faster, just as we saw the tendency to think bigger and higher is better.

"We are a nation in love with speed. We drive fast, eat fast, make love fast. We are obsessed with breaking records and shortening timespans ... While other cultures might believe that haste makes waste, we are convinced that speed reflects alertness, power, success. Americans are always in a hurry" (Rifkin 1987: 71). We see this mania for completing asks as quickly as possible in our educational system. A premium is placed on speed in answering exam questions, in solving maths problems and in getting the right answer first in quiz shows.

The extent to which better has come to mean faster can be seen in a recent book *The Origins of Virtue* by Matt Ridley (1997), where he explains the theory of comparative advantage.

> Suppose there are only two commodities being traded: spears and axes. One tribe, called – for the sake of argument – Japan is good at making spears and very good at making axes; the other, called Britain, is bad at making spears and very bad at making axes. Superficially, it seems to make sense for the first lot to make their own spears and axes and not to indulge in trade at all.
>
> But hold on. A spear is worth a certain number of axes. Let us say that one spear is worth one axe. So every time the first tribe makes a spear, it is making something it could buy from the other tribe by making an axe. <u>Since it takes this tribe less time to make an axe than a spear</u>, it would be sensible to make an extra axe, instead of a spear, and swap it for a spear made by the second tribe. (p. 207, [my underlining])

Reading about Japan being very good at making axes, I assumed Ridley meant that the axes they produced were of higher quality. But, as the underlined clause makes clear, "being very good at making axes" simply means being able to make axes much quicker than average. Quality is here equated with speed, and this is indicative of the way in which we have been constrained in our thinking by the success is speed theme.

The drive for speed and lower costs at the expense of standards of workmanship is well expressed in the classic social documentary novel of the Edwardian era, Robert Tressell's *The Ragged-Trousered Philanthropists*. The workmen are put under pressure to complete a job in the shortest possible time under severe competitive pressure from other companies, which one workman jokingly calls "Pushem and Sloggem, Bluffem and Doemdown, Dodger and Scampit, Snatcham and Graball, Smeeriton and Leavit, Makehaste and Sloggit" (Tressell 1991: 163). Another of the workers, Newman, is fired for taking too much time and care over his work:

> He was at his old tricks. The woodwork of the cupboard he was doing was in a rather damaged condition, and he was facing up the dents with white-lead putty before painting it. He knew quite well that Hunter objected to any but very large holes or cracks being stopped, and yet somehow he could not scamp the work to the extent that he was ordered to; and so, almost by stealth, he was in the habit of doing it – not properly, but as well as he dared. (pp. 161–162).

When the remaining workers, forced to sacrifice their pride in doing their jobs properly, complete the job in as short a time as possible, one of them exclaims:

> "There it stands! A job that if they'd only have let us do it properly, couldn't 'ave been done with the number of 'ands we've 'ad, in less than four months; and there it is, finished, messed up, slobbered over and scamped, in nine weeks!" (p. 283).

Competitive cost-cutting in building and carpentry not only depressed wages, but also undermined a previous culture of "time-consuming" craftsmanship.

Evidence of the degree to which financial transactions have been speeded up is that up-to-the-second on-line trading probably now accounts for a quarter of all transactions by individual investors. This leads to unprecedented market volatility. On October 19th 1987 the computerisation of stock transactions amplified the herd instinct of Wall Street and produced a panic. Investors no longer had the time to consider their decisions, as the pre-programmed computers took over (Rifkin 1987: 117). More recently, during the bursting of the hi-tech bubble, in one three-hour period the NASDAQ lost 13% of its value. When a system is far from equilibrium, the sheer speed of these transactions adds a new dimension to the potential for chaos.

At a personal level, of course, there is pressure to save time by having fast food, rather than a home-cooked meal. McDonalds aim to have a restaurant within four minutes of everyone in the US. More surprisingly, some 21% of customers were willing to pay 35 cents to save themselves two seconds through automatic dialling a number just retrieved through information (Speed Up/Rush to Nowhere 2002).

2.7   Time and space metaphors

A consideration of the equation of success with speed, leads us naturally to a consideration of the way time is metaphorically represented. Time tends to be conceptualised in terms of space, and gives rise to five more specific metaphor themes which are relevant to ideology: TIME ELAPSING IS TRAVEL, and more specifically PERIOD IS SPACE, PERIOD IS LENGTH/DISTANCE, POINT IN TIME IS POSITION and TIME IS MONEY/COMMODITY.

Much has been written in the literature about the way time is conceptualised in terms of space. Time is a space that we are moving forwards through, or time is a moving object coming towards and past us, or time is itself moving forward (Yu 1998, Lakoff and Johnson 1999). What these conceptualisations have in common is the idea of time as linear rather than cyclical, and its association with movement.

Time can **pass**, **go by**, meaning 'elapse' (*time passes/goes by slowly when your boyfriend is away*), or **go on**, **roll by** 'continue to elapse' (*as time goes on/rolls by the memories of that far-off summer begin to fade*), **move on** 'bring changes by elapsing' (*time moves on and we need to change our operating system*), **drag** 'elapse slowly so that it seems long and boring' (*the time dragged while we waited for the results*) and so on.

There is no reason why time should be seen as linear. It is also possible for time's movement to be seen as cyclical, as in William Blake, or, combining the cycle and the line metaphors, as spiral, as in neo-Platonism or Marxism (Crisp 1993). The modern cosmological hypothesis that every big bang is eventually succeeded by a big crunch, giving rise to another big bang, provides some substance to the claim that history repeats itself eternally (Gribbin 1994). It was Judaism, and later Islam and Christianity which introduced the idea of time's linearity – a beginning, a culmination and an eschatological end (Harvey 1996: 214).

It is reported that one of the reasons China was slow to embrace new technology was its conception of time as cyclical rather than linear, lacking the notion of progress. We notice in this claim, which is, by the way, a slightly doubtful generalisation (Crisp 1993: 14), a metaphorical slippage by which movement of time forward becomes associated with progress – a logical sleight of hand whereby multivalent sources produce, if not an equation, at least a cause and effect relation between targets: TIME IS MOVEMENT FORWARD and DEVELOPMENT/SUCCESS IS MOVEMENT FORWARD. But I don't think that necessarily invalidates the claim.

Even people within Western culture may have different psychological attitudes to time. In an experiment conducted by Knapp and Garbutt students were asked to select the most satisfying images of time. One group chose fast moving images, for example, a dashing waterfall, speeding trains, or a spaceship. The second group chose images involving no movement, for instance, an expanse of sky, a motionless ocean, a road or budding leaves. The third group chose human figures, surrogates or artefacts like a string of beads, a winding spool, an old woman spinning, and an old man with a staff. The researchers found a correlation between high achievement in the educational system and the first group. This group saw time as something to defeat or race against, and regarded faster and faster learning as a victory over time. They conceived time as we do in the modern industrial age (Rifkin 1987: 72–73).

We are already beginning to notice, here, a connection between a particular metaphorical conception of time and modern industrial and educational ideology. But this ideological dimension becomes even clearer when we consider the effects of the technological changes in the measurement of time in Europe.

For most of human history, until the modern era, time was measured by observation of natural phenomena, the sun, tides, seasons and so on, the "ecological choreography" of the planet.

> Our ancestors relied on the important temporal events in nature, paying close attention to the changing seasons and the changing constellation of stars in the heavens. Human beings marked time by reference to natural phenomena: the time of the rooster crowing, the time of the passing sun, of the phases of the moon, the time of the in-coming and out-going tides, the time of the snake shedding its skin, the time the sap runs in the trees, the time the bees take to nectar, the time the birds migrate to far off places, and the time they return (pp. 36–37).

Still, in less modern societies than our own, time is measured by these kinds of metonymy. The Trobriand Islanders begin their year when a certain Pacific marine worm spawns. In Madagascar length of time is equated with rice cooking (half an hour), or the time it takes to fry a locust (a moment), in West Africa the time in which maize is not completely roasted (less than fifteen minutes), and in the Sudan the Nuer have "cattle clocks" (Rifkin 1987: 65). In 19th century China short periods of time were indicated by expressions such as "the time it would take to drink a cup of tea", "the time it would take for an incense stick to burn", or " the time it would take to eat a bowl of rice" (Lauer 1973: 461). These natural external rhythms may be parallel to and synchronised with our internal bodily rhythms, the circadian and metabolic pulses of our biological clocks. "Beneath the material surface life is animated and structured by an elaborate set of intricately synchronised rhythms that parallel the frequencies of the larger universe ... all the separate movements pulse in unison to create a single organic whole" (Rifkin 1987: 53).

The first non-natural measurement of time came with the calendar, and here we already see the relationship of time to power and politics. In medieval China the calendar was a prerogative of sovereignty. The knowledge of the right season was power, for it was this knowledge that governed both the acts of everyday life and decisions of state (Landes 1983: 33). The power struggle between French revolutionaries and the Church was manifest in the new calendar of the French Republic, where saints days were abolished, and there was an attempt to re-establish some links with natural rhythms, the names of the months being Vintage, Mist, Frost, Snow, Rain, Wind, Seeds, Flowers. Meadows, Harvest, Heat, and Fruits (Rifkin 1987: 91).

Calendar cultures in Europe began to be replaced by schedule cultures in the late Middle Ages, with the invention of the clock. The main difference between natural and calendar ways of measuring time on the one hand and clock time on the other is that the qualitative measurement (the differences between day and night, autumn and summer, saint's day holiday and a working day) is replaced by a purely quantitative one. And this is, of course, manifest in the conception of time as homogenous linear space, either through metaphor or through the metonymy by which the clock's dial is subdivided into hours, and later minutes and even seconds.

The transformation of quality into quantity appears in a number of English metaphors that equate quality with size or length. 'The general characteristics of a situation' is **the long and the short of it** (*the long and the short of it is we can't afford to send both our children to university*) and a situation with a surprising quality is **nothing short of** (*nothing short of miraculous*), the 'quality of richness or strength of a colour' is **depth** (*the black contrasting with the white gives the painting more depth*), **calibre**, literally 'the width of a gun's barrel' means metaphorically 'quality or standard of ability', **dimension** means 'aspect or quality'(*the harpsichord adds a whole new dimension to the music*). If you 'find out or make a judgement about the quality of something' you **measure**, or **gauge** it (*you can't necessarily measure/gauge career success by the amount of money you accumulate*), and if you do the same to a situation you **size it up** (*he sized up the situation and decided he had better quit his job*). If you 'find out or know someone's character' you **take/have the measure** of them or **have** them **taped** and if their quality is satisfactory they **measure up**. To 'find out the quality of a philosophy, theory or suggestion' you **try it on for size**. A 'standard or specification of quality' is a **benchmark** (*new environmental laws in the EU set a benchmark for other countries to aspire to*). These metaphors are a symptom of our modern mathematical culture, which is obsessed with the need for measurement. In fact, of course, the whole basis of logical quantification depends on the notion of linear scales. If these are in fact metaphors, then mathematics and logic do not represent some transcendental reality but are themselves metaphorically determined (Chilton 1996: 56).

For time to be conceived as continuous, homogenous and measurable, in short, linear, it helps to recruit the metaphors of PERIOD IS LENGTH/DISTANCE. These metaphors are so ingrained in our conception of time that it is sometimes difficult to recognise them. Many figurative expressions refer to time in terms of distances or lengths: **time scale**, **time span**, or **stretch** (*after an 18-month stretch in the navy he gave up*). **Length** means 'amount of time or duration', **long** 'of more than an average period of time', **long lasting** 'remaining or staying fresh for a considerable period of time', **in the long term/run** 'over a considerable period of future time'. If something lasts too long it is **long-winded** or **long-drawn-out**. **A long way off** 'in the far future' and **at length** 'finally, in the end' are the opposite in meaning from **before long** 'quite soon'. To prolong a period of time you **extend** it, **further** means 'for more time' (*I need detain you no further*), whereas **no longer** means 'in the past but not in the present'. By contrast **short** means 'of less than an average time period', **short-lived** 'not lasting for much time', **short range** 'relating to a small amount of time' **in the short run/term** 'over a short period of future time' (*in the short term raising petrol tax is bad for the economy*), **shortly** 'very soon' (*I'll be with you shortly*), and **in a short space of time** 'within or for a little while'. To reduce a period of time you **shorten** or **cut** it (*let's cut/shorten your hours to 6 a week*). If time is a space through which we travel than it can be seen as a path so that **in the course of/along the way/throughout** mean 'during a time or event', **all the way** 'till the completion of a period of time' (*it rained all the way through Monday afternoon*), and **midway** 'half way through a period of time' (*midway through our conversation he took off his glasses*). The **end** literally 'the extreme position or part of an object or space' means 'the last part of a period of time', **endless** 'continuous, repeated (of an activity) without limit (of time)' (*I'm fed up with their endless complaints*). If we think carefully about this lexis we note the confusion brought about by the metonymy of ACTIVITY FOR TIME WHEN IT TAKES PLACE. A vacation or honeymoon or working hours can be seen either from the perspective of the activity occupying that time period, or as the period of time itself.

The first institutions to make use of mechanical clocks in Europe were the Benedictine monasteries, and the division of time that clocks made possible through the metaphor of the division of space, facilitated the rule of obedience to a schedule. "The brethren shall start work in the morning and from the first hour until almost the fourth do the tasks that have to be done. From the fourth until the sixth let them apply themselves to reading. After the sixth hour, having left the table, let them rest on their beds in perfect silence" (Rifkin 1987: 96). The clock was the first automated machine in history and under its influence "the Benedictines helped to give the human enterprise the regular collective beat and rhythms of the machine" (Landes 1983: 69).

In the late Middle Ages clocks became instruments of secular power, and the new bourgeoisie living in towns and their councils often invested in tower clocks such as those today in Munich, Strasbourg and Graz. Besides demonstrating power by fulfilling a kind of totemic function (p. 79), they were related in particular to the regulation of workers within the textile industry.

> As commerce developed and industry expanded, the complexity of life and work required an even larger array of time signals. These were given, as in the monasteries, by bells … Bells sounded for start of work, meal breaks, end of work, closing of gates, start of market, close of market, assembly, emergencies, council meetings, end of drink service, time for street cleaning, curfew and so on through an extraordinary variety of special peals in individual towns and cities (p. 72).

These work bells and clocks steered the conception of time away from the rhythms of nature into something far more mechanical and quantitative, an economic necessity for industrial life. The large amounts of energy used in heating vats in the textile dyeing industry, for example, demanded the synchronisation of the beginnings and ends of the working day. Merchants used the clock as an instrument of economic, social and political domination (Rifkin 1987: 102). "The clock conditioned the human mind to perceive time as external, autonomous, continuous, exacting, quantitative, and divisible. In so doing it prepared the way for a production mode that operated by the same set of temporal standards" (p. 103).

The clock facilitated both empire and industry. The historian David Landes (1983) claims that the clock turned Europe into an imperial hegemonic aggressor, since time measurement was a catalyst in the use of knowledge to increase wealth and power. Industrial production mirrored the rhythm of the clock – in the factories tempo was incessant, unrelenting and exacting. Time sheets and work schedules for employees were established as early as 1700 (Rifkin 1987: 107). No interruption to work, such as talking, was allowed in many factories, witness the rule in John Marshall's flax mills in 1821: "If an overseer of a room be found talking to any person in the mill during working hours, he is dismissed immediately" (pp. 108–9).

Initially this new mechanical tyranny of time and machine was widely resisted by agricultural workers, many of them Irish, more used to the natural rhythms of the farming world. They were consequently labelled lazy, unpunctual, irresponsible, just as Linnaeus labelled Africans who refused the imperial time-style "sluggish, lazy, slow, sly and careless" (see Table 7). Yet the same poverty and desperation that lead the contemporary rural farmer to drift to the urban centre outweighed Irish workers' reluctance to adopt the new industrial time. Moreover, employers overcame resistance by employing children, who were more adaptable, and by encouraging their workers to make and save money and to be loyal to the firm. Significantly enough, it was the gold watch that became the symbol of the loyalty of long service.

The modern attitude to industrial clock-driven time could be summed up as follows: "To be modern was to be punctual, disciplined, fast-paced, and future directed.

Spontaneity, irregularity, laxity, and the unhurried ease that accompanied a less material, more traditional medieval culture was being abandoned in favour of a restless, driving Promethean vision" (Rifkin 1987: 110–12). Every moment was to be filled with a productive task.

Metaphor, we have seen, supported the new industrialised concept of time by constructing it as linear and spatial and therefore, measurable and homogeneous, lacking the distinctive colours of natural or calendar time. But this new industrial time order has connections with metaphorical patterns in several more ways. With the introduction of the work sheet and schedule, time is divided up into spaces to be filled. Hence we note the prevalence of metaphors of PERIOD IS SPACE or CONTAINER to be occupied. **Space** is 'time to do something' (*I need some space to consider my future*) and **place** is the 'stage or time at which to do something' (*this is not the place for a lengthy discussion*). This time may be **vacant, unoccupied** 'free, with nothing to do' (*he spent vacant/ unoccupied moments watching the butterflies*), or with a more ideological evaluation **empty** 'without purpose or meaning' (*my life has been completely empty since my wife died*). For life to be meaningful it should be **full** 'busy (of time)', for **a full life** is 'a life which is busy, extremely active and satisfying' (*though I'm retired I live a very full life with all the charity work I do*). The space of time is something which activities can **fill/ occupy**, meaning 'take up time doing something' (*he filled/occupied his hours writing a novel*). You may wish to **squeeze/pack in** activities 'force into a limited period of time' (*the kids' summer camp was packed with activities*). Consequently your life or schedule may become **crowded** 'containing many interesting events' (*he had a life crowded with incident*) or **overcrowded** 'containing too many events'.

Note that most of the evaluative terms in the above list present the filling of temporal space as positive, reflecting the work ethic ideology behind the Industrial Revolution (Weber 1930/1992). This applies not only to work time, but also to leisure time. When, eventually, workingmen were allowed Saturday afternoons free, association football was introduced to fill this yawning and dangerous gap in their lives. "For idle hands and idle minds the devil finds a work to do". In our modern age: "The more time you have on your hands the less important you must be. So sleep in the office. Never own up to an available lunch slot." (Gleick 1999: 155). This modern view contrasts with Sebastian de Grazia's: "Perhaps you can judge the inner health of a land by the capacity of its people to do nothing – to lie abed musing, to amble about aimlessly, to sit having a coffee – because whoever can do nothing, letting his thoughts go where they may, must be at peace with himself" (quoted in Gleick 1999: 268).

The idea of time as a space or container to fill entails the notion of limits. A **time limit** is 'a period during which something must be completed', and successful adherence to the schedule means finishing **inside** or **within** these limits 'in less than the period of' (*you must complete this project within three weeks*). These metaphors reinforce the notion of deadlines.

A slightly different metaphorical way of looking at the notion of schedule and synchronicity is to combine the analogies of TIME IS MOVEMENT with ACTIVITY/PROCESS

IS MOVEMENT FORWARDS. Then one's activity has to stay level with the time available for performing a task, in a kind of **race against time** 'attempt to complete before time runs out' (*getting the victim to hospital was a race against time*). You can either be **running behind** or **ahead of** time 'spending more/less time than scheduled' (*we're running behind schedule this afternoon, please wait*). If you work more than fast enough you are **ahead of** 'in advance of schedule' (*we're ahead of schedule in completing the building*), but if you cannot **keep up with** your work 'maintain the required rate of activity' you will get **behind with** it 'delayed in schedule' and need to **catch up with** it 'work hard in order to keep to schedule or meet deadlines' (*I took two days holiday and now I must catch up with my work*). (Again there is some conceptual confusion here as to whether you are racing against time itself, or against the activity which is taking place at that time.) Perhaps such a race against time is well symbolised by the moving conveyor belt of factory production. Under this system "the worker became an automaton, no different from the machines he interacted with, his humanity left outside the factory gate" (Rifkin 1987: 130). Remember Charlie Chaplin in *Modern Times*.

Time, being a line, is divisible into smaller and smaller units and exact synchronisation depends on punctuality – happening or arriving at an exact point in time. 'At this moment' is metaphorically **at this point in time** and we are able to synchronise according to these points, in other words to **fix** or **arrange** a time. If we are punctual with our activities or presence we therefore arrive at the exact point in time required – **sharp** or **on the dot** (*unlock the store at 8.00 sharp/on the dot at 8.00*). The smallness of these divisions is apparent in this vocabulary, as also in **split second** 'an extremely short period of time' (*he was back in a split second*). Indeed, the word *punctuality* itself derives from the Latin meaning 'point'. The extent to which the new framing of time and demands for punctuality had been victorious in industrialised clock time is parodied in the following description of suburban life at the beginning of the 20th century:

> In every dormitory suburb, over the length of each road, within the same brief period in the morning, a hundred doors would open, and a hundred breadwinners emerged, like automata from a medieval town clock, to converge on a station where a hundred watches would confirm and a hundred voices agree whether the train was, or was not, on time (Wright 1969: 149).

With computers the measurement of time and of the speed of employees' actions has gone to extraordinary lengths. In the interests of efficiency the temporal space has been subdivided into even smaller units, even for human behaviour.

> The computer reduces time to numbers and turns duration into uniform segments that can be added, subtracted, accumulated, and exchanged. While the computer turns time into a purely manipulable commodity, programs turn humans into instruments to serve the new efficiency time frame. With the computer and program, each person's immediate future can be predetermined down to the tiniest artificial time segments of milliseconds and nanoseconds. Computers present a

new form of social control, more powerful than any previous means used to mar-shal and regiment human energy (Rifkin 1987: 141).

By the 1980s 25% to 30% of all clerical workers found themselves being supervised by a computer in electronic sweatshops doing boring, repetitive, fast-paced work that requires constant alertness and attention to detail (p. 140). The absurdity of the re-sulting studies of time and motion can be seen in the following chart (Table 9) from Systems and Procedures Association of America (pp.131–2).

Table 9. Time and motion study chart for office workers

Open and close	Minutes
File drawer open and close no selection	.04
Folder, open or close flaps	.04
Desk drawer, open side of standard desk	.014
Open centre drawer	.026
Close side	.015
Close center	.027
Chair Activity	
Get up from chair	.033
Sit down in chair	.033
Turn in swivel chair	.009
Move in chair to adjoining desk or file	.05

This kind of study followed the system initiated by Frederick W. Taylor who calibrated a worker's time into fractions of a second (p. 127). The striving for efficiency was, of course, a result of the equation of time with money or with a resource that can be wasted. Ever since the economic system of Adam Smith and the division of labour the emphasis had been on producing more goods in the same amount of time in order to increase wealth, as we noted earlier in Matt Ridley's illustration of comparative advantage. Not only did the division of labour mean more goods were made in less time, but the division of labour led to the division of time into smaller and smaller measurable units (p. 125).

We have seen in this section how the medieval concept of time, "natural" time was superseded by modern industrial time. As Gurevich points out, the new perception of time that began in the Renaissance led to a different way of perceiving the world and a new awareness of man as an individual, the human body as something exclusive and alienated from the world (Gurevich 1985: 28–33, Harvey 1996: 239).

2.8   TIME IS MONEY/COMMODITY

The Italian poet Petrarch at the beginning of the modern period said, "Time is so precious, nay so inestimable a possession, that it is the one thing that the learned agree can justify avarice" (Landes 1983: 91). And "time is money" is the contemporary efficiency expert's mantra. The saying is first attributed to Benjamin Franklin who also said memorably:

> He that can earn ten shillings a day by his labours and goes abroad, or sits idle one half of that day, though he spend but six-pence during his diversion or idleness, ought not to reckon that the only expense; he has really spent, or rather thrown away, five shillings besides (quoted in Gleick 1999: 239).

The equation of time with money, was, of course, cemented in the industrial revolution by the paying of hourly wage rates.

Metaphorically we notice several lexical items under the theme TIME IS MONEY/ COMMODITY. Like money you can **spend time** 'use time or allow it to go past' or in a more focused way **invest** it 'put time into something to achieve a result' (*I invested three years of my life in writing that book*). **Economical** can mean 'using less money', but also mean 'using less time' (*we will have to be more economical with the time we spend on student consultations*). Just as you are forced to pay for something with money, you may have to pay with time: **cost** 'cause to lose (a period of time)' (*shoplifting could cost you your future*).

But time is a commodity too. You may **buy time** 'obtain or be allowed more time'; on the other hand you may not be able to **afford** the time 'have enough time to do', or **spare** the time 'devote time to something when it is difficult for you' (*could you spare the time to write me a reference*), and towards the end of your life you may not have any time left so you **live on borrowed time** 'continue living beyond the time you were expected to die' (*the doctor gave him 3 months to live and since then he's been living on borrowed time*). Once you have time you can **save** it, **waste** or **squander** it 'use time badly', and **use** it **up**, so that you **run out of** it 'have none left'.

The depth of the conceptualising, the reification of time as a commodity, can be seen in the difficulty of providing a meaning which does not itself use the same metaphor. However, this might not be the only way of conceiving time. According to John Mbiti the Ankore of Uganda do not think of *wasting* time but instead **create**, **produce** and **make** time (Gleick 1999: 272).

In the later Middle Ages the Catholic Church resisted the merchant classes' equation of time with money or commodity. Time to them was a gift of God and not to be sold, which was why they also outlawed usury – adding interest on loans according to the time period over which it was lent. However, the new secular Protestant industrial conception won out, so that the accumulation of time in the form of money replaced the accumulation of merit or good works which had been supposed to guarantee you an everlasting life in the hereafter (Rifkin 1987: 160–62). The irony is that our modern rush to save time and make money has actually led to an uncertain future for our children.

Nevertheless, money, in a sense, buys you a future. The middle classes, who tend to have more surplus capital, also have a much more secure notion of the future and tend to plan for far-off goals. (Notice how the higher you are in social status the less frequently you have to be rewarded for your work – hourly pay, or weekly wage packet for the workers, monthly salary for the middle classes, and yearly stipend for priests). By contrast, the poor live a hand to mouth existence, whose immediate uncertainties force them to live in the present. They have no surplus time or money to "invest" in the future. This is, incidentally, quite probably one reason why university fees tend to discourage the working classes more than the middle classes.

Even more extremely, political prisoners undergoing brainwashing are totally deprived of a sense of time – subjected to constant electric light or to darkness, kept away from clocks, deprived of sleep, made to question memories, and denied any hope of the future. Such deprivation is a strategy to produce docility, malleability and obedience (p. 193).

Of course, if time is money, it does not follow that my time is worth the same amount of money as yours. In cultures of inequality we have pyramidal time where the lowest paid workers earn far less than the most highly paid (chief executives earn up to 140 times more than the workers in the same company in the US). This both causes and reinforces class domination.

> Political tyranny in every culture begins by devaluing the time of others. Indeed the exploitation of human beings is only possible in pyramidal time cultures, where rulership is always based on the proposition that some people's time is more valuable and other people's time more expendable (pp. 226–227).

We have long ago lost the idea that quantifiability means equality, the gist of the ancient Greek adage: arithmetic should be taught in democracies, for it teaches relations of equality; geometry alone should be reserved for oligarchies, as it demonstrates the proportions within inequality (Foucault 1972: 219).

2.9 Education, socialisation and time: *Harry Potter and the Philosopher's stone*

Education, as an instrument of socialisation, has a major role in preparing students for the industrialised clockwork time that will be demanded of them in the working world.

> One of the teacher's primary responsibilities is to establish a pace and rhythm in the classroom that mimics the tempo in the larger world for which the children are being prepared. Teachers entrain students to "keep up with their work", keep up with each other, and keep ahead of the game. Students are taught to cram, compartmentalise, and segment their learning to conform with the dictates of clocks, bells, and schedules. Even

the pace and tempo in the hallways, as students move to and from classes, comes to resemble the often frantic rhythms of the larger urban environment (Rifkin 1987: 71).

My recent critical discourse analysis, using concordance data, of the first book of the Harry Potter series throws an interesting light onto the ways in which the Hogwarts school socialises the pupils, the three heroes, and perhaps to some extent the readers, into this modern concept of scheduled time (Goatly 2004).

Table 10. Frequency of lexis for time in Harry Potter and the Philosopher's Stone

TIME	146	SECOND	58	NEW	38
NEXT	96	YEARS	51	YEAR	37
LAST	84	MOMENT	50	WEEK	33
LONG	71	NIGHT	49	MORNING	32
DAY	71	PAST	44	CHRISTMAS	24
OLD	67	MINUTES	44	HOUR	22
LATE	60				

Points and periods of time are extremely frequent in the novel (Table 10). Birthdays and Christmases recur annually. The year is neatly divided into terms, and holidays. The terms, with exams at the end and Quidditch matches punctuating them, are divided into weeks, and the weeks and days into timetabled periods, underlining the importance of scheduled rather than natural time. Moreover, each of the five novels in the Harry Potter sequence represents one year in his school life.

Looking in detail at a selection of concordance lines we are impressed with the sense that there is never enough time to do things, that this commodity is in short supply:

"It's gettin' *late* and we've got lots ter do tomorrow," said
and they were a bit *late* arriving at Hagrid's hut because they'd
staircase if you met him when you were *late* for class. He would drop
"It was you. I feared I might be *too late*." "You nearly were, I couldn't have
around to see if it was a dragon, but *too late* – they plunged even deeper,
leave, saying Ron needed sleep. "It's *too late* to change the plan now,"

Harry and Ron *barely had time* to exchange mystified looks before
out with its own club. They *didn't have time* to come and fetch anyone.
all dry," said Ron. "She *hasn't got much time*," he added quickly, "you
Harry *had even less time* than the other two, because Quidditch
Harry told Hermione. "We *haven't got time* to send Charlie another owl

The emphasis here is often on being too late or not having enough time, as in the last five concordance lines. Where time is a possession it is therefore a highly valued commodity or gift:

> They couldn't afford to waste any more time, Snape might even now be
> out on the window-sill, which gave Harry time to dry his eyes on the sheet.

The frequent and anxious racing against time is demonstrated by its occurrence in the phrase *just in time*, which reminds us of the metaphors of time as an enclosed space on a schedule, with limits and deadlines.

> foot from the ground he caught it, *just in time* to pull his broom straight, and
> He steadied himself *in time* to hear Snape say, " – your little bit
> Snape turned on his broomstick *just in time* to see something scarlet shoot
> Hagrid collected that package *just in time*? Where was it now? And did

In summary, the heroes value time but never seem to have enough of the commodity. And their world is neatly packaged up into bureaucratically divided time periods. This suggests that children reading this book are being asked to accept the tyranny of time as something exciting, even though it is a bureaucratic mechanism of control. As a real student in the States commented, when the gap between lessons in her school was reduced to 4 minutes: "Opening lockers, grabbing books, dodging people and racing across the school are all obstacles students face when trying to switch from class to class in four minutes" (Gleick 1999: 12).

Hogwarts is very like an American or French school in this respect. In fact, the rigidity of the educational tyranny of time was most pronounced in the French system. "The Minister of Education claimed that he could consult his watch at any moment of the day and say whether every child in France, of a given age, would be doing long division, reading Corneille or conjugating Latin verbs" (Rifkin 1987: 112). By contrast "Brazilian students are much less compulsive when conforming to predetermined durational boundaries". On average they define lateness as 33.5 minutes after the scheduled commencement, quite normally turning up "late" and lingering on well after the lesson is scheduled to finish (p. 66).

We have explored how metaphors for time as linear space which can be divided and filled according to schedule, time as movement which has to be kept up with by our activities, and moments of time as points to which we must be punctually synchronised, have reinforced or reproduced a modern conception of time which helped to dominate the industrial worker. We have seen how time metaphorised as money or a commodity has put an emphasis on the need for speed and for efficient sticking to schedule, which too is at the heart of the division of labour and the capitalist industrial enterprise. We might end this section by voicing some objections to this metaphorically-supported ideological conception of time. The first is basically an environmental objection.

> While the new time rebels acknowledge that increased efficiency has resulted in short-term material benefits, they argue that the long-term psychic and environmental damage has outstripped whatever temporary gains might have been wrought by the fanatic obsession with speed at all costs. These time heretics argue that the pace of production and consumption should not grossly exceed nature's ability to recycle wastes and renew basic resources. They argue that the tempo of social and economic life should be made more compatible with nature's own time frame (p. 13).

The second is a humanistic objection:

> If we continue to follow the acceleration of human technological time so that we end in a black hole of oblivion, the Earth and its bacteria will only smile at us as a passing evolutionary folly (Stephen Jay Gould, quoted in Gleick 1999: 275).

And the third is more personal:

> Neither technology nor efficiency can acquire more time for you, because time is not a thing you have lost. It is not a thing you ever had. It is what you live in. You can drift in its currents or you can swim (p. 280).

2.10 ACTIVITY IS FIGHTING

We have explored one major nexus of metaphor themes to do with activity as movement forward. Perhaps the other most prevalent group of metaphor themes in English for constructing activity is to see it as fighting. These exaggerate and intensify the notion of competition, which we observed in the analogy discussed previously ACTIVITY/COMPETITION IS RACE. The metaphor themes we have identified in our database fall into the pattern in Figure 2.

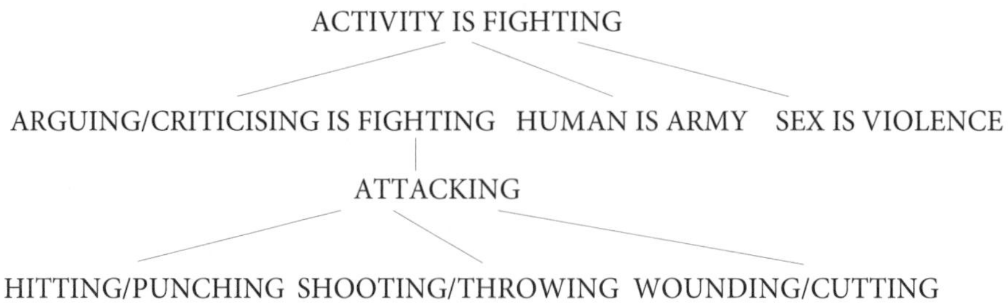

ACTIVITY IS FIGHTING

ARGUING/CRITICISING IS FIGHTING   HUMAN IS ARMY   SEX IS VIOLENCE

ATTACKING

HITTING/PUNCHING SHOOTING/THROWING WOUNDING/CUTTING

Figure 2. The sub-themes of the metaphor theme ACTIVITY IS FIGHTING

(The metaphor theme SEX IS VIOLENCE will be dealt with in the next section)

I do not have the space to give all sixty or so lexical items belonging to the metaphor theme ACTIVITY IS FIGHTING. But many verbs for types of fighting can be applied to other activities: **fight** 'work hard to achieve', **battle** 'attempt to achieve something in a difficult situation', **wrestle, struggle, grapple** 'try hard to do something difficult' (*I've been wrestling/struggling with this maths problem for hours*), **combat** 'attempt to stop something' (*the government needs to take stronger measures to combat crime*). As for nouns we have: **fray** 'energetic or exciting activity', **blitz/assault** 'great effort to do something' (*schools are having a blitz on raising AIDS awareness*), so 'a detailed description of an action or event' is a **blow by blow account**, and **half the battle** 'the most difficult part of the task completed' (*once you ask the right survey questions that's more than half the battle*). Battles can be a series that constitute a **campaign** 'planned group of political or business activities' or **crusade** 'long, determined attempt to achieve what one believes in' (*they are involved in a crusade for racial equality*), a word which George W. Bush found it difficult to use without it evoking its literal meaning in Muslim minds.

To fight these battles you may need a **weapon** 'means of achieving something or opposing someone', **firepower** 'ability to act energetically and successfully' or better still an **arsenal** 'methods or resources available to achieve something' (*our advertisers use a full arsenal of marketing techniques*), and hopefully in your campaign you will have a **spearhead** 'leaders of an activity or campaign' (*the Monday Club are the spearhead for the campaign against immigration*).

A **front** will be 'a particular area of activity' (*she's very creative on the design front*), and those taking initiatives and having the most influence on an activity are in the **vanguard** or the **front-line** (*the minister is in the front line of the drugs awareness campaign*).

Activities can also be seen as (the beginning of) an attack: **come to grips with/square up to** 'confront and deal with effectively and with determination' (*I've finally come to grips with quadratic equations*), **take up the cudgels for** 'support someone strongly' (*the unions took up the cudgels for the retrenched staff*), and in a metaphor from the trenches of the 1st World War, **go over the top** 'behave in an exaggerated excessive and unwise way' (*he went over the top in investing all his savings in Portuguese bonds*).

Activity may be viewed as striking: **tilt at** 'attempt to succeed at or obtain something', **put someone's nose out of joint** 'upset or offend someone by getting what they themselves wanted' (*when I was promoted and he wasn't it put his nose out of joint*), **have/make a stab at** 'make an attempt at' (which if you do 'completely and without limitation' you do **to the hilt**), **knockout blow** 'action that completely destroys an opponent', **knock out** 'very impressive activity' (*the show was a knockout – all the seats were sold for 10 nights*), **strike a blow for** 'do something to support a cause or principle' (*he struck a blow for the cause of handicapped children*). Being struck is 'a setback, problem or disappointment', a **(body) blow** (*the court ruling comes as a blow to environmentalists*), or **one in the eye for** (*our increase in market share was one in the eye for our competitors*).

Successful activity is killing: **execute** 'perform or do a planned action', **close in for the kill** 'take advantage of a changed situation to achieve your aims' (*seeing his chance of a profit John moved in for the kill.*); or having other successes in battle: **take by storm** 'be suddenly and unexpectedly successful and get an enthusiastic response' (*the Beatles took the country by storm in 1964*).

Perseverance is continuation of fighting or resistance: **bash on** 'continue doing something difficult or boring' (*I bashed on with my marking past midnight*), **go the distance** literally 'box until the end of the last round', metaphorically 'manage to continue till the end of something' (*he started an Open University course but was unable to go the distance*), **roll with the punches** 'deal with a series of difficult situations', **hold the fort** 'look after or supervise an activity while someone else is absent'.

Giving up, failure or ceasing an activity is losing a battle: you may **fight a losing battle** 'try to do an impossible task', be **on the ropes** 'doing badly and likely to fail' or in a **no win** situation 'leading to an unsuccessful result whatever happens'. In which case you might as well **give in/admit defeat** 'decide not to continue something before you have successfully completed it', or using the boxing metaphors **throw in the towel/sponge**. This is an admission that an activity **defeats** you – 'proves impossible to solve or carry out' (*this maths problem defeats me*).

If activity is a battle, then people or participants are an **army/host/regiment** 'large group of people' (*when she opened the door there was an army/a host/a regiment of journalists waiting for her*), or the smaller **troop/cohort**. If they are working together on a particular job they are a **task force** (*the health and safety task force have just issued their first report*) and if they represent an organisation or country they are a **contingent** (*the Japanese contingent certainly made their presence known at the World Cup*). If part of an organisation they may be the most important, the **top brass** (*some of the top brass at Enron were fired immediately*), and if 'less important ordinary members of an organisation' the **rank and file/the ranks**, or a **foot soldier** (*she was never promoted much, but over the years she remained one of our most loyal foot soldiers*).

To prepare these people for an activity is to prepare them for war: **mobilize** 'organise or prepare a group for a purpose', **muster** 'gather people together for an activity' (*can we muster enough people for a game of football?*), **enlist** 'ask someone for help or support' (*the prosperous company enlisted several new marketing staff*) or make them a **recruit**.

Max Black's (1962) interaction theory of metaphor claimed that in the metaphor "man is a wolf", not only are men made to seem like wolves, but wolves are also made to seem like men. There is evidence for Black's view in, for example, the objections feminists have to calling God "Father" – it makes fathers like gods too. In the case of these fighting and military metaphors that I have been listing, the interaction view would claim that besides making activities in general look like war in particular, they also make war look like an ordinary activity, rather than an exceptional one.

The extent to which war (or defence) has become a normal activity of government is observed in figures for military expenditure. In the US by far the most important government activity, in terms of expenditure, is now defence/war. As the <u>world socialist website</u> notes, for the year 2003, if you take the normal routine military budget of $368bn add on the $19bn assigned to the Department of Energy for new nuclear weapons, plus the $79bn already passed by Congress to support the war in Iraq, and the extra $87bn that Bush obtained to keep the war going, the total that the US federal government is spending on war/defence is \$543bn – which is as much as it spends on education, public health, housing, employment, pensions, food aid and welfare put together.

The US, in 2003, accounted for 43% of world military expenditure, when currencies are converted at market exchange rates (MERs). The top 5 spenders: the USA, Japan, the UK, France and China, account for 62% of the world total, and the top 15 account for 82%. If, instead of MERs, we use purchasing power parity (PPP) rates, which reflect the actual volume of goods and services that can be purchased in each country with its currency, the US remains the top spender by far, but the next three are China, India and Russia.

In 2002, generally, world military expenditure, which has been increasing since 1998, accelerated sharply, increasing by 6% in real terms to \$794 billion in current prices, accounting for 2.5% of world GDP, and \$128 per capita. Besides the US, the largest increases were in Russia, China and India. While Russia is a strong supporter of the "war on terrorism", to which it links its conflict in Chechnya, its 12% real terms increase also reflects its desire for military reform and the maintenance of defence technological capability. China increased military spending by 18% in real terms, to strengthen its position as a regional and global power. India's 9% real terms increase is the result both of heightened tension with Pakistan and regional power ambitions, where it is in competition with China. France and the UK have also announced substantial increases from 2003, largely to develop "network-centric" warfare, which is seen as important in the "war on terrorism" (Recent Trends in Military Expenditure 5/7/2003).

In fact terrorism has provided a major justification for countries to increase their military expenditure. Why is this? The number of lives lost to terrorists is negligible, compared with, say, the number of lives lost in road accidents or to malaria. The difference must be that the latter do not threaten political power structures whereas the very aim of terrorists is to overthrow the existing political order. At present the USA, UK, France, Russia and China, all of whom are making major increases in expenditure, have a great deal of power to lose – they are all permanent members of the UN Security Council. No doubt India, who now possesses nuclear weapons, will be looking for a permanent seat too in the near future.

Though ACTIVITY IS FIGHTING is very prolific in terms of lexis, ARGUING/CRITICISING IS FIGHTING surpasses it, so much so that to make the lexis manageable our database subdivides it into ARGUING/CRITICISING IS ATTACKING, which itself has subsets for different kinds of attack: HITTING/PUNCHING, SHOOTING/THROWING AT and WOUNDING/CUTTING.

An argument between groups of people or two people is a **battle** or **duel** and a short, sometimes noisy, one is a **skirmish** or a **scrap** in which people **slug it out** 'argue fiercely'. A disagreement is a **conflict** or **war of words**. People eager to argue are **belligerent** or **combative** and criticisms or insults that are unfriendly are **hostile** or **offensive**. If you are 'facing a lot of criticism' you are **embattled**, and may be forced to **retreat from**, 'give up' your opinion in the hope that this will produce a **truce** 'temporary agreement to stop arguing'.

Table 11. Relative military expenditures in 1999
(http://projects.sipri.se/milex/mex trends.html)

	Country	1999 military expenditure	
1.	USA	259.9	
2.	Japan	51.2	
3.	France	46.8	
4.	Germany	39.5	
5.	UK	31.8	
6.	Italy	23.5	
7.	Russia	22.4	
8.	China	18.4	
9.	South Korea	15	
10.	Saudi Arabia	14.5	
11.	Brazil	14.3	
12.	India	10.2	
13.	Turkey	9.6	
14.	Taiwan	9.3	
15.	Spain	8.7	

Figures are in US $bn., at constant 1995 prices and exchange rates.
(Source: Stockholm International Peace Research Institute Yearbook 2000)

Under this schema **attack** means to 'criticise strongly' as do **maul**, **savage**, and **assail**, while 'repeated criticisms or verbal attacks' are an **onslaught.** You may of course **counter attack** 'defend yourself or arguments' or **give as good as you get.**

These criticisms or verbal attacks may be hitting or punching, **hit out at**, **bash** (*he keeps on bashing the weaker students about their English ability*), **knock**, **rap**, **lash**, **lash out**, **take a swipe at**, **hammer**, or **slam**, all meaning 'criticise' or 'criticise severely' (*the spokesman slammed the Taleban for blowing up Buddha statues*), and **hit back at** means 'criticise someone who has criticised you', whereas a **side-swipe** is 'criticism of something which is not the main topic of the conversation'. If a text is **hard-hitting** it is extremely critical. If you are direct in your criticisms or arguments you speak **straight from the shoulder** or **don't pull your punches**. Criticism that is 'harsh and unpleasant' is **bruising** and, pursuing the boxing metaphor, unfair criticism is **below the belt** and may **floor** you 'surprise you so that you are unable to respond' (*he was floored by the suggestion that homosexuality was a good means of population control*). If you argue less seriously you **spar** with a **sparring partner** in a **sparring match** 'friendly argument'.

Metaphors of shooting and throwing can be applied to communication and language in general. **Hurl** means 'shout violently' (*he was hurling drunken abuse at his wife and kids*), **shoot your mouth off** 'talk too much, about something forbidden', while something said **point blank** is said 'directly, abruptly and decisively' (*she asked me point blank to marry her*) and **quick fire** speech is 'very fast with no pauses in it'. You **aim** or **target** your communication at the particular people you want to receive it. Very often shooting and throwing are applied to asking questions, as in **shoot** (*I'm now inviting questions: if you have any, just shoot*), and if you ask a lot of questions in quick succession you **fire** them or **pelt** someone with them (*the kids used to pelt me with questions of the "what if...?" kind*)

Some of these metaphors, **bombard, barrage, volley,** and **fusillade,** are ambiguous, meaning either 'a large number of questions' or 'a large number of criticisms', as are the second-order metaphors **rain, hail** and **shower,** which as first-order metaphors mean 'continuous firing of bullets' (*the children rained questions on their teacher*). Less ambiguously **broadside, pot shot** and **flak** all refer to powerful or strong criticisms (*she took some flak from her brother over her new haircut*). If you criticise someone you **take a shy at, snipe** (*he's always sniping at his elder sister*) or **let fly** (*as soon as I finished my talk the professor let fly with critical comments*). And to direct your criticism towards someone you **level** it at them or **zero in on** them, and they **draw your fire** 'attract criticism' and so they or their behaviour **come under fire** (*the president's tax cuts came under fire from the elderly*).

Lastly, criticism, argument or verbal attack can be seen as wounding or cutting: **tear into, tear to pieces, tear a strip off, flay, dress down** (literally meaning 'cut up a carcass') all mean 'to criticise someone severely or harshly' (*my boss dressed me down/ tore me off a strip for submitting the report late*). **Go for the jugular** (the main vein in the throat) means 'make the maximum effort to defeat in argument or destroy through criticism'. If you are criticised by someone you trust they **stab you in the back,** and this 'malicious secret criticism' is **backstabbing** (*the department will never improve its morale unless we can get rid of this backstabbing*).

The criticism or emotional suffering you experience from criticism is a **wound**. You are more sensitive to criticism if you are **thin-skinned**, and impervious to it if you are **thick-skinned**. The more unkind or forceful the criticism the more **pointed, biting, cutting** or **sharp** it is. If it is nevertheless true it is **close to the bone** (*Galloway's criticism of the PM was so close to the bone he was expelled from the Labour party*).

The weapons involved in such criticism, argument or annoyance are often swords or daggers: if you are **at daggers drawn** with someone 'angry and arguing', or **cross swords with** 'argue with' them, you may be involved in the **cut and thrust** 'debate and repartee' of argument and will be well-served if you have a **rapier tongue/wit** 'the ability to be intelligently and impressively satirical'. However, while arguing you should avoid evidence or facts that **cut both ways** 'are capable of being used on both sides of an argument' (*the correlation between unemployment and health cuts both ways in the public spending debate*).

One of the problems of using these metaphors is that, though they may have been intended metaphorically, they may be interpreted literally (Charteris-Black 2005: 28). During the Cold War, Keenan from the Moscow US embassy sent a document known as The Long Telegram, which was extremely influential in forming US foreign policy towards the USSR. In this he made comments such as the following:

> They have learnt to seek security only in patient but deadly struggle for total de-struction of rival power, never in pacts and compromises … Soviet propaganda is basically negative and destructive. It should therefore be relatively easy to combat it by any intelligent and really constructive program. (Chilton 1996: 139–140).

These quotations are ambiguous as to whether the "struggle", the "destruction" and the "combat" are or should be about physical fighting or about establishing ascendancy of ideas. A similar ambiguity seems to have arisen lately with the Muslim theological term *jihad,* which is often translated as 'holy war', a literal conflict, whereas in its Arabic form it subsumes the more metaphorical 'spiritual struggle'. In the 2004 US presidential election, Kerry insisted that the "war on terrorism" was simply a meta-phor, like the "war on poverty", though Bush poured scorn on this, and insisted that it was a literal war.

However, the distinction between literal war and the war of ideas could be blurred through the metonymy of might is right, or power is good, suggesting that military or economic supremacy is somehow an index of having the better or the most moral ideological system. The defeat of communism in the Cold War can then be seen as a guarantee that capitalism has won the ideological argument with communism.

Metaphors such as this construct argument and criticism as being between two sides, as in the prototypical war, and as leading to defeat for one side and victory for the other. This is not a very helpful attitude when embarking on negotiations of any kind, ruling out the possibility of compromise and constructive argument in which each side contributes ideas to the benefit of both parties.

2.11 The adversarial system in law, politics, the media and philosophy.

This adversarial system is obviously realised lexically by the kind of vocabulary listed above. However, we can see it as being conceptually structured by a rather more basic schema of force dynamics or Event Structure, which involves CAUSE IS FORCE, ACTIV-ITY/PROCESS IS MOVEMENT FORWARD, PREVENTION IS OBSTACLE, PURPOSE IS DIREC-TION, CONFLICTING PURPOSE IS OPPOSITE DIRECTION. The connection depends on the idea that one exerts force against those who are metaphorically opposed to or resist you, who have different purposes or activities of which you disapprove, and which are contrary to your own beliefs.

In Western nations there are two different systems of law – common law, operating in the US, the UK and other commonwealth nations, and civil law operating in other countries of Europe such as France and Germany. These two systems hold criminal tri-als in different ways, common law using the adversarial system, and civil law using the inquisitorial system. The former has two advocates or counsel, one for the prosecution and one for the defence, and relies on the skill of the advocates in presenting evidence to the judge and jury to persuade them of the guilt or innocence of the accused, with the judge as a kind of referee or chairman running the courtroom, and deciding what evidence can be brought. In the inquisitorial system, the judge or team of judges has the much more active role of investigating the case before them.

From a metaphorical point of view it is interesting that the origin of the adversarial system may be the medieval trial by combat, where knights used physical fighting to resolve guilt or innocence either of themselves, or of a third party whom they championed. This means to say that the metaphors for argument and criticism that I spelt out above might be viewed, in this legal context at least, as a historical metonymical replacement for the real thing – fighting.

The adversarial system has come under increasing criticism in recent years, for example by Lord Woolf who saw it as the basis of most of the litigation problems in the United Kingdom, partly because of its waste of time and money. But even for lay people the system creates obvious problems. The facts that are presented to the jury as evidence are selected by the defence or prosecution, and they may choose evidence that hides the facts, since their role is not to discover the truth but to obtain a favourable verdict. Peter Murphy in his *Practical Guide to Evidence* (2000) gives a damning example. A judge in an English (adversarial) court, frustrated by the contradictory accounts of witnesses, finally asked a barrister, "Am I never to hear the truth?" "No, my lord, merely the evidence". There is also the ethical problem of how, with a clear conscience, counsel can defend someone who they believe to be guilty, or prosecute someone who they believe innocent. Furthermore, in the adversarial, common-law system, the defendant can plead guilty, and enter a plea bargain, to avoid too harsh a punishment. In fact, the vast majority of criminal cases in the US are resolved in this way. This can lead to great injustice when a poor defendant can only afford an unskilled or overworked attorney. It can also encourage the prosecution to bring charges far greater than is merited by the facts of the case and for the defendant to plead guilty even when he believes he is innocent (Adversary System, *Wikipedia*).

It is perhaps no accident that in Western democracies there is a tendency to adversarial contests in parliamentary debates, since lawyers are over-presented as MPs or congressmen. In some ways the adversarial two-party political system is even less satisfactory than the trial system or than a debate. In a law court the judge and jury can be persuaded by the evidence brought by the defending and prosecuting counsels, and in a debate, although the debaters themselves are not free to change their minds, the debate is won or lost according to the numbers in the audience change their previously-held opinions. In both these cases there is the possibility and desirability of reasoned argument and evidence having an effect on changing minds. However, in a two-party parliamentary debate, with whips enforcing party discipline, the primary audience, the MPs in the chamber, are required not to change their mind, but to toe the party line, however reasonable or convincing the arguments on the other side. Consequently, such a parliamentary debate, or parliamentary question time, becomes a kind of gladiatorial contest, in which the debaters strive to show off their rhetorical skills and style, rather than advance the cause of truth and reason. Not surprisingly, many members of the public become disenchanted with political debate. On the other hand, presumably the speakers in a parliamentary debate believe in the case they are making, whereas in the courts it is quite possible for a lawyer to be defending someone whom he suspects of guilt.

The mass media encourages adversarial politics by constructing it in terms of an entertaining contest between rival personalities. After all, headlines in newspapers are the places where one is most likely to find criticism or argument expressed in military metaphors. These are designed to produce a sensational and dramatic effect, for the tool of sensationalism is hyperbole, and the essence of drama is conflict. One might consider the following selection of headlines from *The Guardian Unlimited* (12/10/2004).

> **Howard returns to the fray in the battle of Brixton**
> **First blood to Kerry in TV debate**
> **Running mates clash over Iraq**
> **Job loss figures deliver a blow to Bush**
> **It's time our politicians went head to head**
> (an article calling for TV debates in UK)
> **Sniper fire over captured headlines**
> (an article about the mutual criticisms of newspapers over reporting the capture of Saddam)
> **Savaged by the half-dog half-postman**
> Alan Johnson used to be a postman. Now he has become a cross between a postman and a savage dog, shoving a bundle of facts and opinions into your letter box while yapping angrily around your ankles

Additionally, the entertainment media seem to thrive on courtroom TV dramas, from *Perry Mason*, up to *Ally McBeal*, and *The Practice*, which show exactly how entertaining the adversarial system can be.

Like all metaphors ARGUING/CRITICISING IS FIGHTING highlights some aspects of the target and suppresses others. Truth might be better attained by sharing the perspectives of others which are quite different from one's own, by recognising that progress is cumulative not mutually destructive, and building on other people's insights instead of demolishing them. The problem is that such metaphors are mechanisms of regimes of truth: they create a reality rather than simply describing it. If I win the argument by showing that the metaphor is unhelpful, the irony is that by rejecting the metaphor I have already been drawn into accepting it (Balkin 1998: 246–8).

Adversariality is only one way of responding to difference (Fairclough 2003: 41–2) and alternative attitudes have been apparent in various cultures and sub-cultures. In feminist circles there appears to be some controversy about whether one should participate in argument at all, if argument is constructed in such a militaristic and adversarial fashion as our metaphors suggest.

> A concern about critical thinking and argument evaluation, as practiced by philosophers, is their adversarial nature … People are taught to defend and attack, to argue against opponents, to find strategies and tactics of argument, to buttress their own positions, to be sharp and engage in battles of the wits … Metaphors for argumentative practice are abundantly militaristic, as feminist analysts have pointed out and they seem all too readily to class differences in belief as battles of the wits.

Feminist values see themselves as an alternative to these male militaristic values and, if argument can only be constructed in these terms, the conclusion is that one should not argue at all. However, there are possibilities for other kinds of argument and for other metaphors that construct argument and reasoning differently:

> We can argue for a claim without arguing against a person. There are non-adversarial aspects of argument. And there are non-adversarial metaphors for argument – arguments may help us **build a case**, **explore a topic**, or think through a problem. Evaluating arguments may lead us to change our own minds; a critical analysis of someone else's case is not, by definition, a negative one (Govier 1999: 7–8) [my bolding].

Lakoff and Johnson (1980: 5) suggest one could conceive argument as a dance.

Perhaps because of the financial and emotional costs of the adversarial system there has been an increasing tendency, even in the West, to resolve disputes through mediation or negotiation. The central quality of mediation has been described as "its capacity to reorient the parties towards each other, not by imposing rules on them, but by helping them to achieve a new and shared perception of their relationship, a perception that will redirect their attitudes and dispositions towards one another" (Fuller 1971). By contrast the adversarial system of litigation is often slow and expensive, reinforces conflict between parties and may therefore result in further litigation. The decision reached will be within narrow legal parameters, and the whole process may tend to elude the control of the parties involved.[5] One only needs to remind oneself of the case of *Jarndyce v. Jarndyce* in Dickens' novel *Bleak House,* where the whole inheritance in the will under dispute, is, over the space of many years, completely frittered away in legal costs.

Non-adversarial conflict resolution is quite normal in many non-Western cultures, to which the adversarial system is foreign. The following legal case came to court in California involving a dispute among Chuukee Indians. It was brought by the parents of Ignacio Alafonso, who was alleged to have died as a result of a beating by the defendants, and the plaintiffs made a claim of $100,000 and for transfer of land to them by way of settlement and compensation.

Normally in such a case the Chuukee would have resolved the dispute through a traditional apology and compensation system, "chapen awofich", without recourse

---

5.   Information on the characteristics of non-adversarial dispute resolution mechanisms is taken from http://www.fao.org /docrep/W8440e /W8440e26.htm

to the US courts. However, the defendants had not given such an apology and compensation, so the question before the court was to determine whether they should be required to do so, by intervening in the normally non-adversarial Chuukee system.

At trial the plaintiffs called as their witness Chief Kintoki, an expert in traditional Chuukee procedures.

> He testified in this case that it is not the role of the court to order compensation in the traditional system, if none has been offered by the defendants. This is because the traditional apology and settlement system is non-adversarial and the compensation aspect of the traditional settlement is secondary to restoring harmony in the community. Chief Kintoki emphasized there is no set amount of compensation, as "money is not going to buy the life." Rather the compensation is based on how the victim's family feels and how much the other side wants to give to bring the community back into harmony. The amount of compensation is reached by negotiation, not outside coercion, and is but a part of the process. The family of the wrong doer must initiate the apology to show that they are sorry and to open their hearts. If the responsible ones are forced into providing compensation then it destroys the voluntary nature of the act of making peace. Thus the whole point of the traditional apology and settlement is lost.

The Californian court, after hearing this expert witness, decided it could not intervene and order compensation, since, according to native custom, the compensation must be given voluntarily, and the court was bound by the constitution to abide by native custom in such cases (Findings Of Facts, Conclusion Of Law And Judgment, September 20, 1995).

This case is interesting from several points of view. It shows how two legal systems, the American adversarial and the Chuukee non-adversarial system come into contact, and how the case is resolved according to the latter. It illustrates the non-adversarial and therefore voluntary nature of the traditional justice system in Chuukeee society, even to the extent of the plaintiff's expert witness giving testimony that ends up favouring the defendants. The aim of this system, which seemed to fail in the present case, was for the restoration of harmony within the community, and, when it works, one can see that voluntary compensation and apology is a much better way of achieving this harmony than a punishment enforced by an adversarial trial in a court of law.

> The traditional justice systems ... are not so much concerned with establishing proof and administering justice as with ensuring balance and harmony within the whole group ... The idea is not to reconstruct what happened in the past ... The emphasis rather is on how people are to live their lives at the present moment, the nature of their needs, and how the harmony of the whole group has been disrupted (Peat 1996: 48).

In Chinese culture, too, there is a tradition of attempting to solve disputes by negotiation or conciliation rather than arbitration or legislation, and this tradition has survived into the present. Several Chinese laws encourage non-adversarial dispute resolution. For instance the *Foreign Economic Contract Law* states:

> Any disputes arising over a contract shall be settled, as far as possible, through consultations, or conciliation by a third party. Where the parties concerned are not willing to, or fail to, go through consultation or conciliation, they may submit to China's arbitration agency or other arbitration institutions ... (Isinolaw Research Center, November 2003)

China is, of course, a one-party state. And, despite the bad press that such states have, there is a case for saying that the two-party adversarial political system is not suitable for traditional non-adversarial societies. This was the argument of Julius Nyrere in Tanzania – that traditionally disputes and policies were resolved by discussion and reaching of voluntary consensus, rather than setting up an artificial battle which one side won and the other side lost. However, because of the perceived failure of one-party states in East Africa and elsewhere, whether these failures were due to the one-party system or to external economic factors, these ideas have been largely confined to oblivion.

2.12 SEX IS VIOLENCE and rape

It is remarkable and disturbing to note the number of English metaphors for sex that employ sources of violence. Many are quite recent in origin, though the association can be traced back at least as far as classical times, where **phallus** meant 'sword', **vagina** meant 'sheath or scabbard', an association still preserved in **sheath** meaning 'condom'. As in these examples, the male is usually constructed as the aggressor, so that the penis is a **chopper, weapon**, or, by collocation a gun with which a man can **shoot his load** 'ejaculate semen', or **fire blanks** 'produce semen without any sperm in it'. The weapon might be a sword as in **make a pass at**, literally 'attempt to stab with a rapier' and metaphorically 'speak to or touch to show sexual attraction', or an arrow so **shaft** means 'have penetrative sexual intercourse with' (*he claims he's been shafting 3 different women a week for the last six months*). Even the traditional symbol for male seems to incorporate an arrow: ♂. By this violence men may achieve their **conquests** 'women they have had sexual intercourse with', and be **lady-killers** 'seducers', though notice that women too can be **dressed to kill** 'wearing clothes that attract sexual attention'. Less violently, sex is associated with hitting. Some of this lexis is associated with men as the hitters, too, as in **wham-bang-thank-you-mam** 'a very quick act of sex', **knock up** 'make pregnant', **knock off** 'have sex with a woman', **gang bang** 'group rape of a woman'. Verb lexis that can take either sex as agent includes **hit on** 'indicate your sexual attraction for', or **bang/bonk** 'have sex with'. A sexually attractive person of either sex is a **knockout** and, more gently, playful sex is **slap and tickle**.

I want to suggest a connection between these patterns of metaphors, especially those constructing the sexual act of men as aggression, and the increasing incidence of rape. Firstly, it is obvious that rape, along with other abuses of women, is a serious problem. Around the world at least 1 women in 3 has been beaten, coerced into sex or otherwise abused in her lifetime (John Hopkins School of Public Health 2000). In the States, according to the National Victim Center, 683,000 women are raped each year (1992). A study of 6,000 students at 32 colleges in the US showed that 1 in 4 women had been the victims of rape or attempted rape (Warshaw 1994). One third of American women will be sexually assaulted in their lifetime. The United States has the world's highest rape rate among the countries that publish rape statistics: 4 times higher than Germany, 13 times higher than England, and 20 times higher than Japan. However, the number of rape cases is probably on the increase in the UK.

Table 12. The attrition rate for rape in England and Wales (from: Campaign to End Rape Briefing Pack, Rape Crisis Federation of England and Wales http://www.rapecrisis.co.uk/statistics.htm)

Year	Reported Rapes	Convictions	Convictions Rate
1977	1015	324	32%
1987	2471	453	18%
1993	4589	482	10%
1994	5032	460	9%
1995	3986	578	14%
1996	5759	573	10%

Between 1996 and 1997 the number of women reporting rape increased by over 500%. Yet convictions have remained almost static, meaning that whilst in 1977 1 in 3 women reporting rape saw their rapists convicted, in 1996 less than 1 in 10 did. The criminal justice system is currently failing women, not just those who report rape, but every woman, since the message being sent out is that rape is a low risk, high reward activity.

What patterns of social roles and statuses can we see within this phenomenon of rape, and how do they connect to the patterns that we saw in the lexis of SEX IS VIOLENCE? First of all, as with the metaphors, it is men who are usually constructed as the aggressors. An estimated 91% of victims of rape are female, 9% are male and 99% of offenders are male (Bureau of Justice Statistics 1999). 93% of women and 86% of men who were raped and/or physically assaulted since the age of 18 were assaulted by a male (National Violence Against Women Survey, 1998).

Second, rape is not usually a random act of violence perpetrated by a stranger, like, for example, mugging. In the United States 77% of rapes are committed by someone known to the person raped (Bureau of Justice Statistics 1997). The Rape Crisis Centre of England and Wales report that 97 per cent of callers to their hotlines knew their assailant. Husbands often resort to rape – 1 in 7 married women said they had been raped by their husbands, both in the US and the UK. The most common rapists are partners and ex-partners. These figures suggest that men may regard coercive or violent sex as a quite normal way of relating to somebody close to them, just as it is quite normal for them to use the language of aggression when talking about sex. In fact, what women or the US courts regard as rape, men may simply regard as normal sex. In a survey of college males who committed rape, 84% said what they did was definitely not rape (Warshaw 1994). If we look back at the statistics for convictions in England and Wales in Table 12, there may even be a suspicion that (male) police, juries and judges do not recognise rape for what it is, maybe because of the tendency to conceptualise sex as violence. [6][7]

2.13 Summary

In this chapter we considered several sets of metaphors or metaphor themes and saw how they are related to various cultural beliefs, ideologies and practices. Some human practices such as building high, racing at higher and higher speeds, and urban drift, were viewed as actions symbolising power or its enhancement, and dependent on the metaphors POWER/CONTROL IS ABOVE, IMPORTANCE/STATUS IS HIGH, ACTIVITY IS MOVEMENT FORWARD, SUCCESS IS SPEED, and IMPORTANT IS CENTRAL. With DISEASE IS INVASION, I showed how traditional metaphorical constructions were being abandoned and replaced with others, such as talking to rather than fighting bacteria, and stressing symbiosis rather than conflict, in order to address certain medical problems with appropriate practice – probably a case of replacing one model-theoretic metaphor with another. In the case of ACTIVITY IS FIGHTING and SEX IS VIOLENCE, we noted the tendency to regard activities in general and sexual activities in particular as having violence as a defining feature, and the social consequences of this in terms of defence budgets and gender-differentiated concepts of sex. Similarly, ARGUING-CRITICISING IS FIGHTING encourages the adversarial system of law and politics (though the latter may have grown up as a substitute for literal combat) and there is some practical resistance to this adversarial approach to dispute resolution, especially in non-Western cultures. In the case of RACE IS COLOUR metaphor is used to conjure the optical illusion of race, which has little biological validity, out of nothing. Our explorations of metaphors for TIME IS SPACE demonstrated their indispensability in creating the kinds of homoge-

---

6.   This may also be part of another pattern whereby men hold women responsible for the teasing sexual attraction that they exert, and rape is therefore seen as a kind of revenge for humiliation brought about by this teasing (Lakoff 1987: 412–14).

7.   Statistics in this section are taken from the following web-sites:

(1) http://oak.cats.ohiou.edu/~ad361896/anne/cease.html;

(2) http://www.rapecrisis.co.uk/statistics.htm Rape Crisis Federation of England and Wales;

(3) http://www2.ucsc.edu/rape-prevention/statistics.html UCSC Rape Prevention Education.

neity, measurability and divisibility which allowed the scheduling and synchronicity that produced modern industrial work practices and market capitalism. All these are instances of how metaphorical concepts can be realised, not only linguistically but also in social practice (Kövecses 2002: chapter 2).

Perhaps it will be helpful to recap how these metaphorical effects are implicated in ideology – thought in the service of power. The first group of themes with sources of speed, height/size and centrality lead to symbols of power. Big Ben illustrates their confluence, being a clock-tower, symbolising power by its height, in the centre of a very large city, symbolising power by its centrality, showing us the time by which our lives are regulated. RACE IS COLOUR obviously helped in the stereotyping and discrimination that dogged the 19th and most of the 20th century and was complicit with imperialism and the construction of the other as inferior. Disease as invasion, and its alternative treatment as communication are involved in medical technology, and the power over nature. The replacement metaphor suggests a less dominant and more co-operative ideology than the germ-zapping one. Our time metaphors played their part in the servitude to the machine and the industrial process for many workers, and TIME IS MONEY/COMMODITY has become one of the most important strands in the process of commodification by which natural objects are brought within the sphere of the market and under economic control. Time as money showed that people's time is unequal in worth, and IMPORTANT IS CENTRAL represents different parts of the country, and metonymically their inhabitants, as of different value, so both are implicated in structures of inequality. The idea that fighting is a normal activity has led to the huge military budgets of the US by which they maintain their domination as the sole superpower. The adversarial system of politics, which sees argument as a battle to be won, is enormously wasteful of disputants' time and money, and a way by which the legal profession and rich defendants maintain their power. Sex is violence metaphors seem a most obvious way by which men achieve a physical domination of women.

A quote from *M. Butterfly* relates three of these ideological themes: power as size/height, military force, and sexuality.

> But, like, it just hangs there. This little ... flap of flesh. And there's so much fuss that we make about it. Like, I think the reason we fight wars is because we wear clothes. Because no one knows – between the men, I mean – who has the bigger ... weenie. So, if I'm a guy with a small one, I'm going to build a really big building or take over a really big piece of land or write a really long book so the other men don't know, right? But, see, it never really works, that's the problem. I mean, you conquer the whole country, or whatever, but you're still wearing clothes, so there's no way to prove absolutely whose is bigger or smaller. And that's what we call a civilised society (Hwang 1989: 55).

(Unfortunately, this is a rather long book!)

Besides sex, the phenomenon of modern urbanisation depends upon a nexus of these metaphors of power. The "unnatural" speeds with which consumer goods and food supplies are transported around the globe, the urge to build higher and higher, especially to symbolise concentrations of capital in the (banks of) large urban centres, with the result that cities are conceived of as central and important hubs, all these participate in the "global process of capitalist urbanization or uneven spatio-temporal development" (Harvey 1996: 414).

It is worth noting how many such metaphors are implicated in the attempt to control or exert power over nature and to transform it. We found it in the attempt to kill bacteria according to the DISEASE IS INVASION metaphor, in the attempts to replace natural time with clock time, time whose source now becomes linear rather than cyclical (despite the absence of straight lines in nature), in the attempts to defy the natural forces of gravity by building higher, and to travel and transport at faster speeds. As Harvey puts it:

> We harness sources of energy to turn night into day, as we use an international division of labour to put fresh produce in our shops at all times of the year, as we speed up the lifecycles of chickens and pigs through genetic engineering and as human life expectancy rises with improved living standards and medical knowledge (Harvey 1996: 211).

This is a theme we return to in Chapter 7 where we explore how grammar in European languages predisposes us to exert our power over and thereby change nature.

After acknowledging the power of these metaphors we might heed Schumacher's warning: "The direction that modern technology has taken and is continuing to pursue – towards ever greater size, ever higher-speeds, and ever increased violence, in defiance of all laws of natural harmony – is the opposite of progress" (Schumacher 1973/1999: 129).

CHAPTER 3

Metaphors for humans and the living world

"I am not yet born; O fill me
with strength against those who would freeze my
humanity, would dragoon me into a lethal automaton
would make me a cog in a machine, a thing with
one face, a thing..."

Louis MacNiece 'Prayer before Birth'

"Money is a leveller and a cynic, reducing a wondrous multidimensional
ecosystemic world of use values, of human desires and needs, as well as of subjective
meanings, to a common objective denominator which everyone can understand."
(Harvey 1996: 151)

3.1 Introduction

The last chapter considered metaphors implicated in power relations in modern Western societies and economies. In this we concentrate more specifically on themes which construct conceptions of humanity, considering the metaphorical conceptualisation of humans as machines or computers, as food, and as commodities in general. I show how commodification applies not only to human bodies, but relationships, knowledge and thought, as increasingly the quality of (human) life is measured in terms of money and wealth, a measurement going hand in hand with privatisation.

3.2 HUMAN IS FOOD

We ended the last chapter with a discussion of the construction of sex as a violent activity. We shift now to other metaphors that structure our concept of sexual activity, the themes (SEXUAL) DESIRE IS APPETITE within which the object of the appetite is a person, so that HUMAN IS FOOD (Lakoff 1987: 409).

Several lexical items construct desire in general, including sexual desire, as appetite for food. These include **appetite, hunger, hungry; mouth-watering** 'extremely attractive', **drool** 'show extreme or foolish pleasure or desire', and **luscious** 'extremely attractive, pleasant or desirable'. In this schema humans are often characterised as the food that will satisfy this appetite.

Food metaphors constructing humans as sexually desirable are disproportionately used of females. The following group is exclusively applied to women: **cheesecake** 'half-naked, female, photographic models', **crackling** and **crumpet** both meaning 'sexually attractive woman', **tart** 'sexually immoral/attractive woman', **mutton dressed as lamb** 'older woman trying to look young' and **lollipop** 'attractive young girl'. The next group, though sometimes referring to men, more often apply to women: **peach** 'good, attractive person or girl', **arm-candy** 'attractive companion at social events', **honey** 'pleasant person', **sugar** 'person you are fond of', **sweetie** 'pleasant, kind person' and **past their sell-by-date** 'no longer attractive'. This compares with relatively few used more of men than women: **dish, dishy** 'sexually attractive (person)'. Only two in my list – **beefcake** 'man or male models with a muscular body which is attractive to women', and **stud-muffin** 'sexually attractive young man' – are used exclusively for men.

What features from the schema of eating do these metaphor themes transfer to the schema for sex? The schemas differ in that if we do not eat we die, whereas, if we have no sex, we simply fail to reproduce, and the human race eventually dies. Equating sex with eating might suggest that sex is essential for our life, and therefore we are entitled to obtain it by **any** means, just as a starving man would be entitled to steal food. By applying these metaphors mainly to women, men imply they are entitled to have sex with them, even by force or illegal means. More obviously, they suggest that the sole purpose of the women is to satisfy the appetites of men, just as food is produced for the sole purpose of eating, with women, like food, passive in this process (Hiraga 1991).

3.3   Life as a commodity

Food is just one kind of commodity and HUMAN IS FOOD is part of a larger pattern that has serious consequences for the future shape of human life. Human beings are constructed metaphorically as different kinds of commodity. They may be a **product** 'person created' (*these children are the first products of the new school system*). Like products they may be **genuine** 'sincere' or a **fake** 'impersonator, dishonest person', but the genuine ones will have a **trademark** 'typical and identifying characteristic'.

Their characteristics and value are conceptualised as different kinds of metal: **brass** 'confidence, courage' (*how did these chief executives have the brass to award themselves such pay increases?*), **brazen** 'bold and unashamed' (*a brazen attempt at bribery*), or **tin god** 'person considered more important than they really are' (*Catholic priests in Ireland are often tin gods*). All these suggest little value or negative valuation, as does **unrefined** 'rough, impolite', in contrast with the more positive **refined** 'extremely polite and cultured' and **golden-hearted** 'generous, kind'. More positively still, people can be a **treasure, jewel** or **gem** 'kind, helpful or useful person' (*my cleaning lady is a real treasure – she'll do anything I need*) or **asset**, 'person with a useful or valuable quality or skill for an organisation'. They are commodities or products to **sell** 'promote, praise' (*at this interview you must try to sell yourself*), **oversell** 'praise excessively', or **undersell** 'underestimate the value of yourself or others' (*don't undersell yourself by applying to a second-rate university*). It follows that they may be **past their sell-by-date** or **left on the shelf** 'unmarried, without a partner'. This means of evaluation by monetary value even seems to extend to the frequent **dear**, 'beloved', (*she's a dear mother to all of us*) and **dearly**, 'with great affection'.

If people are **undervalued** 'considered less important than they really are', this may be because there is a **glut** or **oversupply** of that type of person (*we now have a glut of IT graduates*). The person themselves can be valued metonymically in money terms, **be worth a million dollars**, and their bodies can **look like a million dollars** 'look wonderful', with sexual organs being particularly valuable parts of the body: **family jewels** 'male genitals' (*you'd better wear a protector – we don't want to ruin the family jewels*); **well-endowed** 'having larger than average sexual organs' (*she's very well-endowed – she'll need at least a D cup bra*).

Parts of the body are treated like money since *bank* is a storage facility for donated body parts giving us **blood bank**, **sperm bank**, **stem-cell bank**, **organ bank** along with the supplier – **blood donor**, **sperm donor** and **organ donor**. While these are donated free in many countries, in others, because of shortages, they are increasingly sold and bought. One such case is rural China, and the selling of blood has led to HIV-infected blood being used in transfusions, and an epidemic of AIDS – a scandal made even more serious by a government cover-up.

Hidden from the world, a village dies of AIDS while China refuses to face a growing crisis

Jonathan Watts in Xiongqiao village, Henan province, the ground zero of an epidemic threatening millions

Saturday October 25, 2003
<u>The Guardian</u>

Chang Sun's wife is HIV positive. So is his mother. So is his aunt. So is his cousin and his cousin's wife. So is the woman next door and, probably, so is her husband. In fact, it is quite possible that almost every adult and many of the children in his small, remote village are infected.

And then, there are those who lie in the flat, brown vegetable fields, which are steadily filling with mossy green burial mounds.

Among them is Chang's father, who died of AIDS last year, and his three-year-old daughter, who succumbed the year before that. His first wife is there too – she threw herself down the village well in 2000 after a doctor told her she was no longer worth treating because she had the virus.

This is Xiongqiao village in Henan province, the ground zero of arguably the world's worst HIV/AIDS epidemic, with up to a million people infected in this single province through a vast, largely unregulated blood-selling operation.

The situation is already a catastrophe, but the risks are growing. The medical treatment is inadequate and the authorities are trying to cover up the truth with a lethal mix of censorship and police intimidation.

One consequence of the commodification of scarce body parts or fluids is that they will be expensive, and therefore likely to be available only to the rich, and to be sold by the poor and desperate. There is already widespread selling of organs by the poor in the Indian subcontinent.

Recently, John Harris, a bioethicist at the University of Manchester, has called for the establishment of a legal and ethical market in organs in which the National Health Service "would purchase live organs and tissues as it does other goods such as dialysis machines or drugs. It would make them available as needed on the basis of urgency at no cost to the recipient." This view is opposed by Alastair Campbell, Professor of Ethics and Medicine at Bristol University, who argues that this would simply expand the opportunities of exploiting the poor. "The consequences of a market in human organs is inevitably exploitation, as studies of the market in kidneys in India has shown." The Chinese government already exploits the demand for organs by offering the body-parts of executed prisoners for sale, and a Norwegian newspaper recently told of a village near Manila where 150 men had each sold a kidney for less than $2000 to raise money for their families. The Council of Europe found that young men from Moldova and Romania were paid $2,500 for a kidney that would be transplanted into a patient who was paying between $100,000 and $200,000. In response to examples such as this professor Campbell objects: "Far from improving the lot of the poor, it worsens their situation, including their health prospects" ('Sale of human organs for profit reignites debate on ban' 2002).

Stem cell therapy is another field where the commodification of human body parts is likely to develop, and to discriminate against the poor. In a comment article in *New Scientist* Ruth Faden points out some of the possibilities and ethical problems. Embryonic stem cells can turn into virtually any body tissue, which raises hopes of using them to treat diseases like Parkinson's or spinal cord injuries. However the problem of rejection can be overcome only if stems cells are taken from the patient or a clone of the patient.

At present, however, both these potential methods are extremely expensive and time-consuming. The worry is that for the foreseeable future only the wealthy may be able to afford this kind of **bespoke** cell therapy. The ideal way to expand access might be to create "universal" stem cell **lines**. These cells, genetically modified to evade immune attack, would enable doctors to offer patients cheaper "**off the shelf**" therapy (Faden 2002: 27) [my bolding].

We note in the bolded phrases the metaphorical construction of stem cells as commodities, through the ambiguous word "line" ('genetic inheritance' or 'product type'), and more obviously as clothes that you can either have tailor-made "bespoke" or buy ready-made "off the shelf".

On a lighter note, the latest kind of "bank" to be suggested is a tooth bank (Wilson 2002: 35). This reminds one of the Western custom of exchanging children's milk teeth, when they fall out, for money, pretending that the tooth fairy visits the children at night and trades the tooth from under the pillow.

Turning to the whole person rather than body parts, the extent to which humans are seen as commodities is particularly repugnant if it leads to the conclusion that some are better or worth more than others, as this affronts ethical and religious notions of equality. This nasty tendency probably originates in the metonymy by which we equate people with their possessions of goods or money, and respect them accordingly (Kövecses 1990: 112). It has become quite widespread in the media to say that "X is worth 30 million dollars" – which literally means something different from "X possesses 30 million dollars", but the metonymy blurs the distinction between being and having. However, this is not a particularly modern phenomenon (there are plenty of examples in Adam Smith, discussed in chapter 8).

The following report of an interview with a Singaporean military historian illustrates the tendency to equate people with their wealth or possessions, particularly the beginning of the last paragraph: "the home … is the sum of a determined woman".

> When you step into the home of [X] you enter a world of charmed gracious living.
> The black and white marble-tiled foyer of the Cluny Park bungalow leads to a drawing room. Here floor-to-ceiling French windows overlook a pool outside.
> Broad white sofas line one side of the airy room, showing off a costly Persian carpet on the maple parquet floor. At one corner is a gleaming baby grand piano, at another a French-Vietnamese cabinet displays figurines of geisha girls, samurai, and Chinese deities-all carved from ivory….
> The home, you realise, is the sum of a determined woman, who took four years to tear it down and build it up again, until she could get it just so.

In his book *To Be or To Have* Erich Fromm noted the idioms **to be one's own person** or **on one's own** which suggest an intimate psychological tendency to equate ownership with identity. This links to and is perhaps a reversal of the Lakoffian conceptual metaphor ATTRIBUTES ARE POSSESSIONS (Lakoff 1993: 206), reinforced by the ambiguity of the English word *property*, meaning both 'attribute' and 'possession'.

One of the predictable and nasty consequences of the inequalities reinforced by this equation is kidnapping. If the purpose is exchange of prisoners, then usually the wealthy person kidnapped will be worth a good deal more than the prisoners they are exchanged for, so one kidnap victim can be exchanged for many prisoners. If the motive is money, this is a crude method of income redistribution, since relatives of the rich victim transfer money to the relatively poor kidnappers. And yet, even the poor can be valued as "kidnap" victims, witness the spread of human trafficking.

Some of the most disturbing aspects of the commodification of humans are in the area of human reproduction and genetics. The former Archbishop of York, John Habgood inveighs against the buying of eggs and sperm:

> There are reports that for some citizens [in the US] procreation has already been commodified to the point at which it is possible and legal to make bids of tens of thousands of dollars on the Internet for the eggs and sperm produced by glamour models. "We bid for everything else in this society," said the owner of the website, "so why not eggs?" (Habgood 2002: 128).

His objection is that manipulating the characteristics of a child subtly changes the relationship between child and parent. A child needs to be loved, accepted and respected as a gift, regardless of imperfections. This opinion is echoed by Tom Shakespeare "Children should be accepted for themselves, not to the extent that they fulfil our wishes or desires. We should be more tolerant of disability and all imperfections, let alone imbalances of sex within a family" (Shakespeare 2002: 23). Habgood regards reproductive manipulation as a kind of magic – an attempt to control forces that we do not understand, and as idolatry – the escape from the reality of what is genuinely other than ourselves by the worshipping of things created with our own hands and minds. He believes reproduction is ideally an act of creation, the endowing of another creature, the other, with the freedom to be itself (2002: 126–27).

Possibly the most important kind of commodification of humans is the patenting of DNA and gene sequences. It was a close run thing whether the entire human genome would be in the public or private domain. The publicly-funded Human Genome Project (HGP), who wanted this knowledge to be public, was competing with Celera Genomics, who planned to commercialise it by charging fees for licenses. John Sulston, the leader of the British part of the HGP project, pointed out, "We were in a position of responsibility... without us, the human genome would be privatized." (Sulston & Ferry 2002, Godrej 2002)

However, although HGP worked as fast as Celera, and they jointly announced completion of the human genome draft in June 2000, the patenting of DNA material and gene sequences went ahead at frantic speed. By December 2000, there were already 9,364 applications for patents covering 126,672 genes and small sub-gene fragments. Applications were growing at the rate of 34,500 every month. Just one company, Genset of France, had applied for patents on 36,083 human gene sequences ('Patenting life: special report' 2000). By 2002 the number of patents on human genetic material may have been as high as 4 million ('Why Should I be Concerned About Human Genetics?').

Many people believe that the knowledge of gene sequences in human cells should remain the common property of humanity. As the law now stands if you can describe a genetic sequence and suggest a use for it, you are entitled to take out a patent, not simply for the novel use you have discovered, but for the genetic material itself. For example, the company Myriad has patented the genetic sequence BRCA1 and 2, having shown, through a diagnostic test, its use in predicting breast cancer (Pagan-Westphal 2002).

We have noted the large number of metaphors which construct humans as commodities and an increasing trend for commodification in the areas of reproduction and genetics. But we can widen our field to consider how the equation of quality with wealth both explains this trend towards commodification and allows us to see it applying to other areas of the natural world besides human beings.

3.4   QUALITY IS MONEY/WEALTH

We noted in chapter 2 in relation to time, that modern science and economic theory attempt to reduce qualitative differences to quantitative ones, through the equation QUALITY IS QUANTITY. Perhaps the most obvious way in which this is done in modern bourgeois political economy is to use money as a common measure of the "heterogeneities of human desires, of use values, and of elements and processes 'in nature'". It thus becomes a means of maximizing utility through market mechanisms that determine the rational allocation of resources. As Marx noted, money reduces the use values of the multidimensional ecosystem, human desires and needs, and subjective meanings to a common measurable objective standard which everyone can understand (Harvey 1996: 150–1).

> In the market place, for practical reasons, the innumerable qualitative distinctions which are of vital importance for man and society are suppressed; they are not allowed to surface. Thus the reign of quantity celebrates its greatest triumphs in "The Market". Everything is equated with everything else. To equate things means to give them a price and make them exchangeable. (Schumacher 1973/1999: 30).

So QUALITY IS QUANTITY becomes the more specific QUALITY IS MONEY/WEALTH

Positive qualities are frequently metaphorised in terms of wealth and money. **Wealth** 'large amount of desirable things' (*he uses a wealth of effective teaching techniques*), **asset** 'useful or valuable quality' or **capital**, **sterling** 'admirable in quality' (*he made sterling efforts to walk again after his car accident*), **fortune** 'set of good events that happen to you and affect your life' (*he had the good fortune to stand in for Pavarotti who was sick*), **bonus** 'pleasant additional quality', **dividend** 'advantage', and **credit** 'honour, pride'.

The degree of something's positive qualities, benefits or importance then becomes its **value/worth** (*he is of great value to the school*), so it is **valued/valuable** (*swimming is a valuable skill*); to 'overestimate/underestimate importance' is to **overvalue/undervalue**, an 'estimate on the basis of immediate appearances' is **face value**, and to 'make less important' is to **devalue**. 'To have extremely important or positive qualities' is to be **priceless** or **precious.**

If things are found to be beneficial and advantageous it is as though they go up in value: **appreciate/appreciation** 'recognise/recognition that something is important or positive' (*I didn't appreciate the importance of contraception until it was too late*), **profitable** 'beneficial, useful' (*arguments at this point are not likely to be profitable), **profit from, make capital out of** 'get an advantage from' (*Thatcher made political capital out of the Falklands War*).

Hence experiences are depicted in terms of money transactions, for example payments. If you are on the receiving end of the payment it is to your advantage: **pay** 'give a benefit or advantage' (*it never pays to take risks with safety*), **payment** 'reward or outcome which one deserves', **payoff, payback** 'useful result or advantage received for something' (*his success was a payoff for hard training*), **earn** 'get a benefit or positive result' (*after five hard weeks I've earned a break*), **repay** 'be worthwhile (of interest/effort/ attention)' (*reading stories to your young child will repay the effort in their later education*) and **compensate** 'make up for, be an advantage that cancels out a disadvantage'. Payment then is often constructed as a **return** for something you have already done or paid and if you expect a good result from this time and effort you can **bank on** it. Even without an expectation of proportionate advantage you may be disappointed **not to get any change out of** it 'get no return result or satisfaction from' (*I got no change out of the three hours I spent with him*). On the other hand you should not miss opportunities to have a **rewarding** experience, and there are just some things that you can **not afford to** 'not allow oneself to' miss.

Alternatively, experience can be a negative result of past behaviour, in which case you are the one paying in the present or future. The **price, cost** is the 'effort or negative effect of doing or obtaining something' (*the price for the war in Iraq should have been Bush's rejection at the next election*), **at any price** means 'whatever the unpleasant consequences may be' (*he was determined to go to war at any price*), **pay (the price) for** 'experience the bad results of what you do', results which you **count the cost of**, 'realise the negative effects of', and a cost or effect which may 'be very negative' will **cost you dearly** (*Clinton's sexual misbehaviour cost him and his party dearly*). Sometimes you pay for your achievements **at the expense of** 'with negative effects on' something else, usually some quality or area of your life you have sacrificed or neglected (*his success as a novelist was at the expense of his family life*).

This quality as money/wealth analogy extends its sources into other transactions such as investing, trade and tax/accounting: **lend** means 'add a desirable quality to' (*his membership lends a touch of class to the club*), or more particularly **invest with** 'give power, importance or value to' (*in his stories everyday reality is invested with a sense of fascination and joy*). You can **trade on** 'exploit to your own advantage' a characteristic or quality you possess (*Blatter traded on his popularity with developing nations to get re-elected*). If something is **more than you bargained for** it turns out to be 'more onerous than you at first thought', and may **tax** 'strain or demand effort from' you. You may be called to **account for** 'defend or explain your actions'.

If we take these metaphors seriously, we increasingly establish the quality or value of anything by conceptualising it in money terms. One symptom is the tendency to equate standard of living with quality of life, suggesting that your quality of life depends on how much you can buy or consume – a doubtful proposition with very harmful effects on the environment as resources are wasted on unnecessary products, and the manufacturing process itself uses up energy and causes pollution.

Heidegger warns that

the humanness of man and the thingness of things dissolve into the calculated market value of a market which ... trades in the nature of Being and thus subjects all beings to the trade of a calculation that dominates most tenaciously in those areas where there is no need of numbers (Heidegger 1971: 114–5).

As an instance of this, Lakoff has explored how even morality seems to be seen as a transaction (Lakoff 1996: ch. 4). For example the lexis in RELATIONSHIP/AFFECTION IS MONEY/WEALTH can be seen in terms of Reciprocation: **indebted to**, 'grateful for help given', **debt**, 'appreciation, gratitude' (*I can never repay the debt I owe him*), with the result that you **owe**, 'feel gratitude and the need to reciprocate' (*I owe him for babysitting so often*) and will need to **repay**, 'do something good to somebody in return for past favours' (*how can I ever repay you for your kindness*) or, more contractually **pay your dues**, 'do your duty' (*I've paid my dues by looking after the children for four years-now it's your turn!*). And if acting according to morality you will be careful not to **short-change**, 'give inferior or inadequate service or treatment to' (*on taking the job I was promised promotion at the first opportunity – I think I've been short-changed in the present personnel actions*). Or moral accounting might take the form of Retribution: **pay back**, 'take revenge on someone who has treated you badly'; **settle accounts/old scores**, 'take revenge by repaying an insult or harm' (*I've finally settled accounts with her for refusing me a job*).

If one behaves well one builds up **credit**, 'honour, pride, reputation' (*his credit is high with the President*) so that people **appreciate** 'feel gratitude for' you or your actions. If you are lucky, when you behave badly people may **make allowances**, 'refrain from criticism or judgement' (*we should make allowances for him – he's just lost his wife*).

There is an intrinsic link between money and relationships of trust. When money is used as a means of exchange, trust and faith has to be put in the relationship between the signifier, money, and the signified, wealth, and that depends upon the ability of users to credit others – credit therefore lies at the root of money exchange even before systems of credit and debt were invented (Harvey 1996: 235).

3.4.1 Privatisation of natural "resources".

A further offshoot of the ideology that quality is wealth is the trend towards privatisation – the bringing of commonly-owned utilities and resources within the economic sphere, and making them subservient to the forces of the market, as we saw with genetic sequences. What value does anything have, unless we can buy it and sell it? As Wayne Ellwood puts it, somewhat cynically:

> This faith in the market as the ultimate measure of human relations is carving out new markets where once there were none – what is sometimes called the "second enclosure" movement. Just as the aristocracy in Britain dispossessed peasants and claimed common lands for their own 300 years ago, giant transnational corporations are aiming to control essential human needs – water, education, healthcare,

the atmosphere, even the genetic structure of life itself – and sell them back to us (Ellwood 2002).

Commonly-owned "resources" and knowledge have been progressively brought within the sphere of economics. The idea of ownership of land was foreign to native Americans and Africans – land was held in common. For example, though native American villages in New England when the English arrived had sovereign rights which defined political and ecological territory, they were not permanent rights nor individual rights. Because of their mobility they only claimed the rights of use for a limited period of time and there was no attempt to prevent others gathering from their land or any concept of trespass or rent (Harvey 1996: 223). The notion of private property relies on one of the grounds of the container schema – the notion of a dividing line between inside and outside. This make possible the idea of exclusivity – what is mine cannot be ours, and what is yours cannot be mine. The idea of property rights and sovereignty evidently grew up together, and as we saw with categorization (1.7), it is the ruler whose boundaries and divisions are respected and validated (see also Ruggie 1986).

Water used to be a national asset which the government managed for the sake of the whole community, or which local communities managed for themselves. The ideology of privatisation assumes that, if brought within private ownership and "floated" on the stock-market, water resource management will automatically be more efficient. Much of the evidence suggests however, quite the contrary, that public companies in the Netherlands, Japan and the US are more efficient than private water companies in France and England (Blokland, Braadbaart and Schwarz 1999).

There seems to be some consensus that many natural resources are best managed by small communities at the local level, rather than at the government level or, worse still, owned at the multinational level. Rajendra Singh tells, for example, of a very successful initiative in water management in India, in which small-scale dams and ponds – *johads* – are built by villagers to harvest rainwater. But the villagers do not claim to own the ponds or the water in them. He points out that no king in history has ever claimed to own water, and that government cannot own water either, since it belongs to nature. Before rights to common land and forest disappeared the villagers had a rich tradition of building *johads*, one which is now being taken up again. He warns: "If multinationals gain control of water, they will squash the rights of the poor" (Tata 2002: 50)

Plants known to, used, or cultivated by indigenous people are increasingly under attack from companies wishing to patent them in acts of "biopiracy". A famous case is the *neem* tree whose anti-bacterial and insecticidal properties have been well known to countless generations of Indians. US and Japanese companies tried to take out eighty patents on the tree and the substances it produces, though not all have been successful. In 1999 Larry Proctor, owner of a seed company POD-NERS LLC, won a US patent on Enola beans of a certain shade of yellow and then began suing Mexican bean exporters to the US for patent infringement of the yellow variety, though again the patent is being challenged by an international agricultural body (www.etcgroup.org). According to Dinyar Godrej (2002: 1–2):

> The ultimate goal is nothing short of the takeover of the world's food supply through the means of patented seed which cannot be saved by farmers and must be bought anew each year. This is achieved by using dubious technologies like Monsanto's Terminator, which make plants bear sterile seed, and by enforcing contracts and prosecutions of farmers who don't comply. In 1998 the Co-President of Monsanto's agricultural division said: "This is not just a consolidation of seed companies, it's really a consolidation of the entire food chain" (Anderson 1999 quoted in Godrej 2002: 2)

Problems of the environment are thought by some within the ecological modernization movement to be soluble by bringing it more thoroughly into the economic area so that eco-tourism is seen as one answer, and putting a price on pollution, for example, by emissions trading, is another. It is often only when the environment can be valued in money terms that those in power take notice. E.P. Odum only managed to secure wetland protection in Georgia by putting some rather arbitrary money figure on the value of these wetlands to the state economy (Harvey 1996: 151). However, Harvey points out various problems associated with this approach: money value may become unstable; it is equivalent to the market price of goods and services but many natural "assets" do not directly provide such services or goods; the ecological organic whole of nature cannot be broken down into parts that are valued separately; the future benefits of natural goods are impossible to calculate since natural phenomena are often chaotic and unpredictable; and monetary valuation of the environment tends to view the ecosystem as an "externality" rather than internalised through respect for nature in religious or cultural terms, presumably taking a little further the idea that if IMPORTANT IS CENTRAL then the environment is marginal. Harvey concludes "it is hard, in the light of these problems not to conclude that there is something about money valuations that makes them inherently *anti-ecological* confining the field of thinking and of action to instrumental environmental management" (1996: 152–155). Nevertheless, putting money value on nature may be one necessary tactic for preventing some kinds of environmental destruction in our late capitalist society, but we should be aware of the change of ideology that this has entailed over the years since land was first enclosed. It amounts to something of a prostitution, and apparently the best things in life are no longer free.

The process of regarding nature as primarily a commodity has already gone a long way. The normal way to characterise "nature" in the media is in terms of its use for humans. In a study of the representation of nature in the BBC World Service, I investigated the common collocations of various classes of natural objects. For minerals such as oil and coal *produce* and *production* are very common, and *burning* collocates with coal while *prices* is a common collocate of oil; all of these suggest their human use and marketisation. *Animal* itself collocates most importantly with *breeding* and *livestock*, underlining the importance of farming, and the same is true of birds where we have *feed, keeping/keepers* along with *egg/poultry production.* The most significant collocate of *bird* is *killed,* presumably for later consumption. Similarly, farming determines the main collocates of plants, where *trees* collocate with *fruit,* giving the very common semi-fixed expression *fruit-bearing trees. Wheat's* collocates, *production, growth, hundred, tons,* focus on its cultivation and economic measurement. Forests, too, with their common collocates *resource, value, output, crops* and *products* are commodities for human use. *Water,* if *clean,* is represented mainly as an essential human resource: *supply, supplies, drinking, running, sanitation.* Issues of *pollution, purification* and *contamination* seem paramount, precisely because they threaten the supplies used by humans. Lastly, there is the land, which is, in the news media, seen predominantly as a possession occasioning battles, as indicated by the collocates *return, dispute, forced, rights, ownership/owners, claims* (Goatly 2002a).

Even environmentalist texts such as the Worldwatch Institute's, 'A New Era Unfolds' (Brown 1993), tend to take this anthropocentric human resource attitude to nature. Analysis of the semantics of the grammar identifies a widespread use of the verbs or nouns *yield, supply* and *carry/support* when nature is an agent, so that nature *supplies/yields* a product or resource for humans, or *supports/carries* a human population. Accordingly, the destruction of nature is regarded not as intrinsically regrettable, but as negative because it reduces the supplies or capital for human use or ownership, which explains the frequency of the verbs *lose, loss, degradation* and *depletion.* The main lament of the chapter is that "natural capital is consumed".

One can conceive commodification as a question of distinguishing ends and the means to ends. Is the living environment just a means of production, or an end in itself? If a means of production, then presumably there is no harm in commodifying it. Things which we do as an end in themselves do not need to be brought within utilitarian calculation and commodified. Especially things which we have not made ourselves, like animals or humans, should not be treated like artefacts as commodities (Schumacher 1973/1999: 83–86).

3.5 ORGANISATION/SYSTEM IS MACHINE

We saw in the previous section that humans have tended to be commodified in terms of organ donation, especially when this is done on a commercial basis. The phrase *spare part* used in this context provides us with a link to a series of metaphor themes that represent humans and social organisations as tools or machines of various kinds. In the Metalude database we have several of these: HUMAN IS IMPLEMENT/UTENSIL, HUMAN IS MACHINE/APPLIANCE, HUMAN IS VEHICLE and ORGANISATION/SYSTEM IS MACHINE. We begin with a discussion of the latter.

Aspects of social organisation or the economy are given a mechanistic construction: **machine** 'group of people who control or organise something' (*the Labour Party machine is running at full speed),* **machinery** 'functioning (of an organisation)' (*the* *machinery of government could be more efficient*), **mechanism** 'methods of dealing with' (*the appeals mechanism needs reforming*), **mechanics** 'practical aspects of a system or organisation' (*the mechanics of the Zimbabwe elections were seriously flawed*), and **tool/instrument** 'plan, organisation or system used to achieve a particular result' (*the World Bank has for too long been an instrument/tool of repression*). If society is a machine or engine then **social engineering** is 'artificial control of or change to the groupings within society' (*the campaign to persuade graduates to have more children is a blatant piece of social engineering*).

Parts of an organisation are parts of a machine: the important and powerful parts are the **kingpin** 'most important person in an organisation', or the **panel** (like a control panel) 'small-decision making group within an organisation' (*the selection panel were interviewing candidates all morning*), whereas the **nuts and bolts** are the 'practical facts of an organisation rather than theories'. Inside the engine are the **workings** 'the way a system or organisation functions', and if these go **like clockwork** they function 'exactly in the way planned' (*the sales promotion went like clockwork and we quickly sold half the flats*). These workings are often conceived of as **wheels** 'the way an organization operates' (*he knows the wheels of administration turn slowly*), hence **oil/grease the wheels** 'help society or an organisation to operate successfully' (*government investment will oil the wheels of reform*), or the **wheels … grind** '(the organisation) functions but with difficulty or inefficiently' (*the wheels of the law grind slowly*), maybe because you **throw a spanner/wrench in the works** 'spoil a plan' or **gum up** the machinery 'prevent a system from operating correctly' (*the house buying system is gummed up*).

Like a vehicle engine an organisation or system may function more or less effectively, **sputter** 'develop unsteadily or intermittently' (*the economy has shown signs of sputtering to life but they have been short-lived*), or **tick over** 'continue basic functions but without expansion or improvement' (*the company is ticking over and profits are steady but not spectacular*), **shift/change gear** 'move from one system of working to another' (*computerization meant the printing industry had to shift gear*), since organisations must be **geared to** 'adapted to' their aims (*tobacco companies are geared to making profits and ignoring moral questions*), though it is impossible to be geared to anything if you are **in neutral** 'not developing or changing' (*after nearly a decade in neutral the Japanese economy is showing signs of growth*).

If a system or organisation is not functioning or running efficiently, then one can, like an engine, either **service** members of it 'provide a person or group with something they need in order to function' (*there are over 500 staff at head office, servicing our global telephone network*), **overhaul** it 'examine and improve' (*the NHS needs to be urgently overhauled*), **dismantle** it 'get rid of a system or organisation' or **scrap** it 'abandon or close down' (*FIFA had failed so badly that they decided to scrap the whole organization and start again*).

Unlike the animal metaphors we look at in the next chapter, most of these metaphors seem either neutral or positive about machines, as though the efficient functioning of an organisation in the manner of a machine is something desirable: it goes like clockwork, and if only the wheels would go more smoothly everything would be fine. This is probably because the main meaning focus of the machine metaphor is appropriate functioning (Kövecses 2002). Only in the metaphor of the wheels grinding do we get the impression that humans might suffer in the process.

The idea that society or the economy was a machine was behind Adam Smith's metaphor of the invisible hand of the market. Clocks have visible hands, but they have invisible "hands" too, in the form of a pendulum. "Just as a pendulum regulates the proper functioning of a clock, the invisible hand of nature operates in a similar fashion, assuring the proper regulation of supply and demand in the economic market place" (Rifkin 1987: 205). Inspired by Galileo, Hobbes, too, saw both humans as machines and human society, the "body" politic, as consequently a machine. "Life is but a motion of limbs, the beginning whereof is some principal part within" (Hobbes 1651/1983: 118–9). The mechanistic metaphor has also been used as though the system of power relations is itself like a clock, with a regulator to keep it functioning in a balanced way:

> The idea of balance among a number of nations for the purpose of preventing one of them becoming strong enough to threaten the independence of the other is a metaphor taken from the field of mechanics. It was appropriate to the way of thinking of the sixteenth and seventeenth and eighteenth centuries, which led to picture society and the whole universe as a gigantic mechanism, a machine or a clockwork, created and kept in motion by the divine watchmaker (Morgenthau 1973: 203).

In the industrial factory age the factory workers or "hands" became subject to the machines, as we saw in the last chapter. Time keeping and enslavement to machines went "hand in hand":

> In the mechanized factory men are synchronized to machines, which in general have more regular habits than men … materials too have to flow to feed the machines, and thus a synchronisation of men, machines and materials develops, more impersonal and complex than anything before. Most men today may not be aware that they are geared to machines – even while they are being awakened by the ringing of a bell and gulping down their coffee in a race with the clock. (Sebastian de Grazia, quoted in Gleick 1991: 35)

"Geared" is an apt metaphor recognising that humans themselves have turned into machines too.

The pattern into which ORGANISATION IS MACHINE fits seems to be as follows. Those with capital can make and own the new technology, but in order for the new technology to be successfully implemented the humans interacting with it must themselves behave as though they were parts of machines. The division of labour was the great driving force behind this mechanisation – "the dividing of every complete process of production into minute parts, so that the final product can be produced at great speed without anyone having had to contribute more than a totally insignificant and, in most cases, unskilled movement of the limbs" (Schumacher 1973/1999: 38). Such a mechanisation of humans, whether in interaction with clocks, steam engines, convey-or belts or computers, is legitimised by the humans themselves being metaphorically redefined as clockwork or steam engine or information-processing systems, according to the latest biological or psychological model. Following this logic, the work they do does not in fact reduce or dehumanise them, but simply allows them to operate according to their nature. It is an opposite view to that of the philosopher Whitehead who saw life as "an offensive directed against the repetitious mechanism of the universe" and modern mechanised industry as "an offensive against the unpredictability, unpunctuality, general waywardness and cussedness of living nature, including man" (quoted in Schumacher 1973/1999: 87–88).

3.6   HUMAN IS MACHINE

Societies, industries and organisations may be metaphorised as a machine, but so may individuals, whether their minds or bodies (witness *L'homme machine* by the 18th century French doctor and philosopher La Mettrie). I devote considerable space to the discussion of this metaphor, for, like HUMAN IS ANIMAL discussed in the next chapter, it is the locus for a critical debate about human identity since the industrial and, particularly, information technology revolutions. I begin by giving evidence of how prevalent the vocabulary is within the metaphor themes HUMAN IS IMPLEMENT/UTENSIL, HUMAN IS MACHINE/APPLIANCE, HUMAN IS VEHICLE. I proceed to demonstrate the strong tendency among certain reductionist scientists to assert or assume the truth of the mechanical/computer model of humans. I briefly consider some objections to this assertion and its consequences in social and ethical practice. Finally, I discuss two theories which have an important bearing on the questions raised by the metaphor, the Santiago theory of cognition, and Donna Haraway's 'Cyborg Manifesto'.

3.6.1   Lexical evidence for the prevalence of the metaphor

At the most general humans can be seen as a **tool** 'slave, servant' (*the president is just the tool of big business*), and therefore **instrumental** 'most important influence causing something to happen' (*he was instrumental in helping Picasso when he was a young artist*). More specifically they are other kinds of instruments or utensils: **whip** 'member of political party who persuades its MPs to vote for the government', **anchor** 'presenter of a TV or radio broadcast consisting of several items', **new broom** 'newcomer to a job who is expected to make changes', **blunderbuss** 'blunderer', **crook**, literally 'staff with a hook at one end used by shepherds and ceremonially by bishops', metaphorically 'criminal or cheat', **rake** 'immoral man who indulges in excessive drinking gambling or sex' (*my elder brother liked to think of himself as bit of a rake*), **crock**, literally 'piece of crockery', metaphorically 'old, weak person' (*there were a few old crocks sitting knit-*

ting in the library), **basket case** 'person who is mad or insane'. Note that many of these, especially the last five, are used pejoratively.

Next there is a group in which a body part is compared with a whole implement or utensil: here we have again **tool** 'penis' (*when he got his tool out I really panicked*), **bag** 'dark, loose or swollen skin under the eyes caused by tiredness or age', **six-pack**, literally a pack of six cans of beer, metaphorically 'six abdominal muscles' (*if you use this exercise machine you'll develop a great six-pack*), **bread basket** 'stomach', **blood vessel** 'capillary, vein or artery'; and compounds, phrases or idioms that imply body part is a tool: **hatchet-faced** 'with a thin, cruel, hard and unpleasant face', **put lead in your pencil** 'cause an erection of the penis', **scissors kick** 'kick in which the legs are brought together quickly'(*with a clever scissor kick the winger deceived the back and ran in for a try*). Verbs constructing part of the body as an implement include **screw** 'have sex with', **flail**, literally 'thresh', metaphorically 'move your limbs in a violent uncontrolled way' (*his limbs were flailing as though he was suffering an epileptic fit*), **rasping** 'producing an unpleasant effect on, like the sound of a file on metal' (*she had a rasping voice which gave me a headache after a while*).

Other metaphors compare a body part with the part of an implement or utensil: **shoulder blade** 'flat triangular bone in upper part of the back', **shank** 'leg', **windpipe** 'trachea, pipe which takes air from mouth to lungs', **butt**, literally 'the blunt end of an arrow', metaphorically 'bottom or backside'.

Humans are compared with various kinds of machines: **automaton** or **robot** 'person who acts like a machine without thinking about what they are doing', i.e. **mechanically**, and **dynamo** 'extremely energetic person'; or parts of machines: **crank** 'strange, eccentric or odd person', **mouthpiece** 'spokesperson', **cog** 'unimportant person in an organisation' (*at IBM I felt like a small cog in a huge machine*). Next there are the metaphors where the source is part of the body: **motormouth** 'person who speaks fast and continuously', **socket** 'part of the body into which another part fits' (*the eye ball had been completely removed from its socket*), **waterworks** 'urinary tract' (*"I've got some trouble with my waterworks, doctor"*), **valve** 'part of the heart that controls the flow of blood', **spare part** 'organ of the body which is transplanted to replace one that doesn't function well' (*he underwent spare-part surgery to replace one of his kidneys*).

The many verbs which are quite specific in selecting machines or appliances as their subjects/agents provide a number of metaphors in this group. These include: **process** 'understand, read', **seize up** (literally of an engine 'to stop working through excess friction') 'become stiff or unable to work (of body parts)' (*in cold weather my joints tend to seize up*), **engage with**, based on the literal idea of one gear engaging with another 'become involved in', **discharge** 'produce pus from a wound', like a factory discharging pollutants (*the scar discharged a thick yellow liquid*). Additionally there are nominalizations: **output** 'rate of working', **input** 'comment, suggestion' (*can I have your input on the new plans?*), **drive**, literally 'mechanical force for powering an engine', metaphorically 'motivation' (*our new head has enormous drive but few brains*), **resistance**, as literally in an electrical circuit, 'rebellion or opposition to change', **breakdown** 'serious mental or physical illness' (*he suffered a nervous breakdown because of stress*), **workings**, literally 'the interior moving parts of a machine or clock', metaphorically 'way of thinking and making decisions' (*it's difficult to understand the workings of his mind in rejecting the job offer*), **burnout** 'extreme tiredness caused by overwork', as in an engine or circuit (*if you don't cut down on overtime you're in danger of burnout*). And there are idioms and phrases which imply mechanistic views of humans: **what makes you tick** 'what motivates you', **run out of steam** 'lose energy'.

Another group comprises verbs metaphorically applied to humans that literally take machines as objects or affecteds. First we have to start up a machine: **turn on/ switch on** means 'start behaving in some way' (*the boss came in and he turned on his posh accent*), and **turn on** can alternatively mean 'attract, excite sexually' (*seeing her in a swimsuit really turned me on*). And when we have finished our task we stop the machine/appliance: **turn off** 'fail to interest or excite, bore, diminish interest' (*I found her pink underwear really turned me off*); **switch off** 'stop paying attention' (*after the first 10 minutes I just switched off*). While the machine is in operation you may have to **adjust** 'change behaviour/ideas' or **readjust** 'change behaviour again' (*will I be able to readjust to life in England?*). You may have to **maintain** it 'provide with food and other basic necessities' or give **maintenance** 'resources for the basic living needs' (*he's divorced and has to make maintenance payments to his first wife*) or mend it: **mend** 'recover from illness/injury' (*it will take 8 weeks for your broken foot to mend*). More specifically the appliance may be a boiler – **stoke up** 'eat a lot of food to avoid hunger later' (*as the morning was cold, they stoked up on waffles, eggs and pancakes*), or a computer – **programmed** 'trained' (*our workers are programmed to reject faulty goods*). A nominalisation which belongs in this group is **genetic engineering** 'changing the structure of genes to "improve" or make more healthy'.

Incidentally this group nicely illustrates the tendency for the literal meaning and the metaphorical meaning to belong to different grammatical structures: *switch off, adjust, readjust, mend* and *stoke up* are all used transitively in their literal meanings and intransitively in their metaphorical meanings. Compare *he switched off the fan* with *I just switched off*. This does something to reduce the de-personification – when used with human subjects they allow a higher degree of agency than when they are used with machines as objects.

Next there are adjectives and adverbs that are applied to humans, mainly taken from the field of engines: **turbocharged** 'made more strong or powerful' (*she was a tiny girl but with a turbo-charged voice*), **high-powered** 'having status, responsibility, energy, skill and knowledge', **high octane** 'exciting, energetic and intense' (*it was a high octane performance that left the audience stunned*), **at full throttle** 'using all your efforts and energies', **high-maintenance** 'requiring a lot of expense to satisfy their lifestyle demands' (*John's girlfriend is a rather high-maintenance partner, I couldn't afford her!*) and **rusty** 'lacking recent experience in practising a skill'. And other miscellaneous idioms remain: **have your head screwed on right** 'be clever in a practical commonsense way', **the penny has dropped** 'some has suddenly understood what they had failed to understand' as if they are a slot machine, and **on the scrap-heap** 'redundant, dismissed from work' (*it's hard to be put on the scrap-heap at 40*).

Finally there are metaphors which specifically construct humans as vehicles. From the field of cars: **spare tyre** 'roll of belly fat', **in the fast lane** 'having a glamorous, busy and exciting life', **in tow** 'following' (*she arrived with her three kids in tow*), **park** 'position your body' (*why do you have to park yourself there – you're in the way*); from cars/ships: **hulk** 'heavy awkward person' (*although he's a great hulk he's very kind*); from other road transport, **carriage** 'way of holding the body when walking', **handlebar moustache** 'long moustache with curled ends'; and aeroplanes, **on automatic pilot** 'acting without thinking' (*I'm bored – I can do my job on automatic pilot*).

To some extent the metaphorical vocabulary of HUMAN IS MACHINE represents a resistance against reducing humans to machines, because the number of pejorative terms outnumbers the positive 2 to 1. This is in contrast to the lexis we observed when machines represents organisations, which are mainly positive (Table 13).

Table 13. Positive and pejorative metaphors in HUMAN IS MACHINE/IMPLEMENT

PEJORATIVE METAPHORS	POSITIVE METAPHORS
crook, crock, rake, basket-case, hatchet-faced, flail, rasping; mechanically, automaton, motormouth, cog, crank, hulk	new-broom, dynamo, drive, turbocharged, high-powered, high-octane

Nevertheless most of the lexis is neutral, and the extent to which it seems natural to use mechanical and vehicular metaphors for the human body can be seen in the following extracts from an article in the American teen magazine *Seventeen* [my boldings].

The Stress Code

How to look and feel a whole lot better when the pressure is on

…. All aspects of your life are changing. Friendships shift; dating – whether it's nonexistent, too intense or just right – can cause your head to spin; your parents may not be as easy to get along with as they were just a few months ago; and **your body is doing a heavy duty transformation** before your very eyes. The bottom line: You're moving into unknown territory, and your brain has a lot of serious stuff to deal with.

Stress, however, involves a lot more than anxiety. (Get ready – here comes the conspiracy theory part.) When you're emotionally strung out, your body reacts with uncool moves that make matters worse. Stress signals **the adrenal glands to pump up the volume of adrenaline**, a hormone that can make you feel jittery and restless. It can also cause digestion to get weird, with upset stomach and constipation being common complaints. Avoiding spicy and fried foods will help; so will eating high-fiber fruits, vegetables and whole grains.

> **Your skin also responds to the extra glandular action by increasing oil pro-
> duction**, which can lead to acne breakouts. You can fight back by using a gentle
> cleanser and an acne cream (or try Noxzema 2-in-1 Pads that do the job in one
> step). Also, check out our five-point make-up routine at night; it'll tell you how to
> brighten up when you're feeling especially pale and pasty. Since **your scalp tends
> to go into the same oil overdrive as your skin,** wash hair every day when stressed,
> using a specially formulated shampoo (we like Nexxus Exx/Oil shampoo).
>
> But beyond dealing with these specific problems, try to get over stress in gen-
> eral. Yes, a hot bath or a massage will soothe your spirits, but our favorite stress-
> busting **tool** is exercise. Serious movement **triggers** the release of endorphins, you
> body's natural feel-good chemicals – for free and with no special equipment; it can
> also help distract you from your worries. Sounds like a good deal to us.
>
> Rev Up your looks when stress has you down. Our five-step make-up plan:
> 1 Choose foundation that's a shade darker than usual to give skin some extra
>   color.
> 2 Do we need to mention that under-eye concealer is a must? ...

The female teenage body here is constructed as a machine which is working independently of the person, who has little or no control over it, unless helped to by such an
advertorial, which suggests some tools to tinker with the mechanism. Not only is the
body here a curiously distanced machine, but it is reduced to its parts – scalp, skin, adrenal glands – and there is little sense of a unified person whose whole makes up more
than her parts. This mirrors the results of Martin's ethnographic research, in which
she found in her subjects a feeling of the "unimaginably small and the unimaginably
large coalesced in the same image, agency residing in cells, the person becoming an
observer of the agency of others inside him or herself" (Martin 1992: 125).

The philosophical debate about whether the human body is a machine, and whether the human mind (soul) is also a machine has a long history, going back at least as far
as Descartes and Hobbes, a tradition explored more in our last chapter (8.2.6). From
a contemporary standpoint, I shall, in the present chapter, demonstrate the degree to
which many scientists and technologists assume in their research and experiments
that the body and mind are no more and no less than machines. I will then proceed to
show some of the ideological forces that have led to this view and this technology, and
perhaps hint at dangers involved in this mechanistic model of humanity.

3.6.2 Science, technology and the mind/body as machine

The literature of popular science reports much scientific research and experimentation
that views and treats the mind and body as simply a machine or, more specifically, the favourite machine of our age, a computer (cf. Lakoff and Johnson 1999: 251–60). A glance
through the latest editions of *New Scientist* will give you a taste. Besides "the **plumbing**
theory of heart disease" and the routine mention of brain "**circuitry**", there is currently,

in some quarters, a drive to produce more human-like robots, which presumes that this is less of a metaphor than we think. Rodney Brooks declares "so the brain is a machine, but it's not necessarily a computing machine", admitting that there is a great deal more that has to be found out before the human-machine, the intelligent and emotional robot can be built (Graham-Rowe 2002a). One solution to this is to admit that our present machines are relatively impotent compared with the components of our nervous system, and to hook up robots or computers to neurons or brain stems of animals in order to enhance the robot's power to learn or computer's power to operate.

In an interesting and disturbing article 'Mind over Metal' (Ananthaswamy 2002) we learn of Steve Potter who has connected brain cells from a real rat to a virtual rat on a computer, and of other researchers who have taken brainstems from fish to control robots, or are using the brain of a monkey to move an artificial arm. Neuro-engineers are confident that the first neuro-computers will be built within five years, which would be a combination of living cells from the nervous system or brain and inorganic machines. Evidently we need to incorporate neurons into computers because conventional computers cannot cope with tasks such as recognising handwriting, speech and faces, and the silicon versions of neurons have not turned out as effective as hoped. "We are nowhere near emulating one cell, let alone a network of neurons," according to Joel Davis.

On the one hand, this kind of development can be seen as a recognition that living tissue is different from machinery, quantitatively at least, in the efficiency of processing information – taking thousand of inputs and outputs and combining and modulating signals in extremely complex ways. On the other hand, by making an interface between neural tissues and machine, it is suggesting that ultimately the neural tissue's output can be understood in mechanical terms. In another article there is a suggestion that machines could be linked up to the brain in order to improve or replace memory; a "surrogate brain that never forgets anything" is the hype for *My Life Bits* by Microsoft (Sample 2002: 21).

Chapter 4 will show that, according to one kind of biological reductionism, the similarity of species can be measured in terms of the amount of DNA shared. But computational capacity seems to provide another field which lends itself to reductionism. Helen Phillips (2002: 40–42) questions the division between humans, animals and plants: "Plants seem to respond in a variety of ways to subtly different sensory inputs. Does this equate to intelligence? A plant's computational capacity can probably match that of many animals".

"What distinguishes us from more primitive creatures? We've got a better operating system", claims Melanie Cooper in the subtitle of an article "Life 2.0". This article reports on the research and theories of John Mattick, developing the idea that RNA is some kind of software. Let me quote some extracts from the article:

> Microsoft does it every few years. So does Apple. But how often does Mother Nature release a new **operating system**?

...

We're talking about a genetic **operating system** where the lines of code are embedded in a genome rather than in **silicon**. And at the heart of this system ... is a motley collection of RNA molecules widely derided as useless.

...

The complete genetic **operating system** that Mattick and Gagen propose regulates both the gene expression and the proteins that carry out structural and functional roles in the cells. Introns provide the additional connections, with each RNA molecule doing different tasks at the same time – an example of **parallel processing** similar to what happens in your brain or a **supercomputer**.

...

Mattick and Gagen suggest that evolution too, may have found a way to exploit **multi-tasking**, by **rewiring** its molecular networks on the fly. It did this by changing the **control codes** – introns and other non-coding RNAs – thus altering which genes are **turned on** at which times. "Changing the **sequence of codes** changes the **stored program**. An infinity of different **programs** is now instantly available," says Gagen. And all without changing the underlying **hardware**: the basic suite of genes. Effectively, evolution got on an **upgrade** that allowed it to race ahead.

The operating systems of modern desktop computers have millions of lines of code. Likewise, a genetic **operating system capable of multitasking and parallel processing** must have stacks of control molecules. And these couldn't just appear out of the blue. Gagen says they are most likely to come from the part of the eukaryotic genome that has grown in size with increasing complexity – in other words the introns (Cooper 2002: 30–32, my bolding).

Apparently scientists in the biological field are changing and redefining the terminology of their discipline to match the underlying principles of information theory and cybernetics. For example, William Thorpe looks upon living things as systems that

> absorb and store information, change their behaviour as a result of that information ... and have special organs for detecting, sorting, and organizing this information ... The most important biological discovery of recent years is that the processes of life are directed by programs ... and that life is not merely programmed activity, but self-programmed activity (Thorpe 1997: 6).

In this world computer programs and genetic codes are both governed by the principles of information theory and cybernetics. Genes contain information programmed into specific sequences. One branch of neo-Darwinianism sees evolution as dependent on the survival of the better informed – being fitter means being more adept at processing greater stores of information in a shorter time, so that successful organisms are simply well-designed programs (Rifkin 1987: 214).

The mind and personality (and even the "immortal soul", if you believe in such a thing) is also being viewed as capable of reduction to computer programs. Since the late 1980s computer scientists in the United States and Japan have been actively engaged in an area of cognitive research called "downloading", an attempt to scan parts of the human brain so as to map a three dimensional picture of its chemistry. Once mapped, a computer program can be written that will simulate the behaviour of each section of the brain, and this can be transferred to a computerised brain which will then think and act just like the original, with an identical set of memories. As Marvin Minsky says, "If a person is a machine, and you get a wiring diagram of it, then you can make copies". Since the computer programs and their data can be copied, even if the computer wears out, the "person" can achieve immortality. Gerald Jay Sussman boasts, "if you can make a machine that contains the contents of your mind then that machine is you. The hell with the rest of your physical body. Now the machine can last forever" (Rifkin 1987: 183–4). Such a program of research hopes to achieve immortality for the first time in history! Marvin Minsky is quite enthusiastic about converting human personality into computer programs to be downloaded into machines, because this would allow us to indulge in otherwise dangerous activities like LSD or religious faith, which might otherwise damage the brain – we would have a back-up copy! (Horgan 1998: 187).

An evolutionary psychologist such as Steven Pinker believes that all psychological behaviour and the physical behaviour it gives rise to can be explained by this computer paradigm.

> Mental life can be explained in terms of information, computation, and feedback. Beliefs and memories are collections of information – like facts in a database, but residing in patterns of activity and structure in the brain. Thinking and planning are systematic transformations of these patterns, like the operation of a computer program. Wanting and trying are feedback loops, like the principle behind a thermostat: they receive information about the discrepancy between a goal and the current state of the world, and then they execute operations that tend to reduce the difference. The mind is connected to the world by the sense organs, which transduce physical energy into data structures in the brain, and by motor programs, by which the brain controls the muscles (Pinker 2003:32).

Pinker even extends mechanism into our morality. "The moral sense is a gadget, like stereo vision or intuitions about number. It is an assembly of neural circuits cobbled together from older parts of the primate brain and shaped by natural selection to do a job" (p. 270).

Many psychologists regard as common-sense the idea that men and computers are merely two different species of a more abstract life-forms called information processing systems. But George Miller perceives some perils in this new common-sense.

> The real danger in this new marriage between the computer sciences and psychology rests in its perception of psyche. It used to be that people thought of the computer in human terms. Increasingly, however, people are beginning to think of themselves in computational terms (Rifkin 1987: 216).

Thus the personifying metaphor COMPUTER IS HUMAN has been reversed to the depersonifying HUMAN IS COMPUTER.

3.6.3   Objections to mechanistic views of humans

We ought to stop and take some historical perspective on the HUMAN IS COMPUTER theme, by recognising a tendency for every age to take its latest technology and apply it as a metaphorical model to biology and physiology, if not cosmology. In *Novum Organum* Francis Bacon exclaimed, "the making of clocks is certainly a subtle and exact work; their wheels seem to imitate the celestial orbs, and their alternating with orderly motion, the pulse of animals". Descartes compared animals to "soulless automata", whose whimpers or screams are not caused by pain, but are emissions of sounds from their internal gears and mechanisms. "It seems reasonable that since art copies nature and men can make various automata which move without thought, that Nature should produce its own automata, much more splendid than the artificial ones." Just as the "clockwork universe" legitimised the operations of the clock and schedule culture of the industrial age, now, in the computer age, intellectuals are tending to redefine the cosmos as an "information universe" of which the body and the brain are a part. Since the physical and biological universe seems to behave just like computers this in turn legitimises information technology and its social effects (Rifkin 1987: 209).

What are the dangers we can detect in this mechanistic and computer view of humans and their brains? Taken to extremes there is the danger that humans like young Japanese computer addicts or *hikikomori* may exchange all human contact for contact with the computer. A less extreme effect might be that people through their interactions with computers begin to behave like computers in non-human ways. According to Craig Brod computer compulsives tend to be intolerant of behaviour that is at all ambiguous, digressive or tangential, preferring simple yes-no responses, to be impatient with open-ended conversations and uncomfortable with people who are reflective or meditative. Other compulsives have been shown to be socially inept because of the way they multi-task, with a tendency to break off conversations and then resume them some days later (pp. 29–30).

Secondly, a mechanistic view of the mind does not seem to allow any space for free-will and the responsibility that goes with it. According to one student at MIT, "you have to stop talking about your mind as though it were thinking. It's not. It's just doing". "Emotions are decision-making programs developed through evolution" (p. 217). This is the kind of science that Prigogine objects to:

> Descartes, Einstein and the other great determinists were "all pessimistic people. They wanted to go to another world, a world of eternal beatitude." But a deterministic world would not be a utopia but a dystopia ... That was the message of Aldous Huxley in *Brave New World*, of George Orwell in *1984*, of Milan Kundera in *The Unbearable Lightness of Being*. When a state tries to suppress evolution, change, flux, by brutal force, by violence ... it destroys the meaning of life, it creates a society of "timeless robots" (Horgan 1998: 239).

In any case, there have been some very strong refutations of the idea that human consciousness can be reduced to a machine or a computer (O'Halloran 2003: 88). Roger Penrose in *The Emperor's New Clothes*, denies the claim of artificial intelligence that computers could replicate all the attributes of the human mind including consciousness. He cites as evidence Gödel's incompleteness theorem – any consistent system of axioms beyond a certain level of complexity gives rise to statements that can be neither proved nor disproved with those axioms; therefore the system will always be incomplete, so no computer system will be able to replicate the mind's creative or intuitive powers (Horgan 1998: 174).

Science's inability to grasp the mind is also reflected in the record of artificial intelligence, the effort to create computers that mimic human thought. The chess matches between IBM computer Deep Blue and world champion Gary Kasparov in 1996 and 1997 showed what a failure artificial intelligence has been. Deep Blue only won the first game of the first match before finally losing by a score of four points to two, though it did win a highly controversial later match in 1997. One would expect the computer to perform much better since chess has straightforward rules and a small, completely symmetrical and standardised playing field, ideal for computers to excel in. And Deep Blue, with a back-up team of five of the best chess programmers in the world, is exceptionally powerful, with 32 parallel processors capable of examining 200 million positions per second (Horgan 1998: 276).

As for functional machines which incorporate the computer, such as aeroplanes, Antonio Damasio puts forward a detailed and conclusive analysis of the differences between the body with a mind as part of it and the plane with the computer in it.

> The physical matter of the aircraft is not alive, its parts aren't made of living cells possessed of a genetic inheritance, a biological destiny, and a life risk. … The plane's integrated cockpit computers have a concern for the execution of its flying function. Our brains and minds have a global concern for our entire living real estate, every nook and cranny of it, and underneath it all, every nook and cranny has a local, automated concern with itself. These distinctions are chronically glossed over whenever living organisms and intelligent machines, e.g. robots, are compared.

The airplane's animation is equivalent to the animation when we look, listen, walk, run, jump, or swim.

> But note how that part of human animation is merely the tip of the iceberg when I talk about emotions and their underpinnings. The hidden part of the iceberg concerns the animation whose purpose is solely the managing of the life state in the part and whole of the organism … There is no equivalent for that part of the animation in current intelligent machines … the 777 is unable to feel anything like human feelings because, among many other reasons, it does not have an equivalent to our interior life to be managed, let alone be portrayed (Damasio 2003: 187–189).

What is interesting and important in Damasio is his insistence that human emotion and thought derives from, grows out of and reflects the homeostatic drive of the body, including the needs of the cells transmitting information. This is important from the perspective of the experiential hypothesis that cognition derives metaphorically from the embodiment of the mind, the experiences of the body. Damasio goes on to underline that

> [t]he mind arises from or in a brain situated within a body-proper with which it interacts; that due to the mediation of the brain, the mind is grounded in the body-proper; that the mind has prevailed in evolution because it helps to maintain the body-proper; and that the mind arises from it in biological tissue – nerve cells – that share the same characteristics that define other living tissues in the body-proper (Damasio 2003: 191).

However developed artificial brains become, they will never be real brains because they will not have human sensual experiences. One could design a computer to become an expert in restaurants, "but this machine would never know what a steak tastes like"-(Horgan 1998: 15). This must be precisely the point to be made if one believes Lakoff's experiential hypothesis – most of our thinking is driven by metaphors based on our bodily experience, and if that experience is lacking, one cannot even contemplate the possibility of non-experiential machines thinking like humans. We return to Damasio in chapter 6.

3.6.4 The Santiago theory of cognition

One revolutionary theory of the relationship between mind and brain is known as the Santiago theory of cognition, which originated with Gregory Bateson and was elaborated more extensively by Humberto Maturana and Francisco Varela. What is interesting in this theory for our purposes is, first, the emphasis which is put on the mind as process, in keeping with the process philosophies which we briefly mention in chapter 7 (7.12), second its compatibility with *Gaia* theory, explored in the next chapter (4.2 and 4.3.2), and third, the way in which the theory relates to the challenges to the theme DISEASE IS INVASION, which we discussed in chapter 2 (2.5).

One of the aspects of the emerging systems theory of life is that cognition is the activity involved in the self-genesis and self-perpetuation of living systems, the process of life itself, including perception, emotion, and behaviour. Cognition, in this theory, does not necessarily require a brain and a nervous system. Because of this one is perhaps entitled to think of the whole biosphere including the rocks, atmosphere, seas as a decision-making mechanism with feedback, as conceived by *Gaia* theory. At the level of human life, however, cognition includes language, conceptual thought, and all the other features of human consciousness.

The theory sees mind and matter/brain not as two separate categories but as complementary aspects of the phenomenon of life – mind is the process of cognition, and the brain is a specific structure through which this process operates. At all levels, from the simplest cell upwards, mind and matter, process and structure, are inseparably connected.

The brain is not the only structure involved in the process of cognition. The immune system is recognized as a network as complex and interconnected as the nervous system, performing equally important co-ordinating functions, though its self-regulatory and self-organising properties are so far not well understood. As we have seen in the last chapter (2.5), new ways of treating diseases have been posited which depend more on the metaphor of communication, rather than on the metaphor of military resistance (Capra n.d., 1996, Varela and Coutinho 1991).

Though this emerging theory seems, in some respects, to be allied to the mind is computer metaphor, since it sees life in terms of information processing, it is not entirely reductionist, as it gives weight to the capacity for self-genesis and self-perpetuation as distinctive features of living systems, a capacity not possessed by computers. Nevertheless, it is worth noting with Martin that Capra's view is an instance of our scientific and metaphorical ways of conceiving the body changing in step with changes in political economy. She notes that the metaphors used to understand the body have shifted from the centralised and hierarchical structured control system of cell biology (a Fordist-style conception) to depictions of an immune system in which the body is seen as "an engineered communications system, ordered by a fluid and dispersed command-control-intelligence network" to which objectives of "specificity, flexibility, and rapid response are attributed (a metaphor grounded in the political economy of flexible accumulation)" (Martin 1992:121, Harvey 1996: 281). One might also want to add that this metaphor also reflects/constructs current views on military deployment in the post cold-War era – with highly flexible, less-localised rapid response forces to counter the ubiquitous threat of terrorism or fundamentalist Islam.

3.6.5 Haraway's cyborg manifesto.

In the 1980s Donna Haraway wrote "A Manifesto for Cyborgs", and it is worth discussing since it locates the IT revolution clearly in an ideological (feminist-socialist) context. Haraway ignored objections like Damasio's, was perhaps too early to be aware of the failures of artificial intelligence, and accepted that the boundary between human and machine is now entirely blurred.

> The second leaky distinction is between animal-human (organism) and machine. Pre-cybernetic machines could be haunted; there was always the spectre of the ghost in the machine. This dualism structured the dialogue between materialism and idealism that was settled by a dialectical progeny called spirit or history, according to taste. But basically machines were not self-moving, self-designing, autonomous ... Now we are not so sure. Late twentieth century machines have made thoroughly ambiguous the difference between natural and artificial, mind and body, self-developing and externally designed, and many other distinctions

that used to apply to organisms and machines. Our machines are disturbingly lively, and we ourselves frighteningly inert (Haraway 1990: 193–4).

The great dangers she identifies in the increasing blurring of humans and machines recapitulate some of our dominant ideological metaphor themes, not only the obvious HUMAN IS MACHINE, but also the discussion of Taylorism as part of industrial time, and the themes of competition and war.

> Contemporary science fiction is full of cyborgs – creatures simultaneously animal and machine, who populate worlds ambiguously natural and crafted. Modern medicine is also full of cyborgs, of couplings between organism and machine, each conceived as coded devices, in an intimacy and with a power that was not generated in the history of sexuality …. Modern production seems like a dream of cyborg colonisation of work, a dream that makes the nightmare of Taylorism seem idyllic. Modern war is a cyborg orgy, coded by C^3I, command-control-communication-intelligence, an 84 billion item in 1984's U.S. defense budget (Haraway 1990: 191).

This new industrial revolution is also implicated in privatisation, if not commodification, militarism, and the imaginations of escape which provide an alibi for destruction of the environment, itself dependent upon the idea that successful activity is movement:

> The new technologies seem deeply involved in the forms of "privatisation" … in which militarization, right-wing family ideologies and policies, and intensified definitions of corporate (and state) property as private synergistically interact. The new communication technologies are fundamental to the eradication of "public life" for everyone. This facilitates the mushrooming of a permanent high-tech military establishment at the cultural and economic expense of most people, but especially of women. Technologies like video games and highly miniaturised television seem crucial to production of modern forms of "private life". The culture of video games is heavily oriented to individual competition and extraterrestrial warfare. High-tech gendered imaginations are produced here, imaginations that can contemplate destruction of the planet and a sci-fi escape from its consequences. More than our imaginations is militarised, and the other realities of electronic and nuclear warfare are inescapable. These are the technologies that promise ultimate mobility and perfect exchange – and incidentally enable tourism, that perfect practice of mobility and exchange, to emerge as one of the world's largest single industries (Haraway 1990: 210–11).

What blurs the boundary between humans and machines, and also humans and animals, is that both or all three can be reduced to information processing systems. As we saw earlier in discussing QUALITY IS MONEY/WEALTH, money is the means of reducing quality to quantity. In much the same way but even more thoroughly, if humans, animals and machines are all reducible to electronically coded information systems, then they are exchangeable and interchangeable.

> Furthermore, communications sciences and modern biologies are constructed by a common move – the translation of the world into a common problem of coding, a search for a common language in which all resistance to instrumental control disappears and all heterogeneity can be submitted to disassembly, reassembly, investment and exchange (Haraway 1990: 206–207).

In developing her argument, Haraway recapitulates some of the ideas of Capra on immunobiology summarised above (3.6.4), and our discussion of auto-immune diseases (2.5).

> The organism has been translated into problems of genetic coding and read-out. Biotechnology, a writing technology, informs research broadly. In a sense organisms have ceased to exist as objects of knowledge, giving way to biotic components, that is special kinds of information-processing devices (Haraway 1990: 207).

She also foreshadows discussions of socio-biology in our next chapter:

> The close ties of sexuality and instrumentality, of views of the body as a kind of private satisfaction and utility-maximising machine, are described nicely in sociobiological origin stories that stress a genetic calculus and explain the inevitable dialectic of domination of male and female gender roles. These sociobiological stories depend on a high-tech view of the body as a biotic component or cybernetic communication system (Haraway 1990: 210–11).

Up to this point I have cited extracts from her manifesto which might seem rather negative about the social consequences of human-machine hybridity. However, Haraway sees this electronic revolution as opening a space for new areas of liberation, for undermining structures of exploitation and domination. Indeed, far from contesting the reduction of human to machine, Haraway accepts it, and welcomes it as an opportunity to dispense with many of the harmful dualisms of Western thought, especially in relation to the "Other":

> To recapitulate, certain dualisms have been persistent in Western traditions; they have all been systemic to the logics and practices of domination of women, people of colour, nature, workers, animals – in short, domination of all constituted as others, whose task is to mirror the self. Chief among these troubling dualisms are self/other, mind/body, culture/nature, male/female, civilised/primitive, reality/appearance, whole/part, agent/resource, maker/made, active/passive, right/wrong, truth/illusion, total/partial, God/man ... High-tech culture challenges these dualisms in intriguing ways. It is not clear who makes and who is made in the relation between human and machine. It is not clear what is mind and what is body in machines that resolve into coding practices. ... we find ourselves to be cyborgs, hybrids, mosaics, chimeras. Biological systems have become biotic systems, communications devices like others. There is no fundamental, ontological separation in our formal knowledge of machine and organism, of technical and organic (Haraway 1990: 219–220).

The solution to ideological structures of domination is, it seems, for Haraway, to undo the categorisation which distinguishes us from the other in the first place. We have something more radical here than metaphor – a re-drawing of literal boundaries and categories, so that we can no longer *katogerein* or "accuse" the Other. Interestingly, her thinking may be subconsciously determined by the themes CATEGORY IS A DIVIDED AREA and RELATIONSHIP IS COHESION. According to the metaphorical logic different categories will be divided from other categories, and division is the end of a relationship, so that we can only have a relationship if we belong to the same category. Similar kinds of metaphorical logic created by the interplay of themes are explored in chapter 5.

We will discuss this attitude to HUMAN IS ANIMAL in the next chapter. I tend to believe that the reductionist approach – we are in the same class as animals because we are information processing machines, therefore we should not dominate and exploit animals, and we cannot anyway without exploiting and dominating ourselves – is only one approach, and perhaps a dangerous one. The challenge is to acknowledge diversity and to respect it – different, but with equal rights and respect, rather than the same therefore with equal rights to respect.

In the penultimate chapter I shall discuss another of the dualisms represented in this last quotation – "agent/resource" and "active/passive" in relation to English and Blackfoot grammar.

3.7   Summary

Let's summarise how the various metaphor themes we have explored in this chapter are related to ideology, the exercise of power and the reinforcement of inequality. We saw that the majority of metaphors in HUMAN IS FOOD, depicting sex as eating, apply to women, with the implication that men's entitlement to food is matched by an entitlement to sex, that women exist for the satisfaction of men's appetites and that they are passive in the process.

The idea that humans are commodities and that some are worth more than others clearly reinforces inequality, though kidnapping for ransom or exchange of prisoners does a little to redress this. The market in human organs and blood militates against the poor, who by desperation are likely to be implicated in their own exploitation in the cause of making the rich healthier.

Genetic engineering represents the exercise of power over our offspring, and the buying of genetic material, sperms or eggs, a commodification that works in favour of those with the greatest buying power. Gene sequences, which should be the common property of humanity, are increasingly being privatised.

Such commodification of knowledge and everything else in nature – body-parts, genes, countryside, water by privatisation, and plants in biopiracy – have as their aim the profits for shareholders who have capital to invest in privatised industries. Turning nature and knowledge of nature into a commodity for human use brings it within the power of the market and reduces qualitative difference to the quantitative differences of measurement by money. This relates to Marx's fetishism thesis, in which commodity market exchange transforms relations between people into relations between things (Harvey 1996: 221). Or as De Botton points out, the inputs to industry – raw materials, machines and labour – will be equally regarded as commodities (De Botton 2004: 107).

Turning, then, to the themes of humans as machine, we note the power of technologists to create or download a human brain in the quest for (an illusory) immortality. Thinking of humans as machines is also an excuse for forcing people to behave like machines as part of the industrial enterprise. Capitalist society itself can be conceived as a machine regulated by the invisible hand of free-trade and the market economy. Regarding humans as computers is a further attempt at control, though paradoxically, the denial of free-will implied by the metaphor could in fact be a license for unethical behaviour. The reduction of humans and animals to information-processing machines provides a further way, besides money, of turning qualitative into quantitative difference, a common denominator which implicates capitalism and commodification. More obviously, such a reduction, whether by wiring humans up to computational machines or insisting the human mind is only a computer, accords great power to those who can make sophisticated machines: they become like gods, and if we worship their products we indulge in idolatry. On the other hand, we might, with Haraway, see this hybridisation of humans and machines, this cyborg world, as an opportunity to challenge the traditional power structures of society, though it equally provides an opportunity for the reassertion of the private and the militaristic.

CHAPTER 4

Humans as animals, literal or metaphorical?

"TOM: Man is by instinct a lover, a hunter, a fighter, and none of those instincts are given much play at the warehouse.
AMANDA: Man is by instinct! Don't quote instinct to me. Instinct is something that people have got away from. It belongs to animals! Christian adults don't want it!"
Tennessee Williams – 'The Glass Menagerie'

4.1 Impositive metaphors and subjective metaphors

In this chapter we consider a particular complication to the interpretation of metaphors, when what is at issue is whether a particular statement is literal or metaphorical, and to what extent. There are well known cases of what was once considered to be literally true later becoming reinterpreted as a metaphor. An interesting example is with the vocabulary of the four humours. "When we describe somebody as having hot blood, or a cold heart, or a dry wit we realise that we are talking metaphorically, whereas in the past we would have believed ourselves to have been talking about physical qualities" (Pope 1985: 179). The word *germ* which originally meant 'seed' (as still detectable in the compound *wheatgerm*, the embryo within the seed), was once used quite literally when referring to disease – it was believed that disease was actually caused by seeds. What happened was that the seed theory of disease died out, and the meaning of *germ* also narrowed to mean microbe, so that we only have left the originally literal, then metaphorical, and now newly literal meaning.

But language users are by no means always unanimous about what is literal and metaphorical. As I have discussed elsewhere (Goatly 1997: 127–30), there is a species of metaphors that one might call asymmetrical, in that the speaker may regard them as metaphorical and the hearer as literal, or vice versa. The speaker may believe a statement is (more or less) literally true, but hearers belonging to different sub-cultures within the same language-speaking community may only interpret this metaphorically. Put more formally, in these cases, there is no metaphorical intention on the part of the speaker, and it is not assumed by the hearer that there was a metaphorical intention; nevertheless the hearer refuses to accept the truth of the assertion as a literal statement and therefore interprets it metaphorically.

We can generally call these metaphors "subjective". Some may arise because of different perceptions of physical reality, as in the case of illusions: you may mistakenly think you have seen a swallow and say "look at that swallow", whereas your interlocutor knows that it is a bat, but can interpret your statement metaphorically, because he realises the similarities between swallows and bats which created your illusion. But those discussed in this chapter are more ideological than perceptual in their origins, and have been called "impositives" (Mack 1975: 248). Take for example the statement "Property is theft." This utterance is an attempt, by the French socialist/anarchist Proudhon, to re-draw semantic boundaries, to redefine the concept of property. One may, of course, reject it outright; but one is still free to attempt a metaphorical interpretation: property resembles theft because both deprive others of the use or enjoyment of an object. Another example, closer to the concerns of this chapter, is Desmond Morris's contention that "A human is a naked ape" (Morris 1967: 9). This utterance is an attempt to re-draw semantic boundaries, to redefine the concept of humanity. Even if one rejects it one might interpret it metaphorically: humans resemble apes in various ways, such as their upright gait.

For Morris this "metaphor" actually draws attention to a false dichotomy, and in this chapter I discuss how the metaphor theme HUMAN IS ANIMAL and LANDSCAPE/WEATHER IS HUMAN BODY might disappear into the literal, depending on one's ideological viewpoint. In theory they can disappear into the literal in two ways, either as synonymy statements, in which case the semantic distinction disappears completely, e.g. "Humans and animals are the same thing", or as statements of hyponymy "Humans are one kind of animal", though the hyponymic statement is the more likely in practice. The hyponymic relationship suggests the hyponym has features not possessed by the superordinate, which distinguish it from other hyponyms in the class, but still insists that these features are not important enough to exclude it from the superordinate class and so not important enough to demand a metaphorical interpretation. Even if we opt for a metaphorical interpretation, there are still distinctions to be made. Depending on one's beliefs and ideology, one might see more or less grounds of similarity between the target and source. So if one were to see many salient and important grounds the metaphor would, perhaps, approximate to a literal statement, paraphrased "X is more or less Y". At the other extreme the differences would be seen as more important than the similarities so the interpretation would be "X is in a few minor respects similar to Y". There are, of course, various mid-points between these two extremes.

So, according to traditional semantic logic, there are at least four interpretations of impositive metaphors: X and Y are the same; X is one kind of Y; X is more or less Y; X is not Y but is in some or few respects like Y. But there are two complications to this scheme. Although one may agree that there are important similarities between X and Y one may disagree about what these similarities are. Secondly, impositive metaphors can be expressions of desirability and idealism, rather than statements of a perceived reality.

In this chapter we will consider the statements "The landscape/weather is a human body", and "humans are animals", in order to explore what creative or destructive blurrings of categories these statements might produce, whether they can be interpreted literally or metaphorically and if the latter, the extent and nature of their grounds. We will also, of course, explore some of the ideological consequences that the different interpretations may lead to.

4.2 LANDSCAPE/WEATHER IS A HUMAN BODY?

It is quite common to use personifying or animalising metaphors for places and especially natural landscapes. The sources are often parts of the human body, and I present them in order from top of the body downwards: **head** 'upper part' (*the head of the valley*), **fringe** 'edge of an area', **crown/brow** 'summit' (*as we came over the brow of the hill we saw a dog*), **face** 'front slope of a hill or mountain', **mouth** either 'estuary' or 'entrance to a cave', **tongue** 'promontory' (*at the end of the tongue of land is a small town*), **neck** 'isthmus' (*the neck of land links to a peninsula*), **shoulder** 'more steeply inclined slope' (*we climbed round the hill's shoulder to the waterfalls*), **arm/finger** 'promontory' (*the arm/finger of land extends out into the ocean*), **backbone/spine** 'central row of hills or mountains' (*a backbone of limestone stretches from China to Siam*), **heart** 'centre' (*the bombing destroyed the heart of the capital*), **artery** 'important road or railway', **vein** 'narrow layer of mineral in rock' (*there are veins of gold in this quartz*), **bowels** 'deep parts, recesses (of the earth)', **flank** 'edge or side of a hill or mountain' (*we proceeded along the flank of the mountain until we reached a road*) and **foot** 'lower part' (*the foot of the mountain is five miles from town*).

Actions performed on the landscape or countryside can be conceived as actions performed on a human body. Some are violent, not **environmentally-friendly**: **gash** 'deep trench' (*the bombs have left deep gashes on the landscape*), **scar** 'scrape the vegetation off' (*the crashed plane had scarred the jungle clearing*), **rape** 'environmental destruction', **denude** 'remove covering of the earth' (*the deforestation had denuded the hills*). Others are more cosmetic: **comb** 'search carefully' (*police are combing the countryside for the escapee*), **manicure** 'look after a garden and make it neat and tidy' (*the lawns around the hotel were beautifully manicured*), **shroud** 'cover a building or place with darkness, fog or mist' (*mist shrouded the mountains and the valley below*).

We can use verbs which normally take humans/animals as subject and apply them metaphorically to the landscape: **lie**, **sit** and **stand** can all mean 'be situated or positioned' (*the Sierra Nevada lies/stands to the east of California*), (*Istanbul is sitting on extensive coal deposits*). Besides standing, hills and mountains can **lean** 'slope' (*the cliff leaned backwards beyond the waterfall*) and **dominate** 'tower above' (*the lake is dominated by a mountain range*). Soil can **release** gas 'give off, let escape' (*chalk releases carbon dioxide when put in acid*) and volcanoes can **spew/belch** 'emit in large quantities' (*the volcano belched/spewed out ash and lava*).

Intransitive verbs can take the form of present participles, and behave more like adjectives: **sprawling** 'extending in an unplanned way' (*London spreads out into sprawling suburbs*), **yawning/gaping** 'extremely wide' (*there was a yawning/gaping chasm in front of the explorers*). There are also adjectives describing the appearance of the body which are applied to the landscape: **bald/bare** 'without vegetation' (*the hillside was bald/bare with only a little grass*), and **gaunt** 'bare and unattractive' (*gaunt hills dominated the equally gaunt cathedral*).

Some adjectives for evaluating human character or behaviour are also applied to soil and landscape: **hospitable** 'with good living and growing conditions' and its opposites, **inhospitable/hostile** (*hardly anything grows in the inhospitable soil*). This kind of soil may remain **virgin** 'unused, uncultivated' (*Costa Rica still boasts many virgin forests*). Landscape can also be **tame** 'not exciting' (*most mountains seem tame after seeing the Alps*) or alternatively **treacherous** 'very dangerous' (*this swamp is very treacherous, keep to the path*).

The metaphor also works in the opposite direction, with the metaphor theme HU-MAN BODY IS EARTH, the reversibility of a statement perhaps suggesting synonymy or identity rather than attribution (cf. *John is the Prime Minister* and *the Prime Minister is John* v. *John is a teacher* and **A teacher is John*). Types of soil or rock can be applied to humans as nouns or adjectives. These are often evaluative, in keeping with the theme MINERAL/METAL IS RANK/CHARACTER/VALUE: **grit** 'bravery', **clod** 'stupid person', **slag** 'sexually immoral woman', **skinflint** 'mean person who hates spending money', **earthy** 'connected with taboo subjects' (*my uncle had an earthy sense of humour*), **flinty** 'severe and hostile' (*the headmaster gave me a flinty stare*), **craggy** 'strong rough and attractive' (*Julia was attracted by his craggy jaws and chin*), **glassy** 'fixed and vacant expression of the eyes', **gravelly** 'rough and low (of a voice)' (*he has a handsome face, blue eyes, black hair and a sexy, gravelly voice*). Some are less evaluative: **carbuncle** 'large painful pimple that swells under the skin', **shingles** 'viral disease that attacks the nerves and produces a rash of red spots'.

The shape and area of land can also be applied either to human society: **stratum** 'group of people sharing the same social status' (*prisoners come largely from the poorest least educated stratum of society*); or human character: **fault**, literally 'line of geological weakness between tectonic plates', metaphorically 'mistake or weakness for which you are to blame' – or is it the other way around?; or human body and its parts: **contour** 'shape of the body' (*your bikini shows off your contours wonderfully*), **tract** 'connected tubes in the body' (*he suffered from irritation of the digestive tract*), **furrow** 'lines or wrinkles in the forehead' and, by implication, **stubble** 'short growth of beard', which grows out of the skin as cereal crops from the ground.

The physiological processes or behaviour may be associated with earthquakes and volcanoes: **eruption** 'pimple or spot, such as acne, that suddenly appears on the skin' (*the eruptions of adolescent acne are caused by blocked hair follicles*), **quake** 'shake with fear', **tremor** 'nervous shaking of the body' (*the disease causes tremors in the hands*). Or actions on the body can be compared with actions on the soil: **irrigate** 'wash part of a person's body with a flow of liquid' (*first we had better irrigate the cut on your shin with disinfectant*), **dig** 'push hard into someone's flesh' (*he dug his elbow into my ribs and I squealed*), **plant... on** 'do something to someone's body' (*he planted a kick on my* *backside*) like plants in the soil, and **bury your face in your hands** 'completely cover your face with your hands' in which case the hands take the place of soil.

Participles of these transitive verbs then become adjectival, whether indicating physical appearance and state: **furrowed** (of a face or forehead) 'with deep folds or lines in it', **weathered** 'tanned, dried or wrinkled by the wind or sun' (of human faces), **parched** 'extremely thirsty', **rugged** 'rough and strong' (*the sweat streamed down his rugged face*); or referring to mental states: **cultivated** 'educated and cultured' (*my great aunt was a very cultivated lady who had been to university*), **devastated** 'emotionally overcome' (*he was devastated by his son's death*) and **harrowing** 'extremely upsetting because connected with suffering' (*Phuong told me a harrowing story of her escape from Vietnam*).

Both these sets of metaphors blur the boundaries between humans and the landscape, though only the first overtly personifies the landscape as something human. However, unlike other themes with the human body as source, there is little emphasis on the functioning of the landscape/body (Kövecses, personal communication). One of the advantages of such personifications for the environmental justice movements is that it allows environmental destruction to be seen in terms of morality, immune to attacks from scientific, rationalistic or legal discourses (for example *rape of the countryside*) (Harvey 1996: 389).

In another metaphor theme human activity or human qualities are ascribed to weather. It can be **treacherous** 'extremely dangerous', **fickle** 'changing suddenly without warning', **hostile** 'not suitable or comfortable for living in', **biting** 'extremely cold so as to cause pain' (*there was a biting east wind which made the beach unpleasant*), **violent** 'strong in effect' (*violent storms have increased in frequency due to global warming*), **raging** 'very hot or violent', and **pitiless** 'very extreme or severe' (*animals were dying in the pitiless drought*). The sounds made by weather are metaphorically compared with human sounds: thunder – **grumble** 'rumble continuously', **clap** 'sudden loud noise made by thunder'; wind – **howl** 'blow hard and make a loud noise (of wind), **whistle** 'make a high sound by blowing hard', **moan** 'make a long low sound'. And other meteorological processes are like human actions: **spit** 'rain very slightly', **piss** 'rain heavily' (*it's really pissing down here at the moment*), **kiss** 'shine or blow on gently' (of sun or wind) (*the sun kissed her bare shoulders*) and **nip** 'coldness in the air' (*he felt the first nip of autumn*).

Traditionally landscape and weather have been viewed as inanimate and incapable of agency, landscape especially. When I investigated patterns of agency – verbs of action and communication in natural objects in *The Times* of London and in Wordsworth's *The Prelude*, I found that in both cases weather was the most and landscape the least active (see Table 14) (Goatly 2000: chapter 10). And certainly from a scientific point of view, they are not regarded as having life. However, Lovelock's *Gaia* theory questions this traditional classification.

Table 14. Percentages of Actors and Sayers by each category of natural participants as a percentage of the total for that category in The Times and The Prelude

	TIMES	*PRELUDE*
Weather	19%	50%
Animals	13%	21%
Lakes Seas Rivers etc.	8%	18%
Plants	10%	17%
Landscape	0%	9%

Gaia, the Greek earth goddess, is the name for the hypothesis that the world, including the atmosphere, the oceans, the biota, the rocks and minerals of the crust, functions as one large self-regulating organism, though one of *Gaia* theory's leading lights, Lynn Margulis, denies that it is exactly a live organism, "because no single organism cycles its waste" (Horgan 1998: 130). According to Lovelock the world can be compared to a giant redwood tree, which, although made up of a core of 99% dead wood with only a thin layer of living cells on its surface, nevertheless functions as one living entity. The rocks, soil and the earth, and the weather in the atmosphere, are, then, according to this theory, part of a living being. Specifically the *Gaia* hypothesis says that

> the temperature, oxidation state, acidity, and certain aspects of the rocks and waters are at any time kept constant, and that this homeostasis is maintained by active feedback processes operated automatically and unconsciously by the biota ... Life and its environment are so closely coupled that evolution concerns *Gaia*, not the organisms or the environment taken separately (Lovelock 1988: 19).

This is how life on earth defies the second law of thermodynamics, which posits entropy, the inexorable flow towards disorder and loss of energy. It evolves into structures of more and more complex order and inter-relation. One would expect, for example, that the oxygen and methane in the atmosphere would react in sunlight to produce carbon dioxide and water vapour and that the atmosphere would revert inexorably to a state of stable equilibrium. The only explanation for the persistence on earth of this unstable atmosphere at a constant composition is the influence of a control system, *Gaia*.

> I see the earth and the life it bears as a system... that has the capacity to regulate the temperature and the composition of the earth's surface and to keep it comfortable for living organisms. The self-regulation of the system is an active process driven by the free energy available from sunlight (p. 31).

Two particular examples of this self-regulation might be cited. The first comes from the phenomenon of "isostatic rebound". As the ice-caps melt, due to global warming, the land mass tends to rise. Besides the direct effect of marginally helping to prevent flooding, this has the indirect effect of causing more earthquakes and volcanoes, which, by throwing large masses of dust up into the atmosphere, prevents a certain amount of the radiation from sunlight reaching the earth's surface, and therefore cools the earth. ('The word: isostatic rebound': 2003). Second, some recent evidence suggests that as a consequence of global warming the salinity of the water near the North Pole is being reduced by the melting Greenland ice sheet and by rainfall increase doubling the amount of water flowing from Siberian rivers into the Arctic Ocean. This salinity is vital for the operation of the Gulf Stream – the warm water current flowing from the Gulf of Mexico northward past Western Europe that keeps it relatively mild. When the stream reaches the Arctic Circle it sinks because its salinity makes it dense, and the water returns to the tropics at great depths in a kind of conveyor belt motion. The consequence of global warming will therefore be, paradoxically, that the Gulf Stream may stop quite suddenly, and plunge Western Europe into the kinds of severe winters we find at comparable latitudes in Canada. In both these cases we see the geological earth responding to stimuli, as if it were a living being, and regulating its own temperature. But lest we become complacent, we should realise that the resulting climactic adjustments are likely to have catastrophic consequences for humanity, though not for the much longer-lived *Gaia* and more primitive living organisms (*Horizon, The Big Chill*: 2003).

Weather's important role in the homeostasis of the *Gaia* organism is observable in the various cycles, such as the water, and nitrogen cycles. But let's look at the more recently discovered sulphur cycle. Sulphur is washed in large quantities by rivers into the sea. Here, especially in the temperate climates near the continental shelves, certain forms of algal seaweed produce dimethyl-sulphide. The sulphur element is then carried upward into the atmosphere, where it is oxidised into sulphuric acid, which in turn provides the condensation nuclei, the seeds, for cloud formation and consequently the rain, which then washes it back to earth. This is a good example of how the weather functions as part of a larger organism, of which only one part, the algae, are traditionally viewed as living. Most telling from our point of view is Lovelock's observation: "There is no clear distinction anywhere on the earth's surface between living and non-living matter" (Lovelock 1989: 40).

If we entertain Gaia theory, I suggest, we can actually see these metaphors personifying weather and the landscape as less metaphorical, or not metaphorical at all. At least the distance of transfer is lessened from the gap between non-living thing and human to the gap between living thing and human, and inter-relatedness and wholeness are emphasised, in the kind of creative blurring that we noted in Haraway (3.6.5). We will say more about the scientific status of Gaia theory in the next section (4.3.2), and chapter 7 (7.5).

4.3 HUMAN IS ANIMAL?

At this point I wish to devote a considerable amount of discussion to the question of the "metaphor" HUMAN IS ANIMAL, not simply because it is interesting from the point of view of metaphorical theory, but because this question promises to be one of the major ideological battlegrounds in the 21st century. One reason that it is such a problematic metaphor is that the nature of animals is only partially known. When we illustrated and discussed the metaphor HUMAN IS MACHINE in the last chapter, we were on less problematic ground, precisely because machines are man-made and therefore reasonably well understood. In fact humans and animals can be used as models for constructing machines in the process of reverse engineering, and in that case there is little doubt that some aspect of humans/animals has been comprehended in machine terms. However, the nature of animals is much less certain. So HUMAN IS ANIMAL compares two phenomena, neither of which is fully known. This opens the way for conflicting ideologies about human and animal nature to exert an influence on "scientific" theorising around this metaphor.

At one extreme people see this as an approximative metaphor "Humans are more or less the same as animals" or a literal hyponymic statement, "A human is one kind of animal", suggesting that what we share with animals is much more important than what we don't share – a somewhat extreme position, with obvious ecological attractions in terms of animal rights. Once one has decided that animal and human nature is more or less, or in the most important respects, the same, one then has to decide which characteristics of animals we share with them. Some see animals as fiercely competitive and aggressive, and their evolution as based upon the struggle for existence. However, this has lately been challenged, and zoologists are now putting much more stress on the symbiotic nature of evolution.

Slightly further away from this extreme is a view of humans as evolved animals and therefore superior to animals: "Human is a superior kind of animal". This might lead to a tendency to think of humans themselves as in a hierarchy, and to espouse eugenic theories of social Darwinism.

At the other end of the spectrum human nature can be regarded as much more dependent on culture, society, discourse, language, symbolism, indeed metaphor itself for its characteristics, and biological theories of human nature as flawed by their reductionism: "Humans are in few respects like animals". One can see that this latter view might have tendencies to an idealistic view "Humans are ideally in only a few minor respects like animals". We will present the metaphorical evidence that it has been common in Western philosophy to regard humans behaving like animals as reprehensible, however much attempts to deny animal ancestry to humans might conflict with science (Darwin), or attempts to repress our animal instincts might lead to hypocrisy and neurosis (Freud). But the idealistic view can also be associated with the other positions too "Humans are ideally like animals". This in known as the "naturalistic fallacy", the idea that what is true must also be good, a version of the confusion between the descriptive and the normative identified by Hume (Gaarder 1996).

One might at this point quote Matt Ridley:

The burgeoning of primatology in the 1970s and 1980s laid bare a plethora of so-phisticated social set-ups throughout the family to which humankind belongs. An-ybody who thinks this is irrelevant to the study of human beings must be a Martian. We are primates, and we can learn about our roots by studying our relatives…

This premise can lead to two fallacies. The first is that primatologists are some-how claiming that human beings are the same as monkeys in every respect and detail, which is clearly nonsense. Each monkey and each ape has its own social system, unique to that species; but there are still common threads … all primate species behave in different ways that are recognisably primate-like. The second fallacy is to suppose that monkeys are somehow more primitive than people socially. Monkeys are not our ancestors any more than we are theirs. We share a common ancestor with all monkeys, but we have altered the body plan and the social habits of that ancestor in idiosyncratic ways. So has each species of monkey.

Deriving lessons from nature is a tricky feat. You must steer your craft carefully between two terrifying temptations. On one side Scylla cries out to you to look for direct animal parallels, ways in which we are just like our cousins. Thus Kropotkin argued that because ants were nice to each other, so we must be instinctively virtu-ous. Thus Spencer argued that because nature is a pitiless struggle, pitiless struggles must be virtuous. But we are not like animals in every respect. We are unique, we are different, just as every species is unique and different from every other; biology is a science of exceptions, not rules; of diversity, not grand unified theories. That ants are communitarian says nothing about whether man is virtuous. That natural selection is cruel says nothing about whether cruelty is moral.

Yet beware of steering your craft too far the other way. Charybdis cries **seduc-tively** from that side to emphasise human uniqueness. Nothing, she says, can be learnt from nature. We are ourselves in the image of god or of culture (**depending on taste**). We have sex drives because we are taught to have them, not because of instinct. We speak languages because we teach each other to speak. We are conscious, rational and free-willed, not like **those inferior things called animals**. Virtually every **high priest** of the humanities, of anthropology and of psychology preaches **the same old defensive sermon** of human uniqueness **that theologians clung to when Darwin first shook their tree** … Today anthropologists demand the existence of culture, reason or language exempts us from biology (Ridley 1997: 154–155) [my bolding].

Like many of the scientists and zoologists discussed in this section, Ridley actually himself steers towards the Scylla he warns us of. It is quite clear from his characterisa-tion of Charybdis that he thinks it the more dangerous. The bolded phrases involve rhetorical persuasion rather than logical argument. "Seductively" (THOUGHT IS RELA-TIONSHIP) has negative connotations. "Depending on taste" (LANGUAGE QUALITY IS TASTE) suggests that there are no arguments to back up the relative importance of cul-ture or religion as distinguishing human characteristics, but that deciding on either is a matter of whim. There is no logic behind the presumption that because we recognise our extreme difference from animals that we necessarily regard them as "those inferior things". The metaphor of the sermon-giving "high priest", for scholars within the humanities, suggests that they are superstitious in their beliefs and hold an undeserved authority. And those insisting on the importance of culture and language, literature, art, music and symbolisation are somehow equated with the narrow-minded bigots who opposed Darwin.

The discourse of evolutionary biology of the past fifty years has powerfully attacked traditional theories of distinctiveness of humans and animals:

> By the late twentieth century in United States scientific culture, the boundary between human and animal is thoroughly breached. ... Nothing really convincingly settles the separation of human and animal. <u>Many people no longer feel the need of such a separation; indeed many branches of feminist culture affirm the pleasure of connection with human and other living creatures.</u> ... Biology and evolutionary theory over the last two centuries have simultaneously produced modern organisms as objects of knowledge and reduced the line between humans and animals to a faint trace re-etched in ideological struggle or professional disputes between life and social sciences (Haraway 1990: 193–4) [my underlining].

But it is interesting here that Haraway's standpoint, especially in the underlined sentence, borders on the idealistic – what we feel a need for and what we get pleasure from seem to have equal validity with scientific theory.

4.3.1 Human as more or less/a kind of animal – selfish, competitive and aggressive.

The recent analysis of DNA has given enormous impetus to the view that humans are more or less animals, provided we consider humans' nature as determined exclusively by genes. After all 99% of the total of our genes are to be found in the mouse genome (Coghlan and Cohen 2002). This human-animal identification has been going strong for a hundred or more years, especially since Darwin, and has been co-opted to support immoral population policies, so it is worth serious discussion.

Table 15. What are human beings? (Laland and Brown 2002: 302)

THEORY	Human sociobiology	Human behavioural ecology	Evolutionary psychology	Memetics	Gene-culture evolution
VIEW OF HUMANS	Sophisticated animals	Sophisticated animals characterised by extreme adaptability	Sophisticated animals guided by psychological adaptations	Sophisticated animals manipulated by cultural parasites	Sophisticated animals guided by genetic and cultural information

Laland and Brown in their book *Sense and Nonsense* (2002) give a table (Table 15) summarising the various attempts within zoology and evolutionary social theory to impose HUMAN IS ANIMAL as a more or less literal hyponymic statement. All these approaches regard humans as sophisticated animals, though we appear to see a gradual move away from this view as the theories to the right incorporate psychology and culture as distinctive human characteristics.

4.3.1.1 *Sociobiology*

Sociobiology, from which most of these theories stem, sees humans simply as sophisticated animals, so that the ways in which animals behave are natural to humans. It has been associated with theories of competition and violence. Lorenz in his book *On Aggression* (1963) claimed "fighting and war are the natural expression of human instinctive aggression" (Laland and Brown 2002: 60). If animals are competitive and aggressive, and humans are simply sophisticated animals, then humans are by nature competitive and aggressive in sophisticated ways. It follows that any political decisions which run against human/animal nature are misguided. Sociobiology has been the starting point for influential work by "realist" theorists of international relations, such as Morgenthau, who claimed "the struggle for power is universal in time and space and ... it is an undeniable fact of experience with its roots in 'elemental bio-psychological drives'" (quoted in Chilton 1996: 92). Herbert Spencer advanced the view that, since the natural world is governed by unfettered competition, "competition unrestrained by governmental intervention in the form of poor laws, or welfare, or social safety nets, is the most natural form of human society" (Marks 2002: 161). This was later exposed by G. E. Moore as one manifestation of the naturalistic fallacy – the argument that what happens in nature is good. "This conduct is more evolutionarily successful, but is it good?"

Sociobiologists have not been slow to link aggression to DNA. In *Demonic Males: apes and the origins of human violence*, Richard Wrangham and Dale Peterson (1996) find a natural inclination of the human male to be aggressive – to be "demonic". This inclination is "written in the molecular chemistry of DNA" (p. 63). Marks parodies this kind of logic, "Chimpanzee males are intrinsically demonic. Humans are genetically almost identical to chimpanzees. Therefore human males must naturally be innately demonic as well!" (Marks 2002: 159). From a slightly different perspective, there has even been a claim to have found the gene for aggression in the form of monoamine oxidase A deficiency. E. O. Wilson, in *Consilience* cites this, quite illogically, as an example of the influence of genes on behaviour, despite the fact that normal people also become violent, not only those with this deficiency (p. 107). Such is the determination, within socio-biology, to account for human behaviour in terms of our genes.

This emphasis on competitiveness, if not outright aggression, runs through virtually all the theories in Table 15, many of which are very fond of using game theory as a model of human behaviour. From our linguistic perspective, we should be aware of the ways in which activity in general is metaphorically referred to by sources of competition and aggression. We gave extensive examples of some such metaphors in chapter

2 (2.6), where we showed that the relatively uncompetitive concept of DEVELOPMENT/ SUCCESS IS MOVEMENT FORWARD, is transformed into the more competitive ACTIVITY/ COMPETITION IS A RACE. But there is a very prolific set in English which construct activity as competition which can go under the heading ACTIVITY IS GAME with the subheadings ACTIVITY IS BALL GAME, ACTIVITY IS CARD GAME, ACTIVITY IS BOARD GAME, ACTIVITY IS GAMBLING GAME. On the aggression side we also gave details of ACTIVITY IS FIGHTING (2.10) (where we might also have mentioned ACTIVITY IS SHOOTING) and SEX IS VIOLENCE. It is likely that these extremely widespread and frequent metaphors have influenced or at least reinforced sociobiological theories.

Many of these theories, predicated on Darwinism, tend to accept the notion that life is a struggle in which only the fittest survive. This idea has also been used as a justification of imperialism, and a spur to eugenics, despite Pinker's attempt to argue otherwise (Pinker 2003). In *The Descent of Man* Darwin (1871/2004) advised against vaccination in the following terms:

> There is reason to believe that vaccination has preserved thousands, who from a weak constitution would formerly have succumbed to smallpox. Thus the weak members of civilised societies propagate their kind. No one who has attended the breeding of domestic animals will doubt that this must be highly injurious to the race of man. … Excepting in the case of man himself, hardly anyone is so ignorant as to allow his worst animals to breed (quoted in Ryan, 2002: 37)

Taking the cue from Darwin, Sollas in *Ancient Hunters and their Modern Representatives* (1924) claimed that "Justice belongs to the strong, and has been meted out to each race according to its strength; each has received as much justice as it deserved … it is not priority of occupation, but the power to utilise, which establishes a claim to the land …" (quoted in Marks 2002: 260). Herbert Spencer concluded that eliminating "unfit" individuals would benefit the human race, and so governments should not take any trouble to relieve the conditions of the poor and needy (Ryan 2002: 35). Madison Grant in *The Passing of the Great Race* (1916) advocated the sterilisation of social failures "beginning always with the criminal, the diseased, and the insane, and extending gradually to types which may be called weaklings rather than defectives, and perhaps ultimately to worthless race types" (Marks 2002: 286). This book was read in translation by Hitler who himself claimed, "It is the struggle for existence that produces the selection of the fittest" (Ryan 2002: 46). Eugenics and the racist imperialist agenda reinforced each other, since it was the duty of the higher races to ensure that future generations were not made more degenerate by the more reproductively successful "lower races".

Eugenics obviously got a bad name in the mid-20th century, but the present possibility of genetic modification or engineering has given it a new impetus. The following frightening idea is critiqued in the New Scientist: "The horizons of the new eugenics are, in principle, boundless. For the first time in all time, a living creature understands its origin and can undertake to design its future" (Midgeley 1998: 56). This is one of the dangerous consequences of pretending that human nature is simply a matter of genes, and of ignoring the enormous cultural and societal influences which go to make up human "nature". Eugenics also ultimately derives from the notion that humans are simply highly evolved animals.

According to Dawkins' *The Selfish Gene* (1990) human behaviour can in fact be explained by the drive to pass on our genes, and this will account for why we favour relatives who share more genes with us, over others who share less genetic material. Every living creature, from the simple bacterium to humans themselves, is designed to act in ways that boost the chances of its genes being reproduced. "If you accept that evolution is all about selfish genes, the group has no role to play. Survival of the fittest means survival of the fittest DNA. There is no such thing as society. You and I are mere vehicles in which our genes are hitching a lift on the road to posterity." (Lynn Dicks, quoted in Ryan, 2002: 242). Selfish gene theory attempts to explain "parts of the psyche that were previously inscrutable" such as the sense of beauty – we look for mates that are good looking because they are healthy and fertile; or a reputation for being tough and a thirst for revenge – these were the best defences against aggression (Pinker 2003: 53).

4.3.1.2 *Animal is a man?*

Selfish gene theory has been developed into sophisticated mathematical models, in an attempt to explain, or explain away, altruistic behaviour. The theory quite clearly echoes the economic and political philosophies of Reaganism-Thatcherism (Chase-Dunn and Gills 2003). Since animals only look after their own genes – themselves and those closely related to them, and since we are simply sophisticated and adaptable animals, we can reach conclusions such as the following: "There's no such thing as society. There are individual men and women, and there are families" (Thatcher 2002: 426).[1] This belief led Thatcher to attempt to abolish the "nanny state"; nannies are not related to us, and therefore make unnatural carers (Yergin, & Stanislaw 1998). We have seen how theories of human as animal have a tendency to justify social policies, whether of the racist and fascist kind in the case of eugenics or the liberal-conservative in terms of cutting tax and reducing welfare provision. ("Liberal" in the English 19th century sense, not the current US sense.) More disturbing still is the extrapolation of the Selfish Gene idea to explain, if not condone, rape in *The Natural History of Rape* (Thornhill & Palmer 2001): "rape ... should be viewed as a natural, biological phenomenon that is a product of the human evolutionary heritage" (quoted in Ryan, 2002: 254).

Instead of seeing humans as animals, there is a subconscious tendency to reverse the metaphorical equation, so that animals are viewed through the lens of human society. Remember Max Black's (1962) claims in his interaction theory that metaphor

---

1.   It is here that I would like to qualify Lakoff's thesis that both conservatives and liberals use the Nation as Family metaphor, the first interpreting it in terms of Strict Father morality, and the latter Nurturant Parent morality (Lakoff 1996:13). At least one strand of conservatism, based on neo-Darwinianism, rejects the idea that our responsibility extends to social groups beyond the family, so that for such conservatives regarding society as a family would be totally misleading.

involves a two-way transfer, not only from source to target, but also from target to source: "Man is a wolf" makes wolves become more like men, as well as vice versa. Within our HUMAN IS ANIMAL impositive metaphor we can see this in operation: traits of human societies are projected onto the animal groups under consideration, to create a hyponymic relationship, if not a synonymous one, maximising the comparison into something more literal. For example, observational studies of chimp "societies" have had various fashionable views of contemporary western society projected on to them. According to Jonathan Marks, in the 1960s Goodall perceived chimps as gentle, by 1971 in *In the Shadow of Man* like a hippie commune, but by the 1980s chimps were being seen as selfish strategists and more violent, sometimes infanticidal, though by the 1990s they had become multicultural. Perhaps such studies tell us as much about ourselves and our (ideal) society as about chimps. Frans de Waal, probably a very nice man, argues from the bonobo that humans are naturally good-natured (Marks 2002: 163ff.).

Projection of philosophical, political and economic theories onto the animals that are being studied does not simply apply to the way chimp society is conceived – it applies to Darwin's evolutionary theories in general. According to Matt Ridley, "Hobbes begat David Hume, who begat Adam Smith who begat Thomas Robert Malthus, who begat Charles Darwin" a genealogy we trace in chapter 8. He points out that, after reading Malthus, Darwin shifted to a more individualistic approach to evolution, and that "the Hobbesian diagnosis – though not the prescription– still lies at the heart of both economics and modern evolutionary biology (Smith begat Friedman, Darwin begat Dawkins)". He notes that Keynes described the *Origin of Species* as "simply Ricardian economics couched in scientific language" and Stephen Jay Gould has said that natural selection "was essentially Adam Smith's economics read into nature". Karl Marx made much the same point: "It is remarkable … how Darwin recognises among beasts and plants his own English society with its division of labour, competition, opening up of new markets, 'inventions', and the Malthusian struggle for existence. It is Hobbes' *bellum omnium contra omnes*" (Ridley 1997: 252).

Following John McGinnis, Steven Pinker makes an explicit connection between the nature of US society and its constitution and theories in evolutionary psychology, identifying five links: (1) The idea of self-interest is enshrined in the right to "life, liberty and the pursuit of happiness". (2) The emphasis upon trade, reflecting the evolutionary biologists' theory of reciprocal altruism, was emphasised in the Commerce Clause of the constitution, which allowed congress to remove trade barriers imposed by the states. (3) The idea in evolutionary game theory that cheaters should be discouraged led to the Contracts Clause. (4) The Takings Clause prevented the government from "cheating" by confiscating property from the more productive citizens. (5) The drive for human aggression was counteracted by the War Powers Clause, giving Congress and not the President the power to declare war. (6) Freedom of speech, assembly and the press was guaranteed in order to prevent tyranny. "The primatologists Frans de Waal, Robin Dunbar and Chrisopher Boehm have shown how a coalition of lower ranking primates can depose a single alpha male. Like McGinnis, they suggest that this might be a crude analogue of political democracy" (Pinker 2003: 296–298).

Damasio, too, links the US constitution to human psychology and emotions:

> Paraphrased in deeply American terms I would rewrite Spinoza's proposition as follows: I hold these truths to be self evident, that all humans are created such that they tend to preserve their life and seek-well-being, that their happiness comes from successful endeavour to do so, and that the foundation of virtue rests on these facts. Perhaps these resonances are not a coincidence (Damasio 2003: 171).

Perhaps not, indeed, given the Protestant ideological origins of both capitalism and neo-Darwinianism. Spinoza, Damasio's mentor, lived in a Netherlands whose liberal social policy the latter describes as follows:

> The Dutch introduced the makings of contemporary justice and modern capitalism. Commerce was respected. Money was supremely valued. The government created laws to permit citizens to buy and sell freely and to best advantage. A large bourgeoisie flourished and devoted itself to the pursuit of property and a life of comfort. The more enlightened Calvinist leaders welcomed the contributions Portuguese Jewish merchants made to those pursuits (p. 231).

We see here a confluence between the Judaeo-Protestant ethic that business success and the accumulation of wealth are signs of God's blessings, the respect for property rights, and free-market capitalism.

Sexist aspects of current society also tend to be projected upon biology, whether it is Francis Bacon setting forth the foundations of the experimental method and representing nature as a female body to be explored or a female spirit to be dominated and tamed, or the representation of human fertilisation as an active sperm going on a brave and arduous quest and eventually claiming as its prize the passive ovum – whereas in fact the egg plays an active role in the fertilisation process (Harvey 1996: 159).

Apparently, in our tendency to project our social theories upon animals, we have become what Yann Martel calls "the most dangerous animal in the zoo ... *animalus anthropomorphicus*, the animal as seen through human eyes ... the obsession with putting ourselves at the centre of everything is the bane not only of theologians but also of zoologists" (Martel 2002: 112–113). The making of nature in the image of society mirrors a phenomenon we noted when discussing HUMAN IS MACHINE – the tendency for cosmologies to be built around the most powerful current technology. In the industrial age cosmologists presented a clockwork universe, and in the computer age we now redefine the cosmos as an information universe. "Cosmologies, then, serve as the ultimate justification for our day-to-day temporal activity. They allow the social order to continue the fiction that its behaviour conforms with 'the natural order of things'" (Rifkin 1987: 201–202). The danger might be, of course, that this leads to an abdication of responsibility for ultra-competitiveness, violence and war.

4.3.1.3   *Game theory*

I said before that the further we proceed to the right in Table 15, the more other aspects of human life besides genetic inheritance and animal nature tend to be taken into account. This might in fact be misleading, because many of the theories are reductionist, explaining culture and psychology in terms of genetic disposition, social Darwinism and the aggressive struggle to pass on one's genes. Indeed, they often go further, reducing not only evolution but also morality and altruism to mathematics by using game theory.

For example, Trivers (1971) argues that reciprocal altruism evolved to reap the benefits of altruistic exchanges and that moralistic aggression evolved to punish cheaters, supporting his argument by the mathematical models of game theory used by economists (Laland and Brown 2002: 83–84). Trivers thought that we behave apparently unselfishly to those who do not share our genes because we calculate that at some time in the future they may repay the favour. This theory has more recently been the basis of a natural history of the emotions which make up the moral sense.

> Other-condemning emotions – contempt, anger, disgust – prompt one to punish cheaters. The other-praising emotions – gratitude and … elevation, moral awe or being moved – prompt one to reward altruists. The other-suffering emotions – sympathy, compassion and empathy – prompt one to help a needy beneficiary. And the self-conscious emotions – guilt, shame and embarrassment – prompt one to avoid cheating and to repair its effects (Pinker 2003: 271).

However, as Lakoff points out, there is a large body of psychological evidence that "people do not reason all the time, or even primarily, in terms of maximizing clear and unequivocal rewards and punishments", and this game-theory model of human behaviour is a function of right-wing ideology (Lakoff 1996: 373–374). Bourdieu also maintains that the habitual forms of action are culturally and historically determined, and so often beyond conscious calculation.

> To view action as the outcome of conscious calculation – a perspective implicit in some forms of game theory – is to neglect the fact that, by virtue of the habitus, individuals are *already predisposed* to act in certain ways, pursue certain goals, avow certain tastes, and so on (Thompson 1991: 17).

"Game" theory is, also, by the way, a rather infelicitous metaphor – though there is some attempt in evolutionary game theory to allow for win-win situations, this contradicts the metaphor in which real competitive games are always zero-sum.

Game theory, in its widespread use as a model by evolutionary biologists, assumes that statistical likelihoods of benefits to the self are what consciously drive decision-making among players of games like the Prisoner's Dilemma, and subconsciously drive apparently altruistic social behaviour amongst evolving populations. I think one of the reasons for the persistence of this theory, or maybe also one of its effects, are the metaphor themes which regard both thought as a process of calculation (THINKING/

CONSIDERING IS CALCULATING) morality as a kind of accountancy, and relationships in monetary terms (AFFECTION/RELATIONSHIP IS MONEY/WEALTH, see 3.4).

Using reason to understand or reach a logical conclusion is often conceived in terms of calculation: **work out** (literally, 'use calculation to solve a mathematical problem') 'use reasoning to discover or understand' (*I've been spending ages trying to work out why he did what he did*), **deduction** (literally, 'taking away a number from a total') 'reaching an answer by thinking carefully about the facts' (*I found out the culprit by a process of logical deduction*). Calculation is also used to refer to how judgements are made more or less accurately: **put two and two together** 'form a judgement hastily using evidence you think is obvious' (*I put two and two together and decided they must be lovers*), **gauge** (literally, 'calculate an amount with a measuring device') 'make a judgement about people's feelings' (*I stood there trying to gauge his reaction*), **miscalculate** 'make a misjudgement' (*unfortunately he miscalculated the opponents grinding determination to win the fight*). The original problem can be conceived as algebra: **equation** 'difficult problem that depends on considering many interacting variables for its solution' (*managing the committee is a complex equation of enforcing school policy and keeping pupils happy*), which involves at least one **factor** (literally, 'whole number produced when you divide a larger number by a whole number') 'fact or situation which explains the result of something' (*heavy snow was a contributing factor in the accident*), and when every variable is factored in we can arrive at a **formula** 'way of doing something that is considered acceptable and efficient' (*playing together is a formula for a successful family*).

Explanation is thus conceived in terms of adding up accounts: **add up** 'have or give a reasonable explanation' (*the evidence all adds up if we assume that James was the murderer*), **account for** 'explain' (*it's difficult to account for the low levels of* AIDS *infection amongst these prostitutes*).

Counting can refer more generally to thinking, believing or considering: **count, account, reckon,** (*I count/account/reckon myself lucky to have a well-paid job that I enjoy*). You introduce a summary of everything that has been thought about by the phrase **in sum**, and the most important things to be considered are **the bottom line** (*the bottom line is – will the new policy actually persuade more people to switch to public transport?*). Expectations, especially important for reciprocal altruism, are also calculations: **calculate on, count on** 'expect or depend on' (*I'm calculating/counting on your presence at the meeting*).

Comparison is conceptualised by counting in order to match totals, as in **amount to** 'be the same as something else', (*the levy on the employment of maids amounts to taxation*), **tally** (literally, 'count or calculate the number of items'), 'agree or match something else' (*the confessions of the two suspects don't tally*), so that when something does not match our expectations, it is like the remainder of one after dividing by two, that is, **odd** (*that was a real odd thing you said, I don't get you*).

Various more specific mathematical concepts are used when talking about comparison and variation: **proportion**, 'relative importance or seriousness' (*worry about* *work is very natural but you've got to keep it in proportion*), **disproportionate** 'not deserving its importance or influence' (*terrorism attracts a disproportionate amount of media attention, because it threatens those in power*), **inverse**, (literally 'getting larger as another number gets smaller') 'exact opposite' (*city dwellers complain about too much rain but they rarely ever complain about the inverse*), **lowest common denominator**, (literally 'smallest number divisible by the bottom numbers in a group of fractions') 'the most basic thing that different groups/people are thought to share in common' (*the need for shelter and food are the lowest common denominators of humanity*), **negative, positive** 'confirming the presence/absence of a disease or a condition' (*he tested negative/ positive for* AIDS), and **plus** 'an advantage or good feature' (*fluency in Mandarin is a plus for this job*).

This is not a particularly new metaphor theme, and is strongly represented in Hobbes: his metaphor for reason and language is, at the threshold of capitalist modernity, an accountancy metaphor, since they "give accounts" of things. Accounts are sums, multiplications and "subtractions" of "items". Accountants make mistakes when the items are not properly defined, not properly counted, not set in the right order, not properly reckoned.

> For there can be no certainty of the last conclusion, without a certainty of all those Affirmations and Negations, on which it was grounded and inferred. As when a master of a family, in taking an account, casteth up the sums of all the bills of expense, into one sum; and not regarding how each bill is summed up, by those that give them in account; nor what it is he pays for; he advantages himself no more, than if he allowed the account in gross, trusting to every of the accountants skill and honesty: so also in Reasoning of all other things, he that takes up conclusions on the trust of Authors, and does not fetch them from the first items in every reckoning (which are the significations of names settled by definitions), loses his labour; and does not know any thing; but only believeth (Hobbes 1651/1983, chapter 5:112).

As Lakoff explores in his book *Moral Politics: What Conservatives Know that Liberals Don't,* we can also use accounting metaphors to conceptualise morality, a link which we already explored (3.4): **credit** 'honour, pride, reputation' **pay your dues**, 'do your duty' **debt**, **indebtedness** 'appreciation gratitude and moral obligation', **repay** 'do something good to somebody in return for past favours', **pay back**, **settle accounts/old scores**, 'take revenge by repaying an insult or harm', etc.

4.3.1.4 *Evolutionary psychology*
Passing to column 3 of Table 15, we find that evolutionary psychology attempts to explain, among other things, how psychological mechanisms have evolved to make men more aggressive and take more risks than women, and to desire more sexual partners (Trivers 1972). Females make the most biological investment in parenting and are therefore a crucial resource, so men compete for them in order to reproduce with

them; polygamy favours males if they are successful in this competition, so they have to take the risk of being aggressive. However, aggressively fighting for mates would be unfavourable and unnecessarily risky for females as, even with many male partners, they would not be able to mother as many children as a man with many wives (Laland and Brown 2002: 175). As Daly and Brown conclude, "the risks that males take may reflect a past history of selection that has fashioned their minds for competition" (p. 176). This is also thought to explain why there are more homicides perpetrated by men than by women (p. 174). Pinker has announced the discovery of "the universality of dominance and violence across human societies and the existence of genetic and neurological mechanisms that underlie it" (Pinker 2003: 294).

In a more measured way, Hinde (1997) has suggested that psychological predispositions have evolved which do not cause war, but which can be exploited for war propaganda. Laland and Brown (2002: 297) summarise his thesis:

> Biological predispositions such as fear of strangers, aggressiveness, and a tendency to distinguish in and out groups do not cause war. However the predispositions do play an important role as they are exploited, for instance in the propaganda of mobilizing and abusive leaders, in ways that lead to the image of the enemy as different or evil and sanctify aggression against adversaries.

4.3.1.5 *Meme theory*

Meme theory, in column 4 of Table 15, is not so centrally concerned as the previous theories with the truth or otherwise of "human is animal", though it builds on the notion that psychology evolves by considering how thoughts evolve, and is still concerned with competitive reproductive success. However, it is worth discussing in passing, since it illustrates the power of the analogy IDEA/EMOTION IS DISEASE. The theory poses the question "what can evolution tell us about how human beings think or what they believe?" Dawkins (1990) believes that in the same way as genes reproduce and propagate by transferring from body to body through sperms and ova, so memes reproduce by spreading from brain to brain. Catchy concepts and fashionable ideas are like genes trying to reproduce themselves in the human mind, establishing cultural traits advantageous to themselves (Laland and Brown 2002). And in ways reminiscent of Capra (chapter 3), Dawkins compares this process with infection by parasitic viruses, since both viruses and ideas are carriers of information (cf. Aaron Lynch's *Thought Contagion* and Richard Brodie's *Virus of the Mind*). When someone introduces a meme into your mind it is like a parasite on your brain, which becomes a vehicle for the meme's further reproduction in the same way that a virus is a parasite on the genetic mechanism of a host cell. The analogy is pursued further: "If our bodies have an immune system to quell biological viruses, then shouldn't we expect our minds to have analogous defences to suppress rogue memes?" (p. 230). And three factors are thought to be important in the spread of these (harmful) ideas: infectiousness, susceptibility and social environment. The first two are already captured in the vocabulary **virulent**, **infectious** and **immune**, detailed below.

There are several conventional metaphors in English which already manifest the metaphor theme, IDEA IS DISEASE, though they tend to be associated with emotions as well as ideas as their targets;[2] or perhaps one could say they imply an emotional attitude (not always negative by the way) to the ideas communicated. Ideas and emotions can be a **bug** 'enthusiasm' that is **contagious, catching** or **infectious** 'easily communicated to many people' (*China can no longer protect itself from the contagious foreign ideas on the internet*), and the emotions associated with ideas can be more or less strong – **virulent** 'full of hate and fierce opposition' (*virulent criticisms of the Prime Minister are not uncommon*), **pathological** 'showing extreme uncontrolled feelings' (*he suffered from fits of pathological resentment*). The effects of these ideas and the accompanying emotions can often cause harm – **poison** 'introduce a harmful idea into the mind' (*young minds all over the world are being poisoned by consumerism*) or be harmful – **noxious** 'harmful and unpleasant' (*these noxious attitudes towards Moslems are a danger to peace*), **poisonous/venomous** 'very unpleasant, negative' (*the venomous written attacks annoyed him*), **inflammatory** 'intentionally causing negative feelings' (*the politician's speech was full of inflammatory ideas about race*) or **jaundiced** 'pessimistic'(*his article represents a jaundiced view*), and negative ideas may **fester** 'become more intense', like an infected wound.

Resisting ideas can be seen in terms of preventing disease: **sanitize** 'change in order to make it less strongly expressed or offensive' (*the committee sanitized the ideas in the document by removing most of the strong adjectives*), **immune** 'unable to be influenced by an idea or emotion' (*he was quite immune to the latest economic orthodoxies*); or of its treatment: **cure of** 'get rid of a bad idea or emotion' (*the displays on Auschwitz in the Imperial War Museum cured him of his anti-Semitism*).

Interestingly enough, we have this metaphor theme reversed so that DISEASE IS AN IDEA appears in the lexis: **transmit** literally 'send a message' metaphorically 'pass on a disease' (*AIDS is a sexually transmitted disease*), **communicable** 'infectious, easily spread' (*TB is communicable through drinking raw milk*), and **respond to** 'be treatable by' (*TB used to respond to drugs*).

One might wonder why Dawkins compares these ideas with a disease. In the metaphor theme they are often seen as such because of the negative emotions with which they are associated. Are they, for Dawkins, ideologies, in the pejorative sense of that term – false ideas hiding a basic material reality? The theme IDEA IS DISEASE does activate the associated themes of DISEASE IS INVASION and ARGUMENT IS FIGHTING:

---

2.   Sontag has pointed out the widespread association between TB, cancer and emotion in 19th century Europe and the US. "Fever in TB was a sign of an inward burning; the tubercular is someone 'consumed' by ardour, that ardour leading to the dissolution of the body" (Sontag 1991: 21). The TB sufferer was supposed to be a sensitive melancholy type (pp. 32-3). Cancer was thought to be caused either by too much excited activity, or from the repression of passion (p. 54).

our reason is like an immune defence against wrong ideas; these wrong ideas have to be eliminated, according to the adversarial system, in which only one side can win (see 2.11). Allowing different perspectives on the same phenomenon to co-exist in harmony or symbiosis is not a possible ground in this metaphor. Presumably only the right ideas should survive – right should be mighty.

These metaphors become exceedingly dangerous once we start to think not just of the ideas, but of the people who hold these ideas as a disease. As Sontag points out, it is quite common to use cancer as a metaphor for opposed political ideologies: Trotsky called Stalinism the cancer of Marxism, Simon Leys spoke of "the Maoist cancer that is gnawing away at the face of China", John Dean referred to Watergate as "a cancer – close to the presidency – that's growing". But such denunciations quite easily slip over into attacks on groups of people: Sontag herself confesses to writing "the white race is the cancer of human history"; the Gang of Four were referred to as "the cancer of China"; in August 1976 a Christian Lebanese rightist officer besieging the Tal Zatar Palestinian refugee camp called it "a cancer in the Lebanese body". Since most treatments of cancer involve aggressive attempts to destroy tumours through radiation or chemotherapy, calling groups a cancer is implicitly genocidal (Sontag 1991: 84).

Leaving this danger to one side, Dawkins has an interesting "germ" of an idea, here, especially that some ideas are maladaptive to human development (for example the economic models which prize the growth of consumerism). But he seems unaware of work in discourse analysis by scholars and thinkers such as Foucault, Bourdieu, Kristeva, Fowler, Kress, Fairclough, Van Dijk, which would give him a clearer picture of "transmission chains for memes" (Laland and Brown 2002: 237). In these writers he would discover how discourse can create cultural categories, such as that of the homosexual, and self-fulfilling regimes of truth, and how the power structures of society, through control of intertextuality, determine whose voices, and whose viruses get the chance to infect all of us. Fortunately, Balkin in *Cultural Software,* by acknowledging, respecting, and critiquing the theories of Foucault, has incorporated meme theory into a theory of discourse and ideology (Balkin 1998, especially chapter 3). He distances himself from sociobiological ideas that genes control memes and suggests that social conventions and institutions are memes which may be useful (symbiotic), neutral, or harmful (parasitic) for their hosts (pp. 67ff). Interestingly, he characterises conceptual metaphors as endemic viruses (pp. 60–62).

4.3.1.6 *Gene-culture evolutionary theory*

The lack of a real social and cultural dimension to most of these theories and the reductionism to neo-Darwinism are equally apparent in gene-culture evolutionary theory, the last column in Table 15. Boyd and Richerson, for example, claim that "fortunately onerous and all-encompassing definitions of culture have had their day. More cognitive perspectives are in the ascendancy which restrict culture to learned information stored in the brain and transmitted between individuals" (p. 272). To any sociolinguist or discourse analyst, of course, this is nonsensical. Discourses, in which ideas are created, passed on and negotiated, take place within genres as expressions of social contexts, which are, in turn, determined institutionally and by the orders of discourse within a culture (Fairclough 2001: 122). Ideas are not simply transmitted from one mind to another in a social and cultural vacuum. The underlying reductionsim of even those theories to the right of Table 15 can be seen in the following quote: "Borrowing Darwinian concepts and methods, suitably adjusted to the structural peculiarities of human culture, is the quickest and easiest path to a reasonable theory of human nature and thus to an improved understanding of human behaviour" (Laland and Brown 2002: 275, Boyd and Richerson 1985).

We have now finished our survey of theories which adopt the naturalistic fallacy, and generally assume that nature is competitive, if not aggressive and violent. One problem with these theories is their potential to be used as an abdication of responsibility (perhaps in the same way as the Augustinian doctrine of original sin): "Evolutionary theory says that the ultimate rationality for our motives is that they perpetuated our ancestors' genes in the environment in which we evolved. Since none of us are aware of that rationale, none of us can be blamed for pursuing it" (Laland and Brown 2002: 175).

According to George Williams, the evolutionary biologist, the immorality of the natural world is obvious: natural selection is a mechanism for maximising short-sighted selfishness – infanticide, siblicide and rape are observed in many types of animals, cannibalism is common except among vegetarians, death from fighting is more common in most animal species than in the most violent of American cities (Ridley 1996: 215).

4.3.2   Humans as more or less animals – but co-operative and symbiotic.

Most of the theories mentioned above, with their impositive statements that (HU)MAN IS ANIMAL, stress the competitive struggle for survival. However, there have been interesting challenges to the Darwinian account of evolution, notable Frank Ryan's *Darwin's Blind Spot: Evolution beyond Natural Selection* (2002). This theory not only puts a new co-operative and symbiotic slant on (animal) nature, and therefore, perhaps human nature, but ties in interestingly with *Gaia* theory.

This book sounds a clear note of warning about neo-Darwinian theories which maintain "that complex adaptations, including behavioural strategies, evolved to benefit the individual (indeed the genes for those traits within an individual) not the community, species, or ecosystem" (Pinker 2003: 285). Though accepting the "naturalistic" view that human nature shares a great deal with animal nature, unlike the neo-Darwinians, Ryan perceives co-operative qualities and principles in animal nature, manifest in symbiotic relationships.

> Symbiosis ... brings a wonderful new perspective on life in general and human society in particular. From the very beginning evolutionary theory has been applied to many fields of human affairs, such as sociology, psychology and even politics. Such interpretations, viewed from a Darwinian perspective alone, lead to an

excessive emphasis on competition and struggle. Most damaging of all, the social Darwinism of the first half of the twentieth century led directly to the horrors of eugenics. The rise, once more of social Darwinism is therefore a source of worry to many scientists, philosophers, and sociologists (Ryan 2002: 6).

There are two kinds of symbiosis: exosymbiosis and endosymbiosis. Exosymbiosis is a relationship of mutual benefit between two separate organisms, a quite familiar concept in biology. More important for evolutionary theory is endosymbiosis, where one organism lives inside another, or actually becomes part of it. Frederick Keeble in the 19th century investigated two types of non-segmented worms *Convoluta roscoffensis* and *C. paradoxa* and found that they were an odd combination of animal and plant. The worms contained large numbers of *Platymonas*, brilliantly-coloured algae living symbiotically in their tissues. The algae produced products of photosynthesis for the worms, who in turn gave their waste products to the algae (p. 48). This kind of symbiotic union was extremely important to plant evolution.

> In the early stages of plant life on earth an amoeboid protist was infected by or ingested a cyanobacterium – the ingestion or infection failed and a new endosymbiosis took place which incorporated the cyanobacterium as a chloroplast, leading to the forerunner of all plant cells – the green alga (p. 147).

The contribution of symbiosis to plant and animal life and their evolution is enormous. The first basic point is that only one living organism can feed independently, that is without relying on other organisms to pre-process its food, and this is the bacterium. Therefore "all life must ultimately depend on the prior existence and continuing presence of these autotrophic bacteria" (p. 68). The result is that "every herbivore, including plant-eating lizards, birds, marsupials, and a wide variety of mammals, such as cattle, hippopotami, and giraffes ... could have evolved only in symbiotic partnership with its gut-based internal zoo of cellulose-degrading microbes" (p. 167). The crucial point about some kinds of endosymbiosis is that they can be a means of transferring genetic material from one organism to another. For instance, in 2001 scientists at the Pasteur Institute discovered that resistance to the drug streptomycin had been transferred from one plague bacillus to another and that this was mediated by a mobile genetic unit, or plasmid (p. 141).

Recognition of endosymbiosis as a mechanism of genetic transfer demands reassessment of traditional evolutionary theory. "Today the majority of Darwinians perceive evolution as arising exclusively from the gradual accumulation of mutations and from sexual recombination, under the controlling influence of natural selection". But

> in symbiosis the mechanism of change is radically different from this Darwinian model. When two or more life-forms interact they bring together genomic and metabolic abilities that have already been honed by evolution. This interaction can involve a major evolutionary jump or saltation. Moreover, for Darwinians the mechanism of change (mutation) is essentially random and non-creative, while

for a symbiologist, the mechanism of change is not random but a creative force in itself (pp. 64–5).

Unlike natural selection, which acts on gene mutations to modify existing genes over a long period, formative symbiotic unions can merge together thousands of genes into a new hybrid organism very quickly. And the creative force of these symbiotic mergings, perhaps a good metaphor for original metaphor, is one which leads towards ever more biological and genetic complexity, a complexity not predicted by natural selection (p. 92).

The complexity also involves increasing interdependence. In a sense the boundaries between classes of organisms become blurred.

> The interdependence of organisms in symbiotic associations … blurred the boundaries of taxonomic definition: where did the individual organism begin and end if genetic material could arrive from beyond the cell walls and change an organism's heredity? (p. 82)

Sorin Sonea (1983) has suggested that the individual kinds of bacteria can be thought of as the cells of a "global super-organism", which has evolved over years of fluid symbiotic relationships. This idea can be combined with the recognition of the important role that bacteria play in changing the environment within which they live to lead us to the conclusions of *Gaia* theory.

> As Lovelock has shown, all life forms interact with and change the ecosystem. For instance, the metabolic activities of bacteria change the rock, soil, water, or air in which they live. If the changes enhance the organism's fitness, it prospers, if the changes pollute its ecology, thereby reducing fitness, the organism declines. A small local change that improves fitness for one life form can, by degrees, influence other life forms in the same ecosystem through the interplay of parasitism, predation, food webs, and the myriad possibilities of exosymbiosis and endosymbiosis. In Sonea's view the bacterial superorganism alters the environment in which its component strains evolve and colonize. This, as he suggests, "is a perfect example of the Gaia hypothesis of how life modifies the environment" (Ryan 2002: 142–3).

For many years *Gaia* theory was marginalized, dismissed or deliberately ignored. But it now seems to have come of age, as a viable theory. In July 2001, at the conclusion of a meeting of the European and American Geophysical Unions in Amsterdam, roughly a thousand scientists subscribed to the following declaration:

> The Earth System behaves as a single, self-regulating system comprised of physical, chemical, biological and human components. The interactions and feedbacks between the component parts are complex and exhibit multi-scale temporal and spatial variability. The understanding of the natural dynamics of the Earth System has advanced greatly in recent years and provides a sound basis for evaluating the effects and consequences of human-driven change (Ryan 2002: 186–7).

Gaia theory has something in common with Stuart Kaufmann's ideas as expressed in the book *The Origins of Order: Self-Organisation and Selection in Evolution* (1997). According to Horgan he showed that

> [w]hen a system of simple chemicals reaches a certain level of complexity, it undergoes a dramatic transition, akin to the phase change that occurs when liquid water freezes. The molecules begin spontaneously combining to create larger molecules of increasing complexity and catalytic capability. Kauffman argued that this process of self-organisation or autocatalysis, rather than the fortuitous formation of a molecule with the ability to replicate and evolve, led to life. According to Kauffman complex arrays of interacting genes subject to random mutations do not evolve randomly. Instead they tend to converge toward a relatively small number of patterns, or attractors, to use the term favoured by chaos theorists. Much of the order displayed by biological systems results "not from the hard-won success of natural selection" but from these pervasive order-generating effects. "The whole point of it is that it's spontaneous order" (Horgan 1998: 133).

In this view evolution is an antichaos phenomenon – a defiance of the second law of thermodynamics and of entropy.

We have already seen that Ryan wrote his book partly as a riposte to neo-Darwinians, and he too draws conclusions about human nature from the scientific theories. For example he dismisses the reciprocal altruism theory of Trivers because he believes we have discovered a deep-seated instinct for co-operation and even self-sacrifice, born out of symbiosis:

> Does anybody seriously believe that a man breaking into a blazing house to save the lives of the screaming children inside does so because he stops to think that one day those children might rescue him? …. Does the boy or the girl who dies trying to save a dog from drowning under the ice on a wintry lake really calculate that, once rescued, the dog might one day pad to his or her rescue? … It seems more likely that important co-operative behaviours, embedded in our human genome – such as love, friendship, and "togetherness" – carry a potential for self-sacrifice in extreme circumstances (Ryan 2002: 248).

He sums up his view of human/animal nature and their impact on culture, as follows:

> To deny the reality of our cultures of war, selfishness, and aggression would be foolish. But these forces are counterbalanced by the curiosity and caring about other people and nature, and especially by the most cherished human quality of all, the one that, along with sentience, defines us as human: our capacity to love (p. 267).

One organism giving up its identity, in order to become part of another so as to bring about its survival and creative improvement, is as good a metaphor as we can get for self-less love.

If, adopting the naturalistic fallacy, we wish to draw conclusions from this retort to neo-Darwinism, we will find that the grounds of comparison become rather different from those in the Darwinian theories. We are not programmed by our animal inheritance to participate in an ineluctable struggle for existence with the aggression which that entails, but are equally inclined towards symbiotic co-operation, not only between ourselves and others in society, but between ourselves and the rest of the living and non-living universe. This is a view quite different from Ridley's in the next book we will consider, who identifies the instinct to co-operation as a distinctive human trait, distancing us from the rest of animal life.

4.3.3   Humans as in many respects animals

Ridley's *The Origins of Virtue* (1997) takes as one step further away from the impositive statement that humans are more or less animals or are kinds of animals, towards a recognition that HUMAN IS ANIMAL is more metaphorical – we share certain qualities with animals, but other traits make us distinctive and unique.

> Our minds have been built by selfish genes but they have been built to be social, trustworthy and co-operative ... Human beings have social instincts. They come into the world with predispositions to learn how to co-operate, to discriminate the trustworthy from the treacherous, to commit themselves to be trustworthy, to earn good reputations, to exchange goods and information, and to divide labour. In this we are on our own. No other species has been so far down this evolutionary path before us, for no species has built a truly integrated society ... Far from being a universal feature of animal life ... this instinctive co-operativeness is the very hallmark of humanity and what sets us apart from other animals (Ridley 1997: 249).

On the other hand Ridley also emphasises the Darwinian basis of this inheritance in terms similar to Dawkins, stressing self-interest. Consider his dismissal of group selection theory: "Most of the examples I have discussed are cases where individuals are co-operating to further their self-interest ... We are designed not to sacrifice ourselves for the group but to exploit the group for ourselves" (p. 188).

Ridley tries to steer the course between the Scylla of reductionism of humans to animals and the Charybdis of cultural determinism by advocating restriction of cultural influences largely to the economic sphere – trade, and property. This is not perhaps surprising, since mathematical models such as game theory are used both in sociobiological theories and in the current anti-humanistic economic orthodoxies which go under the name of economic theory, but which are really no more than econometrics (Pinker 2003: 285).

"Human beings have some instincts that favour the greater good and others that foster self-interested and anti-social behaviour. We must design a society that encourages the former and discourages the latter" (Ridley 1997: 260). How then would he design such a society? The first plank is trade, based on the division of labour. "Trade is the beneficent side of human groupishness" (p. 200). Because of the division of labour trade is a non zero-sum game, that is to say, both parties benefit (p. 207). As the division of labour creates comparative advantages, trade becomes worthwhile: "There is simply no other group that exploits the law of comparative advantage between groups ... the law of comparative advantage is one of the ecological aces that our species holds" (p. 210). Note the card-game metaphor.

A second way of designing a good and sustainable society is through spreading property rights. Ridley believes that, once everything has been commodified, the principles of game theory will operate to everyone's advantage (p. 225). Third World poverty can be cured by establishing secure property rights, without which, according to the Peruvian economist Hernando de Soto, people have no chance to build their own prosperity (p. 239). Ridley further suggests that property owned in common by fairly small groups (not nationalised) provides the best model for preservation of the environment, using the neo-conservative terms "re-privatisation", rather than "small-scale communism", and "handing over to small committees", rather than "worker co-operatives". His invective against government intervention is not balanced by any mention of the power of trans-national corporations (pp. 234–6).

Other aspects of culture besides economic property and trade seem to be dismissed, or seen as dangerous, particularly religion, romanticism and politics. With a provocativeness which borders on the arrogance of a reductionist sociobiologist, he pronounces: "For St. Augustine the source of social order lay in the teachings of Christ. For Hobbes it lay in the sovereign. For Rousseau it lay in solitude. For Lenin it lay in the party. They were all wrong." He goes on:

> The roots of social order are in our heads, where we possess the instinctive capacities for creating not a perfectly harmonious and virtuous society, but a better one than we have at present ...We must encourage social and material exchange between equals, for that is the raw material of trust, and trust is the foundation of virtue (pp. 264–5).

We see here again his tendency to sail towards Scylla, to regard the "instinctive capacities" as the most important.

Although Ridley warns us against the perils of the naturalistic fallacy, that what is natural must be right (pp. 253–257), he often "falls prey" to it himself by underestimating the extent to which he has disregarded cultural factors. He has what he would call a realistic view of human nature, that we are basically selfish, and that people who are not are exceptional.

> Just as we wish other people to turn the other cheek when hurt, but seek revenge on behalf of close relatives and friends, just as we urge morality far more than we act on it, so environmentalism is something we prefer to preach than to practise. Everybody, it seems, wants a new road for themselves, but less road-building. Everybody wants another car, but wishes there were fewer on the road. Everybody wants two kids, but lower population growth (p. 216).

In this vein he discusses the father of Jung Chang, the author of *Wild Swans*, who, putting his belief in the Chinese revolution before his zoological instincts to favour only those with whom he shared genes, refused to show any favouritism towards relatives. (See also the dedication of this book.) "Communism would have worked if there were more such men … but most people are not like Wang Shou-yu" (pp. 258–9). He does not ask what cultural or religious forces create such men and such selflessness. Similarly he is extremely pessimistic about appeals to religious values to combat human greed, as for example in the ecological movement. He regards such appeals as a challenge to his theories: "If such eco-optimism is well-founded then the argument of this book falls, and people are not calculating machines intricately designed to find co-operative strategies only when they assist enlightened self-interest" (p. 214). He concludes: "Environmental ethics are therefore to be taught in spite of human nature, not in concert with it" (p. 225).

Religions, for Ridley, at least Judaism and Christianity, are undesirable aspects of human culture, because of their tribalism, which means punishing the out-group, and setting up moral codes which only apply to the in-group (p. 192). (The examples of Blair, Olmert and Bush and their war on Islam would appear to be evidence to support Ridley here). However, he misses crucial developments in the New Testament. The Good Samaritan was a story Jesus specifically told in order to dissociate truth and morality from genetic or ethnic identity: it is the Jews in the story who behave badly, and the Samaritan who behaves well. Despite the painting of the Good Samaritan on the cover of his book, Ridley misses the point. Later, as Christianity begins to spread, Peter, through a vision, becomes convinced that the gospel is to be preached to non-Jews as well as Jews, and converts the Roman centurion, Cornelius. In the Old Testament, morality and truth were tied to genetics, so that to eradicate falsehood you have to eradicate people, such as when Elijah exterminates the prophets of Baal. But in the New there is the possibility of religious conversion, and not only for those who belong to your ethnic or genetic group. This was one of the great advances made in human development: cultural transmission of knowledge gained ascendancy over genetic transmission (see row 3 of Table 16 below).

One might contrast Ridley's ideas on religion with those of Frank Ryan:

> The Christians who accepted martyrdom had no vested interest in the genes of their fellow humans only faith in their religious belief. When one examines all the great religions, including Judaism, Hinduism, Taoism, and Islam one discovers a similar level of caring and co-operation in their tenets and commandments. What applies to religions also applies to the great majority of human communities, from tribes to nations (p. 246).

Is it its outright challenge to the naturalistic fallacy that makes Ridley reject religion in general and Christianity in particular? The idea that Christ/God became a perfect man in order to make selfish sinful men become perfect, is quite the opposite from Ridley's idea that "sins" (such as greed and covetousness) are our natural human instincts for self-interest, and that the only way to develop society is in step with our instinctual nature through property rights and trade.

However, there are occasions where Ridley moves away from the naturalistic fallacy to suggest that humans can, through cultural intervention, defy their instinctual nature. In fact, towards the end of the book, unless he is being ironic, there is a rather contradictory note, "The first thing we should do to create a good society is to conceal the truth about mankind's propensity for self-interest, the better to delude our fellows into thinking that they are noble savages inside" (p. 261). Though Stevie Smith would not agree:

> I think if we do not learn quickly, and learn to teach children,
> To be good without enchantment, without the help
> Of beautiful painted stories pretending to be true,
> Then I think it will be too much for us, the dishonesty,
> And, armed as we are now, we shall kill everybody. (Smith 1975: 521)

Table 16. Leech (Popper)'s 4 (3) worlds of knowledge (Leech 1983:52)

	World 1	World 2	World 3	World 4
Inmates of these worlds are:	Physical and biological objects /states	Mental (subjective) objects/states	Societal (intersubjective) objects/states	Objective facts, existing independently of particular objects, minds, societies
Communication functions:	Expressive	'Signalling' or conative	Descriptive	Argumentative or metalingual
Historical transmission & accumulation of information:	Genetic	Learning	Cultural transmission	Linguistic transmission by TEXTS
Unit of transmission:	Species	Individual	Society, tribe, culture	Linguistic (scientific?) community
Adaptation to environment by:	Natural selection	Conditioning	Social and technological advance	Error elimination through argument (scientific method)

Perhaps Ridley is feeling his way to the conclusion presented by Antonio Damasio –

> This is the time to introduce the reminder that the best of human behaviour is not necessarily wired under the control of the genome. The history of our civilisation

is, to some extent, the history of a persuasive effort to extend the best of "moral sentiments" to wider and wider circles of humanity, beyond the restrictions of inner groups, eventually encompassing the whole of humanity (Damasio 2003: 163).

It might be interesting to locate this argument within the framework of the 4 worlds of knowledge postulated by Leech (1983) (based on the earlier 3 worlds postulated by Popper) (See Table 16). Those within the sociobiological tradition stress the importance of World 1, through evolutionary psychology attempting to make World 2 dependent upon it. Ridley is marginally more inclusive, celebrating trade and property which are two, minor, parts of World 3, the societal world. In both cases there is an attempt to reduce psychology (World 2) and society (World 3) to explanation in terms of biology (World 1). We shall have more to say about this reductionism in the final chapter.

4.3.4   Humans as possibly like animals in many respects, but ideally as different.

Ridley's latter, contradictory remarks about the need to foster the illusion of non-selfishness leads us to a consideration of ideologies which encourage transcendence of our animal natures. There is a long tradition, in Western philosophy and cosmology, of regarding animals as inferior to humans. The classical and medieval view is well summed up by Tillyard in *The Elizabethan World Picture* (1943). At the top of the hierarchy were purely spiritual beings, God and the angels. Just below them, and in a somewhat ambiguous situation, were humans, partly spiritual and partly animal. They had the free will to choose between their spiritual nature and their animal nature, and the main feature distinguishing them from animals was their ability to use reason to control their will. If humans were to abandon reason and surrender themselves to irrational emotion they would become like animals, and descend in the hierarchy. This notion is not perhaps very distant from popular Buddhism, which claims that if humans behave badly in this life, their karma will dictate rebirth as an animal in the next. (See also Lovejoy 1960 and Lakoff and Turner 1989: 170–171)

> GOD
> ANGELS
> MAN
> ANIMALS
> PLANTS
> MINERALS

The idea of the superiority of humans over animals was boosted by Lamarckian views of evolution, in which later forms were thought superior.

> Each species could then move up the "chain of being", which culminated in human beings ... Lamarck's view of evolution was linear and progressive, with species having an inherent striving to evolve greater complexity, with the pinnacle of creation being human beings (Laland and Brown 2002: 40).

Darwin, too, is constantly using the word "improvement" to talk about natural selection, and readily adopted Spencer's phrase "the survival of the fittest" in later editions of *On the Origin of Species*; indeed, the 5th edition entitled the chapter on natural selection 'Natural Selection or the Survival of the Fittest' (Rogers 1972: 278).

The biologist Romanes, in 1882, made an interesting comparison between phylogenetic development, the evolutionary development of life forms, and ontogenetic development, the development of the individual human during the early stages of its life (Table 17). The implication is that any human development from 15 months onwards distances us from our animal nature.

Table 17. Romanes' comparison between phylogenetic development and ontogenetic development (quoted in Laland and Brown: 45)

Human development	Equivalent to	Psychological ability
Sperm and egg	Protoplasmic organisms	Movement
Embryo	Coelenterate	Nervous system
Birth		Pleasure and pain
1 week	Echinodermata	Memory
3 weeks	Larvae of insects	Basic instincts
10 weeks	Insects and spiders	Complex instincts
12 weeks	Fish	Associative learning
4 months	Reptiles	Recognition of individuals
5 months	Hymenoptera	Communication of ideas
8 months	Birds	Simple language
10 months	Mammals	Understanding of mechanisms
12 months	Monkeys and elephants	Use of tools
15 months	Apes and dogs	Morality

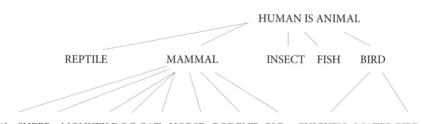

Figure 3. Sub-themes for the metaphor theme HUMAN IS ANIMAL in Metalude

This widespread and persistent view that humans are somehow at the pinnacle of creation has given rise to a general pattern among HUMAN IS ANIMAL metaphors: the great majority are negative and pejorative (Kövecses 2002). Below, I give a fairly comprehensive list of all these derogatory metaphors, divided into the categories in Figure 3, as they are in the Metalude database.

ANIMAL **animal** 'cruel unpleasant person', **beast** 'cruel unpleasant person', **bestial** 'cruel or animal-like', **brute** 'rough, violent man', **bloodsucker** 'parasite who makes no contribution to society', **pest** 'annoying person, especially a child', **predator** 'person who tries to get hold of another's wealth', **predatory** 'grasping, acquisitive', **slug** 'slow-moving, lazy person', **snail** 'slow, lazy person', **worm** 'weak, nasty person not worthy of respect'

MAMMAL **bat** 'silly, annoying or unpleasant person', **bear** 'bad-tempered person', **dumb coyote** 'Indian or mixed-blood person', **elephantine** 'enormous', **goat** 'sexually active man', **hare-brained** 'foolishly impractical', **harelip** 'birth defect of a divided top lip', **herd** 'group of people en masse', **jackal** 'person that takes advantage of what others leave', **mole** 'insider who spies', **runt** 'small weak person', **skunk** 'unpleasant, unkind person', **paw** 'touch roughly, sexually', **fawn** 'flatter, praise insincerely', **weasel out of** 'avoid doing something you don't want to', **keep at bay** 'prevent from attacking or causing harm'

COW **cow** 'unpleasant woman', **bovine** 'slow or stupid', **bull-headed** 'obstinate, without considering other people's feelings', **bull-pen** 'cell or secure area where prisoners are temporarily detained', **calf-love** 'immature love between young people', **cattle-market** 'beauty contest', **beef** 'complain and protest vigorously and persistently'

SHEEP **sheep** 'unthinking imitator or over obedient person', **sheepish** 'shy or ashamed of your embarrassing behaviour', **black sheep** 'someone who brings shame to a family', **mutton dressed as lamb** 'older woman trying to look young', **bleat** 'complain', **pull the wool over someone's eyes** 'deceive someone by giving false information'

MONKEY **monkey** 'mischievous or badly-behaved child', **monkey around with** 'play or interfere with irresponsibly', **monkey business** 'dishonest or bad behaviour', **make a monkey out of** 'make appear foolish', **ape** 'stupid awkward person', **go ape** 'behave in an uncontrolled fashion', **gorilla** 'rough and violent man'

DOG **dog** 'unpleasant untrustworthy person', **dog in the manger** 'person who prevents others enjoying things they don't want themselves', **in the doghouse** 'suffering from disapproval or rebuke', **bitch** 'unpleasant, unkind woman', **cur** 'worthless, cowardly man', **puppy love** 'immature love', **fox** 'clever, cunning and secretive person', **vixen** 'unpleasant woman', **outfox** 'be more cunning than', **wolf** 'sexually predatory man', **wolf down** 'eat greedily', **wolfish** 'sinister or threatening (of a man)', **a wolf in sheep's clothing** 'deceitful and cunning person', **poodle** 'someone who is too willing to support or be controlled by others', **hound** 'follow someone menacingly to obtain something', **bark** 'speak or give orders loudly and roughly', **bay** 'demand greedily', **yap** 'talk continuously and annoyingly'

CAT **alley-cat** 'prostitute or slut', **cat** 'spiteful or backbiting woman', **catty** 'spiteful', **cat-burglar** 'thief who climbs silently to rob houses', **copycat** 'imitator lacking originality', **fat cat** 'greedy and wealthy person', **man-eater** 'promiscuous woman with large sexual appetite', **have kittens** 'get worried or upset', **pussyfoot** 'behave indecisively', **wildcat** 'unofficial, risky'

HORSE **horsy** 'with an ugly face like a horse (of women)', **horse around** 'behave noisily and stupidly', **horseplay** 'rough, noisy behaviour', **ass** 'stupid person', **coltish** 'young, energetic and awkward', **dark horse** 'someone who keeps secrets, especially their own surprising ability', **donkey** 'silly, stupid person', **donkey-work** 'hard, boring part of a job', **mule** 'carrier of illegal drugs', **mulish** 'stubborn'

PIG **pig** 'greedy or fat person', **pigsty** 'dirty, untidy place', **pig** 'unpleasant, difficult person', **swine** 'unpleasant, unkind person', **pig-headed** 'obstinate in support of a plan/idea', **pig out** 'eat excessively', **male chauvinist pig** 'sexist man', **hog** 'greedily monopolise', **roadhog** 'selfish dangerous driver'

RODENT **lemming** 'thoughtless imitator', **rabbit** 'talk continuously and boringly', **rat** 'disloyal, deceitful person', **rat on** 'betray by giving secret information', **rat race** 'ruthless competition for success', **ratty** 'bad tempered, irritable', **pack-rat** 'compulsive collector or hoarder', **shrew** 'bad-tempered woman', **shrewish** 'bad-tempered (of women)', **vermin** 'disgusting people, harmful and dangerous to society'

REPTILE **reptilian** 'unpleasant (of a person)', **snake** 'unpleasant untrustworthy person', **a snake in the grass** 'untrustworthy person', **viper** 'untrustworthy person', **lizard** 'lazy person', **lounge lizard** 'lazy person who likes to socialise and be patronised', **toad** 'unpleasant, unattractive or evil man', **toady** 'flatterer who seeks their own advantage', **tortoise** 'slow-moving person', **chameleon** 'person that changes opinions to please other people', **dinosaur** 'very old-fashioned person', **dragon** 'frightening woman'

INSECT **butterfly** 'person who enjoys social pleasures, especially flirting', **drone** 'unproductive member of society', **gadfly** 'person who deliberately annoys or challenges people in authority', **louse** 'nasty, dishonourable person', **nit** 'foolish, stupid person', **nitwit** 'idiot', **queen bee** 'self-important woman', **sting** 'make hurtful criticisms of', **wasp** 'white anglo-saxon protestant', **waspish** 'angry and unpleasant in manner or harshly critical'

FISH **a cold fish** 'person who is unfriendly or negative in emotions', **an old trout** 'old, ugly woman', **jellyfish** 'cowardly person', **shark** 'dishonest person', **loan shark** 'rapacious money lender', **queer fish** 'strange person', **come the raw prawn** 'try to deceive by pretending ignorance', **urchin** 'small, rough child'

BIRD **bird-brain** 'stupid person', **dolly bird** 'attractive, unintelligent young woman', **jailbird** '(regular) prisoner', **cuckoo** 'foolish, mad', **dodo** 'old fashioned, conventional and inactive person', **jay** 'stupid, over-talkative or showy person', **magpie** 'obsessive collector of worthless items', **mopoke** 'stupid person', **old crow** 'old or ugly girl or woman', **ostrich** 'person who refuses to face unpleasant facts', **parrot** 'repeat without understanding', **peacock** 'man proud of his appearance', **pigeon-chested** 'with a chest that sticks out more than normal', **pigeon-toed** 'walking with the feet pointing inwards', **stool pigeon** 'informer, a criminal who gives information to the police', **turkey** 'foolish, slow and stupid person', **vulture** 'person ready to exploit a situation', **brood** 'think silently about topics with negative feelings', **crow** 'boast noisily', **flap** 'state of anxiety

CHICKEN **chicken** 'coward', **chicken out** 'refrain from through fear', **cock of the walk** 'confident or arrogant man', **cocky** 'unpleasantly and rudely confident', **hen-pecked** 'controlled and a little frightened by your wife'

WATERBIRD **albatross** 'person that causes problems or brings bad luck', **booby** 'dull or stupid person', **booby prize** 'prize given as a joke to the person who comes last in a competition', **booby trap** 'practical joke designed to catch the stupid or unwary', **coot** 'rather silly person', **cormorant** 'greedy, insatiable person', **gaggle** 'group of silly people', **gannet** 'greedy person', **goose** 'silly person', **gull** 'easily deceived person', **lame duck** 'ineffective person', **swan around** 'wander around in a leisurely and irresponsible manner'

The negative metaphorical slant of these metaphors, many connoting unpleasantness, ugliness, pride, uncontrolled appetite and stupidity, reinforces the ideology of human superiority, and makes it very difficult for us to conceive of animals and humans as having equal rights to exist, vital as this is from an ecological point of view. Incidentally, it can be noticed that, according to my count, there are 50% more of these derogatory metaphors that only apply to women (13) rather than only to men (8), a tendency towards mutual reinforcement of the construction of female/animal inferiority.

Ekman has noted the widespread tendency to distance one racial or ethnic group by referring to them as animals:

> Sometimes a person or a group of people – the Bosnian Muslims, the Jews, the American Indians, the African slaves, the Gypsies – may be regarded as not being really human, not like the rest of us. They may be called animals, to show how little they matter, as a defence against sympathy (Ekman 2000: 91).

Charles Kingsley called the Irish "white chimpanzees" (Marks 2002: 69–70).

In an interesting article Santa Ana reports on the metaphors used for immigrants in the *Los Angeles Times*. He identifies animals as providing most important metaphors in the text, even though these are generally the journalists' words, and journalists are supposed to be objective, educated and unprejudiced reporters. In these texts immigrant workers are *lured* by employers, who *pit* them against each other, like fighting dogs, or are the *quarry* of the law enforcement officers who try to *hunt/ferret* them *out* before they *quit the chase*. Women immigrants are accused of coming across the border to *drop their babies* rather than *give birth*, as humans would (Santa Ana 1999: 200–201). He sums up the conceptual scenario or dichotomy that is constructed by this metaphorical use:

> On the hierarchy of living things immigrants are animals. Citizens, by contrast are humans. This hierarchy of life subordinates immigrants to humans. Thus humans are vested by birthright with privileges, such as "human rights" and "human dignity". Animals have no such privileges and are not equal to humans in the estimation of social institutions. Animals can never become humans by legislation or fiat. Their inferiority is inherent. Humans have full control over animals from ownership to use as a food source. Animals are either domesticated or wild and consequently outside the dominion of human society and can be hunted (p. 202).

4.3.5 Humans as in some/few respects like an animal.

One of the more contentious effects of the claim that humans are more or less chimps, because of what they share genetically, is the drive to give primates the same kinds of rights as humans. Steven Wise came forward with the following criterion for giving a creature rights, which he called "practical autonomy". "If a being can desire, can try to achieve what's desired, knows she wants it, and understands self-consciously that she is trying to get it, she is entitled to personhood and basic liberty rights" (Herbert 2002: 54). Oddly enough, he drew parallels with the abolition of slavery, and the according of rights to blacks in the US! The logical fallacies of this drive are twofold. If animals have rights that protect them against humans it is only logical that they should have rights that protect them from each other (Marks 2002: 197). Furthermore, if they have human rights they should have human responsibilities too – "How then do you treat a chimpanzee who steals or murders?" (p. 192). If they are subjects of justice they should be treated as agents of justice (Balkin 1998: 147).

One can see the motive for such rights might be to make people more aware of the abuses chimpanzees often suffer in captivity, to create support for the animal rights movement, or to counter the fundamentalist Christians undermining science education in America (Marks 2002: 185). However, an alternative is biocentrism – the notion that any form of life has an intrinsic worth equal to any of the others – the evolutionary bush rather than the evolutionary tree. We could emulate the Burmese attitude to animals as described by H. Fielding-Hall in *Soul of a People* (1920):

> To him men are men and animals are animals, and men are far the higher. But he does not deduce from this that man's superiority gives him the permission to ill-treat or kill animals. It is just the reverse. It is because man is so much higher that he can and must observe towards animals the very greatest care, feel for them the very greatest compassion, be good to them in every way he can (quoted in Schumacher 1973/1999: 86)

To have rights animals do not have to resemble humans. In fact they have the right not to be humanised, for example in circuses or ads for PG Tips, or in *America's Funniest Home Videos*. For we have seen that, on the whole, in terms of the racist, eugenicist, sexist and individualistic political philosophies it has spawned, the insistence on the near identity of man and animals has been extremely dangerous.

A poem by Edwin Muir is a useful introduction to what separates us from animals.

The animals

They do not live in the world,
Are not in time and space.
From birth to death hurled
No word do they have, not one
To plant a foot upon,
Were never in any place.

For with names the world was called
Out of the empty air,
With names was built and walled,
Line and circle and square,
Dust and emerald;
Snatched from deceiving death
By the articulate breath.
But these have never trod
Twice the familiar track,
Never, never turned back
Into the memoried day.
All is new and near
In the great unchanging Here
Of the fifth great day of God,
That shall remain the same,
Never shall pass away.

On the sixth day we came.

This poem is relevant in two ways. First, language is probably the most important ability that distinguished humans from animals. And second, the world, history and memory are created in our minds by human language, and do not have an existence that we can access except through language. The upshot of this is that people will classify and thereby create experience in various ways, according to their particular interests and cultural and linguistic inheritance. Human classification through language is not value-free, indeed categorization (*kategorein*: 'to accuse') is a function of power.

For example, Linnaeus, one of the great early "scientific" classifiers, favoured breast-feeding by mothers rather than wet-nursing, and so chose the possession of milk-producing breasts as the criterion for his class *mammalia*. He had the additional problem of deciding on how to classify apes and humans, which are very much like us and very much unlike us simultaneously. Traditionally in zoology humans are classified as *hominoidiae* along with great apes (chimps, gorillas and orang-utans). The bases for this classification are teeth, lack of tail, position and mobility of the shoulder, and structure of the trunk. But difference from the apes could have been emphasised: we have two hands rather than four. We have a mental life which is quite distinct, which has led to, among other things, technology, the ability to imagine – to the extent that we may even weep over fictions – and, of course the development of and dependence on language and discourse (Marks 2002: 21–22). Indeed it is language which is the further and necessary means of cultural elaboration and transmission. While there have been attempts to teach chimpanzees and bonobos to use sign language, with some success at the level of individual signs, the syntax they have acquired is extremely limited.

In the conclusion of his book *The Construction of Social Reality* the philosopher John Searle has challenged the dichotomy between biology and culture and suggested that there is a more or less "continuous story that goes from an ontology of biology to an ontology of culture" (Searle 1995: 228). However, he suggests that the brute facts of nature can be distinguished from the institutional facts of culture, and that central to this is the institution of language. Language allows us to impose on brute physical entities, such as sounds or marks on paper, a symbolic function. And language is essential for constructing all other institutional facts such as money, marriage, government and universities. Language creates culture. This reminds of us Hegel's negation of individualism: we are born into the language and culture of a particular society, and depend upon them and it for our identity. Harré, Clarke, and De Carlo (1985) claim the same complementarity between nature and culture centring on language, though their emphasis is more on conversation and the thoughts it gives rise to. Argyle, explains their development of Goffman's social theory as follows:

> The biological innate side of man is incomplete and has to be supplemented by a socially constructed order … there is an instrumental order which deals with the material side of life, and an expressive order which is concerned with the universal quest for respect and reputation. The expressive order is a collective symbolic system, part of society rather than individuals, consisting of a repertoire of meaningful symbolic acts and rules for using them. The system is maintained by public conversation, which becomes internalised as the private thoughts of individuals (Argyle 1988: 102).

The recent trend, as we saw earlier, is to bolster this *hominoidiae* classification by recourse to figures about the amount of DNA shared. But as Marks points out:

> Unfortunately it has become fashionable to stress that chimpanzees and humans must have staggeringly similar psychologies because they share 98.4% of their DNA. But this misses the point: genomes are not like cake recipes … A creature that shares 98.4% of its DNA with humans is not 98.4% human, any more than a fish that shares, say, 40% of its DNA with us is 40% human (Marks 2002: 43).

We are, after all, at least 50% water!

> If we are similar but distinguishable from a gorilla ecologically, demographically, anatomically, mentally – indeed in every way except genetically – does it follow that all the other standards of comparison are irrelevant and the genetic comparison is transcendent? (Marks 2002: 191).

In fact, as Damasio points out, we are cultural beings, too, who have evolved socio-political, religious, and judicial systems to enforce convention and rules of ethical behaviour. These systems become "mechanisms for exerting homeostasis at the level of the group." And hopefully "in turn, activities such as science and technology assist the mechanisms of social homeostasis" (p. 166). This suggests a positive effect on World 3 by World 4 in Table 16.

While Kant and Darwin believed that we are all born with more or less the same innate paradigm, Kuhn argued that our paradigms keep changing as our culture changes. "Different groups and the same group at different times … can have different experiences and therefore in some sense live in different worlds." Whatever is universal in human experience, whatever transcends culture and history is also "ineffable", beyond the reach of language. "Language is not a universal tool. It's not the case that you can say anything in one language that you can say in another" (Horgan 1998: 44). This is an insight that connects well with the Sapir-Whorf hypothesis, and a theme we shall take up at some length in 7.8. where we explore the differing world-views of English and Blackfoot.

Not only are we distinct mentally and culturally from other members of the class *hominoidiae*, but, according to Steve Mithen, remarkably distinct from the other members of the *homo* genus.

> All members of *homo* – other than *H. sapiens* – had domain-specific mentalities, the most advanced appearing in the Neanderthals. *Homo sapiens*, however, had the capacity to make mental links. Not only could they combine different types of knowledge, but they also had the capacity to think in metaphor – a capacity that underlies the whole of science, art and religion … With this extraordinary change in mentality came the ability to create new types of material culture … replete with symbolic meanings … But material culture was no longer simply a product of the mind: it had become a major shaper of the mind. The cultural environments that we humans create around ourselves are of critical importance to the elaboration – if not the origin – of cognitive fluid thought. Paintings on cave walls, written texts and mathematical symbols support the complex ideas that are so important to human minds, but which are difficult to grasp, recall and transmit to others … the earliest modern humans learned to extend their minds beyond their brains. They escaped from the restrictions that biology imposes upon human thought (Mithen 2003: 40–41).

We can create artefacts with symbolic meanings and thereby establish cultural environments that in turn shape the human mind, for example, cave paintings, mathematical symbols and so on. For Mithen we have taken a huge leap beyond our biology, and the fact that we can use metaphor underlines the fact that HUMAN IS ANIMAL is no more than a metaphor with a few grounds. Mithen reminds us that some of the major shapers of the mind are the metaphor themes by which we think.

According to some commentators and historians the whole movement known as social reconstructionism has been seen as an attempt to distance humans from their biology.

> What the available evidence does seem to show is that ideology, or a philosophical belief that the world could be a freer and more just place, played a large part in the shift from biology to culture. ... The main impetus came from the will to establish a social order in which innate and immutable forces of biology played no role in accounting for the behaviour of social groups (Degler 1991: viii).

Fromm also argues that one of the two crucial factors in human evolution and human nature, besides the size of the brain, was the "ever decreasing determination of behaviour by instincts", and he relates this to the development of religion.

> Lacking the capacity to act by the command of instincts while possessing the capacity for self-awareness, reason and imagination – new qualities that go beyond the capacity for instrumental thinking of even the cleverest primates – the human species needed a frame of orientation and an object of devotion in order to survive (Fromm 1983: 122–123).

4.3.6 Human reductionism

The attempt to reduce humans to animals has, as we have seen, had some immoral consequences, especially when it has stressed the competitive and aggressive struggle to pass on genes, seen as the necessary condition for evolutionary improvements to the race. Sociobiological reductionism of human nature and culture to genetics and zoology stems partly from the arrogance of some of the scientists involved, and partly from their ignorance of the history and philosophy of science and of other disciplines within the humanities and social sciences. Francis Crick furnishes the epitome of reductionism at its most virulent. In the opening of his book *The Astonishing Hypothesis* he proclaims:

> The "Astonishing Hypothesis" is that "YOU", your joys and sorrows, your memories and your ambitions, your sense of personal identity and free will, are in fact no more than the behaviour of a vast assembly of nerve cells and associated molecules. As Lewis Carroll might have phrased it "You're just a pack of neurons" (Crick 1994: 3).

Habgood nicely describes such arrogance:

> The point at which it ceases to be right is when a scientific world view dismisses, or denigrates, or tries to explain away, aspects of human nature and human experience which have not first been taken seriously in their own terms. The sciences, when they are true to themselves, are not enemies of religion. What is, is scientific imperialism, "scientism" (Habgood 2002: 144).

Clifford Geertz, like Habgood, objects to reductionism of this kind, narrating how, when he worked at the Institute of Advanced Studies, he would sometimes be confronted by physicists or mathematicians who had developed mathematical models of sociological problems such as race relations. He complains that they arrived at their models without any empirical foundation: "But they don't know anything about what goes on in the inner cities! … They just have a mathematical model … if you want to have a general theory of war and peace, all you have to do is sit down and write an equation without having any knowledge of history or people" (Horgan 1998: 157).

Marks proposes that reductionism is caused by a deficiency in scientific education, the lack of any formal teaching on the interaction between society and scientific theory, on how scientific "facts" are negotiated with culture.[3] This he believes produces "naiveté, xenophobia and intellectual arrogance" (Marks 2002: 286). Many scientists talk as though they are discovering scientific theories, rather than inventing them in a social context, and science students are "simply taught to believe they are reading nature. How sad!" (p. 272). But this could be worse than sad. For sociobiology and the theories developed from it have been outstandingly successful.

> In the study of human behaviour no-one even talks about "sociobiology" or "selfish genes" anymore, because the ideas are part and parcel of the science. In the study of humans there are major spheres of human experience – beauty, motherhood, kinship, morality, cooperation, sexuality, violence – in which evolutionary psychology provides the only coherent theory and has spawned vibrant new areas of empirical research. Behavioural genetics has revivified the study of personality and will only expand with the application of the Human Genome Project. Cognitive neuro-science will not shrink from applying its new tools to every aspect of mind and behaviour, including the emotionally and politically charged ones (Pinker 2003: 135).

Pinker tries elsewhere to argue for good reductionsim which "consists not of replacing one field of knowledge with another but of connecting or unifying them. The building blocks used by one field are put under a microscope by another" (p. 70). But why are those working in the sociobiological tradition happy to put the fields of aesthetics, developmental psychology, the sociology of the family, ethics, and war studies ("beauty, motherhood, kinship, morality, cooperation, sexuality, violence") under

---

3.   Even Lakoff falls prey to this myth. "Cognitive science is, in itself, apolitical." (Lakoff, 1996: 17)

the microscope of their own evolutionary psychology discipline for which they claim unique explanatory power, but unhappy to allow theories of the philosophy or sociology of science to examine theories of evolutionary psychology from outside?

And yet, however much we may wish to reject this reductionism, the opposite reductionism is just as dangerous – "rejecting all material and biological conditions of human behaviour as irrelevant in favour of a triumphalist mode of thought in which human history, economy and culture reign supreme" (Harvey 1996: 166). I concur with Marks' balanced conclusion:

> In sum, the place of the human species in the natural order is predicated on the place of the chimpanzee, and is consequently a contested site on the boundary of animalness and godliness, beast and angel. When genetics provides information bearing on that question, it does so within the contexts of both scientific study of heredity and the study of human systems of meaning. It cannot be divorced either from its intellectual context, social and philosophical implications, or the responsibilities of scientists (Marks 2002: 288).

4.4 Summary

We ought now attempt to sum up this extensive chapter, with the aid of Table 18. The question we concentrated on most was to what extent HUMAN IS ANIMAL is a statement of hyponymy ("a human is a kind of animal"), or whether it is a near identity statement ("humans are more or less animals"), or whether it is a metaphor of some kind ("humans are like animals"), and, if the latter, what the grounds of comparison might be and how extensive they are. We have ranged over theories in socio-biology, which largely stress the identity statement or hyponymy, regarding what distinguishes us from animals as insignificant, to theories such as Ridley's which allow for the desirability of cultural elements such as property and trade, to theories which, while debunking the criterion of the percentage of DNA shared (Marks), stress our difference from our biological ancestors due to the development of symbols, including language and metaphor and institutions (Searle, Mithen), or emphasise our need to escape from our biological heritage, like social-reconstructionism. Most theories which accept HUMAN IS ANIMAL as the best explanatory model take as the grounds of the model/metaphor the aggression and competitiveness on which Darwinian theories of evolution are based, and we saw how this might be related to metaphor themes ACTIVITY IS FIGHTING, THINKING/CONSIDERING IS CALCULATING, and AFFECTION/RELATIONSHIP IS MONEY/WEALTH, or, in Dawkins' meme theory to IDEA/EMOTION IS DISEASE (DISEASE IS INVASION and ARGUMENT IS WAR.) The only exception to this emphasis on competition and aggression is Ryan, who stresses the symbiotic principle behind evolution as an equally important potential ground shared by the source and target in HUMAN IS ANIMAL. We explored how this latter principle is compatible with an increasingly accepted theory of symbiosis and interrelatedness, or *Gaia* theory, a theory that is also supported by themes like PLACE/LANDSCAPE IS BODY, HUMAN BODY IS EARTH, and WEATHER IS HUMAN ACTIVITY/QUALITY.

Table 18. Summary of interpretations of the statement HUMAN IS ANIMAL

Semantics	View of Humans	Grounds	Theory	Supporters
	Sophisticated animals	Competitive & aggressive	*Human Sociobiology*	Wilson Lorenz Wrangham Peterson
	Sophisticated animals characterised by extreme adaptability	Competitive & aggressive	*Human behavioural ecology*	Trivers Winterhalder Smith
"HUMAN IS ANIMAL" AS HYPONYMIC STATEMENT OR APPROXIM- ATIVE METAPHOR	Sophisticated animals guided by psychological adaptations	Competitive & aggressive	*Evolutionary psychology*	Pinker Hinde
	Sophisticated animals?	Co-operative & competitive	*Symbiosis*	Ryan
	Sophisticated animals manipulated by cultural parasites	Competitive & aggressive	*Memetics*	Dawkins
	Sophisticated animals guided by genetic and cultural information	Competitive & aggressive	*Gene-culture evolution*	Boyd and Richerson
	Sophisticated animals redeemed by property, trade and cultural lies	Competitive & aggressive	*"Origins of Virtue"*	Ridley
"HUMAN IS ANI- MAL" AS TRANS- FER METAPHOR	Just as much institutional as animal/biological		*"Construction of social reality"*	Searle Damasio
	Not animal simply because of sharing DNA			Marks
	Cultural being due to symbolic environment			Mithen
	Should become less animal in the cause of a free and just society	Competitive & aggressive	*Social-recon- structionism*	Fromm

As a postscript we can consider the question of metaphors for nature in general and animals in particular in a slightly different way. Let's return to the idea that even scientists who claim some kind of objectivity for their discipline are actually driven by the value-laden metaphors which they use for nature. Man then becomes a source for animal targets rather than vice-versa: Darwin using English bourgeois society, with its division of labour and entrepreneurial competition for resources, as a source for the animal/plant target; or Damasio and Pinker seeing the US Constitution as a model for biological behaviour. In Marxist terms, this is an ideological strategy of naturalisation: "ideology is the reflection in ideas of the material interests of a ruling class, a reflection in which the outward appearances of the economic forms expressing those interests are seen and presented in mystified fashion as naturalised as the product of 'human nature' (in our genes perhaps)" (Jones, P.E. 2000: 236). Or, more generally, as Harvey points out:

> We see in short only those values which our value-laden metaphors allow us to see in our study of the natural world. Harmony and equilibrium; beauty, integrity and stability; co-operation and mutual aid; ugliness and violence; hierarchy and order; competition and the struggle for existence; turbulence and unpredictable dynamic change; atomistic causation; dialectics and principles of complementarity; chaos and disorder; fractals and strange attractors; all of them can be identified as "natural values" not because they are arbitrarily assigned to nature, but because however ruthless, pristine and rigorously "objective" our method of enquiry may be, the framework of interpretation is given in the metaphor rather than the evidence (Harvey 1996: 163).

Indeed Kuhn (1993) and Pylyshyn (1993) have put the same point in slightly different terms, pointing out that scientific models work as metaphors predicting various hypotheses or grounds which may then be tested. The program of research is driven by the metaphor, and different metaphors will highlight or predict different attributes of the phenomenon under investigation. With a target as complex and multi-faceted as "nature" or "animal" there is enormous scope for different metaphor sources derived from different concepts of humanity and different social and cultural systems within which that humanity takes its shape.

CHAPTER 5

Interactions between metaphor themes

Yet dearly I love you, and would be loved fain,
But am betrothed unto your enemy:
Divorce me, untie, or break that knot again;
Take me to you, imprison me, for I
Except you enthral me, never shall be free,
Nor ever chaste, except you ravish me. John Donne.

"Epidemic diseases usually elicit a call to ban the entry of foreigners, immigrants.
And xenophobic propaganda has always depicted immigrants as bearers of disease"
(Sontag 1991: 147).

5.1 Introduction

When the award of the project to build The Freedom Tower in New York on the site of the old World Trade Center was announced, one of the winning architects, David Libeskind, dubbed it "a beacon of light and hope". Underlying this simple phrase was a complex interplay of metaphor themes. This tower is planned to be the tallest in the world. As demonstrated in chapter 2, this would make it a symbol of power. But the metaphorical source of height is multivalent, having within its range other metaphor themes with height as source, such as happiness. Furthermore, the metaphorical target of happiness in general, and hope in particular, is diversely represented, not only by height, but also by light, giving us "beacon". One might even suggest, giving more weight to the source in multivalency, a metaphorical attempt to combine conceptual targets falling within the source's scope, with height representing a super-category merging hope, happiness, health, status and power and a number of other possible targets.

Moreover, behind the tower's name lies the equation of space with freedom, according to the metaphor theme FREEDOM IS SPACE TO MOVE. Building spaces high into the air, in defiance of the laws of gravity, symbolises freedom, in the specific sense of an attempt to overcome the restrictions of our natural physical movement. And yet, by contrast, there are a number of metaphors associating certainty, reliability and security with being low or down. The metonymy behind this, that tall structures more easily fall, is of course underlined by the history of the World Trade Center. So we have here a pair of oppositional metaphors – is it better to take the risks of freedom and of the hubris fed by status and power by building high or to choose certainty and reliability, while respecting gravity, by building low? "Pride goes before a fall." The need to deny the logic of this metonymy, and thereby the opposition, prompted protestations by the other architect, David Childs, that improvements in skyscraper design should make the new tower "the safest building in the world" ('A Tower to Reclaim the NY Skyline' 2003).

This chapter, therefore, is concerned with the ways in which metaphor themes interrelate. As illustrated above, we deal with multivalency (different targets, same source – POWER/CONTROL IS ABOVE, HAPPINESS IS HIGH) and diversification (different sources, same target – HAPPINESS IS HIGH, HAPPINESS IS LIGHT), and oppositional metaphors, where two metaphorical schemata, both with positive evaluations, set up a behavioural or ideological tension (POWER/CONTROL IS ABOVE v. CERTAINTY/RELIABILITY IS LOW). We also suggest cases of the metaphorical merging of the conceptual categories into super-categories, and illustrate a rather complex case of metaphorical theme interaction where theme reversal takes place.

5.2   Multivalency

In *Cultural Software* (1998), when investigating the mechanisms of ideological thinking, Balkin devotes one chapter to homologies (see 2.4) These depend upon analogies, A is to B as C is to D (A : B :: C : D), which produce associations between A and C, and B and D. Multivalency might be thought of as an intermediate process between metaphor and homology since the analogy A : B :: C : B creates even firmer associations between A and C. I hope to show it is a powerful means of achieving cognitive associations, since there is a tendency to equate the different targets, represented by the same source, B. To illustrate it simply, if POWER IS HIGH[1], MORE IS HIGH and GOOD IS HIGH, we might tend to think that power is good and more is better.

POWER = GOOD is manifest in one aspect of contemporary celebrity worship – the myth of the noble Noble. Lady Diana and J.F. Kennedy were not only powerful people who died tragically young, but acquired an aura of virtue probably quite out of proportion to the good they actually achieved, with Diana ranked with Mother Teresa. Michael Owen, the English footballer, contemplating his imminent transfer to Real Madrid, hoped that being in a team of star footballers would make him a better person! Incidentally, an etymological basis for this confusion between power and goodness is found in the ambiguity of the Latin word *virtus* or Middle English *vertue*, which could mean both 'the power to act' (*by virtue of which*), as well as 'goodness' (*virtue*).

---

1.   In Metalude this theme is labelled POWER/CONTROL IS ABOVE.

5.2.1 Multivalency → MORE = GOOD

However, this section concerns the concept MORE = GOOD. GOOD (QUALITY/MORAL-ITY) IS HIGH belongs to a group of metaphor themes that also includes BAD IS LOW, and DETERIORATE IS FALL/LOWER. I will just give details of the first of these, while the others can be consulted in Metalude.

High means 'the best, or extremely good' (*this is high quality jade*), as in **high-class** 'good quality' of produce (*high-class fruit and vegetables*) and **high grade** 'good quality' of substance or mineral (*this is high-grade uranium*), **high fashion** 'best quality fashion', and **high point** 'best part of an experience' (*the high point of the circus was the acrobats*). **Top** and **tops** then mean 'excellent or the best', as in **tip-top** (*in tip-top condition*), **top-notch** (*a top-notch designer*) and **tops** (*York and Bath come out tops as tourist destinations in the UK*).

Up also connotes good quality as in **ups and downs** 'good and bad experiences' (*their marriage had its ups and downs*), **up-market** 'of especially high quality intended for the rich or sophisticated' (of goods or products) (*there are a number of up-market tailors in the Bond Street area*), **upside** 'advantage, good point about something' (*it's cold in winter, but the upside is that the fare's cheaper then*), **upturn** 'improvement' (*an upturn in the economy*), **be up to the mark, live up to** 'be as good as usual or expected' (*he didn't live up to his reputation as the greatest tenor*), and **upkeep** is 'the cost or process of keeping in good condition' (*the upkeep on my properties is less than the rent I charge*). If you are 'a lot better than', you are **head and shoulders above** (*head and shoulders above all the other actors*), and 'the greatest experience or best quality' is associated with the sky as in **heaven** (*I was in cinematic heaven*), and **star** (*he's our star player*).

Not only do these sources of upward orientation express quality in general, but refer more specifically to morality: **high-minded** means 'moralistic' (*he's so high-minded he won't allow them to share a bedroom*), **lofty** 'with strong ideals' (*the lofty ambition of reducing prostitution*), **above** 'too good or honest to do' (*she's not above lying to protect herself*), while **upstanding, upright** mean 'behaving in an honest, moral and responsible way' (*being an upright citizen was important for his sense of self-esteem*).[2] HAPPY IS HIGH, which can be consulted in Metalude, also constructs a more specific kind of goodness as verticality: **on top of the world, on cloud nine, on a high** etc.

The same source is used for a large amount or more, as in MORE IS HIGH, part of a group of other related themes – LESS IS LOW, INCREASE IS RISE, DECREASE IS FALL. **High** means 'costing a large amount' (*food prices are very high this autumn*) so **sky-high, astronomical** mean 'extremely great in amount' (*the prices of property in Hong Kong are sky high*), **the stratosphere** 'an extremely high amount' (*prices have gone into the stratosphere*) and **top** 'largest number or amount' (*our top sales figures are for December*).

---

2. Lakoff relates the idea of Being Good is Being Upright to the idea that Morality is Strength, which forms part of the Strict Father Metaphor and can be used to justify militarism (Lakoff 1996: 72–74)

More specifically **high** can mean 'a great amount' of speed (*he run around the field at high speed*), **high season** 'busiest time for tourism' (*the high season in Australia is November to March*). A high thing can mean metaphorically a 'large amount' as in **mountain** (*there's a mountain of evidence about the dangers of smoking*), **pile, stack** (*I've got a pile/stack of things to do today*), while **peak** means 'highest level' (*house prices are at a peak so don't buy now*), and **ceiling** 'upper limit' (*the government imposed a ceiling on pay increases*). According to this schema **above, over, upwards of** mean 'more than' (*don't drive above/over the speed limit*) or (*upwards of 200 million pounds*), **top**, the verb, means 'be more than' (*the offer I had from Hong Kong topped the one I had from Singapore*), and **on top of** 'in addition to' (*on top of my broken foot I cracked a tooth*). Having a higher position can also be related to excess: **over** 'too much' (*this cake is overcooked*), **overly** 'excessively' (*don't be overly cautious with cyanide*) and **over the top** 'uncontrolled and too much' (*the emphasis on sport in Australia is over the top*).

Because these different targets GOOD (MORALITY/QUALITY), HAPPY and MORE share a multivalent source they may become associated or confused into an equation MORE = GOOD (HAPPY). This is also reinforced by the idea that QUALITY IS SHAPE/SIZE and QUANTITY IS SIZE or LENGTH, so that more in general or larger sizes are desirable, QUALITY = QUANTITY.

This equation drives our orthodox economic thinking, with the result that growth, producing and consuming more is good, whether it leads to increased human happiness and ecological sustainability or not. Capitalism seems to produce accumulation for accumulation's sake, production for production's sake and consumption for consumption's sake. In fact there is little clear correlation between purchasing power and human happiness. Research measuring association between wealth and life-satisfaction shows that the positive correlation disappears once the gross national product exceeds $8,000 per person. In addition, as Table 19 shows, some societies, such as China, India, Ireland and Nigeria, have much higher degrees of satisfaction than predicted on the basis of their wealth or purchasing power (Seligman 2002: 51–55).

Table 19. Comparison of life-satisfaction with purchasing power by country

NATION	LIFE SATISFACTION	PURCHASING POWER
Japan	6.53	87
Nigeria	6.59	6
India	6.70	5
Germany	7.22	89
China	7.29	9
Finland	7.68	69
USA	7.73	100
Ireland	7.88	52
Switzerland	8.36	96

One of the areas of social life where MORE = GOOD is proving a dangerous equation is in the area of nutrition. As of 2003 about 61% of Americans are overweight, and about 20% are obese (Critser 2003: 4). One cause is undoubtedly the consumption of fast food in increasing quantities. As Critser reveals:

> By the end of the century supersizing – the ultimate expression of the value meal revolution – reigned. As of 1996 some 25% of the $97 billion spent on fast food came from items promoted on the basis of either larger size or extra portions. A serving of MacDonald's French fries had ballooned from 200 calories (1960) to 320 calories (late 1970s) to 450 calories (mid-1990s) to 540 calories (late 1990s) to the present 610 calories. In fact everything on the menu had exploded in size. What was once a 590-calorie MacDonald's meal was now ... 1550 calories (p. 28).

The reason for the food industry's success in the marketing campaigns promoting larger size portions was that, according to one commentator, John Peters, "They all know that, by and large, consumers are still stuck with the nineteenth-century notions of 'more for less is better' in their heads" (p. 174).

The mania for more, in terms of size, spread into other areas of life during the 70s, 80s and 90s.

> There was more to this than just eating more. Bigness: the concept seemed to fuel the marketing of just about everything, from cars (SUVs) to homes (mini-manses) to clothes (super-baggy) and then back again to food (as in the Del Taco macho meal, which weighed 4 pounds). The social scientists and the marketing gurus were going crazy trying to keep up with the trend. "Bigness is addictive because it is about power," complained Irma Zall, a teen marketing consultant, in a page one story in *USA Today*. While few teenage boys can actually finish a 64-ounce Double Gulp, she added, "it's empowering to hold one in your hand" (p. 29).

Zall's analysis highlights another possible association through metaphorical multivalency. If MORE IS HIGH, and POWER IS HIGH (POWER/CONTROL IS ABOVE, see the lexical details in 2.2), then MORE = POWER.

The nexus of metaphor themes operating behind this mind-set is quite complicated, because the results of over-eating, obesity, can themselves be interpreted as a statement of freedom, according to FREEDOM/CHOICE IS SPACE TO MOVE. It is interesting to see how this "logic" operates, almost unconsciously, in the following quote from Critser. He has been telling the story of Larry, a customer who complained to a restaurant that he was no longer able to find a chair he could fit into. Critser interprets this longing for extra space as the affirmation of personal and economic freedom:

> Nowhere did this new boundary-free culture of American food consumption thrive better then in the traditional American family, which by the 1980s was undergoing rapid change. The catalyst came in two forms: individual freedom (born of the liberation movements of the '60s and '70s) and entrepreneurial adventurism (born of the economic tumult of the late '70s and early '80s) (p. 31).

Critser uses the belt as the symbol of self-control, instantiating the sub-theme NO FREEDOM IS TYING/BINDING. "Family, school, culture, religion – in the late twentieth century, the figurative belt had not only been loosened, it had come off. What of the most traditional measure – and reminder – of excess girth?" (p. 57). One particular social class, the black community, had quite recently won the battles against, first, slavery, and then, segregation, and they seemed particularly prone to symbolise their new-found freedoms through being overweight: the impact of obesity on black women was disproportionately high (pp. 118–119).

One interesting statistic is that obesity tends to be more severe in those states with high degrees of religious affiliation. Critser suggests that people who believe the soul is more important than the body have no qualms about letting their bodies become unhealthy (p. 56). It would be useful to have more detailed figures about the kind of religious affiliation, but I suspect an equally good explanation is the Judaeo-Protestant endorsement of wealth. From the time of the Old Testament increase in worldly goods and number of descendants has been interpreted as a sign of God's blessing and approval. For example, in Genesis, Abraham, because his and Lot's herds are in competition for pasture, allows Lot to occupy the fertile valley of the Jordan, and moves his flocks to the less fertile land of Canaan. As his reward God promises:

> All the land that you see I will give to you and to your offspring for ever. I will make your offspring like the dust of the earth, so that if anyone could count the dust, then your offspring could be counted. Go, walk through the length and breadth of the land, for I am giving it to you (Genesis, ch. 13, vv. 15–17).

And he made similar promises after Abraham obediently agreed to sacrifice his son Isaac. The equation of GOOD IS MORE is here interpreted as GOOD *has* MORE, an interpretation important for the bourgeois Protestant merchant class which emerged in and after the Reformation in Europe.

Although this Judaeo-Protestant ethic is rather at odds with the Sermon on the Mount, "Blessed are the poor, for theirs is the kingdom of heaven", and the religious traditions that believe in the sanctity of poverty, it is still going strong among the religious fundamentalist right in the US. As Dan Quayle said at a Republican convention, arguing against graduated income tax: "Why should the best people be punished?" (quoted in Lakoff 1996: 29–30). In Buddhism one can observe similar differences and attitudes to goodness and its symbolism in body girth by comparing the differing styles of slim Thai Buddha images and fat Chinese "Buddha" images, actually a popular confusion between Buddha and Tai Tol Fatt. This might be regarded as a Chinese corruption of Buddhism, which traditionally respects moderation and the Middle Way between self-mortification and excess.

A thorough-going and comprehensive critique of the equation of goodness with quantity or size is, obviously enough, E.F. Schumacher's *Small is Beautiful*. Though this first appeared in the 1970s, it is a prophetic book, and most trends he identifies can be observed, often in exaggerated form, in the beginning years of the 21st century.

Schumacher was alarmed by the ecological consequences of the quest for growth and increasing production and consumption. Indeed he advocates a minimalist Buddhist approach, quite distinct from conventional economic thinking.

> The modern economist is used to measuring the "standard of living" by the amount of annual consumption, assuming all the time that a man who consumes more is "better off" than a man who consumes less. A Buddhist economist would consider this approach excessively irrational: since consumption is merely a means to human well-being, the aim should be to obtain the maximum well-being with the minimum of consumption (Schumacher 1973/1999: 41).

He directly challenges the equation of MORE = GOOD.

> The chance of mitigating the rate of resource depletion or of bringing harmony into the relationships between those in possession of wealth and power and those without is non-existent as long as there is no idea anywhere of enough being good and more-than-enough being evil (p. 250).

He regarded the encouragement of greed and envy in order to increase consumption and material growth as antithetical to long-term human and ecological well-being in a finite environment. Particularly harsh criticism is directed at the US industrial economy, especially at its claims to efficiency:

> An industrial system which uses forty per cent of the world's primary resources to supply less than six per cent of the world's population could be called efficient only if it obtained strikingly successful results in terms of human happiness, well-being, culture, peace and harmony. I do not need to dwell on the fact that the American system fails to do this, or that there is not the slightest prospect that it could do so if only it achieved a higher rate of growth of production, associated, as it must be, with an even greater call on the world's finite resources (p. 95).

For Schumacher, not only is the MORE = GOOD equation harmful in its environmental and resource depletion effects, but because the greed and envy it leads to is the main cause of war: "Economically, our wrong living consists primarily in systematically cultivating greed and envy and thus building up a vast array of totally unwarrantable wants" (p. 23). This is potentially catastrophic, because greed and envy are "the very forces that drive men into conflict" (p. 24). Many Iraqis and others believe one main cause of the 2nd Iraq War was the US's attempt to ensure a stable oil supply, in a political situation where relations with Saudi Arabia, its main Middle East supplier, were becoming increasingly strained.

Furthermore, Schumacher thought small-scale organisations both less harmful to the environment and more satisfying for and less exploitative of their workers.

> [T]he greatest danger [to the environment] invariably arises from the ruthless application, on a vast scale, of partial knowledge such as we are currently witnessing

in the application of nuclear energy, of the new chemistry in agriculture, of transportation technology, and countless other things (p. 22).

He believed that "people can be themselves only in small comprehensible groups" (p. 56). Large-scale companies, with shareholders, are necessarily exploitative. Whereas in a small or medium-sized private firm the owner or boss works, in a large listed private company the shareholders take profits without putting in any work. Private ownership then becomes "a fiction for the purpose of enabling functionless owners to live parasitically on the labour of others" (p. 225). To sum up Schumacher's ideas: "Man is small, and, therefore, small is beautiful. To go for giantism is to go for self-destruction" (p. 131).

This call for self-restraint and minimalism is in sharp disagreement with the ideology of those like Ivan Boesky, who eulogized greed in his commencement address at the University of California, Berkeley: "Greed is all right, by the way. I want you to know that. I think greed is healthy. You can be greedy and still feel good about yourself." As soon as he had delivered this encomium, spontaneous applause broke out (Ridley 1997: 260–1). And such an ideology is surely reinforced by the multivalency of HIGH in MORE IS HIGH and GOOD IS HIGH.

5.2.2 Multivalency → CHANGE = SUCCESS/DEVELOPMENT.

In 2.6 I gave detailed lexis for the metaphor theme ACTIVITY IS MOVEMENT FORWARDS, and the related DEVELOPMENT/SUCCESS IS MOVEMENT FORWARD, SUCCESS/EASE IS SPEED. These themselves are offshoots of the very basic metaphor theme CHANGE IS MOVEMENT. If development/success is paired with the source of movement forward, and change shares this source of movement, there is the possibility of equating the two targets into the equation CHANGE = SUCCESS/DEVELOPMENT, which makes change seem a positive thing.

The metaphorical lexis for CHANGE IS MOVEMENT, and its obverses UNCHANGING IS HARD/RIGID and UNCHANGING IS STATIC, betrays a bias in favour of movement/change. If you change your opinion you **shift** (*attitudes to homosexuality shifted during the 90's*), and if your refuse to change it you will not **budge** (*they won't budge on the issue of equal pay*), while **move** can mean both 'change opinion or behaviour' (*old people are moving away from eating meat*). **Move on** means 'start doing a new activity' (*we moved on from painting to wallpapering*), and if you 'keep on changing' activities you **flit** from one to another (*she's always flitting from one hobby to another*). As far as matter is concerned **pass** means 'change, be transformed' (*wax passes from liquid to solid when you cool it*). Sometimes change is metaphorically associated with the movement of liquids: **drift** 'general development or change' (*the drift towards full-scale war*), and **flux** 'constant change' (*in the general flux of politics she stood like the one constant landmark*).

Change in the direction of movement stands for change in general as in **turn** 'change quality, character or colour' (*suddenly my mother turned nasty*), **turn into** 'become, be changed into' (*the witch recited the spell and Peter turned into a frog*) and **twist** 'change in the way something happens' (*the end of Act IV gave the play an unexpected twist*). Rotation through 180° or 360° expresses complete or continuous change: **turnabout** 'complete change from one state or condition to its opposite' (*what accounts for the dramatic turnabout in the University's examination performance this year?*), **revolution** 'complete change in society through force' (*the French Revolution destroyed the aristocracy*), **rotate** 'regularly change the person who does a job' (*the headship of department rotates among senior members*), and if the rotation continues into a spin we have a **gyration** 'frequent and sudden changes' (*the gyrations in government policy are amazing*).

Moving backwards and forwards indicates changes that cancel each other out. These metaphors are generally applied to opinions and attitudes: **swing** 'change significantly' (*her mood can quickly swing from calm to hysterical*), **swing back** 'change back to its original state' (*public opinion swung back behind President Bush*), as does a **pendulum** a 'change from one opinion to an opposite one' (*the pendulum will swing back away from the individualism of the 80s and 90s*), or **oscillate** 'change repeatedly from one attitude to another' (*his feelings were oscillating between desperation and hope*). But movement backwards and forwards applies to states as well as opinions, as in **seesaw** 'continually change from one state to another and back again' (*the Dow-Jones index see-sawed up and down*), **ebb and flow** 'frequently changing situation' (*the ebb and flow of fashion continues unchecked*), **get back to** 'return to a previous state' (*I must try to get back to sleep*), and **reverse** 'change to the opposite' (*the appeal court reversed the lower court's decision*).

Causing change is conceptualised as causing movement: **shake up** 'make major changes in an organisation' (*the reform of institutions is one way of shaking up the country*), **world-shaking** 'very surprising and important in changing perception or behaviour' (*911 was a world-shaking event*), **turn ... upside down/inside out** 'change a system or way of life completely' (*my world was turned upside down by AIDS*), and **turn ... on its head** 'cause to be the opposite of what is was' (*these new discoveries turn the accepted paradigms on their head*).

Sudden and unexpected changes are represented by sudden, violent and unexpected movements: **lurch, jump** 'suddenly change from one activity to another' (*in his spare time he lurches from one hobby to another*), **turbulent, turbulence** 'changing in a confused and disorganised way' (*we must hold on to religion in these turbulent times/times of turbulence*) and **upheaval** 'great change involving much difficulty, activity or trouble' (*emigrating to Australia was a great upheaval for all the family*).

Only in this last group is the lexis consistently pejorative. From the other group only **gyration** and **flit** seem to have negative connotations. This contrasts markedly with the converse metaphorical theme, UNCHANGING IS HARD/RIGID, where ten of the lexical items in our database are strongly pejorative, five mildly pejorative, and only six neutral or positive.

Let's begin with the more obviously pejorative ones. **Unyielding, stiff-necked** and **hard-line** are applied to people who are 'unwilling, stubborn or unable to change their beliefs or behaviour' (*I'm unyielding in my opposition to mobile phone*), (*he is a hard-line* *communist*), (*don't be so stiff-necked and defy the rest of your colleagues*), while **rigid, rigidity** are applied to their beliefs 'not able/inability to be changed or persuaded' (*she had very rigid ideas about bringing up children*). People or institutions that behave 'in old-fashioned and therefore formal ways' are **starchy** (*museums have tried to shake off their starchy image*). Beliefs, habits or customs which do not change or develop are **fossilized** (*environmental needs are changing while policies remain fossilized*), **petrified** (*afternoon tea is a petrified English institution*), or they **ossify** (*years of easy profits had ossified the firm's thinking*), each of these drawing on the notion that being turned to stone or bone makes what was originally living and flexible into something hard and rigid.

Slightly less pejorative are **set** 'unchanging, conservative' (*he's very set in his beliefs*), and **embedded** 'unchanging, permanent' (*Russian working-class culture is notorious for its embedded racism*), **unbending** 'tending to make judgments that cannot be changed' (*his unbending insistence on good grammar annoyed the pupils*), and **set/cast in stone/concrete** 'extremely difficult to change' (*the regulations are now set/cast in stone/concrete – it will be a massive job to get them amended*).

Neutral lexis in this metaphorical theme is **fixed** 'unchangeable, permanent' (*the mortgage rates are fixed at 4% for the duration of the mortgage*), **firm** 'certain in belief or opinion, unlikely to change' (*he remains a firm believer in the positive effects of the market*), and **solidify** 'become certain and less subject to change' (*the ideas they brainstormed solidified into a definite plan*).

Only **stable** 'not likely to change' (*after his heart attack he is now in a stable condition*) and **solid** 'certain, unwavering, loyal' (*the public housing estates give the PAP solid support*) seem to have positive connotations, though as we shall see later, when unchangingness overlaps with reliability there are many more positive metaphors.

A similar pattern, in which lack of change appears negative, is observable in the other converse of CHANGE IS MOVEMENT, i.e. UNCHANGING IS STATIC. Eleven items seem more or less negative, eleven neutral and only six positive. Traditional and un-modernised institutions or people are seen as **stuffy** (literally 'without ventilation, because the air cannot move') 'formal, boring and old-fashioned' (*British Council libraries are still rather stuffy places*), (to be contrasted with **the winds of change, a breath of fresh air**), or such a person is a **stick in the mud** 'someone who is not willing to change or accept new ideas' (*why don't you go abroad for your holiday, you stick in the mud?*), or of wanting to **cling to** 'refuse to give up' a tradition or belief (*old people still cling to superstitious burning of paper money*). People or their opinions that are difficult or impossible to change are **entrenched** (*you'll never change entrenched Chinese attitudes to homosexuality*), **immovable** (*the Israelis are immovable on the status of Jerusalem*) and tend to **dig in/dig their heels in** 'refuse to change your opinions or plans' (*she wanted a mobile phone but her father dug his heels in*). A situation that you have to accept because you cannot change it is something you are **stuck (with)** (*she was stuck with a brutal husband in a loveless marriage*), or **tied to** (*we are tied to taking our vacation in the school holidays*). And situations that fail to change, develop or improve **stagnate** or are **stagnant** (*the IT industry is showing signs of stagnating*).

Neutral items here are the extremely common, and easily overlooked: **still** 'continuing to this or that time' (*I'm still hungry*), and **stay** 'maintain the same state' (*he stayed calm all through the horror movie*). If something is unchanging it is **fixed** 'very difficult to change' (*he has fixed opinions about the need for a balanced budget*), **stationary/static** 'not changing' (*property prices have been stationary for several months now*). If you 'maintain things the same or at the same level' you **freeze** them (*the price of fuel has been frozen*), and if you **stick with/stick to** a situation or activity 'decide not to change to anything else' (*if you're in a job that satisfies you, stick with it*). If you are 'maintaining your opinions in a determined way' you are **tenacious,** literally 'with a tight grip' (*environmentalists were tenacious in their opposition to the new airport*). The idea behind these later metaphors is that to prevent or refuse change you hold, fix or stick something in order to prevent movement.

Lexis which is mildly positive includes **settled** 'permanent and predictable' (*I now live a very settled existence in a small seaside town*), **stick to, adhere to** 'obey rules or regulations' (*the US can't remain in the UN if it doesn't adhere to the rules*), **stick at, apply yourself to** 'keep doing the same thing with determination despite difficulties' (*you will find rock-climbing hard at first, but stick at it*), (*he applied himself to mathematics more than to languages*), and **stick by** 'continue to give help and support to a person' (*he stuck by his wife despite her infidelity*).

The general position here seems to be that the equation CHANGE = SUCCESS/DEVELOPMENT is winning out, in that metaphors for resistance to change are predominantly negative in their connotations. It is quite likely that the metaphorical lexical inheritance of the last four hundred years, the age of Modern English, reflects the modern belief in progress, that change, especially technological, is generally for the good.

However, for much of human history the past has seemed better than the present or the likely future. While discussing the metaphorical structuring of time (2.7) we noted the Chinese traditional longing for a former Golden Age. Hindu cosmology, too, which, although it sees time as cyclical, and the Golden or White Age as eventually returning, locates the present in a degenerate era or yuga. Daniel Bassuk explains as follows:

> As myth reflects man's first awareness of time, so mythic time in India is a never-ending cycle of creation, preservation, and destruction, each complete cycle being a hundred years in the life of Brahma ... Within this division are many divisions and sub-cycles, the most important of which is the Kalpa, equivalent to 4,320 million years on earth or one day in the life of Brahma. The Kalpa is divided into one thousand periods, each of which is further divided into four ages or yugas called Krita, Treta, Dwapara, and Kali. All four yugas are represented by the image of a cow. And each yuga differs from the others in the number of legs that the cow can stand on.

We can summarise the differences between the four ages/yugas in Table 20, (where we notice incidentally the four colours of Linnaeus' racial classification, and the consistent symbolism of white as good and black as evil).

Table 20. Characteristics of the 4 ages (yugas) of Hindu cosmology

Yuga	Duration In Years	Colour of Deity	No. of Legs	Moral Character and Quality Of Life
Krita	1,728,000	White	4	people are contented, healthy, virtuous, and prosperous
Treta	1,296,000	Red	3	men are quarrelsome and often act from ulterior motives; work, suffering and death are common
Dwapara	864,000	Yellow	2	some tread the right path, but lying and quarrelling abound and vice and evil increase
Kali	432,000	Black	1	most people are wicked, quarrelsome, and beggar-like, value what is degraded, eat voraciously and indiscriminately, are oppressed by their rulers and by famine and war; cities are full of thieves

Many Hindus believe that we are at present in the Kali yuga, or age of degeneration, and that our miseries can only end with the coming of a final saviour and Avatar, which will bring to an end the complete cycle in a dissolution called a *pralaya* (Bassuk 1987: 16–17).

For most of the history of Western thought there were similar feelings that the Golden Age had gone, whether it was the Anglo-Saxons looking back to the Roman Empire whose architectural remains they called "the works of the giants", or even the Renaissance looking back to the Golden Age of Ancient Greece. We can observe this in the attitude to scientific and social progress, as described by John Horgan (1998).

The historian J.B. Bury (1920) demonstrated that the concept of progress is only a few hundred years old. From the Roman Empire through the Middle Ages, most thinkers had a degenerative view of history, believing that the high point of mathematical and scientific knowledge was in ancient Greece and that civilisation had deteriorated since. Although the founders of modern experimental science like Isaac Newton, Francis Bacon, René Descartes and Gottfried Leibniz proclaimed that humans could accumulate knowledge through systematic investigation, they thought the process would be finite, that our knowledge of the world would one day be complete, and could then be used to construct a utopia, based on Christian morality.

It was only under the influence of Darwinism that intellectuals began to believe that progress could be never-ending. Gunther Stent wrote in his 1978 book *The Paradox of Progress* that after Darwin's *The Origin of Species* "the idea of progress was raised to the level of a scientific religion" (quoted in Horgan 1998: 21–22). Modern nation states embraced this idea in view of the marvellous inventions of nuclear power, radar, computers, and missiles. Much of this new technology was seen as necessary for national economic and military security as Vannevar Bush proclaimed in *Science; the endless frontier*, a book which encouraged the founding of the National Science Foundation and basic scientific research. The Soviet Union also saw scientific endeavour as essential in the competitive race for political supremacy – perhaps influenced by Engels who in *Dialectics of Nature* regarded science as moving forward at an accelerating pace. However, the end of the cold war has reduced some of the incentives for investment in science.

Because we were born in an era of technological progress, antibiotics, organ transplants, moon landings, jumbo-jets, laptop computers or tests for breast cancer genes, we might assume that it is a natural part of life. "But an historical perspective suggests that such progress is probably an anomaly that will, must end. Belief in the eternality of progress – not in crises and culminations – is the dominant delusion of our culture" (Horgan 1998: 268).

For Oswald Spengler in *The Decline of the West* (1918) science proceeded cyclically not linearly – romantic periods of investigation of nature, followed by periods of consolidation and ossification with scientists becoming more arrogant and less tolerant of other belief systems, such as religious ones, so that society rebels against science and retreats into fundamentalism (pp. 23–24). This seems a reasonable characterisation of a present tendency among scientists, as we saw in the last chapter, and scepticism is growing about the claim that the changes brought about by technology based on scientific discoveries will automatically improve things. No doubt fuelled by technologically-inspired disasters like Chernobyl, Bhopal, and BSE, suspicion of change has now become widespread, detecting in technological and consumerist-inspired developments "a fanaticism of rapid change and a fascination with novelties – technical, organisational, chemical, biological and so forth – which insists on their application long before their long-term consequences are even remotely understood" (Schumacher 1973/1999: 93).

> Common sense, on the contrary, would suggest that the burden of proof should lie on the man who wants to introduce a change; *he* has to demonstrate that there *cannot* be any damaging consequences … "Anything so complicated as a planet, inhabited by more than a million and a half species of plants and animals, all of them living together in a more or less balanced equilibrium in which they continuously use and re-use the same molecules of the soil and the air, cannot be improved by aimless and uninformed tinkering. All changes in a complex mechanism involve some risk and should be undertaken only after a careful study of all the facts available. Changes should be made on a small scale at first so as to provide a test before they are widely applied. When information is incomplete, changes should stay close to the natural processes which have in their favour the indisputable evidence of having supported life for a very long time" (Buchsbaum 1957), (quoted in Schumacher 1973/1999: 109–10).

Schumacher quoted this prophetic critique some 30 years ago, but populations of Western Europe have now begun to match his scepticism. Ulrich Beck in his book *Risk*

Society (1992) suggests the political consequences of disillusion with and scepticism of scientific and technological progress.

Indeed some scientists have never embraced the notion of scientific or evolutionary progress. Thomas Kuhn, for example, sees science, like life on earth, not as evolving towards anything, but away from something (Horgan 1998: 44). He cites as an instance Aristotle's theory of physics, which was founded on the idea that motion was the same thing as change. (Quite incidentally this makes CHANGE IS MOVEMENT literal for Aristotle, or what I have called an asymmetrical impositive metaphor for us.)

> Aristotle used the term *motion* for example to refer not just to change in position but to change in general – the reddening of the sun as well as its descent toward the horizon. Aristotle's physics was simply different from, rather than inferior to, Newtonian physics (p.42).

And Freeman Dyson, with his principle of maximum diversity, sees the universe and life as a series of interesting challenges rather than a steady development.

> The laws of nature and the initial conditions are such as to make the universe as interesting as possible. As a result, life is possible but not too easy. Always when things are dull, something turns up to challenge us and stop us from settling into a rut. Examples of things which make life difficult are all around us: comet impacts, ice ages, weapons, plagues, nuclear fission, computers, sex, sin, and death. Not all challenges can be overcome, and so we have tragedy. Maximum diversity often leads to maximum stress. In the end we survive, but only by the skin of our teeth (Dyson 1988: 398).

The strength of the Darwinian-inspired belief in progress can be seen by the way it has influenced disciplines as remote from it as theology. Perhaps in an attempt to co-opt the theory of evolution, rather than opposing it, the Jesuit philosopher theologian Teilhard de Chardin in *The Phenomenon of Man* claimed evolution moves inexorably to its end-point, the Omega of the glorified Christ, which gives Christianity a rather different evaluation of time from Hinduism or traditional Chinese Taoism. As Hans Küng puts it:

> Thus this God does not exist behind the flux of history but is known as the God of history. Precisely as the God of the beginning is he the God of the end, precisely as alpha is he the omega, and precisely as the creatively primordial One is he also the eschatologically future One, the coming One whom man and human kind, actively progressing in hope, may await as the one who will make all things new and who therefore here and now demands that man and humankind rethink and return from the past to the future of the coming kingdom in which God will not only be in all, but will be all in all (Küng 1987: 464).

Perhaps De Chardin and Küng's views owe something to Aristotle's conception of Nature as *phusis*, the essence of things that have a source of movement in themselves. If we combine this with the teleological theme that PURPOSE IS DIRECTION (or PURPOSES/ DESIRED RESULTS ARE DESTINATIONS) it becomes easy to believe that natural processes are inherently directed towards goals. Living things move to a purpose or end, in both senses of the word. Hence to explain their behaviour it is necessary to think in terms of so-called "final causes", i.e. causes which have goals and purposes, the gathering and consummation of creation up into the Omega-Christ. As Tennyson put it,

> That God, that ever lives and loves,
> One God, one law, one element,
> And one far-off divine event
> To which the whole creation moves. (*In Memoriam*, Epilogue, ll.141–144)

5.3 Evaluative oppositions

We have now considered two cases by which multivalent sources might create extra ideological equations, MORE IS HIGH + GOOD IS HIGH → MORE = GOOD, and CHANGE IS MOVEMENT + DEVELOPMENT/SUCCESS IS MOVEMENT → CHANGE = SUCCESS. I now turn to other kinds of metaphor theme interactions, namely how positively evaluated metaphor themes set up incompatible ideological tensions and oppositions.

There is one set of very basic oppositions which are emerging in the course of this book, which might be typified by the opposed concepts in Table 21, and realised, among others, by the metaphor themes below them.

Table 21. Ideological and metaphorical oppositions

Relationship	Isolation
Unity	Separation
Diversity	Sameness
Quality	Quantity
Co-operation	Competition
ORGANISATION IS MACHINE	QUALITY IS QUANTITY/SIZE
SOCIAL ORGANISATION IS BUILDING	QUALITY IS WEALTH
SOCIAL ORGANISATION IS BODY	ACTIVITY IS GAME/FIGHTING
RELATIONSHIP IS PROXIMITY/COHESION	FREEDOM IS SPACE TO MOVE

The basic distinction is between a structure, in column 1, in which the individual parts are diverse, representing different qualities and therefore incommensurate, and related to each other in a co-operative enterprise. And column 2, where the inidividual entities are seen as similar and therefore quantifiable, free, separate and in competition with each other. We have discussed most of these metaphor themes already. SOCIAL ORGANISATION IS BUILDING is discussed later in this chapter (5.3.2), and SOCIAL OR-

GANISATION IS BODY will be identified as a dominant theme of the medieval social and economic ideology, which in early capitalism came under threat from the ideologies of the second column (8.2.6). The last pair represent the opposition with which I am immediately concerned.

5.3.1 RELATIONSHIP IS PROXIMITY/COHESION V. FREEDOM IS SPACE TO MOVE

Good relationships are represented as physical closeness, physical attachment, or indivisibility of a unit. Undoubtedly these have metonymic connections grounded in our physical bodily experience as Lakoff's theory predicts. In fact, he regards the latter as part of the basic *link* schema based on the physical attachment between bodies and objects (Chilton 1996: 54–55).[3] At the beginning of our bodily experience we are part of our mother before birth, and after birth often cry to demand closer bodily contact, becoming physically attached in the process of breast-feeding. Slightly later, infants are satisfied if their mother is sufficiently near, visible and audible, although they remain quite close in strange environments. Personal space increases from about 0.2 metres nose to nose indoors at 2 ½ years to 0.5 metres at twenty years (Hayduk 1983, quoted in Argyle 1988: 172). We continue to want the security of parental proximity until our teenage years, and then, even though we may not wish to be seen with parents in public, will nevertheless live in the same house.

Our adult bodily experience takes us in the opposite direction, as we establish our own relationships as pubescent teenagers. "Morris (1971) suggests that in western culture couples normally go through twelve stages of intimacy, always in the same order: from (1) eye to body, via (6) arm to waist, and (7) mouth to mouth, to (12) genitals to genitals" (Argyle 1988: 102). We note the increasing proximity or attempt to combine and share surface areas and attachment in a striving for cohesion. At stage 12, teenagers or adults, in most cases, become attached in sexual intercourse, attempting as best we can to achieve a physical union of our bodies which may or may not symbolise the intellectual and emotional union we feel (cf. Kövecses 2000a: 118–122). Psychoanalytically, this adult experience of partnership or marriage might derive its structure from our experiences of proximity with our first caretakers; Freud regarded adult love as a re-finding of infantile love for our first caretaker (Quinn 1991: 57).

In this way physical proximity becomes symbolic of emotional attitude and relationship, and this proximity can be divided into four zones:

1. *Intimate*, from contact to 6–18 ins., for people in intimate relationships they can touch, smell, feel heat, can talk in a whisper, but cannot see very well.

---

3. According to this schema the links are symmetrical (if A is linked to (close to) B, then B is linked to (close to) A), and are constraints or dependency relations (A and B are constrained and dependent on each other). The objects linked may both be seen as static, or one may be seen as movable in relation to the other which is a fixed Ground as with metaphors for tying, fixing and securing etc.

2. *Personal* distances, from 1 ½ – 4 ft; this corresponds to "personal space", closer than which discomfort is commonly experienced; it is possible to touch the other by reaching, and they can now be seen clearly, but not smelt.

3. *Social* distances are from 4 – 12 ft. and are used for formal business purposes, e.g. across a desk. Interactors use a higher level of gaze and need to speak louder; body movements are visible.

4. *Public* distance is over 12 ft and up to 25ft or more and is the distance kept from important public figures. Facial expression is more difficult to see, a louder voice is needed, and bodily movements need to be exaggerated. (Hall 1966: 169–70)

Whether virtual relationships over the internet without physical contact can ever be a satisfactory substitute I doubt, since emotional union has to be expressed by physical proximity, at least.

The metonymies and symbols of relationship as proximity and contact are elaborated into metaphors in the lexicon, which we might label RELATIONSHIP IS PROXIMITY/COHESION. Proximity is an indication of a good relationship. **Close** means 'intimate' and **close circle** 'an intimate group', and the relatives with whom you have the most strong or intimate relationship are *next* **of kin.** Affection towards friends or family is **togetherness,** and if two people are **together** or **go together** they are 'intimately related romantically or sexually'.

Having physical contact or attachment is a metaphor, as well as an index or symbol, of affection and love. In general **be attached to** means 'love, have affection for', and business relationships are **connections** or **contacts.** This attachment may be based on bodily contact, such as **join hands with** 'co-operate, become jointly involved in' or **cling to** 'love possessively' (*she clung to him in her despair and he had no freedom*). Quite often the metaphorical source schema is one of tying with rope or string: **bind** 'make people feel they belong together' (*the English language binds the UK and the US together and encourages political alliances*), **ties** 'friendly feelings or relationships', **tie the knot, get spliced, get hitched,** 'get married' (*when are you going to tie the knot?*), **knit** 'unite people closely', **close-knit** 'united' and the more pejorative **entangled** 'personally involved with' (*he became romantically entangled with a student*). Less easily detachable physical contact, which may make you **inseparable** 'very good friends', is associated with the **glue** or **cement** 'means of strengthening a relationship within a social group' (*poverty used to be the glue that preserved the extended family*), the means to **cement** 'make a relationship stronger' (*their friendship was cemented by a mutual interest in aerobics*), or to, even more strongly, **weld** 'make people into a united organisation' (*he had the personality to weld the party together*). The result is a **bond** 'close relationship' (*the bond between mother and child is enhanced by breast-feeding*), as in **male bonding** 'close friendship between men' (cf. LOVE IS A BOND, Kövecses 2000a: 26).

A social group organisation with strong internal relationships is then seen as an indivisible object or **unit** 'social group working together for a particular purpose', or union 'organisation of workers from a particular profession or trade', or if several countries are involved, a **bloc[k]** 'group of countries that are political, economic or military allies' (*the Soviet bloc had a formidable scientific research programme*). The stronger the relationships between the members, the more they show **solidarity** or **cohesion** 'unity in opinions and support' (*we want to march tomorrow to show solidarity with our leaders*). If a person establishes a relationship with another person or organisation they **join** and hopefully **mesh** 'be suitable for each other' (*I believe our personalities mesh well*), and if two organisations establish a relationship and become 'one' they **merge, coalesce, amalgamate,** or less permanently **combine** 'unite for a particular common purpose'.

The converse of these metaphors is that lack of relationship is distance, not having or breaking of an attachment, and division. **Remote** and **distant** mean 'unfriendly, unemotional', and **distance** is 'lack of an intimate relationship'. If you deliberately avoid intimate relationships you **keep your distance/at a distance** do 'not become very involved with' (*Grant always tended to keep his girlfriends at a distance*) or **keep at arm's length** 'avoid becoming too friendly or involved with' (*I keep my students at arm's length so they show me respect*), with the result that you may get the reputation of being **unapproachable** 'unfriendly and intimidating in manner' (*she was quite a bitch, an unapproachable character, and everyone at school was scared of her*) or **aloof** 'not very friendly or sociable'. On the other hand, you may find yourself without a relationship through no intention of your own: **marooned** 'in a lonely and helpless situation' (*more and more families are marooned in decaying inner-city areas*), **isolated** 'alone or lonely', sometimes deliberately excluded as an **outcast** 'person not accepted into a group'. Moving apart becomes the source for the weakening, ending or failure of a relationship: **part/go their separate ways** 'end a relationship', **separate** 'end the relationship of marriage', **grow apart/drift apart** 'fail or become estranged in a relationship' (*over the years Paul and his wife grew/drifted apart*).

Having no attachment is lacking an involved relationship: **unattached** 'not married, without a partner', **detached** 'not personally or emotionally involved', **cut off** 'lonely or isolated'. To remove an attachment is to weaken or end relationships: **loosen ties** 'make the relationship weaker' (*to get elected they loosened their ties with the communists*), **uncouple,** as one can literally to the carriages of trains, 'separate two organisations or end their relationships' (*Blair has worked hard to uncouple the Labour party from the unions*). Ending relationships can also be seen metaphorically as ending contact: **drop** (*he dropped most of his old friends and made new ones*), **dump** 'suddenly end a relationship with', **brush off** 'reject by refusing to talk or be pleasant to' (*James tried to be friendly but Matt just brushed him off*).

More prolifically, the end of a relationship is seen as a break or division: **break-up, breach** 'ending of a relationship', **break off/split up** 'end a relationship' (*I decided to break off/split up with Sam last night because I'm more interested in Bob*), **rupture** 'damage or end a relationship between people', **sever** 'end a relationship between' (*I severed my relationship with him as soon as I knew he was on heroin*). When the relationships within groups become hostile or argumentative they are divided: **divide/fracture/split** 'cause disunity in' (*FIFA has been fractured by the question of Blatter's financial mis-management*), **divisive** 'causing hostility and argument' (*abortion is often a divisive issue*), **division** 'argument which causes a group to separate into two' (*there were too many divisions within the communist party for it to survive*), **riven** 'violently disunited', **tear... apart** 'cause to be disunited' (*the quarrel tore the party apart*). One part of the organisation may **split off** 'divide into a separate organisation' in a **breakaway** or **splinter group** 'group formed by separation from an original group because of disagreement' (*the SDP formed a breakaway/splinter group from the Labour Party*).

There is however an intrinsic ambiguity in our evaluation of the meanings of proximity and touch, because it as an indication of both "warmth" and dominance. Experiments show, for example, that subjects who see couples in silhouette where one member of the pair touches the other give higher ratings for status, assertiveness and warmth to the toucher compared with the touched (Argyle 1988: 226). Some kinds of bodily contact are, of course, aggressive, which may underlie these findings. This tension could be a manifestation of the approach-avoidance conflict that underlies degrees of proximity – the need for company versus the need for privacy, personal territory and individual freedom (p. 184).

As a result of this ambiguity these generally positive metaphors for friendship, affection, solidarity and belonging conflict with another important set of positively evaluated metaphors, which might be collectively labelled FREEDOM IS SPACE TO MOVE. **Room, latitude, space,** means 'freedom or opportunity for action' and the narrower space of **elbow-room** and **leeway** mean 'freedom to act within certain limits' (*he gave me a certain amount of leeway in the application of the examination mark scheme*), while **loose** means 'sexually free or immoral'. There are a number of adjectives with the negative suffix un- to do with freedom: **unrestricted** 'free to do something in the way you want', **unfettered** 'free to act without being limited by rules or influence' (*pubs are now unfettered by limits on their opening times*), **unbridled** 'not controlled or limited' (*we need to campaign against the unbridled use of cars*), which may also apply to the freedom to express emotion – **unrestrained** (*there was unrestrained joy on the faces of the mothers*). Continuing this idea that the removal of a physical restraint to movement confers freedom we have **give a free rein to** 'allow the freedom to act' (*the young film-makers were given free rein to experiment*), **let loose** 'have complete freedom in a place or situation' (*she has all the excitement of a little girl let loose in a candy store*), and **cut loose** 'behave in a wild, uncontrolled way' (*in the second half of the show the band really cut loose*). Terms that mean literally 'not tight' imply a certain amount of freedom: **loose** means 'not controlled very closely', and **slack** 'undisciplined, not strictly observing or enforcing the rules' (*he has a very slack attitude to bribery and corruption*). These lexical patterns have their non-linguistic realisation in the broken shackles at the foot of the Statue of Liberty (Kövecses 2002: 59).

It follows that lack of freedom is being bound, tied or otherwise physically restrained. **Bind** means 'force by rule, agreement or restriction' (*authorities will be legally bound to arrest any suspects*), and is also a source for the laws of probability as in **bound**

to 'be certain (to happen)' (*there are bound to be price increases next year*), while **bondage** means 'being under the control of' (*Marxism was supposed to free people from the bondage of superstition*). If you are **tied/tied down** you are 'forced to accept limitations to your freedom' (*he didn't have a family as he didn't want to be tied down*), and if one's **hands are tied** one is 'prevented from taking action' (*her hands were tied by the US constitution*). The metaphor theme includes other ways of restraining such as **hobble**, literally 'tie a horse's legs together so it cannot wander away' and metaphorically 'limit or control the freedom of' (*a long list of alterations to its constitution have hobbled the new school management team*), **chained to** 'unhappy with because of lack of freedom to avoid' (*he felt chained to a boring, badly- paid job*), **fettered/shackled** 'prevented from acting or behaving freely' (*a private trust would not be so fettered/shackled by bureaucracy*), and, when prevented by lack of money, **strapped** (*I've long been strapped for cash and still owe him a couple of grand*).

The targets of rules, controls, limits and oppression have as their sources various means of physical restraint: **restraint** 'rules or conditions', **chains** 'oppression or lack of freedom' (*the colonies suffered for years from the chains of economic exploitation*), **straitjacket** 'severe limit to development or activity' (*the national curriculum must be a guide, not a straitjacket*), and **strings attached** 'special demands or limitations' (*look at the small print of the contract to see if there are any strings attached*). And control is associated with reins: **rein in** 'control', **keep on a tight rein** 'have a lot of control over' (*her parents had kept her on a tight rein*), though one may **kick over the traces** 'show no respect for authority by breaking rules' (*on their day off the football team would kick over the traces*). The metaphors even extend into the areas of lack of freedom due to busyness and obsession: **tied up with** 'busy with something (*he's tied up with his new book – you'll be lucky to see him*), **wrapped up in** 'obsessed by to the neglect of other things' (*he's too serious and dedicated, wrapped up in his career*).

Another converse of the analogy FREEDOM IS SPACE TO MOVE is NO FREEDOM IS ENCLOSURE. If you are in a **prison** you feel that you are in 'a situation that it is impossible to change' (*he felt his marriage had become a prison*) and a **trap** is 'a dangerous or unpleasant situation you cannot escape' (*young and friendless people are prone to falling into the trap of strange cults*), while a **prisoner** is 'someone who has no freedom to avoid a situation' (*he's a prisoner of his own addictions*). If you restrict someone's freedom of action they feel **hemmed in** or **hedged about** with rules and conditions. And if they are **besieged** they are too busy to do what they want because they are 'receiving, or subjected to, and with no chance of avoiding' something negative (*the TV company was besieged with phone calls after the sex education programme*). If it is an emotional state that you cannot avoid you may be **locked** in it 'dominated (by negative emotions)' (*survivors of disasters often remain locked in a state of guilt for years*).

FREEDOM IS SPACE TO MOVE, and NO FREEDOM IS TYING/BINDING or ENCLOSURE can be explained at a theoretical level by Talmy's force dynamic theories.

> The Agonist is identified with the self's desires, reflecting an inner psychological state. It is being overcome by an Antagonist acting ... as blockage – in the psychological sense, one might say 'suppression' ... This antagonist represents a sense of responsibility or propriety and appears as an internalisation of external social values. In effect, perhaps, a force-dynamic opposition originating between the self and the surroundings seems here to be interjected into an opposition between parts of the self. Correspondingly the desiring part is understood as more central and the blocking part as more peripheral (Talmy 1988: 71).

Talmy relates this schema to Freudian theory. The desiring part is seen as more central like the id, the deep component of the self that has basic desires, while the superego arises as an internalisation of socially derived values, and the two are in conflict (p. 95). The need for the security of social relationships seems pitted against the demand for independence and the satisfaction of desire (Kövecses 1990).

The conclusion is that we have two basic metaphorical patterns, which are at odds with each other. On the one hand there is the idea that bonding, being attached is a positive thing, through which we establish meaningful relationships within society. And this is related to a metaphorical pattern that we discuss elsewhere (8.2.10.1) that DESIRE IS BENDING/ATTRACTION. On the other hand we have a set of metaphors which suggests that bonding could be bondage, and being tied to a family or entangled in a relationship might be undesirable. The western notion of freedom and individualism seems very much supported by the FREEDOM IS SPACE TO MOVE analogy – one thinks of the metonym of the wide-open spaces of the American West – so that it becomes quite difficult to conceive of someone achieving freedom through a relationship, as though the two are diametrically opposed. But perhaps this is a western tension, less common in other societies.

> Western society is based upon the notion of the primacy of the individual. This is profoundly different from an Indigenous society where each person is first and foremost part of the group, and the group itself is part of the natural world. Rather than people insisting upon individual rights and freedoms, they acknowledge their obligations and relationship to society and the earth. ... From within a worldview that is based upon relationship the threat of banishment is far more serious than life imprisonment or the death penalty, for it means cutting a person off from the whole society, and even from the opportunity to speak and hear his own language. In other words it removes the very context that gives a person's life meaning and identity (Peat 1996: 47, 49).

Many Muslim women claim that they achieve a certain freedom by accepting the clear roles defined by them through marriage, and that this can be liberating, providing it is not abused by men. Similarly, the collectivist, communitarian Confucian values of East Asian societies, which put more stress on relationship rather than the individual, might result in freedom from crime and freedom to walk the streets safely at night, as one can in Singapore, Hong Kong and Tokyo.

The birth rates (and marriage rates) are falling all over Europe and the industrialised world, and perhaps this reflects the ideas suggested by this metaphorical opposition that relationships, for example with children, take away one's freedom. Who wants to tie the knot if it leads you to being tied down? (Don't answer that, perhaps.) In 2003 the birth rate in Japan was 1.29 per woman. According to Junko Sakai "These women have become more individualistic and the men baulk at sacrificing their freedom on the altar of marriage and fatherhood" ('Race to Reverse Declining Birth Rate' 2004). Meanwhile the divorce rates are going up: "In 2004, the number of divorces granted in the UK increased by 0.2 per cent to 167,116, from 166,737 in 2003. This is the highest number of divorces since 1996, and the fourth successive annual increase". (Office for National Statistics; General Register Office for Scotland; Northern Ireland Statistics and Research Agency 2005).

The conflict between relationship and freedom can also be found in religion. Within Christianity there is this paradox that God's "service is perfect freedom". And this paradox is most forcefully expressed in John Donne's sonnet 'Batter my heart three-person'd God'. In lines 8 and 11, he uses the familiar metaphor of loss of freedom being captivity or tying, when the persona of the poem complains that the viceroy, reason, who should govern and defend him (the usurped town), is not free to do so because he has been taken captive; and when he talks of his betrothal to God's enemy, the devil, as a knot that needs to be untied. But the paradox comes in lines 12 and 13, which can be paraphrased as 'Take hold of me and imprison me, for I will never be free unless you make me a prisoner'.

> BATTER my heart, three person'd God; for, you
> As yet but knock, breathe, shine, and seek to mend;
> That I may rise, and stand, o'erthrow me, and bend
> Your force, to break, blow, burn and make me new.
> I, like an usurped town, to another due,   5
> Labour to admit you, but Oh, to no end,
> Reason, your viceroy in me, me should defend,
> But is captived, and proves weak or untrue.
> Yet dearly I love you, and would be loved fain,
> But am betrothed unto your enemy: 10
> Divorce me, untie, or break that knot again;
> Take me to you, imprison me, for I
> Except you enthral me, never shall be free,
> Nor ever chaste, except you ravish me.

Jeremy Rifkin wrestles with the paradox in less successful fashion when he calls to the technologically-obsessed Western world for a change of consciousness in our attitude to time, nature and each other:

> Our highest aim has been to free ourselves from **the fixed bonds** of nature. We have
> long associated free will with the **loosening of** our temporal **ties** with the ecology of

the planet and the **strengthening of our bonds** of social autonomy. So much philosophical literature is taken up with the intimate relationship between free will and autonomy that for all practical purposes they have come to mean the same thing.

We should rethink these assumptions so that

> ... free will is no longer measured by the degree of autonomy one exercises but rather by the degree of communal participation and sharing that one experiences ... There is no reason why freedom need any longer **be bound** to the notion of independence. One can be free to choose relationship over self-**containment** (Rifkin 1987: 241) [my bolding].

In the first two lines of the first quote Rifkin uses the metaphor traditionally, but in the third line he talks about "strengthening the bonds of autonomy", which, in traditional terms, would seem paradoxical. However, he continues with the converse of the traditional metaphor in the second quote by talking about being "bound by independence" and "self-containment", which suggest that independence and self-sufficiency can actually reduce our freedom and make us prisoners of ourselves.

Althusser's and Foucault's notion of subject positioning presents the same paradox though it is not framed in the same metaphorical terms. Subject positioning refers to the roles which we are assigned when we participate in institutional activity, as part of a social group. It has often been regarded as simply a subjection to the power structures of society, but adopting these positionings is equally an empowerment, as Fairclough points out (Fairclough 2001: 31–32), and like all cultural software it enables at the same time as it limits (Balkin 1998: 19, 27). If, for example, children new to school manage to learn the discoursal and bodily practices of the classroom quickly, such as raising the hand, they are enabled to get the teacher's attention when necessary to speak and ask permission to do things. Similarly, Balkin stresses that hermeneutic power, the power of understanding conferred by cultural software, including metaphors, is not a power that denies autonomy.

> The ability to decide, to understand, to interact with others to articulate and express one's values are all hallmarks of individual autonomy. Yet all of these features are developed through cultural software – which means being subject to various forms of hermeneutic power (Balkin 1998: 280).

I suggest that the need to stress the positive empowerment of subject positioning through cultural software derives from the fact that we are inclined to view relationships as diametrically opposed to the freedom of the power to act, rather than the means of achieving it.

On the other hand, as Fromm points out, heroes, and especially spiritual heroes, are those who free themselves by walking out, both literally by becoming wanderers or wandering beggars, and often metaphorically too, by leaving their families. Abraham and Moses are the wandering heroes of the Jewish tradition. The Buddha, Jesus and his disciples left their families and responsibilities for a higher calling. Odysseus and

Hercules are travellers (Fromm 1983: 96). However, these "freedoms" from human relationships are in the service of a higher relationship with God or the Gods.

Some rather sad testimony to the effect of pornography on its addicts attests to the opposite fact. A life of masturbation to pornographic images might be seen as a bid for power, or freedom to take revenge against women's liberation and improved social status. However, it is, in fact, a life of slavery.

Men and porn

Edward Marriott

Saturday November 8, 2003
The Guardian

....

Men, say psychologists, also feel threatened by the "emotional power" they perceive women wielding over them. Unable to feel alive except when in relationships with women, they are at the same time painfully aware that their only salvation from isolation comes in being sexually acceptable to women. This sense of neediness can provoke intense anger that, all too often, finds expression in porn. Unlike real life, the pornographic world is a place in which men find their authority unchallenged and in which women are their willing, even grateful servants. "The illusion is created," as one male writer on pornography puts it, "that women are really in their rightful place and that there is, after all, no real and serious challenge to male authority." Seen in this light, the patently ridiculous pornography scenario of the pretty female flat-hunter (or hitch-hiker, driver with broken-down car, or any number of similar such vulnerable roles) who is happy to let herself be gang-banged by a group of overweight, hairy-shouldered couch potatoes makes perfect psychological sense.

The porn industry, of course, dismisses such talk, yet occasionally comes a glimmer of authenticity. Bill Margold, one of the industry's longest-serving film performers, was interviewed in 1991 by psychoanalyst Robert Stoller for his book Porn: Myths For The Twentieth Century. Margold made no attempt to gloss over the realities. "My whole reason for being in this industry is to satisfy the desire of the men in the world who basically don't care much for women and want to see the men in my industry getting even with the women they couldn't have when they were growing up. So we come on a woman's face or brutalise her sexually: we're getting even for lost dreams."

The myth about porn, as a witness told the 1983 Minneapolis city council public hearings on it, is that "it frees the libido and gives men an outlet for sexual expression. This is truly a myth. I have found pornography not only does not liberate men, but on the contrary is a source of bondage. Men masturbate to pornography only to become addicted to the fantasy. There is no liberation for men in pornography ... [It] becomes a source of addiction, much like alcohol. There is no temporary relief. It is mood-altering. And reinforcing, i.e. 'you want more' because 'you got relief'". …

And the alternative to pornography, says Morgan, is not always easy. "Relationships are difficult. Intimacy, having a good relationship, loving your children, involves work. Pornography is fantasy in the place of reality. But it is just that: fantasy. Pornography is not real, and the only thing human beings get nourishment from is reality: real relationships. And, anyway, what do you want to say when you get to the end of your life? That you wish you'd spent more time wanking on the internet? I hardly think so."

At the end of these extracts the idea emerges that a real relationship, demanding though it is, gives much more freedom than the bondage of pornographic addiction, though the latter masquerades as a kind of escape from the domination of women.

The FREEDOM IS SPACE TO MOVE metaphor also allies itself to the ideal of competition, particularly to COMPETITION IS A RACE (detailed in 2.6). It is obviously incompatible with AFFECTION IS PROXIMITY and RELATIONSHIP IS PROXIMITY/COHESION. If you are attached to somebody else you cannot race *against* them (only *with* them in a three-legged race). This opposition is part of the co-operation v. competition opposition which we discussed in the previous chapter and summarised at the start of this section. Are we all linked co-operatively in a symbiotic relationship as part of *Gaia*? Or are we all individuals trying to distance ourselves from each other and our competitors?

5.3.2   Change v. stability in relationships.

We have noted that one of the obvious ideas of modernity is that change is good and inevitably leads to progress, reinforced by the interaction of CHANGE IS MOVEMENT, and DEVELOPMENT/SUCCESS IS MOVEMENT (FORWARDS). In the last section, however, we found that relationships imply lack of change or movement, since they involve bonds, which restrict us, and that this produces a conceptual tension between freedom to act and relationships. In this section we look at a similar tension, not in the field of personal relationships but in the area of international relations, drawing for much of our findings on Paul Chilton's (1996) book *Security metaphors: cold war discourse from containment to common house.*

For much of the twentieth century in international relations it was the notion of stability, rather than change, that was seen as desirable, via the metaphor of the balance of power or equilibrium. This metaphor did much to shape policy for "the balance of power metaphor can be viewed as part of a discourse – a coherent and institutionalised set of concepts and practices that do not so much describe an objective state of affairs out there, as actively constitute them" (Chilton 1996: 113).

The schema is common in theorists of international relations, such as Morgenthau:

> The concept of equilibrium as a synonym for balance is employed in many sciences – physics, biology, economics, sociology, and political science. Whenever the equilibrium is disturbed either by an outside force or by a change in the other elements composing the system, the system shows a tendency to re-establish either the original or new equilibrium (Morgenthau 1973: 168).

The balancing process can be adjusted either by making the heavier side lighter or the lighter one heavier (p. 178). Imperialism was thought to upset the balance: "the system may consist of two scales, in each of which are to be found the nation or nations identified with the same policy of the status quo or of imperialism" (p. 93).

Moreover the notion of a balance of two forces suggests the mentality of "my enemy's enemy is my friend" – the idea of two blocs, so that multipolar systems tend to resolve themselves into bi-polar ones (Chilton 1996: 113). The history of Vietnam is a case in point, where an independence movement, led by Ho Chi Minh, not particularly interested, initially, in teaming up with the Soviet Union, was forced into the Russian bloc. Eventually, of course, there was an attempt to contest this bi-polarity in the form of the non-aligned movement.

This metaphorical way of thinking is strongly represented in conceptual metaphor themes. Each bloc, wishing to achieve opposite goals, exert force in opposite directions, since a sub-theme of DEVELOPMENT/SUCCESS IS MOVEMENT FORWARD is PURPOSE IS DIRECTION, which in turn has the sub-themes SHARE PURPOSE IS ALIGN and CONFLICTING PURPOSE IS OPPOSITE DIRECTION.

Mutual support and co-operation is alignment, facing in the same direction: **align** 'support because of having a common purpose' (*the prime minister is aligning himself with the liberals*) so that **non-aligned** means 'independent of other powerful countries' aims' (*the Swiss have always tried to remain non-aligned*). The alignment may take the form of facing in the same direction while positioned next to – **side by side, in harness, stand shoulder to shoulder with** '(work) in support of each other' (*China and Russia are working side by side/shoulder to shoulder/in harness to maintain the ABM treaty*). Or it may be facing in the same direction while one is behind the other – **line up behind/ with** 'give support to' (*some surprising names have lined up behind the idea*), **in tandem** 'working together to achieve something' (*we taught the chemistry course in tandem*), and **pull together** 'co-operate' (*the nation pulled together to avoid a slide into complete chaos*). While these metaphors stress common orientation as an expression of support and co-operation, similar metaphors have to do with travel in the same direction and stress agreement: **go with ... all the way, go along with** 'support and agree with completely' (*I'll go with you all the way/go along with you on your reform proposals*), and, **fellow-traveller** 'person who agrees with the beliefs of an organization without joining' (*fellow-travellers of the Soviet Union were badly treated in South Africa*).

In order to achieve stable political balance the forces acting on each other have to push (or pull) in opposite directions, because of their different purposes: **oppose, opposition,** literally 'push/-ing in the opposite direction from or resist/-ing pressure', metaphorically 'disagree/-ment with or reject/-ion of a plan or idea' (*the Article 23 legislation met with great opposition*), **run counter to**, literally 'go/be in the opposite direction to', metaphorically 'be directly in conflict with' (*much of the plan runs counter to the beliefs of the Islamic community*), **go against** 'oppose or disagree with' (*he's always going against his father's advice*), **turn against** 'begin to oppose, stop supporting or liking', and **line up against** 'be opposed to' (*it did give some indication of the forces lined up against Yeltsin*).

The result of this movement in different directions will be that the two groups or ideas hit each other, **collide** 'be opposed (of beliefs, interests, purposes)' (*when public and private interests collide it will make a fascinating spectacle*), are **on a collision course** 'about to fiercely disagree' (*Japan's universities are set on a collision course with their students*), or **clash**, literally 'be hit together and make a lot of noise', metaphorically 'be opposed (of beliefs, ideas, purposes)' (*his proposals for the future of the club clashed with the members' views*). Sometimes the angle of confrontation may not be 180°: **cross** (literally 'intersect') 'oppose, defy' (*if you cross me again I shall lose my temper*), **at cross-purposes** 'having different understandings or aims' (*the two friends are both at cross-purposes with the officials*).

Alternatively the opposing forces are pulling away from each other: **tug of war** 'struggle to achieve different purposes' (*there was a tug of war between avoiding a budget deficit and the desire to keep taxes low*), **tension** 'differences between aims, or arguments' (*the movie explored the tension between public duty and personal loyalty*).

Even the common word **side** 'opposing group or team' participates in the metaphor theme: two sides of a piece of paper or a street face in opposite directions (*the two sides were both without key players for the match*).

The idea of opposing bipolar forces combines the idea of COMPETITION with STABILITY. Often competition is conceived as a race, e.g. the arms race and the space race, but by using the Newtonian mechanistic notion of the balance of forces the idea of competition can be reconciled with stability and lack of change rather than the change implied by movement. This is one way of attempting a compromise between stability and freedom to act. However, the power drives of nations make this compromise inherently unstable because nations are aiming at superiority not balance. Consequently, the tension remains (Chilton 1996).

In the context of international relations it is interesting to explore this tension by relating it to Chilton's discussion of the metaphor of **security**. The literal meaning of the metaphor *security* is ambiguous, leading to diversification. (1) It could belong to the idea of fixing of one object to another, generally with rope or string, as in "If they secure the box to the truck it won't fall off". This first meaning plugs into two metaphor themes: RELATIONSHIP IS PROXIMITY/COHESION along with lexical items such as **bind** 'make people feel they belong together', **ties** 'friendly feelings or relationships', **tie the knot, get spliced, get hitched**, 'get married' **knit** 'unite people closely', **close-knit** 'united' **entangled** 'personally involved with'; and the metaphor theme CERTAINTY/RELIABILITY IS SOLIDITY/FIRMNESS along with lexical items such as **steady** 'reliable, constant', **solid** 'reliable and complete' (of information, knowledge), 'loyal and dependable' (of people), **firm** 'completely reliable', **stable** 'unchangeable, dependable' and so on. (2) The other literal meaning of *security* belongs to the idea of a container that is difficult to break into as in "The house is secure". The first meaning is obviously important to the idea of stability and cohesion in government and power structures as suggested by **bloc**, though the notion of cohesion, specifically impenetrability, links to the second meaning. As far as Chilton's work goes, the second meaning is dominant, since the discourse of international relations is extremely dependent upon the metaphor of the state as a container. This rather abstract container image-schema can be realised at the basic category level as two metaphor themes SOCIAL ORGANISATION IS BODY (ORGANISATION PART IS BODY PART) and SOCIAL ORGANISATION IS BUILDING[4].

The container/building metaphor can be operationalised into a concrete symbol by the building of walls – Hadrian's Wall, The Great Wall of China, the Berlin Wall, and now the Wall/Fence/Barrier in the West Bank, which both provide security, and the lack of freedom, for example, of East Germans to "escape" to the West, or of Palestinians to access their farmland, their jobs and public amenities. The metaphor can also have repercussions for "freedom" of information, as it plugs into the theme KNOWLEDGE/WORDS IS FLUID. Leaking of state secrets, or the spread of dangerous ideology can both be viewed as threats to national security. Ideally, we need a closed container whose contents are invisible to those outside, and whose walls are impenetrable to outside ideas.

The prototypically stable man-made structures are buildings, since, in order for a building to survive, it should not move. It is not, therefore, surprising that states and organisations are also conceptualised as buildings, to stress their stability and durability. Thomas Hobbes was famous for his emphasis on the need for a strong sovereign to provide security at the national level, by preventing the internal conflicts within the state. Hobbes argues for conformity by merging the idea of cohesion into the idea that the state is a building. Those who do not fit in are

> … not unlike to that we see in stones brought together for building of an edifice. For as that stone which by the asperity, and irregularity of figure, takes more room from others, than itself fills, and for the hardness, cannot be easily made plain, and thereby hindereth the building, is by the builders cast away as unprofitable, and troublesome: so also a man that by asperity of nature, will strive to retain those things which to himself are superfluous, and to others necessary and for the stubbornness of his passions, cannot be corrected, is to be left, or cast out of society, as cumbersome thereunto (Hobbes 1651/1997: 209).

Unfortunately, the stability and security of a cohesive and self-contained state is incompatible with Adam Smith's discourse of free exchange and movement of goods.

---

4.   Kövecses 2002 sees these two themes with the sources of BODY and BUILDING as sub-metaphors of ABSTRACT COMPLEX SYSTEMS ARE COMPLEX PHYSICAL OBJECTS.

The tension derives from the idea that a container, such as a body or building, ensures security by controlling what goes on inside the state, and what comes in and out of it, excluding those who do not fit in, and protecting the state from outside attack. However, this allows little scope for freedom, symbolised by movement, and in capitalism enshrined in free trade (Chilton 1996: 89. See also our discussion of Matt Ridley (4.3.3)).

The problem arose in relationships between the US and the USSR towards the end of World War Two. Stalin conceived the USSR as a container tightly closed for security reasons, an understandable conception given the history of invasions of Russia. However, in that era the US was encouraging the opening up of global trade or free trade. "The American emphasis on openness, however, could itself only appear as penetration to someone whose understanding was dominated by the need for a securely bounded space." America was in fact formulating the container schema selectively: the state was a container for security reasons, but should be a space without boundaries for purposes of free trade (Chilton 1996: 133). The same might be said of the contemporary situation as regards the selective application of the container metaphor for immigration but not for capital flows. Immigration is tightly controlled, with policing of boundaries of states to prevent illegal immigration, but the almost instant free flow of capital around the globe has become more and more of a reality.

Churchill's iron curtain metaphor suggests that the Soviets lived behind the curtain, a self-imposed restriction of their freedom. This is a theatrical curtain, hiding with Soviet secrecy what is happening on the stage. Contact and therefore communication is not possible through an iron curtain in either direction, of course. The audience is free to come and go but those enclosed on the stage behind the curtain are denied such freedom. The idea of the open West versus the enclosed East then begins to take shape.

Chilton discusses the use of these container metaphors in the speech with which Truman spelt out the so-called Truman doctrine, given before a joint session of Congress on 12th March 1947. He concludes:

> The structure of concepts that constitute the Truman doctrine speech are thus held together in a kind of bonding of opposite semantic poles that can be summarised as in [Figure 4]. One the one hand "we" are "inside" the space of our identity and security. "Totalitarian" regimes are "outside" (and thus help to define "us"). The container schema contributes in this way to the definition of self and other. On the other hand "we" is also defined by container concepts in the other sense – namely as "free" and "independent". These terms themselves are understood as a function of containment and binding metaphors: to be "free" is to be not contained, bound, imprisoned or constrained. Totalitarian regimes, "outsiders" are characterised by the reverse – that is by acts of imprisoning, preventing, binding (Chilton 1996: 183).

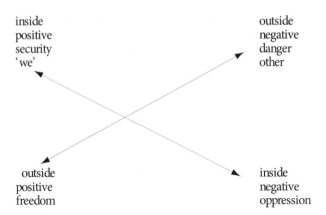

Figure 4. Ideological oppositions in the Truman doctrine speech

This attempt to overcome the tension between containment and freedom, the space to move, does not hold up, of course. According to the logic of the metaphorical opposition, security will always bring with it curtailment of freedom, so that seeing others' inside as negative oppression and ours as positive security is simply disingenuous. Civil liberties groups in the US are quite convinced, for example, that the emphasis on homeland security after the 9/11 attacks has brought considerable diminution of freedoms.

The tension between freedom and relationship is also relevant to George Lakoff's characterisation of the liberal and conservative ideologies in US politics according to the competing metaphors of the nurturing family and the paternalistic "strict father" family respectively. Since freedom, the watchword of the right, involves space to move and is antithetical to relationships, and right-wingers only see their responsibilities as extending to those with whom they share their genes, it is doubtful if the right would ever conceive society in terms of their own family. I discuss his theories at much greater length in 8.3.

5.4   A complex case of metaphor theme interaction

In racist circles there is a myth that the ideal nation is made up of people who are alike – by race, by culture, by language and by shared values. This myth gains support from a number of metaphor themes. One could see it as a reversal of the CATEGORY IS DIVIDED AREA theme, which was illustrated in chapter one (1.7). A divided area then becomes a category – so that everything within the bounded area has to be the same or similar.

Moreover there is the multivalency of the PROXIMITY source to represent both RELATIONSHIP and SIMILARITY. SIMILARITY IS PROXIMITY is a fundamental metaphor theme equating as it does two of the basic psychological Gestalts of perception. Proximity is used for similarity in general: **near to**, 'very similar to' (*the sensation was near to* *nausea*), **close** 'very similar' (*Clare has a close resemblance to her elder sister*), **the nearest thing to** 'most similar thing to something non-existent' (*bonds are the nearest thing to a completely safe investment*), and **verge on** 'be very similar to' (*his was a fury that verged on madness*). **Not far wrong** and **close** mean 'nearly correct' (*you were close/not far wrong: it's 42 not 40*). "Approximation" to a stated amount is conveyed by a number of synonyms to do with closeness: **around, about, close to** (*there are around/about/ close to 6 million people infected*), **near** (*the pound ended last year near its annual low*); or slightly more distantly: **in the region of, in the neighbourhood of, in the vicinity of** (*the number of tigers left in India is in the region/neighbourhood/vicinity of 2000*). Some of this metaphorical lexis is restricted to an approximation which is slightly more than the exact truth: the prepositions **nearly, well-nigh, nigh on** 'a little bit less than' (*I earned nearly/well-nigh/nigh on 3000 dollars in the summer*) or the verbs **nudge, approach** 'be almost at an amount or speed' (*we were approaching/nudging 150 kph*).

Conversely DIFFERENCE IS DISTANCE. **Remote from, far (different)** from mean 'very dissimilar' (*botany might seem remote from engineering*) (*Singapore was far different from what I imagined*), **a long way from** means 'very different from what is desired or expected' (*he's a long way from being a popular prime minister*), **nowhere near** 'very different in amount from' (*they are nowhere near the sales target*) and **wide of the mark** 'very wrong, far from the truth' (*your guess about my age was wide of the mark: I'm only 24*).

Difference can also be conveyed by separation: **separate** means 'different' (*abortion and contraception are two separate issues*), **poles apart** means 'completely different', either in opinions (*the unions and management are still poles apart*) or qualities (*in terms of musicianship Pavarotti and Domingo are poles apart*). And to separate is to make a distinction **set ... apart** 'make different' (*only Peter's accent set him apart*), **tell ... apart**, 'distinguish between' (*facial expressions might help imaging software tell people apart better*).

The extent of difference is measured by distances between: **margin** 'difference between two numbers' (*they won by a margin of two votes*), **gap,** 'considerable difference' (*the poem explores the gap between our hopes and reality*), **gulf/chasm** 'important or significant difference' (*the gulf/chasm between rural and urban life has never been wider*); and these distances/differences may be increased, **the gap widens** (*as the gap widens between the rich and the poor terrorism will increase*), or decreased, **close the gap** (*Malaysia has managed to close the economic gap between itself and its rich neighbour Singapore*), or made irrelevant/non-existent, **bridge the gap** (*Verdi bridged the gap between classical and popular music*).

By association through the multivalency of PROXIMITY, therefore, RELATIONSHIP becomes SIMILARITY and according to this logic the most successful relationships will be with people who are similar to us. This reinforces the notion that those within a bounded space should be similar, the reversal which gives us DIVIDED AREA IS CATEGORY: "Birds of a feather flock together."

But what criterion does one select for similarity or categorisation? One could select colour, of course, as constitutive of race. The largest proportion of immigrants to the UK in the 1980s was the Irish, though, being white, they were not perceived as a "problem". The question brings us back to Bourdieu and his exploration of class and classification.

> The transition from the state of being a practical group to the state of being an instituted group (class, nation etc.), presupposes the construction of the principle of classification capable of producing the set of distinctive properties which characterise the set of members in this group, and capable also of annulling the set of non-pertinent properties which part or all of its members possess in other contexts (e.g. properties of ... age or sex), and which might serve as the basis for other constructions. The struggle lies therefore at the very root of the construction of class (social, ethnic, sexual, etc.): every group is the site of a struggle to impose a legitimate principle of group construction, and every distribution of properties, whether it concerns sex or age, education or wealth, may serve as a basis for specifically political divisions or struggles. .... Indeed, any attempt to institute a new division must reckon with the resistance of those who, occupying a dominant position in the space thus divided, have an interest in perpetuating a doxic relation to the social world which leads to the acceptance of established divisions as natural or to their symbolic denial through the affirmation of a higher unity (national, familial, etc.) (Bourdieu 1991: 130).

Those who defend the existing classifications of society, for example race/colour, in which they are the most powerful group, use the language of nature to justify this classification. This is an exceedingly important motive for the adoption of power-aggression theories of nature, since the celebration of the winners in a competitive struggle is useful to those in power. In other words, it is natural for the dominant group to be dominant, and unnatural for it to in any way voluntarily reduce its dominance, because this dominance is the result of an evolutionary competitive struggle, in which the dominant group is destined to come out on top. And what could be more natural than the process of evolution? Or of the colour of one's skin? As a consequence, the idea that those enclosed in the same space and near to each other should be similar in race supports the drive to ethnic cleansing, and the ghetto mentality.

However, to see the extent of metaphor theme interaction we need to be more specific about divided spaces. Conceiving the territory of a nation state as a divided space or container is a rather abstract notion, and, as already noted, in practice Metalude's favourite metaphors for society are SOCIAL ORGANISATION IS A BUILDING and SOCIAL ORGANISATION IS A BODY. Let's consider these in turn and how they complicate the metaphorical interactions we have begun to explore.

The prototypical building, the one which as young children we first experience and become familiar with, is our house or apartment. As Chilton points out, those inside this secure home are typically family, sharing blood relations, as opposed to outside, alien and threatening beings that have to be faced and challenged. The state or house has control within a clear-cut boundary or wall which is its territory or home, (echoing Benveniste and Bourdieu, 1.7) so that there is no overlapping of homes or territories. The boundary or walls set up a distinction between inclusivity and exclusivity – you are either in or out, and you cannot belong to more than one home or family. The home provides stability and permanence or security, by holding things in place, but also does so "by means of exclusion rather than by any other means that are available to human societies" (Chilton 1996: 64) In modern racist societies this metaphor theme tends to express itself as the exclusion of immigrants. Keeping racial or national categories separate is also, of course, in keeping with the GOOD IS PURE/ UNMIXED (for details see 2.4).

But the nationalist/racist myth also wishes to keep intact and pure the nation's values, uninfluenced by foreign morally-suspect ideas, necessitating the containment of ideas as well as people.[5] This pure-ideas ideology exploits the second favourite source for SOCIAL ORGANISATION, the BODY, by which STATE OF AN ORGANISATION IS HEALTH, a health threatened by ideas, since IDEA IS DISEASE (4.3.1.5) and DISEASE IS INVASION (2.5). An external ideological disease must not be allowed to penetrate our own body politic. "If communism is viewed as … disease it follows metaphorically that its spread needs to be contained. If the Soviet Union is expanding its borders and invading other countries it needs to be contained" (Chilton 1996: 153). This metonymic relation between military invasion and the spread of ideology, symbolised by communist troops, is clear in Dean Acheson's reminiscences on his briefing of Congress about the Truman Doctrine:

> No time was left for appraisal. In the last eighteen months, I said, Soviet pressure on the Straits, on Iran and on northern Greece had brought the Balkans to the point of where a highly possible Soviet breakthrough might open three continents to Soviet penetration. Like apples in a rotten barrel **infected** by one rotten one, the **corruption** of Greece would **infect** Iran and all to the east. It would also **carry infection** through Asia Minor and Egypt, and to Europe through Italy and France, already threatened by the strongest domestic communist parties in Western Europe (Acheson 1987: 219) [my bolding].

This passage reverses the metaphor theme DISEASE IS INVASION into INVASION IS DISEASE.

Given this reversal, and the conception of immigrants as invaders, we are prepared to think of immigrants or other races as a disease. This is a commonplace of racist discourse. "The Nazis repeatedly cited Pasteur and Koch to argue that the Jews were like an infectious bacillus that had to be eradicated to control a contagious disease" (Pinker 2003: 154). Santa Ana found similar references to disease in anti-immigrant discourse and also discovered, like Mehan (1997), immigrants depicted as *invaders*, "footsoldiers in these criminal organisations" (Santa Ana 1999: 205). How this metaphorical association of disease, invasion and immigration can operate in a text is apparent in

---

5.   Lakoff (1996: 93) points out that according to this metaphor immorality can spread through contact, so immoral people must be kept apart form moral people, hence urban flight, segregation, and long sentences.

the following quote: "The report – which recommended a 3-year moratorium on immigration nationwide and linked illegal immigration to a **host** of society's **ills** – has been branded by Latino and Asian leaders as insensitive and one-sided." [my bolding] (*Los Angeles Times*, 29th June, 1993, p B1) (quoted in Santa Ana 1999: 205). Here *ills* meaning 'disease' is directly linked to illegal immigration, and *host* originally meaning 'army' is indirectly linked to immigration by representing disease as an army.

According to Sontag (1991), in medieval Europe associating foreignness and disease was conceived of as less a metaphor and more a metonymy of cause and effect: "Massacres of Jews in unprecedented numbers took place everywhere in plague-stricken Europe of 1347–8, they stopped as soon as the plague receded" (p. 72). But nowadays there are similar reactions to disease. "Authoritarian political ideologies have a vested interest in promoting fear, a sense of the imminence of takeover by aliens – and real diseases are useful material. Epidemic diseases usually elicit a call to ban the entry of foreigners, immigrants. And xenophobic propaganda has always depicted immigrants as bearers of disease" (p. 147). Reinforcing this pattern is the tendency to label diseases with the names of foreign countries – Hong Kong flu, Japanese encephalitis, German measles, Dutch elm disease, and so on. When syphilis first began its spread at the end of the 15th century "it was 'The French pox' to the English, the *morbus Germanicus* to the Parisians, 'the Naples sickness' to the Florentines, 'the Chinese disease' to the Japanese" (p.133). It has, of course, been tragically true in the history of North and South America that invasion of white men has produced disease. For example, by 1805 smallpox and malaria had already killed 90% of the Indian population of the lower Columbia River basin (Josephson 2002: 42).

Perhaps we can sum up the kind of metaphorical logic which the interaction of these themes leads to. Since SIMILARITY IS PROXIMITY + RELATIONSHIP IS PROXIMITY we might feel relationships are preferable between similars, for example those similar in colour; this is a case of multivalency equating targets. Those similar in colour belong to the same category, and since metaphorically CATEGORY IS A DIVIDED AREA, so a divided space or container (e.g. a society, SOCIETY IS BUILDING or BODY) might become a category, with those inside it the same according to the criteria for the category, e.g. colour. This move depends upon the reversal of target and source CATEGORY IS DIVIDED AREA → DIVIDED AREA IS CATEGORY, reinforced by another case of targets equated by multivalency CATEGORY IS DIVIDED AREA/CONTAINER + SOCIETY IS CONTAINER (BUILDING or BODY) → SOCIETY = CATEGORY. Moreover, SOCIETY IS A BUILDING, a kind of divided area, and genetically similar family members share the prototypical building, a house or apartment which, like an ideal category, has clear boundaries/walls to exclude outsiders, those who are different. Therefore society should exclude those who are different genetically (especially if SOCIETY IS A FAMILY). This logical move is internal to the metaphor theme schema. In addition, SOCIAL ORGANISATION IS A BODY and DISEASE IS INVASION, so if immigrants are invaders they are a disease that needs to be kept out. This logic depends upon a source schema, BODY, interacting with or expanding to include a target schema from another theme, DISEASE. And, if an IDEA IS

A DISEASE, it threatens the state of health of the body politic, especially when ideology is represented by an army. This logic depends upon two compatible source schemas, DISEASE and BODY, interrelating or expanding to include each other.

5.5   Diversification

This section discusses some of the range of diverse sources used for conceptualising the targets Emotion and Education. It will emerge that diversification can either share grounds as in EMOTION IS LIQUID and EMOTION IS WEATHER, grounds which both stress the changeability of emotion and help to constitute the very concept of emotion in English, or can have different grounds, as when education is conceptualised as a journey of exploration, or a process of internal growth, or the provision and acquisition of knowledge.

5.5.1   Diverse metaphors for emotion

Before discussing its diverse metaphors, we should locate emotion in opposition to fact and reason. This opposition takes part in the following cultural homology – reason : passion :: cool : hot :: stable : volatile :: permanent : transient (Balkin 1998: 236). We start by giving full details of the metaphor theme already mentioned in relation to security metaphors, that is CERTAINTY/RELIABILITY IS SOLIDITY/FIRMNESS.

There is an ambiguity in the notion of reliability – it can either be applied to facts or people, especially in their relationships with others. So **solid** can mean both 'reliable and complete (of information, knowledge)' (*this course gives a solid basis for a drama degree*), but also 'loyal and dependable' (*he has been a solid friend to me for many years*). **Secure** 'reliable' and **unshakeable** 'certain and unable to be changed or lost' also tends towards this ambiguity.

However, other lexis divides between relationships and facts or ideas. For relationships we have the adjectives **steady** 'reliable, constant' (*they have a steady relationship*), **stable** 'unchangeable, dependable' (*we had a stable six-year relationship together*), and **indissoluble** (literally 'unable to be dissolved) 'impossible to change or end' (*their marriage was indissoluble*). And we have nouns which apply literally to solid objects, **brick** 'trustworthy person' (*my aunt was a real brick*), or to the means of providing stability or solidity: **footing** 'basis for a relationship' (*we have to know on what footing you intend staying with us – lodger or guest?*), **ballast** 'qualities that make a relationship or person's character stable' (*his faith in God has always been a kind of emotional ballast*), and **sheet anchor** 'source of stability or confidence' (*complete honesty is the sheet anchor of marriage*).

As for the reliability or certainty of facts and ideas, there are the adjectives **firm** 'completely reliable' (*this is firm evidence of an improvement*), **sound** 'reliable and reasonable' (*he made many sound investments*), **rock solid** 'very reliable, certain to last' (*this is a rock solid agreement*), **four-square** 'established, determined and unlikely to change' (*party opinion is four-square against the Iraq war*), **substantial** 'reliable, of value' (*there are substantial arguments against this*), the substances involved always being solid – **concrete** 'real, certain and actual' (*until we get some concrete proposals we can't make a definite decision*), **cast iron** '(evidence/argument) impossible to challenge or disprove' (*there are five cast iron arguments for the policy of restricting cars*) or in any case hard: **hard and fast** 'certain, unable to be changed (of a rule or law) (*there's no hard and fast rule against marking while you are invigilating exams*). This adjective also applies to facts **hard facts/evidence** 'proven, certain' (*he has no hard evidence to back up his claims*) and money in a form which one can rely on: **hard currency** 'money that has a value anywhere in the world' (*the Euro is taking over from the dollar as the most important hard currency*), **hard cash** 'money in the form of coins or notes rather than cheques or credit cards' (*I'd be grateful if you could pay me in hard cash*).

Various verb sources to do with making more stable or solid can mean make more certain: **secure** 'obtain for certain' (*he secured a top job in the ministry*), **fix** 'make definite' (*he fixed the time to meet at 8.30*) or 'arrange the result (of a match) in advance' (*he was sent to prison for fixing football matches*), **set** 'establish certainly' (*they have set a definite deadline for the project*), **nail** 'find enough evidence to prove a criminal guilty' (*the evidence from the victim's mother was what finally nailed Jensen*), **nail down** 'obtain certain answers' (*I tried to nail down the reasons for his absence*), **clinch** 'decide or make certain of after much thought or discussion' (*they finally clinched the deal to buy the house they preferred*), **crystallize** 'make thoughts and opinions clear and certain' (*putting your ideas down on paper often helps to crystallize them in your own mind*). 'Remain unchanging or valid' is the meaning of **stabilize** (*the number of applicants has stabilized to around 40 per year*), and **hold** (*but do your results hold in more extreme climates?*), and to 'make something certain or reliable by giving evidence for it' you **support** it (*there are many arguments to support your position*).

It is quite obvious that the above metaphor theme CERTAINTY/RELIABILITY IS SOLIDITY/FIRMNESS is related to RELATIONSHIP IS PROXIMITY/COHESION, as we saw when discussing security metaphors above. Their lexical data shows that both facts and relationships are conceived as depending on stability. This puts both in contrast with emotions, which are conceptualised, at least in English-speaking cultures, as movement: EMOTION IS MOVEMENT.

For Kövecses the main contrast in the metaphorical conceptualisation of relationships and emotions is between the passivity of humans when affected by emotions, and the active rationality of humans in dealing with relationships; perhaps the association of relationships with rationality depends upon their sharing solidity as source. Kövecses identifies different metaphor themes from me: EMOTION IS FORCE and RELATIONSHIP IS COMPLEX PHYSICAL OBJECT (Kövecses 2000a: 113), but we agree that the two seem to be metaphorically opposed to each other, since forces tend to produce movement which threatens the stability of structures. Indeed, more generally, as already noted, CHANGE IS MOVEMENT, and in combination with EMOTION IS MOVEMENT, this suggests inherent changeability. Just like the tension between freedom and belonging (5.3), there is an intrinsic tension between the need for stable lasting relationships and the changeable emotions that we experience as part of these relationships. Fortune – change of power through time – is a whore. Relationships should be stable, but time is movement and therefore unstable.

The folk view of love, enshrined in the themes EMOTION IS FORCE, EMOTION IS WEATHER, EMOTION IS MOVEMENT, EMOTION IS A CURRENT IN A LIQUID sees us as passive in relation to it (Ekman 2000: 216). We experience emotions as happening to us, controlling us, not chosen by us. Romantic love, in its courtly love roots, is a passion beyond the control of the lovers, especially of the young man: a sickness caught involuntarily, an irresistible gravitational force, a "falling" in love. This contrasts with the idea that love can be based on control and rational decision-making. How can such a love be compatible with a long-lasting steady relationship? If we look at the Christian marriage service the couple are asked to promise to love one another until death in an act of will. But in uncontrollable romantic love, we can fall out of love as quickly as falling into it. Therefore marriage or stable long-lasting relationships demand a different kind of love, and to equate the two kinds of love is anomalous if not contradictory. "Its [romance's] central tenet cannot be reconciled with its promise of eternity" (MacRobbie 1991: 98).

Relationships are built, maintained and strengthened like buildings, and can break down, need repair or be dysfunctional. But emotions are a force which makes you explode, sweeps you off your feet, makes you fall in love, all suggesting a threat to this structure. On the other hand, morality is seen as being high or upright, so morality is the strength to resist the downward and destructive forces of gravity. The logic dictates that the emotional person is weak and prey to emotions, whereas the moral person is strong and in control (Kövecses 2000a: 194–5). One could relate this tension, in a similar way to Talmy, to Freudian conceptions of the ego which is the relationship between the id, representing loss of control and the following of emotional drives, and the super-ego, representing morality and the maintenance of control and rational thought or self-mastery (p. 199).

Emotions are normally encoded using mass nouns, and facts are encoded as count nouns. Objects, referred to by count nouns, are, amongst other things, conceptually characterised as being externally bounded and having internal structure, while substances, referred to by mass nouns, are unbounded and unstructured (Langacker 1991: 18–19).

> We experience mental processes such as thoughts, judgments, guesses, doubts etc. as objects we are in control of – we can sit down and start thinking about a problem and stop when we are done, i.e. mental processes are bounded in time. Emotions, by contrast are experienced as being substances beyond our control – we cannot wilfully stop feeling love, hatred or anger, i.e. emotions are unbounded. We also experience mental processes as being subject to our reasoning – we may, for example ask a person to justify his ideas … Emotions, by contrast, appear to us

as being unstructured – we cannot generally ask people to explain their emotions (Radden 2000: 104).

In the next section I compare some major metaphor themes for emotion: EMOTION IS MOVEMENT, EMOTION IS LIQUID (EMOTION IS CURRENT, EMOTIONAL EXPRESSION IS OUTFLOW), EMOTION IS WEATHER. I show that these themes share a number of grounds, among which those suggested above are the most important – uncontrollability, changeability and brevity. In Ekman, for example, hatred and resentment are not classified as emotions as they last too long (Ekman 2000: 113).

5.5.1.1   *EMOTION IS MOVEMENT*

According to most of the lexical evidence, the experience of emotion is metaphorically movement caused by some external force, rather than the force itself.[6] The only clear examples of emotion as the actual force is **pull** 'influence with emotion' (*sad memories of his childhood pulled at his heart*) and **yield to** (literally 'to stop resisting a force') 'give in to an emotion' (*he yielded to sentimentality and tears appeared in his eyes*). Since emotion is the movement itself, **move/moving** means 'cause/causing strong feelings' (*the generosity of the villagers moved me intensely/was very moving*). A force which causes you to go or travel somewhere causes you to have emotion: **send/transport** 'cause delight/extreme happiness in' (*I was transported by the playing of the orchestra*), **get/be carried away** 'become very excited and lose control' (*the crowd of students was carried away by his violent speech*). All the above involve change of location from one place to another.

But emotion may be a slighter movement, or one which does not necessarily permanently change location: **unsettle, disturb, perturb** 'cause anxiety to' (*the prospect of war is unsettling/disturbing/perturbing investors in the stock market*), **excite** (literally 'cause to make frequent small movements') 'make feel happy, eager, or enthusiastic' (*he was excited by the prospect of visiting Thailand*). Emotions may be more violent movements such as shaking: **shake** 'make upset or troubled' (*the news of Wilson's resignation shook the whole country*), **rattle** 'worry or make nervous' (*I was really rattled by the man following me home through the fog*), and a shake of the wings is a **flap** 'state of anxious excitement' (*I'm in a great flap because I haven't prepared tomorrow's lecture yet*). Revolving also indicates emotion: a **whirl** is 'excitement and confusion' (*my head was in a whirl and I lost control of the car*), **flip** 'become very angry' (*my father flipped when he discovered me smoking*), and **turn ... upside down** 'change completely making people too confused or upset to act' (*when Hamlet realises his uncle killed his father his mental world is turned upside down*), suggesting that change causes emotions, a metonymic link with CHANGE IS MOVEMENT; and **throw ... into a spin** 'make anxious and emotional' (*the bad news threw them into a spin*).

As in this last example, emotion can be throwing too: **throw** 'confuse' (*I wasn't expecting any visitors, and I was really thrown*), **throw ... into** 'cause to experience an

---

6.   The same is true even with the lexis in the related theme EMOTION IS TOUCH/IMPACT. The exception is with EMOTION IS CURRENT where emotion tends to be the force itself.

emotion' (*the last song threw the crowd into a frenzy*), and a **fling** is 'a short period of en-joyment and excitement' (*he's out having his last fling before he gets married tomorrow*).

Forces causing an emotion can also move you by their impact: **hit** 'have a strong emotional effect on' (*I was hit by the poverty in which most Rwandans have to struggle to survive*), **hit/knock for six** 'make extremely surprised or upset and unable to speak or act' (*the diagnosis of cancer knocked him for six*), **shock** 'surprise or emotional upset', and **jolt** 'cause a lesser shock' (*failing the exam jolted him out of his complacency*), while **jar** means 'cause unpleasant feelings' (*her rather supercilious comments jar after a while*). **Repel** (literally, 'push away') means 'cause disgust' (*US foreign policy repels me*), **stag-ger,** the transitive verb meaning 'cause to walk unsteadily' means metaphorically 'cause shock or surprise in someone' (*the news that they were going to marry staggered him*), while **whip** means 'cause emotions in' (*Hitler could whip a crowd into hysteria*). This category overlaps slightly with the metaphor theme EMOTION IS TOUCH/IMPACT. [7]

If you are nervously anticipating something that will cause you negative emotion, you are metaphorically in a state where you are likely to move suddenly: **twitchy** 'nerv-ous or anxious', **jumpy** 'nervous and anxious through fear or guilt' (*Blair must be get-ting twitchy/jumpy about the opposition to war with Iraq, and his loss of popularity*), or you may be **like a cat on a hot tin roof** 'in a state of nervous anxiety' (*I guessed he was guilty – he was like a cat on a hot tin roof*), or more generally just **restless** 'worried or bored' (*the kids got restless when it rained as the hotel had no games room*).

Presumably because the physical manifestations of emotion can stand as meto-nyms for the emotion itself, and might be described in everyday discourse by using the metonym (the metonymy of CAUSE AS EFFECT, specifically EMOTION AS SYMPTOM) (Wierzbicka 1999: 295), various kinds of slight shaking tend to metaphorically repre-sent the emotions that cause them, rather than, or as well as, the effect itself: **quiver** 'express your emotion through your voice or appearance' (*the kids were quivering with excitement as Chinese New Year approached*), **a shiver down the spine** 'feeling of ex-citement, pleasure or fright' (*Jessye Norman's singing sends shivers down my spine*), are probably metonymical or literal. But we also have the metonymical or metaphorical **quake** 'feel very frightened' (*he was quaking inside, though he maintained a calm ex-terior*), **tremble** 'be worried or frightened about' (*I tremble to think what will happen when Dad finds out*); a **wobbly** is a 'state of being extremely angry and upset' (*my Dad threw a wobbly when he discovered I hadn't been doing my homework*), **shudder** is 'fear or anxiety' (*Britain's biggest supermarket chain has sent a shudder through its rivals by cutting prices*), while **palpitations** are a 'shock' (*my father will have palpitations when he sees the new puppy*).

---

7. Kövecses 2000a discusses these metaphor themes comprehensively in terms of the idea that EMOTION IS STATE (PLACE), CAUSES ARE FORCES, CHANGES ARE MOVEMENTS, so that BECOMING EMOTIONAL IS MOTION INTO A STATE (PLACE), CAUSING EMOTION IS CAUSING MOTION INTO A STATE (PLACE).

5.5.1.2   *EMOTION IS LIQUID*

EMOTION IS LIQUID belongs to the analogy EMOTION : LIQUID :: FACT/REASON : SOLID. As the prototypical emotion is the prototypical liquid, we are dismissive or suspicious of emotions which are somehow on the borderline between the two categories: **mushy, sloppy, slushy, sappy, soppy** 'sentimental, having too much emotion' (*don't read those mushy/sloppy/slushy/sappy/soppy women's magazine romances*). Perhaps these kinds of text try to make the emotion or liquid unnaturally permanent or solid. But texts which do not express enough emotion are also criticised as being 'boring or unstimulating': **arid, dry** (*I found this article very arid/dry*). Adding liquid can be seen as adding emotion: **infuse** 'fill with an emotion' (*the fall of the USSR infused Germany with optimism*), **inject** 'make more interesting or exciting' (*the star injected some interest into the show*); and taking it away may mean to 'reduce the capacity for emotional response' or **drain** (*all the stress had drained her emotional energies*). To **evaporate** means to 'disappear (of attitude or emotion)' (*she was so charming my resentment evaporated*). The extent to which one experiences an emotion can be associated with fullness: **full of, brim-full of, brimming with** 'experiencing or showing a great deal of an emotion' (*I had met Mrs Allen, who is brimful of energy, enthusiasm and Irish charm*). Intensity of an emotion is **depth** (*I am aware of the depth of feeling that exists in Palestine*). If an emotion decreases in intensity it will **subside** (*all our fears began to subside*). Intensity of emotion or its expression is associated with the concentration of a liquid: **dilute** 'lessen or weaken' (*these measures should dilute the public anger*), or **distil** 'express the essence of an emotion' (*the poems distil feelings of nostalgia*). On the other hand emotion is also conceived of as water: **test the water** 'find out other people's feelings' (*you should test the water of the meeting before making that suggestion*), **pour oil onto troubled waters** 'pacify, calm someone down' (*the counsellor poured oil onto troubled waters*).

While most of these metaphors in the theme EMOTION IS LIQUID merely imply movement and therefore changeability, movement is inherent in the two major metaphorical sub-themes, i.e. EMOTION IS CURRENT/WAVE and EMOTIONAL EXPRESSION IS OUTFLOW.

A 'sudden increase in emotion' is a **wave, surge, swell,** (*there was a surge/wave/swell of sympathy for him*) which, when among a large group, is a **groundswell** (*there was a groundswell of disgust over the Jenin massacre*). A **shock wave** is a 'distressing reaction' (*Bush's death sent shock waves through society*), and **tide** a 'strong uncontrollable experience (of emotion)' (*the tides of my passion left me weak and helpless*). If feelings **ebb and flow,** they 'decrease and increase' (*there is a marked ebb and flow of feelings during the menopause*). On the metaphorical basis that what is unknown is unseen, 'hidden feelings' are an **undercurrent** or **undertow** (*an emotional undertow was present in the political debate*). Often these are negative or dangerous emotions as in a **vortex** (*he got caught up in a vortex of despair*). Feelings can 'be experienced strongly by a group' – **run high** (*passions are running high over the bombing*), or by an individual – **course** (*in that moment a surge of hatred coursed through my blood*). Used transitively the emotion is a force which can affect one intensely: **overwhelm,** (*I'm overwhelmed by your expressions of love*), **flood,** (*he was flooded with joy when his* *daughter was born*), sometimes negatively – **engulf**, (*desperation and disgust engulfed me as I listened to Eminem's songs*). All these metaphors represent a large amount of water coming from the outside, which is therefore difficult to cope with, and stress both lack of control and passivity.

However, if emotion is liquid inside one, and its expression is the flowing out of liquid, then lack of control is emphasised, but passivity less so. An **effusion** is an 'uncontrolled expression of strong emotion', (*I hate his effusions of self-pity*), **outburst**, a 'sudden, violent expression of feeling', (*I hate her unpredictable outbursts*), or a **gush**, **gushing** 'expression of/expressing insincere feeling' (*his performance was a load of gush*). The means by which you express your feelings are thus an **outlet**, (*poetry provided an outlet for her emotions*). The following intransitive verbs indicate that emotion can no longer be controlled: **overflow** 'express strong feelings' (*suddenly her anger overflowed*), **well** 'increase to the point where they have to be expressed' (*feelings of deep sorrow welled up inside me*), **brim over** 'express a feeling without restraint' (*he was brimming over with enthusiasm*), **boil over** 'have such strong uncontrollable feelings that you have to express them' (*many people are boiling over with rage at the support the US gives to Israel*). We also have transitive verbs, but only with the first two of these does the experiencer of the emotion seem relatively in control: **pour out (outpouring)** 'express strongly and uncontrollably' (*she poured out her feelings of resentment*), **express** (literally 'force liquid out by squeezing') 'communicate an emotion' (*this poem expresses Plath's despair as well as any other*). The others could be involuntary: **ooze, exude** 'display an emotion or attitude clearly', (*the second candidate oozed/exuded confidence throughout the interview*). An unexpressed emotion is one you **bottle up**, 'refuse to talk about or express emotions' (*it's bad for your mental health to bottle up your emotions for too long*) or **choke back**, 'prevent the expression of emotion' (*I choked back my anger and tried to remain calm, despite the provocation*).

5.5.1.3   *EMOTION IS WEATHER*

There are a number of general expressions constructing emotion or mood as weather: **weather** 'deal with a distressing emotional experience' (*we weathered that period of anxiety better than expected*), **climate** 'emotional atmosphere or mood' (*the climate of violence and fear in Soweto*); **barometer** 'indicator of opinions or feelings' (*the election will be a barometer of anti-Asian feelings*). Very closely linked are the general items which mean an emotional impression given by a person – **air** (*he walked into the room with an air of diffidence*), or of a place or situation – **atmosphere** (*there's still an atmosphere of tension in the town*). To 'get rid of negative feelings between people' is to **clear the air** (*we had a big row and that seemed to clear the air*).

Equivalent to wave/current in the EMOTION IS LIQUID theme is the idea of wind or air current. To 'test opinions or emotional reactions' you **find out which way the wind is blowing**, **fly a kite** and thereby determine the **prevailing** ones 'the most normal or common opinion or emotion' (*the prevailing mood was one of disappointment rather than anger*). A **gust** is a 'sudden and intense emotional feeling' (*he experienced a small* *gust of delight*). More specifically different types of wind are associated with different emotions: **breezy** 'confident and happy' (*he walked in with a breezy smile and handed out the cakes*), whereas a much stronger wind is overconfidence – **bluster** 'speak aggressively or proudly' (*he blustered, but underneath he was afraid*), while **gales** refers to 'a loud outburst of many people laughing' (*his remarks provoked gales of laughter*).

Negative emotions, especially anger, are associated with storms: **storm/tempest/hurricane** 'strong emotional reaction' (*there was a storm/tempest of protests about the war*), **stormy/tempestuous** 'fiercely emotional' (*ever since they married they've had a stormy/tempestuous relationship*), **storm** 'shout loudly and angrily' (*"don't you dare touch me!" he stormed*), **storm** 'move in or out of a room noisily and angrily' (*the US delegate stormed out of the anti-racism talks*), but a **storm in a teacup** is 'unnecessary anger or anxiety' (*fears of the millennium bug were a storm in a teacup*). The expression of anger is conceptualised as thunder or lightning: **thunder** 'shout loudly and angrily' (*"get out of here!" he thundered*), **fulminate** 'criticize strongly and angrily' (*Castro fulminated against global capitalism*), **black as thunder** 'extremely angry' (*his brother's expression was as black as thunder*). Discontent is the sign of a thunderstorm to come as in **rumblings** 'signs of people's discontent' (*there were rumblings of discontent among the school staff*) and **brew** 'become more intense' (*discontent was brewing in the shanty towns of South Africa cf. a storm is brewing out in the South China Sea*). More generally **rough** weather is an 'emotionally taxing' time or experience (*she has had a rough year with the death of her mother*).

In contrast with stormy we have **calm** 'peaceful' (*after all the excitement life is much calmer now*), **calm down** 'become less emotional' (*calm down – it's still a week until your birthday*), and **temperate** 'restrained in emotions' (*his behaviour was quite temperate*).

Many of the other specific types of weather metaphors, with sources of darkness, light, and cold are doubly determined, not only by EMOTION IS WEATHER, but also EMOTION IS SENSE/IMPRESSION with its sub-themes SADNESS IS DARKNESS, HAPPINESS/HOPE IS LIGHT, HOSTILITY/UNFRIENDLINESS IS COLDNESS: **dark** 'sad or gloomy' (*the period after her death was the darkest period of my life*), **gloom** 'unhappiness or hopelessness' (*'Autumn Sonata' is a film full of gloom*), **cloud** 'show unhappiness or anger' (*John's eyes clouded with disappointment*), **miasma/fog** 'unpleasant general feeling about the character of a situation or place' (*after his wife's suicide he seemed to sink into a miasma of depression*), **glower** 'look very angry annoyed or threatening' (*he glowered at me over the top of his glasses and then started to rant*). For an emotional atmosphere to improve is for it to **lift** like a cloud lifting (*his depression lifted after the birth of his first child*). **Sunny** means 'cheerful' (*he was a nice boy with a sunny disposition*), **a place in the sun** is 'an advantageous or happy position' (*after years of hard work he's finally found his place in the sun*), and to enjoy positive reactions from others is to **bask** (literally 'to sunbathe') (*he was basking in his outstanding annual appraisal*). Whereas an unfriendly and unwelcoming emotional attitude or reaction is **frosty** (*his autobiography had a frosty reception from his family*).

What general conclusions can we draw about the diverse metaphor themes for emotion illustrated above? The ones I have selected here, (and others will be explored in chapter 7), seem to stress the very aspects of emotion that Kövecses mentioned. Lack of conscious control, changeability, and suddenness. Suddenness seems particularly well represented by the weather metaphors, where winds and storms are the most frequent subdivision. The depressions bringing rainstorms and strong winds are much shorter lasting than areas of high pressure, which tend to persist (we are more likely, therefore to talk about a sunny "mood" or "disposition", more permanent than the sudden emotion in a storm of anger). And thunder and lightning are punctual events. Emotion as movement in general and movement of a current of liquid in particular seem to stress change. They all seem to underline lack of control in one way or another.

It is worth considering whether the English concept of emotion, itself culture-bound, with no exact equivalent in German or Russian as we shall see in the next chapter, is not simply reflected by these prevalent metaphors, but rather determined by them. As Wierzbicka points out, one trend in academic psychology, and indeed in physiology, sees emotions as a disruptive force. She quotes the following sentences from psychology textbooks found by Fehr and Russell:

> A state of emotion is recognised by its holder as a departure from his or her normal state of composure; at the same time there are physical changes that can be detected objectively ... When sufficiently intense, motion can seriously impair the processes that control organised behaviour ... Sometimes emotion is difficult to control (Wierzbicka 1999: 7).

This pejorative view of emotion is probably linked to the physiological theory that emotions are partly constituted by changes in the body which threaten its stability (see the discussion of Damasio's theories in 6.3.1). The normal state of a person is regarded as composure or homeostasis, and emotions as forces which disrupt this state. The metaphor sources we have been looking at, liquid, movement, current of liquid and (bad) weather, certainly stress passivity and lack of control. Weather, at least winds and storms, stresses suddenness, too. Ekman, a researcher within the physiological tradition of emotion research, defines emotion as a sudden phenomenon: "it may be that under exceptional circumstances a single emotion endures for more than seconds or minutes, but I think it likely that closer inspection would reveal that the same emotion is being repeatedly evoked" (quoted in Wierzbicka, 1999: 20).

Wierzbicka rightly points out that any such conception of emotion as disruptive and sudden is culture bound (1999: 17–20) and, I would add, constituted and shaped largely by the kinds of metaphors I have detailed in English. She points out that in Russian culture, for instance, to be in an emotional state such as 'joy', 'worry', 'sadness', 'sorrow', 'grief', 'delight' constitutes normality, and that not to be in one or other of these states would indicate that one's soul or *duša* had become dead, rather in the same way as Wordsworth or Coleridge conceived mental health or 'joy' as emotional responsiveness. In addition, these are not passive emotions in Russian, but emotions that one actively engages in, and therefore conveyed by verbs rather than adjectives: *radovat'sja* ('rejoice'), *grustit'* (roughly 'indulge in sadness'), *serdit'sja* ('to rage, be angry') and so on. She also claims that in German, where the closest word we have for emotion is *Gefühle,* one would be much less likely to associate emotion with brief duration, as illustrated by this quote from Victor Klemperer:

> Immer hat man den Druck und das Ekelgefühl auf der Seele und entgeht ihn nur noch auf Minuten.
> One has constantly an oppressive feeling and a feeling of disgust/revulsion [lit. 'on the heart/soul'], which one can only escape for minutes.

Wierzbicka herself relates the lack or control or composure in the English concept 'emotion' to the metaphor 'upset', for which there is no equivalent concept in other European languages,

> The central image in the feeling of upset is one of disorder and disarray. The synonyms for feeling upset all include a sense of confusion, and an interruption of the normal control and orderliness of life … we tend to feel upset when we have a sense that our normal orderly control over our lives is threatened (Wierzbicka 1999: 19, quoting Gaylin 1979: 175).

5.5.2   Diverse metaphors for education

The Lakoffian theory of conceptual metaphor suggests that our thoughts are at least constrained by, if not the prisoners of our body. However, even if we concede this, we still have choices from among the sources we use. This results in diverse metaphors with which to construct the "same" concept differently, and this construction will be more radically different if the grounds of these sources are diverse too. Structuring a field of human activity by one conceptual metaphor theme rather than another may be ontologically and ideologically heretical, because it determines the nature of the field in a radically different way.

In a recent article (Goatly 2002b) I investigated the use of metaphors for education in the Hong Kong SAR's educational reform proposals by analysing the government's *Review of Education System Reform Proposals Consultation Document* (dated May 2000). The reform model is intended to foster internal motivation in students, to encourage them to create knowledge and to develop as well-rounded balanced personalities, and thereby to counter the transmission model, in which knowledge is simply handed down from teacher to student, with undue emphasis on academic learning and memorization. In the document I discovered five or six major diverse metaphorical schemata for education: commodity acquisition, mechanism, building construction, a path or journey of exploration, growth and nurture, with a subschema of catering. (In the following analysis the figures in square brackets indicate the number of occurrences of the metaphor tokens in the consultation document.)

Commodity acquisition can be illustrated by the following:

> Higher education should aim *to give* students a global perspective (p. 4).
> Should there be any change to the way the curriculum is *delivered*? (p. 75).
> To help students *acquire* the most up-to-date knowledge and skills (p. 8).
> Helping students *grasp* important concepts (p. 86).
> The curriculum as a whole will enable students *to have* a good understanding of their country (p. 31).
> Students must also *possess* basic knowledge in different learning areas (p. 4).
> Our knowledge of people and matters are *accumulated* bit by bit from what we see and hear and take part in (p. 11).

Acquisition of education as a commodity or as cultural capital, or as investment hoping for a good return clearly belongs with traditional education, particularly as far as business-oriented Hong Kong is concerned.

The mechanism metaphor is largely a matter of quality control:

> … a quality assurance *mechanism* … *setting* quality *indicators* (p. 21).
> … a sound *mechanism* to ensure that their graduates meet the required standards (p. 97).
> … an external *mechanism* for the evaluation and quality assurance of early childhood education providers (p. 22).

Educational assessment as a mechanical process reflects traditional regimes of thinking about education in Hong Kong, linked as it is to the idea of getting grades and external rewards and qualifications for which assessment is necessary. The major problem is that, if education is creative, outcomes cannot be specified in advance and therefore any mechanical means of assessment or quality assurance may be "wide of the mark". The measuring mechanism also supposes we are comparing like with like, that we can standardize individuals' development and reduce it to numbers (QUALITY IS QUANTITY).

The metaphor of constructing knowledge gives us examples like these:

> Everyone needs to be able to *construct* knowledge on his or her own as well as to *grasp* new concepts and technology promptly (p. 123).
> … so as to *construct* knowledge, develop multiple abilities and enhance their personal quality, thereby *laying a sound foundation* for life, work and life-long learning (p. 125).

We have slipped, in the last example, through apparent multivalency, from building in which students construct/create knowledge for themselves to building as a curriculum in which the knowledge to be acquired is predetermined, i.e. the foundation. The system, materials and curriculum will, in fact be *designed* [7] by the authorities:

> … the *design* of the school curricula (p. 11).
> … to *design* school-based teaching materials (p. 31).

So, although constructing knowledge as a metaphor appears more creative than acquisition, this depends upon the extent to which the knowledge is already available like prefabricated concrete units, or whether the construction starts from scratch. As with pre-determined goals, if the design of the curriculum and its modules is rigid, then this undermines this metaphor's affinity with the reform process.

A metaphor that is most obviously and frequently exploited in the document is the path/course/route metaphor. As a path there is only one best direction to the goal, as is clear from the metaphor *attain* (literally 'reach') [6],

> ... accord due recognition to the qualifications *attained* (p. 101).
> ... enable each student to *attain* all-round development according to his/her own attributes (p.107).
> ... basic *attainment* standards (p. 45).

The teacher will have to give *guidance* [5] to ensure that students reach the correct goal:

> The provision of *guidance* and support to students in need (p. 17).
> The teachers' *guidance* is very important (p. 36).

The metaphor of *exploration* [10] might grow up out of the path/track/journey metaphor, but is more in tune with the "reform" agenda of the document.

> ... students would become more interested in learning and *exploration* (p. 37).
> ... so that he/she is capable of ... *exploratory* thinking (p. 5).
> They [people] must be equipped *to venture into new domains* of knowledge (p. 3).

Although education as a journey/track is slightly more progressive than the construction metaphor, the problem is that it is often a pre-determined track with goals and objectives set by society for society, rather than an exploration into new fields of knowledge.

The emphasis in agricultural and other organic metaphors seem to be on encouraging the inner growth of students, a growth which is either natural of for which they themselves are ultimately responsible.

> ... the attitudes, abilities and knowledge to be *cultivated* (p. 41).
> It is exactly through these learning experiences that important abilities like leadership, communication and organisation skills can be *fostered* (p. 14).
> ... to *nurture* in students ... a global outlook (p. 7).
> ... helping them to *cultivate* an interest in learning, positive values and attitudes, as well as analytical and independent thinking skills (p. 11).
> Schools should make use of the room thus created to help students *foster* attitudes and enhance abilities (p. 30).

This style of education quite obviously belongs to the Nurturant Parent model of society, proposed by Lakoff (1996: 235) and reflects Metalude's DEVELOP IS GROW (cf. Kovecses 2000a: 99).

However the internal nature of the educational process can be partly externalised when the metaphor of nurture is modified into the metaphor of *catering* [6].

> ... assisting all schools to *cater for* students' different needs (p. 108).
> They would need to *cater for* students whose ability range straddles four or five bands
> ... have an adequate understanding and *foretaste* of the career chosen (p. 39).

It seems that the notion of a balanced curriculum is a secondary metaphor based on the notion of a balanced diet (Dearden 1981). We already noted metaphors of providing, but here *provision* can be interpreted in the narrower sense of providing food, to give some evidence of the recursive nature of the metaphor:

> Through the *provision* of all-round and *balanced* learning experiences (p. 19).

These organic and growth metaphors obviously allow more freedom for students to develop and follow their internal motivations according to a progressivist philosophy. However, even this metaphor can be developed along traditional lines with the idea of catering – providing a consumable commodity and limiting the students' activity to chewing and digestion.

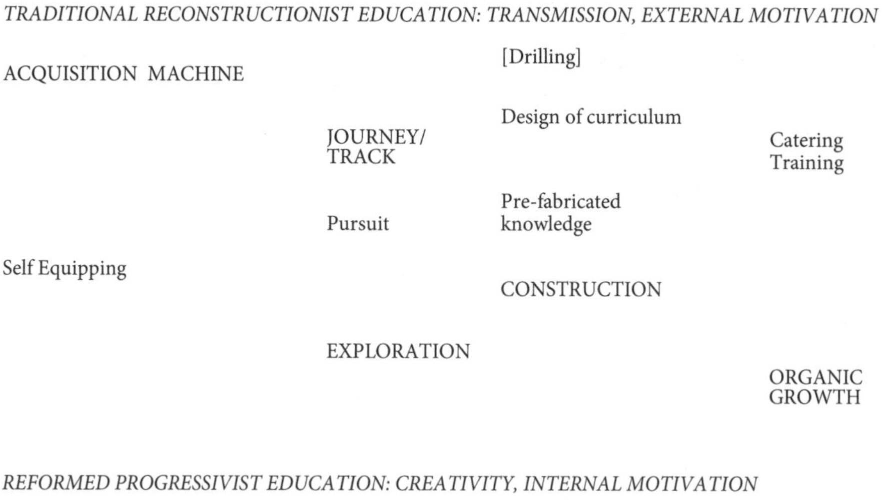

TRADITIONAL RECONSTRUCTIONIST EDUCATION: TRANSMISSION, EXTERNAL MOTIVATION

ACQUISITION MACHINE

[Drilling]

Design of curriculum

JOURNEY/
TRACK

Catering
Training

Pre-fabricated
knowledge

Pursuit

Self Equipping

CONSTRUCTION

EXPLORATION

ORGANIC
GROWTH

REFORMED PROGRESSIVIST EDUCATION: CREATIVITY, INTERNAL MOTIVATION

Figure 5. Position of dominant metaphors in the education reform consultation document in relation to tradition and reform

The conclusion has to be that the progressivist thrust of the reform is often compromised by the metaphors chosen or available. The hypothesis is that these different philosophies of education will lead to or reinforce different practices. If that is the case, then many of the metaphors in the document actually undermine the reform effort, especially those that see education as acquisition and the teacher as the provider. My evaluation of the metaphorical schemata in terms of whether they tend to reinforce or undermine these goals are diagrammed by their position in relation to the upper and lower poles in Figure 5.

One reason for the use of metaphors with the potential for sabotaging the reform might simply be that the writers are using them subconsciously. Where metaphors are used or read consciously, there are a number of options, suggested by Chilton (1996: 58–59) for resisting and contesting them:

1. The speaker may reject the source currently being used for target of the discourse, and then use a different source. If education were to be seen as a chemical reaction either between knowledge or between pupils, the teacher could be constructed as a catalyst setting off interactions without taking part in them or interfering with their outcome, instigating rather than controlling. Knowledge creation could be seen as analogous to the making of new chemical compounds rather than mixtures or accumulation. Another schema could see education as a ball-game in which the teacher is coach or opponent, with an emphasis on argument and contestation as a way of building up mental and emotional muscles. And pupils would form a co-operative team valuing each other's diverse abilities and skills.

2. The speaker may retain the current source but reformulate the target domain. Instead of the teacher being seen as providing resources or knowledge, as in the acquisition of commodities metaphor, the teacher could themselves be seen as a resource, available for the students to use for any educational purpose they choose.

3. The speaker may retain the current metaphor, but re-specify the grounds by rewriting the script. The construction script could be rewritten, in which case the students would be achieving their own aims, rather than meeting pre-determined objectives. I have already suggested the script of education as a journey following a path could be rewritten as a script where students find or make their own paths. So that rather than a guide the teacher could more usefully be a cartographer producing sketch maps, again with the implication that the direction of exploration will be freer, and students would be encouraged to revise or add to the map on their return. Indeed, instead of guiding, teachers might deliberately create obstacles or diversions for students in order to encourage "lateral" thinking, or explorations of unknown areas. In fact, assessment and examination could be seen, not as a mechanism for measuring students according to specifications, but the students' own descriptions of their journeys of exploration. Syllabi could also be retrospective, conceptualized as tracks left behind by the journey rather than a path along which to be guided.

If traditional metaphors are being used unconsciously in this document, and thereby militating against the overt aims of the reforms, then one would expect them to be influenced by certain well-established conceptual metaphor themes and ideologies. There are two or three here which we ought to explore.

Firstly there is the ambiguity of the journey schema, or ACTIVITY IS MOVEMENT FORWARD. Various aspects of the schema might be highlighted. One could focus on all three parts of the schema: (1) the beginning point, where force is applied by the authorities to determine that reformed education takes place (CAUSE IS FORCE); (2) the path – the methodology by which the teacher guides the student, (MEANS IS ROAD/TRACK); and (3) the end point which is predetermined by the objectives of the curriculum (PURPOSE IS DIRECTION/DESTINATION). One might focus simply on the beginning and the end-point, knowing where one will end up, though not precisely the "route" by which one will arrive, being forced to meet the aims or objectives of the syllabus but not knowing how this is to be achieved, like teachers who unthinkingly employ the traditional (successful?) methodologies for achieving their ends. To focus simply on the means of travel would mean putting more emphasis on the learning process rather than results, and would involve devising a methodology. To focus neither on origin nor endpoint gives the concept of exploration. It also implies that the explorer is not selecting a single directed path and that the orientation is toward a process rather than toward an objective, or initiated by an authoritative origin (Chilton 1996: 52). This would be equivalent to making the syllabus a *post facto* document, and allowing students to find their own way of choice through spontaneous and individualised learning. The more liberal the curriculum, the fewer of these three factors will be specified. It is clear that if all three are in operation the journey metaphor remains a traditional one, but exploration and the process curriculum where only one aspect of the journey is controlled fits better with the reformed curriculum.

The mechanism metaphor depends upon the notion of quality assurance, originally applied to manufactured goods, in which only a certain degree of tolerance for different dimensions was allowable, for example, within 0.5 millimetre. The idea that educational outcomes can be measured on a scale, like a manufactured product, is a way of reducing qualities to quantity according to the theme QUALITY IS SIZE/LENGTH, details of which were given in 2.8. in relation to time. Measuring students in this way assumes that like is being compared with like: perhaps grading students is as futile as trying to give oranges and apples marks out of ten for being a fruit.

> Quantitative differences can be more easily grasped and certainly more easily defined than qualitative differences; their concreteness is beguiling and gives them the appearance of scientific precision, even when this precision has been purchased by the suppression of vital differences of quality (Schumacher 1973/1999: 33).

Poincaré defined mathematical generalisation as the art of giving the same name to different things (Bourdieu 1991: 117), presumably so that they could then be counted.

Of course, that the product to be delivered in the education process should be subject to quality control assumes that education is a kind of commodity. This aspect of the commodification of knowledge, which makes it something for the teachers to provide to students and for students to acquire (column 1 of Figure 5), is strongly supported by the metaphor theme: IDEA/INFORMATION IS COMMODITY.

Various kinds of selling cover the giving of information: **sell** 'persuade someone that an idea is a good one' (*we've been trying to sell the president the idea that the business faculty should be reduced in size*), **retail** 'tell or recount a story or piece of information' (*Mr Adams gleefully retailed the story to Mr Anderson in his club over brandy*), **purvey** 'provide information' (*this document purveys all the details of the proposed path of the motorway*), and **peddle,** 'spread around stories information or gossip' (*the US peddled the myth that the Iraqis would welcome their troops enthusiastically*). In order to sell something you may have to **promote,** 'put forward, recommend and persuade people to accept' (*he's promoting a change to the curriculum which would reduce the number of credits to 72*) but be careful not to **oversell** 'promote as better or more important than it really is' (*I think this lobby group have rather oversold the need for reforms*). The person who does the selling of news, gossip, hostile policies and horror stories, like a fishmonger or ironmonger, is respectively a **scandalmonger**, **rumour-monger**, **war-monger**, and **scaremonger**. People who believe the information sold **buy** it (*I don't buy that explanation for global warming*).

Information may, of course, be **exchanged**, like commodities, rather than bought: **swap, trade** 'tell each other information or stories' (*they swapped/traded/exchanged memories of the 2nd World War over lunch*); and it is possible to **import** and **export** ideas or culture habits (*the idea of TV dinners was imported from the US/exported to the UK*). Once you have information it can be kept like a commodity: **store** 'large amount of knowledge, stories, jokes or information available to be told' (*Jessica dipped into her store of theatrical anecdotes*), **storehouse** 'publication where a lot of information can be found' (*Encyclopaedia Britannica is one of the great storehouses of human knowledge*) or you may wish to **recycle** it.

Erich Fromm described the mind-set of students who regard knowledge simply as a commodity to be possessed. They put a great deal of emphasis on noting down, memorizing, rote learning, and storage. Knowledge does not become part of them nor do they become creative by interacting with it or trying to relate it to their existing knowledge. They want everything fixed and penned down. By contrast, the best students come through interest, respond actively, attempt to relate what is said to what they already know or believe: new ideas, perspectives and questions arise in their minds (Fromm 1983: 17–18).

Bourdieu utilises the metaphor theme IDEA/INFORMATION IS COMMODITY in his metaphor of knowledge as cultural capital.

> One of the central ideas of Bourdieu's work … is the idea that there are different forms of capital: not only 'economic capital' in the strict sense (i.e. material wealth in the form of money, stocks and shares, property, etc.), but also 'cultural capital' (i.e. knowledge, skills and other cultural acquisitions), 'symbolic capital' (i.e. accumulated prestige or honour), and so on. One of the most important properties of fields [or markets] is the way in which they allow one form of capital to be converted into another – in the way, for example, that certain educational qualifications can be cashed in for lucrative jobs (Thompson 1999: 14–15)

Thompson believes that Bourdieu's metaphor is just an explanatory or exploratory one, rather than an impositive. However, its potential for misunderstanding is great, and it may be interpreted as reductionist, as though Bourdieu has "bought into" the commodification of knowledge. He might be susceptible to Fromm's criticism that in many education systems the knowledge a student acquires is commensurate with the amount of property and status they are likely to have in later life, and schools are factories that package and deliver knowledge (Fromm 1983: 29).

Bourdieu emphasises that, besides knowledge, linguistic utterances participate in the labour market. Speakers take into account, when reproducing linguistic expressions, the market conditions within which their products will be received and valued by others (Thompson 1999: 17–19). For example, slang is the pursuit of distinction in a dominated market (p. 22). For the linguistic market has its monopolies and oligopolies – it is not a free market. An example would be the reluctance to abandon the teaching of Latin: those in power, who had acquired it as linguistic and cultural capital, insisted on its importance in the curriculum lest it be devalued.

> Linguistic exchange … is also an economic exchange which is established within a particular symbolic relation of power between a producer, endowed with a certain linguistic capital, and a consumer (or a market), and which is capable of procuring a certain material or symbolic profit. Words and utterances are signs of wealth and authority (Bourdieu 1991: 66).

5.5.3   Summary of diversification

We have analysed two concepts, Emotion and Education, diversely structured by a range of metaphorical sources. The first analysis suggests that the various themes for emotion tend to share grounds of: passivity of the experiencer; uncontrollability; unpredictability; and suddenness. In the case of education there is an attempt at more differentiation, though some of the diverse metaphor themes can be modified in order to share grounds, for example, education as construction might be simply fitting together parts provided by the teacher, rather than finding materials and fashioning them together for oneself, and education as a journey might involve following and being guided along a predetermined path rather than exploring, and education as growth can be co-opted to the transmission of knowledge metaphor by talk of catering and a balanced curriculum.

Clearly there is enormous scope for research in exploring the diversity of structuring in relation to other diverse metaphor themes, explaining their ideological and ontological presuppositions, and validating the resulting hypotheses through experimentation, by, for example, testing whether a different metaphorical conception leads to different thought patterns or behaviour.

Diverse metaphors are essential for ideological analysis. Since each metaphor highlights and suppresses certain features of a target, or constructs the target in a particular way it both empowers our understanding and limits it. To counteract this limitation we have to deconstruct the metaphorical model, and this normally involves introducing a competing metaphorical model, which can give us a vantage point from which to assess the limitations and power of the other metaphor (Balkin 1998: 248).

5.6   Summary of metaphorical interactions

In this chapter we have considered three different kinds of metaphor theme interaction: multivalency, where sources are shared, diversification where targets are shared, and evaluative opposition. At the beginning of the chapter we showed how multivalency can lead to association between different targets so that GOOD IS HIGH and MORE IS HIGH taken together suggest MORE = GOOD, which reinforces patterns of excessive wealth accumulation and consumption as part of the Protestant capitalist ethic, despite the objections that Small is Beautiful. We also explored how CHANGE IS MOVEMENT and DEVELOPMENT/SUCCESS IS MOVEMENT FORWARD might suggest that CHANGE = DEVELOPMENT/SUCCESS, again an increasingly doubtful and contentious suggestion, though one which the technologically driven retail economies of the West have espoused in the cause of selling the latest and most fashionable consumer products. We also considered the evaluative oppositions FREEDOM IS SPACE TO MOVE (PURPOSE IS DIRECTION) v. RELATIONSHIP IS PROXIMITY/COHESION and CERTAINTY/RELIABILITY IS SOLIDITY/FIRMNESS. This is a tension which in the West seems to be increasingly, but perhaps erroneously, resolved in the direction of freedom rather than relationship, if statistics on divorce and birth rates are anything to go by. We showed the attempt in the cold war discourse of international relations to reconcile these opposed themes by the metaphor of the balance of forces.

We then exemplified two kinds of diversification. Emotion, constructed in opposition to the certainty/solidity of facts, is diversely structured as movement, liquid, and weather, all sources sharing grounds of uncontrollability, passivity of the experiencer, and brevity. Diverse metaphor themes for education, unlike emotion, were quite varied in their grounds, either undermining attempts at educational reform, through lexis such as **giving, provision, balanced curriculum,** according to an ideology that sees knowledge as a commodity, or encouraging it through lexis such as **exploration,** and **construction,** where the latter metaphors seem to be reducing the power and control of the educational authorities over the educational process and giving more freedom to students.

We also considered a complex nexus of metaphorical interactions implicated in racism: RELATIONSHIP IS PROXIMITY, SIMILARITY IS PROXIMITY, CATEGORY IS DIVIDED AREA, SOCIAL ORGANISATION IS A BUILDING, SOCIAL ORGANISATION IS A BODY, RACE IS COLOUR, IDEA IS DISEASE, DISEASE IS INVASION – a nexus which suggests that the ideal state is one where the inhabitants are the same colour, and constructs immigrants as invaders, or a disease, or as bearing dangerous ideologies.

Introduction to section 2

Section 1 of this book concentrated on the exploration of how metaphor themes are associated with various aspects of contemporary social life. Section 2, while still exploring this topic, becomes rather more theoretical and philosophical in nature. In this section we address the question, first introduced indirectly in Chapter 4, of the relative importance of bodily experience and culture in the patterns and networks of metaphors in the lexicon of contemporary English. Chapter 6 considers much of the persuasive evidence that metaphors for emotions are grounded in bodily experience, showing how these are culturally modified to some extent at more specific levels, though even this bodily experience may be to some extent culturally relative. Chapter 7 takes a perspective on grammar, to show that the most frequently occurring grammatical structures in English, if not most European languages, and those first acquired in childhood, structure the world, and humans' interactions with their environment in ways which are both out of step with modern scientific theories, and potentially destructive. "Grammatical metaphors" of various types may go some way to re-conceptualising in the direction of a more helpful grammar. However, a radically different grammar and worldview, such as that of the Algonquin language Blackfoot, could be even more helpful. Chapter 8 attempts to show that various metaphor themes of competition and conflict, quantification, money and commodification have been created, exploited and nurtured from the early capitalist period onwards, as manifest in the philosophical writings of Hobbes, Hume, Smith, Malthus and Darwin. It concludes with a discussion of the theological concept of incarnation and locates this within a discussion not only of Lakoffian theories of experientialism but also of metaphorical reductionism.

As my arguments about the issue of the experiential hypothesis and metaphoric universals are quite subtle and extend over these three chapters it is desirable at this point to chart the course of the argument in advance. Chapter 6 presents considerable evidence that identical metaphorical patterns are extremely widespread across different languages, if not universal, particularly those in which there is an intimate relationship between what is being conceptualised and bodily experience. The most obvious case is in conceptualising emotion, since emotion is very often defined in terms of disturbance to bodily equilibrium, or is manifest in changes to the body. The strong correlation between emotion and the bodily experience and perception of the body gives a real-world or metonymic basis, which can be elaborated metaphorically. Even here, we find that different languages, though they may share metaphorical patterns at the general level, differ in the particular lexis used to instantiate the general pattern.

Moreover, we have to take account of the fact that the body and bodily experience are affected by culture, so the fact that bodily experience gives an experiential basis for metaphors does not entail that that all kinds of bodily experience are universal.

Furthermore, as chapter 7 makes clear, even at the less specific level there are "exotic" languages such as Blackfoot where even the most general cognitive patterns do not seem to apply, such as the distinction between objects and processes caused by or acting on those objects. The result is that the Event Structure schema, which might seem, from the point of view of Western languages, a candidate for universal general metaphorical patterns (CAUSE IS FORCE, CHANGE IS MOVEMENT, ACTIVITY/PROCESS IS MOVEMENT FORWARD, DIFFICULTY IS OBSTACLE etc. etc.) may not apply to all languages. In other words the paradigm metaphor of activity – that independently existing objects exert a force on other independently existing objects to move them – is not a universal metaphor for actions or events. In addition, ideology has effects on the metaphorical patterns to be observed in the dictionary. The ideology may invent the metaphorical equation, as in TIME IS MONEY/COMMODITY or DISEASE IS INVASION. Or it may recruit existing metaphors and encourage, develop and elaborate them, as when ACTIVITY IS MOVEMENT FORWARD is elaborated, through the ideology of competition into the idea that activity is a competitive race, either against others or against time. In doing this it may attempt to replace or marginalize alternative metaphors, such as disease as imbalance, or activity as the harmonious workings of the body or a machine (cf. Kövecses 2005).

Chapter 8 gives specific examples of how metaphor themes have either been created or exploited and elaborated to express, bolster and strengthen a capitalist ideology which began in the 16th century, under the historical influence of Protestantism, and has become the common-sense dominant ideology in the last twenty-five years. One strand of this ideology, which sees humans, like animals, as competing for scarce resources in order to ensure the survival of themselves and their families, is strengthened by the prolific metaphor themes of competition such as ACTIVITY IS GAME – BALL GAME, CARD GAME, BOARD GAME, GAMBLING GAME or themes of violence ACTIVITY IS FIGHTING, HUMAN IS ARMY, SEX IS VIOLENCE. A second strand equates quality with quantity QUALITY IS QUANTITY, and, more particularly, with wealth QUALITY IS MONEY/WEALTH, assuming that well-being, relationships (AFFECTION/RELATIONSHIP IS MONEY/WEALTH), time (TIME IS MONEY/COMMODITY), indeed virtue itself, can be expressed or recognised in terms of money or material possessions. I hope I show that these metaphors have a continuity in the works of Hobbes, Smith, Hume, Malthus and Darwin and that they were either created or nurtured and espoused in turn by these philosophers.

CHAPTER 6

Are metaphorical themes universal?

"Bodily hexis is political mythology realised, em-bodied, turned into a permanent disposition, a durable way of standing, speaking, walking, and thereby feeling and thinking." (Bourdieu 1991)

6.1 Mind, body and culture

This chapter poses two related questions: (1) To what extent is our thinking and ideology determined by our bodies and the metaphors that they give rise to? (2) What variation is there in the metaphor themes across languages and cultures? These questions are related: if the sets of metaphors are based metonymically on our bodily experiences, then we could hypothesise a degree of universality. For example, the cause-effect metonymy is the basis for EMOTION IS HEAT (strong emotions do cause all of us humans to feel hot).

Connected to this question is the hypothesis that "every metaphorical mapping presupposes a conceptually prior metonymic mapping ... that the seeds for any metaphorical transfer are to be found in a metonymic projection" (Barcelona 2000c: 31).

We shall begin by giving due weight and attention to the evidence for this metonymic hypothesis and to the first hypothesis that these metonyms are based upon our common bodily experiences and are therefore universal. However, notice that the two hypotheses are independent. It would be perfectly possible for conceptual metaphor themes to be dependent upon metonymic relationships without being universal. This might be obvious with metaphorical themes whose sources or targets are culturally specific. For example, MONEY IS FOOD is a well-represented metaphor theme in English, and the metonymic relation is reasonably obvious: you use money to buy food. But for cultures without money this could not be a metaphor theme. Similarly, lack of the source rules out universality, for example, ACTIVITY IS CARD GAME, based on the metonymy of specific for more general, could not be universal since some cultures do not have any experience of card-playing.

But given the present theory it is difficult to see how metaphors could be universal unless they are metonymic, because, in the theory, the only explanation posited for the origin of these metaphors is an experiential correlation giving rise to a metonymical base. However, this does not preclude some other theory emerging with a different explanation for the universality of metaphor themes, perhaps structuralism or Freudian theory or Jungian archetypes of the collective unconscious. Nor should one underestimate the influence of phonology on the accretions of lexis into metaphor themes (See Goatly 1997: 78–79).

We begin by considering probably the best candidate for universality based on experiential correlations and metonymies, that is, metaphor themes for emotions. We summarise Damasio's recent theory of the emotions to show the relationship between bodily responses and emotion, one so intimate that he actually defines emotion as the physical response to a stimulus. We then proceed to build on work by Kövecses detailing the particular physiological responses which account for many specific conceptual metaphor themes, citing scientific evidence for these correlations.

However, in the following section we show that, even with the emotion metaphors based on the metonymies of physical responses, there are important cultural variations. We consider some literature on cultural differences between Japanese and Chinese in the conceptualisation of anger and then proceed to compare European humoral theory with Chinese theories of *qi* and explore their effect on the conceptualisation/lexis of emotion. This is regarded as evidence of the powerful effect of culture and ideology on metaphor. If there are important cultural variations even with metaphors where the target (emotion) and source (bodily response) are intimately connected by cause and effect, if not experientially identical, cultural variations are much more likely in metaphors without such an obvious experiential basis.

Turning from emotion metaphors to metaphor themes in general, we widen our discussion to consider how metaphors might fail to be universal. Discussing Grady's work on primary metaphors, one of the stoutest defences of the experientialist hypothesis, we compare his data with the Metalude database to show that a considerable number of metaphor themes appear to have no experiential metonymic basis, suggesting they may not be universal either.

The chapter's conclusion places our discussion in the context of the debate over the relative importance of biology and culture, explored in relation to the "metaphor" MAN IS ANIMAL in chapter 4. The strong version of the experientialist hypothesis, that all cognition depends upon bodily experience through metonymy/metaphor, might be an attempt at reductionism of culture and ideology in the sociobiological tradition, a reductionism we challenge through the idea that the body is a historical and cultural object as much as a biological one. This prepares the way for the chapter 8, where we trace some of the historical bases of the metaphor themes contributing to the dominant ideologies of modern western society.

6.2   Metonymy as basis of all conceptual metaphor themes

First we should consider the various definitions of metaphor and metonymy. "Metonym-based metaphor is a mapping involving two conceptual domains which are grounded in, or can be traced back to, one conceptual domain" (Radden 2000: 93).

Though this definition sounds fine, it depends upon an independent definition of what constitutes one conceptual domain rather than another. For example, one might ask, as we did in a previous chapter, whether humans and animals are part of the same conceptual domain or distinct domains.

One approach is to specify the domain as an idealised cognitive model (ICM), under which one might include schemas/scripts, and frames. A script/schema is a stereotypical or default sequence of actions in a number of scenes involving actors in defined roles, associated props, entry conditions and results. Shank and Abelson (1979) famously described the restaurant script:

Props:	tables, chairs, cutlery, food, plates, menu etc.
Roles:	customer, owner, cook, waiter, (cashier)
Entry conditions:	customer is hungry; customer has money
Results:	customer has less money; customer is not hungry; owner has more money
Scene 1. <u>Entering</u>:	going in, deciding where to sit, sitting
Scene 2. <u>Ordering</u>:	(asking for menu, waiter bringing menu) choosing, signalling to waiter, giving order, waiter telling cook the order
Scene 3. <u>Eating</u>:	cook giving waiter food, waiter bringing customer food; customer eating food
Scene 4. <u>Exiting</u>:	customer asking for bill, waiter writing bill, taking bill to customer, (customer tipping waiter), customer going to cashier, paying cashier, leaving restaurant.

According to the current theory, emotions have scripts too.

> Just as, say the "restaurant script" evokes the series of events which typically occur in going to a restaurant, so the "anger script" activates knowledge of the sequence of events associated with anger (such as provocation, desire for retribution, attempts at suppression, acts of retribution, return of equilibrium ...). Knowledge of the script makes it possible to assign "default values" to unobserved episodes. Thus, by observing certain outward signs, a person can infer the entire pattern of events, including the mental state of the angry person (Taylor 1995: 11).

This both explains how we can stereotypically or prototypically infer the existence of mental states in others analogous to our own, and points out the basis for and bias towards metonymic links in conceptualising anger, as the other parts of the script are metonyms of the anger inferred.

What kinds of relationship within domains might be the basis for metonymy, which is in turn the basis for metaphor? Traditionally, common metonymies have been identified such as CONTAINER FOR CONTENTS (e.g. "I drank two bottles of wine"), PLACE FOR INHABITANTS (e.g. "Paris is in an uproar"), PLACE FOR ACTIVITY (e.g. "I've been watching Wimbledon all afternoon"), CAUSE FOR EFFECT (e.g. "Henman, you are my sorrow"), PART FOR WHOLE ("Tickets cost $6 per head") and so on. How far to

extend the notion of metonymy remains a difficult question. And in seeking metonymic causes how far back does one go? Kövecses and Radden (1998) have given an
exhaustive list of metonymical relationships. They extend the notion of metonymy to
the relationship between form and meaning: FORM FOR CONCEPT (p. 42). This means
the symbolic representation has a metonymic link with the concept, for example a
word form with its meaning. But this kind of metonymy would automatically come
into play with any conventional metaphorical lexical item. And the continued use of
that item metaphorically would then depend upon a metonymy. However, we surely
have to go back beyond this kind of metonymy if we are going to use it as an explanation for conceptual metaphor themes. There is a problem of directionality in this
move. For example, do we think in terms of POWER/STATUS IS UP because we see people of status/power in higher physical positions, or because being high allows us to
have gravity working on our side? The symbolic expression of the conceptual metaphor theme which puts powerful people in more elevated positions could be seen as
a FORM FOR CONCEPT metonymy, and it provides new metonymic motivation for the
metaphor reproducing it. Moreover, this motivation is probably more important than
any original metonymic motivation. But this amounts to no more than saying that
symbolic systems, including language, reproduce their meanings.

Because I believe the metonymies which involve form-meaning relationships
draw the boundaries of metonymy too widely and thereby confuse the theory, I set
these aside and list the remainder that Kövecses and Radden have identified in Table
22. For the purposes of our analysis not all these metonymies seem to be equally useful
as explanations for origins of metaphor themes. The importance of some will become
apparent in the course of the chapter. However, it is worth illustrating those more obviously important in Metalude.

Table 22a. Metonymic categories: part to whole ICMs (after Kovecses and Radden 1998)

WHOLE ICM AND ITS PARTS	
WHOLE THING FOR PART OF A THING	PART OF A THING FOR A WHOLE THING
MORE SPECIFICALLY	
CONSTITUTION ICM	
OBJECT FOR MATERIAL CONSTITUTING THE OBJECT	
MATERIAL CONSTITUTING THE OBJECT FOR THE OBJECT	
COMPLEX EVENT ICM	**CATEGORY AND MEMBER ICM**
SUCCESSIVE SUBEVENTS FOR COMPLEX EVENT	CATEGORY FOR MEMBER OF A CATEGORY
CO-PRESENT SUB-EVENTS FOR COMPLEX EVENTS	*MEMBER OF A CATEGORY FOR THE CATEGORY

Table 22b. Metonymic categories: parts of an ICM (after Kovecses and Radden 1998)

ACTION ICM

INSTRUMENT FOR ACTION	RESULT FOR ACTION
AGENT FOR ACTION	ACTION FOR RESULT
ACTION FOR AGENT	MEANS FOR ACTION
OBJECT INVOLVED IN THE ACTION FOR THE AC-TION	MANNER OF ACTION FOR ACTION
	*TIME PERIOD OF ACTION FOR ACTION
ACTION FOR OBJECT INVOLVED IN THE ACTION	DESTINATION FOR MOTION
*LOCATION OF ACTION FOR ACTION	TIME OF MOTION FOR ENTITY INOLVED IN MOTION

PERCEPTION ICM

PERCEPTION FOR THING PERCEIVED	THING PERCEIVED FOR THE PERCEPTION

CAUSATION ICM

STATE/EVENT FOR THE ENTITY THAT CAUSED IT

MORE SPECIFICALLY

*EMOTION FOR CAUSE OF EMOTION	*PHYSIOLOGICAL/BEHAVIOURAL EFFECT FOR EMOTION
MENTAL STATE FOR OBJECT/PERSON CAUSING IT	SOUND CAUSED FOR THE EVENT THAT CAUSED IT

PRODUCTION ICM

PRODUCER FOR PRODUCT

MORE SPECIFICALLY

AUTHOR FOR WORK	PLACE FOR PRODUCT MADE THERE

CONTROL ICM

CONTROLLER FOR CONTROLLED	OBJECT FOR USER OF THE OBJECT
CONTROLLED FOR CONTROLLER	

POSSESSION ICM

POSSESSOR FOR POSSESSED	POSSESSED FOR POSSESSOR

CONTAINMENT ICM

CONTAINER FOR CONTAINED

First a point about notation. From now on, in order to use the same order for Target and Source in metonymy and metaphor theme labelling, I shall use the formula TAR-GET AS SOURCE. So Kövecses and Radden's WHOLE THING FOR PART OF THING becomes in my notation PART OF THING AS WHOLE THING, short for "conceptualising part of a thing as a whole thing". In Table 22 the relevant metonymies which are discussed here are asterisked.

A glance at the Metalude "Map of Root Analogies" will show the importance of CATEGORY AS MEMBER OF A CATEGORY. We have a superordinate metaphor class ACTIV-ITY IS SPECIFIC ACTIVITY in which we include ACTIVITY IS GAME, ACTIVITY IS SAILING, ACTIVITY IS COMPETITION, ACTIVITY IS PERFORMANCE, etc. etc. There are other more local metonymically-based metaphor themes in Metalude. ACTIVITY IS PLACE (ACTION AS LOCATION FOR ACTION) is based on the fact that to perform a particular action we often have to be in a particular place, e.g. in a squash court to play squash. Already in 2.7. we have encountered some of the confusion brought about by ACTION AS TIME PERIOD OF ACTION. As for this chapter, we will be particularly interested in EMOTION AS CAUSE OF EMOTION, and EMOTION AS PHYSIOLOGICAL/BEHAVIOURAL EFFECT.

It may be possible to integrate this cognitive approach to the more linguistic distinction between metaphor and metonymy given by Roman Jakobson (1990). He defined metaphor as substitution on the paradigmatic axis of the language system, and metonymy as a matter of deletion on the syntagmatic axis of the message or text. Since the items on the syntagmatic axis are in grammatical relations with each other, we could generalise these relationships to semantic relationships between grammatical categories, such as EXPERIENCE (OBJECT) AS LOCATION CIRCUMSTANCE (ADVERBIAL): "I've been watching Wimbledon all afternoon". In other words, since metonyms depend upon contiguity in experience, and since the literal referent and the metonymic referent are part of the same ICM, one would expect this contiguity to be reflected in textual contiguity such as collocation and colligation. This approach also accounts for the fact that word-formation processes, especially compounds which count as a shorthand for a longer phrase (e.g. *washing machine* 'machine for washing clothes'), are identified by Kövecses and Radden as manifestations of metonymy.

The point of concentrating on metonymy as a possible basis for metaphors is to highlight the experiential basis of metaphor themes, especially conceptual metaphor themes. Grady (1997), for example, in the appendix to his Ph. D dissertation, makes a list of primary metaphor themes, and stresses their experiential basis. The experiential basis can be seen as a regular co-occurrence and a resulting correlation (or what in my definition of metaphor I call "analogy"). For example he explains the basis of the primary metaphor theme MORE IS HIGH (QUANTITY IS ELEVATION) as the experience of a pile, or objects/fluids in a container. Many of the experiential bases he cites seem convincing, but others are quite doubtful; he suggests that AFFECTION IS MOISTURE (a sub-category of my EMOTION IS LIQUID) is based on "the correlation between sympathetic relations and physical proximity, leading to contact with tears, sweat, saliva, etc.?", which he rightly ends with a question mark.

Barcelona states clearly the claim we are testing in this chapter.

> As Kövecses demonstrated long ago (1986) most metaphors for emotions are, to a very large extent, based on metonymies, which encapsulate the conventional beliefs (folk models) about the effects – physiological or behavioural – of emotions on people (people are believed to go red if they are angry, walk erect if they are proud etc.). These metonymies provide an array of inherent dynamic image-schematic structures for the target domains of emotions. A large part of their inherent image-schematic structure seems to have been built on the basis of EMOTION-DRIVEN BEHAVIOUR/PHYSIOLOGY and other experientially accessible and contiguous (sub) domains (Barcelona 2000c: 47).

What makes emotions especially involved with metonymy is that people are most concerned with their causes and effects, and their physiological effects are fairly consistent (Radden 2000: 104).

Wierzbicka, too, with her remarkable and extensive studies in anthropological semantics, identifies three kinds of universals in the language of feelings/emotions, relevant to the study of emotion metonymies and metaphors:

1. In all languages, people can describe cognitively-based feelings via observable "bodily symptoms" (that is, via some bodily events regarded as characteristic of these feelings).
2. In all languages, cognitively-based feelings can be described with reference to bodily sensations.
3. In all languages, cognitively based feelings can be described via figurative "bodily images" (Wierzbicka, 1999: 276).

Under 1, it is important to note that the metonymy EMOTION AS PHYSIOLOGICAL/ BEHAVIOURAL EFFECT may be learned and culturally-specific rather than universal (Kövecses 2000a: 171). In Chinese, the bodily-perceived symptoms of anger are different from English: *la chiang lian,* (lit. "pull long face"), *la xia lian,* are both used to describe becoming angry (Chun 1997: 3–4).

Under 2, it is debatable whether the emotion and the bodily sensation is caused by the emotion or simply concurrent with it – Damasio says it is not only concurrent but also part of the emotion (WHOLE OF A THING AS PART OF A THING). In any case there will be a metonymic relationship. However, note here, again, that there is a great deal of cultural relativity in the way bodily sensations are matched with emotions. In Russian one can say "it cuts one's breath from ecstasy" but in Tajik a similar sensation is linked not with ecstasy but with fright "his breathing stopped from fright". Conversely, similar emotions may be associated with different bodily experiences: in Russian one's eyes "flash from anger", in Kuria they can "shake from anger" (Wierzbicka 1999: 297).

Strictly speaking, 3 is not so relevant to our introduction to metonymy, since the examples are counterfactual and therefore similes or metaphors: the speaker does not actually believe, for example, that their heart is broken, when they say "she broke my heart", or that her blood is boiling when they say "I was boiling with rage" (p. 297). However, historically, it may be difficult to know whether a speaker from an earlier period actually believed what was said, in which case it is metonymy or even literal language, or did not believe it, in which case we have metaphor.

The first part of this chapter examines emotion metaphors that might be based on universal metonymy-based experiences, explores one psycho-physiological theory of the emotions and gives scientific evidence to prove experiential connections.

6.3   EMOTION IS SENSE IMPRESSION

A glance at Metalude shows that one of the overarching metaphor themes for emotion is EMOTION/IDEA IS SENSE IMPRESSION. Various sub-themes are contained under this general theme as in Figure 6.

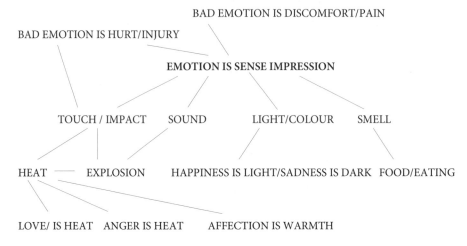

Figure 6. Sub-themes for EMOTION IS SENSE IMPRESSION

6.3.1   Damasio's theory of the emotions

The main theory of emotion and feeling under consideration is Antonio Damasio's in *Looking for Spinoza: Joy, Sorrow and the Feeling of the Brain* (2003). This provides some explanation for these emotion metaphors and explicit support for conceptual metaphor theory and the experiential hypothesis which regards cognition as embodied. Damasio's theory is, however, just one of a number of expert theories that have emerged in the 20th century as summarised by Kövecses (2000a: 131–33).

> Emotion as physical agitation or bodily disturbance (Young 1943).
> Emotion as a kind of force or drive that impels the person to respond (Plutchik 1980).
> Emotions as subjective physical sensations (Schachter 1971).

The first and second of these correspond to the metaphor theme we already looked at in Chapter 5: EMOTION IS MOVEMENT. The first and the third relate to the idea of bodily homeostasis, as we shall see in Damasio, and the third, clearly plugs in nicely to EMOTION IS SENSE IMPRESSION. One question we might bear in mind is whether these theories are driven by the conceptual/linguistic metaphors or whether they are models as close to the literal truth as science at present allows us to come. If the latter, our conceptual metaphor themes targeting emotion have a firm metonymical basis.

We can summarise Damasio's book as follows: he begins with the definition of emotions, which are, for him, the physiological reactions to bodily states and the disturbances to them; proceeds to a discussion of feelings, which are conceptualisations or perceptions of these emotions; and finally suggests the basis of all thought and even religious belief and experience is in embodied emotion/feeling.

6.3.1.1 *What triggers an emotion?*

Emotions are set off by what Damasio calls an ECS, an emotionally competent stimulus, the object or event whose presence, actual or in mental recall, triggers the emotion. For example, the taste or smell of bad food or bodily waste induces the emotional response of disgust. Emotion-triggering sites in the brain are activated by an ECS, as though the ECS is a key which fits the lock on the emotion-triggering device, or the emotion-triggering device selects the ECS. Interestingly, Damasio likens the ECS to a virus:

> These descriptions sound a lot like that of an antigen (e.g. a virus) entering the bloodstream and leading to an immune response (consisting of a large number of antibodies capable of neutralising the antigen). And well they should because the processes are formally similar. In the case of emotion the "antigen" is presented through the sensory system and the "antibody" is the emotional response. The "selection" is made at one of several brain sites equipped to trigger an emotion (Damasio 2003: 58).

This reminds one of the theme (IDEA)/EMOTION IS DISEASE. Is this conceptualisation of an ECS driven or reinforced by the metaphor theme? Or does the metaphor theme reflect some kind of basic reality?

Also germane to our larger discussion of the interplay between the universal body and culture is Damasio's contention that the ECS may be innate or may be learned:

> The brain is prepared by evolution to respond to certain ECS's with specific repertoires of action. However, the list of ECS's is not confined to those prescribed by evolution. It includes many others learned in a lifetime of experience (p. 3).

The biologically-determined and the socially-learned emotions may be related, the second developing from the first: "think how the social emotion 'contempt' borrows the facial expression of 'disgust', a primary emotion that evolved in association with the automatic and beneficial rejection of potentially toxic foods" (pp. 45–6) (cf. Kövecses 1990).

6.3.1.2 *What is an emotion?*

An emotion then is an automatic response to an ECS. "An emotion-proper, such as happiness, sadness, embarrassment, or sympathy, is a complex collection of chemical and neural responses forming a distinctive pattern" (p. 53). These emotional responses are constituted by internal or external movements and actions of the body. "Emotions are actions or movements, many of them public, visible to others as they occur in the face, in the voice, in specific behaviours", though some are not perceptible, e.g. hormonal changes and electrophysiological wave patterns (p. 28).

> In all emotions, multiple volleys of neural and chemical responses change the internal milieu, the viscera, and the musculo-skeletal system for a certain period and in a particular pattern. Facial expressions, vocalisations, body postures, and specific patterns of behaviour (running, freezing, courting, or parenting) are thus enacted. The body chemistries as well as viscera such as the heart and lungs help along. Emotion is all about transition and commotion, sometimes real bodily upheaval (p. 63).

This description of emotions, which relates to the expert theory 1 above, reflects the metaphor theme EMOTION IS MOVEMENT including mainly movements of the body, rather than changes of location, or motion. Change and specifically movement is the essence of emotion, according to this description (though Damasio may be using movement as a metaphor for change). It also reflects the shared grounds of changeability inherent in EMOTION IS WEATHER, and EMOTION IS LIQUID (see 5.5.1).

As evidence for the connection between emotion and movement/action Damasio cites the case of a female patient being treated for Parkinson's disease (pp. 68ff). Because she had poor control of her movements, electrodes were inserted in her brain stem in a part known as the mesencephalon, one electrode on each side of the brain stem, with four contact points on each electrode. One contact in a position on the left side of the brain improved her condition greatly, but a contact two millimetres below induced emotions of great sadness and depression, so she cast her eyes down, leaned to the right and started to cry uncontrollably. Asked what was happening she said: "I'm falling down in my head, I no longer wish to live, to see anything, to hear anything, feel anything … I want to hide in a corner …"

The electrical current had not passed into the general motor control structures as intended, but had flowed instead into one of the brain stem nuclei that control particular types of action. Those actions, as an ensemble, produced the emotion sadness. This repertoire included movements of the facial musculature, movements of the mouth, pharynx, larynx, and diaphragm, which are necessary for crying and sobbing; and the varied actions that result in the production and elimination of tears.

What is the significance of this report for metaphor theory? It claims that emotions are certainly grounded in bodily experience because they are constituted by bodily reactions to brain stimuli. We note too that in order to avoid the painful emotions she experiences the woman desires to avoid all sense impressions, suggesting the association apparent in our overarching metaphor theme EMOTION IS SENSE/IMPRESSION: "I'm falling down in my head, I no longer wish to live, to see anything, to hear anything, feel anything … I want to hide in a corner … ". More specifically we see that various imaginary bodily experiences are felt as part of this emotion. These experiences, in this particular case, are associated with positions in space, explaining the origin of orientational sources for emotion themes such as HAPPY IS HIGH, SAD IS LOW. Evidently the electrode contact in this position activated structures in

> the right parietal lobe, a region involved in the mapping of the body state and particularly of the mapping of the body in space. This activation probably related to the patient's consistent report during stimulation of marked changes in her body state, including the sensation of falling through a hole (p. 73).

6.3.1.3 *What is the point of an emotion?*

Emotions are the responses to well-being, to threats to it, or to the absence of it. So the ultimate result of the emotional responses, directly or indirectly, is the placement of the organism in circumstances conducive to survival and well-being, whether this is inner regulation of the body to maintain a state of homeostasis, or the well-being of the person in their physical and social environment (p. 53).

> From chemical homeostatic processes to emotions proper, life regulation phenomena, without exception, have to do … with the integrity and health of the organism. Without exception, all of these phenomena are related to adaptive adjustments in the body-state and eventually lead to the changes in the brain mapping of the body-states, which form the basis for feelings (p. 49).

When the body is functioning efficiently or even optimally, both internally and in its environment, in a free-flowing and easy way, this is the basis for the feeling of happiness and pleasure, but when the body is struggling to maintain a balance of the life processes this is the basis of the negative feelings of sadness or pain (p. 131). So, the satisfaction of drives – for example, hunger, thirst and sex – causes happiness; but thwarting the satisfaction of those drives can cause anger or despair or sadness (p. 50).

6.3.1.4 *How are emotions different from feelings?*

In compiling my list of metaphor themes in Metalude, I did not make the fine or technical distinction that Damasio does between emotion and feeling, so that his description and theory of feelings and how they arise can also be applied to my diverse metaphor themes for emotion.

Emotional responses are often observable, in that they are physiological. "Feelings, on the other hand, are always hidden, like all mental images necessarily are, unseen to anyone other than their rightful owner, the most private property of the organism in whose brain they occur" (p. 28). Feelings have a conscious element for their owners, a perceptual and cognitive element "the idea of the body being in a certain way", whether this awareness is of emotional responses or other homeostatic reactions (p. 85).

Most interesting for experiential theories of emotion metaphor is Damasio's contention that feelings are perceptions of varied bodily states and changes:

As I see it, the origin of the perceptions that constitute the essence of feeling is clear. There is a general object, the body, and there are many parts to that object that are continuously mapped in a number of brain structures. The contents of those perceptions are also clear: varied body states portrayed by the body-representing maps along a range of possibilities.

As examples of these body states Damasio cites tensed muscles and relaxed muscles, the beating of the heart fast or slow, the respiratory and digestive processes and the composition of chemical molecules in the blood.

The particular state of those body components, as portrayed in the brain's body maps, is a content of the perceptions that constitute feelings. The immediate substrates of feelings are the mappings of myriad aspects of body states in the sensory regions designed to receive signals from the body (p. 87).

Feeling is a perception of these body states, rather like sense perceptions, and like them depends both on the object of perception and the brain's interpretation of this object. The difference is that "in the case of feelings, the objects and events at the origin are well inside the body rather than outside it. Feelings may be just as mental as any other perceptions, but the objects being mapped are parts and states of the living organism in which feelings arise" (p. 91).

Damasio has substantial evidence for this theory that feelings amount to the perceptions of bodily states. "When feelings occur there is a significant engagement of the areas of the brain that receive signals from varied parts of the body and thus map the ongoing state of the organism." Experimental subjects were asked to re-enact an emotion by imagining an experience that produced it, and brain activity was monitored.

All the body-sensing areas under scrutiny – the cingulated cortex, the somatosensory cortices of insula and SII, the nuclei in the brain stem tegmentum – showed a statistically significant pattern of activation or deactivation. This indicated that the mapping of body states had been significantly modified during the process of feeling (pp. 97ff).

When subjects, with electrodes attached to them to measure skin conductivity variation, were asked to give a signal that they were experiencing a certain feeling, these changes always preceded the signal. This indicates that emotional states and responses come first and feelings after.

Besides experimental evidence for the idea that feeling is a perception of emotional response, there is physiological evidence from the structure of the brain. The peripheral nerve fibres and neural pathways which convey information from the body's interior to the brain terminate in their own dedicated region, the insular cortex, the identical region whose activity patterns are disturbed by feelings of emotions.

The very same region that both theoretical proposals and functional imaging studies relate to feelings turns out to be the recipient of the class of signals most likely to represent the content of feelings: signals related to pain states; body temperature; flush; **itch**; tickle; **shudder**; **visceral** and genital sensations; the state of the smooth musculature in blood vessels and other viscera; local Ph; glucose; osmolality; presence of **inflammatory** agents; and so forth (pp. 106ff.) [my bolding].

(Notice, incidentally, how what might have been regarded as lexis for the metaphor theme for emotion, especially the bolded items here, are, according to Damasio's theory, literal emotional responses.) Similarly Ryan reports that the locus coeruleus in the upper mid-brain is involved in registering complex sensations and emotions, an area which is linked to "such visceral functions as adrenaline release, heartbeat, skin pallor, and sweating – in fact the physical symptoms we associate with powerful emotion" (Ryan 2002: 253).

Ekman provides more remarkable evidence that bodily responses (Damasio's emotions) create feelings when they are perceived or registered, and that the bodily activity or movement precedes feeling. He found that facial movements which "express" particular universal feelings, can actually create those feelings:

> I found that when I made certain expressions, I was flooded with strong emotional sensations [Damasio's "feelings"]. It wasn't just any expression, only the ones I had already identified as universal to all human beings … Simply making an expression would produce changes in people's autonomic nervous systems. Over the next ten years we did four experiments, including one in a non-Western culture, the Minangkabau of Western Sumatra. When people followed our instructions about which muscles to move, their physiology changed and most reported feeling the emotion [feeling] (Ekman 2000: 36).

We should note that feelings are not necessarily the perceptions of real or genuine bodily sensations, but potentially of false, filtered or imaginary states too (Damasio 2003: 117). This, probably, is one of the distinctive human characteristics, the ability to respond with feeling to works of fiction and the imagination, and leaves open the door for the cultural products of the human brain to act as ECSs and form the basis of emotional response and feeling.

6.3.1.5 *What is the relation between feeling and thought?*
Damasio also makes a controversial link between feelings and thoughts. Feeling encompasses

> the body states that are the essence of the feeling and give it a distinctive content, the altered mode of thinking that accompanies the perception of that altered body state; and the sort of thoughts that agree, in terms of theme, with the kind of emotion being felt … the mind also represents "well-thinking" as well as well-being (p. 89).

He uses the kind of linguistic data that we are interested in to give evidence for this link between feelings and thoughts/decisions.

> The hunches that steer our behaviour in the proper direction are often referred to as the gut or the heart – as in "I know in my heart that this is the right thing to do". The Portuguese word for hunch, by the way, is *palpite*, a close neighbour of "palpitation" 'a skipped heartbeat' (p. 150).

The suggestion here is that emotions are inherently rational, so that removing the mental presence of the body is like pulling the rug from under the mind (p. 192).

> I believe that the foundational images in the stream of mind are images of some kind of body event, whether the event happens in the depth of the body or in some specialised sensory device near its periphery. The basis for those foundational images is a collection of brain maps, that is, a collection of patterns of neuron activity and inactivity in a variety of sensory regions. Those brain maps represent, comprehensively, the structure and the state of the body at any given time. Some maps relate to the world within, the organism's interior. Other maps relate to the world outside, the physical world of objects that interact with the organism at specific regions of its shell. In either case what ends up being mapped in the sensory regions of the brain and what emerges in the mind, in the form of an idea, corresponds to some structure of the body, in a particular state and set of circumstances (p. 197).

It should be obvious why I have quoted Damasio at such great length. The last paragraph indicates that he sees bodily experience as the foundation for thinking, which gives support to the general experiential hypothesis. More particularly, of course, he shows that feeling arises from perceptions of body states and changes to body states, whether internal or external. This "fact" then becomes the metonymic, if not literal, basis of the theme EMOTION IS SENSE/IMPRESSION, with all its sub-themes (see Figure 6).

We can diagram Damasio's theory as follows:

ECS → EMOTION/BODILY RESPONSE → FEELING

In the next sections we will use this diagram to systematically consider the various kinds of metonymical relationships that determine important metaphor themes for feelings. Let's begin with the cause-effect relationship between the ECS and the emotion/bodily response.

6.3.2 EMOTION AS CAUSE OF EMOTION metonymy

Presumably the ECS is the cause of the emotional bodily response, so that the ECS might provide the source for any metaphor themes which have the formula EMOTION IS CAUSE OF THAT EMOTION. Kövecses, for example, suggested the metaphor themes HAPPINESS IS PLEASURABLE PHYSICAL SENSATION and SHAME IS HAVING NO CLOTHES ON (Kövecses 2000a: 40, 134). One likely candidate for a CAUSE OF EMOTION AS EMOTION metonymy comes from the phenomenon of colours creating certain moods. This could be the basis for the metaphor theme EMOTION IS COLOUR. Research on colour has given us the findings in Table 23.

Table 23. The moods created by colour (from Burgoon & Saine 1978)

Colour	Moods
Red	Hot, affectionate, angry, defiant, contrary, hostile, full of vitality, excitement, love
Blue	Cool, pleasant, leisurely, distant, infinite, secure, transcendent, calm, tender
Yellow	Unpleasant, exciting, hostile, cheerful, joyful, jovial
Orange	Unpleasant, exciting, disturbed, distressed, upset, defiant, contrary, hostile, stimulating
Purple	Depressed, sad, dignified, stately
Green	Cool, pleasant, leisurely, in control
Black	Sad, intense, anxiety, fear, despondent, dejected, melancholy, unhappy
Brown	Sad, not tender, despondent, dejected, melancholy, unhappy, neutral
White	Joy, lightness, neutral, cold

We have already explored one sub-theme of EMOTION IS LIGHT/COLOUR in chapter 2, namely, EXCITEMENT IS LIGHT/COLOUR, which might relate to the fact that in the research reported white gives the mood values neutral and cold. But let's have a look at the details of the more general metaphor theme here, restricting ourselves to colour.

6.3.2.1 Colours as metonymic sources for emotion targets
General colour words can apply to emotions in general: **spectrum** 'range (of opinions/feelings)', **tinge** 'slight amount of an emotion or idea' (*there was a tinge of sadness in his greeting*). Emotions which decrease **fade** 'become less intense or strong' (*sympathy for the refugees is beginning to fade*), whereas descriptions that involve too many disturbing details are like colours that are too bright – **lurid*** 'shocking because of sex, violence or immorality' (*newspapers contained lurid accounts of the murders*).

Going through the colour spectrum we can start with red, which seems to be associated with strong uncontrollable emotion especially anger: **see red** 'become very angry' (*she saw red when she caught him stealing*), **a red rag to a bull*** 'something certain to produce a violent and angry reaction' (*arguing for nationalisation is like a red rag to a bull to him*), **ruddy*** literally 'reddish', a weaker form of the swear word 'bloody', indicating annoyance rather than anger (*when are they going to fix this ruddy light?*); though red can also apply to strong-sexual feelings **red-blooded** (*he was a red-blooded male teenager*). Pinkish colours tend to represent optimism and positive emotions **rosy** 'hopeful' (*the economic situation is quite rosy at the moment*), **rose-tinted/-coloured glasses** or **spectacles*** 'tendency to see things optimistically' (*my uncle thought I could get into Oxford, but he always looks at me through rose-tinted glasses*), while **tickled pink** means 'very pleased', (*when she praised his leadership he was tickled pink*). Yellow is rather negative: **yellow** 'nervous to the extent of being cowardly' (*go on jump – don't be so yellow*) and **jaundiced** (from the French *jaune*) 'pessimistic, unfairly critical' (*she had a jaundiced view of psychiatrists*). **Green with envy** means 'extremely envious', **blue** 'sad' (*he's been very blue since failing his exams*) and **purple*** 'shocking or offensive' (of writing) (*the novella 'The Lover' is full of purple prose*). Not on the spectrum at all we have **brown study** 'very serious mood' and **black humour/comedy*** 'comedy that involves frightening or unpleasant things' (*black humour is used as a defence against the horrors of the war*). Note that with the asterisked items above, strictly speaking we do not have EMOTION AS CAUSE OF EMOTION, because it is the cause of the emotion, the ECS, to which the word applies, not the emotion itself.

It is interesting to look for any correspondences with Burgoon and Saine's findings in Table 23, and what they might tell us about metaphor theory. For red 'angry' and 'full of vitality' seem to correspond to the metaphorical meanings; for yellow 'unpleasant' corresponds to some extent; for black 'anxiety', 'fear'; and for brown 'melancholy'. The moods evoked by blue, purple and green apparently correspond to none of the metaphorical meanings, indeed sometimes contradict them, as with purple 'dignified' and blue 'pleasant'. The moods for white and black do seem to correspond quite strongly to another pair of metaphor themes: HAPPINESS/HOPE IS LIGHT and SADNESS/PESSIMISM is dark – of which more later.

Given the extensive and varied moods created by each of the colours in Table 23, the degree of correspondence is quite low. This suggests that, though the general metaphor theme EMOTION IS COLOUR could be motivated by the metonymy of EFFECT-AS-CAUSE, the semantics of the lexical items are quite unpredictable and result from the vagaries of culture and lexicalisation processes, rather than from universals. Alternatively, although only a few of the lexical meanings seem to be motivated by this particular EFFECT-AS-CAUSE metonymy, there may be other particular or different metonymical explanations for the lexis. For example, red for the emotion of anger might be motivated by the emotional response of going red in the face, more exactly, in Damasio's terms, COMPLEX EVENTS AS CO-PRESENT SUB-EVENTS; or, in traditional commonsense terms, which sees redness in the face as the result of anger rather than constituting anger, the EMOTION AS PHYSIOLOGICAL/BEHAVIOURAL EFFECT. It has even been suggested that the blue colour of a decaying corpse of a plague victim, which induces negative feelings, could be the EMOTION AS CAUSE OF EMOTION metonymy behind the "depression" meaning of *blue*, cited in the Shorter Oxford English Dictionary as "the colour of plagues and all things hurtful" (Ling 2003: 25).

6.3.2.2 *Light as metonymic source for emotion target*
Much more likely as a plausible EMOTION AS CAUSE OF EMOTION metonymy are the pair of metaphor themes HAPPINESS/HOPE IS LIGHT and SADNESS/PESSIMISM IS DARK. Evidence comes from the phenomenon of Seasonal Affective Disorder, abbreviated, appropriately enough, as SAD. Although this disorder affects people in other seasons, it is largely associated with winter depression. A study in Alaska reported around 9% of those screened as suffering to some extent from SAD. 20% of patients treated for recurrent depression at a northern Canadian mental health centre seemed to be suffering from winter depression. A large-scale longitudinal study of young adults in Zu-

rich found that 10.4% had SAD, defined as at least two consecutive years of seasonal depression in the three-year study period.

The brain measures the length of each day and regulates accordingly the secretion of specific brain hormones that affect mood and behaviour. In winter less serotonin and more melatonin are secreted, which brings on depression, and towards early spring, more serotonin is produced and less melatonin, alleviating the sense of depression brought on by the latter hormone (Rifkin 1987: 42–53). This explanation is not a total explanation of SAD, but, since SAD patients have consistently different behavioural responses to the serotonergic agent, m-CPP, it suggests that serotonin dysregulation may be partly responsible. Whatever the doubts about the causes, light therapy seems to have a beneficial effect. In two studies 60% of the depressed patients responded positively to light therapy, and in another study which involved simulating a summer dawn during the winter, there were significant improvements (http://www.mentalhealth.com/book/p40-sad.html 2003).

The effect of the different degrees of light on mood, at different seasons and in different weathers, does provide a causal metonymic motivation for the metaphor themes SADNESS/PESSIMISM IS DARKNESS, HAPPINESS/HOPE IS LIGHT and EMOTION IS WEATHER. The ECS becomes the source for the metaphor theme.

We have already given evidence for EMOTION IS WEATHER (chapter 5). However, the image of a cloud seems to unite EMOTION IS WEATHER with SADNESS/PESSIMISM IS DARK: **cloud** 'negative thoughts or emotions' (*when he took his life he was suffering under a cloud of despair about his future*), **cloud (over)** 'show sadness, worry or anger' (*John's face clouded with despair*), **cast a cloud/shadow over** 'make less hopeful or optimistic' (*the rise in interest rates cast a cloud over the property market*), and, as in the last example, shadows are similar to clouds in their metaphorical meanings: **in the shadow of** 'being made unhappy by' (*he lived the rest of his life in the shadow of a second possible heart attack*), **overshadow** 'cause to seem or be less happy' (*news of his father's death overshadowed his winning the gold*).

Generally the concept of darkness is a source for sadness or lack of hope: **dark** 'sad or desperate' (*redundancy was a dark experience in my life*), **darken** 'make unhappy' (*the mood was darkened by news of their grandfather's death*), **darkest hour** 'worst or most unhappy period' (*my darkest hour was when my wife attempted suicide*), **black** 'very miserable and depressed' (*his mood was even blacker than the day before*), **gloomy/ gloom** 'unhappy and without hope/unhappiness and pessimism' (*I'm gloomy about the future of poetry in this coming century*), **dim** 'hopeless', (*his chances of getting into university are rather dim*). Vocabulary used for dull colours can also be used for moderate unhappiness or for lack of humour and enthusiasm: **subdued** 'not as happy as usual', (*subdued, he sat in the corner of the room*), **sombre** 'without humour or amusement' (*the sombre mothers are waiting for the bodies of their drowned children*), **muted** 'not enthusiastic' (*his plan received a muted response*), and **lacklustre** 'lacking enthusiasm or liveliness' (*the tenor gave a lacklustre performance*). Hopeful expectations are lights during darkness, whether **a false dawn** 'signs of hope for improvement which are deceptive' (*he went through rehab and we thought he'd lost his addiction, but it was a false dawn*), or **light at the end of the tunnel** 'hopes of a pleasant future situation in an unpleasant one' (*sometimes he doubted there was any light at the end of the tunnel and despaired*).

So, conversely, HAPPINESS/HOPE IS LIGHT. **Bright** means 'full of hope or happiness' (*with these exam results you have very bright prospects*), **brightly** 'happily, optimistically' (*Senegal began brightly by beating France 1–0*), **on the bright side** 'considering the positive aspects' (*let's try and look on the bright side – one of the twins survived*), and **radiance** (**radiant**) '(with) joy showing in the face' (*the bride looked radiant as she kissed the bridegroom*). The source can be an association with heavenly bodies which emit light: **starry-eyed** 'unrealistically optimistic or idealistic' (*these starry-eyed students have never done a hard day's work in their lives*), or **sunny** 'cheerful and happy' (*the Disneyland staff are supposed to wear big sunny smiles*), or **ray of sunshine** 'very happy person or person that gives happiness to others' (*John is a ray of sunshine in our office*). **Ray** and **glimmer** mean 'small amount of positive emotion' (*these results are a ray/glimmer of hope in a gloomy situation*). If people's moods become happier they **brighten** 'become more pleasant, happy or optimistic' (*their spirits brightened when they saw the lights of a farmhouse in the distance*), **lighten** 'become happier and less anxious' (*on Friday afternoon the atmosphere in the office lightened*). When faces and eyes express happiness they **light up** 'suddenly look surprised or happy' (*when I mentioned food his eyes lit up with pleasure*), **shine** 'express happiness' (*his face shone with joy*) or **glow** 'look attractive with happiness and health' (*the schoolchildren's faces were glowing with excitement*).

6.3.2.3   *Metonymic sources for the disgust target*

It is interesting to look at a number of emotion triggers or ECSs for disgust as potential sources for metaphorical themes, or as related to them in some way. Ekman identifies the most potent triggers of disgust, the bodily products – mucus, faeces, vomit, urine and blood (Ekman 2000: 174). It is obvious enough that urine and faeces are used as sources of the metaphorical theme EVIL/WORTHLESSNESS IS WASTE; faeces metaphorise disgust and contempt for something because of its low quality: **shit, turd** 'contemptible, nasty person' (*he's a real shit*), **shitty** 'nasty, of low quality' (*that magazine is shit*), **shit on** 'treat very badly and unkindly' (*if he goes on shitting on me I'm going to quit the job*), **pooh-pooh** 'show scorn for something' (*he pooh-poohed my attempts to play the piano*). They are also associated with disgust for immorality: **mucky** 'pornographic' (*there are so many mucky TV shows after 11p.m*), **cesspit** or **cesspool** 'unpleasant or immoral situation' (*illegal immigrants often get stuck in a cesspit of prostitution and other illegal activities*). Waste may also be associated with contempt for nonsense and uselessness: **crap** 'something useless, worthless, nonsensical or bad quality' (*my financial advisor gave me all that crap about buying when stocks are low*), **horseshit** and **bullshit** 'nonsense' (*don't give me any of this horseshit about GM crops being essential to prevent starvation in Africa*), **bumf** (literally 'toilet paper') 'written material such as advertisements, or documents that are unwanted or boring' (*I get so much junk mail* *through the post – I don't need all that bumf*). The same sense of pointlessness or insignificance can be conveyed by urine: **piss around** 'waste time doing things without any particular purpose or plan' (*if you'll stop pissing around we can begin the task*), **piddling** 'insignificant' (*$5 is a piddling amount*).

Interestingly enough, Ekman points out that these sources of disgust, bodily fluids and wastes, are not so disgusting when they are part of our own bodies: people will swallow their own saliva or even own phlegm, but not if you first ask them to spit it into a glass of water. Similarly we do not feel disgust about exchanging bodily fluids with lovers, or even changing nappies/diapers or clearing up the vomit of babies for whom we have affection (Ekman 2000: 177). I would suggest that somehow the principle behind RELATIONSHIP IS PROXIMITY/COHESION is overriding the natural disgust normally triggered by these ECSs, so that when they are internal to us or associated with people who are either literally or metaphorically close to us, the disgust disappears.

Disgust is, for obvious evolutionary reasons to do with the avoidance of poisoning, associated with the offensive smells that warn us against eating bad food. Metalude suggests that EXPERIENCE IS EATING or EXPERIENCE IS FOOD (both very prolific themes), and therefore it is not surprising that BAD IS SMELLY. "Tastes and smells may be among the most natural source of concepts for good and bad, because they are among the simplest and most prototypical examples of stimuli that we have evaluative reactions to" (Grady 1997: 88): **odour** 'sign of some thing bad or of wrongdoing' (*the odour of corruption hung about everything*), **stench** 'atmosphere connected with bad behaviour' (*the stench of scandal surrounded the minister*), **stink** and **stinking** '(be) extremely bad or unpleasant', (*I don't want your stinking job*), **reek** 'be the sign of something unpleasant or immoral' (*her promotion reeks of sexual favouritism*), **whiff** 'slight sign of something bad or harmful' (*the politician's speech had the whiff of hypocrisy and arrogance*), **putrid** 'causing moral offence by being unfair' (*it was a putrid joke to play on him*), **malodorous** 'morally offensive' (*he invents his own malodorous fantasies about cannibalism*), **rank** (literally 'having a strong unpleasant smell') 'complete or extreme' (of something bad) (*it was rank nepotism to make his son director*).

Ekman suggests an interesting experiment (that you can try at home, given the result of the 2004 US Presidential election) of thinking of some morally repugnant act or person and then of paying "attention to the feelings in your throat, the beginning of a light gagging. The sensations in your upper lip and nostrils are increased, as if the sensitivity to these parts of your face has been turned up so you feel them more" (Ekman 2000: 183). If this works for you, then it indicates the power of the metaphoric transfer of disgust triggers to morally repugnant acts.

6.3.2.4 *Facial expressions as metonyms and metaphors*

Ekman has done considerable research on the reading of facial expressions, and Wierzbicka claims that if these facial movements are analysed structurally along with a semantic analysis we can identify eight as minimal meaningful units:

1. Brow furrowed – eyebrows drawn together
2. Eyebrows raised
3. Eyes wide open
4. Corners of the mouth raised
5. Corners of the mouth lowered
6. Mouth open (while not speaking)
7. Lips pressed together
8. Nose wrinkled

She continues, underlining the intertwining of the metonymic (indexical) and metaphoric (iconic):

> Since the facial expressions … are presumed to be universal rather than culture-specific… it is reasonable to expect that their basis will turn out to be either iconic or indexical … rather than symbolic and conventional. For example, if we attribute to wide opened eyes the semantic component "I want to know more about it" it is clear how such a meaning could be gleaned, universally, from the gesture itself (with its implied message "I want to see more"), without the help of any local conventions. Similarly if we attribute to an open yet silent mouth the semantic component "I don't know what I can say", it is clear how this meaning could be "figured out", without the help of any local conventions.
>
> What I mean by "iconic" and "indexical" is that the basis for decoding lies either in similarity ("like") or in co-occurrence ("when"). For example the wrinkling of the nose (usually linked in the literature with "disgust") can convey that I feel "something bad" *like* a person *when* she has to smell something bad that she doesn't want to smell. The gesture … looks like a rather futile attempt to remove one's nose (or at least the bottom part of one's nose) from contact with something malodorous … (Wierzbicka 1999: 183–4).

6.3.3   Specific emotional/bodily responses

Having considered the cause-effect metonymy between ECS and emotion in which the metaphor theme formula is EMOTION IS ECS, or EMOTION IS CAUSE OF EMOTION we turn now to the middle part of the diagram.

ECS → <u>EMOTION/BODILY RESPONSE</u> → FEELING

How we interpret this depends on whether we accept Damasio's theory of emotion, in which bodily response constitutes the emotion, or the more traditional notion that the bodily response is caused by the emotion – anger causes you to feel hot. In either

Table 24.   An overview of physiological metonymies for basic emotions, based on Kovecses (2000a: 123-4, 134)

PHYSIOLOGICAL PHENOMENA	EXAMPLE	CORRESPONDING METAPHOR THEME
Change in body temperature	Drop in body temperature for FEAR	FEAR/UNPLEASANT EMOTION IS COLD
	Rise in body temperature for ANGER	ANGER IS HEAT
	Rise in body temperature for PASSION	LOVE/PASSION IS HEAT
Change in skin colour/ skin condition	Redness in face and neck area for ANGER	(EMOTION IS LIGHT/COLOUR)
Release of sweat, tears, saliva	Moist hands for FEAR, tears for SADNESS	EMOTION IS LIQUID?
Change of respiration and heart rate	Quickening of heartbeat for ANGER	(EMOTION/CHARACTER IS BODY-PART/ FLUID?)
Unnatural condition of stomach/bowels	Feeling nauseated for DISGUST, FEAR	? BAD IS SMELLY (BAD EMOTION IS DISCOMFORT/PAIN) (EXPERIENCE IS FOOD/ EATING)
Bodily tension/release of tension	Fists and teeth clenched for ANGER	ANTAGONISM/ANNOYANCE IS FRICTION
	Relaxation of body and lungs (sighing) for RELIEF	NERVOUSNESS IS TENSION
	Tension of muscles for ANXIETY	NERVOUSNESS IS TENSION
Specific kinds of physical movements	Slow shuffling movements for SADNESS	? SAD IS LOW
	Heavy walk, stomping for ANGER	(CONTROL IS PUSH/PUT DOWN??)
	Being startled for FEAR	(EMOTION IS MOVEMENT)
	Jumping up and down for JOY	HAPPY IS HIGH
	Touching, hugging, kissing for LOVE	RELATIONSHIP IS PROXIMITY/COHESION
	Grabbing for DESIRE	DESIRE IS ATTRACTION
	Approach for ENJOYMENT, PLEASURE	DESIRE IS ATTRACTION
	Approach for ANGER	ANTAGONISM/ANNOYANCE IS FRICTION
	Moving away for FEAR	(NO RELATIONSHIP IS DISTANCE/ SEPARATION)
	Slumping for SADNESS	SAD IS LOW
	Looking down for SADNESS	SAD IS LOW
	Looking with fixed gaze for WONDER	AWARENESS/INTEREST IS FIXING/ CAPTURE

case, we are considering the second element in the flowchart: the metonymic relationship, in traditional terms EVENT AS THE EFFECT OF THE EVENT, will be in Damasio's framework WHOLE AS PART, since one of the physiological responses that constitutes the emotion stands for all those physiological responses. Kövecses points out that the question whether the physiological phenomena are the effect or the cause of the emotion has never really been decided, maybe because the physiological responses are in fact the emotion.

In Table 24 I have modified a list first put forward by Kövecses (2000a: 123–4, 134), which illustrates the metonymy EMOTION AS PHYSIOLOGICAL/BEHAVIOURAL EF-FECT. (Kövecses adopts the traditional language-based folk view of emotion rather than the expert view (Kövecses 2000a: 130–31)). I have added more examples of physi-ological responses (Ekman 2000: 61, 103, 135; Ungerer 2000: 324) and indicated, in the third column, metaphor themes which correspond to the physiological responses. Those metaphor themes that have a doubtful metonymic relationship with the phsysi-ological response are accompanied by a question mark. Those that provide part of the metaphorical lexis for a more general theme are put in parentheses.

Many of the metaphor themes in the table are spelt out at length elsewhere in this book (see index of metaphor themes), but the first in the third column FEAR/UNPLEAS-ANT EMOTION IS COLD gives a very neat illustration of the effect of physiological re-sponse on metaphorical lexis: **cold feet, in a cold sweat, chilling/spine-chilling, make your blood freeze, make your blood run cold.**

6.3.3.1   Body heat metonymies as metaphoric basis

I do not have the space here to discuss or give evidence for all the suggestions made in Table 24 about correlations between physiological response and emotion/feeling, though, as we have seen, Damasio's theory gives us some general evidence. In the next sections I shall concentrate on the scientific evidence for the metonymies at the basis of LOVE/PASSION IS HEAT, AFFECTION IS WARMTH, and its related RELATIONSHIP IS PROXIMITY/COHESION. A discussion of ANGER IS HEAT will be postponed until a later section, where we will look at some of the literature on cultural modifications of "uni-versal metonymy-based metaphors".

The first complication to the metaphorical lexical patterns in Metalude is the ob-servation that a number of metaphors with HEAT as a source, though they prototypi-cally have ANGER or PASSION as targets, can have both as targets, as well as a number of other strong emotions, such as resentment, hatred, enthusiasm, or excitement. Hence, these metaphors have to be listed under a more general category EMOTION IS HEAT.[1] Among them we find those mentioning heat generally: **heatedly** 'with anger or very strong feelings' (*the question of privatisation was heatedly debated*), **in the heat of the moment** 'when angry and excited' (*he apologised for shouting at her in the heat of the moment*), **hot-blooded** 'very quick to express or feel emotions' (*he was a hot-blooded*

---

1.   Kövecses (2000a, 2002: 202-6) even suggests that heat as a source applies very generally beyond the field of emotions, indeed that few, if any sources are specific to emotions as targets.

boxer, but lacked skill and control), **white heat** 'very strong feelings' (*in the white heat of the moment we made regrettable comments*). Extreme heat, especially of water (combining with EMOTION IS LIQUID) gives us **scalding** 'expressing strong and fierce emotions' (*his scalding rejection of my novel upset me for months*), **boil over** 'have such strong uncontrollable feelings that you have to express them' (*many people are boiling over with rage at the support the US gives to Israel*) and **searing** 'emotional and powerful' (*his latest play is a searing story of love and desperation*).

Burning and fire are the typical manifestations of extreme heat: **fiery** 'showing very strong feeling' (*he made a fiery speech in support of Trade Unions*), **the fires of** 'the very strong emotions associated with' (*his speeches fuelled the fires of protest*), **flame** 'strong feelings' (*flames of passion surged through Paul's veins*), **burning** 'strong and persistent' emotions (*he had a burning desire to sail around the world*), which may be expressed as in **blaze** 'express a strong emotion' (*Pauline's eyes blazed with enthusiasm*), or unexpressed as in **smoulder** 'feel strong, unexpressed emotions'(*his eyes were full of smouldering passion*), or difficult to get rid of as in **inextinguishable** 'impossible to stop feeling' (*her inextinguishable love for her daughter will never disappear*). In this script for fire, causing or encouraging the emotion is lighting, fanning and fuelling it: **kindle** 'start an emotion or feeling' (*the book kindled his desire to visit India*), **rekindle** 'renew positive feelings or friendship' (*his poems and letters rekindled my love for him*), **fan** 'encourage or enhance an emotion' (*Powell's remarks fanned the flames of racial hatred*), **fuel** 'increase or create an emotion' (*positive discrimination fuelled resentment among poor whites*), **add fuel to** 'make more intense' (*his antifeminism added fuel to the anger of the opposition*), **stoke (up)** 'encourage an emotion to develop' (*politicians have been stoking up racial hatred*).

There is plenty of scientific evidence, at least from other mammals, of a metonymic basis for the conceptual metaphor theme LOVE/PASSION IS HEAT. Blumberg (2002) reports some of the research on rats:

> Male rats heat up during sex … As soon as the female was introduced into the male's cage, his body and brain temperatures began to increase. By the time the male ejaculated, his body temperature had risen more than 1 degree C … but his brain, though not necessarily his body, cooled down following ejaculation, only to heat up again when copulation resumed … Exercise could not account for all the thermal changes that accompany sex. Rather … rats exhibit massive constriction of the peripheral blood vessels in the head (and probably elsewhere) immediately on exposure to females, before physical contact is made and before the male's activity increases. Such constriction reduces the flow of the cool blood from the skin surface of the head and face to the brain, thereby causing a rise in brain temperature … The constriction of the rat's blood vessels during sex is probably a part of the general strategy to direct blood flow to the genitalia … Female rats also heat up during sex although they do not exhibit rapid brain cooling when the male ejaculates, nor do they sprawl or exhibit other signs of being overheated (Blumberg 2002: 163–165).

Interestingly enough, because we are imaginative, the emotional response can become detached from the actual act of sex, and by a process of classical Pavlovian conditioning we can heat up in anticipation of sex, much as we learn to salivate when we see candy (pp. 167–8). One might suggest that this facilitates the separation of the concept of passion/love from the act of sex. Metaphorically it makes it easier to use HEAT as metaphorical source for love as well as for sexual activity.

Besides the more general lexis given above, which applies heat to both love, anger, and to a lesser extent hatred and resentment, we have more particular heat metaphors referring to passion, LOVE /PASSION IS HEAT. Again we have heat in general **have the hots for** 'be sexually attracted to' (*as soon as I saw him I had the hots for him*), which by a transferred epithet gives us **hot stuff** 'exciting or sexually attractive' (*I think Maria is really hot stuff*). Fire is also found here in **smoulder** 'have a sexually passionate nature' (*Alan Rickman seems to smoulder intensely in this latest movie*), **aflame** 'sexually excited' (*her appearance in a swim suit set his desires aflame*) and similarly with another transferred epithet **old flame** 'former lover or sexual partner' (*he had several old flames from Loughton High School*). Hot liquids also figure as sources – **sizzling** 'exciting' (often sexually) (*she was a blonde girl with a sizzling figure*), **steamy** 'erotic or passionate' (*we saw a steamy film and then went back to Paul's flat*) as does hot climate – **torrid** 'showing strong (sexual) feelings' (*the movie ends with a torrid love scene*).

These heat metaphors for passion conceptualise the source of heat as largely internal to the experiencer. But heat may also be applied externally. Mammals tend to raise or maintain their body heat by huddling or cuddling together.

> Mammals are noteworthy for the degree to which their social interactions involve close body contact … Huddling among littermates is one of the earliest social experiences of altricial infants. Even more fundamental to all mammals is the close body contact that derives from the mammalian way of feeding young, that is the attachment of the infant either continuously (as in kangaroos) or intermittently, (as in humans) to a maternal nipple. Because suckling necessarily entails close physical proximity to the mother, the infant also receives heat from the mother's chest and abdomen (Blumberg 2002: 126).

Blumberg even sees the impulse to cry, at least in young rats, as a physiological response to lowered body temperature. When infant rats experience extreme cooling this decreases cardiac function and thickens the blood. Threatened with a heart attack, the pup experiences considerable emotional distress. But to counter this cooling the pup contracts its abdominal muscles while at the same time closing its larynx, which squeezes blood from its peripheral circulation system back towards the heart. This squeezing and closure of the larynx produces the rat's cry. So "the cry is simply an acoustic by-product of a physiological process that serves to maintain cardio-vascular function when times are bad" (pp. 124–125). This suggests a physiological basis for what is traditionally viewed as an expression of emotion or feeling, and perhaps that even human cries may, partially at least, originate in the need for warmth rather than for affection.

Certainly this primal experience of shared body heat with a mother gives a strong metonymic basis for the theme AFFECTION IS WARMTH. This theme is represented by **warm (warm to)** '(become) friendly and affection ate' (*they are a very warm family*), **warmth** 'affection', **warm-hearted** 'generous and affectionate' (*my mother-in-law is a kind, warm-hearted woman*). If people's affection becomes very strong they **get on like a house on fire** 'quickly become close friends' (*they only met by chance but they got on like a house on fire*). An increase in temperature which melts ice is a metaphor for increased friendliness as in **break the ice** 'create a friendly atmosphere amongst people who have never met before' (*I've devised a few games to break the ice at the beginning of the meeting*), **thaw** 'become friendlier' (*she was distant at first but soon her attitude began to thaw*), which is slightly more specific as a noun, **thaw** 'improvement and increasing friendliness between countries' (*there has been a marked thaw in US-Russian relations over the last 10 years*), and, perhaps, **melt** 'become less harsh in emotion' (*I only have to gaze into her eyes and she melts*).

Conversely, there is the theme UNFRIENDLY IS COLD: all the following, though with slight variations, indicate unfriendliness. On a descending temperature scale we have **cool** 'unfriendly but polite' (*she's been very cool to me since I criticised her hairstyle*), **chilly** 'unfriendly or unwelcoming' (*I was put off by their chilly politeness*), **cold** 'unfriendly or unkind' (*she looked hard into his cold eyes*), and **coldly** 'in an unfriendly or unemotional way' (*the children received their new step-father rather coldly*), along with the idioms **cold shoulder** 'intentional unfriendliness' (*he looked for support, but Smith gave him the cold shoulder*), and **cold fish** 'person who is unfriendly or negative in emotions' (*he was a cold fish – I never really got to know him*). More extreme cold gives us **icy** 'with a controlled lack of affection or friendliness' (*his reaction was icy*), **frigid** 'unfriendly or very formal' (*he gave me a frigid look*), **frost** 'hostile attitude which is polite on the surface' (*there was a certain frost in his attitude ever since I criticised him*) and **frosty** 'unfriendly' (*I suffered under his frosty stares*), **wintry** 'unfriendly or hostile (of expression)' (*she gave me a wintry smile and didn't return my greeting*), and **glacial** 'very unfriendly or hostile' (*the Queen's gaze was glacial*). There are also idioms which convey unfriendliness to the point of exclusion: **left out in the cold** 'excluded from an activity in an unfriendly way' (*I didn't get to know about the meeting, and felt left out in the cold*), **freeze out** 'ignore in an unfriendly way so as to exclude' (*the EU are trying to freeze Zimbabwe out by applying sanctions*).

Moreover, this analogy AFFECTION : UNFRIENDLINESS :: WARMTH : COLD is not just observed in English. "Jeffrey Alberts and Gyula Decsy of Indiana University examined two groups of languages that have not shared a common ancestor for many thousands of years: Indo-European … and Proto-Uralic. The same pattern emerged in all the languages they examined: 'warmth carries with it an affective connotation of closeness and, well, warmth'" (Blumberg 2002: 132).

Blumberg also points out the theme's reversal into PROXIMITY IS WARMTH.

Given the paramount importance of maternal contact for the provisioning of warmth to mammalian infants, it is not surprising that our language has come to reflect these early thermal needs. It seems likely that the infant's dependence on maternal warmth gave rise to the linguistic pattern in which *warm* typically denotes physical closeness and *cold* typically denotes physical distance (p.130).

As, for example, when playing games involving a hidden object the player looking for it may ask "Am I warm?" And in Hungarian when the finder is close to the hidden object the hiders may cry "Fire! Fire!" (Kövecses, personal communication)

6.3.3.2   *Metonymies of proximity as metaphoric basis*

We noted the possibility that sharing maternal warmth during breastfeeding might be the metonymic basis of this metaphor. This suggests that it shares a metonymic basis with RELATIONSHIP IS PROXIMITY/COHESION (for lexical details see 5.3.1, where we had a preliminary discussion of some of the experiential bases or effects for the theme). More scientifically, there is experimental evidence of the metonymy underlying the symbolism of proximity and cohesion, namely, people sit and stand closer to those they like (Argyle 1988: 173–4). Rosenfield found that female subjects who are seeking approval stood at 57 in., compared with 94 in. when attempting to avoid approval (Rosenfield 1966). A study by Mehrabiam (1968) discovered that sitting distance varied between 68 ½ in. for a person who was liked, to 110 in. for a person who was disliked. Willis (1966) showed that people stood at different distances in real life with the following order of closeness: Parents; Close friends; Friends; Acquaintances; Strangers. There may be a regressive significance in the fact that parents come closest.

People also interpreted closeness in terms of liking and disliking. Patterson (1968) found that people who stood closer to experimental subjects were rated as "warmer" and liking the subjects more. People who are mentally disturbed in some way, such as schizophrenics and violent prisoners, who have difficulty in establishing emotional relationships, tend to have larger personal spaces than "normal" (Argyle 1988). This highlights the ambiguity in the direction of the metonymy. As a sign of our affection or as a bodily response that partly constitutes it, we move or position ourselves close to others. And if people sit closer to us or touch us this becomes an ECS for affection, as reported in the following experiments. "In an ESP experiment which gave the confederate the opportunity or excuse to touch the face of the subject, the subject rated the confederate more favourably than without touch" (Boderman, Freed, & Kinnucan 1972), though this could have been because the confederate also became warmer. In another experiment librarians touched borrowers for half a second when returning their library tickets, and this increased the liking for the library and the librarian amongst female subjects, but not males (Fisher, Rytting, and Heslin 1975).

The tendency to move towards those we like is an experiential basis for another theme in Table 24, DESIRE IS ATTRACTION. The scientific evidence of the physiological connection between pleasure and approach comes in research on dopamine. Evidently this hormone not only controls pleasure, but also movement forwards (Szalavitz 2002). This seems a very natural metonymic link: "When you think about it, it makes sense that when you are attracted to things, your natural instinct is to move towards them" (Jim Pfaus, quoted in Szalavitz 2002: 40).

The lexis for DESIRE (LIKING, INTEREST) IS ATTRACTION is given below. Note that such is the difficulty of talking about a degree of emotion between desire and interest without using the metaphor *attraction* that many of the dictionary definitions quoted below cannot avoid using it, or are not aware of its ambiguity and literal meaning. **Attract**, **pull** and **draw** (literally meaning 'cause to move towards') all mean metaphorically to 'stimulate interest pleasure or desire in' (*it was her sense of humour that first attracted me*). As a result of this interest or desire people will **gravitate towards** 'be interested by and attracted to' (*I always gravitate to the quick crossword rather than the cryptic one*), **fall for** 'start to love someone because you find them desirable' (*she fell for Mat when they were both undergraduate students on a field trip together*) or **come on** 'make your sexual interest known to someone' (*when we went clubbing Alex was coming on to her* (**come** implying 'movement towards')). The 'object of your desire or interest' is a **magnet** (*the school kids couldn't avoid the magnet of the ice-cream van*), with its derived adjective and noun **magnetic** 'attractive and popular' (*he is the most magnetic male dancer in the Royal Ballet*) and **magnetism** 'charm, attraction' (*he won the election due to the magnetism of his personality*).

Desire and interest can also be conveyed by bending: from the perpendicular – **inclined to** 'tending towards, preferring' (*I'm inclined to stay at home during the holiday*), **inclination** 'the wish to do something' (*I never had the inclination to ski*), **lean towards** 'tend to be interested in' (*he's always leaned towards Socialism*), **leanings** 'interests, desires' (*I think his paedophile leanings disqualify him*); or from a straight line – **bias** 'preference for' (*hiring practice shows a bias towards whites*), and **bent** 'attachment to particular beliefs or activities' (*government advisers are all economists of a socialist bent*).[2]

6.4 The cultural influences on emotion metaphors

I have now given an overview of some of the general experiential metonymic bases for emotion metaphors, and looked in more detail at experiential bases for specific emotion metaphors based on body heat. In this section I will concentrate on metaphors for anger, ANGER IS HEAT, ANGER IS EXPLOSION, which typically combine into ANGER IS HOT LIQUID/GAS IN A CONTAINER, with a view to discussing the evidence that, though these are universal metaphors, they undergo interesting cultural modifications.

---

2. Incidentally, since one moves towards what one is interested in, and can therefore perceive it more clearly as one approaches, proximity also provides the metonymic basis for AWARENESS /INTEREST IS PROXIMITY, details of which may be found in Metalude.

6.4.1   Metaphor themes for anger in English

One might think that the most obvious metonymic explanation of the metaphor theme
ANGER IS HEAT would be the body temperature rise, or experience of feeling hot that
arises from anger (or, in Damasio's terms, partly constitutes it). However, interestingly,
as well as the EMOTION AS PHYSIOLOGICAL/BEHAVIOURAL EFFECT metonymy the EMO-
TION AS CAUSE OF EMOTION metonymy may come into play. Research by the psychologist Craig Anderson shows that aggression and violence increase in high temperatures.
Baseball pitchers have a greater tendency to hit the batter with a ball on hot days, mo-
torists without air-conditioning honk their horns more. Anderson even suggests that
if global warming raises temperatures by 1 degree centigrade in the US this will lead
to 24,000 additional murders! (Blumberg 2002: 157). This is not an entirely new idea.
Montesquieu thought that in southerly climes "the strongest passions multiply all manner of crimes … in northern climates scarce has the animal part of love a power of making itself felt … In warmer climates love is liked for its own sake, it is the only cause of
happiness, it is life itself" (p. 158). Or as Benvolio puts it in *Romeo and Juliet*:

> I pray thee, good Mercutio let's retire,
> The day is hot, the Capulets are abroad:
> And if we meet we shall not 'scape a brawl,
> For now these hot days is the mad blood stirring.
>
> (Act 3, Scene1, ll.1–4)

ANGER IS HEAT is a fairly prolific theme. Someone with a **hot temper** or **hot tempered** has a 'tendency to get angry easily' (*he seems very charming but he actually has
a hot temper*), if you speak **hotly** you talk 'in an angry way' (*he hotly denied taking any
bribes*), or get involved in a **heated** 'angry or emotional' situation or discussion, (*there
was a heated argument between the Prime Minister and his deputy*), while if you are
'very annoyed' you are **hot under the collar** (*he gets very hot under the collar when I
criticise his novel*). Extreme heat makes something glow white or **incandescent** 'extremely angry' (*he was incandescent with rage*).

Anger is also associated with the prototypical source of heat, fire or flames: **flaming** 'angry' (*we had a flaming argument about religion*), **incendiary** 'likely to cause anger or violence' (*Smith's incendiary speech led to furious riots*). To 'become suddenly
angry' is to **flare, flare up** (*she flared up when she found out I'd been gambling*). Burning
even more strongly one has a **blazing row** 'noisy excited and intensely angry argument'
(*the murder was preceded by a blazing row we could hear through the wall*), while, by
contrast, 'anger which increases slowly' is a **slow burn** (*when he walks around like that
you know he's on a slow burn*).

ANGER IS HEAT also connects with CRITICISM IS HEAT, suggesting that the criticism
is angry: **blistering** 'angry and unkind' (*blistering remarks came from the delegates*),
roasting 'severe criticism' (*I got a roasting for coming back late*) or **scalding** 'strong or
fierce' (*I'm trying to recover from her scalding criticism*).

This last illustrates the combination of two source schemas for emotion, HEAT and WATER (the second having been already exemplified and discussed in 5.5.1.2). Heating water until it boils is a doubly determined schema for anger: **boil** 'be angry' (*all the time I was boiling with rage, but dare not object*), **boiling point** 'state of anger which is likely to get out of control and become violent' (*the crowd was at boiling point, and the police started firing tear gas*), but slightly more controlled anger is less vigorous boiling: **simmer** 'be almost unable to control anger' (*she was simmering with rage when I left the room*), **seethe** 'experience unexpressed anger' (*she is seething at all the bad reviews she received*). Conversion of liquid into vapour is associated with the expression of emotion: **steamed up** 'very annoyed and showing your anger' (*he got very steamed up about his boss's mistreatment of him*), **fume** 'express impatience and anger' ("*that's you last chance," he fumed*). Someone who is 'easily angered' is therefore **volatile** (*she has a volatile temper*).

Note, however, that a mixture of gas and liquid can be used as an expression of anger and intense emotional upset even if it does not involve heat: **froth at the mouth** (*the customer was frothing at the mouth over the terrible service*) or **in a lather** (*he got in a lather when his car wouldn't start*).

It is now a platitude in the conceptual metaphor literature to say that the most important metaphor theme for anger in English is ANGER IS HOT LIQUID IN A CONTAINER. This may be something of a distortion of the lexical evidence. For a start, the previous examples in which anger is a boiling liquid do not exploit the container part of the liquid schema, though, of course, liquids are usually encountered in vessels. Secondly, several of the lexical items which might be thought to belong to that theme can actually be used for negative emotions in general such as stress rather than just anger: **let off steam** 'get rid of strong feelings by behaving noisily' (*singing opera is a way for me to let off steam*), **safety-valve** is 'a means to release negative emotions' (*doing exercise is a good safety valve for stress*) and **pressure cooker** 'an emotionally stressful situation' (*playing in the pressure cooker of the European Cup finals is a mental challenge*). The one exception, which does seem to apply almost uniquely to anger, is **boil over** 'have such strong uncontrollable feelings that you have to express them' (*many people are boiling over with rage at the support the US gives to Israel*).

Thirdly, most of the lexis which is cited to support this platitude is better covered by the more prolific metaphor theme EMOTION IS EXPLOSION: **explosion** 'outburst of strong feeling' (*the teacher's explosion of anger shocked the pupils*), **explode** 'show sudden and strong emotion' (*I didn't want to explode with anger, so I left the room*), **explosive** 'tending to express strong and sudden anger' (*my son has an explosive temper*), **blow up** 'lose your temper' (*I blew up when I discovered how two-faced she'd been*), **blow a gasket** and **flip your lid** 'lose your temper or control' (*when I told him I was resigning he blew a gasket*), **blow your stack/top** 'become extremely angry' (*he blew his stack when she threatened to walk out on him*), **erupt** 'become angry and violent' (*the Asian districts of the city erupted*), **fireworks** 'strong expression of anger' (*if my parents know I was home late there will be fireworks*), **outburst** 'expression of anger' (*my outburst yesterday was unforgivable*). Part of the schema is what leads up to the explosion, which is equivalent to the cause of the anger, what might **spark** it **off** 'cause an emotional reaction' (*the speech sparked off an angry protest*), or the fact that such an explosion is quick with people who have a **short fuse** 'tendency to get angry easily' (*he has a very short fuse – try not to annoy him*), and the need to 'calm a dangerous or emotional situation' to **defuse** it (*the TV broadcast was an attempt to defuse the situation*). In none of these lexical items is there any suggestion of a heated liquid, but rather a sudden violent outwards movement, implying, if anything, an expanding or hot gas.

Fourthly, in the equally prolific metaphor theme EMOTIONAL EXPRESSION IS OUT-FLOW there is seldom any mention of heat, and the emotions concerned are of many kinds, not always or just including anger. Emotion in this theme is certainly a liquid, sometimes understood to be in a container as any schema for liquids would predict, but not hot: **ooze** 'display an emotion or attitude very strongly' (*the second candidate oozed confidence throughout the interview*), **gushing** 'expressing feelings insincerely' (*she's a very gushing person*), **gush** 'empty expression of feeling' (*his performance was a load of gush*), **outpouring** 'uncontrollable expression of feeling' (*I was amazed by his outpourings of adoration*), **pour out** 'express strongly and uncontrollably' (*she poured out her feelings of resentment*), **effusion** 'uncontrolled expression of strong emotion' (*I hate his effusions of self-pity*), **outlet** 'way in which emotion can be expressed' (*poetry provided an outlet for her emotions*), **overflow** 'express strong feelings' (*suddenly her anger overflowed*), **well** 'increase to the point where they have to be expressed' (*feelings of deep sorrow welled up inside me*), **brim over** 'express a feeling without restraint' (*he was brimming over with enthusiasm*), **exude** 'display an emotion or attitude' (*Tiger Woods exudes confidence at every hole*), **express** 'communicate an emotion' (*this poem expresses Plath's despair as well as any other*). Refusal to express an emotion involves exerting pressure to stop it flowing out, but this is not normally a pressure caused by heat: **bottle up** 'refuse to talk about or express emotions' (*it's bad for your mental health to bottle up your emotions for too long*), **choke back** 'prevent the expression of emotion' (*I choked back my anger and tried to remain calm, despite the provocation*).

There may be a way in which these more basic metaphor themes can be combined into a compound metaphor in order to corroborate Kövecses' intuitions and Gibbs and O'Brien's (1990) experimental evidence about the importance of ANGER IS A HOT LIQUID IN A CONTAINER (See Figure 7). We might construct a schema in which anger heats the liquid in a container to produce a gas until the pressure of the gas causes an explosion. But we need to change the metaphor theme to ANGER IS HOT FLUID IN A CONTAINER, which, if we take *fluid* to mean 'not solid', includes gas and allows us to think of the expression of anger as an explosion of a gas, which may or may not, before heating, have been a liquid.

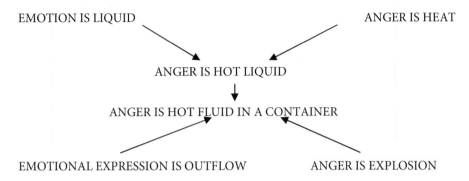

Figure 7. Inter-relations of metaphor themes to produce ANGER IS HOT FLUID IN CONTAINER

Table 25. Cultural comparisons in the conceptualisation of anger (based on Kövecses 2000a pp. 148-154)

STAGES	ENGLISH	HUNGARIAN	CHINESE	JAPANESE
Cause	Rising of fluid	Same	Excess *qi* wells up	Same as E
	Production of steam	Same		Same as E
Anger	Production of pressure	Same		Same as E
Attempt to control anger	Attempt to resist pressure	Same	Attempt to hold back qi in stomach or spleen	Same as E
Loss of control	Explosion	Same	Explosion	Same as E
	Up in the air	Same		
Expression	Comes out in expression	Same		

For Hungarian Container can be head

For Chinese Present in breast, heart, stomach or spleen — pressure is in a particular body organ. *Qi* calms down afterwards

For Japanese Stomach/bowels seen as principle container. Hara (stomach) can also be seen as a container, but not one under pressure. Idea of *hara* rising reaching the chest *mune* and then the head *atama*. Reaching the head it can no longer be hidden

Kövecses states that ANGER IS HOT LIQUID IN A CONTAINER obtains in English, Hungarian, Japanese, and that ANGER IS LIQUID IN A CONTAINER obtains for Chinese as well. This metaphor structures anger as follows in all four cultures, exploiting the metaphor theme THE BODY IS THE CONTAINER FOR THE EMOTIONS, ANGER IS FLUID IN CONTAINER or the more general THE ANGRY PERSON IS A PRESSURISED CONTAINER. On the basis of his data (summarised in Table 25) Kövecses claims:

> Without the constraining effect of embodiment it is difficult to see how such a surprisingly uniform category (of metaphors) could have emerged for the conceptualisation of anger. The widely different cultures we have examined should have produced a great deal more diversity in (metaphorical) conceptualisation than what appears to be the case on the basis of the data available to me in this study (Kövecses 2000a: 160).

6.4.2 Cultural variations in metaphor themes for anger

What mainly concerns us in the following paragraphs is the comparison between the two European languages and Chinese/Japanese. Firstly, according to Kövecses' data, in Chinese there are no metaphors to do with anger that suggest the heating of the fluid to produce pressure. This might be thought to be evidence against the metonymic account of metaphorical origins, but Kövecses suggests that Chinese does not seem to have metonymical expressions that mention the bodily heat effects of anger, lacking, for example equivalents to *get hot under the collar*. This is a sign that the conceptualisation of the physiology of anger is slightly different. However, he maintains that there is a real embodiment which involves blood-pressure rising and body heating up when anger occurs for Chinese as for the rest of us (Lakoff 1987, Johnson 1987, Kövecses 2000a: 159) and it is simply that the literal or metonymic expressions in Chinese do not conceptualise this. Another difference between Chinese and the other languages' metaphors is that when *qi* is blocked there is the possibility of its diversion.

There are important cultural differences between Japanese and English as well. For a start the expression of anger *hara/ikara* which represents true feelings, is complicated by *tatemae*, the need to preserve one's outward face. Matsuki suggests that Kövecses third stage of the anger model needs modification for Japanese since *ikari/hara* allows the angry person more chance to exercise control than seems to be the case in English. She represents the model thus:

1. Offending event
2. Anger
3. Attempt at control
4. Loss of control
5. Act of retribution

(Incidentally stage 5 seems to be significantly different from Kövecses stage 5 in column 1 of Table 25 – possible allowing for the fact that in "revenge" cultures the expression of anger is seen as an act of retribution).

The Japanese stage three has subdivided stages, *hara, mune*, and *atama*. The ontology of Japanese anger includes an ascending scale based on the three body zones, metaphors not found in American English. When a Japanese person gets angry *hara* rises up from the belly/navel/womb. When a person tries to control anger he tries to keep it in *hara*. When a person needs to control his anger to show *taemae*, but still experiences the anger, conflicts go beyond the container of *hara* and move to *mune*, the chest. *Mune* is the container for anger overflowing from *hara*. *Mune* is the seat of nausea, so conflicts and frustration caused by efforts to control anger cause nausea. When about to lose control anger comes to *atama* (the head). Anger that could be controlled in *hara* and *mune* cannot be rationalised in *atama*.

Matsuki (1995) concludes that we must look at a social context in order to better understand culture-specific structures of anger, in particular social relationships. Non-prototypical cases of anger differ from one another depending on a person's situation in their social milieu. Social factors account for some variation in the choice of metaphor, although systematic correlation between social factors and use of specific metaphors remain unexplored, a lack I hope this book goes some way towards remedying (see also Kövecses 2005: chapter 10).

Although Matsuki's analysis is persuasive in arguing for the uniqueness of the cultural situation in which metaphors are generated and used, it may be that she underestimates the commonality between English and Japanese emotion metaphors. The source of overflowing, rather than explosion, seems very important in her account, and this source, as we demonstrated, is also extremely important in English for emotion in general, though not for anger in particular, as part of the theme EMOTIONAL EXPRESSION IS OUTFLOW (cf. Kövecses 2000a: 65–68). For example, **overflow**, **well**, **brim over**, **exude**, and **ooze** all seem to refer to the involuntary movement beyond the edges or walls of a container in the same way that anger wells up and brims over from *hara* to *mune* to *atama*.

Besides accepting the cultural modifications in Japanese and Chinese of ANGER IS (HOT) FLUID IN A CONTAINER, Kövecses also entertains suggestions that there are significant cultural differences in metaphor themes for anger and that they are by no means uniform. For example Lutz (1988) suggests that the Ifaluk on a Micronesian atoll emphasise the prosocial, moral ideological aspects of anger, not the antisocial, individualistic and physical aspects manifest in the HOT FLUID IN A CONTAINER metaphor (Kövecses 1995: 161). English anger in its expression stage is directed at the offending party, but in Zulu ANGER IS HUNGER prompts them to devour everything indiscriminately, not to direct anger towards a specific target (pp. 166–168).

It is worth looking more closely at the concept of 'song' in Ifaluk and contrasting it with 'anger'. The English concept of anger (as in *angry with*) is linked with a cognitive scenario which includes the following components: a) this person did something bad, b) I don't want this person to do things like this, c) I want to do something to this person because of this. By contrast, the cognitive scenario linked with the Ifaluk concept 'song' includes components a) and b) above but not c); on the other hand it includes an additional component d), which it shares with concepts embodied in the meaning of English words such as *reproach* and *admonition* "I want this person to know this"…. "'song' may manifest itself in sulking, refusal to eat, or even attempted suicide, whereas 'anger' normally manifests itself in an action aimed at the offender, not at oneself" (Wierzbicka 1999: 273–4).

Similarly, the Ilongot word *liget* lacks component c), but includes a component rather more general "I want to do something because of this", and a further "I do not want people to think I am not as good as other people". As a result *liget* can be applied to "fierce work in one's garden" (p. 287).

Even so, Kövecses conclusion, in defence of the experiential hypothesis, is that "given universal real physiology, members of different cultures cannot conceptualise their emotions in a way that contradicts universal physiology: but nevertheless they can choose to conceptualise their emotions in many different ways within the constraints imposed on them by universal physiology" (Kövecses 1995: 165), though he has modified his views somewhat recently (Kövecses 2005: 47).

6.4.3 Humoral theory and the body-cultural history debate

One interesting and important challenge to Kövecses' (1989) analysis of emotional expressions in terms of universal, metonymy-based metaphors comes form Geeraerts and Grondelaers (1995). They claim that his analysis is flawed because it is ahistorical, and therefore obscures the influence of cultural traditions as a source of emotion concepts. In their discussion of the effect of the theory of the four humours on emotion metaphors they emphasise two aspects usually absent from cognitive theories of metaphor, the diachronic and the cultural, though recently Kövecses has recognised their importance (2005: parts III and IV, 103–5).

Before investigating this debate, I think it is worthwhile to adopt refinements to our theoretical framework suggested by Kövecses, as well as explicitly representing his standpoint. Discussing metaphors for anger, he distinguishes between various kinds of motivation for metaphor themes or conceptual metaphors. Existential motivation, which creates theoretical linguistic expressions, as for example in the humoral theory of anger. Conceptual or cognitive motivation, as for example when we perceive a correlation between pouring more liquid into a container and the level of the fluid rising, enabling the conceptual metaphor MORE IS HIGH. And bodily motivation, when the meaning of an expression or concept can be embodied, reflected in our experience of our bodies, as when increased body heat gives rise metonymically to ANGER IS HEAT. Kövecses (1995) believes that bodily and conceptual motivation (which we might call experiential motivation) can influence existential motivation, though he doesn't believe that the influence can be the other way around. Indeed, he suggests that bodily and conceptual motivation puts constraints on ways of understanding, that is, the existential motivation provided by theorising anger.

The metaphors seem to conform to the patterns defined by the physiology-based metonymies. In short physiology can be seen as setting boundaries to the range of possible conceptualisations ... What is claimed, then, is that if a language does have this metaphor, it is likely to also have expressions that describe physiological responses, which in turn provide bodily (and cognitive) motivation for this way of conceptualising anger (p. 191).

Geeraerts and Grondelaers' discussion reminds us of Damasio whose conception of emotion is perhaps closer to the humoral theories than to the mechanistic ideas which followed them. Stearns (1994: 66–67) gives a historical perspective:

Prior to the nineteenth century, dominant beliefs, medical and popular alike, attached anger, joy and sadness to bodily functions. Hearts, for example, could shake, tremble, expand, grow cold. Because emotions were embodied, they had clear somatic qualities: people were gripped by rage (which could, it was held, stop menstruation), hot blood was the essence of anger, fear had cold sweats. Emotions, in other words, had physical stuff. But during the eighteenth century, historians increasingly realise, the humoral conception of the body, in which fluids and emotions alike could pulse, gave way to a mechanistic picture. And in the body-machine emotions were harder to pin down, the symptoms harder to convey. Of course, physical symptoms could still be invoked, but now only metaphorically.

Table 26. The four humours and their correspondences in medieval medicine

	PHLEGM	BLACK BILE	YELLOW BILE	BLOOD
Characteristic	Cold and moist	Cold and dry	Warm and dry	Warm and moist
Element	Water	Earth	Fire	Air
Temperament	Phlegmatic	Melancholic	Choleric	Sanguine
Organ	Brain/bladder	Spleen	Liver/stomach	Heart
Color	White	Black	Yellow	Red
Taste	Salty	Sour	Bitter	Sweet
Season	Winter	Autumn	Summer	Spring
Wind	North	West	South	East
Planet	Moon	Saturn	Mars	Jupiter
Animal	Turtle	Sparrow	Lion	Goat

Geeraerts and Grondelaers (1995) sketch the theory of the four humours in Western medicine, which amounted to an elaborate system of correspondences, as shown in Table 26, between the elements and their characteristics, temperament, organs of the body, tastes, seasons, winds, planets and animals, and colours (reminding us of our discussion of racial colour-coding in 2.4). They go on to show how metaphors for emotions were influenced by an explicit, existential model and have left their vestiges in the vocabulary of English.

What vestiges have they in fact left? The theme EMOTION IS BODY-PART/BODY-FLUID, provides a number of items connected with body liquids which bear some relation to the medieval medicine categories: *phlegm *phlegmatic 'ability or characteristic of remaining calm in anxious circumstances' (*with his normal phlegm he worked on steadily as the rain splashed down*), *bile *bilious 'bitterness/bitter' or 'anger/angry' (*he reserves his bile for his much hated colleagues*), *gall *galling 'rudeness/rude, cheekiness/cheek' (*I didn't have the gall to ask him for a 20 mile lift*), and bad *blood 'negative feelings towards others' (*there had been bad blood between them for years*). However another item which does not seem to fit in is spunk (literally 'semen') 'bravery and determination' (*don't give up now – where's your spunk!*).

As far as body organs are concerned we have references to the heart: *heart-warming 'encouraging, inspiring confidence' (*it's a heart-warming tale of self-sacrifice*), take/lose *heart 'become more/less courageous' (*when he gained consciousness we began to take heart*), *heart 'sympathetic and kind feelings' (*he has a good heart and gives generously to charity*), change of *heart 'change of feelings or ideas' (*the government had a change of heart on tax increases*), break someone's *heart 'make someone feel very unhappy or disappointed' (*when his wife left him it broke his heart*). And *spleen 'feeling of anger and dissatisfaction' (*in a fit of spleen he walked out of the house, slamming the door*), *stomach 'courage or inclination for something difficult' (*Syria has no stomach for a war with the US*), *guts 'courage' (*I don't have the guts to criticise the boss*), *gut reaction/feeling 'deeply felt instinctive response without evidence or reason to back it up' (*my gut reaction is that the US should stop subsidising Israeli defence spending*). But we also have visceral 'based on deep feeling and emotional reactions rather than on reason or thought' (*my students' approach to literature is visceral rather than analytical*), and balls 'courage' (*he doesn't have the balls to argue with his boss*).

In addition, there are a number of items which seem unrelated to humoral theory, to do with the spine and nervous system: backbone 'courage to do what is necessary' (*the headmaster didn't have enough backbone to expel the bullies from school*), spineless 'lacking in strength and courage' (*the new president is completely spineless*), nerve 'bravery or confidence necessary to do something difficult, unpleasant or rude' (*it takes a lot of nerve to be a racing driver*), and fibre 'strength of character or emotional commitment' (*society lacks the moral fibre to resist the greed encouraged by advertisers*).

Furthermore, we have items to do with face: face 'pride, respect, reputation' (*he refused to change his plan despite criticisms as he need to preserve his face*), put a brave face on 'pretend publicly not to be upset or unhappy about' (*his daughter didn't get into university, but he put a brave face on it*), cheek 'rudeness or lack of respect' (*after ditching us at the party, she had the cheek to come and ask us for help*), turn your nose up at 'reject as inferior' (*don't turn your nose up at the newer universities – they still give you an opportunity to study*), snub 'insult (someone) by not giving them any attention or treating them as if they are not important' (*I didn't notice her and apparently she thought I had snubbed her*).

Let's look at the asterisked items above, which seem to correspond to or be synonymous with elements in the humour correspondence chart (Table 26). While some have kept the traditional metaphorical/metonymic meaning predicted by the existential humoral theory, e.g. *phlegm* and perhaps *bile* (if referring to yellow bile), many seem to have different meanings, e.g. *spleen* which means 'anger' not 'melancholy', *stomach/guts* which mean 'bravery' not 'anger' as *choleric* would suggest, and *gall* (if this is a synonym for *bile*) meaning 'rudeness, misplaced confidence' not 'anger'.

A possible way of looking at the problem would be to say that "the physiological factors have a marked influence on the reinterpretation process that expressions with a humoral origin undergo in the course of time" (Geeraerts & Grondelaers 1995: 170). They would suggest, then, that the physiological factors that Kövecses concentrates on could be crucial in this reinterpretation process.

> As the original literal motivation gradually disappears, the elements of our emotional vocabulary could receive a new interpretation as figurative expressions of the physiological effects of particular emotions. Such a physiological reinterpretation would not be automatic, however; in some cases the expression could lose all transparency, while in others the new figurative meaning could be purely metaphorical rather than metonymical along the "physiological effects" line. For instance, taking for granted that the origins of *fiery* in the sense "irascible" are humoral, and also taking for granted that the expression has not become totally opaque … its contemporary reinterpreted meaning could be based on the physiological metonymy that anger causes body heat, but it could also be the case that *fiery* is synchronically interpreted on the basis of a metaphorical image; the propensity of the irascible person to burst out abruptly could be compared with the fire's tendency to flare up suddenly (Geeraerts & Grondelaers 1995: 171).

However, though this might account for the use of words like *fiery*, it appears not to apply to the items we listed above taken from body-parts and bodily liquids. More than likely their meanings have drifted away from the original meaning because the disappearance of the theoretical system of physiology/medicine removed all motivation for their specific meanings. This would imply that most are now arbitrary and opaque, and the only original motivation for them was theoretical or existential rather than experiential or bodily. However, they still belong to the more general metaphor theme EMOTION IS BODY-PART/BODY-FLUID, which, because of some kind of cognitive presence, can motivate them, and can produce new lexical items like *spunk* and *balls*. A bodily explanation here would, anyway, seem unlikely in most cases. Though some organs or parts of the body, such as the heart and the face, we can associate metonymically with emotions, we have no conscious awareness of the operation of other internal organs like the spleen and possibly the liver (at least in English, though this may depend upon the way the workings of these organs is conceptualised in different languages and cultures). And there is nothing much within our experience to metonymically associate emotion with liquid, at least, as we saw earlier, Grady (1997), could find nothing convincing.

Kövecses raises the question of whether the humour theory itself may be grounded in the very same range of physiological experiences as the hot fluid metaphor. So an expression like "my blood is boiling" was, in former times at least, multiply motivated – by physiological experience and by the expert cultural theory of the four humours (Taylor 1995: 14). He suggests that "a generic-level … schema seems to be motivated by physiology and the details of the schema at the specific level seem to be filled out by the cultural system" (Kövecses 1995: 193). Geeraerts and Grondelaers suggest that this claim could be tested by diachronic historical research: we could find out if the physiological conceptualisation of anger precedes theory by investigating whether pre-Hippocratic Greece had the same metaphors/concepts, before the humoral theory was propounded (1995: 172–3).

Research could also be carried out in other languages, since the tendency for languages to link feeling/emotion with insides, generally the stomach or the liver, seems to be widespread. Whether these are existential/folk-theoretical and hence literal, and whether they were metaphorically/metonymically used before the theory came into being could perhaps be established (Wierzbicka 1999: 277). For example, the Austronesian language Mbula (Table 27) and Chinese (Table 28) conceptualise emotions in this way.

Table 27. Emotions and the liver in Mbula (Bugenhagen 1990: 205)

Expression	Gloss	Literal meaning
Kete- (i)malmal	'angry'	'liver fight'
Kete- (i)bayou	'very angry'	'liver hot'
Kete- (i)beleu	'uncontrollably angry'	'liver swirl'
Kete- pitpit	'get excited too quickly'	'liver jumps'
Kete- ikam ken	'startled'	'liver does snapping'
Kete- biibi	'too slow'	'liver is big'
Kete- kutkut	'anxious'	'liver beats'
Kete- iluumu	'at peace'	'liver cool'
Kete- pas	'out of breath' 'lose one's temper'	'liver removes'
Kete- paNana	'calm, unmoved, longsuffering'	'liver is rock-like'
Kete- ise	'aroused'	'liver goes up'
Kete- isu	'take a rest'	'liver goes down'
Kete- pakpak	'very angry'	'liver is sour'

It is likely that Chinese terms are linked to the system of folk medicine and physiology:

Table 28. Emotion and internal organs in Chinese (Chun (1997) quoted in Wierzbicka, 1999, 300-302)

Expression	Literal meaning	Comments on meaning
Chang duan	'broken intestine'	In great grief misery or sadness e.g. 'one is crying like chang duan'
Xin ru dao ge	'heart is like cut by a knife'	In a very painful situation because of sadness, grief, misery
Wu zhang ju lie	'five organs all broken'	In great anger, therefore his or her internal organs are broken
Xin ji ru fen	'one's heart is like burning'	In great anxiety, like fire burning
Xia po dan	'gallbladder is broken from fear'	The gallbladder is linked with courage by the Chinese. If one is terrified badly he or she is said to be *Xia po dan*

In drawing this section to a close, I have to agree with Wierzbicka on the equal importance of the innate physiological and the learned cultural bases for explaining emotion and the metaphors used to describe and express it.

> In all languages there … seem to be ways of speaking that link feelings based on thoughts with events and processes involving the body – a fact strikingly consistent with the emphasis placed by many scholars, especially psychologists, on the biological aspects of "emotions". First of all these ways of speaking suggest that some externally observable bodily behaviours (in particular facial behaviours) are seen universally as voluntary or semi-voluntary modes of expressing and communicating cognitively based feelings … Second they suggest that some visible and/or audible (that is externally observable) bodily events and processes may be seen, universally, as involuntary symptoms of cognitively based feelings (such as example *blush* in English). Third, all languages also appear to have conventional bodily images, that is expressions referring to imaginary events taking place inside the body, used as a basis for describing the subjective experience of feelings assumed to be based on thoughts (Wierzbicka 1999: 305).

The first part of this chapter has shown how such bodily expressions of emotion and symptoms of emotion form the basis of the imaginary metaphorical vocabulary used for emotions, though within this universality we have seen that there are considerable cultural variations in the specifics of expression, symptoms and particularly imaginary metaphorical concepts. So we have to balance these claims with the importance of culture:

> Although human emotional endowment is no doubt largely innate and universal, people's emotional lives are shaped, to a considerable extent by their culture. Every culture offers not only a linguistically embodied grid for the conceptualisation of emotions, but also a set of "scripts" suggesting to people how to feel. How to express their feelings, how to think about their own and other people's feelings, and so on (Wierzbicka 1999: 240).

6.5   Challenges to the universality of conceptual metaphor themes.

So far in this chapter, especially when dealing with metaphors for emotion, we have adopted a rather universalist approach, except where we presented Geeraerts and Grondelaers' (1995) more historical and diachronic discussion of emotion metaphor in the last section. However, there are many reasons to question claims of universality in conceptual metaphors and metaphor themes. The universalist theory of emotions derives jointly from naïve objectivist science, and a linguistic imperialism which assumes that the English vocabulary for emotion and specific emotions can be used unproblematically to refer to emotion concepts in other cultures speaking other languages. Given that I adopt a weak version of the Sapir-Whorf hypothesis, I cannot accept that any language, let alone English in particular, cuts up nature at its joints, that is, reflects pre-existing divisions and classifications present in nature or in human experience. As we shall see, even the concept of 'emotion' is language specific, and therefore, probably even more so, are more specific emotions. To explore this question further we should look more systematically at the reasons why conceptual metaphors and metaphor themes may be local rather than universal.

There are various possible reasons for non-universality in metaphors and metaphor themes, some of which we can list as follows, with the section of the chapter where they are discussed in parenthesis:

-   No such target concept exists in one culture/language as exists in another, or the target concept is not quite identical in the two cultures (6.5.1) (cf. Kövecses 2005: 121, 253–7).
-   No such source concept exists in one culture/language as exists in another, or the prototypical source concept has cultural variation at the basic category level in different cultures (6.5.2) (cf. Kövecses 2005: 118–9, 253–7).
-   Source and target both co-vary, and apparently identical sources and targets in fact differ (6.5.3).
-   The same target and source concepts exist in both/all cultures, but they are paired differently, or paired in one language and not in another (6.5.4) (cf. Kövecses 2005: 70–87).
-   Although there is an identity, because the mappings are only partial, different grounds are explored in different languages, including different emotional grounds (6.5.5) (cf. Kövecses 2005: 123–25).
-   Though source and target are paired similarly at some general level, they are differentiated at a more specific level (6.5.6) (cf. Kövecses 2005: 68–70).

While this book was nearing completion Kövecses published *Metaphor in Culture: universality and variation* (2005), whose chapters 4 –7 are a necessary complement to this section. It is worth making a comparison between the two, and I have listed the parts of his book which are relevant to the items on the list above. Besides the categories that I use below, he also stresses that even when in two different languages/cultures there exist metaphor themes with identical diverse sources for the same target, different cultures may prefer one of the sources to another. Taking an intra-cultural example from 5.5.2, one sub-culture may prefer to see education as growth, while another may see it primarily as acquisition. Another difference is that he stresses that the range of targets, roughly my multivalency, and the scope of sources, roughly my diversification, may vary from culture to culture (pp. 70–79, 122–23). A major difference is perhaps that I do not make such a distinction between thought and language as he does, which accounts for the fact that 6.5.3 has no counterpart in his book.

6.5.1 No such exact target concept exists in one culture/language as exists in another.

Wierzbicka gives plenty of evidence that 'emotion' is a concept in English which does not have equivalents even in languages which are closely related to English culturally and genetically, let alone more "exotic" languages (Wierzbicka 1999: 3). To explore this evidence we first of all have to understand what the word *emotion* means for English speakers.

> The English word *emotion* combines in its meaning a reference to 'feeling', a reference to 'thinking' and a reference to a person's body. For example, one can talk about "a feeling of hunger", or a "feeling of heartburn", but not about an "emotion of hunger", because the feelings in question are not thought related. One can also talk about a "feeling of loneliness" or a "feeling of alienation" but not "an emotion of loneliness" or an "emotion of alienation", because, while these feelings are clearly related to thoughts (such as "I am all alone", "I don't belong", etc.) they do not suggest any associated bodily events or processes (such as rising blood pressure, a rush of blood to the head, tears, and so on) (1999: 2).

We notice that Wierzbicka, by identifying the English meanings for feelings and emotions, arrives at a rather different classificatory scheme from Damasio. What Wierzbicka and normal English usage calls 'emotions' is more like what Damasio calls 'feelings' – i.e. bodily responses plus thoughts of them. However, the reverse is not true: what is an emotion for Damasio is not the same as a feeling in ordinary English/Wierzbicka, because feelings may have no bodily basis, as in 'alienation' and 'loneliness' above. (There is an additional inconsistency that some of the ordinary English feelings, such as itchiness or heartburn, because they are bodily responses, ought to be, but are not, included in Damasio's 'emotions'.)

The ordinary English concept of 'emotion' as explained by Wierzbicka, has no equivalent in German, Russian or Samoan:

> The word usually used as the translation equivalent of the English *emotion*, *Gefühl* (from *fühlen* 'to feel') makes no distinction between mental and physical feelings, although contemporary scientific German uses increasingly the word *emotion*, borrowed from scientific English, while in older academic German the compound *Gemütsbewegung*, roughly 'movement of the mind', was often used in

a similar sense ... At the same time the plural form – *Gefühle* – is restricted to thought related feelings, although – unlike English – it does not imply any "bodily disturbances" or processes of any kind. The same is true of Russian, where there is no word corresponding to *emotion* and where the noun *čuvstvo* (from *čuvstvovat* 'to feel') corresponds to *feeling* whereas the plural form *čuvstva* suggests cognitively-based feelings. To take a non-European example, Gerber (1985) notes that Samoan has no word corresponding to the English term *emotion* and relies instead on the notion of *lagona* 'feeling' ... thus while the concept of 'feeling' is universal and can be safely used in the investigation of human experience and human nature, the concept of 'emotion' is culture-bound and cannot be similarly relied on (1999: 3–4).

Not only, of course, may general abstract categories like 'emotion' be language and culture specific, but also more specific kinds of feelings or 'emotions'. The Russian *toska*, roughly 'melancholy-cum-yearning', and *zalet*, roughly 'to lovingly pity someone' or the Ifaluk concept *fago* (roughly 'sadness/compassion/love'), the German *Schadenfreude* or English *embarrassment* seem to be culture-bound concepts (Wierzbicka, 1999: 8, 11, 103–4, 112–116). The Polish terms *tęsknota, tęsknić*, which now represent a key emotional concept, can only be glossed in a very roundabout way: 'a combination of nostalgia, painfully missing someone and a longing to be reunited with them'. They can be traced historically and culturally as growing out of Polish émigré literature.

> Speakers of English use categories such as *sad, angry, disgusted* and *happy* whereas the speakers of Ifaluk use different, non-matching categories such as *fago, song, waires* and *ker*... while speakers of Malay use categories such as *sedih, marah, jijik* and *gembira*, which are different again (p. 24).

Tahitians do not appear to have a word for *sadness* (pp. 26–27). The modern meaning of the word *anger* in English is only partially equivalent to the two closest terms in Polish – *złość*, ('temper tantrum, feeling cross'), *gniew*, ('outward expression of anger, scolding') so that neither could be used to translate "some people feel angry at God for allowing them to get sick, at their doctors for not being able to find a cure, at the government for putting money into weapons rather than medical research, or at the world in general" (p. 32).

Not only is this diversity clear across languages, but even within the same language emotion concepts like 'anger' change from one historical period to another under cultural influences. The modern English view of anger as something that can be manipulated, controlled, vented, released, left unresolved, directed at a target, stirred up, repressed, expressed, suppressed and so on is quite different in its semantic range from anger found in Shakespeare (p. 31). This diversity challenges the claim of universalists like Ekman, and those who relate emotions to basic evolutionary survival, that there are six basic emotions: happiness, sadness, anger, fear, disgust and surprise. Not all languages have these. Human beings from different cultures may not be essentially alike in their emotional lives.

Wierzbicka elaborates on how the importance of various emotions can vary over time as a culture changes. For example she shows how *happy* is now a much more frequently used word and therefore a more important concept than *joy* in contemporary culture. 'Joy' being more intense and 'happy' less so, she sees this as part of a cultural tendency to dampen emotions in contemporary Anglo culture (cf. Kövecses 1991). On the other hand the predominance of *happy* would reflect the climate of positive thinking, cheerfulness and fun (p. 54). Similarly, 'frustration' is a highly culture-specific concept associated with a society which emphasises goals, plans and expected achievements, and it is has spread, as a loan word, to Polish, German and Bahasa Indonesia, who had no such lexicalised concept before (p. 72). She also demonstrates, at some length, how the German concept of *Angst*

> is a cultural creation, and that the boundaries between 'different emotions' such as 'Angst', 'anxiety', or 'fear' … are imposed by different cognitive scenarios with which the words in question are associated, and the cognitive scenarios themselves are shaped, not just by universal human biology but by culture, which in turn is shaped by history, religion and way of life (p. 167).

In particular she traces the meaning of 'Angst' back to its uses by Martin Luther's influential theological writings, and his translation of the Bible (chapter 3).

In fact, we can agree with Argyle, in his explanation of Harré's development of Goffman's social theory:

> The biological innate side of man is incomplete and has to be supplemented by a socially constructed order … there is an instrumental order which deals with the material side of life, and an expressive order which is concerned with the universal quest for respect and reputation. The expressive order is a collective symbolic system, part of society rather than individuals, consisting of a repertoire of meaningful symbolic acts and rules for using them. The system is maintained by public conversation, which becomes internalised as the private thoughts of individuals (Harré 1979).

Under this theory emotions are seen not only as physiological reactions but as part of the shared symbolic order. For example, pride includes the belief that one has been worthy of victory. This accounts for historical and cultural variation in emotions. We no longer have 'melancholy', an Elizabethan emotion, more positive than depression, and a valued aesthetic state. We do not have the Japanese 'amae', a relation of childish dependence on another adult (Harré, Clarke & De Carlo 1985). To this extent emotions are not just brute facts but institutional facts too (cf. Searle's distinction discussed in 4.3.5).

In a more straightforward and perhaps trivial way, we can observe that certain of the targets in Metalude simply do not exist for some cultures. In societies where there are no electricity, engines or machines, then ELECTRICITY IS LIQUID, ENGINE IS

ANIMAL or HUMAN, MACHINE IS ANIMAL or HUMAN cannot exist. Where there is no vehicle or traffic there will be no metaphor themes TRAFFIC IS LIQUID/BLOOD, VEHICLE IS ANIMAL/HUMAN. Where there is no money there are no themes such as MONEY IS FOOD, and in non-literate cultures it would be pointless to try to locate the themes TEXT IS BUILDING/CONTAINER, TEXT IS PATH or TEXT IS STRUCTURE.

6.5.2   No such exact source concept exists in one culture/language as exists in another

The source domains arising from social interaction may obviously be culturally specific. Social activities – rituals, games, even interactions with buildings – appear as sources both for complex or remote forms of social organisation and activity, as well as for abstract concepts which may not be primarily social. For example, we may talk of time as money, use baseball metaphors for American and cricket metaphors for British politics, and poker metaphors for international politics, but it should be obvious that the use of money, the playing of baseball, cricket and poker are social activities which are culturally specific, and may not exist in certain cultures (despite the premier baseball competition being labelled "the World Series"!) (Chilton 1996).

This is observable, even in relation to sub-cultures, where sources for a number of metaphorical idioms, like **off the wall**, and **on/in the bread line**, might be differently identified. *Off the wall* means something like 'in an improvised fashion', but it depends upon the experience within a certain culture or sub-culture of either squash or film projection, since the source is unclear: does it derive from the speed with which one has to react to the unpredictable as the ball comes off the wall in squash, or the improvisation of using a wall on which to project films if no screen is available? With the second idiom the fact that the original **in the bread line** has been changed to **on the bread line** (Randolph Quirk, personal communication) indicates an ambiguity about and change in the metonymic experiential basis. The original meaning depended on a STATE AS BEHAVIOUR CAUSED BY IT metonymy: if you are at or below subsistence level you have to wait in a queue for handouts of bread. But the phenomenon of bread queues no longer being salient, it was reinterpreted experientially within a statistically bureaucratic culture as referring to the line of a graph or chart, marking the boundary between those who had insufficient food to survive (below the bread line) and those who had more than sufficient (above the bread line). This is metonymic, in terms of CONCEPT AS EXPRESSION. These examples indicate that, even across the sub-cultures of a language community, and through time, the experiential basis can disappear and need reinterpreting to make sense of an expression, even though both interpretations depend upon metonymy. It is very likely, therefore, that many isolated metaphors such as this will not be universal.

We introduced in chapter 1 Lakoff's theory that the sources of metaphor themes derive from our infant experience of our bodies and their interaction with objects in space. Hence, we would expect such sources to be universal features of bodily human experience. However, concepts of body and of self in a given culture are an integral part of the cultural model of person in that culture. As Chilton points out, "social organisation, architecture and religious belief, for example, might be held to affect the physical environment and thus an individual's physical experience of body and motion. How much is universal, how much culturally relative is an open question" (Chilton 1996: 49–50).

Let's consider the case of buildings, and how, following Chilton's account, the cultural specificity of source concepts of "house" might lead to metaphorical miscommunication in international politics. Buildings are culturally specific, whereas containers (not a basic–level category and therefore probably less psychologically salient) are not. The cultural specificity of *dom* in Russian, translated as *house* in English, is, when used as a metaphorical source, capable of leading to misunderstandings or at least different interpretations. Russians prototypically see a house as an apartment building in which access is restricted between the separate apartments, though they share the same common entrance. When Gorbachev, the Russian leader and architect of *perestroika*, used the metaphor of the common house of Europe, he obviously had in mind the Russian concept of an apartment block.

> The home is common, that is true, but each family has its own apartment, and there are different entrances too … It is only together, collectively and by following the sensible norms of co-existence that the Europeans can save their home, protect it against a conflagration and other calamities, make it better and safer, and maintain it in proper order (quoted in Chilton 1996: 266).

According to Chilton, Gorbachev lighted on this particular metaphor because

> his problem was to combine the concept of security-sovereignty with some kind of collective, all-European inter-state concept. How could the Soviet Union enter the European continent, yet also remain securely separate? Since the Russian *dom* is communal yet contains separate sovereign spaces, the metaphor is apt for the purposes of Gorbachevian foreign policy (p. 272).

However, because the Western idea of the unitary *house* is different from the Russian subdivided *dom*, there is the possibility of misunderstanding. "The Western unitary house model, by contrast, makes the idea of maintaining different social systems (socialist and capitalist) in the same 'house' at best paradoxical and at worst meaningless" (p. 275). While on the one hand the common house metaphor allowed some useful ambiguity in discussions with East Germany and West Germany about the future of the East, where apartment block houses were just as common as in Russia, talk of a common European home alarmed the Americans, who saw it as a metaphor representing the idea of a united Europe, with a common social organisation, without internally impermeable boundaries, whose secure outer wall excluded them.

As for metaphor themes, it is quite obvious that certain sources found in Metalude will be culture-bound. A hunter-gatherer stone-age culture, for example would not be familiar with the sources in RANK/VALUE/CHARACTER IS METAL, ACTIVITY IS BOARD GAME,

ACTIVITY IS CARD GAME, ACTIVITY/LIFE IS WRITING, COMPREHENSIBLITY IS STRAIGHT-
NESS, EMOTION IS ELECTRICITY, HUMAN IS MACHINE/APPLIANCE, ORGANISATION/SYSTEM
IS MACHINE, or MEANS/OPPORTUNITY IS TRANSPORT. Nomadic peoples of the Sahara
desert are unlikely to use sources such as those in HUMAN IS SHIP, ORGANISATION IS SHIP,
ACTIVITY IS BOAT TRAVEL, ACTIVITY IS SAILING, or FAILURE IS SHIPWRECK.

6.5.3   Target varies with the source

In this case of non-universality the target varies with the source because it is defined
by the source or sources used to conceptualise it. Thus, although targets might appear
to be identical, because they are determined metaphorically by different sources, they
are in fact different.

Indeed, one problem which arises from the way I have framed the possibilities for
kinds of non-universality is the assumption that source and target are independent
variables, inherent in the terminology of "mapping" and the invariance hypothesis.
This latter claims that features and structures are mapped across target and source domains, and are preserved in the mapping. But, as Brugman points out, Lakoff is often
unclear whether features and structures in the target domain are preserved in the same
way as features from the source domain are preserved in the transfer; and many abstract target domains are "structured entirely by one or more metaphorical mappings"
(Brugman 1990: 258–59). Supposing therefore that, instead of simply mapping pre-
existing features of a well-defined target, a source actually structures and constitutes
that target. In that case whenever the sources vary the target too will vary. In discussing the diverse metaphor themes for education in Chapter 5, we saw, for example, that
education and the learning process is not so much mapped onto a source, but that the
different themes constitute the rather vague or ambiguous notion of education differently. Even when we looked at emotion, we noted that the particularly modern English
concept seemed to be constituted by the metaphors of bad weather, movement, current in a liquid, to produce or reinforce the culturally-specific idea that emotions are
beyond human control, disruptive and brief.

We have already come across examples of how different subcultures might have
apparently identical sources and targets, though in fact, on closer inspection the target
is different precisely because the source is conceived differently. Supposing we assume
that HUMAN IS ANIMAL is a shared metaphor – there are certain respects in which humans resemble animals. As chapter 4 demonstrated, a sub-culture that characterises
animals as aggressive has a different concept of animals than one which conceptualises
them as symbiotic, and it will follow from this that the different subcultures will also
have different conceptions of the nature of humans. Similarly, in *Moral Politics* Lakoff
discusses US liberal and conservative ideologies in terms of the metaphor THE NATION
IS A FAMILY. However, the Strict Father family (conservative) is a different source from
the Nurturant Parent family (liberal). The upshot of this is, of course, that society too
is conceived differently.

6.5.3.1 *Chinese attitudes to time*

Another example is furnished by differences in the traditional Chinese and the Western post-Enlightenment notions of time. For both there appears to be a similar conceptual metaphor theme TIME IS MOVEMENT IN SPACE. However, unlike post-Darwinian westerners who tend to see time as linear and progressive, for the traditional Taoist and Buddhist Chinese the movement in space is a quite different kind of movement – cyclical and with potential for deterioration.

Chinese temporality was, for the most part, cyclic. A prominent belief of Chinese religions – including Taoism and Neo-Taoism, Confucianism and Neo-Confucianism, and Buddhism – is that the universe is in a constant state of flux. This state of flux is either an oscillation between two poles or a circular movement, but in both cases time returns to its starting point, and hence is relative rather than absolute (Bodde 1953: 21).

The cyclical view of time is also reflected in the tendency of Chinese philosophy to clearly differentiate the "three worlds" of past, present and future. As in Hindu attitudes to time (2.7, 5.2.2) the present may be seen as degraded and corrupted, and this creates an orientation to the past, veneration of antiquity, and an emphasis on precedent. Conformity rather than deviation from the past may become the deciding factor in intellectual debates, since the future is just an opportunity to work to restore the past and to relive it (Lauer 1973: 454). In order to do so academic endeavour must be oriented to history, so the etymology of *chi-ku*, meaning "learning", can be traced back (historically!) to the meaning 'searching out the ancient ways'.

The scholar Yen Fu saw in this aspect of Chinese temporality a significant difference from the West, which, in part, accounted for Western superiority in material benefits. He pointed out that the Chinese neglect the present in their fondness for antiquity, and that, in contrast with the Western idea of progress, the Chinese view cycles of order and disorder, prosperity and decline "as the natural course of heavenly conduct of human affairs" (Teng and Fairbank 1967: 151, Lauer 1973: 453–4). It follows that history is not oriented to any particular future goal; rather the aim of society must be an attempt to arrest decay. Kuan Tzu, in the 1st century BC, uses the predetermined cyclical movements of the planets and seasons as a model for orderly activity in time.

> Heaven does not change its constant activities. Covering all things, regulating cold and heat, setting in motion the sun and the moon, maintaining the orderly sequence of the stars and the planets – such are the constant activities of heaven … When constant activities function, there is order; when they are neglected, there is disorder (Rickett 1956: 122–3).

"Change, therefore, follows and should follow a predictable, knowable, and fixed repetitive pattern" (Lauer 1973: 455).

The traditional Chinese view was never quite as monolithic as these scholars claim, since though "sectarian Daoist and Buddhist eschatology possessed no linearism, Confucianism did" (Crisp 1993: 14; Needham 1969). Moreover, the Chinese conception of time, change and progress has now come under the influence of Darwinism and especially Marxism, Maoism and the concepts of modernisation. Nevertheless, one might expect the traditional attitudes to time to have left their mark on the metaphors through which time is conceptualised.

The cyclical nature of Chinese traditional time is apparent in the structure of novels. According to Timothy Mo in *An Insular Possession*, while the Western novel proceeds as a series of causes and effects in linear time, the Chinese novel

> moves in a path which is altogether circular. It is made up of separate episodes, pretty generally of chapter length, which may refer only to themselves and be joined by the loosest of threads. ... The one [the Western novel] is the form adapted for bearing the fictional wares of a civilisation committed to progress and advance, through the Scientific Explanation of phenomena from an analysis of cause and effect. The other [the Chinese] is the cast of a society which looks in upon itself and has no notion of progress but a spiral decline from a golden age to a brazen one, in letters as well as all else ...

Mo acknowledges the important influence of language on this different literary conceptualisation of time.

> Chinese is uninflected: that is to say, it lacks tenses. The events which, in our own novels are, according to custom, conceived of as having already taken place, however recently, and are as much recorded by the writer as described ... are in the native mode conceived of as occurring in an immediate present which (however remote the past in which they are known to have happened) unfolds directly and without mediation before the reader's very eyes (Mo 1986: 316–7).

Interestingly enough, according to Mo, if in his novel he is speaking in his own voice, the sub-theme of TIME IS MOVEMENT IN SPACE, PERIOD OF TIME IS LENGTH has a stronger metonymic basis in traditional Chinese culture than in the West, one which, as with many metonymies, allows reversal into LENGTH IS PERIOD OF TIME, and in fact is more or less literal.

> We have known a distance walked in one direction from a certain spot to another to be described as four *li*. To walk between these same very points but in the opposite direction, or retracing one's steps, the same informant would describe the distance as 15 *li*. How can this be? Why, going the one way is all downhill, returning the other is all uphill! ... Thus to elicit a more nearly correct and nice answer, it might be more appropriate to ascertain the duration of the journey, rather than its extent. The Chinese confuse TIME and DISTANCE (pp. 319–320).

This would indicate that apparently similar metaphor themes might in fact co-vary because both source and target are mutually defined and, despite the appearances of the identical target-source labels, defined differently in different cultures. But, further, that they may co-vary by being still interpreted as metonymic or even literal, rather than metaphorical. This was the case where HUMAN IS ANIMAL is interpreted, in one sub-culture, as a more or less literal statement, in the other as a mere metaphor.

6.5.4 Sources and targets are paired differently

The same target and source concepts exist in the different cultures, but they are paired differently, or paired in one language and not another.

How does this relate to the double hypothesis that all metaphor themes have a metonymic base, and that this metonymic base is universal? If the hypothesis is true, then there should be quite severe constraints on the different pairings. There are only a limited number of experiential correlates for a given target.

Radden lists under cultural models of metonymy or metaphor those like western conceptualisation of physical force – the impetus model, (see our discussion of Langacker's canonical event in chapter 7), communication and the conduit metaphor as suggested by Reddy (1993), and the distinction between ideas and emotions – ideas are encoded in English as countable nouns, whereas emotions are coded as mass nouns (Radden 2000: 102–104).

But let's see if we can find some more explicit examples from an "exotic" language such as Chinese. While both Chinese and English have more or less similar concepts of emotion and plant, and there may be a couple of English lexical items which link them as target and source, EMOTION IS PLANT comprises a much more important metaphor theme in Chinese, with at least six lexical items or expressions:

> 1. 心花怒放 [xin hua nu fang]
> Literal meaning = 'heart flower in full bloom'
> Metaphorical meaning = 'be elated, be wild with joy'
> 2. 花心 [hua xin]
> Literal meaning = 'flower heart'
> Metaphorical meaning = 'inconstancy in love, a change of heart'
> 3. 芒刺在背 [mángcì-zàibèi]
> Literal meaning = 'prickle in one's back'
> Metaphorical meaning = 'feel uneasy and nervous'
> 4. 心乱如麻 [xin luan ru ma]
> Literal meaning = 'heart confused like a bundle of flax'
> Metaphorical meaning = 'utter confusion'
> 5. 粗枝大叶 [cūzhī-dàyè]
> Literal meaning = 'thick branches and large leaves'
> Metaphorical meaning = 'carelessness'
> 6. 柳性 [liu xing]
> Literal meaning = 'the nature of willow'
> Metaphorical meaning = 'carnal pleasure'

And perhaps, via a metonymy, the following, though they might equally be part of HUMAN IS PLANT:

> 7. 杨柳依依 [yang liu yi yi]
> Literal meaning = 'poplar and willow are reluctant to be separated'
> Metaphorical meaning = (of a man and a woman) 'feel deeply attached to each other, experience ardent love'
> 8. 柳啼花怨 [liu ti hua yuan]
> Literal meaning = 'the willow trees weep and the flowers complain'
> Metaphorical meaning = 'the sadness of parting lovers'

Though in English we have a number of lexical items which link status with position or direction, such as *right-hand man*, *sinister*, this is more common in Chinese, and in particular there is no correspondence between the east and importance in English as there is in Chinese:

> 1. 做东 [zuòdōng]
> Literal meanin = 'to do in the east'
> Metaphorical meaning = 'act as the host (to somebody)'
> 2. 东家 [dōng jia]
> Literal meaning = 'the person in the east'
> Metaphorical meaning = 'master, landlord, boss'
> 3. 房东 [fángdōng]
> Literal meaning = 'the east of the house'
> Metaphorical meaning = 'landlord or landlady'
> 4. 股东 [gǔdōng]
> Literal meaning = 'the east of the stock'
> Metaphorical meaning = 'shareholder; stockholder'

Whether under the influence of communism or not, there are also a number of Chinese metaphors suggesting a theme BAD IS PRIVATE:

> 1. 私心 [sīxīn]
> Literal meaning = 'private heart'
> Metaphorical meaning = 'selfish motives (or ideas)'
> 2. 徇私 [xun sī]
> Literal meaning = 'for private purpose'
> Metaphorical meaning = 'jobbery, corruption'
> 3. 走私 [zǒusī]
> Literal meaning = 'walk privately'
> Metaphorical meaning = 'smuggle'
> 4. 私通 [sītōng]
> Literal meaning = 'private communication'
> Metaphorical meaning = (1) 'fornicate, have illicit sexual intercourse'
> (2) 'communicate secretly with the enemy'

5. 私情 [sīqíng]
Literal meaning = 'private relation'
Metaphorical meaning = 'illicit sexual relations'

6.5.5 Different grounds or partial mapping of potential correspondences.

In this case of non-universality, although there is an identity in pairing, because the mappings are only partial then different grounds or aspects of the source schema are mapped or explored in different cultures/languages. In terms of the individual lexical item this would mean that the target and source are identical, but the ground is different. In terms of metaphor themes with the same target and source this would mean that different aspects of the ICM or schema are elaborated by the lexical items found under that metaphor theme. In either case, but particularly the latter, this represents a challenge to the universal experientialist hypothesis.

A comparison between Chinese and English gives us an example of more or less identical metaphors but where the specific vocabulary of English explores different aspects of the ICM or script from Chinese. Yu Ning shows how HAPPY IS HIGH is a metaphor theme common to Chinese and English, but that parts of this metaphor are elaborated in English but not Chinese. In English height is a source for happiness: **high** 'extreme excitement and happiness' (*exercise always gives me a high*), **high** 'extremely happy due to drug-taking' (*he was high on cocaine when I tried to interview him*), and **in high spirits** 'extremely happy and enjoying oneself' (*he was in very high spirits at the wedding reception*). If you become happier or something makes you happier you move or are moved upwards: **lift** 'make feel happier' (*the sunshine lifted my spirits*), **perk up** 'suddenly become happier' (*when I reminded him of his upcoming holiday he perked up a bit*), **jump for joy** 'be very pleased and show your pleasure/excitement' (*when he saw his exam results he jumped for joy*), **bouncy** 'happy and energetic' (*4 year olds are always bouncy in the morning, a bit too bouncy, really*), **buoyant** 'cheerful' (*after his concert he was in buoyant mood*), **spirits rise/raise spirits** 'improve to a happier mood' (*though disappointed with the election result news of Patten's defeat raised his spirits a little*). As a result of being moved upwards you are happy: **uplifted** 'inspired to be happy and cheerful' (*her smile was so radiant that he felt uplifted by it*), **exalted** 'experiencing great happiness' (*when she finished playing the Rachmaninov and received such applause she was exalted*), and **exaltation** means 'very strong feeling of happiness' (*they had the exaltation of knocking out Man Utd.*). Something that makes you happier is an **upper** 'stimulating anti-depressant drug' (*I was so depressed I took an upper*), and you are more likely to move upwards easily if you are not heavy: **light-hearted** 'happy and not serious' (*they had a light-hearted discussion over drinks*). You can regain your happiness by going up after being down: **bounce back** 'return to you usual state of happiness after an unpleasant experience' (*she soon bounced back after the death of her father*), or ride on an **emotional roller-coaster** 'sudden changes of mood from happiness to sadness and despair or vice versa' (*the match was an emotional roller coaster for fans when Italy came back to win from 3–0 down*).

Chinese metaphors explore more or less the same areas of the metaphor theme, where being high is happiness, and rising/raising is being/making happier.

Ta   hen   gao-xing
'He very high-spirit'
'He is in high spirits/happy'

Ta   hen   xing-fen
'He very spirit-lift'
'He is very spirit-lifted/excited'

Ta   chu-yu   kang-fen zhuangtai zhizhong
'He situate-in high-lift state   inside'
'He is in a state of high-liftedness/extreme excitement'

Tamen qingxu gao-zhang
'They mood high-rise'
'They are in an exalted mood'

Tamen gege   qingxu gao-yang
'They everyone mood high-raise'
'They are all in high-spirits'

Tamen gege   xing-gao cai-lie
'They everyone spirit-high colour-strong'
'They are all glowing with high spirits'

Ta xing congcong de
'He spirit rise-rise PRT'
'He's pleased and excited'

Ta xing-tou   hen gao
'He spirit-head very high'
'He's in very high spirits'

Zhe-xia   tiqi le   wo-de xingzhi
'This moment raise ASP my   mood'
'This time it lifted my mood'

(Yu Ning 1995: 71–72).

Yu Ning also suggests that the idea of happiness being off the ground temporarily gives us metonymies (metaphors?) such as:

Tamen xi-yue   *bian-wu*
'They   happy-leap glad-dance'
'They were jumping and dancing for joy' (p. 78).

However, there is no equivalent in Chinese for the idea of being off the ground and up in the air more permanently than in jumping or dancing, which is an important aspect of English HAPPY IS HIGH: **over the moon** 'very pleased' (*she was over the moon about her new baby*), **on cloud nine** 'extremely happy and excited' (*she was on cloud nine after getting the job*), **walk/float on air** 'be extremely excited and happy' (*when I got into Oxford University I was walking on air for several days*), **on the crest of a wave** 'very happy and confident' (*now my book's been published I'm on the crest of a wave*). To these Yu Ning adds, 'I was flying high', 'I'm six feet off the ground' 'We were in the clouds' (though whether these are attested as conventional metaphors in any dictionary or corpus I am not sure).

The reason Yu Ning gives for this difference between the parts of the source ICM explored in English and Chinese is that in Chinese culture being permanently off the ground symbolises the undesirable qualities of smugness, complacency, and frivolity (p. 74). (It can of course, also be used in a similarly pejorative way in English, though with more connotations of pomposity and impracticality: **lofty**, **high-flown**, **high-sounding**, and **airy-fairy** rather than **down to earth**.)

An interesting example of differing grounds for an individual lexical item is when a human target is conventionally referred to using the source word *banana*. Apparently, though the pairing is identical, the grounds are different in different languages and language varieties. In British and American English this conventional metaphor always takes the plural form as in "he is bananas" meaning 'he is crazy'. In Singaporean English "he is a banana" means 'he is Chinese by race, but has Western values'. In Portuguese, the word *banana*, when applied to a human target means 'a conformist'. This is an interesting case, because the three language communities have chosen different features of bananas as a basis of their meanings. British/American speakers have, at least in the past, selected the curved shape of the banana as the basis for their metaphorical meaning, because it plugs into the conceptual metaphor theme SANITY/NORMALITY IS STRAIGHTNESS. Singaporeans have noticed the colour contrast between the outside and the inside of a banana, which plugs into the metaphor theme RACE IS COLOUR, and exploited a number of other metaphor themes such as UNDERSTANDING IS PENETRATION. The Portuguese speaker has a different image for bananas – thinking of a bunch or hand growing on the tree. Seen in this perspective bananas look quite similar and all point in the same direction, (SHARE PURPOSE IS ALIGN), and are packed tightly together (SIMILARITY IS PROXIMITY). This example might furnish evidence for Grady's primary metaphor theory, which we explore later.

6.5.6   General identity of pairing with specific differences

We need to put some question marks over the rather neat way of framing the problem of universality in the previous sections. The main problem concerns the levels of specificity. One might be tempted to agree with Barcelona: metaphors and metonymies are to a large extent culture specific, because the domains of experience are not necessarily the same in all cultures, but the most abstract over-arching metaphors and metonymies seem to have as input or source domains universal physical notions like "verticality", "container" etc. known as image schemas, which are acquired on the basis of our earliest bodily experiences (Barcelona 2000b: 6). According to this theory, at some general level we may be able to discount the problems discussed in 6.5.2 above, if not 6.5.1.

However, one major difficulty with conceptual metaphor theory is that there has been no concerted effort among researchers to sit down together and work out the criteria for positing a conceptual metaphor theme. It's like doing Chemistry without a periodic table. This is a problem with Metalude itself. From the perspective of 6.5.2 only a small proportion of the sources would be culture specific, because the vast majority of them are quite general – MOVEMENT, PLACE – or are qualities of things – STABILITY, PROXIMITY, WEIGHT, HARDNESS, HIGH – rather than things, such as MONKEY, CHICKEN. However, not all sources are conceived so generally, and there are a number of superordinate categories of things as sources e.g. VEHICLE, MACHINE, PREY, FOOD, and even basic-level sources such as SHIP. One of the reasons that there is so much multivalency in the Metalude themes, might be that, from a cognitive theory point of view, I have tended to work at too low a level of specificity in these last cases. However, there is a tension between theoretical explanatory elegance and the psychological power and salience of images in language processing and memory: only when one descends to the basic level can the imagery which enhances memory operate. And this could be important both for the productivity of the metaphor theme, and for any use it may have in teaching vocabulary, one desired by-product of my lexicographical project.

The most interesting attempt to be more systematic about metaphor theme categories is work by Grady (1997) on primary metaphors, which we will consider in the next section.

6.6   Grady primary metaphors and multivalency

Grady (1997) elaborates a theory which attempts a better account than the traditional Lakoffian one for why some metaphor themes are inadequately explained experientially, why grounds are only partially explored (6.5.5). His theory also attempts to show how ascending to a higher level of generality (6.5.6) is more explanatorily elegant.

He starts by defining primary scenes as the metonymic basis for metaphor.

Primary scenes are minimal (temporally-delimited) episodes of subjective experience, characterised by tight correlations between physical circumstance and cognitive response. They are universal elements of human experience, defined by basic cognitive mechanisms and abilities, which relate in some salient sense to goal-oriented interaction with the world.

For example, warmth and emotional intimacy, heaviness and strain become closely associated in various primary scenes (p. 24). Source concepts for primary metaphors have a content tied to physical perception or sensation and have image content, though this may not be very rich. Primary target concepts are not abstract. They are very real and fully experienced, but they have no image content (p. 26). He suggests that there is a grounding, a correlation in experience of primary scenes that provides the motivation for the primary metaphors: e.g. DIFFICULTY IS HEAVINESS – difficulty of lifting heavy objects; KNOWING/UNDERSTANDING IS SEEING – experiences where information is gathered through the visual channel; AFFECTION IS WARMTH – correlation between affection and body warmth (produced by proximity); CAUSAL RELATEDNESS IS PHYSICAL CONNECTION (Metalude's CAUSE IS LINK/LINE/CONNECTION) – the joint motion of objects which are physically connected; HAPPINESS IS BRIGHTNESS – the correlation between bright light and safety, warmth etc. (Grady 1997: 27).

Primary targets reflect the operations of extremely basic cognitive mechanisms, and they are simpler and more universal than, for example, abstract culturally-created concepts such as Justice (p. 28). And primary metaphors are universal because the sources are more general than basic level categories, and experientially simple. For example, UNDERSTANDING IS GRASPING (cf. Metalude's UNDERSTAND/CONTROL IS HANDLE) is a primary metaphor, since grasping "is one of our most basic tools for controlling, moving, and maintaining possession of objects ... a self-contained routine – an experiential gestalt". Similarly, ACTIVITY IS MOTION is a primary metaphor, whereas MARRIAGE IS DRIVING A CAR is not. Not only does the latter involve many different actions, unlike motion and grasping, but the source and target scripts also create the potential for many details that are not metaphorically mapped, and the richness of their scripts reflects the fact that both target and source are culturally-specific concepts (pp. 144–148).

Grady convincingly takes a conventionally touted conceptual metaphor THEORIES ARE BUILDINGS and shows it is unsatisfactory because there are unused parts of the metaphor which cannot be explained, and there are overlaps, that is, in my terms, multivalency and diversification. We can build societies and marriages as well as theories, so the source, building, is mulitivalent. Similarly, theories can be textiles, so we have diverse sources for the same target. Grady's conclusion is that this metaphor theme is too specific, so he prefers the general and image-poor primary metaphors ORGANISATION IS PHYSICAL STRUCTURE and VIABILITY IS ERECTNESS, "metaphors which have a direct experiential basis, and which motivate highly predictable sets of data (i.e. sets without gaps)". He claims that complex metaphors such as THEORIES ARE BUILDINGS are actually compounds of these primary metaphors, so that a better account would be VIABLE ORGANISATION IS ERECT PHYSICAL STRUCTURE, which gives a plausible grounding in primary scenes of our experience (pp. 47–53). We can see how these primary metaphors can cut across several more specific metaphor themes and simplify what would otherwise be cases of multivalency and diversification. Or one could consider these rather sparse primary metaphors as the common grounds of various diverse or multivalent sources.

Grady shows how metaphorical elaboration can take place, by combining primary metaphors, for example with the item *buttress*.

> The language suggesting that a theory can be buttressed reflects two distinct underlying images: an image of logical organisation as the relation between physical parts, and an image of functionality as erectness. These metaphors are independently motivated by distinct primary scenes, and they license independent sets of linguistic data. Since they are compatible with one another, however, they may be combined, or unified, into a single mapping which refers both to physical part-whole structure and to erectness. An emergent feature of the more elaborate mapping which this unification yields is that certain parts are in asymmetrical relationships with each other: some parts are supported by others (pp. 200–201).

Grady concludes:

> A decompositional approach shows that innovative usages of the [this] sort are most profitably understood as combinations of independent but compatible metaphors which each add detail and specificity to the compound which they make up (p. 63).

Given the rather general nature of the primary metaphors their grounding would appear to be different from that given in traditional conceptual metaphor theory, which is quite specific: they cannot be said to derive from experiences in one particular domain, they are more like the kinds of cognitive phenomena which structure grammatical meaning discussed in the next chapter. For example, Grady is often forced to a very abstract level in identifying primary metaphors, e.g. "scenes involving a feeling of need plus a focus on some particular physical object are recurrent and salient in our experience" (p. 91).

To sum up, Grady has attempted to simplify and "shore up" the metonymic basis of metaphor theory by resorting to one-dimensional sources and targets which cross-cut basic-level categories (such as dogs, trees, and even buildings), which one might designate by nouns, by using concepts which could be referred to by adjectives or verbs or their nominalizations. By reducing the fecundity of an imagery-rich basic-level category, with all its accrued cultural connotations, to a sparse simple feature, he has of course managed to explain away the cultural variation in the different elaboration of grounds (6.5.5), and some of the linguistic relativity of sources, targets and their pairings (6.5.1–4).[3]

However, despite his efforts, we might still have doubts about the metonymic basis for metaphor themes and primary metaphors. Undoubtedly many metaphor themes and primary metaphors have as grounds or grounding a metonymic base with which they correlate, sometimes involving analogy. These are constrained because they have to reflect specific recurring experience types. But many metaphor themes may also depend on the CATEGORY AS MEMBER OF A CATEGORY metonymy with a source concept which is a specific instance of a target concept (pp. 223–226). Moreover, in many cases there is some kind of loose analogy or similarity across domains that would appear to have little if any metonymical and experiential basis.[4]

6.7 Questioning the metonymic basis of metaphor themes

Taylor points out that not all metaphor themes or conceptual metaphors seem to be motivated by metonymy. In particular he concentrates on various synaesthetic metaphors such as loud music/loud colour; sweet cake/sweet music, where "the metaphor does not really develop out of the metonymy. It is simply motivated and constrained by the metonymic model of the target" (Barcelona 2000c: 42).

I labelled my metaphor themes in Metalude "Root Analogies", because what appears important to me is the analogical nature of their structure – the relation of A : B : C in one domain was construed as analogous to X : Y : Z in another. Whether these analogies developed out of metonymies in experience of one domain was not important to me. There appear to be cases, suggested by Taylor, where such analogical metaphor themes cannot have been derived from the same domain metonymically, even by primary metaphors.

One such case is SIGHT IS SOUND: **loud** not only means 'producing or consisting of a large amount of sound', but metaphorically 'having unpleasantly bright colours or patterns' (*he was a quiet man but always wore loud ties*). When a voice makes a loud unpleasant sound it **screams** 'makes a horrible impression of non-matching colours' (*if you wear that pink jacket with your orange skirt, they'll scream at each other*), and when a percussion instrument makes a loud metallic noise it **clashes,** in terms of colour 'looks ugly or wrong together' (*the green curtains clash with the orange carpet*). By

---

3.   For a similar critique, see Kovecses 2005: 4, 11.

4.   Kövecses (2000b, 2002) presents a solution where the fully-embodied concept (perhaps at the basic level of conceptualisation), a "simple" rather than a "primary" metaphor, will have certain salient grounds or convey central knowledge, for example in the case of BUILDING it would be 'abstract construction', 'abstract stability' and 'abstract structure'. Multivalent sources would tend to have identical grounds.

contrast, colours that 'match or combine pleasantly' **harmonize** (*the blue of the walls and the green of the curtains harmonize effectively*).

At the other end of the scale of volume we have colours that are **quiet** 'not very bright or noticeable' (*he wanted to wear quiet colours so that he'd blend in with the crowd*), or **muted** 'soft and gentle, not bright and strong' (*I prefer sombre, muted colours – but my wife likes to dress brightly*). The quality of sound gives us a metaphor for 'quality of colour' in **tone** (*the flat was decorated in pastel tones*). By analogy of 1:2 a **halftone** will have minimal colour 'picture made up from a pattern of very small black spots' (*black-and-white newspaper pictures are usually produced in halftone*), but particularly exciting colours will be **jazzy** 'very bright and colourful' (*he wore a dark suit but a jazzy tie*).

There is no particular recurrent experience, which I can think of, which would make us associate loud music or sound with bright colours, and so provide an experiential basis for these metaphors. Rather, one would have to seek for some abstract ground like 'conspicuousness' to link them.

Even more "arbitrary" seem to be the lexical items in metaphor themes such as EMOTION IS COLOUR (illustrated above in Table 23). Though some might have a metonymic basis, others, namely *blue, purple* and *green*, seem to contradict the experimentally-determined association with mood, and neither do they seem motivated by analogy, except for the trivial analogy of difference: as yellow is different from green, so cowardice is different from envy. There simply seems to be an association between the two domains, which encourages the "metaphorical" use of the vocabulary from one domain in the other. Much the same was seen to be true with EMOTION IS BODY/PART or FLUID. What is the experiential basis for associating spunk and balls with bravery and determination? Perhaps, in these cases, it is enough for one lexical item to colonise metonymically, as source, a target domain, in order to set up an association between the two domains, so that other lexical items from the source set can follow, but without any metonymic basis. If someone goes white with shock or red with anger, as a metonymic basis for *appalled* and *see red*, then *yellow* 'cowardly', *green* 'envious' etc. can follow the original coloniser, without metonymic motivation (though perhaps with an existential motivation).

After glancing through Metalude I have come up with a number of metaphor themes which, on the face of it, would not appear to have an experiential metonymical basis either as internal bodily or cognitively motivated metaphors. It might be worthwhile comparing them with Grady's list in the appendix of his thesis. Of course, the list from Metalude may not be primary metaphors in Grady's sense, so it might be unfair to blame him for not considering them. However, they are attested by a considerable amount of lexical evidence. At least we can ask ourselves the following questions.

Are there any metaphor themes in Metalude which are primary metaphors, because they deal with the same sparse universal semantic concepts, but which do not appear in Grady? These may or may not be amenable to an experientialist motivation.

COMPREHENSIBILITY IS STRAIGHTNESS (but he has NORMAL IS STRAIGHT)

GOODNESS (HONESTY) IS STRAIGHTNESS

CONSIDER IS TRAVEL OVER/INTO

TOPIC/SUBJECT IS PLACE

EMOTION IS LIQUID

GOOD IS HIGH

IDEA/EMOTION IS LIQUID (but he has CIRCUMSTANCES ARE LIQUIDS)

SANITY/CALM IS BALANCE

SOUND IS LIQUID

and all synaesthetic metaphor themes.

Are there metaphor themes in Metalude that Grady also mentions for which he gives a convincing experiential motivation?

NON-OPERATIONAL/INACTIVE IS LOW

TEXT IS STRUCTURE

Are there any which can be convincingly explained in relation to primary metaphors, although they themselves are not primary metaphors, in the way in which he attempted to do with THEORIES ARE BUILDINGS?

ARGUMENT/IDEA IS BUILDING

COMMUNICATING IS COOKING/SERVING

CREATE IDEA/TEXT IS MAKE CLOTH

IDEA/EMOTION IS FOOD

SOCIAL ORGANISATION IS BODY

TEXT IS BUILDING/CONTAINER

TEXT IS PATH

THINKING/BELIEVING IS WALKING/TRAVELLING

COMMUNICATING IS LEADING

VERBAL COMMUNICATION IS TRAVEL/MOVEMENT

What examples can we give of metaphor themes where there is little scope for reducing them to primary metaphors to account for all the vocabulary associated with them? These are extremely numerous. Just taking those which have liquid as their source gives a fair number.

CROWD/HUMANS IS LIQUID

KNOWLEDGE/WORDS IS FLUID

LIGHT IS LIQUID

MONEY IS LIQUID/BLOOD

TRAFFIC IS LIQUID/BLOOD

ELECTRICITY IS LIQUID/WATER

The latter is a case where an experiential basis is unlikely: it so happens that when they are paired in experience the experiencer is electrocuted!

Our conclusion has to be that many metaphorical themes may be traced ingeniously to a metonymic base, but they seem to have taken on a life of their own, quite independent of the original primary metaphor. This might be achieved by imagery operating at the basic category level, not through single features at a more general and image-poor level. Grady would say they are complex metaphors which are motivated by combinations of primary metaphors. But, in addition, there are many metaphor themes depending upon an association between two distinct domains, where it is difficult to conceive of one experiential domain in which they were metonymically related. Indeed Grady (1999) later conceded this point. An explanation here might be that one lexical transfer based on metonymy, or based on existential theory, creates a cognitive association paving the way for further lexical transfers unmotivated by the original metonymy. But culture, history and ideology also have a large part to play in producing or nurturing and elaborating many of the metaphor themes found in Metalude.

6.8   The body as biological or historical and cultural?

I would like now to turn our ideological lenses upon what Lakoff calls "*The* Contemporary Theory of Metaphor". This grew up in a particular historical context, among linguists heavily influenced by, though ultimately distancing themselves from, Chomskyan notions of language. Two aspects of Chomsky's theory seem to have been inherited. The emphasis on linguistic universals or universal grammar, and the notion that language is an innate genetically-determined faculty, though for Chomsky's mental faculty Lakoff and his followers substitute the biological (Lakoff and Johnson 1999: 476). Others starting in this tradition, such as Steven Pinker, have gone on to emphasise the biological and chemical aspects of reality, to the exclusion of all else, in the kind of reductionist statements we cited in 4.3.6.

There is quite a large dose of reductionism to biology in the experiential hypothesis itself: that it is our universal bodily experience which is the important determinant of our cognition, and that culture and history are at most some variations upon the biological theme. Some might even go further, and see the universality of emotions like *anger* as biologically derived through some kind of evolutionary advantage or through aggression genes. But we have seen that Ifaluk *song* and Ilongot *liget* precisely lack this concept of aggressive retaliation against the offending party. I'm not even sure it's very strong in English *anger* either.

I believe I have demonstrated a number of points in this chapter. Firstly there is, indeed, especially in the conceptualisation of emotion, a bodily and metonymic base which explains many metaphor themes. But this bodily experiential basis is influenced by culture even in areas where the body is intimately linked with the concept itself, i.e. emotion in Damasio's and Wierzbicka's definitions of it. When we come to consider metaphor themes where the bodily basis is less obviously related to the target, we see that many such themes resist explanation in terms of the experiential metonymic hypotheses, and are certainly not universal. Attempts like Grady's to boost the metonymic hypothesis by shifting to a higher level of generality are convincing in some cases, but even these theories suggest the possibility that, at the more specific level of the basic-level category, where imagery operates, cultural modifications are important. And in many cases it is difficult to see a metonymic basis at all. Even in cases where metonymy suggests universal metaphorical patterns, we can see that target concepts and source concepts are only loosely similar in meaning in different languages, cultures and sub-cultures, and that, indeed, the target concept may vary in step with the source concept.

The strong experientialist theory of metonymy-based conceptual metaphor, with its universalist tendencies, depends upon the idea that the body is in turn universal and purely biological. However, both our bodily movements and the way we conceive of our bodies are as much a product of culture. Bourdieu, for example, sees the body and the sense and disposition of our body as a cultural and historical product.

> Bourdieu speaks ... of a bodily or corporeal "hexis", by which he means a certain durable organisation of one's body and of its deployment in the world. "Bodily hexis is political mythology realised, em-bodied, turned into a permanent disposition, a durable way of standing, speaking, walking, and thereby feeling and thinking." The importance of bodily hexis can be seen in the differing ways in which men and women carry themselves in the world, in their differing postures, their differing ways of walking and speaking, of eating and laughing, as well as the differing ways that men and women deploy themselves in the more intimate aspects of life. "The body is the site of incorporated history. The practical schemes through which the body is organised are the product of history and, at the same time, the source of practices and perceptions which reproduce that history" (Thompson 1991: 13).

Bourdieu makes the link between language and the body, not just at the semantic level, but at the phonetic level too, where different articulatory movements, such as those creating different accents, have differing values as cultural capital in the linguistic market.

> It is no coincidence that bourgeois distinction invests the same intention in its relation to language as it invests in its relation to the body. The sense of acceptability which orients linguistic practices is inscribed in the most deep-rooted of bodily dispositions: it is the whole body which responds by its posture, but also by its inner reactions or, more specifically, the articulatory ones, to the tension of the market. Language is a body technique, and specifically linguistic, especially phonetic, competence is a dimension of bodily hexis in which one's whole relation to the social world, and one's whole socially informed relation to the world, are expressed (Bourdieu 1991: 86).

Bourdieu identifies specific articulatory metaphors in French, which belong to EMO-TION/CHARACTER IS BODY-PART, especially the lips: *bouche fine, pincée, levres pincés, serrées, du bout des lèvres, bouche en cul-de-poule* 'to be fastidious, supercilious, tight lipped', *faire la fine bouche, la petite bouche* 'to be fussy about food, hard to please'. The articulation of the word *bouche* is symbolic of tension (articulatory self-censorship), while *gueule* is, by contrast, open and relaxed: *faire la gueule* 'sulk', *fort en gueule, coup de gueule, grande gueule, engueuler, s'engueuler, gueuler, aller gueuler* 'loud mouthed', 'dressing down', 'bawl', 'have a slanging match', 'mouth off' – all to do with strength of voice. *Gueule* also participates in idioms for violent insults: *casser la gueule, mon poing sur la gueule, ferme ta gueule* 'smash your face', 'a punch in the mouth', 'shut your face'. In addition it is associated with identity: *bonne gueule, sale gueule* 'nice guy', 'ugly mug' by way of the expression *ouvrir sa gueule* 'say one's piece'. It also connotes frank accept-ance of pleasure from food: *s'en foutre plein la gueule, se rincer la gueule* 'stuff oneself with food and drink'.

> On the one hand domesticated language, censoring made natural, which pro-scribes gross remarks, coarse jokes, and thick accents, goes hand in hand with domestication of the body which excludes all excessive manifestations of appe-tites or feelings (exclamations as much as tears or sweeping gestures), and which subjects the body to all kinds of discipline and censorship aimed at denaturalising it. On the other hand the "relaxation of articulatory tension", which leads to the dropping of the final "r" and "l" … is associated with rejection of the censorship which propriety imposes, particularly on the tabooed body, and with the outspo-keness whose daring is less innocent than it seems since, in reducing humanity to its common nature – belly, bum, bollocks, grub, guts and shit – it tends to turn the social world upside down, arse over head (pp. 87–88).

Harvey, too, stresses the socially determined nature of our bodies, which makes a return to the natural biological body as a means of liberation and challenge futile.

> [N]o human body is outside of the social processes of determination of space-time. To return to it may well be to instantiate the space and time of the very social processes being purportedly rebelled against. If, for example, workers are transformed into appendages of capital in both the workplace and the consump-tion sphere (or, as Foucault prefers it, bodies are made over into docile bodies by the rise of a powerful disciplinary apparatus from the eighteenth century on) then how can their bodies be a measure of anything outside of the circulation of capital or of the various mechanisms that discipline them? Or, to take a more contempo-rary version of the same argument, if we are now all cyborgs (as Haraway in her celebrated manifesto on the topic suggests) then how can we measure anything outside of that deadly embrace of the machine as extension of our own body and body as extension of the machine? (Harvey 1996: 276–7).

Here Harvey reminds us of the discussion in chapter 3, which, quoting Haraway, ex-plored the HUMAN IS MACHINE theme, and pointed out that, in order for humans to become an efficient part of the industrial manufacturing enterprise they were best conceived and taught to behave as mechanical, predictable and time-governed. In fact, as this example shows, instead of metaphor themes simply reflecting an experiential basis, they may be ideologically constructed in order to produce particular bodily experiences and control certain physical behaviours (consider also TIME IS MONEY, QUALITY IS MONEY/WEALTH). The theoretical or existential metaphor *produces* a metonymy – CAUSE AS EFFECT. Moreover, the social and cultural construction of the body means that any metonymic experiential basis is no longer simply biological and local:

> Sensuous interaction between the body and its environs can certainly carry with it a wide range of psychic as well as social meanings; the difficulty is that our relations as organisms embedded in nature extend far further into a chain of commodity production and exchange that reaches into every corner of the globe (p. 303).

I hope that in this chapter I have given a fair account of theories of metaphor that attempt to base it upon metonymy, and which may even go further and claim a universal metonymic biological or experiential basis for metaphor themes. Doubtless these theories can account for some of the lexical metaphorical evidence, especially in domains like emotion. But I intend, in the next chapter to show that, despite claims by Barcelona and Grady, culture and linguistic categories interact even at high levels of generality such as grammar. And in the final chapter, that many of the English metaphor themes we have explored in this book owe their frequency, popularity and strength, if not their origins, to specific historical theories in economic philosophy.

CHAPTER 7

Grammar, metaphor and ecology

When you have an effective enough technology so that you can really act upon your epistemological errors and can create havoc in the world in which you live, then the error is lethal. (Bateson 1975: 460)

7.1   Introduction

So far in this book, when considering the influence that metaphor has on our thinking and ideology, we have limited ourselves to words – the patterns of vocabulary in the dictionary that we have called metaphor themes. This chapter extends our discussion into the area of grammar.

In chapter 1 I suggested that, as language users, we are more aware of the influence on thought of original metaphors, less of conventional metaphors, and less still of literal vocabulary. Grammar, however, lies at a level even less accessible to our conscious awareness: partly because it is less changeable than vocabulary – while new words are being invented every day, grammar is very resistant to new structures; and partly because the metalanguage for grammar, the vocabulary used for speaking about it, is much more complex and technical than that for talking about words. As we have seen, metaphorical vocabulary and metaphor themes structure our experience of concepts such as emotion, education, disease, time or success. Similarly, but in an even more fundamental way, the grammatical clauses of the languages we speak structure how we understand, experience and act on our material, social and mental worlds. And just as there are levels of conventionality in our use of vocabulary, whether the highly conventionalised literal vocabulary, or the kinds of conventional metaphors we have been dealing with in this book, so there are usual or conventional clause patterns for conceptualising and constructing events, and rather less typical clause patterns, known variously as "marked clause structure" or "grammatical metaphor". For example, the usual way to refer to a Thing is by a noun, and to a Process by a verb. A marked or metaphorical grammar would use a noun to refer to a process, as in – "John's eating of the banana" rather than "John ate the banana".

The rigid distinction between nouns and verbs and between things and processes imposed by literal grammar of English and other Standard Average European (SAE) languages will be one area of discussion in this chapter. Another wider concern is the way in which transitivity constructions – the relationships between subjects, verbs and objects and so on – structure what has been called a canonical event, the most typical way of conceptualising events in the West. The reason for considering these particular features of grammar is that they build a model of our experience, especially our experience of the natural world, which is by no means ideologically neutral. I will discuss how the world-view created by these grammatical structures, a simplified Newtonian worldview, is out of step with modern scientific thinking about our physical and biological environment, notably the thinking among physicists that matter is fundamentally process. Further, I will try to show how dangerous this world-view is in its implications about our relationships with nature – especially that humans can dominate nature by acting on it/her/him in a one-sided way as actors in an asymmetrical process. I discuss the 19th and 20th century's attempts to dominate and control nature, through dams, hydro-electric projects, road-building and fisheries, as detailed by Josephson (2002) in *Industrialised Nature*.

Having discussed "literal" grammar and its possible effects, in the latter parts of the chapter we will consider grammatical "metaphor" – those structures available in English grammar which deviate from the typical clause structure, and in so doing construct a view of the world which may be more sympathetic to the findings of modern physics and to ecology. We will find, however, that what we can do with English is rather limited. Consequently the chapter proceeds to look at an "exotic" language radically different from English or SAE in the way in which it constructs the world. This language is the North American Algonquin language, Niitsi'powahsin (Blackfoot). The degree to which the grammar of this language constructs a radically different view of the world from English is perhaps no better illustrated than by the claim of native speakers that they can speak Niitsi'powahsin for a whole day without using a noun!

Moving from transitivity in general, we will briefly explore the grammatical expression of possession, showing the general tendency, as capitalism developed in the West, for possession to be metaphorically equated with taking, getting, grabbing or holding.

The chapter will end with some reference to process philosophies more in step with modern scientific thought, and more conducive to the survival of the world we inhabit. The irony is that just like the species that are under threat as a result of a worldview and an industrial practice based on simplified Newtonian dynamics, Niitsi'powahsin is one of the 27% of the world's 6,809 languages that are either critically endangered, endangered or vulnerable (Sutherland 2003: 22; see also Crystal 2000: chapter 1). The radically different view of the world which Niitsi'powahsin represents is one we desperately need to prevent ecological disaster and ultimately our own degradation and endangerment.

7.2   The Noun-Verb/Thing-Process construction

Many, if not most, of the world's languages reflect a distinction between processes and things by the grammatical differentiation between verbs and nouns. There is also a tendency, at least in SAE languages, to conceptualise events in terms of one energetic thing exerting force through some process on another less energetic thing. This conceptualisation of events has been well expressed by Langacker, who calls it "the billiard-ball model", which is also referred to as the Event Structure metaphor (Lakoff 1993, Lakoff and Johnson 1999, Kövecses 2005: 43–47).

> We think of our world as being populated by discrete physical objects. These objects are capable of moving about through space and making contact with one another. Motion is driven by energy, which some objects draw from internal resources and others receive from the exterior. When motion results in forceful physical contact, energy is transmitted from the mover to the impacted object, which may thereby be set in motion to participate in further interactions. Let us refer to this way of thinking as the **billiard-ball model.** This archetypal folk model exerts a powerful influence on both everyday and scientific thought, and no doubt reflects fundamental aspects of cognitive organization. Our concern here is with its linguistic import, particularly its role in providing the conceptual basis for certain grammatical constructs. Among these constructs are the universal categories of **noun** and **verb.** Aspects of the billiard ball model correspond directly to the noun and verb prototypes: discrete physical objects are clearly prototypical for the class of nouns, and their energetic interactions for the class of verbs (Langacker 1991: 13–14).

Table 29. Contrasts between objects and processes

	Object	Energetic Interactions
Instantiated	In space	In time
Extension	Spatially compact	Temporally compact
	Temporally unbounded	Spatially unbounded
Autonomy/Dependence	Autonomous	Dependent
Word Class	Noun	Verb

Things-Objects and Processes-Energetic Interactions can be distinguished by four criteria: their domain of instantiation, their extension, their autonomy and the word class used to refer to them, as in Table 29. Space is the domain of instantiation for typical noun referents and time is the domain of instantiation for typical verb referents. Noun referents do not typically extend infinitely in space and are continuous in their extensions – hence rocks and balls are more typical than ropes or a flock of geese. But they are conceived as temporally of infinite extension, i.e. relatively permanent. Also, noun referents are typically conceptualized as autonomous – the billiard ball exists independent of any process it is involved in. By contrast verb referents – interactions or processes – have a temporal domain of instantiation – they are compact and continuous along the temporal axis, but spatially expansive (at least involving the locations and trajectories of the billiard balls). Processes are not autonomous – we cannot conceptualise an interaction without some reference to the entities interacting; for example, one cannot conceive of or imagine kicking without imagining a foot. Therefore processes are conceptually dependent (pp. 13–14).

The autonomy of nouns can be observed by contrasting what happens semantically when verbs are turned into nouns, a technique known as nominalization, with what happens when nouns are turned into verbs, verbalization. Nominalization adds nothing to the conceptual content of the verb, because nouns are autonomous, e.g. *explode/explosion*. But verbalization of nouns generally is accompanied by adding conceptual content: 'add N' – *salt, water, beautify*; 'remove N' – *weed, peel*; 'use N as instrument' – *glue*; 'turn into N' – *coil, liquefy, vaporise* (1991: 25).

7.3   The Typical Clause and Canonical Events

Not only does the billiard ball model insist on the distinction between Thing-Noun and Process-Verb, it is also the basis of the prototypical finite clause describing an action performed by an agent on some affected thing, also known as a transactive clause (Hodge and Kress 1992: 8–9). The billiard ball model is a metaphor for what Langacker calls an action chain (Figure 8), which can be used to model many aspects of clause structure.

head   tail

Figure 8. The action chain

The billiard-ball or action-chain model combines with a stage model which idealises the observation of external events, each event comprising the interactions of participants within a setting. This combination gives us the Canonical Event Model (Figure 9).

What the stage model contributes to the canonical model is the notion of an event or action occurring within a setting and a viewer observing it from an external vantage point. At the same time, inherited from the billiard-ball model is the minimal conception of an action chain, in which one discrete object transmits energy to another through forceful physical contact. Moreover, the action-chain head is characterised as an agent, and its tail as a patient that undergoes a resultant change of state (indicated by the squiggly arrow). The canonical event model represents the normal observation of a prototypical action (pp. 285–286, Lakoff 1987: 54–5, O'Halloran 2003: 122–123).

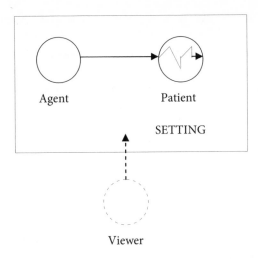

Figure 9. The canonical event model

Langacker points out that the typical transitive clause seems to reflect the billiard-ball model in its semantics.

> Already we can see emerging an extensive parallelism between the canonical event model and the structure of a finite clause. Not only does a prototypical clause reflect the model overall, but various clausal elements correspond to particular facets of it: the speaker and hearer correspond to the viewer; their construal of the scene as the viewing relationship; and the grounded verb to the energetic interaction. Other grammatical constructs pertain to the participants in the interaction or to the setting. As idealised by the model, these notions are sharply distinct – the setting is stable and inclusive, whereas the participants are mobile, discrete and small by comparison. Moreover, participants interact with each other but merely occupy the setting ... Rough grammatical correlates of the setting/participant opposition include the distinction ... between circumstantials and actants and the contrast between certain adverbial expressions [clause level adverbs] and the nominal complements (p. 299).

Let's give an example to make Langacker 1991's observations clearer (Table 30).

Table 30. Grammar, expressions and meanings in the clause (1)

Traditionally	*fishermen*	*caught*	*100,000 tons of fish*	*a year*	*in the North Sea*
Setting (temporal) Adverbial	Participant (Actor) Nominal Subject	Energetic Interaction Finite Verb	Participant (Affected) Nominal Object	Setting (temporal) Adverbial	Setting (locational) Adverbial

There are certain properties of the semantic structuring of the clause which it is worth underlining here.

1. It describes an event (as opposed to a static situation), namely, the fishermen's catching of the fish.
2. It has two participants expressed by overt nominals that function as subject and object, in our case *fishermen* and *100,000 tons of fish*.
3. These represent discrete physical entities which are individuated and distinct from the setting or environment in which they are located, i.e. from *the North Sea*.
4. These entities (*fishermen* and *fish*) already exist when the event occurs (i.e. they are not products of the event).
5. The subject (*fishermen*) and object (*100,000 tons of fish*) are fully distinct from each other.
6. They participate in a strongly asymmetrical relationship: the fishermen are viewed as doing something to the fish, which are totally affected by their action and are passive.
7. The participant referred to by the subject (*the fishermen*) performs the action volitionally, while that referred to by the object (*fish*) is non-volitional (pp. 302, 307).

This last point needs more explanation, being independent of the canonical event model. The choice of subject participant is partly determined by the empathy hierarchy, according to which the following kinds of entity take the role of subject participant with decreasing degrees of likelihood:

speaker > hearer > human > animal > physical object > abstract entity

It is such a hierarchy which accounts for the following grammatical data:

> The dog chased me.   I was chased by the dog.
> I chased the dog.   ?? The dog was chased by me.

"The dog was chased by me" is unlikely because the subject referent, the dog, is not very high in the empathy hierarchy compared with the speaker. Speakers, hearers, humans and animals, the most likely subject agents, are capable of volition, whereas, at least according to commonsense view of the world, physical objects and abstract entities are incapable of volition. This increases the likelihood that subject referents (Actors) will be exercising volition.

Consequently, by imposing the empathy hierarchy and the correlation between energy sources and animacy onto the canonical event we arrive at the construal of the prototypical clause in which a human agent provides the energy to act upon a passive (perhaps non-human) affected in a setting/environment which is marginalized as unimportant. As I argue later, this typical construal of material events is one which is out of step with the insights of modern scientific thinking and is environmentally dangerous. It suggests humans can dominate or ignore a passive nature.

The question remains why we feel that the canonical event model is a natural or commonsense way of conceptualising events, or to put the question another way, what is its origin? The canonical model might be a reflection of the already discussed conceptual metaphor theme CHANGE IS MOVEMENT (see 5.2.2), since events are one kind of change. Grady gives some reason for equating change with motion:

> The metaphorical association between changes and motion could arise from the fact that the motion of objects in our surroundings is a prototypical case of change in our environment. When we detect spatial motion – e.g. by visual means – we are also conscious of the fact that our environment has changed in a more general sense. If we are in a sense programmed to be alert to the changes in the scene around us, then spatial motion is certainly one of the most important triggers for this sense (Grady 1997: 107).

This might suggest, echoing Lakoff in his Experientialist Hypothesis (1987: 267–268), that it is our infant experience that lays the foundation for the equation between change and movement and for the canonical event model. Not only are types of change involving movement probably the earliest we notice, but our very conception of a Thing, a discrete object that can be detached from its environmental circumstances or settings, derives, in large measure, from the infant's ability to move objects relative to these circumstances. And, of course, on the human time scale, these things are relatively permanent, compared with the actions that the baby performs on them by manipulation, pushing and so on. I think an argument can be made for saying that the canonical event model, which divides the world into things and processes and settings, and models events as one energetic thing imparting force and motion to a relatively inert one, derives from pre-conceptual material experiences of this kind.

The pervasiveness of this billiard-ball model, incorporating as it does infantile conceptions of change, emerges in the metaphor themes from Metalude which conceptualise cause as force exerting impact and pressure, and activity/process as movement (forwards). As an extension of the CHANGE IS MOVEMENT theme, CAUSE IS FORCE (EFFECT IS IMPACT/PRESSURE). As a particular example of the change-motion equation, ACTIVITY/PROCESS IS MOVEMENT (FORWARD) (SO INACTIVITY IS IMMOBILITY, BEGIN IS START MOVING, CONTINUE IS GO ON and CEASE IS STOP etc.). As part of this schema MEANS IS ROAD/TRACK (path) or TRANSPORT and DIFFICULTY/PREVENTION IS OBSTACLE, while SOLUTION IS WAY ROUND/OVER/THROUGH, and OPPORTUNITY/POSSIBILITY IS OPENING. The schema also relies on the idea that STATE IS A LOCATION/PLACE. "A metaphorical correspondence between states and locations would arise as a corollary of the mapping between change and motion, since motion, by definition, involves locations, in the same way that change involves states" (Grady 1997: 107). According to this aspect of the canonical event we have three stages: a prior state or location of the billiard balls, a transition phase of energetic movement and interaction when the event "takes place", and a final static state when the billiard balls are in new positions and therefore new states. Lexical details of some of these metaphor themes can be found in earlier chapters, or from Metalude.

To sum up, the lexical evidence from metaphor themes suggests that our bodily pre-conceptual experiences of movement are the basis of our lexical metaphors for change/process/activity that determine the billiard-ball element in the canonical event model. The naturalness of this model is reinforced by the typical grammar of finite clauses of action which sees the Actor/Agent (Subject) as causing the Process (Verb) which affects the Affected (Object), within a Setting (Adverbial of Location/Time) just as an external agent applies a force to an object to set it in motion against a static and unaffected background.

7.4   Canonical events, the Newtonian world-view and industrialisation

The canonical event model originating from infant experience, and reinforced by the linguistic structures of the typical clause, is the basis for Newtonian and pre-Newtonian dynamics/mechanics or what Talmy (1988: 92) calls "naïve physics". The reason is that both of them see physical changes of all kinds in terms of motion, imparted by some external force.

> There is only one type of change surviving in dynamics, one process, and that is motion. The qualitative diversity of changes in nature is reduced to the study of the relative displacement of material bodies (Prigogine and Stengers 1985: 62).

Dynamics/mechanics is best summarized in the statement of Newton's three laws of motion:

1) A body remains in its state of rest unless it is compelled to change that state by a force impressed on it.

2) The change of motion (the change of velocity times the mass of the body) is proportional to the force impressed.

3) To every action there is an equal and opposite reaction.

To these may be added the law of universal gravitation: "every particle of matter in the universe attracts every other particle with a force that is proportional to the product of their masses and inversely proportional to the square of the distance between their centers" (www.phy.bg.ac.yu/web_projects/giants/newton.html).

Obviously it is the first two of these laws which most readily fit the canonical event model (though note that "state of rest" in the sense of 1) does not preclude that the body is already in steady motion). Law 3) and the law of gravitation allow for reciprocity of actions, and unlike the naïve billiard-ball model, allow for force to be exerted from a distance. Nevertheless, in terms of the mechanics of industrial development and civil engineering it is arguable that the first two laws have been the most influential.

Moreover, there is a correspondence between the setting of the canonical event and Newton's conception of space and time. This was radically different from the medieval view, or the view expressed by Leibniz. Newton saw space and time as existing in their own right, content-neutral containers indifferent with respect to whatever it was that was placed within them, as in the temporal and spatial setting of the canonical event. By contrast, Leibniz argued that that space was always contingent on substance or matter. He developed a relational view in which space and time are nothing apart from the things in them and owe their existence to the ordering relations that exist among them. Situatedness, positionality and condition provide a multiplicity of temporal and spatial perspectives on a single actual universe (Harvey 1996: 250–251). In opposition to this, the canonical event model has the observer in one fixed position.

This overcoming of the particularity of the local introduces a final important aspect of Newton's science – the emphasis put upon quantification at the expense of qualitative difference. Descartes and Newton's theories were in contradistinction to Aristotelian theories, "which rested on a geocentric view of the universe and dealt with nature in qualitative rather than quantitative terms" (Westfall 2005: 2). Newton saw attractions between particles and bodies, for example surface tension and capillary action, as well as gravitation, as capable of quantitative definition, within a Pythagorean tradition which insisted on the mathematical nature of reality. Mathematics is, as we have seen, the great enterprise in reductionism through quantification, whether in musical pitch, or the grading of students (see chapters 4, 5 and 8).

While there has been some controversy over the direct influence of Newtonian mechanics/dynamics on the Industrial Revolution, there is persuasive evidence that the latter would have been impossible without the former. Newton was not only a scientist for scientists, but his ideas became part of the popular culture in the century after the publication of *Principia* (1687). His laws of motion gave a mechanical explanation of the behaviour of all bodies or particles in the universe, and gave an intellectual basis to the Industrial Revolution:

> Brought together by a shared technical vocabulary of Newtonian origin, engineers, and entrepreneurs – like Boulton and Watt – negotiated, in some instances battled their way through the mechanization of workshops or the improvement of canals, mines and harbours … By 1750 British engineers could talk the same mechanical talk. They could objectify the physical world, see its operations mechanically and factor their common interests and values into their partnerships. What they said and did changed the Western world for ever (Jacob 1997: 115).

Newton's science and mathematics were spread by the Royal Society, which included lay people as well as scientists, and were, moreover, popularized by teaching in schools, by lectures throughout the length of Britain, by the publication of textbooks, and even by inclusion in popular journals. The result of this was that the industrial inventor, no less than the experimental scientist, became fundamentally dependent upon Newtonian science and mathematics for exploiting and transforming nature. Indeed, the pervasiveness of Newtonian mechanics provided Britain with the knowledge base that underlay the mechanics of the Industrial Revolution (Bekar and Lipsey 2001), because Newtonianism was represented to the public world as providing the solution to a wide range of problems in mechanics, mining, and hydraulics (Stewart 1992: xxxiv). The result of the dissemination of Newton's science was the creation of

> in Britain by 1750 a new person, generally, but not exclusively, a male entrepreneur, who approached the productive process mechanically, literally by seeing it as something to be mastered by machines, or, on a more abstract level to be conceptualized in terms of weight, motion, and the principles of force and inertia (Jacob 1997: 6–7).

The emergence of the entrepreneur reminds us that Newton's ideas were technologised with utilitarian economic goals in mind, which, of course involved the exploitation of nature as a human resource. This continued a tradition going back to 17th and 18th century Europe, which advocated the dominion, control and mastery of nature. Francis Bacon was one such philosopher, as was Descartes, the latter arguing that the general good of mankind could be best pursued by gaining knowledge that is useful in life in order to "render ourselves the masters and possessors of nature". Marx later argued that this attitude to the natural world was due to the economic mind-set of a manufacturing economy and led to the practical subjugation of Nature by Man. These ideas of dominating nature were a package of thought which gained force in the political economy of Western Europe as the Industrial Revolution progressed (Harvey 1996: 121).

This idea of domination could be perhaps related to the twin Enlightenment goals of emancipation and self-realisation, which, however, tended to isolate the individual from both nature and social bonds. We recall our analysis in chapter 5 of the conflicting metaphors of RELATIONSHIP IS TYING/BINDING and FREEDOM IS SPACE TO MOVE, and note that the observer in the canonical event is separate from and independent of the action chain being observed. The Enlightenment with its emphasis on freedom in general and free trade in particular favoured FREEDOM IS SPACE TO MOVE. In classical political economy Locke, Hume and Smith advocating the freedom of the market and its hidden guiding hand, had a highly instrumental view of nature – as capital assets or resources for human exploitation, so that domination of nature was necessary for both emancipation and self-realisation. Sophisticated, often Newtonian, knowledge of nature was necessary in order to best exploit the natural world for human purposes and for market exchange (pp. 124–5).

7.4.1   Industrialising nature

Let's fast forward to the 20th Century to observe some of the devastating consequences of the Industrial Revolution as applied to mastery over nature. Evidence of these can be seen in the recent book by Paul Josephson, *Industrialised Nature*. This is a historical investigation of the effects of large scale projects using "brute force technology", that is the confluence of science, engineering, finance, politics and arrogance to produce large-scale technological systems to manage natural resources (Josephson 2002: 3).

> In each aspect of the management process – growing, harvesting, processing, storing, studying, understanding, buying, selling, importing, exporting, building, excavating, channelling, funnelling, bulldozing, exploding, imploding, distributing and consuming – we have gained extraordinary power to transform nature into something increasingly orderly, rational, and machine-like – in a word, industrial. The hydropower stations that turn the seasonality of rivers into a regulated year-round flow for agricultural irrigation, power generation and transport; the railroads, roads, and highways that enable penetration of the so-called wilderness or frontier; the extraction of mineral wealth; the harvesting of wood, fish, fruit, and vegetable products and the transport of these raw materials to cities for processing and consumption; and the machines that repetitively grind, level, move, push, power, snip, cut, debark, prune, pulverize, grade, terrace, dig, drill, pump, open, close, purée, mix, seal, snip, behead, descale, and freeze have all contributed to the illusion – ultimately fleeting – of inexhaustibility of natural resources (p. 4).

Attitudes of contempt for nature and worship of the machine were important factors in this industrialisation process. Josephson clearly relates large-scale engineering and forestry projects in Russia, as well as the US, to the Enlightenment ideology of natural domination, an attitude that the advent of communism did little to change "for scientists already accepted the view that it was their place to secure human supremacy. Now, however, a state-sponsored modernisation technology vigorously supported their efforts" (Josephson 2002: 24).

7.4.1.1 *Dam building*

Josephson starts with a consideration of the large dam building projects in both the US and the USSR, in which the control and exploitation of nature as a necessary resource was achieved through the combined forces of science, technology, capital investment and bureaucratic dictat.

> The cascades of hydropower stations and irrigation systems on the Volga and Columbia Rivers required extensive capital investment, unbounded organisational reach, and scientific certainty. They required a vision of nature that was at once utopian and utilitarian. The former came from the belief that nature ought to be controlled – indeed could be controlled – through the melding of scientific study, large-scale technology, and appropriate government structures. The utilitarian aspects ... came from a deeply ingrained belief among specialists in both countries that water had an obligation to humanity, indeed, a moral duty, to fulfil many missions before it flowed wastefully into the sea (p. 68).

These projects both in the capitalist USA and the communist USSR were also a matter of national pride, a precursor of the space race, demonstrating an obsession with speed of completion (SUCCESS IS SPEED) and with building bigger as a measure of importance (IMPORTANT IS BIG), "a battle of hydroelectric envy" (ACTIVITY IS WAR/COMPETITION) (Josephson 2002: 18). Consequently they sometimes had more symbolic, nationalistic significance than practical use.

Some of the consequences of dam building on this scale were beneficial, but at too high a cost. Indeed the whole of the Volga fishing industry was virtually destroyed by the the Kuibyshev dam. And although the dam projects on the Columbia River basin provided year-round cheap electricity, turned desert to farmland, regulated floods and supported the aluminium, logging and nuclear industries, they changed human culture and destroyed flora and fauna. Eleven towns sufficiently sizeable to have post-offices disappeared under reservoir water, displacing thousands of people. Indians' burial grounds were flooded and the rapids at Kettle Falls with their Chinook salmon runs vanished in the effort to prevent water "wastage" (p. 53).

7.4.1.2   Forestry

Next Josephson investigates the transformation of the pine forests of New England and northwestern Russia into factories producing wood-products.

> The advantages of this technological approach … were higher productivity per acre, per unit of capital and per unit of labour input. The environmental and social costs were the destruction of first growth forests, the ruin of rivers and streams, and the creation of an industry with low wages, high accident rates, and rapid labour turnover – a pattern for technological revolution, environmental change and social disruption encountered throughout the world (p. 78).

The Industrial Revolution was clearly the precondition for these practices – when technology was limited, bringing down a fir tree, moving it to the river for the spring thaw, and getting it down river to the sawmills and markets was so labour-intensive and expensive that logging was forced to be selective. But with the technological advances in transport, harvesting and processing, foresters and manufacturers could fell everything indiscriminately and make products from everything they cut (p. 81). New advanced machinery proliferated – chain-saws, feller-bunchers, skidders, harvesters, delimners and yarders. The result is that "No longer the tree, never the operator, but now the brute force machine dictates the nature and extent of lumbering operations" (p. 92).

The environmental human and cultural effects were devastating.

> The forests have disappeared hectare by hectare, and with them have gone endemic species and indigenous people. The earth has been scarred by mining and oil extraction. Hazardous wastes associated with industrial manufacturing now fill soils, lakes, rivers, and valleys even in the centre of 'undeveloped' regions (p. 195).

7.4.1.3 *Transportation and electric power*

Moving on from forestry Josephson explores the development of transportation and electrical power grids, essential prerequisites for the enterprises of industrialising nature. To serve the centres of population, industry and political power "corridors of modernisation", that is roads, powerlines, and railways, were necessary for the "opening up" of the "remote" regions of Brazil and the USSR, the Amazon basin and Siberia.

Interestingly, from a metaphor standpoint, Josephson describes some of the mistaken attempts at resource development in the Amazon in the 60s by the Brazilian general Golberg do Couto e Silva. In his development effort the general combined racism and centralisation, the belief that the white man would civilise the indigenous peoples of the interior, with commodification and militarism – the exploitation of the resources by colonisers who resorted to violence when their domination was resisted (p. 143). It is significant that these attitudes combine four metaphor themes: IMPORTANT IS CENTRAL, ACTIVITY IS FIGHTING, QUALITY/VALUE IS WEALTH/MONEY and GOOD IS CLEAN/WHITE. These corridors of modernisation tend to become coercive and concentrate political power in the centre. They were the basis for industrialisation, militarization, integration and colonisation in Brazil (p. 153), and the motive for their development was clearly exploitation of resources. Just as in the American West, government officials considered Indian lands of marginal value until the discovery of some commodity or resource important to the centres of power (p. 152).

7.4.1.4 *Fishing*

Finally, Josephson shows how in the North Atlantic there has been an attempt to turn the fish and the ocean into a "cold-blooded machine". Under Stalin in the 1920s and 30s industrial metaphors began to replace biological concepts in scientific journals. Fish became an industrial machine, and resource scientists were referred to as engineers (p. 209). "It is necessary to transform [fishing] from a backward into a progressive, technically advanced, socialist industry. We need to make the forces of nature serve the interests of socialism, not be a slave to nature" (p. 209). But fish stocks declined in dammed lakes because of the frequent changes in water level, in chemistry and in temperature, and lack of preparation of the beds of the lake with the kind of smooth gravel necessary for spawning (p. 214).

Science in fishing was ambiguous – it could be the basis for environmentally sensitive regulation of fisheries, but instead became the tool of modernisation and industrialisation (p. 251). This would indicate that it is not the scientific or even technological advances which by themselves cause problems but rather their subjection to ideologies of nature as resource, capitalism and nationalism. But we may also see that the kind of reductionism we noted in chapter 4 is also a powerful force, reducing biology to physics and the mechanics of production, an organic 'machine', orderly and well-oiled, part of the Stalinist vision of changing nature into a giant factory.

The results of the industrialisation of fishing have been both sad and devastating for the environment and the small-scale local fisherman.

Given government support, universal scientific knowledge, and brute force technology, it is not surprising that Soviet fisheries bureaucrats in Murmanbrya, executives of Norwegian canning and refrigeration factories, and representatives of US and Canadian corporate trawling and processing industries have been able to pursue single-mindedly their goals of harvesting, processing and marketing whatever comes their way. At the same time the traditional fisherman remains increasingly powerless to survive the pressures of brute force technology. He finds the stocks of fish disappearing, his access to them restricted, and his community and way of life endangered. Because of brute force technologies, all that remains is the myth of the yeoman farmer, the Gloucester fisherman and Maine lobsterman, the Murman sailor, and the Lofoten cod fisherman (p. 253).

7.4.1.5   *General effects of technological "improvements"*
In general, the effects of the industrialisation of nature have been and promise to be politically, economically and socially disruptive.

According to some estimates, in the last two decades of the 20th century at least 80 million people were displaced by dam construction and urban transportation projects worldwide, and perhaps 10 million more are uprooted annually by development projects generally. As southern tier countries turn to large-scale industrialisation, electrification, and urbanisation projects, more dislocation will result, with increased landlessness, joblessness, homelessness, political and economic marginalisation, and morbidity and mortality (p. 161).

In many cases there has even been a more obvious tragic irony about the attempts to improve nature. For example, flood control led to urbanisation, which involved covering the earth with tarmac, which in turn exacerbated the problems of flooding. This suggests that technological applications to nature often have unpredictable consequences.

Nature tends towards complexity, so the effort to understand and to plan on the basis of that understanding is fraught with pitfalls. The most obvious of these is the tendency to exploit natural resources rapidly and with full confidence that plans will not go awry, but if they do, science and technology will provide a way out (pp. 131–2).

In fact the "way out", the attempt at a technological fix, is usually partial and inadequate, whether in forestry or fisheries. The high-yield "forest-farms" do attempt reforestation, but it is haphazard and uses chemical fertilisers, herbicides and insecticides. Salmon ladders and fishways did not compensate for the problems caused by dams, since the latter caused changes in water temperature, oxygen and nitrogen loads, and seasonal flow patterns, which prevented the salmon's natural behaviour.

7.4.2 The role of ideological metaphors in the industrialisation of nature

We cannot solely blame Newtonian mechanics for the industrialisation of nature and its environmental consequences, but we have seen that its development was a contributory factor by enabling the Industrial Revolution in the first place and the industrialisation of nature we have witnessed in the 20th century. I also contend that Newtonian conceptions and their technological aftermath were in dynamic relationship with a canonical event version of reality, reproduced by the grammar of English and of other Standard Average European languages. Moreover, besides these scientific and cognitive causes, there is an equally important social and political dimension to the development of the brute force technologies that overwhelm nature. They are a product of the hubris of scientists and technologists, economic aspirations of the populations and political power. They are also no doubt facilitated by certain kinds of metaphorical thinking.

Throughout Josephson's book various key metaphor themes and the ideologies they foster recur. I have alluded to some already, especially in the behaviour of the Brazilian general, but their implications are worth exploring further. Their prevalence suggests that the grammatical metaphor of the canonical event and its link to science and technology had to be boosted by other lexical metaphorical themes already discussed, and the ideologies they represent before technology could really achieve its most harmful effects. Population pressure (MORE = GOOD), capitalist conceptions of property which led to obsessive greed for profits (QUALITY IS WEALTH, HUMAN IS COMMODITY), the reliance of central governments (IMPORTANT IS CENTRAL) on economic indicators like GDP, which are easily quantifiable, as a measure of economic well-being, while ignoring less easily quantifiable factors, equally important to the quality of life (QUALITY IS QUANTITY). Below I shall consider how the drive towards commodification, quantification and standardisation, centralisation and the control of time and seasonality, all made their contribution to the industrialisation of nature and degradation of the environment.

7.4.2.1 *Commodification and private property*
Private ownership of forests seems, in many cases, to have speeded up their destruction.

> The industrial landowners [in Maine] undertake 48% of all the cutting in terms of acreage but are responsible for 77 % of the shelterwood cutting, 83% of the clear-cuts, 84% of the habitat destroying brush-clearing (to create tree farms), 90% of the tree planting, and 97% of the herbicide use (p. 95).

In the time of Catherine the Great public forests did much better than private forests – private forests were exploited without regard for the future (p. 98). Lenin's Decree on the Forests in 1918 seized all the private forests and recognised that the forests had an impact on climate, water, soil and agriculture, public health and aesthetics (p. 103). Native Amazonians, who had no concept of ownership of forests and land, did deforest but on a small scale with less obtrusive technologies, and with a world view that saw nature as something to live in rather than as a commodity (p. 137).

7.4.2.2   Time and seasonality

One of the major enterprises of technology has been to replace natural time with industrialised time. All of the technological interventions explored by Josephson, the building of dams and transportation corridors, forestry and the industrialisation of fishing, were either deliberate attempts to reduce seasonality, or were shaped by these attempts, or ignored the qualitative yearly cycles of the natural world in order for time to become a homogenous quantitatively measurable space for "industrial" production.

Dam building projects reduce seasonality and alter time in two ways. They provide electricity, which replaces the natural alternation of dark and light and "brings the radiance of sunshine to our hours of darkness" (Josephson 2002: 45). Second, they are designed to reduce the seasonality of river flows for agricultural purposes. "'Is it possible to capture a huge quantity of water, which is uselessly carried off in the spring into the Caspian sea? Is it possible to redistribute the yearly flow of the Volga, to divert the ruinous spring run-off of the river … '"(p. 28). Forestry was shaped into becoming less seasonal by transport technology. First roads, and then railways, enabled logging to proceed year round at a steady space, whereas previously the timber trade was reliant on the spring thaw to move logs down the river to the mills (pp. 81–82). Fisheries have attempted to ignore the seasonality of fishes' life cycles, and have reduced the variety of activities distributed throughout the fisherman's year. Originally New England fishermen-farmers varied their work according to the seasons, fixing nets, planting crops, baiting trawl lines, digging clams, and tending lobster traps when fishing was not possible because of weather or lack of mature fish, but coastal fishing expanded and lost its seasonality from the 1870s onwards. Similarly, in the USSR by 1955 the trawling fleet of 2.7 million metric tons was fishing all year round, with no consideration for the spawning season.

7.4.2.3   Standardisation and mass-production: quantity and quality

The industrialisation of nature meant that Taylorism and Fordism were applied to agricultural production, in the same way as they were to industry, where the product, the time in which it was made, and the industrial worker were standardised and quantified (see 2.7). Standardising of the agricultural product led to monocultures, such as in Fordlandia [sic], a massive rubber plantation in the Amazon, planted very densely in rows, which made the trees vulnerable to leaf eating insects and plant disease. Similarly the result of standardisation of hydrolelectric projects was "a gray, uniform countryside; a gray, uniform series of dams; and a gray, uniform quality of life for workers and engineers alike" (p. 31). Through a grave flaw in economic theory, the standardised output of these technologies is much easier to quantify than the costs of making nature more predictable. Unfortunately "when balancing costs and benefits, so long as the benefits we can quantify are greater than the costs we cannot, we ignore the incalculables" (p. 11).

7.4.2.4 *The quantified control of space and centralisation*

The quantification of industrialised nature's output works hand in hand with the measurement, control and quantification of the land itself. We saw in 1.7 how the king, the ruler, draws and regulates the boundaries, not only the metaphorical category boundaries, but also the literal boundaries of the state, the area under his control. Humans who see themselves as the rulers over their environment

> strive to impose a Cartesian grid of regularity and structure on nature. One can see this in the patchwork of rectangular fields visible in aerial photographs of agricultural regions. … the imposition of regularity helps us meet the two-fold need of understanding how nature functions and developing long range plans to transform it (pp. 131–2).

But as we saw in chapter 2, because IMPORTANT IS CENTRAL, the spaces so divided and controlled are not equal in value. Josephson's "corridors of modernisation", the railways, highways, bridges, and canals, the massive power generation, transmission and distribution systems, and the extravagant irrigation networks facilitate the rapid movement of people and machines into the interior to establish outposts of technological civilisation and to harness resources to meet the demands of urban residents (p. 132). The highly centralised nation of Brazil provides a good example, since massive volumes of water in the Amazon tributaries generate megawatts of electricity for urban population centres, despite high transmission costs.

Cases of industrialised nature projects being undertaken in remote regions to meet the needs of the centre are still current. One is The Three Gorges Dam which will have twenty-six 500MW turbines for a total of 13,000MW, will create a reservoir 600km long, flood 710 sq. km of land, and displace between 1 and 2 million people to satisfy the demand of urban and manufacturing centres. There are efforts in the United States to open the North Slope of Alaska and federal lands in Utah to oil and gas exploration. These projects inevitably reinforce the disparity in wealth between the rural poor and the urban rich. For example, in all, Soviet dams flooded 2,600 villages and 165 cities – and nearly 31,000 sq km. of agricultural land and a similar area of forestland (p. 31). All this benefited Moscow at the expense of the countryside and its inhabitants.

Another consequence is that the centre imposes state-organised universal scientific knowledge and ignores local indigenous knowledge (p. 194) through a Cartesian and Newtonian conceptualisation of space which ignores Leibnizian positionality. The central thereby becomes the universal and the peripheral becomes local and contingent, even though "universal scientific findings that ignore local knowledge will be fraught with costly and crucial inaccuracies" (p. 195). One might locate this tendency within the larger tendency to globalisation at the expense of the local (Fairclough 2003: 45).

We can end this section with a different view of the pre-industrial forest, before the technological revolution was inflicted upon it. In the following passage nature is not construed by the grammar as passive, but as an active provider, though still as a means to human ends. I have underlined the phrases construing forest as Actor.

> In the Middle Ages, <u>the forests</u> **provided** a buffer for Russia against nomadic Mongols and Turks who fought Slavs for control of Eurasia. <u>The forests</u> **offered** animals and birds for the hunt, not only a sport but as essential industry, **providing** commoners with food, furs for clothing, hides for leather, tax payments and commerce. The forest was the site of honey and beeswax industries. And <u>it</u> **insulated** scores of rivers and lakes from overfishing.

7.5   Modern scientific challenges to Newtonian dynamics

The Newtonian paradigm, intertwined as it is with the canonical event model, or at least the parts of it important to industrialisation, which made possible the misconceived projects listed above and their ecological destructiveness, is now a reactionary one. Modern physics has moved on, and our thinking has to if we are to avoid further destruction of the world's ecological network.

There are at least four important elements of the Newtonian world view or canonical event model which later scientific theory was to challenge: (A) that nature is passive and controllable "the mythical science of a simple passive world"; (B) that the basic building blocks of matter are permanent rigid bodies with an extension in space; (C) that the human observer is outside the nature or matter he describes and acts on. (D) that a clear distinction can be made between agents and participants on the one hand, and the spatial setting on the other. Let us consider these in turn:

(A)
The Affected participant in a physical process/canonical event is seen as passive and controllable: the billiard-ball which is hit. But the notions of the controllability of natural objects were undermined by thermodynamics and the theory of entropy, which allows for the dissipation of energy:

> Thus the "negative" property of dissipation shows that, unlike dynamic objects, thermodynamic objects can only be partially controlled. Occasionally they "break loose" into spontaneous change (Prigogine and Stengers 1985: 120).

The study of fluid dynamics and the investigation of convection suggest a spontaneity that Newtonian dynamic systems deny.

(B)

The canonical event or billiard-ball model depends upon the absolute distinction between things and energetic interactions, typically designated by nouns and verbs. The languages we speak reinforce this illusion of permanent things:

> The words [for table and lamp] indicate that we are speaking of fixed substances, although things are nothing but a process of energy that causes certain sensations in our bodily system. But these sensations are not perceptions of specific things like table or lamp; these perceptions are the result of a cultural process of learning, a process that makes certain sensations assume the form of specific percepts. We naively believe that things like tables and chairs exist as such, and we fail to see that society teaches us to transform sensations into perceptions that permit us to manipulate the world around us in order to enable us to survive in a given culture. Once we have given such perceptions a name, the name seems to guarantee the final and unchangeable reality of the percept (Fromm 1983: 69).

This illusory belief in the existence of permanent rigid bodies that could be acted upon was undermined by relativity theory:

> Indeed it is not possible in relativity to obtain a consistent definition of an extended rigid body, because this would imply signals faster than light. In order to try to accommodate this new feature of relativity theory within the older notions of structure, physicists were driven to the notion of a particle that is an extensionless point … Actually, relativity implies that neither the point particles nor the quasi-rigid body can be taken as primary concepts. Rather these have to be expressed in terms of events and processes (Bohm 1980:123–124).

Defining particles as points creates persistent problems in particle physics. Calculations involving point-like particles often culminate in nonsense, just as division by zero yields an infinite and hence meaningless result. In the early 1980s many physicists came to believe that superstring theory might overcome this problem. The theory replaced point-like particles with minute loops of energy; in the same way as the vibrations of a violin string create different notes, so the vibrations of these strings might generate all the forces and particles of the physical universe (Horgan 1998: 61). As Rifkin puts it: "What we perceive as solid, material forms, may be a macro-expression of rhythms, vibrations, pulsations, and fields that give rise to and order all physical phenomena" (Rifkin 1987: 44).

Whitehead developed a philosophy of space and time which recognised the importance of the primacy of process and interaction. Arguing against the canonical event entities he proposed that we should not see physical bodies as if they are first in space and then act upon each other. Bodies are in space only because they interact so that space is the expression of their interaction (Harvey 1996: 256). This applies to human bodies too, and consequently creates problems for the notion of a detached observer in a canonical event.

(C)
In the canonical event the viewer is outside the setting within which the participants interact. However, modern physics demonstrates that the supposition that humankind is outside the world it observes and acts on is an illusion.

Firstly, scientific experimentation and observation depend on an experimenter/observer who is alive and they are always time-oriented. But life is the manifestation of a far-from-equilibrium system, and time depends on entropy within this system. Therefore the living observer and his/her time-based measurements are inescapably part of the system being observed and not external to it (Prigogine and Stengers 1985: 300).

Secondly, the implication of quantum mechanics is that the observed object and observing instrument can no longer be regarded as separate, a point demonstrated by Heisenberg. Rather the primary emphasis now is on undivided wholeness not separation (Bohm 1980: 134). Bohr, during the 1920s, developed the idea that subatomic entities such as electrons have no real independent existence. They exist in a probabilistic indeterminate state of many superposed states until they are forced into a single state by the act of observation. These electrons or photons sometimes act like waves, sometimes like particles, depending on how they are observed during the experimental process.

Building on Bohr's insights, Wheeler proposed that reality might not be wholly physical; in some sense, our cosmos might be a participatory phenomenon, requiring the act of observation – and thus consciousness itself. In the 1960s he helped to popularize "the anthropic principle" – the universe must be the way it is, because, otherwise, we might not be here to observe it. Wheeler found evidence for this hypothesis in his delayed choice experiment, a variation on the well-known two-slit experiment. When electrons are aimed at a barrier incorporating two slits, the electrons act like waves: they go through both slits at once and, when they strike a detector on the far side of the barrier, form an "interference pattern", created by the overlapping of the "waves". However, when the experimenter closes one slit the electrons travel through the other open slit like simple particles and the interference pattern disappears. In the delayed choice experiment, the physicist decides whether to leave both slits open or to close one off *after the electrons have already passed through the barrier* – with the same results. The electrons seem to know in advance how the physicists will choose to observe them. This experiment was carried out in the early 1990s and confirmed Wheeler's prediction (Horgan 1998: 81–82).

I find this experiment strange, and difficult to understand, but it would suggest that the metaphors and frameworks we choose for modeling the physical universe determine the nature of that universe in quite radical ways – perhaps something even more radical then Foucault's idea of "regimes of truth". We saw something of this in Chapter 4 where the "truth" about chimpanzee society seemed to vary according to the ideological fashions of the society from which the observer views it.

Within physics, therefore, there has been a progressive movement away from models approximating the canonical event, and the billiard-ball model as represented by Newtonian dynamics. It is noteworthy, too that the models that modern physics proposes for understanding the nature of matter might also be a function of the "objects" under investigation, as well as the process of observation. The progression within physics from the investigation of the motion of bodies, to heat transfer, to the movement of fluids will generate their own dominant metaphors. For a sample of the latter:

> The best image of process is perhaps that of the flowing stream whose substance is never the same. On this stream one may see an ever-changing pattern of vortices, ripples, waves, splashes etc., which evidently have no independent existence as such. Rather they are abstracted from the flowing movement, arising and vanishing in the total process of the flow (Bohm 1980: 48).

Besides the changes of subject matter within physics there was, in the nineteenth century, the more fundamental change in scientific field, the greater attention given to evolutionary biology. This new emphasis was important since it revealed that the tendency of thermodynamic systems to increasing disorder did not apply to open systems; quite the contrary – biological evolution showed an increase of order and complexity over time. The shift of subject matter was decisive, then, in giving more priority to open systems, rather than the closed Newtonian ones, thereby suggesting the interrelatedness, if not wholeness, of matter.

If the models we have of reality are functions of the latest fashionable "objects" and processes of observation in physics, then this has profound consequences for cognitive metaphorical theory and its relationship to ontology and ideology. In physics we have moved from a naïve or "infantile" Newtonian physics, based on the most salient kinds of changes, physical movements, to the less accessible models based on the study of convection and fluid dynamics or of quantum particles. One could either say that these represent an advance on Newtonian physics because they explain more of physical reality, or that, in either case, the portion of physical reality being described, by providing a source for a metaphoric model, in a sense determines that model. However, when it comes to evaluating models, one should perhaps judge them by their technological consequences, in which case the Newtonian model seems dangerous.

(D) So there is a further ecological challenge to the canonical event model. The latter makes clear a separation between setting and environment, and participants and their energetic interactions. This is challenged by *Gaia* theory (see 4.2, 4.3.2), which lately has become more widely respected and accepted (Ryan 2002:186–7). The theory claims that the world, including the atmosphere, the oceans, the biota, the rocks and minerals of the crust, functions as one large self-regulating system (Lovelock 1988: 19). *Gaia* suggests that this open system works against the inexorable march of entropy and energy loss, predicted by the second law of thermodynamics and, on the contrary, evolves into structures of more and more complex order and inter-relation. The theory emphasises wholeness and interrelatedness, so that the idea we can separate ourselves from our environment, suggested by the distinction between agents and settings in the canonical event, becomes a dangerous illusion, as does the idea that the agent and patient are totally distinct. Mining the earth for minerals becomes about as sensible as eating one's liver for nutrients.

7.6 Congruent language and grammatical metaphor

We have discussed the canonical event model, its origins in infant cognition and its reproduction in patterns of metaphor themes, and have suggested its relationship to the Newtonian world-view and the technological consequences of that world-view. I have also shown how that Newtonian world-view has been called into question, not only by its technological consequences, but also by the "findings" and theories of modern physics and ecology.

If the typical finite clause of an SAE language constructs and reproduces a canonical-event model of physical processes, then our typical SAE languages tend to conflict with modern scientific theory in the way they construct versions of reality. This inadequacy of language to reflect scientific emphases on the active process of matter, or the inseparability of life and its environment, was pointed out quite eloquently by David Bohm (1980) in *Wholeness and the Implicate Order*. But, not being a linguist, he was unable to give a useful discussion of resources available in the language for re-representing the all-embracing world of process. The remainder of this chapter will be precisely concerned with this question of how linguistic resources can be marshalled to undermine the canonical-event model and those (7) aspects of the clause which Langacker enumerated, and to produce a grammar which reflects modern scientific theory, a grammar that I shall call hereafter "consonant".

In order to do this we have to become more linguistic in our analysis, and to do this I shall rely on the grammatical theory known as Systemic-Functional Grammar (SFG), associated primarily with the work of Michael Halliday, which furnishes a better and more elegant account of the semantics of the clause than Langacker's cognitive grammar. As far as the conceptual or ideational meanings of the clause are concerned, Halliday identifies 5 process types, typically expressed by the Verb:

1. Existential: representing what exists in the world.
2. Relational: representing what is the state of the things which exist and what relations they have to each other.
3. Material: representing what is happening in the world, what actions and events are going on.
4. Mental: representing how people are perceiving, feeling and thinking.
5. Verbal: representing how people are communicating or expressing their perceptions, feelings and thoughts.

Each of these process types is typically associated with different participants (underlined) (Figure 10). (I omit the participants of Verbal processes below, as I do not discuss them). Circumstances, temporal or locational (which include Langacker's "settings") are optional extras.

Existential: Existent

There are *six moons of Uranus*

Relational: Token Value

John is *stupid*

The chair is *in the garden*

Material: Actor Beneficiary Affected Circumstance

John killed *an elephant* in Africa

John gave *Mary* *the tusks*

Mental: Experiencer Experience Circumstance

John noticed *the bird* in the morning

Figure 10. Processes and their participants in the clause

The clause realises ideational or conceptual meaning by the selection of process type, which is realised as a transitivity configuration, which in turn translates into a group sequence (Halliday 1985: 321).

(1) PROCESS TYPE → (2) TRANSITIVITY CONFIGURATION → (3) GROUP SEQUENCE.

For example, a typical transitive declarative clause realizes a Material process as in Figure 11.

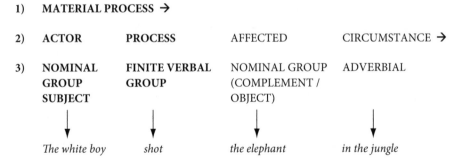

1) **MATERIAL PROCESS** →

2) **ACTOR** **PROCESS** AFFECTED CIRCUMSTANCE →

3) **NOMINAL** **FINITE VERBAL** NOMINAL GROUP ADVERBIAL
GROUP **GROUP** (COMPLEMENT /
SUBJECT OBJECT)

The white boy *shot* *the elephant* *in the jungle*

Figure 11. Processes, participants, circumstances and their realisation in the clause (bold type for compulsory elements, timid type for optional elements)

When the semantic structure of the clause corresponds unproblematically with the structure of a canonical event, as in the above example, we have what Halliday calls "congruent" grammar. When there is a lack of correspondence, Halliday calls it "grammatical metaphor" (Fairclough 2003: 143–4). Although grammatical metaphor is very common in writing, congruent grammar is primary in the sense that it is the first grammar we learn to speak, and the grammar most commonly found in conversation.

It is therefore likely to have enormous influence as the foundation of our cognition as we learn language. Grammatical metaphor tends to be a product of literacy and to be mastered in the early years of secondary school (Derewianka 1995).

Grammatical metaphor can occur at various levels in the series diagrammed in Figure 11, which are in principle independent, though they often co-occur. I shall be concentrating on two of these in this chapter:

(Type 1) Unconventional syntactic roles for participants/circumstances. For example, in the passive construction the Affected becomes the Nominal Group Subject. In sentences such as *the next day saw them at the summit* the Temporal Circumstance becomes the Nominal Group Subject.

(Type 2) Unconventional mapping of Actors and Affecteds, Circumstances and Processes onto groups. For example in nominalization, e.g. *many complaints* in "they received many complaints", the Process becomes a Nominal Group.

One might ask why incongruence is called *metaphor*. There are a number of important ways in which grammatical metaphor resembles lexical metaphor. Firstly there is the tension they both produce, the feeling of conceptual and emotional mismatch or incompatibility between target concept and source concept, a tension which forms the basis of Berggren's (1962) theory of lexical metaphor. Similarly, Halliday and Martin recognize this tension in grammatical metaphor between the wording (literal) and meaning (transferred) (Halliday and Martin 1993: 31). Black claimed, in his interaction theory of metaphor, that this tension, and the transfer that resolves it, operate simultaneously in opposite directions, so that in "man is a wolf" men seem more like wolves, but also wolves come to resemble men (Black 1962). I will show that this kind of interactive interpretation, and the possibility of two directions for resolving metaphorical tension, make the grammatical metaphor of nominalization, the turning of verbs into nouns, ambiguous in relation to consonance.

Secondly, one obvious function of both lexical and grammatical metaphor is to make new meanings possible, or to expand the meaning potential of the system. This is especially clear with metaphors used to provide a label for a new thing/concept, e.g. *mouse* for the computer keyboard attachment. The kind of tension created by such metaphors will result in an expansion of the system rather than resolving the tension in one particular direction. It's more like stretching chewing gum, than pulling on a rubber band. I suggest we often need this kind of metaphorically-induced expansion of meaning potential in grammar in order to achieve more consonant representation.

Thirdly, crucial to both kinds of metaphor is the sense that the norms are being flouted: in the case of lexical metaphors the lexical item has an unusual referent; in the case of grammatical metaphor (types 1 and 2) processes and participants are being recoded through unconventional, marked, syntax and groups.

In both types of metaphor, the choice of which features to regard as critical is what determines whether a use is literal or metaphorical. In the lexical *mouse* metaphor, the usual conceptual features [+animal, +mammal, +rodent] are abandoned in favour of [shape, resemblance of wire to a tail, the tendency for sudden spurts of movement] to bring about a metaphorical change of meaning. In grammatical metaphor Type 2, e.g. nominalization, the usual criteria for noun phrase reference [spatial compactness, permanence, and autonomy of existence] have been abandoned also.

But decisions on what conceptual features are criterial, the distinction between literalness and metaphoricity, is a social convention. The congruent wordings which represent things as nouns and second-order entities/processes as verbs are no more natural or consonant with some kind of external reality than, say, the representation of things with verbs would be or, in the case of nominalization of verbs, representing processes with nouns. Indeed, as discussed, according to the latest theories in physics, they are probably less consonant. Of course, our normal use of nouns to refer to things and verbs to refer to processes reinforces this permanence-based categorization, for wordings after all "confer" a reality, simultaneously constructing and referring to our world.

A further crucial construction of reality is involved when we consider transitivity and Type 1 grammatical metaphor. Here the congruent or at least usual structure for material processes has Actor as Subject, Process as Verb, and Affected as Complement (Object). To make the point again, such material process transitive constructions ontologically represent, with their congruent wordings, a world in which cause and effect are separable, in which one relatively permanent entity causes a process which has an effect on another relatively permanent entity in an asymmetric way.

The congruent/metaphorical distinction is, then, in a sense, arbitrary. Clearly the same processes of selecting some kinds of similarities and ignoring other kinds operates in normal classification or reference, just as much as it does in metaphorical classification or reference. Remember our classification of boxes in Chapter 1 (1.5). The literal and congruent might simply be seen as conventional·metaphor.

7.7 Grammatical metaphors for modern science

I now discuss the ways in which congruent language use for describing material processes often represents the world in ways which are inconsonant with modern scientific theory, and *Gaia* theory in particular. We can exemplify this by reconsidering the sentence we analysed earlier (Table 31):

Table 31. Grammar, expressions and meanings in the clause (2)

Traditionally	fishermen	caught	100,000 tons of fish	a year	in the North Sea
Circumstance (temporal)	Participant (Actor)	Process	Participant (Affected)	Circumstance (temporal)	Circumstance (locational)
Adverbial	Nominal Subject	Finite Verb	Nominal Object	Adverbial	Adverbial

1) A division into agentive participants, affected participants and circumstances, which is not consonant with modern scientific theory in general or Gaia theory in particular. Such structures are an obstacle in conceiving the notion of undivided wholeness.

2) The particular division into (volitional) agent and (passive) affected, which is not in keeping with the notion of matter being active or with feedback within the mechanism which is Gaia. The fish, for instance, are not thought to have any effect on the fisherman, though it is the fishes' presence and value on the market which causes the fishermen to catch them. This division represents a false unidirectionality or asymmetry of cause and effect. In the longer term the agent will always be affected by the consequences of his/her actions: if I drive a car the car will produce sulphur dioxide and nitrogen dioxide which may contribute to my suffering from asthma, or to global warming which will directly affect me.

3) The division into agent/affected participants, discrete and individuated physical entities, on the one hand, and location circumstances on the other. This can misguidedly suggest that the environment, represented by circumstantial elements, is either powerless, or is not affected. For example "The North Sea" is seen as a circumstance, part of the setting, rather than involved in or affected by the process, as it must inevitably be from an environmental point of view.

4) The categorization of phenomena into processes and things, which is doubtful given the insights of modern physics. In a typical congruent clause the things already exist when the event occurs (i.e. they are not products of the event). The catching is seen as a process, but the fishermen and the tons of fish and the North Sea are constructed as relatively permanent things or substances. And the catching is dependent on the prior existence of the fishermen and the fish.

We can now look at various resources available in the language for undermining the construction of a reality that is inconsonant in the above four ways. We shall see that several of them involve grammatical metaphors. We discussed in chapter 4 (4.2) metaphorical lexis already in the dictionary of English which might blur the distinction between humans and the landscape. However, there are various ways in which grammar too can be systematically modified to represent nature as less than inert, as animate. Most of the structures below have to do with material process clauses, but we begin by considering the transformation of Relational and Mental Processes into Material ones. The first two structures that we look at also involve conventionalised lexical metaphors.

7.7.1   Activation of tokens

Firstly, we can metaphorically reconstruct relational processes into material ones, so that instead of nature being static it is seen as active. For example

> *There are five trees in the valley/five trees are in the valley → Five trees stand in the valley;*
> *There is a boulder on top of the hill → a boulder tops the hill.*

Let's call this "activation of tokens". Wordsworth in *The Prelude* is fond of this kind of grammatical metaphor:

> The visionary dreariness.....
> **Invested** moorland waste, and naked pool,
> The beacon **crowning** the lone eminence
>
> The garden **lay**
> Upon a slope **surmounted** by a plain
> Of a small bowling-green; beneath us **stood**
> A grove
>
> There **rose** a crag,
> That, from the meeting-point of two highways
> Ascending, **overlooked** them both

Instead of "being at the top of" an eminence or slope or two highways, the plain or beacon or crag "surmounts" or "crowns" or "overlooks" them. And in this environment of active existence even the quite normal *stood* seems to take on more material energy than usual.

7.7.2   Activation of experiences (phenomena)

Secondly we can metaphorically reconstruct Experiences in mental process clauses as though they were Actors in material processes.

> *We noticed the river → the river arrested our gaze,*
> *I love the forest → the forest touches my heart.*

Let's call this "activation of experiences". Again, examples in Wordsworth's *Prelude* are quite common.

> Till <u>the whole cave</u>, so late a senseless mass,
> **Busies** the eye with images and forms
> Boldly assembled

(cf. I saw the many images and forms in the whole cave…)

> Yet, hail to you
> <u>Moors, mountains, headlands, and ye hollow vales,</u>
> <u>Ye long deep channels</u> for the Atlantic's voice,
> Powers of my native region! <u>Ye</u> that **seize**
> The heart with firmer grasp!

(cf.? My heart adores/loves/worships/the moors, mountains, headlands etc.)

7.7.3   Ambient structures or dummy subjects: prop *it* and existential *there*

Halliday suggests the possibility, generally unrealised, of perceiving phenomena as wholes without distinguishing participants and circumstances from processes. Instead of saying *birds are flying in the sky*, "we might have said something like *it's winging*; after all we say *it's raining*" (Halliday 1985: 101–2). One could either see this as the Actor being conflated with the process, or the process existing completely without an Actor. This is potentially a very consonant structure, reversing the tendency of division, 1), and also reducing things to processes, so undermining 4).

Bolinger and Langacker see this structure rather differently. In "It is raining" *it* refers to "ambience or all encompassing environment … It embraces weather, time, circumstance, whatever is obvious by the nature of reality or the implications of context" (Bolinger 1977: 84–5). The *it* in this construction, therefore, "neutralises the setting/participant distinction…" (Langacker 1991: 377). According to Langacker, this neutralisation undermines 3), the distinction between location circumstance and participant.

Existential *there* is a more widespread option for a "dummy" subject, often in conjunction with nominalization, turning a verb into a noun, and the grammatically metaphorical choice of a relational process instead of a material one.

> someone in the family has died → there's been a death in the family

This structure makes it possible to state a proposition involving a process, without mentioning the participant (Actor) involved. It makes 1) unnecessary, and avoids 4). Langacker regards this construction, in addition, as something like a conflation of setting/location circumstance and participant, an undermining of 3), as though the place ("there"), hosts some kind of relationship, e.g. "There is a vase on the table" (p. 352).

7.7.4 Activation of circumstances

A more obvious blurring of the distinction 3) between "a stable inclusive setting and the smaller more mobile participant" (p. 34) occurs in grammatical structures where what is congruently a Location Circumstance becomes the Subject/Actor.

> The bed is crawling with ants. (cf. Ants are crawling all over the bed.)
> The flowers are glistening with dew. (cf. Dew is glistening on the flowers.)

The literal setting/circumstance, the bed and the flowers, seem to be responding actively to the process, if not controlling it. The ants and dew, the literal Actors, are metaphorically either an accompaniment, if we take the *with* literally, or a means/instrument. Such structures suggest the setting or circumstance and the participant, the ants/dew and the bed/flowers, adopt a common relationship to the process, mutually participating in it. Or that the literal Circumstance/environment and the literal Actor co-operate in causality. In either case the parallels between environment and Actor make for some felicitous blurring or interchangeability. By its metaphoric tension it enables the transfer of features of agency to the environment, so resisting the tendency of 3) to separate participants from environmental setting. We might think that this is not a very productive structure, but a poet like Wordsworth puts it to novel uses: "And all the pastures dance with lambs".

7.7.5 Creative processes and cognate objects

When the material process verbs chosen somehow create the second participant, there is some degree of blurring of the distinction between process and participant 4), by making the participant dependent on the process, e.g. *light a fire, write a letter, knit a sweater*. In cognate object constructions, e.g. *sing a song, live a hard life, fight a good fight*, the permanence/transitoriness feature which typically distinguishes things from processes is undermined because the thing referred to by the noun lasts only as long as the process indicated by the verb (p. 363).

The reified process is not really the tail of an action chain – since there is no sense that there is a transfer of energy affecting another participant, the end of the path of energy flow (p. 364). In our normal way of thinking about nouns and verbs, it is the thing referred to by a noun that has an independent existence or autonomy, and the verb is dependent upon it. These structures go some way towards reversing this canonical autonomy/dependence relationship.

7.7.6 Reciprocal and reflexive verbs

The next three structures seem to be ways of blurring the distinction between Actors and Affecteds, and their congruent asymmetrical relationships, distinction 2) of congruent grammar. Reciprocal verbs, such as *meet, touch, interact, collide, fight, clash,* and *marry,* emphasize the mutuality of cause and effect. The plural Subjects of such verbs are simultaneously Actors and Affecteds. One wonders whether other verbs that are now used transitively could acquire the grammatical option of being reciprocal. At present, with most verbs, if we want to convey a similar meaning we have the rather clumsy and prolix option of adding *each other* to achieve a kind of reflexivity, but with the semantic difference that the phenomenon is then being construed as two separate processes.

> John and the car hit each other
> The two men hit each other

Compare this with

> John and the car collided
> The two men fought

Though somewhat clumsy, reflexives such as *washed himself, killed himself* also blur the distinction between Actor and Affected. Their dual roles are conflated in a single participant, which undermines the typical asymmetry of the typical congruent clause. The same is true, but even more so, of ergative verb constructions.

7.7.7   Ergativity

The label "ergative" was originally applied to a certain language type that has a distinctive kind of case marking. In these languages the subject of transitive clauses is specially marked (with ergative case), while intransitive subject and transitive object have the same (generally zero-marked) form (or absolutive case). Halliday adopted this label for certain verbs in English where the participant designated by the intransitive (or middle) subject is identical to the participant designated by the transitive (or effective) object. The intimation here is that what seems to be the Actor in an intransitive clause becomes the Affected in a transitive clause.

The Ergative paradigm centres on pairs of clauses like those in Table 32 from Halliday (1985: 146), in which he dispenses with the terms "Actor" and "Goal" (or "Affected"), using instead the terms "Instigator" and "Medium", and replaces the terms "transitive" and "intransitive" with "effective" and "middle".

Table 32. Patterns of ergative verbs

MEDIUM	PROCESS		INSTIGATOR	PROCESS	MEDIUM
The boat	sailed	v.	Mary	sailed	the boat
The cloth	tore	v.	The nail	tore	the cloth
The rice	cooked	v.	Pat	cooked	the rice
MIDDLE		v.	EFFECTIVE		

These verbs, such as *sail, tear* and *cook* can be contrasted with verbs of the non-ergative type, such as *eat, swallow*. The difference is that when the middle version is transformed into the effective version by the addition of another participant, the added participant becomes the Subject of the effective version. By contrast, when the intransitive transforms into the transitive by the addition of another participant the added participant becomes Object of the transitive version, as in Table 33.

Table 33. Patterns of non-ergative verbs

ACTOR	PROCESS		ACTOR	PROCESS	AFFECTED
John	ate	v.	John	ate	a grape
John	swallowed	v.	John	swallowed	a coin
INTRANSITIVE		v.	TRANSITIVE		

Halliday claims that the English Language has, over the last hundreds of years, increased the number of verbs like *sail, tear* and *cook* which display the ergative middle and ergative effective opposition (p. 146). Could it be that the emergence of these patterns is some kind of adaptive response to the insights of modern scientific thinking which, though not entirely consonant with it, at least pave the way for a more consonant grammar? Davidse draws attention to the fundamental difference between the transitive and ergative systems:

> Within the transitive paradigm, the Goal [Affected] has no relation of its own – grammatical or semantic – to the process: the process is being done to it, but the Goal [Affected] itself does not "do" the process. It is, as it were, a totally "inert" affected. Within the ergative system something is being done to the Medium AS WELL AS the Medium itself "doing" the process. It is characteristic of the central ergative participant that it co-participates in the process;..... [In *John opened the door* (ergative)] Instigator *John* "affects" the door by instigating its opening, but the door co-participates in the process of opening (Davidse 1992: 118). [my insertions in brackets]

It is worth juxtaposing the earlier quote from Prigogine and Stengers:

> Thus the "negative" property of dissipation shows that, unlike dynamic objects, thermodynamic objects can only be partially controlled. Occasionally they "break loose" into spontaneous change (Prigogine and Stengers 1985: 120).

The use of the ergative clause type can construe a reality in which energy is not simply imposed on an inert nature from the outside to produce change, as in the transitive Newtonian model, but in which nature provides its own energy, and its own propensity for spontaneous change. The middle ergative option is quite consonant with modern physics' view of nature, suggesting, at least, that the state of an entity is the result of some self-generating process. Since no Actor/Instigator or chain head is specifically mentioned, and cannot be assumed to exist, the causal element must reside either in the Medium, or perhaps even be ascribed to the process itself. This is closer to the modern scientific notion of reality as process, the idea that any state or succession of states where we find ourselves are abstractions from a process.

Langacker points out that the ergative system reverses the action-chain canonical event path of energy flow. In a material process with non-ergative verbs the comparison between intransitive and transitive versions shows that the Actor and Process are independent of the Affected, whereas with ergative verbs the comparison of the middle version with the effective version shows that the Instigator is dependent on the Medium and Process. The kind of dependency path is as follows

1. The ice cracked.
2. A rock cracked the ice.
3. The waiter cracked the ice with a rock.
4. The manager made the waiter crack the ice with a rock.
5. The owner had the manager make the waiter crack the ice with a rock.

Through ergative structures the asymmetry of Actor and Affected is undermined, because the Medium in intransitive clauses appears to be the source of energy, rather like an Actor.

In this famous passage from Book 1 of *The Prelude* the boy Wordsworth describes the experience of ice-skating. The frequent use of ergative verbs (in bold) give the natural objects an energy, mirrored by the impression that the cliffs appear to go on moving in arcs even after the boy has come to a sudden halt.

> So through the darkness and the cold we flew,
> And not a voice was idle; with the din
> Smitten, <u>the precipices</u> **rang** aloud;
> The leafless trees and <u>every icy crag</u>
> **Tinkled** like iron; ………
> ………………..and oftentimes,
> When we had given our bodies to the wind,
> And <u>all the shadowy banks</u> on either side
> Came **sweeping** through the darkness, **spinning** still
> The rapid line of motion, then at once
> Have I reclining back upon my heels,
> Stopped short; yet still <u>the solitary cliffs</u>
> **Wheeled** by me even as if the earth had **rolled**
> With visible motion her diurnal round!
> Behind me did they **stretch** in solemn train,
> Feebler and feebler, and I stood and watched
> Till all was tranquil as a dreamless sleep.

7.7.8 Nominalization

In "proper" nominalization a nominalized form represents qualities and processes as "abstracted" from things and time respectively. We can talk of orders of entities in terms of existence in space, and existence in time. First-order entities/things are temporally unbounded and exist bounded in space, second-order entities/processes are temporally bounded and exist in time, and third-order entities/abstractions are unbounded and have existence in neither (see Table 29).

Nominalizations properly refer to third-order entities, e.g. "Cooking involves irreversible chemical changes", in which cooking refers to the process as a generic type, "abstracted" from a particular token instance at a specific time. A second kind of nominalization involves reference to second-order entities. Here reference is to particular countable tokens of processes, e.g. "The cooking took five hours". The third kind of nominalization has been called improper (Vendler 1968). This refers to first-order entities, things with physical substance and often extended in space, e.g. "I like John's cooking", which refers to the food which results from the cooking, (the RESULT OF ACTION AS ACTION metonymy).

What relation does nominalization have to consonance? Apparently, nominalization is the species of grammatical metaphor that, *par excellence*, is neither congruent nor consonant. After all, by using a noun it metaphorises processes as things and therefore suggests that they have a kind of permanence, an existence outside time. This is especially true of improper nominalization.

However, returning to proper nominalization, it is important to remember the interactive, tensive nature of grammatical as well as lexical metaphors. Interaction would mean, in the case of proper nominalization, that the target (Process) is made to resemble the source (Thing), but that simultaneously the source (Thing) is made to seem more like the target (Process). Thus nominalization can give rise to the following reasoning: if, in the case of nominalizations, nouns can realize processes, may it not be the case that all nouns really refer to processes? At least the distinction between process and thing seems blurred.

Furthermore, proper nominalization displays a crucial feature tending towards consonance. Even more than middle ergative clauses, nominalizations can exclude any reference to an agent or cause external to the process, so the same effect of suggesting a self-generated process is achieved.

We can illustrate with an example from a Geography textbook. Instead of the congruent *water condenses* we have the nominalized wording "condensation" which, later in the text, is re-coded as a process with a dummy process verb: "condensation occurs" (Wignell, Martin, and Eggins 1993:159). What is of interest in this sequence is its graphic demonstration of the absorption of the Medium into the Process. Such is the extent of this absorption that, when the discourse demands a clause rather than a nominal group, the possibility of "squeezing" the Medium out again is resisted.

The increasing use of nominalization in modern scientific texts (Halliday 1988) could, therefore, be related to the sense of the primacy of process, undermining 4), as could the kind of non-congruent structure in history texts which nominalizes verbs both as Actor and Affected: "Competition for individual wealth stimulated the growth of trade" (Eggins et al. 1993: 90) or "[Economic] growth causes [environmental] pollution".

The possibilities for a more consonant grammar opened up by nominalization should not be underestimated. Indeed the following listed choices of wordings (Table 34) give progressively higher profile to process in the options which they allow for ignoring "Things". (Optional reference to participant Things is indicated in parentheses.)

Table 34. Grammar and the relative profiles of things and processes

Participant thing Profile	Linguistic Structure Choice	Participants	Process profile
HIGH	Transitive Effective	Actor + Affected	LOW
	Passive	Actor (+ Affected)	
	Ergative Middle	Medium	
	Nominalisation	(Actor/Affected)	
LOW	Dummy *it*		HIGH

We have now explored at some length certain grammatical structures or "metaphors" that can be used in the English language to undermine the canonical event model expressed by the typical clause, and make it more consonant with modern scientific theory. Some of these involved the change to a material process from a relational or mental process, namely activation of tokens and activation of experiences, which is possible too with activation of circumstances. In the case of activation of experiences and circumstances what would be an Object/Complement in a literal clause becomes the Subject in the metaphorical one. Ambient structures, like the activation of circumstances seem to abolish the distinction between participant and setting by choosing the setting as subject/actor, or as dispensing with a subject/actor altogether. Creative processes/cognate object constructions, reciprocal and reflexive verbs, and ergatives seem to problematise the idea of Affected, by having as their objects nouns which are not at the tail of an action chain. Nominalisations code processes as nouns, but can thereby, paradoxically remove participants from the original "literal" clause.

Interesting as these grammatical resources are they still represent the atypical, metaphorical or marked clause structure, one which we acquire quite late in our language development. For a language whose grammatical structures are more typically consonant with modern scientific theory we turn to Niitsi'powahsin (Blackfoot), a seriously endangered Algonquin language, which is, however, still spoken by thousands of people in Alberta and Montana. If we are native English speakers we might regard the grammar of

Niitsi'powahsin as metaphorical compared with the "literal" English, or, if Niitsi'powahsin is our native language, think of English grammar as metaphorical by comparison.

Hutton (2000) suggests that there are two ways of relating Whorf's discussion of the native American language Hopi to ideology. One can take the objectivist/universalist view, which he associates with cognitive linguistics/metaphor theory, and celebrate languages like Hopi and Blackfoot as being closer to "objective truth" as, for example revealed by modern scientific theory, particularly physics. Or one could take the relativist view, and, forgetting the Holy Grail of objectivity, celebrate the diversity of world-views represented by different, particularly exotic, non-SAE (Standard Average European) languages. In fact, in what follows, I hope to do both, and do not see them as contradictory, since I believe the current models of modern physics are themselves metaphorical and non-objective. We have to try out different models and see which best ensure our survival: since out experience of reality is mediated by models and metaphors, "truth" becomes relative to purpose.

7.8   Niitsi'powahsin (Blackfoot) grammar as radical metaphor

David Peat in *Blackfoot Physics* (1996) identified Niitsi'powahsin and other Algonquian languages and cultures as structuring the world in ways that are closer to the insights of modern theoretical physics. In terms we are already familiar with Peat, himself a physicist, points out:

> In modern physics the essential stuff of the universe cannot be reduced to billiard-ball atoms, but exists as relationships and fluctuations at the boundary of what we call matter and energy. Indigenous science teaches that all that exists is an expression of relationships, alliances, and balances between what, for lack of better words, we could call energies, powers or spirits.

Peat claims that the emphasis on nature and matter as a flux of processes is also a notion that is fundamental to the "scientific" world-view of Algonquin-speaking peoples, such as the Cheyenne, Cree, Ojibwaj, Mic Maq, and Blackfoot (Peat 1996: 7). In terms of metaphor theory the existence of such a language, which does not use the canonical event structure in its semantics, represents a challenge to claims like the following that Event Structure is a good candidate for universality: "All this suggests that the Event Structure probably exists around the world and that it must have developed independently everywhere" (Kövecses 2005: 46–7).

Peat was particularly interested in the theories of David Bohm who saw reality as processes and activities in a continuous movement of folding and unfolding. Bohm did not limit this movement to external reality but extended it to thoughts, feelings and emotions unfolding within the brain and the body. For Bohm this meant that the objective outer world and the subjective inner world are aspects of one underlying movement. We noted earlier Bohm's realisation in *Wholeness and the Implicate Order*

(1980) that the English language was particularly badly equipped for expressing the process nature of inner and outer reality and of their interpenetration. This realisation we have already explored at some length in this chapter by showing that the canonical event model imposes an objective/subjective dichotomy in its use of the stage model, and stresses the separation of things and energetic interactions. Peat claims that the kind of language Bohm was looking for (his "rheomode") actually existed already in the language of the Algonquin peoples.

Evidently Bohm met several Algonquin speakers shortly before his death and was impressed by the correspondence between their language/world-view and his own philosophy based on the findings of modern physics. "What to Bohm had been a major breakthrough in human thought – quantum theory, relativity, his implicate order and rheomode – were part of the everyday life and speech of the Blackfoot, Mic Maq, Cree and Ojibwaj" (pp. 237–238).

Peat presents some interesting observations and informant evidence on the nature of the Niitsi'powahsin language.

> Sa'ke'j Henderson has said that he can go for a whole day without ever speaking a noun, just dealing in the rhythms and vibrations of process. Nouns do exist within the language but, like the vortex that forms in a fast flowing river, the nouns are not primary in themselves but are temporary aspects of the everflowing process (p. 237).

Verbs, therefore, or something like them, dominate the grammar of the Algonquin peoples, some of them having more than a thousand different inflections or endings because, they "are concerned with the animation of all things within their process-vision of the cosmos" (p. 222).

In one passage Peat describes the Montaignais conceptualisation of a healer's singing in terms which remind us of our earlier analysis of the dependency of things on processes in English cognate noun constructions such as *sing a song*, and which are also reminiscent of our characterisation of superstring theory which sees matter as energetic vibration.

> What is really happening is "singing" – the action, the process. The healer cannot really say that it is "he" who is singing, rather the process of singing is going on. Within our Western worldview agents carry out actions, nouns/objects interact and bring about changes in each other. The author of a process is a noun; an object and the verb is its action. But for the Montaignais reality is profoundly different; it is flux, process and change within which individual human beings are transitory forms, and manifest expression of temporary alliances and powers, spirits and energies. Thus, no human being can bring the song into existence. Rather the singing itself is the primary reality, the vibrational process that floods across the world (pp. 144–5).

The sounds of the language itself are felt to be manifestations of this vibrational process, so that the language is not just a medium, but the energetic operation of this living force (p. 224).

7.8.1   Emphasis on "verbs" in Niitsi'powahsin

In order to find further evidence for Peat's claims about Niitsi'powahsin, we now look at certain aspects of its grammar. For this purpose I begin with Donald G. Frantz's *Blackfoot Grammar*, though, as we shall see later, many of the grammatical categories he uses are of doubtful validity when applied to Niitsi'powahsin, including the distinction between noun and verb. Where these terms have been challenged I have indicated the doubts with scare quotes "...".

It is certainly true that "verbs" are extremely important in the language. Prefixes and suffixes, and other formal variations of "verb stems" are numerous, reflecting distinctions such as: transitive-intransitive; "animate-inanimate"; independent-conjunctive-subjunctive-imperative-unreal; "singular-plural"; "first-first+second-second-third-fourth person"; "present-future-past tense"; and durative-perfective "aspect", giving well over a hundred possible inflexions. In addition "verb stems" are often complex:

> Many morphemes, the closest equivalents of which are separate words in most other languages, are part of the verb in Blackfoot. These include negatives, quantifiers, intensifiers, all kinds of adverbials, and many many others, including numerous morphemes which would be main or auxiliary verbs in other languages (Frantz 1991: 84).

Apart form these general features of Niitsi'powahsin we can take a superficial look at some of the specific areas of the grammar which make it possible to do without nouns.

7.8.1.1   *Incorporation and omission of pronouns/nouns*
Incorporating a noun or a pronoun into the verb is a common feature of many languages. In Latin, for example, it is unusual to use pronouns – the ending of the verb indicates whether the verb is first, second or third person, e.g. *amo* 'I love', *amas* 'you love', *amat* 'he/she loves'. In the language Tetelcingo Nahuatl nouns rather than pronouns are incorporated, e.g *tonal-kiisa* [sun-emerge] 'sun come out' and *lapis-kʷilowa* [pencil-write] 'write with pencil' (Langacker 1991: 374–5).

There is pronoun incorporation in Niitsi'powahsin too. "When speaker or addressee is subject there is usually no separate *word* to indicate that fact, e.g.

> Nitáakahkayi.
> Nit-áak-ahkayi
> I-will-go^home   'I'm going home'" (Frantz 1991: 21).

The English meteorological verbs discussed earlier under "ambient" structures, have their counterparts in Niitsi'powahsin. Here Frantz claims that the pronoun is incorporated in the verb by use of "the third person singular suffix *-wa*: *Áísootawa* 'It's raining'" (p. 23). Leroy and Ryan point out that – *wa* is actually used to indicate the relative importance of a human related event, rather than a third person marker. So "there is no objectification in this Blackfoot utterance, no noun or verb – just an observance of event manifestation" (Leroy and Ryan 2004: 38).

They also point out that the subject often does not need to be stated. A whole sentence translation like 'he will run very fast' becomes "áaksiiksikkamokska'siwa", 'expected-very^fast-running' (p. 38). Similarly where nominal objects would have to be mentioned in an SAE language they are often left unspecified in Blackfoot: "Nítohpommaa" 'I purchased (something unspecified)'" (Frantz 1991: 41).

7.8.1.2 *Verbalisation of "nouns"*

According to Frantz another way of incorporating "nouns" into "verbs" is called verbalisation, which is achieved in Niitsi'powahsin by adding suffixes. By adding the suffix *-yi*, intransitive verbs can be derived from "nouns" to give a meaning which seems equivalent to the English Relational process plus Value, or in more traditional syntactic terms predicate noun phrases: ínaa (chief) → ikitáaksinaayi "you will be chief". By adding *-wa'si* one can convey the meaning of "turning into"

> nítohkiáayowa'si
> nít-ohkiáayo-wa'si   "I became enraged" (p.108)
> I – bear – became

The suffix *hkaa/-Ihkaa* carries the meaning "acquire"

> iimííhkaayaawa
> iimíí-   hkaa-   yi-aawa   "they fished"
> past:fish-acquire(AI)-3p-PRO

And *-hko/-Ihko* adds the meaning "provide for"

> Nitsináánsskoayaawa
> Nit-inaan- Ihko-   a: -yi-aawa   "I got something for them"
> I-possession-provide(TA)-dir-3p-PRO

However, Niitsi'powahsin speakers, like Ryan Heavy Head (personal communication) would dispute Frantz's analytical categories.

> It's apparent to me that there were never any 'nouns' here to begin with. *Ohkiaayo* is not literally a "bear", nor *mamii* a "fish", nor *inaan* a "possession" – each of these supposed nouns are really just describing characteristics, events, processes, and such.

He goes on to give examples such as

> the word for 'otter' *aimmoniisi*, which just means 'sliding' (referring to its movement). Or there's *ksisskstaki*, the "noun" for beaver, which just means 'grating'

(referring to how it eats) ... *Ohkiaayo* is not verbalized with the addition of *-waʼsi*, instead, *-waʼsi* just describes the state of its manifestation, the early stage of transformation toward ohkiaayo-ness (which includes rage, the practice of violently seizing, gestures of intimidation, etc) ... There really are no nouns that I can find in Niitsiʼpowahsin [Blackfoot] to verbalise.[1]

7.8.2 "Nominalisations"

Perhaps the most important contribution to the verbiness or processual aspect of Niitsiʼpowahsin is, paradoxically, what Frantz calls "nominalisation". Given claims that one can speak Niitsiʼpowahsin all day without using a noun, and doubts whether nouns even exist in the language, its native speakers would not regard these as true nominalizations, in the cognitive sense of turning a process into a thing. Rather it seems to be that what Western languages might refer to with nouns Niitsiʼpowahsin refers to with verbs or clauses, or, in a more radical view, Niitsiʼpowahsin seems to undermine the distinction between verb and noun completely. Frantz admits that these "nominalisations" are the functional equivalent of English relative clauses (Frantz 1991: 116). "Clauses which modify a noun are relatively rare in Blackfoot. It is perhaps a typological characteristic of the language that free relatives are used to the near exclusion of relative clauses which modify a noun." (p. 129).

First we have conversions in which we find an "intransitive verb used as a noun stem referring to the subject of the underlying verb" (Frantz 116 ff.). For example,

> Áyoʼkaa ʼsleepʼ→
> omiksi áyoʼkaiksi
> om-iksi á- Iyoʼka-iksi   ʼwho sleepʼ ʼthose sleepersʼ
> that-3p dur-sleep -3p

In associated instrument nominalizations *aʼtsiS* is added to "Animate" Intransitive stems, for instance:

> Sináákiaʼtsisi
> Sinááki -aʼtsiS-yi   ʼwhich makes an imageʼ ʼbookʼ
> Make^image-instr -in.s

Paraphrases of other examples can give us an idea of how widespread these free relative clauses are in everyday vocabulary; ʼcut in strips-instrumentʼ: ʼwhich cut in stripsʼ or ʼscissorsʼ; ʼcover instrumentʼ: ʼwhich coversʼ or ʼlidʼ.

Another class of such "nominalisations" are known as "conjunctive nominals". Conjunctives are one class of verb that are used in subordinate clauses. When discussing

---

1.   It is, incidentally, worth pointing out that European languages might, historically, have had a similar emphasis on process in what now we would identify as nouns: *gold* originally meant ʼthat which shines or glittersʼ (Kövecses, personal communication).

these Frantz admits that this is "clause nominalization for not only do the verbs agree with subject and object but all other elements which normally accompany verbs in clauses may be present" (p. 120). Among this class we have instrumental nominals involving the 'instrument/means' prefix: *omoht-/iiht-/oht-*, e.g.

> iihtáóoyo'pa
> iiht -á -ooyi-o'p -wa   'that one eats with' or 'fork'
> instr-dur-eat -2l:nom-3s

Other examples include 'that one speaks with' or 'telephone', 'that one buys with' or 'money', 'that one sees afar with' or 'telescope'. We also have Locational nominals, formed with the prefix *it-/iit* ('there'), e.g

> iitáóoyo'pi
> iit -á -ooyi-o'p -yi   'where one eats/restaurant'
> there-dur-eat -21:nom-in.s

Other examples are 'that one eats on/table', 'where one washes clothes/laundry', 'where one washes dishes/sink'.

We can see how, unlike SAE languages, there is more of a tendency to make the "verb" the compulsory element which can stand alone, and that any "nouns" which might occur are dependent upon the "verb". So that, in this case, unlike English, it is not true to say that "nominalization adds nothing to the conceptual content of the verb, because nouns are autonomous, e.g. *explode/explosion*" (Langacker 1991: 25). Nouns seem to be verbalised out of existence, or what we would refer to as things are referred to by one-word clauses, misleadingly called nominalizations. All these are no doubt factors in the emphasis that Blackfoot culture puts upon process and flux.

As Bohm recognised, Niitsi'powahsin, through its grammar, appears to offer a better linguistic instrument for representing the quantum world of process. This it does, mainly, by its emphasis on verbs, and by the ways in which "nouns" are made dependent on them or "incorporated" into them in various ways. However, this may be a misleading way of putting it. One cannot help thinking that Frantz, in his grammar of Blackfoot, has been viewing and describing the language through the lens of SAE grammar. This is especially evident in his use of the concept of nominalisation, but inevitably in the English glosses that he gives to Niitsi'powahsin vocabulary. In what sense, to a Niitsi'powahsin speaker, is the pronoun incorporated into the verb, or in what sense is there an "unspecified object" in *Nítohpommaa* 'I purchased (something unspecified)' (Frantz 1991: 41). These nominals, perhaps, only seem to be "missing" from an English perspective.

7.8.3   Niitsi'powahsin (Blackfoot) speakers' perspectives

So let's attempt to abandon, for the moment, the lenses of Western grammar, which has colonised linguistic description, and, if Whorf is correct, will be inadequate to the description of languages like Niitsi'powahsin, and let's take Niitsi'powahsin speakers' insider view of the semantics of their grammar. For these following insights I am indebted to Leroy Little Bear and Ryan Heavy Head, and their radical, fascinating article 'A Conceptual Anatomy of the Blackfoot Word' (2004).

These writers urge us to abandon many of the linguistic categories we are accustomed to work with, and which underpin a grammatical analysis such as Frantz's. As we have seen above, the distinction between word and clause seems to disappear in the case of "nominalisations", and, in that of verbalisation of "nouns", the distinction between noun and verb seems problematic. A linguistic unit can be both a verb and a noun simultaneously, just as quantum matter can be both a particle and a wave. So Leroy and Ryan abandon much of the traditional linguistic terminology and posit three levels of structure for which they use Niitsi'powahsin terms.

At the first level, the smallest meaningful unit is called *aóhtakoistsi*, or "sounding", which might come close to what in traditional linguistics is called a bound morpheme, rather like the *-ing* of English. Unlike morphemes in English these units "suggest only a potential to contribute to transitional meaning, to mark a temporary aspect of a view, quality, process or essence associated with an event not yet delineated". The aóhtakoistsi does not have a clearly delineated meaning or definition but rather a "*relationship-dependent-meaning-emergent trait.*" (Leroy and Ryan 2004: 33)

At the second level aóhtakoistsi can be joined together to convey the experience of an event, "marking a perceptible happening that issues from a more all-encompassing dimension of reality as constant flux". This combination can be called *aanissin* or "the completed saying." (p. 33) While English conveys a conceptual structure based on generic-specific categorisations, Niitsi'powahsin addresses different aspects of an event that English might label with the same noun or its hyponyms.

> For instance, an English speaker has, in his vocabulary collection, the generic word *book* and a small group of specific type-terminology like *text, novel, journal* etc. The Blackfoot speaker, on the other hand, might talk of *sinaakia'tsisi* ('facilitates the generation of images'), *iihtáísinaakio'pi* ('means of generating images'), *okstakia'tsisi* ('facilitates recording'), *áípá'sókinnihpi* ('held wide open and flat'). The Blackfoot aanissin is not conceptually organised as an abstract or generic word, nor is it a specific type-term, inferring its taxonomic membership in a wider category. It is, rather, constructed on the basis of the event that is manifesting and being referenced ... thus it is at this transition from aóhtakoistsi to aanissin, that the conceptual divide between the English and Blackfoot language structures becomes most apparent. If positioned alongside the traditional Western taxonomy of the utterance, aanissin bridges the space between lexeme and sentence. Of course, presented here as its own grammatical category, it is neither. But if one attempts to translate the English lexeme or sentence into Blackfoot, he will inevitably arrive at aanissin ... The referent of aanissin is not understood as descriptive of either a subject or an object. Nor is the aanissin suggestive of a relationship between such agents and those acted upon. Rather aanissin is action alone, or the manifestation

of form, where anything that might – in another language – be portrayed as actor or recipient is here inseparable from, arising within, or the essence *of* the event. It can therefore be seen that the distinction between noun and verb entirely dissolves in the Blackfoot language, as one cannot exist without the other (p. 33).

We can contrast the English noun *chair* with one Niitsi'powahsin translation equivalent. In English this is both a morpheme and a word and a lexical item, and can be the subject or object of a sentence, in which case it can either be an Actor or Affected or Circumstance ("The chair squashed the cat's tail", "I pushed the chair away" "I sat on the chair"). One common translation equivalent of *chair* in Blackfoot is *asóópa'tsisi*, a compound of four áóhtakoyi, which might be glossed as *become-sit-facilitate-ing*.

> There is nothing in this breakdown which could be equated with the static quality of the 'chair' as known to the English speaker, and no indication of its concrete existence in a real world outside of human experience. It is not a noun (*thing*) nor a verb (an *interaction* between a subject and either himself or an object). Instead what we register in "asóópa'tsisi" is a facilitating event, logically interrelated and dependent upon a human event, that is in fact cited as an aspect of "asóópa'tsisi" as a happening (p.34).

Leroy and Ryan show the quadripartite semantic structure of the aanissin such as *asóópa'tsisi*, which they gloss roughly as view + quality + process/change + manner^of^state = event. Under *view* we might locate various kinds of deixis such as tense, aspect and person. However these terms would be misleading since, for the Blackfoot, with their emphasis on the present human life event which becomes manifest out of a wider reality of constant flux, the concept of time is quite radically different from the European. And "first and second person markers" mean respectively the exclusion of the addressee from the event or the inextricable connection of the addressee to the event.

Under the second position, *quality*, are included adjectives, intensifiers, and other descriptors which enhance or clarify the process referred to in the third position. Notice, however, that these qualifiers can take the form of what Western linguists might call verbs, as in the example of asóópa'tsisi, where *opii* is the second element. It is a quality related to a happening, as if one process qualifies another. "Instead of seeing a world comprised of bodies within bodies, agents and subjects, nouns and verbs, actors and actions, the Blackfoot simply registers event manifestation simultaneous with other event manifestation, all emerging from, returning into, and defining an unbound universal state of constant flux" (p. 36).

In the third position we have what is glossed *process* or *change*. "This process/change is not of the type forced upon an object by an agent, but is rather an aspect of the interrelatedness and interdependence of simultaneous events." (p. 36) This position signifies the means by which events are understood to become manifest, in the particular case of our example – facilitation.

In the fourth position, *manner^of^state*, there is the opportunity to mark number, and to indicate whether the event is the predominant or dependent event. The event conveyed by the aanissin is unbounded, more like a mass than a thing, in its unmarked form. For example the simpler sounding *asóópa'tsii* conveys the notion 'chairness'. So that "please get me a chair" would normally come out in Niitsi'powahsin as "wishing-given-there, chairness". When the Niitsi'powahsin speaker specifies number he is, unlike English, "delimiting a portion of a wider event experience ... What is primordial, and therefore most important is the eventing itself, not the individual body" (p. 37).

At the third and highest level we have áíkia'pii. From an English perspective we might think that 'chair' cannot be a complete idea, and that therefore we are obliged to combine it with something else to make a clause or sentence. However, this is not the case with Niitsi'powahsin. As we saw in our analysis of an aanissin like asóópa'tsisi, and from Frantz's free relative clauses, the event is already in a sense complete, like a clause. Nevertheless it is possible to produce more complex áíkia'pii structures, when multiple happenings occur simultaneously or when one event is dependent upon another. Leroy and Ryan's example (p. 38) is the Niitsi'powahsin equivalent of *that boy brought a chair* (Table 35).

Table 35. The Blackfoot equivalent of "that boy brought a chair"

iihpommaatooma anna saahkómaapiwa amoyi asóópa'tsisi

iih	pommaat	oom	wa	ann	wa	saahk	oma	a'pii	wa	amo	yi	a's	opii	a'tsis	yi
by way of	transfer	move	ing	that familiar	ing	young	yet	state of	ing	this near	ing	bec-ome	sit	facil-itate	ing

This is indeed an excellent example of the process emphasis of Niitsi'powahsin grammar and thought, where three manifesting events are interrelated. The authors have certainly

> illustrated that not all cultures generate a perception of reality as comprised of a fragmented landscape of solids within solids, acting as agents of change in the world, but that some – like Blackfoot culture – produce experiences of fluid event manifestation, arising and returning into a holistic state of constant flux (p. 38).

7.9 Other relevant aspects of Blackfoot world-view

There are a number of other aspects of Blackfoot and North American Indigenous culture, as discussed by Peat, that are of particular interest to us because they relate to metaphor themes that we have observed in earlier chapters, namely LANDSCAPE IS HUMAN BODY, and TIME IS (cyclical) MOVEMENT IN SPACE. In addition, Peat himself interprets the influx of European ideas in terms of the metaphor, in fact the metonymy, of IDEA IS DISEASE.

According to Peat, North American indigenous peoples' practice and ritual emphasise, as does *Gaia* theory, the interconnectedness of nature and the sensitivity and complexity of natural systems. For example, in their traditional Thanksgiving address the Iroquois people acknowledge the wholeness inherent within all of life. Moreover, whenever arriving at a decision they consider its implications right down to the seventh generation of their descendants (Peat 1996: 7). This sense of interconnectedness is found in the myths of the creator Napi:

> Napi created this land, his body is to be found imprinted upon it, and his name is found in its many features – here is his belly, over there his chin, elsewhere his elbow, and flowing through the land are his rivers. The Oldman River is a contemporary geographer's corruption of the Old Man's river, for Napi is also called the Old Man (p. 24).

> Land is said to be Napi's body. As one hears the story of Napi and his various actions, one begins to realise that Napi is also the people, and Napi's body is The People's body. The land is the body of the People, and the land is contained within the body of each Blackfoot man, woman and child (p. 107).

The sense of interconnectedness or even identity between landscape and humans means that LANDSCAPE IS HUMAN BODY is more like a literal belief for the Blackfoot than the kind of fanciful residual metaphor which we find in a few lexical items of English. Ryan Heavy Head has also pointed out (personal communication) that the landscape is not only Napi's body, but, exploiting an interaction with the metaphor theme SOCIAL ORGANISATION IS BODY, Napi's body, the landscape, is also the social body, the body-politic.

As in traditional Hindu and Chinese culture, so in the Blackfoot world-view, time is seen as cyclical.

> From this world of flux, many patterns or cycles or happenings are recognised to occur, with some variation, at fairly predictable intervals. These are wide, all-encompassing changes (day to night, summer to winter, life to death, and back again) by which all events are seen to contribute cooperatively towards a kind of homeostasis of the cycles.

However, circular Blackfoot time is even more radically different from the Western linear concept in its sense of simultaneity.

> Within this metaphysics of time and reality the buffalo are still present. It is as if, to use images from our own western view of science, other places and other times interpenetrate and coexist with our own. To traditional people this is no mere metaphor or poetic image but the reality in which they live, and since to The People time is a great circle, the time of the buffalo will return again... But it has always seemed to me that the Blackfoot did not so much "chase" or "follow" the buffalo as that they were partners in a mutual movement, one aspect of a relationship

> of time and motion in which the transformations of life and death, increase and depletion, light and dark, and the cycle of the seasons all had their part to play... so it is that humans and animals are locked together in a cooperative movement, in a complex dance of time and season (pp. 26–27).

What I find interesting here are the echoes of Rifkin's disquisition on the attitude to time of less industrialised societies, how, before the invention of modern time-measuring instruments, humans were necessarily more attuned to the rhythms and vibrations of the external natural world. These rhythms could be calibrated with our internal bodily circadian and metabolic pulses of our biological clocks. "Beneath the material surface life is animated and structured by an elaborate set of intricately synchronised rhythms that parallel the frequencies of the larger universe ... all the separate movements pulse in unison to create a single organic whole" (Rifkin 1987: 53).

Leroy and Ryan (2004) relate the attitude to time as simultaneous and present to the conceptualisation of the grammar. The Blackfoot view of time and events is as unbounded flux rather than discrete areas of past, present and future.

> From the Blackfoot perspective, no whole is bounded. Thus there are no words, only an infinite range of aanissiistsi [free "relative" clauses]. A single saying is understood as complete when it follows the quadripartite formula ... but even then it is subject to further transformation. And aóhtakoisti [bound morphemes] are not separable from the context of these aanissiistsi, they are not atomistic individuals which build into greater wholes, but are rather aspects of these unbounded aanissiistsi, where the latter signifies the notation of perceptible happenings of the source flux. From this world view, one can very easily rationalize that only the present is of any significance, because this present is no less than the sum of all events passed, those in various stages of becoming, and those expected or hoped (p. 35).

Moreover, Peat sees in the recent history of the Blackfoot a clash between a more real, wholesome and sustainable ideology and a sick Western Newtonian industrialised ideology. He characterises it thus:

> It was the clash between an open system, a society that sought balance and harmony, that maintained a cyclic time renewal, as well as an alliance of dreams and spirits and one that sought security through control – a society that had accepted the sacrifice of disease in return for mastery over matter and time and the accumulation of wealth. Like a cancer, new perceptions, worldviews, political and economic ways of thinking spread throughout Turtle Island (Peat 1996: 122).

This leads Peat to an interesting development of Dawkins' meme theory, which, as we saw in chapter 4, uses the metaphor IDEA IS DISEASE. The development is achieved by turning this metaphor into a metonymy. Not only can we think of ideas as disease metaphorically, there is a metonymic link of cause and effect which means that Western peoples suffer from disease as a direct result of their ideological obsessions with "progress, growth and increase" (p. 112) (Our discussion in chapter 5 of the link between obesity and the equation MORE = GOOD would appear to be a small instance of this). When these ideologies were imported to North America the diseases that developed with them were imported too, with the well-known devastating effects on the North American Indigenous population.

In ways which link interestingly with our discussion of EMOTION/IDEA IS DISEASE (chapter 4) and DISEASE IS INVASION (chapter 2) and their interaction to form negative metaphors for immigration (chapter 5), Peat points out that viruses are a form of information, just like ideologies.

> A virus is information, a segment of DNA that enters into the cells of a healthy body and instructs them to operate in a different way, manufacturing more viruses and, in the process causing the host to sicken. Healthy bodies, however, have their own system of defence, the immune system, that recognises the pattern of an intruder and manufactures antibodies that act to destroy viruses and bacteria … Thus, at the level of an individual, disease could be thought of as a battle between systems of information. This image also applies at the social level because the conditions under which viruses mutate and are passed on, as well as the conditions under which human immune systems become debilitated, are the direct result of social conditions. Disease is a manifestation of human thought because it is ideas, worldviews and beliefs that create the conditions in which a society can be riddled with disease strife and poverty, or can continue in health and harmony (pp. 116–117).

This passage not only claims that the metonymy of cause and effect is in operation by which ideas and ideologies produce disease, but it borders on suggesting that disease itself is simply one kind of information system, so that there is a kind of hyponymic reversal of the metaphor theme: IDEA/EMOTION IS DISEASE→ DISEASE IS ONE KIND OF IDEA. We also note the way in which Peat, with his military metaphors, seems to swallow wholesale the theme DISEASE IS INVASION.

7.10 Possession

Having discussed at length the relationship between ecological destruction, the congruent clause and simplified Newtonian mechanics, and held out possibilities of a more consonant grammar, either with English or better still Niitsi'powahsin, I now turn to a relatively local grammatical phenomenon, the grammaticalisation of possession.

The most comprehensive account is that of Heine, who has surveyed the different schemas adopted in the world's languages for conveying possession (Heine 1997: 47–67) (See Table 36). I summarise these below.

Table 36. A formulaic description of schemas used for the expression of predicative possession (Heine 1997: 47)

Formula	Label of event schema
X takes Y	Action
Y is located at X	Location
X is with Y	Companion
X's Y exists	Genitive
Y exists for/to X	Goal
Y exists from X	Source
As for X, Y exists	Topic
Y is X's property	Equation

7.10.1 Action schema

In this schema predicative possession is derived conceptually from a transitive structure of Actor – Material Process – Affected.

> Most commonly a 'have' verb arises out of the semantic bleaching of active possession verbs such as 'get', 'grab', 'seize', 'take', 'obtain' etc. whereby the sense of 'acting to take possession' has been bleached, leaving behind only its *implied result* of 'having possession' (Givon 1984: 103, quoted in Heine 1997: 47).

For example, "*gagner* 'gain, win' has become the 'have' verb in some French-based Creoles and African varieties of French" (p. 48) 'Have' constructions in Germanic and romance languages are ultimately derived from verbs like *take, catch, get hold of, hold, grasp, lift,* e.g. the German verb *haben* still had the concept of 'hold' or 'keep' as part of its meaning in Middle High German (p. 50). A current example is in Hawaiian Creole:

> Get   wan wahini shi get wan data
> "There is a   woman who has a   daughter" (p. 49).

This mirrors the ambiguity of the English *possess*: "he possessed the two cows" meaning either 'he took the two cows' or 'he owned two cows'.

7.10.2 Location, existence and other schemas

Location is equivalent to 'Y is at X's place', where the possession is the Subject/Token and the possessor is Locative Circumstance Complement. Sometimes the equivalent of the English "I have a book" involves a relational process verb, as in the case of Modern Irish, and sometimes without, as in Modern Russian (p. 51).

> Tá leabhar agam
> Is book   at:me

> U menya kniga
> At me   book

This schema is difficult to distinguish, in many cases, from the Goal schema, 'Y exists to/ for X', when the preposition is ambiguous between location and direction, as in French

> Le livre est à moi
> The book is at me

Closely related to the location schema is the Companion or Accompaniment schema 'X is with Y', perhaps reflecting a conceptual metaphor A POSSESSION IS A COMPANION, as in the Bantu language Venda:

> Ndi na   modhoro
> I.be with motor-car

The Genitive schema, can be conveyed by 'X's Y exists', as in Turkish:

> Kitab-im var
> Book-my   existent

The Source schema, 'Y exists (away) from X' is often a template for attributive, rather than predicative possession, but occurs predicatively in the Athabaskan language Slave:

> Tsét'ú   nets'e
> Cigarette   you.from
> "Do you have cigarettes?"

The Target schema involves the thematisation of the possessor, 'As for X, Y (of X) exists' as in the Western Nilotic language Lango

> Òkélò gwók'ɛrɛ pé
> Okele dog.his 3.NEG.exist
> "Okelo doesn't have a dog"

The Equation schema conveys 'Y is X's (property)' as in English "the book is mine" and Mandarin Chinese

> Shū   shì, wǒ-de
> Book be   me-of
> "The book is mine"

7.10.3 Ideology and the action schema

While these different ways of conceptualising possession may be to a greater or lesser extent available in any one language, different languages are likely to favour one or another schema over the others. As Heine points out: "Languages in Europe, for example, have, at least over the last two millennia, drawn primarily on the Action Schema for developing 'have'-constructions, while people in central and Southern Africa have preferred the Companion Schema" (p. 72). In fact, the situation with European languages makes them rather "exotic" and exceptional in favouring the Action Schema as the origin of possessive constructions (p. 229).

The question that concerns me is whether this has any relation to ideology. One of the major differences between the Action Schema and the others is that in the former the Possessor is the Subject (an Actor) of a transitive clause, and the Possession is the direct Object (Goal/Affected) although when adopted for possession it no longer behaves like a typical action verb, being resistant to passivisation, and imperfective aspect (*the book was had by John, *John is having a book). By contrast, in the other major schemas the Possessor is likely to be a Complement, syntactically less prominent, and impossible to conceptualise even remotely as an Actor (pp. 229, 231).

Isačenko (1974) and Orr (1992) have produced evidence that possessive constructions in Russian and other Slavic languages were originally based on Location Schemas, and only more recently, under the influence of Germanic and Romance languages, have they developed an action schema verb. Heine disputes this, claiming that locative *u* constructions, in, for example, Bulgarian, are used only for physical and temporary possession rather than inalienable and abstract possession, which is conveyed by the action schema-based *imam* constructions. He argues that, since the general pattern of semantic development in possessive constructions is from physical via temporary to inalienable to abstract, *imam* constructions must have pre-dated *u* constructions in order to have arrived to the point where they express inalienable and abstract possession (p. 233). This is a debatable argument. One could equally well see the *u* construction as the basic one, and the *imam* construction as becoming more dominant under the influence of different ideologies expressed by Germanic and Romance grammar.

Isačenko claims that the modern notion of possession or property is not one known to "primitive" societies, who therefore conceptualised and grammaticised possession differently, presumably with more Locative-type Schemas.

> Possession proper, or 'ownership' is a legal institution appearing in societies after they have reached a certain stage of development. It is instructive to compare the verbs related to ownership in H[ave]-languages with those in B[e]-languages ... English *to own* German *besitzen*, Czech *vlastnit* are transitive verbs belonging to the domestic stock of the vocabulary. Russian, a typical B-language, has no domestic transitive verb meaning 'to own, to possess'. The verbs *vladet* and *obladat* used as equivalents of 'possess' mean primarily 'to be master of, to govern', derived from the stem *vlad-* 'reign'. Both words are borrowings from Slavonian (Isačenko 1974: 64).

The more active forms of possession associated with capitalist acquisition, accumulation and property rights were reflected in, reinforced or perhaps even determined by the use of Action-Schema based grammatical constructions. The general linguistic development seems to be in this direction, which suggests that the verb *have* develops in connection with the concept of private property, rather than functional property or property for use (Fromm 1983: 11).

Not only the literal domain of possession is affected by this, but the metaphorical too, by which, through nominalisation, we can metaphorically think of possessing actions, qualities, feelings, thoughts. Fromm (1983), following Marx, Engels and Du Marais has contested this move to the metaphorical.

> To express an activity by *to have* in connection with a noun is an erroneous use of language because processes and activities cannot be possessed; they can only be experienced. Du Marais recognised this: 'I have an idea', 'I have a longing', 'I have the will' = I think, I desire, I want.

In *The Holy Family* Marx and Engels point out that Bauer's notion of the goddess of love that possesses man turns love into a thing, a man who loves into an alienated man of love.

> "I have great love for you" is meaningless. Love is not a thing that one can have, but a process, an inner activity that one is the subject of. I can love, I can be in love, but in loving, I have … nothing. In fact the less I have, the more I can love (p. 10).

7.11 Conclusion and summary: process philosophies and ideologies

In our final chapter I will attempt to trace some of the ideological roots of the metaphor themes with which we have been brainwashed, and which have led us into an ecological, if not spiritual, crisis. But before doing so, and to conclude this chapter, I would like to suggest other counter-ideologies, besides Blackfoot culture, which put emphasis on process and thereby undermine the idea of anything but transitory possession.

The problem is, as I have partially demonstrated, that the billiard-ball model and the canonical event model are the commonsense cognitive schemas acquired from our infant experience, though not in Blackfoot language and culture. As part of our bodily and cultural inheritance, reproduced by our early childhood learning of the congruent grammar of SAE languages, which expresses these models, we are very attached to the notions of the existence, possession and permanence of things, including, of course, ourselves.

These models seem to have dominated, for the most part, Western philosophy, a dominance traced by Hans Küng (1987). Although Heraclitus developed "a radical philosophy of becoming according to which *everything* is fluid in the contradictoriness of all appearances" this was resisted by Parmenides who insisted on the illusoriness of becoming and the reality of being: "an absolutely rigid kind of immovableness and unchangeableness: being is and cannot not be". Greek and later philosophy for the most part continued in the tradition of Parmenides: the philosophy of nature (Empedocles, Anaxagoras, Leucippus, and Democritus) with its conception of unchangeable substance, whether made up of elements or atoms; Plato's ontology, and Plato's theory of ideas, which devalued a changing world of appearance; Aristotle's *energia* philosophy, which explained movement in terms of the motionless *nous*; Plotinus' dynamic philosophy of emanation with its conception of the non-living primordial One; and the metaphysics of medieval scholasticism. It was only after Descartes had developed his novel theory of motion, that Leibniz joined Hobbes under the influence of the natural sciences and the calculus to embrace a basically dynamic monadology. Following them Kant interested himself in the becoming of the cosmos and Lessing in the history of both nature and humankind as a sustained process of development. Drawing on Fichte and Schelling,

> Hegel then moulded a consistent and comprehensive metaphysic of becoming, development, history and life. It is chiefly due to him that the nineteenth century became a historical century, with the philosophy of becoming exerting an especially strong influence on Nietsche, Bergson, Whitehead and, finally, Heidegger (Küng 1987: 434–435).

We might say more about the rejection of reification, and the primacy of process and interrelatedness in the philosophy of Whitehead, and also of Peirce. Whitehead explores how reality is created from one moment to the next and inherited in its interrelatedness in memory and perception (Sherburne 1981). He rejects Newton's autonomous space and time and construes them as "simply abstractions from the totality of prehensive unifications as mutually patterned in each other ... space-time is nothing else than a system of pulling together of assemblages into unities" (Harvey 1996: 258). Peirce in his category of Firstness conceives the world as it was to Adam "before he had drawn any distinctions, or had become conscious of his own existence, that is first, present, immediate, fresh, new, initiative, original, spontaneous, free, vivid, conscious, evanescent" (Peirce 1958: Vol. 1 paragraph 357).

One can also find a strong emphasis upon process and impermanence in Buddhist philosophy, probably the major world religion most in tune with the theories of modern physics.

> Heraclitus' and Hegel's radical concept of life as a process and not as a substance is paralleled in the Eastern world by the philosophy of the Buddha. There is no room in Buddhist thought for the concept of any enduring permanent substance, neither things nor the self. Nothing is real but processes. Contemporary scientific thought has brought about a renaissance of the philosophical concepts of process thinking by discovering and applying them to the natural sciences (Fromm 1983: 13).

For Buddhism, impermanence encompasses the self as well as the world of things, and thereby deconstructs the notion of possession and independent action. Our illusory sense of identity is shored up through domination: we construct a self through the exercise of power over humans in political and social domination; or through the use of technology to dominate the environment, in order to produce and possess property, consumer goods, and other ultimately unsatisfying symbols of status and identity.

> Until our own time, the West has been unable to free itself from non-process perspectives – philosophies of consciousness – which turn their backs on the immediately experienced, aesthetically breathtaking, rich and intense momentary nows. Non-Buddhist orientations of this kind generate the subject-object duality of thought and thing, mind and body, self and world, spirit and matter, man and nature, time and eternity, fact and value, that no amount of dialectic has ever been able to heal. This is another reason why, as Whitehead told Northrop when the latter was a graduate student in London, "we cannot be too suspicious of ordinary language, whether in philosophy or everyday life" (Jacobson 1988: 74).

> To make the concept [of process] possible many careless habits of the Western tradition had to be overcome: its thingification of the world, its simple-minded submission to ordinary language and common-sense assumptions (p. 29).

Metaphor, especially original metaphor, is, par excellence, the means of de/reconstructing common-sense ordinary language categories. I have tried to demonstrate in this chapter how grammatical metaphor, in so far as it resembles the lexical, has a vital role to play in this denaturalization. I have also attempted to show, in a rather cursory manner, how the commonsense world of Blackfoot might be less nonsensical than that of SAE cultures, and how the grammaticalisation of possession is a relatively recent phenomenon.

Some models one is willing to accept in the quest for truth. But we have to recognize that truth is relative to purpose. For architects the earth is flat, for astronauts it is, more or less, spherical. If our purpose is the long-term survival of the planet then truth will be whatever promotes that survival, and the metaphorical models will be selected accordingly. Semiosis certainly is grounded in our interaction with a real world. We have no direct access to this world, since perception, cognition and language intervene between the world and us. But we evolve those models of thinking and perceiving which are positively adaptive to our environment. For example, our perceptual faculties construct interpretative models based on sensation which, among other things, invert the images on our retina, often interpret the size of the image in terms of distance rather than absolute size of the imaged object, and these perceptual models serve us well in most cases. They are tested against experience, through feedback, and if the model is more or less true for our purposes we can cross the road safely without being run over. If these models are wrong we don't survive. We have, in the last two hundred and fifty years, evolved a model, an ideology in which we can dominate and exploit nature, increasingly to serve the purposes of international consumer capitalism, and this model is being tested against our experience through negative and positive feedback.

> We have chosen to sever our participatory union with the rest of creation, and to redefine the world as a binary field where only subject and objects exist. We have chosen autonomy over participation, isolation over communion, and have used power to turn the world's phenomena into objects for manipulation and expropriation (Rifkin 1987: 223).

If this model is wrong, and it looks as though it is, we may collectively fail to survive. If that threatens to happen, we must abandon urgently those modes of infantile perception and cognition which are often associated with canonical events and congruent grammar.

Whether the message of the new physics, the theory of Gaia, the gospel of inter-relatedness, will have an impact in time on the ideology of the future is a vital question. The Newtonian-inspired ideology, the ideology of the triumph of technology, of applying external forces to exploit an inert nature, may, if there is to be a future, give way to a world-view represented by a different grammar. Meanwhile congruent transitive material process clauses, and action schemas for possession militate against a new world-view.

> When you have an effective enough technology so that you can really act upon your epistemological errors and can create havoc in the world in which you live, then the error is lethal. Epistemological error is all right, it's fine up to the point at which you create around yourself a universe in which that error becomes immanent in monstrous changes of the universe that you have created and now try to live in (Bateson 1975: 460–461).

Ironically, of course, it is the indigenous marginalised people, like the Blackfoot, along with others such as the Saami of northern Scandinavia, the Chuckchi of Siberia and the Parkana of Brazil, who find it most difficult to survive the implementation of these brute force possessive technologies, to live with these monstrous changes of the universe (Josephson 2002: 7).

CHAPTER 8

Capitalism and the development of ideological metaphors

London, New York, Los Angeles, Sydney, 2004. The category of the successful person comprises both men and women, of any race, who have been able to accumulate money, power and renown through their own activities in one of the myriad branches of the commercial world ... The ability to accumulate wealth is prized for reflecting the presence of at least four cardinal virtues: creativity, courage, intelligence and stamina. The presence of other virtues – humility or godliness, for example – rarely detains attention ... Money is imbued with an ethical quality. Its presence indicates the virtue of its owner, as do the material goods it can buy (De Botton 2004: 193–4).

8.1 Introduction

In this final chapter I consider the historical and cultural factors behind many of the metaphor themes so far discussed and exemplified, themes which have become so widespread and influential in our cognition, and in the mental and ideological construction of our biological, social, economic and ecological worlds. While some of these metaphors depend for their source and, perhaps, targets, on our bodily experiences, even these have been selected, emphasised and elaborated under cultural influences; some have been co-opted to support particular economic and social ideologies, while others, indeed, are deliberate theoretical constructs (what Kövecses labels "existential"). I wish to show that many of the most significant metaphor themes have been created by, nurtured by, or used to express and reinforce a philosophical tradition which can be traced back at least as far as the first part of the capitalist era, the dawn of the Scientific and Industrial Revolutions in 17th century Britain. Beginning with Thomas Hobbes this tradition can be followed, with variations, through Hume, Adam Smith, Thomas Malthus, who, in turn, had considerable influence on Darwin, and represents ideologies which have begun to acquire a new ascendancy since the last quarter of the 20th century. In some ways this journey of exploration provides a historical background to and partial genealogy for the socio-biological theories already discussed in chapter 4, and also relates to the discussion of time and industrialisation in chapter 2.

The ideological connections between these philosophers, were, in some cases, underpinned by social connections and friendships, notably that between Hume and

Adam Smith. Hume and his sister entertained a large circle of Scottish friends, including Adam Smith, and occasional guests from overseas, such as Benjamin Franklin, who stayed with Hume for a month. Such was Hume's admiration for Smith that, during a serious illness, he joked with Boswell about death and the possibility of an afterlife, and then changed the subject to recommend that Boswell read Smith's *Wealth of Nations* (Baier 1998).

As it is essential to my argument to show that the ideologies of these early capitalist philosophers represent a departure from the late Middle Ages, and can be located in a specific historical period and culture, I shall, during my exploration, from time to time refer to Tawney's and Weber's critical accounts of Protestantism and the rise of capitalism. These writers show, better than I ever could, what a revolution in orthodoxy these economic philosophers brought about.

Finally I summarise the ideologies under critique and objections to them by discussing Lakoff's metaphorically-informed analysis of right-wing ideology in *Moral Politics* (1996). The chapter, and book, ends with a self-reflexive discussion of reductionism and with a theological speculation on the relationship between truth, incarnation and contemporary metaphorical theory.

8.2 The ideological tradition of capitalist economic philosophy

A simplified summary of the ideological consensus might represent it as a confluence of two strands. The first strand starts with the idea that humans, along with animals, are basically competitive and selfish, their altruism extending, naturally, only to include family and close friends. Given this fact, and the scarcity of resources, humans, like animals, are involved in a competition for survival of themselves and their progeny, which, unless checked, results in violence and war. There are various ways in which this competition might be checked: a strong sovereign or government guaranteeing property rights; the division of labour and trade; or moral restraint, which prevents the overpopulation that intensifies competition. A second strand, perhaps bolstered by Newtonian mathematics, begins with the idea that quality can be expressed as quantity, and, more particularly, that well-being, relationships, time, indeed virtue itself, can be expressed or recognised in terms of money or material possessions. Combining the two strands we have the economic virtues, the most salient of which is "industry", making sure that one's time, being equivalent to money, is not wasted, and that one therefore accumulates enough capital to ensure one's survival and the survival of one's children.

8.2.1   Competition and conflict

In chapter 2 I gave details of the numerous metaphor themes in English which construct the activities of our lives in terms of competition:

- COMPETITION IS RACE, COMPETITIVE SUCCESS IS WINNING A RACE, IMPORTANT IS FIRST
- ACTIVITY IS FIGHTING, HUMANS ARE ARMY, SEX IS VIOLENCE
- ARGUMENT IS WAR, ARGUING/CRITICISING IS FIGHTING, ARGUING/CRITICISING IS ATTACKING – HITTING/PUNCHING or SHOOTING/THROWING or WOUNDING/CUTTING
- ACTIVITY IS GAME – BALL GAME, CARD GAME, BOARD GAME, GAMBLING GAME.

These vary from the relatively playful, where activities are various sorts of games, to the violent, where activity is war. What the schemas share is that there are winners and losers in these games and battles, despite the anomalous coinage "a win-win situation".

The emphasis on competition which we observe in our philosophers, and which is reflected and reinforced by these metaphor themes, was a relatively new historical development, directly in conflict with the medieval conception of society as a symbiotic inter-related organism. From a medieval perspective "every social movement or personal motive which sets group against group, or individual against individual, appears, not the irrepressible energy of life, but the mutterings of chaos" and "self-interest is a demon which leads the individual to struggle for riches and advancement." (Tawney 1926/1938: 175, quoting Laud 1847: 167)

8.2.1.1   *Competition and conflict in Hobbes*

Hobbes is probably most famous for his claim that by nature society is in a state of war caused by lack of trust, glory, but principally competitiveness:

> ... so that in the nature of man, we find three principal causes of quarrel. First competition; secondly diffidence; thirdly, glory ... Hereby it is manifest that during the time men live without a common power to keep them all in awe, they are in that condition which is called war; and such a war as is of every man, against every man.

War, a period in which "every man is enemy to every man", is destructive of civilisation. In such conditions there will be "continual fear, and danger of violent death; and the life of man, solitary, poor, nasty, brutish and short" (Hobbes 1651/1997: 70). This "miserable condition of war" is a consequence of "the natural passions of men", which "carry us to partiality, pride, revenge and the like". Thus each family and indeed each nation is naturally disposed to compete or fight against its neighbours, and the winners in the struggle are celebrated (p. 93).

In the debate over the HUMAN IS ANIMAL metaphor, Hobbes refuses a comparison with symbiotic and co-operative bees and ants, because, unlike these insects, men are always in competition for honour and dignity, and make a distinction between the private good and the common good. Most important, bees and ants agree and co-operate naturally, whereas humans only agree and co-operate artificially, that is by contract – so some higher power is necessary to make them keep their covenant (pp. 94–95).

Hobbes, as is well-known, regarded the power of the sovereign as the guarantee of laws and covenants to restrain man's natural competitiveness and hostility. But the sovereign state which results, though bringing about an artificial co-operation, is still likely to be hostile to other nation states – indeed fear of other external states may be a main motive for internal co-operation: "And law was brought into the world for nothing else but to limit the natural liberty of particular men, in such manner, as they might not hurt, but assist one another, and join together against a common enemy" (p. 134).

It was perhaps not surprising that Hobbes saw war as the natural state of humankind. For, quite apart from his experience of civil war in England, the wealth created by the initial stages of capitalism in Europe was used to finance wars, which ravaged Europe for three quarters of the sixteenth and seventeenth centuries and led to economic and financial ruin in Spain, the southern Netherlands, Antwerp, the greater part of France and large parts of Germany (Tawney 1926/1938: 86–87).

8.2.1.2   *Competition and conflict in Hume*

Humans' natural competitiveness rather than co-operativeness, and the need for government to restrain it through justice are themes taken up by Hume. "Anger and hatred are passions inherent in our very frame and constitution. The want of them, on some occasions, may even be proof of weakness and imbecility" (Hume 1740/1969: 655). Humans, being naturally selfish, are inevitably in conflict with each other, "as the self-love of one person is naturally contrary to that of another", a conflict only to be prevented through the property-owning justice system (p. 581).

In Hume we already have the opposition between the desire for freedom (FREEDOM IS SPACE TO MOVE) and the desire for security (RELATIONSHIP IS PROXIMITY/COHESION), familiar from chapter 5 (5.3.1). The idea is that we voluntarily give up freedom in exchange for security – "the security and protection which we enjoy in political society, and which we can never attain, when perfectly free and independent". The need for this security is predicated upon the natural "wickedness and injustice of men, who are perpetually carried, by their unruly passions, and by their present and immediate interest, to the violation of all the laws of society" (p. 602).

Like Hobbes, Hume saw a foreign threat as the origin of the civil society of sovereign nation states: "I assert the first rudiments of government to arise from quarrels, not among men of the same society, but among those of different societies" (p. 591). Hume, in a rather surprising passage, asserts that increases of riches or possessions leads to war and fighting which thereby leads to government, and this is a reason why monarchies are the first form of government. "Camps are the true mothers of cities; and as war cannot be administered, by reason of the suddenness of every exigency, without some authority in a single person, that same kind of authority naturally takes place in that civil government, which succeeds the military" (p. 592). War then seems to be a *felix culpa*, a cloud with a silver lining.

We might wonder, however, by what means sovereigns are established. It is naturally by war and military might that the sovereign first takes power. Most races of kings or dynasties, in their origin, were founded on usurpation and rebellion. "'Twas by the sword, therefore, that every emperor acquired, as well as defended, his right ... [T]he right of the stronger, in public affairs, is to be received as legitimate, and authorized by morality, when not opposed by any other title". For the monarchy to be inherited is also understandable.

> The presumed consent of the father, the imitation of the succession to private families, the interest that the state has in choosing the person, who is most powerful, and has the most numerous followers; all these reasons lead men to prefer the son of their late monarch to any other person (p. 610).

We notice here the doctrine of might is right, or, foreshadowing Darwin and Spencer, the survival of the fittest, genetically determined. In terms of metaphor themes the equation GOOD = POWER, is derived from the multivalency GOOD IS HIGH and POWER IS ABOVE.

8.2.1.3 *Competition and conflict in Adam Smith*

The importance of the restraining power of the sovereign is accepted too in Adam Smith as a precondition of civilisation. Due to man's innate warlike nature, before the division of labour "among the nations of hunters, the lowest and rudest state of society, such as we find it among the native tribes of North America, every man is a warrior as well as a hunter." So in modern civilised sovereign states "the first duty of the sovereign, that of protecting the society from the violence and invasion of other independent societies, can be performed only by means of military force..." (Smith 1776/1991: 468).

In a paradoxical turn, Smith suggests that a powerful standing army allows freedom of speech and action, because it guarantees that no action can represent a real threat to the sovereign power. A standing army therefore becomes necessary even in times of peace to protect the government from internal dissent. The result is that the provision of a military force grows gradually more and more expensive as that society advances in civilisation (p. 470).

The inevitable result is that the richer and more civilised the nation, the more it can afford to spend on the military. For Smith, wealth, military expenditure and civilisation, (and presumably the spread of civilisation through empire) go hand in hand, quite unproblematically:

> In modern war the great expense of fire-arms gives an evident advantage to the nation which can best afford that expense; and consequently to an opulent and civilised, over a poor and barbarous nation. ... The invention of fire-arms, an invention which at first sight appears to be so pernicious, is certainly favourable to the permanency and to the extension of civilisation. (p. 471).

This telling passage twists various ideological strands and metaphor themes together. It gives respectability to the idea that ACTIVITY IS FIGHTING, a natural metaphor, bordering on the literal when fighting becomes the most important activity of government. It does this partly by exploiting, like Hobbes, the equation, military POWER = GOOD, but it also anticipates discussion below of QUALITY IS WEALTH.

Smith did most among the philosophers under discussion to elaborate the idea that innate competitive drives could and should be harnessed for economic development. Competition is clearly behind the theory of supply and demand. When the supply to buyers is less than effectual demand

> a competition will immediately begin among them, and the market price will rise more or less above the natural price, according either as the greatness of the deficiency, or the wealth and wanton luxury of the competitors, happen to animate more or less the eagerness of the competition (pp. 59–60).

Anything which interferes with competition will therefore distort the supply and demand mechanism of the market. The regulation of wages is one means of preventing competition: "For if people in the same kind of work were to receive equal wages, there would be no emulation, and no room left for industry or ingenuity". And regulation of prices is ideally avoided too: "Where there is an exclusive corporation, it may perhaps be proper to regulate the price for the first necessary of life. But where there is none, the competition will regulate it much better than any assize" (p. 151). (Notice the favourite clock or machine metaphor of "regulation".)

Monopoly is perhaps the most obvious form of anti-competitive behaviour. Smith criticises restraints on imports since these produce monopolies at home and therefore decrease competition and make goods more expensive. He similarly opposes bounties (export subsidies) and trade treaties which restrict price-cutting competition. For "in every country it always is and must be the interest of the great body of the people to buy whatever they want of those that sell it cheapest" (p. 383).

8.2.1.4 *Competition and conflict in Malthus*

Malthus shifted the focus of competition to the biological, even though the dependency of population upon the available means of subsistence is also mentioned in Hume and Smith. The instinct to reproduce inevitably leads to competition for resources, which in turn leads to hostility, violence and predation:

> In plants and animals the view of the subject is simple. They are all impelled by a powerful instinct to the increase of their species; and this instinct is interrupted by no reasoning or doubts about providing for their offspring. Wherever, therefore, there is liberty, the power of increase is exerted; and the superabundant effects are repressed afterwards by want of room and nourishment, which is common to plants and animals; and among animals, by their becoming prey of each other (Malthus 1992: 14).

The most important preventive check on population growth is therefore, as with animals, war.

Whereas Hobbes and Hume emphasised the importance of the sovereign power as an antidote to war, Malthus, sounding rather like George Bush on AIDS prevention, looks to female sexual abstinence as a means of preventing population growth and the ensuing war and starvation which would otherwise naturally occur.

> A much larger proportion of women pass a considerable part of their lives in the exercise of this virtue than in past times and among civilised nations … [I]t may be considered in this light as the most powerful of the checks which in modern Europe keep down the population to the level of the means of subsistence (p. 43).

However, Malthus wishes to avoid the extremes of self-restraint as well as extremes of self-gratification:

> But placing this evil in the most formidable point of view, we should evidently purchase a diminution of it at a very high price, by the extinction or diminution of the passion which causes it; a change which would probably convert human life either into a cold and cheerless blank or a scene of savage and merciless ferocity (pp. 212–213).

There is no doubt that Malthus perceives animal life and uncivilised human societies as in a natural state of ferocious competitiveness and hostility.

8.2.1.5 *Competition and conflict in Darwin*
Charles Darwin re-read Malthus' *Essay* in 1838, and borrowed the Malthusian biological theme of limits to the constant geometrical progression of population growth, depicting life as an inevitable struggle for survival, due to an unrelenting insufficiency of food supply.

> In the next chapter the struggle for Existence amongst all organic beings throughout the world, which inevitable follows from the high geometrical ratio of their increase, will be considered. This is the doctrine of Malthus, applied to the whole animal and vegetable kingdoms (Darwin 1859/1991: 3).

However, the possibility of increased production and sexual restraint does not exist in the animal and plant worlds "for in this case there can be no artificial increase of food, and no prudential restraint from marriage" (p. 48).

The exact relationship between Malthus and Darwin has been a matter of some discussion. According to Rogers (1972) Darwin had already developed a basic theory of natural selection before reading Malthus in 1838. What Darwin did was to express his theory using metaphors taken from Spencer and Malthus, "the survival of the fittest" and "the struggle for existence" respectively. These were in Spencer and Malthus literal concepts applied to society, so that later social Darwinists simply took them as literal when used by Darwin, another example of asymmetric metaphor (Goatly 1997):

"although Darwin in no way encouraged such social interpretations of his theory, his use of metaphorical concepts from Malthus and Spencer made possible the social interpretation of what Darwin intended only to be a biological theory of evolution" (Rogers 1972: 269)

Darwin, while acknowledging the interdependence of species, nevertheless tends to emphasise the competition between members of the same species.

> I should premise that I use this term [struggle for existence] in a large and met-aphorical sense, including dependence of one being on another, and including (which is more important) not only the life of the individual, but success in leav-ing progeny. Two canine animals, in a time of dearth, may be truly said to struggle with each other which shall get food and live. But a plant on the edge of a desert is said to struggle for life against the drought, though more properly it should be said to be dependent on the moisture. A plant which annually produces a thou-sand seeds, of which only one on average comes to maturity, may be more truly said to struggle with the plants of the same and other kinds which already clothe the ground ... As the mistletoe is disseminated by birds, its existence depends on them, and it may metaphorically be said to struggle with other fruit-bearing plants, in tempting the birds to devour and thus disseminate its seeds. In these several senses, which pass into each other, I use for convenience' sake the general term of Struggle for Existence (pp. 47–48).

Despite Darwin's claims that he is using the last phrase in a metaphorical sense, he develops the military metaphors [my boldings] throughout *The Origin of Species.*

> **Battle** within **battle** must continually be recurring with varying success; and yet, in the long run, the forces are so nicely balanced, that the face of nature remains for long periods of time uniform, though assuredly the merest trifle would give the **victory** of one organic being over another ... What a **struggle** must have gone on during long centuries between the several kinds of trees, each annually scat-tering its seeds by the thousand; what **war** between insect and insect – between insects, snails and other animals with birds and beasts of prey (p. 55).

> We forget that each species, even when it most abounds, is constantly suffering enormous destruction at some period of its life, from **enemies** or from competi-tors for the same place and food (p. 51).

Since life is constructed as a battle there will inevitably be winners and losers. Those with the competitive advantage will win the battle and defeat the inferior by driving it to extinction.

> [T]he theory of natural selection is grounded on the belief that each new vari-ety and ultimately each new species, is produced and maintained by having some advantage over those with which it comes into competition; and the consequent extinction of the less-favoured forms almost inevitably follows (p. 281).

An important ideological feature of the theory is that competition determines structural traits.

> The structure of every organic being is related, in the most essential yet often hidden manner, to that of all the other organic beings, with which it comes into competition for food or residence, or from which it has to escape, or on which it preys (p. 57).

Success in competition among males, for example, depends upon "some advantage over other males in their weapons, means of defence, or charms" (p. 66). If character depends largely upon competition and predation, it follows that human nature depends on the traits that guarantee success in competition or war.

Despite some claims to the contrary, there is plenty of evidence that Darwin accepted progressivism, that the inferior forms or species were those which became extinct.

> In another and more general manner, new species become superior to their predecessors: for they have to beat in the struggle for life all the older forms, with which they come into close competition ... so that by this fundamental test of victory in the battle for life, as well as by the standard of the specialisation of organs, modern forms ought, on the theory of natural selection, to stand higher than ancient forms (p. 293).

If we accept that our fundamental structural traits are determined by success in the war of competition for survival, and that the best win the war, the logical conclusion is that the best are the most warlike. The multivalency of POWER/CONTROL IS ABOVE, ACHIEVEMENT/SUCCES IS HIGH and GOOD (MORALITY/QUALITY) IS HIGH (while BAD IS LOW, IMPROVE STATUS IS RAISE, DETERIORATE IS FALL/LOWER), suggests that POWER/ACHIEVEMENT/SUCCESS = GOOD. This reminds us of Smith's argument, that, given the high cost of weaponry, the most wealthy and civilised are those who survive. These conclusions make a fundamental mistake in concluding that those that are best at surviving are ethically the best. They may be the worst, as Thomas Huxley suggested (Rogers 1972: 278).

Competition will be fiercest among members of the same or similar species, where the competition is more direct, "for they frequent the same districts, require the same food, and are exposed to the same dangers" (p. 56). In words suggesting the naturalness of genocide he reveals "consequently each variety or species, during the progress of its formation, will generally press hardest on its nearest kindred, and tend to exterminate them." It follows that positively adaptive specialisation will not only lead to success but also to less competition. "The inhabitants of the world have beaten their predecessors in the race for life and are, in so far, higher in the scale, and their structure has generally become more specialised". In this sense competition is an extremely positive force, and the life forms which have survived in a low state of specialisation and organisation have done so because of lack of competition. These ideas are reminiscent of Hume's theory that civilisation and systems of justice developed out of war and greed for property. The idea of specialisation, too, has a clear economic correlate in the division of labour and trade. More specialisation and more trade lead to less war.

Competition being a positive force for development, the more dense the population, and the more intense the competition, the stronger and better suited for survival the resulting species (p. 324). Moreover, the resultant forms are also better suited for conquest and imperial domination over the less powerful.

> In each well stocked country, natural selection acts through the competition of the inhabitants and consequently leads to success in the battle for life, only in accordance with the standard for that particular country. Hence the inhabitants of one country, generally the smaller one, often yield to the inhabitants of another and generally the larger country (p. 157–8).

Imperial conquest thus becomes natural, unsurprising and even a virtuous circle:

> Widely-ranging species, abounding in individuals, which have already triumphed over many competitors in their own widely-extended homes, will have the best chance of seizing on new places, when they spread into new countries. In their new homes they will be exposed to new conditions, and will frequently undergo further modification and improvement; and thus they will become still further victorious, and will produce groups of modified descendants (p. 303).

8.2.2   Self-interest, individualism and the family

This second element of early capitalist ideology relates back to our discussion of neo-Darwinism and socio-biology in chapter 4, where we discussed the proposition HUMAN IS ANIMAL. The competitive drive, which we have identified as a common ideological theme in our five philosophers, is founded on the idea of individualism, and a self-interested desire for preservation, only mitigated by a concern for one's immediate family. It is quite striking how prevalent the idea is that in our natural state the only social group that we instinctively favour is the family with whom we share our genes. This idea was obviously not invented by sociobiologists or Richard Dawkins following Darwin, but seems to have been recognised in our economic philosophers.

8.2.2.1   *The self, the individual and the family in Hobbes*
Like later biologists Hobbes insists that self-preservation is the driving force, and indeed the right of every individual.

> The right of nature ... is the liberty each man hath, to use his own power, as he will himself, for the preservation of his own nature; that is to say, of his own life, and consequently of doing any thing, which in his own judgment, and reason, he shall conceive to be the aptest means thereunto (Hobbes 1651/1997: 72).

This is the rule governing social behaviour, for Hobbes sees all voluntary acts as having for their object good to the actor. Thus he cannot understand any acts of complete selflessness, or martyrdom or self-sacrifice for others, any more than Matt Ridley can (4.3.3). "For no man giveth, but with the intention of good to himself: because gift is voluntary; and of all voluntary acts the object is to every man his own good." (p. 83).

When Hobbes recommends the transferring of right to a sovereign, the motive for this is "nothing else but the security of a man's person, in his life, and in the means of so preserving life, as not to be weary of it." In line with economic metaphors he talks of the mutual transferring of right as a contract or covenant – one of the ideas behind the American constitution (p. 74). He writes of covenants in terms foreshadowing the game theory beloved of evolutionary psychologists, but insists that the co-ercive power of the sovereign is essential to guarantee their observance:

> [F]or he that performeth first hath no assurance the other will perform after; because the bonds of words are too weak to bridle men's ambition, avarice, anger, and other passions, without the fear of some coercive power; which in the condition of mere nature, where all men are equal, and judges of the justness of their own fears, cannot possibly be supposed (p. 76).

The similarity with game theory can be highlighted by comparing this problem of cheating and non-performance of covenants or promises to the game known as the "The Prisoners' Dilemma". Here the best outcome for both of two prisoners is for the other to confess and take the sole punishment for a crime, but, in terms of calculated rationality, it is best for both to confess and receive a punishment less harsh than the maximum. This second outcome is better because keeping one's promises and sharing the punishment provides more long-term security; if you break your promise you betray trust and will therefore never be trusted in the future, and will also provoke opposition amongst those whom you have cheated or betrayed.

With further premonitions of socio-biology and Dawkins, Hobbes recognises that this selfishness is tempered somewhat by love of one's family, those with whom one shares genes. "Let the civil law ... be once abandoned or but negligently guarded and there is nothing that any man can be sure to receive from his ancestor, or leave to his children" (p. 121). Monarchy passes to children "because men are presumed to be more inclined by nature to favour their own children, than the children of other men" (p. 109).

8.2.2.2 *The self, the individual and the family in Hume*
Hume saw humans motivated by advantage or disadvantage to themselves, the former producing pleasant sensations and the latter unpleasant. Selfish pleasure thereby becomes the basis of morality:

> Every passion or turn of character which has a tendency to our advantage or prejudice, gives a delight or uneasiness; and 'tis from thence the approbation or disapprobation arises ... [A]ll morality [is] founded on pain or pleasure (Hume 1740/1969: 346–7).

We must always proceed cautiously beyond individualism for

> all beings in the universe, considered in themselves, appear entirely loose and in-
> dependent of each other. 'Tis only by experience we learn their influence and con-
> nection; and this influence we ought never to extend beyond experience (p. 518).

Self-interest is something we can count on.

With a remarkable anticipation of Dawkins, Hume points out that we are inclined to benevolence towards those with whom we share genes, the more so the greater proportion of genes shared.

> A man naturally loves his children better than his nephews, his nephews bet-
> ter than his cousins, his cousins better than strangers, where everything else is
> equal. Hence arise our common measures of duty, in preferring the one to the
> other. Our sense of duty always follows the common and natural course of our
> passions (p. 535).

This fact dictates, for Hume, the double standards of sexual morality. Women must be faithful to their partners, in order to convince them that the children they bear are the male partner's offspring with whom genes are shared. Since the mother can be sure that the child she bears is her own, there is less necessity for faithfulness in men.

> Whoever considers the length and feebleness of human infancy, with the concern
> which both sexes naturally have for their offspring, will easily perceive, that there
> must be an union of male and female for the education of the young, and that this
> union must be of considerable duration. But in order to induce men to impose on
> themselves this restraint, and undergo cheerfully all the fatigues and expenses to
> which it subjects them, they must believe, that the children are their own, and that
> their natural instinct is not directed to a wrong object, when they give a loose to
> love and tenderness (p. 621).

This passage suggests that in our natural state we need only show love and tenderness to relatives, and that kindness to others besides our kin is misplaced. In thus justifying the importance of female chastity he enjoins women to restraint and passivity in relation to sex, an attitude we remarked when discussing the metaphor theme HUMAN IS FOOD (3.2).

However, we should notice the counterbalancing importance that Hume gives to sympathy as the foundation of morality and which supplements the interest we have in our friends and family:

> When any quality or character has a tendency to the good of mankind, we are
> pleased with it, and approve of it; because it presents the lively idea of pleasure;
> which idea affects us by sympathy, and is itself a kind of pleasure. But as this
> sympathy is very variable, it may be thought that our sentiments of morals must
> admit of the same variations. We sympathise more with persons contiguous with
> us, than with persons remote from us; with our acquaintance than with strangers;
> with our countrymen than with foreigners. But, notwithstanding this variation of

our sympathy, we give the same approbation to the same moral qualities in China as in England (pp. 631–2).

We might take note here of the literalisation of the metaphor themes RELATIONSHIP IS PROXIMITY/COHESION – we have least affection for those we have never met – and perhaps SIMILARITY IS PROXIMITY, foreigners being different.

8.2.2.3 *The self, the individual and the family in Smith*
For Smith, too, self-interest was a basic feature of human nature and therefore at work in any form of society, and the market economy develops as its expression. However, Smith regards the commercial society produced by the market as catering more to the self-interest of the poor, by fostering their individual liberty. In feudalism the poor are personally dependent on the rich, but in capitalism they are free from this kind of serfdom.

The most famous of Smith's comments on man's innate selfishness, one which was a product of bourgeois capitalism and might not have applied to feudal society (De Botton 2004: 105–6), runs as follows:

> It is not from the benevolence of the butcher, the brewer or the baker that we expect our dinner, but from their regard to their own interest. We address ourselves, not to their humanity but to their self-love, and never talk to them of their own necessities but of their advantages. Nobody but a beggar chooses to depend chiefly upon the benevolence of his fellow citizens (Smith 1776/1991: 20).

But besides this, Smith suggests that the selfish use of goods is sane behaviour and anything else is madness: "A man must be perfectly crazy who where there is tolerable security, does not employ all the stock which he commands". One way of employing stock is by consumption or spending. In an attack on the squirearchy, Smith argues against the consumption of perishable goods and spending on menial servants, dogs and horses and recommends spending on durable goods, because this encourages employment of labourers and the increase of capital. Furthermore, the goods bought remain as a stock or capital, whereas the former expenditure leaves nothing behind (p. 287). However, he also admits the kind of selfishness this can lead to.

> When a man of fortune spends his revenue chiefly in hospitality, he shares the greater part of it with his friends and companions; but when he employs it in purchasing such durable commodities he often spends the whole upon his own person, and gives nothing to any body without an equivalent. The latter species of expense, therefore, especially when directed towards frivolous objects … frequently indicates, not only a trifling, but a base and selfish disposition (p. 290).

Apparently to be a good capitalist consumer one should indulge in selfish accumulation of goods.

We have traced the self-interested individualism that operated in the economic field during the 17th and 18th centuries. This was accompanied, if not formed, by a corresponding emphasis on the individual in the religious thought of Protestantism.

God speaks to the soul, not through the mediation of the priesthood or of social institutions built up by man, but *solus cum solo*, as a voice in the heart and in the heart alone. Thus the bridges between the worlds of spirit and of sense are broken, and the soul is isolated from the society of men, that it may enter into communion with its Maker (Tawney 1926/1938: 105).

No one could help lonely sinful man achieve salvation. No priest, no Church (since the damned also belonged to the Church), no sacraments, which were simply an outward symbol, not even Christ, since only the elect were saved (Weber 1930/1992: 104–5).

Under these circumstances Puritan capitalists threw themselves into intense business activity as a way of achieving self-confidence and avoiding anxiety (p. 112). Success in one's worldly calling is an indispensable sign of election (p. 115). "Mind your own business" might have been their catchphrase.

8.2.2.4 *The self, the individual and the family in Malthus*

For Malthus self-love was an inescapable fact of social existence. Indeed, the *Essay on Population* was written partly as a riposte to Godwin's socialism, which Malthus rejected on the basis that humans are naturally self-interested rather than benevolent, and if shown benevolence would simply breed themselves back into misery:

> Thus it appears that a society constituted according to the most beautiful form that imagination can conceive, with benevolence for its moving principle, instead of self-love, and with every evil disposition in all its members corrected by reason, not force, would, from the inevitable laws of nature [i.e. population growth if goods are given to the poor indiscriminately], and not from any original depravity of man or of human institutions, degenerate in a very short period into a society constructed upon a plan not essentially different from that which prevails in every known state at present: a society divided into a class of proprietors and a class of labourers, and with self-love the mainspring of the great machine (Malthus 1992: 66–67).

Notice how this recognition of self-love goes hand in hand with a dehumanisation of society into a lifeless machine obeying mechanical rules. Malthus believes that duty is a much weaker force than self-interest, and that socialism is therefore bound to fail: "If we were to remove or weaken the motive of interest, which would be the case under Mr Godwin's system, I fear we should have but a weak substitute in a sense of duty" (p. 53). Even if benevolence were a strong motive, population growth would inevitably threaten it and make self-love reassert itself (p. 61).

Like Hume, Malthus wishes to tap into the natural affection that men have for their offspring, by insisting on the institution of marriage, and women's chastity within it. Malthus' major project of controlling population growth can be achieved by making every man responsible for the support of his own children, because man would not bring into the world children which he had not the means to support (p. 64). However, this natural check against large families would not work without the existence of the laws of property and succession (p. 79). This suggests that the inheritance of property is essential and natural, since any efforts made during our lives to accumulate wealth and property would be wasted if that wealth could not be handed on to those who bear our genes.

8.2.2.5 *The self in Darwin*

We have already spent some time discussing neo-Darwinian ideas, such as Dawkins' selfish genes (4.3). The theory of sexual selection is of course predicated on the idea that we are struggling to pass on our genes to the next generation:

> This form of selection depends, not on a struggle for existence in relation to other organic beings or to external conditions, but between the individuals of one sex, generally the males, for the possession of the other sex. The result is not death to the unsuccessful competitor, but few or no offspring. … Generally the most vigorous males, those which are best fitted for their places in nature, will leave most progeny (Darwin 1859/1991: 65).

8.2.3 Man is animal

The idea that humans are driven by basically biological drives, and have an innate nature shared with animals surfaces from time to time in the philosophers under consideration, though with varying degrees of prominence and approval. In Hobbes and Smith and even Malthus there is an attempt to avoid the naturalistic fallacy, emphasising the importance of civilising our behaviour so that it becomes less like that of animals. Hobbes recognises the need to escape the "brutish", and Smith points out the civilising nature of human institutions:

> If human institutions had never thwarted those natural inclinations, the towns could nowhere have increased beyond what the improvement and cultivation of the territory in which they were situated could support (Smith 1776/1991: 321).

Malthus, of course, shifted the argument away from institutions to focus on the biological tendency for populations to multiply to the level where subsistence was threatened, which was, for him, a fundamental law of nature. For him human misery was not simply a result of inadequate social and political institutions, which could be reformed or changed through revolution. "The checks on population growth are misery and fear of misery, the necessary and inevitable effects of the law of nature, which human institutions, so far from aggravating, have tended considerably to mitigate, though they can never remove" (Malthus 1992: 62). However, he did recommend distancing ourselves from animal behaviour through education and prudent restraint in the production of children.

Probably the most interesting of our philosophers, in this respect, apart from Darwin, already discussed in chapter 4, is David Hume. In his theory of the passions and the emotions he emphasises our commonality with animals:

> Thus, all the internal principles, that are necessary to us to produce either pride or humility, are common to all creatures; and since the causes, which excite these passions, are likewise the same, we may justly conclude that these causes operate after the same *manner* through the whole animal creation (Hume 1740/1969: 378).

Hume believed that though animals may lack moral "sentiments", they do feel, love, hate, experience pride and shame, as well as desire, enjoyment, suffering, hope, and fear, on which our morality is based (Baier 1998).

Indeed, Hume insists that our moral systems are based on passion rather than reason, the principle that we approve of what gives us pleasure, and disapprove of what gives us pain. "Virtue is distinguished by the pleasure, and vice by the pain, that any action, sentiment or character gives us by the mere view and contemplation" (Hume 1740/1969: 527) (which reflects BAD EMOTION IS DISCOMFORT/PAIN or HURT /INJURY). Since we share these passions with animals we are less different from them than the traditionalists assert, who regard reason as what distinguishes us from animals. "Morals excite passions, and produce or prevent actions. Reason of itself is utterly impotent in this particular. The rules of morality, therefore, are not conclusions of our reason" (p. 509).

Hume links the principle of pleasure/moral approval and displeasure/moral disapproval to the question of sexual attractiveness. In section IV of Book 3 *Of Morals* he seems to acquiesce to the following pattern: genetic inheritance leads to power which leads to admiration. Pride and humility, love and hatred are stimulated by advantages of mind, body or fortune (the first two of which are genetic endowments), because they excite pain or pleasure. Thus, for example, a handsome, sexually attractive man is loved and esteemed by women because of his capacity to give enjoyment (p. 665). In what sound rather socio-biological terms, though lacking in a genetic explanation, Hume underlines the idea that we look for healthy, strong and attractive mates, that "An air of health, as well as of strength and agility, makes a considerable part of beauty; and that a sickly air in another is always disagreeable, upon account of that idea of pain and uneasiness which it conveys to us." (p. 665).

Hume's naturalistic account of reason, morality, politics, culture, and religion made him a precursor of Darwin and Darwinians. It goes without saying that Darwin established the connection between man and animal, by his revolutionary idea that humans were descended from apes (chapter 4). It is perhaps useful here to stress that the sociobiological ideas discussed have firm antecedents in much of Darwin's later thinking. If humans are merely advanced animals, their mental and moral faculties have to be explained as extensions of those faculties found in animals. In the *Descent of Man* (1871) and *The Expression of the Emotions in Man and Animals* (1872), Darwin attempted to show that many mental activities derive from instincts imprinted by evolution, and especially that the way we express emotions is an inheritance from our animal ancestors. He also proposed that the social behaviour of higher animals is the foundation for human moral values. Since our animal ancestors evolved as part of social groups, it follows that instinctual traits were selected which promoted socially useful behavioural patterns. We have inherited these instinctive traits, and our moral values are simply rationalisations of these automatic behaviours.

8.2.4 Property

In chapter 3 (3.3) we discussed contemporary trends in the commodification of humans, natural resources like water, genetic information and knowledge, linking our discussion with the themes HUMAN IS VALUABLE OBJECT/COMMODITY, IDEA/INFORMATION IS COMMODITY (IDEA/INFORMATION IS MINERAL), TIME IS MONEY/COMMODITY. In chapter 7 (7.10), we also explored the progressive grammaticalisation of the action schema for possession in European languages. This trend towards increasing appropriation and property rights has an emphasis, if not an origin, in our economic philosophers.

8.2.4.1 *Property in Hobbes*
According to Hobbes the driving force to competition and the war he so feared and suffered from was the desire for and the power of acquisition, whether riches, reputation or friends (Hobbes 1651/1997: 48). "[B]ecause the way of one competitor to the attaining of his desire is to kill, subdue, supplant, or repel the other" (p. 56). However, this desire and power are insatiable and the very motives of life.

> Nor can a man any more live whose desires are at an end, than he whose senses and imaginations are at a stand. Felicity is a continual progress of the desire from one object to another; the attaining of the former, being still but the way to the later (p. 55).

In Hobbes' thinking, the advantage of handing over power and sacrificing our freedoms to a sovereign were precisely to establish property rights, in order to regulate the human desire for power and possessions.

> For before constitution of sovereign power all men had right to all things; which necessarily causeth war; and therefore this propriety [property], being necessary to peace, and depending on sovereign power, is the act of that power, in order to the public peace (p. 99).

The war of every man against every man threatens justice, but particularly the notion of property: "It is consequent also to the same condition, that there be no propriety [property], no dominion, no mine and thine distinct; but only that to be every man's, that he can get; and for so long, as he can keep it" (pp. 71–72). For only with the advent of the notion of private property does the concept of justice take form:

> And this is also to be gathered out of the ordinary definition of justice in the schools: for they say that justice is the constant will of giving to every man his own. And therefore, where there is no own, that is no propriety; there is no injustice.

Furthermore, the coercive power of the sovereign is necessary to maintain this justice, and property rights become the reward for giving up power to the sovereign (pp. 79–80).

8.2.4.2 *Property and trade in Hume*

Hume seems to accept more or less wholesale Hobbes' views on the threat to society posed by the insatiable and ubiquitous desires for possessions: "this avidity alone, of acquiring goods and possessions for ourselves and our nearest friends is insatiable, perpetual, universal, and directly destructive of society". He also accepts the relationship between property and justice, but extends property's influence to other social rights and obligations. Indeed, Hume sees property rights and their guarantee as a panacea:

> No one can doubt, that the convention for the distinction of property, and for the stability of possession, is of all circumstances the most necessary for the establishment of human society, and that after the agreement for the fixing and observing of this rule, there remains little or nothing to be done towards settling a perfect harmony and concord.

If we allow property rights, man's innate self-interest will be redirected towards increasing the wealth of all members of society. Reciprocally, in preserving society we make much greater advances in acquiring possessions than "in the solitary and forlorn condition which must follow upon violence and an universal licence" (p. 544). Additionally, property rights and the justice system transform our innate selfishness into social relations, which may then, through politics and education, in turn produce the virtue of sympathy.

Antitcipating Malthus, Hume links this theory of the interdependence of self-interest, property and justice to the idea that humans are not benevolent and that there is scarcity in nature. Ironically, from a modern perspective where water is being increasingly privatised, he cites air and water as examples of commodities that are in such plentiful supply that they do not need to be owned:

> When there is such a plenty of any thing as satisfies all the desires of men: in which case the distinction of property is lost, and everything remains in common. This we may observe with regard to air and water, though the most valuable of all external objects (p. 546).

Hume defines possessions in terms which might ring alarm bells in our more ecologically-conscious age, which has seen widespread privatisation, and reminds us of the grammar of the location schema and the action schema for possession (7.10).

> We are said to be in possession of any thing, not only when we immediately touch it, but also when we are so situated in respect to it, as to have it in our power to

use it; and may move, alter and destroy it, according to our present pleasure or advantage (p. 557).

He also anticipates or echoes his friend Smith in emphasising the need for the legal transfer of goods in commerce and trade.

> Different parts of the earth produce different commodities; and not only so, but different men are by nature fitted for different employments and attain to greater perfection in any one, when they confine themselves to it alone. All this requires a mutual exchange and commerce; for which reason the translation of property by consent is founded on a law of nature, as well as its stability without such a consent (Hume 1740/1969: 567).

Like Matt Ridley (4.3.3) he considers the division of labour, trade and commerce to be the main planks of civilisation, and also as natural, thus prefiguring Darwin with his idea of the biological division of labour.

8.2.4.3 *Property and trade in Smith*

Smith is not quite so sure that the love of trade is natural, "one of the original principles of human nature", or whether it is "the consequence of the faculties of reason and speech" (Smith 1776/1991: 19). In fact, Smith makes an important distinction between human society and animal co-existence. Varieties in nature, for example among dogs, are of no use to each separate species, whereas humans' varieties of labour, through its division, are beneficial to the different kinds of workers, by making possible trade and barter. "Each animal is still obliged to support and defend itself, separately and independently, and derives no sort of advantage from that variety of talents with which nature has distinguished its fellows" (p. 22). In Smith's view mutually beneficial symbiosis is therefore only possible for human society, not for animals or nature. To maximise this symbiotic tendency and the division of labour the trading market must be extended as far as possible through good communications, those ecologically destructive corridors of development described by Josephson (7.4.1).

We also note Smith's treatment of the commodification of labour and land. Smith equates labour with commodities, indeed it is the ultimate and real standard for estimating and comparing the value of commodities – their real price, whereas money is simply their nominal price (p. 39). Labour is viewed as a further form of capital, exchangeable for and dependent upon circulating capital: "Land however improved will yield no revenue without a circulating capital which maintains the labourers who cultivate and collect its produce" (p. 229).

Smith, like Malthus after him, saw that subsistence was the deciding factor on both population size and the demand for labour. When labour is oversupplied wages fall and fewer children are born or survive, thereby reducing the labour pool. When labour is well rewarded, children are better provided for and more survive, so the number of labourers increases.

> The market would soon be much understocked with labour in the one case, and so much overstocked in the other, as would soon force back its price to that proper rate which the circumstances of society required. It is in this manner that *the demand for men, like that for any other commodity*, necessarily regulates the production of men; quickens it when it goes on too slowly, and stops it when it advances too fast (p. 84) [my italics].

Here labour is clearly treated as a commodity, and one that is no more important than any other kind. In fact, the purpose of labour is to supply the market in order to serve the circumstances of society, the economic system.

For Smith, human progress and social development could be measured in terms of the increasing scope of property rights. In the hunter gatherer stage few rights are recognised besides what are needed to support one physically and morally, namely food and shelter, personal freedom and the recognition of social status. In the next stage, that of the nomadic herdsmen, property rights cover food and tools far in excess of what is needed to satisfy each individual and their immediate family. The third agricultural stage extends rights of property to include land. In commercial society property rights are extended to cover contractual entitlements and ownership of purely symbolic property (paper money, credits). Smith not only saw this progression as an extension of the scope of property, but also an extension of personality (Haakonssen 1998).

The novelty of these ideas about property is apparent when contrasted with the preceding age. For the medieval world and the early Puritans property was a necessary evil. Tawney sums up this attitude:

> It is right for man to seek such wealth as is necessary for a livelihood in his station. To seek more is not enterprise, but avarice, and avarice is a deadly sin. Trade is legitimate: the different resources of different countries show that is was intended by providence. But it is a dangerous business. A man must be sure that he carries it on for the public benefit, and that the profits he takes are no more than the wages of his labour. Private property is a necessary institution, at least in a fallen world; men work more and dispute less when goods are private than when they are common. But it is to be tolerated as a concession to human frailty, not applauded as desirable in itself: the ideal – if only man's nature could rise to it – is communism (Tawney 1926/1938: 44–45).

But the ideology of the sanctity of private property was already well established by the time of Hobbes, Hume and Smith. "In the 15th century if a man practised extortion he was told that is was wrong. A century later he was told that it was right and in accordance with the law of nature" (p. 167).

This insistence on private property was an ideology which went hand in hand with the depopulation of the English countryside between 1489 and 1640, and the enclosure movement which forced villeins off the land (p. 152). The justification for enclosures was that property is a right anterior to the existence of the State and that the latter has no right to take property from any man without his consent. Cromwell himself had accepted that it was only freeholders who constituted the body politic and that they could use their own property as they wished, without taking into account superiors or the mass of men or peasantry. "Enclosures will increase the output of wool and grain. Each man knows best what his land is suited to produce, and the general interest will be best served by leaving him free to produce it ... the advancement of private persons will be the advantage of the public." (Joseph Lee *A Vindication of a Regulated Enclosure*, quoted in Tawney 1926/1938: 256–57).

But this ideology of the sanctity of property was not achieved without objections. It produced "men that live as though there were no God at all, and that would have all in their own hands, men that would leave nothing to others, men that would be alone on the earth, men that be never satisfied" (Crowley 1872: 132). For critics property rights did not seem to go with the normal traditional responsibilities to the community and the obligations of charity (p. 153). Prayers like the following were heartfelt pleas against the unrestrained workings of the ascendant ideology:

> We heartily pray thee to send thy Holy Spirit into them that possess the grounds, pastures, and dwelling-places of the earth, that they, remembering themselves to be thy tenants, may not rack and stretch out the rents of their houses and lands, nor yet take unreasonable fines and incomes, after the manner of covetous worldlings ... but so behave themselves in letting out their tenements, lands and pastures, that after this life they may be received into everlasting dwelling places ('A Prayer for Landlords' *A Book of Private Prayer Set Forth by Order of King Edward VI*)

8.2.4.4 *Property in Malthus*

Emphasis on the importance of property in Malthus' *The Essay on Population* is a riposte to the socialism and revolutionary writings of Godwin, who had denounced property in the following terms:

> The spirit of oppression, the spirit of servility, and the spirit of fraud, these are the immediate growth of the established administration of property ... The other vices of envy, malice, and revenge, are their inseparable companions. In a state of society where men lived in the midst of plenty, and where all shared alike the bounties of nature, these sentiments would inevitably expire. The narrow principle of selfishness would vanish. No man being obliged to guard his little store, or provide with anxiety and pain for his restless wants, each would lose his individual existence in the thought of the general good. No man would be an enemy to his neighbours, for they would have no subject of contention: and of consequence philanthropy would resume the empire which reason assigns her (Malthus 1992: 57–8).

As we have seen, our economic philosophers, by contrast, considered human nature as basically self-centred, avaricious and competitive, if not war-like.

Echoing them, Malthus makes the highly reductionist claim that property along with self-restraint within marriage are the foundations of human civilisation:

> To the laws of property and marriage, and to the apparently narrow principle of
> self-love, which prompts each individual to exert himself in bettering his condi-
> tion, we are indebted for all the noblest exertions of human genius, for everything
> that distinguishes the civilised from the savage state (p. 331).

Enforced privatisation of as much land as possible by dividing it into individually owned
plots is a means of increasing production and therefore reducing human misery:

> A yearly increase of produce should, if possible, be obtained at all events; that in
> order to effect this first great and indispensable purpose, it would be advisable to
> make a more complete division of land, and to secure every man's property against
> violation, by the most powerful sanctions (p. 63).

The inevitable inequalities in a property owning society can be mitigated according
to Malthus' theory of effective demand: the demand for and purchase of goods by the
upper classes will generate wealth in the lower classes. This seems hypocritical when
lower classes are being asked to restrain themselves because of lack of resources to feed
a growing population.

Malthus' philosophy, and attitude is still going strong, as Harvey reminds us:

> Internationally this same opposition arises as advanced capitalist countries preach
> to the rest of the world about how the latter's population growth is putting pressure
> on resources while urging their own upper classes to an orgy of conspicuous con-
> sumption as a necessary condition to "sustainable" growth (Harvey 1996: 144).

8.2.4.5 *Darwin, trade and the division of labour*

As Darwin was not an economist, it might seem odd to associate him with the division of labour and trade, and the market. But, his farming background and marriage
into the Wedgewood pottery manufacturing family provided him with metaphors: the
selective stock breeding practices of the farmer give us "natural selection"; and his notion of species diversification into niches mirrored the ideas of division of labour, and
the roundaboutness of production in the factory system. His theory and his metaphors
are a good example of the interpenetration of the social and the "natural" (Harvey
1996: 160–61): one's personal and social history, interests and concerns determine
one's choice of metaphors, thereby working against any universalising tendencies in
metaphorical patterning (Kövecses 2005).

Natural selection is a metaphor derived from the practice of selective breeding by
farmers and horticulturalists.

> It may be metaphorically said that natural selection is daily and hourly scrutinis-
> ing, throughout the world, the slightest variations; rejecting those that are bad,
> preserving and adding up all those that are good; silently and insensibly work-
> ing, whenever and wherever opportunity offers, at the improvement of each or-
> ganic being in relation to its organic and inorganic conditions of life (Darwin
> 1859/1991: 62).

Though this could be a stockbreeding metaphor in origin, it sounds equally like a manufacturer exercising quality control, or a shopper comparing and costing goods in the market place. In any case, it seems to be a metaphor in the spirit of utilitarian economics:

> If man can by patience select variations useful to him, why, under changing and complex conditions of life, should not variations useful to nature's living products often arise, and be preserved or selected? ... I can see no limit to this power, in slowly and beautifully adapting each form to the most complex relations of life (p. 392).

The economic metaphor is pursued when Darwin himself uses the phrase "physiological division of labour" (p. 70). He believes that natural selection tends towards more specialisation and a higher level of organisation, which can be measured by

> the amount of differentiation of the parts of the same organic being, in the adult state ... and their specialisation for different functions; or as Milne Edwards would express it, the completeness of the division of physiological labour (p. 93).

Indeed, the phrase "the economy of nature" occurs several times in the *Origin of Species*. Species become "more diversified in habits and structure, so as to be able to seize on many and widely different places in the economy of nature" (p. 393). We note the wording suggesting a land grab, with overtones of enclosure or imperial conquest. Darwin elaborates some of the grounds of this metaphor, to include distribution, supply and scarcity: "Yet, unless it [the universal struggle for life] be thoroughly ingrained in the mind, the whole economy of nature, with every fact of distribution, rarity, abundance, extinction and variation, will be dimly seen or quite misunderstood" (p. 47). Nature then is an economic actor: "In order to spend on one side, nature is forced to economise on the other side" (p. 111).

8.2.5   Summary

We have now come to the end of one ideological strand running through our four economic philosophers and our biologist. This is the ideology of competition or war caused by scarcity, predicated on human self-interested desires to possess property for themselves or their kindred. The rights to property depend variously in our philosophers upon the institutions of a sovereign monarchy or a justice system, or moral restraint, and can lead to the benefits of trade with its division of labour.

The following passage from Hume sums up the different filaments in this strand and how they entwine.

> Men being naturally selfish, or endow'd only with a confined generosity, they are not easily induced to perform any action for the interest of strangers, except with the view to some reciprocal advantage, which they had no hope of obtaining without such a performance. ... The invention of the law of nature, concerning the stability of possession, has already rendered men tolerable to each other; that of

the transference of property and possession by consent has begun to render them mutually advantageous: But still these laws of nature, however strictly observed, are not sufficient to render them serviceable to each other, as by nature they are fitted to become. … Your corn is ripe today; mine will be so tomorrow. 'Tis profitable for us both, that I should labour with you today, and that you should aid me tomorrow. I have no kindness for you, and know you have as little for me. I will, therefore, not take any pains on your account; and should I labour with you upon my own account, in expectation of a return, I know I should be disappointed, and that I should in vain depend upon your gratitude. Here then I leave you to labour alone: you treat me in the same manner. The seasons change; and both of us lose our harvests for want of mutual confidence and security.

All this is the effect of the natural and inherent principles and passions of human nature; and as these passions and principles are inalterable, it may be thought that our conduct, which depends on them, must be so too, and that 'twould be in vain, either for moralists or politicians, to attempt to tamper with us, or attempt to change the usual course of our actions, with a view to public interest. And indeed, did the success of their designs depend upon their success in correcting the selfishness and ingratitude of men, they would never make any progress, unless aided by omnipotence, which is alone able to mould the human mind and change its character in such fundamental articles… Hence I learn to do a service to another without bearing him any real kindness; because I foresee that he will return my service, in expectation of another of the same kind, and in order to maintain the same correspondence of good offices with me or with others …

In order, therefore to distinguish these two different forms of commerce the interested and the disinterested [for those we love or have affection for to whom we perform kindness without thought of reward] there is a certain form of words invented for the former, by which we bind ourselves to the performance of any action. This form of words constitutes what we call a promise, which is the sanction of the interested commerce of mankind … [T]hey [the forms of words of a promise] are the conventions of men, which create a new motive, when experience has taught us, that human affairs would be conducted much more for mutual advantage, were there certain symbols or signs instituted, by which we might give each other security of our conduct in any particular incident. After these signs are instituted, whoever uses them is immediately bound by his interest to execute his engagements, and must never expect to be trusted any more, if he refuse to perform what he promised (Hume 1740/1969: 572–4).

In this key passage we encounter first the idea that naturally selfish men can be taught to behave well both by the institution of property rights and commercial transactions and by the expectation of future repayment, the kind of calculated reciprocal altruism touted by Trivers (see 4.3.1). But we also find the idea that promises or covenants are an essential institution (institutional facts according to Searle – 4.3.4). A person's social standing depends upon his keeping his promises – his credit – the theme of relationship as transaction, elaborated later (8.2.8.5). Morality grows out of self-interest and the institution of the promise that accompanies non-simultaneous exchange "becomes a new obligation upon mankind" (p. 575). In short, we have an expansion on "the three fundamental laws of nature, that of the stability of possession, of its transference by consent, and of the performance of promises" (p. 578)

8.2.6 Newtonian influence on economic philosophers

In chapter 7 we argued that the canonical event structure corresponding to congruent English grammar reinforced and reflected, even if it did not determine, aspects of Newtonian physics, especially the first two laws of motion and the law of universal gravitation. Newtonian physics made possible through machines the Industrial Revolution and its mechanical attitudes to nature. It is worth, therefore, making the point that Newton had a profound influence on our economic philosophers, most directly on Hume and Malthus.

Hobbes seems to anticipate Newton, in the emphasis he gave to motion, and in his tendency to reduce qualitative change to motion, in step with CHANGE IS MOVEMENT and the canonical event model. For example in Part Two of *De Corpore*, he considers the causes of qualitative change, and concludes by demonstrating the thesis that all change is motion, that motion is the only cause of motion, and that power (potentia) is nothing but motion in so far as it is a cause of motion (Sorell 1998). However, for Hobbes this was no metaphor.

In dismissing the metaphor FREEDOM IS SPACE TO MOVE, Hobbes foreshadows Newton's laws of motion:

> Liberty or freedom signifieth (properly) the absence of opposition (by opposition, I mean external impediments of motion) and may be applied no less to irrational and inanimate creatures than to rational. For whatsoever is so tied or environed as it cannot move but within a certain space which space is determined by the opposition of some external body, we say it hath not liberty to go further. And so of all living creatures whilst they are imprisoned or restrained with walls or chains; and of the water whilst it is kept in by banks or vessels that otherwise would spread it self into a larger space we use to say they are not at liberty to move in such a manner as without those external impediments they would ... but when the words free and liberty are applied to any thing but bodies they are abused; for that which is not subject to motion is not subject to impediment (Hobbes 1651/1997: 115).

Hume was much less hesitant about adopting the canonical event Newtonian model as a metaphor for causation in general. In *An Abstract of a Book Lately Published; Entitled a Treatise of Human Nature* he states that the Chief Argument of Book 1 is causation. "The movement gained by a billiard ball when struck by another ball provides Hume with his illustration. 'This is as perfect an instance of the relationship of cause and effect as any which we know, either by sensation or reflection'" (Mossner 1969: 17).

Hume targets social behaviour with Newton-based metaphors:

> We may carry this further and remark, not only that two objects are connected
> by the relation of cause and effect, when one produces a motion or action in the
> other, but also when it has a power of producing it. And this we may observe to
> be the source of all the relations of interest and duty, by which men influence
> each other in society, and are placed in the ties of government and subordination
> (Hume 1740/1969: 59).

He also extends the metaphor to the mental world. Union or cohesion amongst ideas
"is a kind of attraction which in the mental world will be found to have as extraordinary effects as in the natural..." (p. 60). Indeed, the Newtonian law of universal gravitation, with proximity as a factor in the force of attraction (Westfall 2005), might well,
at least for Hume, underpin RELATIONSHIP IS PROXIMITY or DESIRE IS BENDING/AT-
TRACTION. For "the generosity of men is very limited and ... seldom extends beyond
their friends and family" (Hume 1740/1969: 652). We have more generosity towards
those who are closest to us physically.

More generally Hume's project was to show that human passion and emotion was
subject to the same kind of laws as Newton had discovered in the natural sciences. He
ends the *Dissertation* by expressing the hope that "in the production and conduct of
the passions, there is a certain regular mechanism, which is as susceptible of as ac-
curate a disquisition, as the laws of motion, optics, hydrostatics, or any part of natural
philosophy" (Baier 1998: 550).

Smith too, though more sanguine about the analogy between Newton and economic philosophy, recognises a common project of discovering the real connections
which make a coherent theory:

> [Newton's] principles, it must be acknowledged, have a degree of firmness and
> solidity that we should in vain look for in any other system. The most scepti-
> cal cannot avoid feeling this ... And even we, while we have been endeavouring
> to represent all philosophical systems as mere inventions of the imagination, to
> connect together the otherwise disjointed and discordant phenomena of nature,
> have insensibly been drawn in, to make use of language expressing the connect-
> ing principles of this one, as if they were the real chains which Nature makes use
> of to bring together her several operations ([1795] 1980, IV.76: 105, quoted in
> Haakonssen 1998: 817–8).

Malthus was a mathematician in the Newtonian tradition, with a good degree in
mathematics from Cambridge, and he adopted the scientific method of testing through
experiment and observation. He was an avid and conscientious collector of statistical
data, who criticised Godwin for infringing Newtonian principles by arriving at conclusions based on extrapolation from causes to possible effects, rather from observed
effects to possible causes. One such example was the hypothesis that lifespan could be
increased, which he regarded as mere conjecture and prejudice:

> If this be the case, there is at once an end of all human science. The whole train of
> reasonings from effects to causes will be destroyed … We may return again to the old
> mode of philosophising, and make facts bend to systems, instead of establishing sys-
> tems upon facts. The grand and consistent theory of Newton, will be placed upon the
> same footing as the wild and eccentric hypotheses of Descartes (Malthus 1992: 50)

Malthus was particularly fond of reducing social problems to mathematics and mathematical variables, which to him were as universally applicable as Newton's laws.
Growth in population will be proportionate to the increase in the means of subsistence; "the only true criterion of a real and permanent increase in the population of any
country is the increase of the means of subsistence" (p. 41), since sexual passion is a
mathematical constant "the passion between the sexes has appeared in every age to be
so nearly the same that it may always be considered, in algebraic language, as a given
quantity". In computing population growth Malthus quotes from Sir William Petty's
aptly titled *"Political Arithmetic"*, where by pure mathematics if the ratio of births to
deaths is 3 :1 doubling of population occurs in 12.8 years (p. 17).

The possibility of a redistribution of the means of subsistence to the poor is rejected since this would reduce the amount of subsistence available to the skilled working classes, in an exact mathematical proportion (pp. 92–3). This argument was part of
Malthus' famous opposition to the poor laws, that they depress the purchasing power
of those above the poverty line who have superior skills to paupers. According to
Malthus' mathematical calculations, if you pay workers more prices will rise, and they
will be no better off (p. 97); in fact raising wages produces famine (p. 99). The convenient corollary of this, for employers, is that if you pay workers less prices will fall and
they will be no worse off!

Just as Newton discovered universal forces, so Malthus reduced the checks on
population to three universal forces "moral restraint, vice, and misery" (pp. 28–9).
Misery (and vice) takes the form of "terrible correctives of the redundance of mankind" – plagues, pestilences, and famines, which display a "universality of their operation" (p. 35).

8.2.7 Man and society as machines

In chapter 3 (3.6) we discussed the contemporary cultural effects of the machine metaphor
themes HUMAN IS IMPLEMENT/UTENSIL, HUMAN IS MACHINE/APPLIANCE, ORGANISATION/
SYSTEM IS MACHINE and the following section explores their ideological roots.

Tawney makes an interesting metaphorical observation contrasting the medieval
view of society with that of the Enlightenment. From the twelfth to the sixteenth centuries in England the metaphor by which society is described is the human body.

> The facts of class status and inequality were rationalised in the Middle Ages by a
> functional theory of society, as the facts of competition were rationalised in the
> eighteenth by the theory of economic harmonies … society, like the human body,

is an organism composed of different members. Each member has its own function, prayer, or defence, or merchandise, or tilling the soil. Each must receive the
means suited to its station, and must claim no more. Within classes there must be
equality; if one takes into one's hand the living of two, his neighbour will go short.
Between classes there must be inequality; for otherwise a class cannot perform its
function, or … enjoy its rights. Peasants must not encroach on those above them.
Lords must not despoil peasants. Craftsmen and merchants must receive what
will maintain them in their calling, and no more (Tawney 1926/1938: 35–36).

In fact the SOCIETY IS HUMAN BODY metaphor, famously expressed in *Coriolanus* (Act
1. Scene 1. ll. 94–156), can be traced back at least as far as Plato, the Roman orator
Cicero, and St Paul (I Corinthians, chapter 12, vv. 12–21). Just as in the Hippocratic
tradition health in the body was achieved by harmonious balance, so the health of
society would be achieved by harmonious working and balance between the parts of
the body politic. However, our economic philosophers substituted the body metaphor
preferring to see society as an economic machine, with economics no longer simply a
means to an end within a more complex body (p. 73).

In Table 21 (5.3) I placed SOCIETY IS A HUMAN BODY and SOCIETY/ORGANISA-
TION IS MACHINE on the same side of the opposition. The reason for this was that
both emphasise the idea of parts belonging to the whole, and the diverse functions of
the parts. However, because machines produce standardised products the latter theme
becomes a stepping stone for equating QUALITY with QUANTITY on the other side of
the opposition.

As we saw in chapter 7 (7.4), there is plenty of evidence that a widespread understanding of Newtonian physics lay behind the development of machines in the Industrial Revolution. And the same Newtonian principles became a metaphor for the
working of economics. Political "arithmetic" after the Restoration, was deeply influenced by the progress of mechanical natural science. Economists, like mathematicians
and physicists, attempted the exact measurement of natural conditions, the calculations of forces and strains, and the reduction of the complex to the operation of simple,
constant, and measurable forces. Economic, no less than scientific theory, aimed "to
express itself in terms of number, weight, or measure, to use only arguments of sense,
and to consider only such causes as have visible foundations in nature; leaving those
that depend upon the mutable minds, opinions, appetites, and passions of particular
men to the consideration of others" (Preface to Petty's *Political Arithmetic* quoted in
Tawney 1926/1938: 248–249). Understandably, then, the machine metaphor is quite
consciously used both of humans and society.

Let's begin with Hobbes, who, though still partly dependent on the medieval metaphor of the body-politic, (ORGANISATION/SOCIETY IS HUMAN BODY) makes both the
human body and the commonwealth targets of the multivalent MACHINE source. The
conceptualisation might proceed as follows: HUMAN IS MACHINE → (ORGANISATION/
SOCIETY IS HUMAN BODY →) ORGANISATION/SYSTEM IS MACHINE.

Nature (the Art whereby God hath made and governs the world) is by the *Art* of man, as in many other things, so in this also imitated, that it can make an artificial animal. For seeing that life is but a motion of limbs, the beginning whereof is in some principal part within; why may we not say that all *Automata* (engines that move themselves by springs and wheels as doth a watch) have an artificial life? For what is the heart but a spring; and the nerves but so many strings; and the joints but so many wheels, giving motion to the whole body, such as was intended by the artificer? Art goes yet further, imitating that rational and most excellent work of nature, man. For by art is created that great LEVIATHAN called a commonwealth, or state which is but an artificial man; though of greater statures and strength than the natural, for whose protection and defence it was intended; and in which the sovereignty is an artifical soul, as giving life and motion to the whole body; the magistrates and other officers of judicature and execution artificial joints; reward and punishment (by which fastened to the seat of sovereignty, every joint and member is moved to perform his duty) are the nerves, that do the same in the body natural; the wealth and riches of all the particular members are the strength; *salus populi* (the people's safety) its business; counsellors, by whom all things needful for it to know, are suggested unto it, are the memory; equity and laws, an artificial reason and will; concord, health; sedition, sickness; and civil war, death. Lastly the pacts and covenants, by which the parts of this body politic were at first made, set together and united, resemble that fiat, or let us make man, pronounced by God in the creation (Hobbes 1651/1997: 9).

Hobbes, perhaps thinking like Smith of clockwork, sees mankind, and the state as characterised by motion which will keep going until something stops it dead. The movement of the clock leads him to the conclusion that "the general inclination of all mankind" is "a perpetual and restless desire of power for power, that ceaseth only in death" (quoted in Chilton 1996: 83).

Hume thought he had discovered the kinds of uniformity and regularity in human decision-making and behaviour expected of a machine. Any "liberty of spontaneity" we may appear to have is determined by internal psychological causes (Enquiries: 94) (Baier 1998). We suggested in chapter 7 that Newtonian physics, with roots in the canonical event model, led to a view of nature as passive and amenable to control by fixed laws of physics and mathematics, reducing Nature, as Josephson demonstrates, to an industrial machine, with disastrous ecological consequences. Machines were regarded as a manifestation of the application of regular laws of physics to material objects, and, being designed by humans were even more predictable and amenable to regulation than nature. If the machine metaphor is applied to humans and society, as the data we gave in chapter 2 makes clear, it is humans, as well as the larger nature, who become passive and have their behaviour determined by fixed laws, in which even personal liberty is something of a myth.

When we consider Adam Smith we find this interesting comparison between humans and machines:

> When any expensive machine is erected, the extraordinary work to be performed by it before it is worn out, it must be expected, will replace the capital laid out upon it, with at least the ordinary profits. A man educated at the expense of much labour and time to any of those employments which require extraordinary dexterity and skill, may be compared to one of these expensive machines. The work which he learns to perform, it must be expected, over and above the usual wages of common labour, will replace to him the whole expense of his education, with at least the ordinary profits of an equally valuable capital. It must do this too in a reasonable time, regard being had to the very uncertain duration of human life, in the same manner as to the more certain duration of the machine (Smith 1776/1991: 107).

Smith here discusses human labourers in terms of the capital-generating work output of the machine over a period of time, and in terms of the capital invested in machines, while indicating some disquiet about humans' relative unpredictability. Time is money, as well as men being machines, as we saw in chapter 2.

Unpredictable variables in nature do much to complicate economics for a Newtonian-based mathematician or economist, and Smith sometimes regrets this unpredictability. For example, the variability in soil and climate might lead to unforeseen price increases: "Such enhancements of the market price are evidently the effect of natural causes which may hinder the effectual demand from ever being fully supplied, and which may continue, therefore, to operate for ever" (pp. 64–5). On the other hand Smith recognised that the agricultural worker, who had a variety of jobs depending on the natural seasons – ploughman, harrower, sower and reaper – and had to be intelligent enough to cope with the variability of the natural world, was increasingly becoming the industrial manufacturing worker, doing one mindless, repetitive and monotonous job in step with machines. Smith lamented the fact that, because of labour unions in the town, workers employing less skill and intelligence in factories received artificially high wages (pp. 134–6).

Many Enlightenment philosophers were interested in establishing imaginative order in an otherwise chaotic world. Machines were a means of achieving this, and were therefore an apt metaphor for the working of economics and the money markets. "We see how one thing driveth another, like as in a clock where there are many wheels, the first wheel being stirred driveth the next and that the third and forth till the last that moveth the instrument that striketh the clock" (Malynes 1662: 98). As noted earlier, Smith's "invisible hand" of the market is a metaphor drawn from the pendulum of a clock with its mechanical regulation and precision. The clock is one of the recurring machine analogies for the natural world and for society. It also assumes a creator of the machine, like a divine watchmaker, the remote god of deism that does not need to intervene in its workings (Haakonssen 1998).

Malthus was fond of Newtonian analogies based on mathematics, ballistics, weights, springs, and opposing forces. When social problems are posed as being analogous to those of the infinitesimal calculus, the choices involved in the maximization or minimisation becomes one of balancing opposed forces, or marginal rather than all-or-nothing adjustments. In this respect Malthus' *Essay* can be read as an applied treatise on the proper methods of reasoning in the moral and social sciences (Winch in Malthus 1992: xxii, Malthus 1992: 347).

Malthus questions the sustainability of Godwin's socialism, because for him self-love is "the mainspring of the great machine" (Malthus, 1992: 66–67). Even words like "motive" now so thoroughly lexicalised that in everyday use we forget its origin, may, in Malthus, belong to the machine metaphor: "If we were to remove or weaken the motive of interest, which would be the case under Mr Godwin's system, I fear we should have but a weak substitute in a sense of duty" (p. 73).

Darwin too used the mechanical metaphor from time to time, speaking as though the organic changes caused by evolution were like gradual changes and improvements in machines brought about by engineers and craftsmen.

> When we regard every production of nature as one which has had a long history; when we contemplate every complex structure and instinct as the summing up of many contrivances, each useful to the possessor, in the same way as any great mechanical invention is the summing up of the labour, the experience, the reason, and even the blunders of numerous workmen; when we thus view each organic being, how far more interesting – I speak from experience – does the study of natural history become (Darwin 1859/1991: 405–6).

8.2.8 Quality and quantity

In earlier chapters we suggested that mathematical reductions are ways of ignoring qualitative differences in order to measure and count, tying in with metaphor themes such as QUALITY IS SHAPE/SIZE, and IMPORTANT IS BIG. This reduction, as we have shown, has now spread into many areas of our lives particularly our conception of time (2.7) and educational performance (5.5.2). We also noted that, at least in the Edwardian times of the *Ragged-trousered Philanthropists*, output was measured in quantity not quality. Furthermore, machines make standardised products, ideally with little variation, so the idea of quality is swallowed up in quantity.

The advantages that Smith sees in the division of labour are that, by specialising in one particular task, the workman will be able to do it faster, and produce more in the same amount of time.

> The improvement of the dexterity of the workman necessarily increases the quantity of work he can perform; and the division of labour, by reducing everyman's business to some simple operation, and by making this simple operation the sole employment of his life, necessarily increases very much the dexterity of the workman (Smith 1776/1991: 13).

Work, too becomes standardised.

The main reason that Smith dislikes the apprenticeship system, and the trade unions (the crafts and the mysteries) is that they are a restrictive practice and artificially increase the cost of labour by restricting competition. If they were abolished

> the same increase of competition would reduce the profits of the masters as well as the wages of the workmen. The trades, the crafts, the mysteries would all be losers. But the public would be a gainer, the work of all artificers coming in this way much cheaper to market (p. 131).

Presumably one of the reasons to set up unions and professional bodies for doctors, chartered accountants, lawyers, and so on, is to provide quality assurance for their members' work. This, however, seems beside the point for a mindset that thinks in terms of quantity not quality.

A further aspect of the QUALITY IS QUANTITY theme is the idea that GOOD = MORE. Smith, representative of our philosophers, was a great believer in economic growth, the increase in production, wages, consumption and, contra Malthus, population. Increases in wages and population bring prosperity: "The liberal reward of labour, therefore, as it is the effect of increasing wealth, so it is the cause of the increasing population. To complain of it, is to lament over the necessary effect and cause of the greatest public prosperity" (p. 85). High wages correlate with the rate of increase in wealth, rather than wealth itself, which explains why wages in New York are higher than those in London (p. 73).

Using a collection of familiar metaphor themes, Smith associates the progressive state of high growth rates with human happiness: "The progressive state is in reality the cheerful and the hearty state to all the different orders of the society. The stationary is dull; the declining melancholy" (p. 86). Besides the theme DEVELOPING/SUCCEEDING IS MOVING FORWARD ("stationary", "progressive"), we note particularly the multivalency of "declining" 'in deteriorating health' (HEALTH/LIFE IS HIGH) and 'decreasing' (MORE IS HIGH), which suggests the metonymy, or metaphor, MORE = HEALTH.

More is certainly good and healthy in Smith's economic vision. "To maintain and augment the stock which may be reserved for immediate consumption, is the sole end and purpose both of the fixed and circulating capitals" (p. 230). In order to increase production we must increase the number of those involved in productive labour. Menial servants, civil servants, the sovereign, the military, and entertainers are unproductive labour, and, in too large numbers are dangerous to the economy (p. 283). By contrast, saving and investing money increases productive labour.

> That portion of his revenue which a rich man annually spends, is in most cases consumed by idle guests, and menial servants, who leave nothing behind them in return for their consumption. That portion which he annually saves, as for the sake of the profit it is immediately employed as a capital is consumed in the same manner, and nearly in the same time too, but by a different set of people, by labourers, manufacturers and artificers, who re-produce with a profit the value of their annual consumption (p. 278).

In this obsession with increased production, Smith seems to ignore the effects on the environment, or to assume natural resources are limitless. When circulating capital needs to be replenished, this is done quite simply by exploiting the land, mines and oceans:

> So great a part of the circulating capital being continually withdrawn from it, in order to be placed in the other two branches of the general stock of the society, it must in its turn require continual supplies, without which it would soon cease to exist. These supplies are principally drawn from three sources, the produce of land, of mines, and of fisheries (p. 230).

8.2.9 QUALITY IS WEALTH/MONEY

A specific version of equating quality with quantity is QUALITY IS WEALTH or MONEY and the corollary BAD/UNIMPORTANT IS POOR/CHEAP. In terms of ideology this is one of the most important metaphor themes generated by the economic philosophers here considered, partly because it sets itself up against traditional medieval Christian values of the sanctity of poverty, by celebrating acquisitiveness as a sign of God's favour, and partly because evaluation in money terms is the most outrageous form of reductionism, reinforcing commodification and thereby measuring human value in narrow economic terms.

8.2.9.1 *QUALITY IS WEALTH/MONEY in Hobbes and Hume*
Hobbes is already in the habit of reducing humans to the monetary value determined by supply and demand, based on the price the buyer is willing to pay.

> The value or the worth of a man, is as of all other things, his price; that is to say, so much as would be given for the use of his power; and therefore is not absolute; but a thing dependent on the need and judgment of another. ... For let a man rate themselves at the highest value they can; yet their true value is no more than it is esteemed by others (Hobbes 1651/1997: 50).

Wealth is, apparently, not only a worldly measure of the quality of humans but also a kind of measure used by God – a metonymic symbol of God's favour, as in the Old Testament ethic (5.2.1). "Good fortune, if lasting, honourable; as a sign of the favour of God. Ill fortune and losses, dishonourable" (pp. 52–53).

Hobbes sees anxiety about future security, for example about the after-life, as a cause of religion, as well as the cause of the accumulation of wealth in this life. In fact, in an increasingly secular society the latter kind of material wealth might substitute for the former spiritual hope of heaven.

> [I]t is impossible for a man, who continually endeavoureth to secure himself against the evil he fears, and procure the good he desireth, not to be in a perpetual solicitude of the time to come; ... So that man, which looks too far before him, in the care of

> future time, hath his heart all day long, gnawed on by fear of death, poverty or other calamity; and has no repose, nor pause of his anxiety, but in sleep (pp. 60–61)

It is almost as though wealth in this life and salvation in the next are interchangeable in reducing anxiety.

Hume asks what causes us to value our fellow creatures. Among the list of desirable attributes he puts the external advantages of possessions and clothes. So that "a prince that is possess'd of a stately palace, commands the esteem of the people on that account; and that, first, by the beauty of the palace, and second by the relation of property, which connects it with him." (Hume 1740/1969: 380). Human wealth thereby becomes the index of human value. Hume gives three reasons why a man's fortune should make us value and admire him: pleasure in viewing a rich man's beautiful possessions; the prospect of gaining some advantage from his generosity and liberality; and our sympathetic pleasure in seeing him enjoy his wealth (p. 666).

8.2.9.2   QUALITY IS WEALTH/MONEY *in Smith*

Echoing Hobbes, Smith has no difficulty in equating a man's worth with the money he owns, bearing in mind that "wealth" in the following passage means 'well-being' rather than 'possessions':

> We say of a rich man that he is worth a great deal, and of a poor man that he is worth very little money. A frugal man, or a man eager to be rich, is said to love money; and wealth and money, in short, are, in common language, considered in every respect synonymous (p. 326)

Indeed Smith gives the whole 5th section of Book 2 of *The Wealth of Nations*, the title: "Of our Esteem of the Rich and Powerful" and remarks "nothing has a greater tendency to give us an esteem for any person, than his power and riches; or a contempt, than his poverty and meanness."

It seems to follow from this equation that increasing one's capital by saving is a way of satisfying the instinct of improving or "bettering" oneself, "a desire which, though generally calm and dispassionate, comes with us from the womb, and never leaves us till we go to the grave". Conversely loss of riches, in particular bankruptcy, is shameful, if not equivalent to a hanging offence. "Bankruptcy is perhaps the greatest and most humiliating calamity which can befall an innocent man. The greater part of men, therefore, are sufficiently careful to avoid it. Some indeed do not avoid it; as some do not avoid the gallows" (p. 282).

Quite apart from equating humans' worth with their possessions, the QUALITY IS WEALTH/MONEY theme often seems to be distorted since use value and exchange value are not the same. Measuring the importance or quality of something in money terms quite often ignores use value and simply concentrates on exchange value:

> The things which have the greatest value in use have frequently little or no value in exchange; and on the contrary, those which have the greatest value in exchange

> have frequently little or no value in use. Nothing is more useful than water: but it will purchase scarce anything; scarce anything can be had in exchange for it. A diamond, on the contrary, has scarce any value in use; but a very great quantity of other goods can be had in exchange for it (p. 35).

Indeed, exchange value and use value are often inversely related. This suggests the basis of one of the distortions in economics by which economic measures of wealth (exchange value) are out of step with human needs, happiness and well-being (use value). Perversely, some economists celebrated the stimuli to Japanese and US GDP of the Kobe earthquake in 1995 and the Florida hurricanes in 2004.

For Smith's economic model it was vital that wealth be equated with virtue rather than vice, that the quantity of one's possessions should be an index of morality not evil. Avarice needs to be made harmless in the eyes of society, in order for the market to operate effectively. For only in this way can labour be liberated from slavery. In pre-capitalist society property owners are forced to consume their property by maintaining dependents, whether family or servants. But in capitalist society they can spend the riches which they have accumulated in the public market through money, an anonymous form of exchange. Such exchanges will lead to a redistribution of goods. Thus for Smith accumulation of wealth and the freedom of the poor are inextricably linked (Haakonssen 1998).

8.2.9.3 *QUALITY IS WEALTH/MONEY in Malthus*

Most of Malthus' remarks concerning the correlation between riches and morality focus on showing that the poor are morally worthless, or that poverty and vice correlate. As Tawney puts it, "A society which reverences the attainment of riches as the supreme felicity will naturally be disposed to regard the poor as damned in the next world, if only to justify itself for making their life a hell in this" (Tawney 1926/1938: 265). Beggars are morally repugnant, so that "dependent poverty ought to be held disgraceful" (Malthus 1992: 101). Exploiting a metonymy of cause and effect, skilled workers, who produce more value, are more valuable than the unskilled poor, and therefore spending money on the poor, as the Poor Laws did, is actually rewarding worthlessness, and undervaluing the more worthy skilled artisan (p. 100).

The poor "themselves are the cause of their own poverty" (p. 228), and there are various reasons why they can be blamed for it. First, the labouring poor have a tendency to think in the present, not to save for the future, and spend their money in alehouses, whereas petty tradesmen and small farmers are more careful and frugal. "The poor laws may therefore [by discouraging frugality and saving] be said to diminish both the power and the will to save among the common people, and thus to weaken one of the strongest incentives to sobriety and industry, and consequently to happiness" (p. 101).

Secondly, and famously in Malthus, the poor become or remain poor by overbreeding: "When the wages of labour are hardly sufficient to maintain two children, a man marries and has five or six. He of course finds himself miserably distressed." This husband

and father then proceeds to blame low wages, the parish's lack of help, the avarice of the rich, and even God for his distress. "In searching for objects of accusation, he never adverts to the quarter from which all his misfortunes originate. The last person he would think of accusing is himself, on whom, in fact, the whole of the blame lies" (p. 227).

If vice, in the form of lack of sexual restraint, causes poverty, in a vicious circle poverty produces more vice.

> The continued temptations which beset helpless poverty, and the strong sense of injustice that generally accompanies it from an ignorance of its true cause, tend so powerfully to sour the disposition, to harden the heart, and deaden the moral sense that, generally speaking, virtue takes the flight clear away from the tainted spot and does not often return (p. 234).

In particular, poverty produces the vice of sexual licence: "There is a degree of squalid poverty, in which, if a girl was so brought up, I should say her being really modest at twenty was an absolute miracle" (p. 235). There is no accident in the presumption behind the proverb "She was poor but she was honest". In fact, for Malthus, chastity was more important than public health improvements in reducing poverty (p. 239).

Not only does Malthus talk of the "the disease of poverty" (p. 229), as a metaphor, but also suggests that the poor cause disease, as a metonymy, perhaps another reason to blame them. These comments remind us of the racist associations between disease and "the other", principally foreigners, explored in chapter 5.

> We know from constant experience that fevers are generated in our jails, our manufactories, our crowded workhouses, and in the narrow and close streets of our large towns; all which situations appear to be similar in their effects to squalid poverty: and we cannot doubt that the causes of this kind, aggravated in degree, contributed to the production and prevalence of those great and wasting plagues formerly so common in Europe (p. 36).

The logical conclusion is that the poor have no right to exist, having entirely negative value.

> But there is one right which man has generally been thought to possess, which I am confident that he neither does, nor can possess – a right to subsistence ... If the society do not want his labour he has no claim of right to the smallest portion of food, and, in fact, has no business to be where he is (pp. 248–9).

Especially this seems true of the children of the poor as Malthus suggests when considering those who have been abandoned:

> <u>The infant is, comparatively speaking of no value to the society</u>, as others will immediately supply its place. ... At present the child is taken under the protection of the parish, and generally dies, at least in London, within the first year. <u>The loss to the society, if it be one</u>, is the same... (pp. 263–4). [my underlining]

8.2.9.4 *Protestantism and wealth*

Malthus, if we can believe it from the previous underlined comments, was a Christian priest, and the equation of goodness with wealth would not be possible without a sea change in attitudes to wealth within Protestant Christianity, a change charted in detail by Tawney and Weber. The 17th century Puritan minister Richard Baxter indicates that increasing one's wealth is part of one's religious vocation:

> If God show you a way in which you may lawfully get more than in another way (without wrong to your soul or any other), if you refuse this and choose the less gainful way, you cross one of the ends of your calling, and you refuse to be God's steward, and to accept his gifts and use them for Him when He requiretyh it: you may labour to be rich for God, though not for the flesh and sin (Baxter 1678: vol.1, ch. X, 1, 9, pgph. 24).

Wealth is thus bad ethically only in so far as it is a temptation to idleness and sinful enjoyment of life, and its acquisition is sinful only when it is with the purpose of living merrily and without care. Here combined we have the idea of the good steward, and the Old Testament hero like Abraham, whom God rewards materially for his obedience (Weber 1930/1992: 162–3).

Weber sums up the general attitude, and its importance for the development of capitalism:

> For in conformity with the Old Testament and in analogy to the ethical valuation of good works, asceticism looked upon the pursuit of wealth as an end in itself as highly reprehensible; but the attainment of it as a fruit of labour in a calling was a sign of God's blessing. And even more important: the religious evaluation of restless, continuous, systematic work in a worldly calling, as the highest means to asceticism, and at the same time the surest and most evident proof of rebirth and genuine faith, must have been the most powerful conceivable lever for the expansion of that attitude toward life which we have here called the spirit of capitalism. When the limitation of consumption is combined with this release of acquisitive activity, the inevitable practical result is obvious: accumulation of capital through ascetic compulsion to save. The restraints that were imposed on the consumption of wealth naturally served to increase it by making possible the productive investment of capital (p. 172).

However, the dangers to pure religion of this Protestant belief in God's material blessings were apparent to none other than John Wesley, the founder of Methodism:

> I fear, wherever riches have increased, the essence of religion has decreased in the same proportion. Therefore I do not see how it is possible, in the nature of things, for any revival of true religion to continue long. For religion must necessarily produce both industry and frugality, and these cannot but produce riches. But as riches increase, so will pride, anger, and love of the world in all its branches (quoted in Weber 1930/1992: 175).

8.2.9.5   *Thoughts and relationships as money*

We have seen that quantity, in the form of money, becomes, in these philosophers, the yardstick by which to measure the quality and value of humans. But it can also become a metaphorical source for measuring human relationships, thought processes, and, of course, time. Human relationships are viewed in terms of money exchange, according to the theme AFFECTION/RELATIONSHIP IS MONEY/WEALTH.[1] The basis for this equation is probably metonymic. Reputation, according to these economic philosophers, lies mainly in having good credit, in meeting one's promises or covenants in returning loans or in trading. "There is nothing which touches us more nearly than our reputation, and nothing on which our reputation more depends than our conduct with relation to the property of others" (Hume 1740/1969: 552). While one's immediate interest might be served by breaking a promise or contract, the more important remote interest derived from avoiding unjust transactions is to be found in good character, credit and reputation, which are the pillars of social order and security (Baier 1998).

Benjamin Franklin makes clear the metonymic economic basis for relationships in a commerce-driven society where, as in the following passage, "credit" ceases to be a metaphor:

> The most trifling actions that affect a man's credit are to be regarded. The sound of your hammer at five in the morning, or eight at night, heard by a creditor, makes him easy six months longer; but if he sees you at a billiard table, or hears your voice at a tavern, when you should be at work, he sends for his money the next day; demands it, before he can receive it, in a lump. It shows, besides that you are mindful of what you owe; it makes you appear a careful as well as an honest man, and that still increases your credit…. (quoted in Weber 1930/1992: 49–50).

The metonymy lies in the fact that *credit* means 'trustworthiness in repaying money' before it widens to mean general 'trustworthiness'; or one could say that trustworthiness in general causes or is caused by the ability to borrow and repay money.

But the metaphor theme also had a religious basis, or could be applied to man's relationship with God. Religious account books recording sins, temptations and progress made in grace were kept by all the moralists and theologians and Benjamin Franklin tabulated book-keeping statistics of his progress in the different virtues. Bunyan compares the relationship between a sinner and his God with that of a customer and shopkeeper (p. 124).

Phrases like "the commerce of the sexes" are quite widespread, especially in Malthus (1992: 59). Sometimes we are not sure whether he is speaking metaphorically of sex, or literally of money:

> The only mode, consistent with the laws of morality and religion, of giving to the poor the largest share of the property of the rich, without sinking the whole com-

---

1.   Kövecses (2000a), perhaps more elegantly, labels this INTERACTION IN A RELATIONSHIP IS ECONOMIC EXCHANGE.

munity in misery, is the exercise on the part of the poor of prudence in marriage, and of economy both before and after it (p. 120).

One is reminded of Miss Prism in Oscar Wilde's *The Importance of Being Earnest* enjoining the lower classes metaphorically to "thrift". Malthus even suggests that the more sex is delayed the greater pleasure it gives (pp. 220–22). The strong possibility that the money metaphor might be misapplied to love and sex is ignored. Against Malthus, Juliet says "My bounty is as boundless as the sea/My love as deep, the more I give to thee/The more I have," (*Romeo and Juliet* Act 2, Scene 2, ll.141–143), whereas with money transactions the more you give the less you have to give. In this respect love and money are incommensurate.

Thought itself, most notably in Hobbes, is also constructed by an accounting metaphor, and the quality of reasoning the quality of calculation, taking up the themes VERBAL COMMUNICATION IS TRANSACTION or THINKING/CONSIDERING IS CALCULATING (see 5.5.2).

> For words are wise men's counters, they do but reckon by them; … Subject to names is whatsoever can enter into, or be considered in an account; and be added to another to make a sum; or subtracted one from another and leave a remainder. The Latins called accounts of money *rationes* and accounting *ratiocinatio*: and that which we in bills or books of account call items, they called *nomina*; that is names: and thence it seems to proceed, that they extended the word *ratio* to the faculty of reckoning in all other things … In Sum, in what matter soever there is place for addition and subtraction, there is also a place for reason; and where these have no place, there reason has nothing at all to do … for reason in this sense is nothing but reckoning (that is, adding and subtracting) of the consequences of general names agreed upon, for the marking and signifying of our thoughts (Hobbes 1651/1997: 26).

8.2.10 Economic virtues and TIME IS MONEY/COMMODITY

We have already noted, in chapter 2, Benjamin Franklin's equation of time with money, the metaphor theme TIME IS MONEY/COMMODITY. This idea was soon taken up, especially by Adam Smith. Efficiency in the use of time brings efficiency in production and profits, and this is one reason why he advocates the division of labour.

> The habit of sauntering and of indolent careless application, which is naturally, or rather necessarily acquired by every country workman who is obliged to change his work every half hour and to apply his hand in twenty different ways almost every day of his life renders him almost always slothful and lazy, and incapable of any vigorous application even on the most pressing occasions.

Such practices "must lose a good deal of time" (Smith 1776/1991: 14). Capital expenditure allows and necessitates this division of labour and constant employment:

> It is by means of an additional capital only that the undertaker of any work can either provide his workmen with better machinery, or make a more proper distribution of employment among them. When the work to be done consists of a number of parts to keep every man constantly employed in one way requires a much greater capital than when every man is employed in every different part of the work (p. 234).

For Smith labour, or the time spent on labour, is the measure of money, as we can see in the use of the "cost" metaphor in the following. "If among a nation of hunters ... it usually costs twice the labour to kill a beaver which it does to kill a deer, one beaver should naturally exchange for, or be worth two deer." And acquiring dexterity and skill over long periods of time in training allows one to charge more for one's labour. If time is money, and money is the measure of well-being, any time spent not making money is wasted. Indolence, therefore, becomes the worst vice.

This leads us to consider what are known as the economic virtues, which recognise the value of time and oppose themselves to idleness. They are famously championed by all our philosophers, but especially Hume, Smith and Malthus. What they have in common is the endorsement of "virtues" which lead to economic productivity, capital savings and investment, all of which suggest QUALITY IS QUANTITY or MORE = GOOD. Hume is perhaps distinctive in the emphasising pride as a positive virtue, and Malthus in advocating chastity, as we have already seen.

8.2.10.1 Economic virtues in Hume

Hume associated the following virtues with great men: "Their prudence, temperance, frugality, industry, assiduity, enterprise, dexterity are celebrated as well as their generosity and humanity" (Hume 1740/1969: 637). Generosity and humanity are perhaps taken for granted here, but the emphasis is precisely on those abilities such as hard work, perseverance, initiative, and dexterity which fit great men to be successful entrepreneurs and workers, along with the frugality which allows them to accumulate capital for investment. Hume famously rejects "celibacy, fasting, penance, mortification, self-denial, humility, silence, solitude, and the whole train of monkish virtues" (Baier 1998: 552). Indeed, what Hume teaches us to admire most is worldly success, especially in business. We should consider

> which of those qualities capacitates man best for the world, and carries him farthest in any of his undertakings. There are many other qualities of the mind whose merit is derived from the same origin. Industry, perseverance, patience, activity, vigilance, application, constancy, with other virtues of that kind... are esteemed valuable upon no other account than their advantage in the conduct of life. 'Tis the same case with temperance, frugality, economy, resolution. As on the other hand prodigality, luxury, irresolution, uncertainty are vicious, merely because they draw ruin upon us, and incapacitate us for business and action (p. 660).

The virtues Hume espouses inevitably lead to inequality, a fact for which he is quite un-apologetic, since without them all would be poor: "Render possession ever so equal, men's different degrees of art, care, and industry will immediately break that equality. Or, if you check these virtues, you reduce society to the most extreme indigence" (Enquiries: 194)

Regarding wealth and possessions as a sign of moral worth, Hume re-evaluates pride, not as the mother of the Seven Deadly Sins, as in Catholic theology, but as an admirable virtue, only wrong when it is insufficiently disguised and thereby provokes envy and contention (p. 650). His argument in favour of pride goes as follows:

> Vices give us pain, and virtues give us pleasure. Now, since every quality in our-selves or others, which gives pleasure, always causes pride or love; as every one that produces uneasiness, excites humility or hatred; it follows that these two par-ticulars are to be considered as equivalent, with regard to our mental qualities, virtue and the power of producing love or pride, vice and the power of producing humility and hatred ... We may observe, that a genuine and hearty pride or self-esteem, if well concealed and well-founded is essential to the character of a man of honour, and that there is no quality of the mind, which is more indispensably requisite to procure the esteem and approbation of mankind (pp. 647–9).

I suspect some logical slippage through metaphorical multivalency in Hume's think-ing here. IMPORTANCE/STATUS IS HIGH, GOOD (QUALITY/MORALITY) IS HIGH, MORE IS HIGH, and POWER/CONTROL IS ABOVE. IMPORTANCE/STATUS would therefore equal GOOD, as would abundance of possessions. Indeed Hume also seems to subscribe to POWER = GOOD, admiring the destructive hero who gains military glory: "But when we fix our view on the person himself, who is the author of all this mischief, there is something so dazzling in his character, the mere contemplation of it so elevates the mind, that we cannot refuse it our admiration" (p. 651).

8.2.10.2 *Economic virtues in Smith*

Since TIME IS MONEY/COMMODITY Smith seems to celebrate most the virtues of frugali-ty and savings, while denouncing profligacy, and in admiring "industry", meaning 'hard work', while disapproving of idleness. Smith's dislike of the apprenticeship system is based on the idleness it produces: "An apprentice is likely to be idle, and almost always is so, because he has no immediate benefit to be otherwise ... a young man naturally conceives an aversion to labour, when for a long time he receives no benefit from it" (Smith 1776/1991: 130). (Sadly there seems no possibility that an apprentice will enjoy learning and employing his skill for its own sake, and so has to be bribed to work.)

Smith sees the advances in the British economy over the previous few centuries as precisely due to the decrease in idleness through the investment of capital in labour: rich countries devote a larger proportion of their produce to maintaining productive labour.

> We are more industrious than our forefathers; because in the present times the funds destined for the maintenance of industry are much greater in proportion to those which are likely to be employed in the maintenance of idleness, than they

> were two or three centuries ago. … In the mercantile and manufacturing towns, where the inferior ranks of people are chiefly maintained by the employment of capital, they are in general industrious, sober, and thriving; as in many English, and in most Dutch towns (pp. 275–6).

Smith even admits that the influence of capital in increasing industriousness of the workers may become tyrannical: "Workmen, when they are liberally paid by the piece, are very apt to over-work themselves, and to ruin their health and constitution in a few years" (p. 86).

Industry links with Smith's other predominant economic virtue, frugality or parsimony. London, Lisbon and Copehagen are, he claims, superior to Paris, because the latter consumes what it produces, while the others have a surplus, which can be used in trade and investment in commerce and manufacture. "The idleness of the greater part of the people who are maintained by the expense of revenue, corrupts, it is probable, the industry of those who ought to be maintained by the employment of capital…" (p. 277). Smith even goes so far as to proclaim "every prodigal appears to be a public enemy, and every frugal man a public benefactor" (p. 281).

8.2.10.3 *Economic virtues in Malthus*

What Malthus emphasises, when compared with Smith and Hume, is the idea that scarcity of resources was part of the divine system designed to put pressure on humans to overcome their natural tendency towards indolence and laziness, and to advance the cause of economic prosperity and civilisation.[2] Providing state pensions and social security, as suggested by Condercet, would undermine this spur to industry.

> [I]f the idle and negligent be placed upon the same footing with regard to their credit, and the future support of their wives and families, as the active and industrious, can we expect to see men exert that animated capacity in bettering their condition, which now forms the master-spring of public prosperity? (Malthus 1992: 47)

Similarly, he denounces the egalitarianism of the revolutionaries in France, and the social experiments of Robert Owen and Thomas Spence,

> the unsuitability of the state of equality, to the production of those stimulants to exertion which can alone overcome the natural indolence of man, and prompt him to the proper cultivation of the earth and the fabrication of those conveniences and comforts which are necessary to happiness (Malthus 1992: 76).

According to Malthus' system, the more dire the consequences of failure in society and falling into a lower class, and the greater the rewards of success and rising in status, the greater the incentives to industrious work habits.

---

2.   Perhaps a spiritual corollary of this can be observed in George Herbert's poem "The Pulley", where God deliberately makes man restless.

> A state in which an inequality of conditions offers the natural rewards of good conduct, and inspires widely and generally the hopes of rising and the fears of falling in society, is unquestionably the best calculated to develop the energies and faculties of man, and the best suited to the exercise and improvement of human virtue.

Despite his theory that overpopulation produced misery, Malthus even rejected birth control within marriage, since it reduced the stimulus to industry produced by scarcity (p. 369).

One of the advantages that Malthus saw in this enforced industriousness was that, once the basic requirements for food had been met, the habits of industry would be employed for further work so that the workers could buy luxuries. In this way the consumer society would be born.

> It is under these circumstances, particularly when combined with a good government, that the lower classes of society are most likely to acquire a decided taste for the conveniences and comforts of life ... which, at the same time that they gratify a natural or acquired want, tend unquestionably to improve the mind and elevate the character (p. 190).

Malthus, as we saw, insisted on a further economic virtue as an antidote to the miseries of war and poverty, namely restraint on sexual gratification by delaying marriage until we can support our children. He even suggests this as a pre-eminent virtue.

> If it can be proved that an attention to this obligation is of more effect in the prevention of misery than all the other virtues combined; and that, in violation of this duty, it were the general custom to follow the first impulse of nature, and marry at the age of puberty, the universal prevalence of every known virtue in the greatest conceivable degree would fail of rescuing society from the most wretched and desperate state of want, and all the diseases and famines which usually accompany it (p. 216).

A period of abstinence would allow scope for the other economic virtues, sobriety, industry, and economy, which would enable a man to get married without fear of the consequences (p. 218).

8.2.10.4 *The economic virtues and Protestantism*

The virtues which our economic philosophers celebrate represent an ideological revolution. The moral theologians of the Middle Ages regarded labour as honourable and necessary, trade as perilous, finance as sordid, if not disreputable, values which we find reversed in modern economic theory (Tawney 1926/1938: 45).

> The medieval theorist condemned as a sin precisely that effort to achieve a continuous and unlimited increase in material wealth which modern societies applaud as meritorious, and the vices for which he reserved his most merciless denunciations were the more refined and subtle of economic virtues (p. 48).

Usury was regarded as contrary to scripture for it was

> to sell time, which belongs to God, for the advantage of wicked men; it is to rob those who use the money lent, and to whom, since they make it profitable, the profits should belong; it is unjust in itself, for the benefit of the loan to the borrower cannot exceed the value of the principal sum lent him; it is in defiance of sound juristic principles, for when a loan of money is made, the property in the thing lent passes to the borrower, and why should the creditor demand payment from a man who is merely using what is now his own? (p. 55).

In short, TIME SHOULD NOT BE MONEY, QUALITY IS NOT WEALTH/MONEY, and MORE IS NOT NECESSARILY GOOD.

By stages, beginning with Luther and Calvin, these medieval views on capitalism, investment and the acquisition of wealth were gradually undermined.

> Early Calvinism no longer suspects the whole world of economic motives as alien to the life of the spirit, or distrusts the capitalist as one who has necessarily grown rich on the misfortunes of his neighbour or regards poverty as in itself meritorious, and it is perhaps the first systematic body of religious teaching which can be said to recognise and applaud the economic virtues (p. 114).

Though for the reformers salvation was by faith not works, both Luther and Calvin emphasised the idea of a calling. Success in this calling becomes a proof of one's salvation so that Christians must carry on their business with a high seriousness, as though it were itself a kind of religion (p. 119).

> The valuation of the fulfilment of duty in worldly affairs [is] the highest form that the moral activity of the individual could assume ... The renunciation of the duties of the world are seen as selfishness and ... the division of labour forces everyone to work for everyone else (Weber 1930/1992: 80–81).

According to Weber the idea of a calling was absolutely necessary for the success of capitalism, because it guaranteed a hard-working and disciplined workforce, justified exploitation, and sanctified the acquisition of wealth among the bosses.

> A specifically economic ethic had grown up. With the consciousness of standing in the fullness of God's grace and being visibly blessed by Him, the bourgeois businessman, as long as he remained within the bounds of formal correctness, as long as his moral conduct was spotless, and the use to which he put his wealth was not objectionable, could follow his pecuniary interests as he would and feel that he was fulfilling his duty in doing so. The power of religious asceticism provided him in addition with sober, conscientious and unusually industrious workmen, who clung to their work as to a life purpose willed by God ... Finally it gave him the comforting assurance that the unequal distribution of the goods of this world was a special dispensation of Divine Providence ... Calvin himself had made the much-quoted statement that only when the people, i.e. the mass of labourers and craftsmen, were poor did they remain obedient to God (p. 177).

Tawney pithily sums up the revolution in morality:

> The insistence among men of pecuniary motives, the strength of economic egotism, the appetite for gain – these are the commonplaces of every age and need no emphasis. What is significant is that change of standards which converted a natural frailty into a resounding virtue (Tawney 1926/1938: 245).

8.2.11 Progressivism in Darwin: CHANGE = GOOD

This revolution in moral values preceded a revolution in attitudes to time and progress, predicated on Darwinism. Darwin's theory was interpreted, rightly or not, to suggest that evolutionary changes were improvements, that CHANGE = GOOD. There seems to be some debate as to whether Darwin believed this himself. Certainly there is plenty in *The Origin of Species* to suggest this belief, though perhaps in his later work, *The Descent of Man* he is more equivocal. Of course, better for survival, and better at passing on one's genes may not necessarily mean morally better, even in Darwin's theory.

Throughout the *Origin* Darwin talks in terms of improvement. In later editions of the Origin (1869) he readily adopted Spencer's phrase "the survival of the fittest" instead of the original "natural selection". In step with CHANGE = GOOD evolution generally meant improvement so that "the vigorous, the healthy, and the happy survive and multiply" (p. 58). Here are some quite conclusive quotations:

> Old forms are supplanted by new and improved forms (Darwin 1859/1991: 397).

> Recent forms are generally looked upon as being, on the whole, higher in the scale of organisation than ancient forms; and they must be higher, in so far as the later and more improved forms have conquered the older and less improved forms in the struggle for life (p. 397).

> Hence we may look with some confidence to a secure future of great length. And as a natural selection works solely by and for the good of each being, all corporeal and mental endowments will tend to progress towards perfection (p. 408).

Darwin seems to see man as the apex of the evolutionary tree, the yardstick against which improvements are measured:

> The ultimate result is that each creature tends to become more and more improved in relation to its conditions. This improvement inevitably leads to the gradual advancement of the organisation of the greater number of living beings throughout the world. But here we enter on a very intricate subject, for naturalists have not defined to each other's satisfaction what is meant by an advance in organisation. Amongst the vertebrata the degree of intellect and an approach in structure to man clearly come into play (p. 92).

As far as man is concerned, therefore, evolution was progressive, but Darwin, in *The Descent of Man*, contended that evolution was not necessarily so. He therefore felt the need to explain why the evolutionary branch leading to humans became much more intelligent than our nearest relatives the great apes, postulating that the decisive factor was the upright posture acquired when we descended from the trees to walk on the savannahs, which freed the hands and allowed them more control over the environment.

Darwin also laid the foundations for a racist form of social Darwinism, believing that amongst humans Europeans were more advanced on the evolutionary scale, and that amongst Europeans those which had developed a modern industrial capability were the highest expression of social evolution (Bowler 1990). The idea that societies competing against each other for supremacy was a realisation of the evolutionary struggle for survival clearly provided an apologia for imperialism.

> The more civilised so-called Caucasian races have beaten the Turkish hollow in the struggle for existence. Looking to the world at no very distant date, what an endless number of lower races will have been eliminated by the higher civilised races throughout the world. (Letter of Darwin July 3, 1881 quoted in Rogers (1972: 274))

But we have already discussed many of these ideas and their legacy in chapter 4.

8.2.12 Capitalist economic philosophers, experientialism and the contemporary theory of metaphor

We have begun this chapter with a demonstration that many of the major metaphor themes in Metalude were promoted into their dominant ideological positions by the economic philosophy of 17th to mid-19th century Britain. What I was not so prepared for, when embarking on this voyage of exploration, was to find in philosophers such as Hobbes and Hume some of the roots of the experientialist theory of metaphor.

8.2.12.1 Relations to Lakoff and Damasio in Hobbes.

We saw in chapter 7 that Newton's theory reduced all types of change to the metaphor of motion (CHANGE IS MOVEMENT). As we have noted, Hobbes believed that natural science could be understood entirely as matter in motion. Hobbes conducted a thought experiment in which the world was annihilated, following which all that remained was the corporeal body, or perhaps the brain in whose internal parts were preserved motions produced in the past by the impacts of the external world on the sense-organs (Sorell 1998). He saw the origin of thought and reasoning in the motions occurring in various parts of our organic body, which produced imagination, which then produced named categories. "Reasoning will depend on names, names will depend on the imagination, and imagination will depend (as I believe it does) merely on the motions of our bodily organs; and so the mind will be nothing more than motion occurring in various parts of an organic body" (quoted in Sorell 1998: 467)

In keeping with the metaphor theme DESIRE IS BENDING/ATTRACTION (EMOTION IS MOVEMENT) Hobbes insisted that these motions of our body are not simply sense impressions, they are also emotions, particularly of appetite and aversion which in Latin, like the Greek *horme* and *aphorme* mean approaching and retiring.

> As in sense, that which is really within us, is only motion, caused by the action of external objects, but in appearance; to the sight, light and colour; to the ear, sound; to the nostril, odour etc: so when the action of the same object is continued from the eyes, ears and other organs to the heart; the real effect is nothing but motion, or endeavour; which consisteth in appetite or aversion, to, or from, the object moving (Hobbes 1651/1997: 31–32).

When motion derived from sense perception encourages vital motion, the sensor experiences pleasure at the sight, smell or taste of the object and tends to move its body so as to prolong or increase the pleasure. If the pleasure-giving object is distant, then the sensor typically moves towards it. By contrast, displeasure is an after-effect of the act of perception which hinders vital motion. A creature experiencing this hindrance attempts to counteract it, typically by moving away from the perceived object. Aversion is constituted by the small inner movements that initiate the avoidance action, just as "appetite" names the internal beginnings of approaching behaviour (Sorell 1998).

In terms which recall Damasio's claims about the intimate relationship between thought and emotion Hobbes continues: "The origin of them all [all thoughts] is that which we call sense; (For there is no conception in a man's mind, which hath not at first, totally, or by parts, been begotten upon the organs of sense). The rest are derived from that original" (Hobbes 1651/1997: 11). Hobbes's theory is remarkably like the experiential metonymic theory we discussed in chapter 6:

> ... as anger causeth heat in some parts of the body, when we are awake; so when we sleep, the overheating of the same parts causeth anger, and raiseth up in the brain the imagination of an enemy. In the same manner; as natural kindness, when we are awake causeth desire; and desire makes heat in certain other parts of the body; so also, too much heat in those parts, while we sleep, raiseth in the brain an imagination of some kindness shown (p. 14).

We see here, then, a relation to emotion metaphor themes based on EMOTION IS SENSE IMPRESSION (TOUCH, IMPACT, SMELL, SOUND, LIGHT/COLOUR) and BAD EMOTION IS DISCOMFORT/PAIN or HURT/INJURY.

8.2.12.2 *Relations to Damasio and Lakoff in Hume*

Following Hobbes, Hume's most general thesis is that all ideas, what we think about, originate in impressions, either from sense experience or emotional experience (Baier 1998). "That all our simple ideas in their first appearance are derived from simple impressions, which are correspondent to them, and which they exactly represent" (Hume 1740/1969: 52). The means by which ideas and sense impressions are related are resemblance, which we might call metaphor, and spatial contiguity and cause and effect, which are both kinds of metonymy. In a rather modern way, which anticipates

Damasio, Hume prophesies that "anatomists" will find some physiological explanation, in terms of our nervous system and the physical proximity of memory traces in the brain, to account for the psychological phenomena.

Like Hobbes, again, he gives particular importance to the sense impressions of pain and pleasure, (BAD EMOTION IS DISCOMFORT/PAIN or HURT/INJURY) as these are the cornerstones of his philosophy of morality. "Bodily pains and pleasures are the source of many passions, both when felt and considered by the mind; but arise originally in the soul, or in the body, whichever you please to call it, without any preceding thought or perception" (p. 328). Like Damasio Hume conceives bodily sensations as an Emotionally Competent Stimulus, or ECS (6.3.1).

He summarises his theory of morals, obviously building on Hobbes, in the following way:

> The chief spring or actuating principle of the human mind is pleasure or pain; and when these sensations are removed, both from our thought and feeling, we are, in great measure, incapable of passion or action, of desire or volition. The most immediate effects of pleasure and pain are the propense and adverse motions of the mind; which are diversified into volition, into desire and aversion, grief and joy, hope and fear, according as the pleasure or pain changes its situation, and becomes probable or improbable, certain or uncertain, or is considered as out of our power for the present moment. But when, along with this, the objects that cause pleasure or pain, acquire a relation to ourselves or others; they continue to excite desire and aversion, grief and joy. But cause, at the same time, the indirect passions of pride and humility, love or hatred, which in this case have a double relation of impressions and ideas to the pain or pleasure ... Vices give us pain, and virtues give us pleasure (p. 625).

This hedonistic philosophy, again remarkably reminiscent of Damasio, explains why, as we saw earlier, he regards pride as a virtue, and is quite obviously consistent with the doctrine that the accumulation of goods in the form of property and wealth, in which we can take pride and pleasure, is an indication of virtue rather than vice. This is a theme taken up in Malthus, who regards goodness as leading to pleasure and evil to pain.

> Natural and moral evil seem to be the instruments employed by the Deity in admonishing us to avoid any mode of conduct which is not suited to our being, and will consequently injure our happiness. If we be intemperate in eating and drinking, we are disordered; if we indulge the transports of anger, we seldom fail to commit acts of which we afterwards repent (Malthus 1992: 208).

And if we multiply too fast, we die miserably of poverty and contagious diseases. Again, this hedonism suggests that the pleasures enjoyed by the rich are the results of their virtue.

It is worth emphasising that Hume's philosophy also gives a basis for Lakoff's experientialist ideas and Grady's view of primary scenes. He emphasizes the influence of experienced repetition on our beliefs and our passions. For him the perception of cause and effect is the more or less instinctive extrapolation into the future of regularities and frequencies that have been experienced in the past, along with the mind's projections of causal inferences, onto the subject matter of those inferences (Baier 1998).

We also find in Hume reference to what Lakoff and Johnson call an "image schema", an idea of a class of objects more general than the image of individual objects. For Lakoff and Johnson the image schema is an idea at precisely the right level of generality for identifying conceptual metaphor sources. Since ideas are based on sense impressions which we have had or may have, Hume takes every idea to be "individual", and to refer to something of which we have had or might have an impression. However, in thinking we need something rather more abstract than this particular idea. Hume's example of triangles is one which Johnson takes up in his explanation of image schema: if we wish to consider a claim about all triangles, we might begin with an "image" before our minds of, say, a particular equilateral triangle, but we may and should substitute other ideas of other types and sizes of triangles to test the claim (Johnson 1987).

8.3   A critique of Lakoff's *Moral Politics*

I have, I hope, both in this chapter, and in chapters 6 and 7, demonstrated the ideological forces which account for the prevalence of many of the important metaphors in Metalude, and shown that they have become so prolific because they are as much historical and cultural constructs as reflections of bodily experience. It is essential, however, at this point, to compare my attempts to link metaphor themes with ideology with a similar attempt by George Lakoff in *Moral Politics*.

Lakoff claims that political thinking in the US is dominated by the metaphor of Society as a Family. Right-wing political thinking invokes a set of metaphors centred on the Strict Father Family, whereas left wing or liberal thinking relies on a rather less well-developed set of metaphors centred on the Nurturant Parent Family. He suggests that many quite reasonable US citizens think in right-wing or conservative ways, simply because their cognition is dominated by the Strict Father Family metaphors, not because they are involved in any ideological competitive struggle for power or wealth or privilege. He laments the fact that liberals have a less-developed set of conceptual metaphors (metaphor themes), which means the odds are stacked against them in political argument, since this argument is fundamentally metaphorical in nature.

There is much of value in Lakoff's book which clarifies and succinctly summarises many of the links we have already explored between metaphor and right-wing ideology, and shows the interconnections between the strands of this ideology. Perhaps most importantly, he shows how dominant these neo-conservative strands are in contemporary American and global post cold-war politics.

Lakoff nicely summarises the QUALITY IS MONEY/WEALTH ideology whose roots we have traced, recognising too its reduction of quality to quantity.

> There is a fundamental economic metaphor behind much of morality, the ubiquitous conception of Well-Being As Wealth, which brings quantitative reasoning into the qualitative realm of morality. It is so fundamental a metaphor that it is rarely even noticed as being metaphoric …

But, instead of rejecting this metaphor, as a right-wing capitalist one, he distinguishes a right wing and a left wing interpretation of it:

> There are two distinct general uses of the Well-Being as Wealth metaphor, one concerning the results of the interaction and the other the results of distribution. The former is the Moral Accounting metaphor … the latter is the Moral Action as Fair Distribution (Lakoff 1996: 63).

The implication of the moral accounting metaphor is that moral qualities are equated with wealth, indeed, as the Protestant ethic tells us, wealth is produced by moral behaviour and is therefore a metonymic index of it. According to Lakoff, if we combine Adam Smith's view of the marketplace with this moral accounting metaphor we arrive at the conclusion that the pursuit of wealth/self-interest creates the most well-being for everyone through the invisible hand of the market. When everyone pursues their own self-interest unimpeded, this works for the good of all. From this point of view a moral citizen

> is someone who, through self-discipline and the pursuit of self-interest, has become self-reliant. This means that rich people and successful corporations are model citizens from a conservative perspective. To encourage and reward such model citizens, conservatives support tax breaks for them and oppose environmental and other regulations that get in their way. After all, since large corporations are model citizens, we have nothing to fear from them (Lakoff 1995).

Lakoff also convincingly shows a link between the economic virtues, success in competition and the Strict Father metaphor, and Morality is Strength, even, like us, tracing this back to Hobbes (1996: 78).

> Competition is a crucial ingredient in such a moral system. It is through competition that we discover who is moral, that is, who has been properly self-disciplined and therefore deserves success, and who is fit enough to survive and even thrive in a difficult world (p. 68).

Under this system competition is a condition for the development and sustenance of the right kind of person. And inequality is inevitable, because the people who are better off than others deserve to be (p. 69). If Morality is Strength then poverty, illegitimacy and drug addiction are simply the just rewards for moral weakness (p. 75).

Lakoff sees the American Dream as a manifestation of the economic virtues: the myth that, as America is a land of opportunity, anyone can, through hard work, climb the social ladder to prosperity, and if you fail to you are lazy or not talented enough. The poor show moral weakness or moral inferiority, while the rich deserve their wealth, because of self-discipline and hard work (p. 83). In fact they are philanthropists, because, by reinvesting their earnings, they provide jobs for others.

Lakoff shows that the Strict Father model "metaphorically" equates morality with discipline, authority, order, boundaries, homogeneity, purity, and self-interest. This list of qualities brings together many themes we have explored in this chapter: discipline in the Puritan economic virtues; authority and order in Hobbes' desire for strong government, and Hume and Smith's emphasis on property rights to prevent an anarchic free-for-all; self-interest as the overriding motive for economic development and favouring of our progeny. The need for boundaries links back to our exploration of the theme CATEGORY IS A DIVIDED AREA (1.7), a theme which interacted dangerously, as we saw in chapter 5, with ideas of SIMILARITY IS PROXIMITY, RELATIONSHIP IS PROXIMITY/COHESION, GOODNES IS PURITY. Lakoff points out that this morality breeds a divisive culture of exclusion and blame, appealing to the worst human instincts, stereotyping, demonizing and punishing the Other simply for being different, and leading to racism, militarism and the horrors of Bosnia, Rwanda, Somalia, and the Ku Klux Klan (p. 383).

According to Lakoff, the Nurturant parent model insists that "what children need to learn most is empathy for others, the capacity for nurturance, co-operation and the maintenance of social ties." It instils an understanding of the nature of interdependence – that the bonds of affection and earned mutual respect are stronger than the bonds of dominance, and that nurturance is something that is provided by the natural environment and should be returned (pp. 109–11). In this respect the Strict Father and the Nurturant parent moralities line up quite neatly with the (neo-) Darwinian emphasis on competition versus the more modern Gaian emphasis on interdependence and symbiosis.

So Lakoff, too, recognises the influence of Darwin and Lamarck on right-wing Strict Father notions of the natural order. The progressivism which can be read in(to) evolutionary theory, "people are naturally more powerful than animals and plants and natural objects", can lead to a conclusion that "people have moral authority over nature". Progressivism focuses on questions of natural superiority, apparent in books such as *The Bell Curve*, with its implication that if whites are more advanced in evolutionary terms they are therefore better morally (pp. 81–83).

Progressivism interpreted in terms of moral superiority and power fosters right-wing attitudes to the environment. Among these Lakoff lists at least six Strict Father morality propositions about nature (p. 213). Nature is God's Dominion, (given to man to steward wisely), encouraging the kind of power over nature, reproduced in transitive material process clauses with humans as actors and nature as affecteds, that we explored at length in chapter 7; Nature is a Mechanical System (to be figured out and put to use), which is a main theme of the industrialisation of nature (chapter 7), and of time (chapter 2); Nature is an adversary (to be conquered and made to serve us), reflecting the general theme of competition, war and the struggle for survival found in Darwinism, and explored in chapter 4; Nature is a Resource (for immediate human use), which matches the notion that nature is only valuable or important in so far is it provides for or affects humans, an emphasis detected in my research on nature in the

BBC, reported in chapter 3; Nature is Property (for the use of the owner and for sale and purchase), which fits with the theme of the commodification of nature (chapter 3), itself part of the larger theme of the importance of property rights for the economic philosophers discussed in this chapter.

By contrast, left-wing, Nurturant Parent attitudes to the environment (pp. 215-6) seem to reflect *Gaia* theory as discussed in chapters 4 and 7: Nature is a whole (of which we are inseparable parts), so *Gaia* behaves like an indivisible organism; Nature is a divine being (to be revered and respected), so *Gaia* is the earth goddess; Nature is a living organism (whose needs need to be met if it is to survive), hence the self-regulating homeostatic nature of *Gaia*; Nature is a mother and Nature is a victim of injury (who has been harmed and needs to be healed), are represented in the metaphor themes LANDSCAPE IS HUMAN BODY, and HUMAN BODY IS EARTH (for details see 4.2).

Lakoff's book, therefore, both gives a summary of many of the important themes of right-wing ideology which are created, reinforced and enacted through the metaphor themes in my book. Just as important, he demonstrates how contemporary and dominant are many of the ideologies whose sources we have attempted to trace back to the 17th century.

However I take issue with Lakoff's argument over two points – I do not believe it is possible to apply the Strict Father/Nurturant Parent distinction to account for conservative and liberal policies with any consistency. Nor do I believe that those who espouse conservative views are ideologically innocent. At the least they are seduced by latent ideology inherent in the metaphors they think with, but in addition they are implicated in ideology, as we all are, simply by the subject positions we take and the economic relations we practise in society.

The very metaphor which is the foundation of Lakoff's argument, NATION IS A FAMILY, is problematic for right-wing thinkers. As we saw in chapter 4, the New Right thinking and sociobiological traditions of the selfish-gene reinforce each other, issuing dicta like "there is no such thing as society" (responsibilities only extend to families with whom we share genes), and issuing denunciations of the "nanny" state. Consequently there is a contradiction in saying that the government is regarded as a strict father – because the right sees government control as illegitimate authority, and believes in small government, free enterprise without government regulation. By contrast the patriarch in the family has legitimate authority and is highly regulatory (*pace* Lakoff 1996: 78-7). Lakoff admits that right-wing ideology supports the pursuit of self-interest (p. 35). But surely the strict father precisely restricts the pursuit of individual self-interest, by reining in the undisciplined individualism of the less dominant family members with the motive of maintaining power and control! Lakoff, in fact admits a contradiction between Strict Father morality and the "no-meddling condition".

One would expect the strict father to want to control guns since you do not allow your children guns, even more perhaps in the case of a strict father family. Nor would even a strict father, except in extreme cases such as Abraham or Jephtha, inflict death on their children. If the death penalty amounts to infanticide, then this suggests that the nation as family metaphor does not hold for conservatives (p. 209). Lakoff claims this is because the strict father's main duty is protection (p. 192), but this does not apply to the "children" it sacrifices. More likely the right to bear arms and the death penalty are advocated because the idea of the survival of the fittest fits into the notion of military solutions – eliminating ideology through violence, as Elijah did with the prophets of Baal. The right's military expenditure is another manifestation of this ideology of the desire to dominate and the military survival of the fittest. Lakoff talks about moral systems when he should perhaps be talking about ideological systems.

High military expenditure is one of various particular right-wing policies which are, in any case, inconsistent with the idea of small government. In an interesting passage Lakoff mentions Reich's concept of "corporate welfare"; despite protestations against welfarism by the conservative right, government actually supports big corporations. "They receive huge amounts of money that they do not earn: money from inordinately cheap grazing rights, mineral and timber rights, infrastructure development that supports their businesses, agricultural price supports" (p. 172). This is further evidence of a flaw in Lakoff's neat Strict Father v. Nurturant Parent opposition; the right-wing government is acting like a nurturant parent rather than a strict father. The fact that these two family metaphors are not consistently applied, suggests that at the heart of political decision-making are power and ideology rather than simply Lakoff's two metaphor complexes.

Right wing attitudes to eugenics, poor parenting, AIDS, immigration and homosexuality, expose further inconsistencies. Lakoff claims that the priority given to Moral Strength, Moral Authority and Moral Order in the Strict Father version of the Nation as Family metaphor puts it out of touch with the priority given to human flourishing and empathy in the Nurturant Parent version (p. 382). However, as we have seen, right-wing, sociobiology-based theories see the nurturing of the race as more important than the nurturing of individuals, so they do not give up the nurturing parent value, simply apply it differently. The right wing advocate orphanages to prevent the cycle of poor parenting continuing – but, this too is a kind of nurturing and welfarism. To be consistent the right would let them fail as punishment for irresponsible parents. Similarly, demanding abstinence to prevent the spread of AIDS contradicts the basic freedom to pursue one's happiness and give rein to one's natural desires, which is advocated in the economic sphere in the encouragement of spending, accumulation and greed. And if immigrants are part of the nation then they should be helped, because they are guests, if not members, of the family (pp. 186–88). Gays see their sexual orientation as essence, but left-wing liberals believe in nurture rather than nature (p. 226).

But there are probably more fundamental weaknesses in Lakoff's argument. For him morality is the promotion of the well-being of ourselves and others, and is grounded experientially (1996: ch. 3). To be well is to be healthy, wealthy, strong, free, cared for, happy, whole, clean, beautiful, in the light, standing upright, socially integrated. These experiences provide the grounding for our system of moral metaphors (pp. 41–2).

There are various problems here: some of these aspects of well-being are contradictory; social integration and freedom, as we discussed at length (5.3.1), are constructed metaphorically as in opposition. More important, as this chapter has shown, systems of Christian (rather than Judaeo-Protestant) morality deny them: as far as wealth is concerned, Christianity preaches that the kingdom of God belongs to the poor, not the rich, and that power and strength are temptations to be resisted, as Christ did. The moral accounting metaphor escapes the Christian notion of grace: "(the wages of sin is death, but) the gift of God is eternal life" (p. 53).

In fact, the more we consider these experientially-grounded, metonymically-based metaphors for morality, the more we realise just how much they owe to the ideologies of the economic philosophers we have been discussing, particularly Hume, with his claim that morality is based on the pleasure principle. In an interview with Lakoff, Pires de Oliveira (2000: 32–33), comes close to pointing this out, and provokes a spirited and defensive response. The final irony is that Lakoff, a professed liberal, says the left-wing prefers the nurture model to the nature model (p. 32). But cognitive linguistics and contemporary metaphor theories were strongly influenced in their origins by the nature model – language and conceptual metaphor is a universal property of body/mind, provoking Kövecses' (2005) correction of this imbalance to take culture, if not ideology, more seriously. Lakoff is a little more like a liberal in the 19th century or European sense, exemplified by Thatcherism, than in the modern US sense, which equates with (mild) socialism. He ignores the ideological and historical basis of MO-RALITY IS PLEASURE.

8.4   Reductionism or not?

The topic of reductionism has surfaced from time to time in this book, most notably in Chapter 4, with Crick and Pinker. But we need to revisit it, both as a summary of the economic philosophy in this chapter, and because the question mark of reductionism hangs over contemporary metaphor theory, indeed over metaphor itself.

We saw that one of the influences of Newton was to reduce change to movement, and the physical universe to mathematics. Our economic philosophers influenced by him tended to reduce man to an economic animal by equating quality of life and morality with the accumulation and investment of capital, measurable in money terms. Tawney is quick to point out the perils of such economic reductionism:

> Economic efficiency is a necessary element in the life of any sane and vigorous society, and only the incorrigible sentimentalist will depreciate its significance. But to convert efficiency from an instrument into a primary object is to destroy efficiency itself. For the condition of effective action in a complex civilisation is cooperation. And the condition of cooperation is agreement, both as to the ends to which effort should be applied, and the criteria by which its success is to be

judged. Agreement as to the ends implies the acceptance of a standard of values, by which the position to be assigned to different objects may be determined. In a world of limited resources, where nature yields a return only to prolonged and systematic effort, such a standard must take account of economic possibilities. But it cannot itself be merely economic, since the comparative importance of economic and other interests – the sacrifice, for example, of material goods worth incurring in order to extend leisure, or develop education, or humanise toil – is precisely the point on which it is needed to throw light. It must be based on some conception of human nature as a whole, to which the satisfaction of economic needs is evidently vital, but which demands the satisfaction of other needs as well, and which can organise its activities on a rational system only in so far as it has a clear apprehension of their relative significance (Tawney 1926/1938: 277–8).

This important passage makes us realise that it is the conception of human nature which is what will determine social and economic policy – and a conception of human nature which reduces humans to animals in the neo-Darwinian mode, or economic machines in the industrial mode, might be thought to abolish any tension between the economic virtues and human nature. However "a reasonable estimate of economic organisation must allow for the fact that, unless industry is to be paralysed by recurrent revolts on the part of outraged human nature, it must satisfy criteria which are not purely economic" (p. 278).

The wider world of nature, our environment, can not be ignored either, otherwise we will succumb to "the smiling illusion of progress won from the mastery of the material environment by a race too selfish and superficial to determine the purpose its triumphs shall be applied. Mankind may wring her secrets from nature, and use their knowledge to destroy themselves..." (p. 279)

Reduction to mathematics follows a long tradition which began with Pythagoras:

> Curiously enough it was music that provided the clue. They [Pythagorean philosophers] reflected on the fact that the differences between musical notes from a single vibrating string depend on the length of the string. There is a simple mathematical relationship between them; the shorter the string the higher the note. Here then was a difference in quality which could be accounted for by a difference in quantity. It is not too much of an exaggeration to say that in this mathematical discovery lay the seeds of all future science. If the ultimate nature of things depends on mathematical relationships, then it follows that the world as perceived by our senses must be logical and intelligible as mathematics (Habgood 2002: 6–7).

Ever since, mathematics has tended to set the benchmark for science. Galileo boosted the tradition with his injunction "measure what can be measured, and make measurable what cannot be measured", for to him the book of nature was written in the language of mathematics (Gaarder 1996: 203). And Descartes believed that only quantitative properties can define an outer reality, an idea which Locke took up with his concept of objective 'primary qualities' such as extension, weight, motion and number. In his essay 'Beliefs' Aldous Huxley pointed out that the scientist selects "from the whole of experience only those elements which can be weighed, measured, numbered, or which lend themselves in any other way to mathematical treatment" (Peat 1996: 239).

Countability, however, ignores the idiosyncratic, the context-dependent, the individual and the singular. In Western science

> what is considered to be pre-eminent about the universe could perhaps be classified as the general, the abstract, the repeatable, the context-independent, and the all-embracing. By contrast the individual, the idiosyncratic, and the singular event are considered to be of less importance, or as being particular and superficial cases of something deeper and more embracing (p. 255).

As a consequence, some fields of knowledge lend themselves to mathematical and numerical treatments more than others. They are useful for astronomy and particle physics, where the forces and "objects" under consideration fit mathematical definitions very precisely. Indeed, some concepts in these fields are purely mathematical constructs, for example the properties of quark – charm, colour and strangeness. But mathematics is less useful for complex phenomena, like those found in biology, where each organism is unique, and changes irreversibly from moment to moment (Mayr 1988, quoted in Horgan 1998: 203).

A fundamental weakness with mathematical reductionsim, according to Oreskes, Blitz, and Frechette, is that the only mathematical propositions that can be verified are those dealing with pure logic and pure mathematics. $2 + 2 = 4$ is an analytic statement, true by definition and conventional agreement, not because it matches an external reality. It therefore becomes problematic to attempt to use numerical models to measure nature, and ecological crises such as resource depletion and global warming: "verification and validation of numerical models of natural systems is impossible." Natural systems are always open, so our knowledge of them is incomplete, approximate and factors out the unknown and unmeasurable. These mathematical models might be thought of as a work of fiction (Oreskes, Belitz, & Frechette 1994, quoted in Horgan 1998: 202–203).

8.4.1   Feyerabend, Prigogine and reductionism

Prigogine's chaos theory represents a reaction to a mathematical reductionism. In fact Prigogine tends to want to take physics in an opposite direction, instead of explaining it in terms of mathematics to ally it to biology. "What we have to do is to include evolutionary patterns in our descriptions. What we need is a Darwinian view of physics, a biological view of physics … You cannot on the one side believe you are part of an automaton and on the other hand believe in humanism" (Horgan 1998: 218). But Prigogine, perhaps, does not go far enough, even though his chaos theory somehow chimes with the relativism and uncertainty of modern thought.

We might think of a hierarchy of academic disciplines investigating different kinds of reality, (whether one includes theology in the hierarchy is a matter of belief):

(theology)
philosophy
arts and humanities
social sciences
economics
psychology
biology
chemistry
physics
mathematics

Any attempts to explain, metaphorically, one level in the hierarchy in terms of another is limited and represents some kind of distortion, because each level is to an extent independent. "At each stage entirely new laws, concepts and generalisations are necessary, requiring inspiration and creativity to just as great a degree as in the previous one ... Psychology is not applied biology, nor is biology applied chemistry" (Anderson 1972: 393).

One of the fiercest critics of reductionism was Feyerabend. Though he didn't live long enough to write the book he planned, entitled *The Conquest of Abundance*, he hoped to show that all human enterprise, in an attempt to make sense of reality, reduces its abundance. For purposes of survival our perceptual systems cut down abundance and so do academic disciplines such as religion, science, politics and philosophy. Any discipline's construction or representation of reality is inadequate, not to say presumptuous:

> You think that this one-day fly, this little bit of nothing, a human being – according to today's cosmology! – can figure it all out? This to me seems so crazy! It cannot possibly be true! What they figured out is one particular response to their actions, and this response gives this universe, and the reality that is behind this is laughing "Ha! Ha! They think they have found me out!"

For Feyerabend, reductionsism leads to a kind of modern cultural totalitarianism, not to say, fascism, which is far from laughable:

> I say that Auschwitz is an extreme manifestation of an attitude that still thrives in our midst. It shows itself in the treatment of minorities in industrial democracies; in education, education to a humanitarian point of view included, which most of the time consists in turning wonderful young people into colorless and self-righteous copies of their teachers; it becomes manifest in the nuclear threat, the constant increase in the number and power of deadly weapons and the readiness of some so-called patriots to start a war compared with which the holocaust will shrink into insignificance. It shows itself in the killing of nature and of "primitive" cultures with never a thought for those thus deprived of meaning for their lives; in the colossal conceit of our intellectuals, their belief that they know precisely what humanity needs and their relentless efforts to recreate people in their own sorry image; in the infantile megalomania of some of our physicians who blackmail their patients with fear, mutilate them and then persecute them with large bills; in

the lack of feeling of many so-called searchers for truth who systematically torture animals, study their discomfort and receive prizes for their cruelty. As far as I am concerned there exists no difference between the henchmen of Auschwitz and these "benefactors of mankind" (Feyerabend 1987: 309).

Besides their social consequences the effects of reductionism can be seen in the psychology of the individual. The division of labour which Darwin himself practised, devoting himself single-mindedly to his biological theories and researches, produces the antithesis of the Renaissance Man, or the Faustian generalist. Darwin laments that as a schoolboy and up to the age of thirty he took intense delight in poetry, Shakespeare, visual art and music

> but now for many years I cannot endure to read a line of poetry: I have tried lately to read Shakespeare, and found it so intolerably dull that it nauseated me. I have also lost almost any taste for pictures or music … my mind seems to have become a machine for grinding general laws out of large collections of fact … The loss of these talents is a loss of happiness, and may possibly be injurious to the intellect, and more probably to the moral character, by enfeebling the emotional part of our nature (Darwin 1958, quoted in Shumacher 1973/1999: 76).

8.4.2 Experiential cognitive science as reductionism

An important question is to what extent modern cognitive science and cognitive linguistics, and Lakoff's cognitive theory of metaphor located within it, represents a form of reductionism. The mere fact that Lakoff calls it "*The* Contemporary Theory of Metaphor" might already make us suspicious. This theory confines itself largely to the cognitive effects of metaphor, ignoring its textual, interpersonal or emotional effects (in contrast to Berggren 1962, MacCormac 1990, Goatly 1997), and concentrates on conventional rather than original metaphors.

Some grand celebrations of the scope of a biologically-based cognitive science and linguistics are also disquieting. Here is Langacker, prophesying the emergence of a unifying theory:

> As we enter the last decade of the twentieth century, one can see emerging in many disciplines – linguistics, psychology, cognitive science, semiotics, anthropology, computer science, artificial intelligence, philosophy, neuroscience, and others – a constellation of ideas, outlooks, methods and empirical findings that seem on the verge of coalescing to form a coherent, comprehensive, and biologically natural conception of language and mind (Langacker 1991: 538–9).

More specifically Grady makes tremendous claims about metaphor theory:

> The concepts that are linked by primary metaphor are ones that relate in meaningful ways to our goals and our actions in the world. These findings lend additional detail and substance to the general understanding of cognition as a tool

well-adapted to helping us survive in the physical world: our loftiest intellectual constructs are ultimately based on our most basic responses to our immediate environment (Grady 1997: 135).

There is a strong tendency for some researchers in cognitive metaphor theory such as Grady and Lakoff, with their notion that all or most thought can be reduced to experiential metaphors, to become, without being too dogmatic about it, quite possibly, reductionist. However, as we have seen, researchers like Kövecses are honourable exceptions to this tendency.

8.4.3 Literalisation, reductionism and ideology

At the beginning of chapter 1 I introduced the notion of "literalisation of vehicles (sources)", by which I meant the literal use of lexis or literal reference to a schema when the same lexis or schema is used or referred to metaphorically in the same context. My example was a playful one from advertising: "buying a new bathroom from Graham means you won't have to splash out too much". However, it is worth extending this notion of literalisation, to include the non-linguistic application of metaphors, so that it can be discussed in relation to reductionism and related to ideology. We have already seen that the literal and actual dominant technology, which is uppermost in the minds of scientists and technologists, has provided metaphors for nature, humans and society. The natural world may be seen as an industrial machine, animals may be automata, humans may be machines or computers, that is sophisticated information processors, economies may be clocks. A step further is when, instead of simply regarding these as metaphors we make them into impositives. Instead of being explanatory metaphors they become model-theoretic metaphors. The result of this is that humans may, for example, be thought of as nothing but information processing machines. This is a more radical form of literalisation, especially when it justifies, for example, treating humans as machines to further the cause of industrialisation and mass-production in factories according to a Fordist or Taylorist model. What was a metaphor is turned, through ideology, into a something literal by metonymy.

Such reductionist literalisations operate between various levels in the hierarchy of disciplines. We have seen extensively how through money social relations and economics have been reduced to mathematics or arithmetic. Chaos theory within physics has become a model for society and economics. Brain chemistry has attempted to explain psychology. Mechanics, as part of physics, has tried to turn nature into an industrial machine.

8.4.4 A less-reductionist model of discourse

If we are ourselves to avoid reductionism, any model we make of discourse and language, and metaphors within it, must be as inclusive as possible. In fact, we might attempt to treat language and discourse and their metaphors as part of a complex system, which is context dependent, open, non-linear and adaptive. (For a useful summary of complex systems see Cameron 2003: 40–55). This is how we saw *Gaia* in chapter 4, as a complex biological-chemical-physical system, where one part is always seen as interacting with the other parts of the whole which are its context, as well as being open to the free-energy given by the sun, which changes in a non-linear, i.e. unpredictable, way, and which adapts in order to preserve some kind of homeostasis. The following diagram (Figure 12) is a sketch representing three essential dimensions that I feel need to be taken into account for anything resembling a theory of language and discourse. (I have tried to make some connections between Leech/Popper's 4 Worlds of Knowledge 4.3.3, Table 16). Various linguistic schools and theories have emphasised one of the lines of the triangle, at the expense of the others. Chomsky (and even more so Pinker) might be seen as emphasising the base line of the triangle, by insisting on the genetically-inherited innate language capacity, presumably located in the brain. Michael Halliday might be thought of as emphasising the society and culture relationship with language and discourse, for language is a social semiotic, and discourse is encountered in discourse types or genres which are determined by culture and ideology. Psycholinguists, and pragmaticians such as Grice and Sperber and Wilson emphasise the psychology line, seeing communication as inferential and a matter of making manifest evidence for and hypothesising intended meanings and effects.

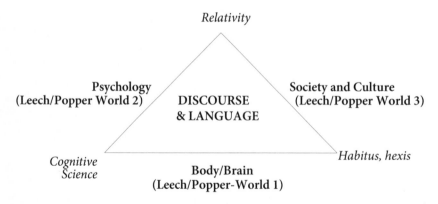

Figure 12. A model of language, discourse, mind, body and culture

Much could be written to illustrate these different approaches. What is of interest to me, in drawing this book to a close, is the relation of our exploration of metaphor themes to this diagram. Metaphor theory has, since the 1980's, been heavily biased towards Cognitive Science, which mediates between Body/Brain and Psychology, but through lexicalised metaphors to be found within the triangle. The main purpose of this book, pursuing a trend already manifest in Kövecses (2005), has been to show the equally important societal and cultural determinations and dependencies behind our metaphor themes. As a shorthand I have labelled the mediating factor here Relativity, capturing Whorfian notions of the influence of society and culture via language on thought (see chapter 1). Some of our "existential" metaphor themes might be thought to originate in Society and Culture and pass through the Body before reaching Psychology. But others, such as TIME IS MONEY/COMMODITY would appear to go more directly from Society and Culture to Psychology. Both pass through the triangle of language and discourse as metaphors discoursally instantiatied and/or conventionalised in lexis, and grammar (chapter 7). The other corner of the triangle I have labelled "Habitus/Hexis", terms from Bourdieu (see 2.7 and 6.8). Language and discourse, within the triangle, are a path by which our bodies are disciplined, as for example in the shapes and movements our vocal apparatus takes in producing the sounds of our language, language which may or may not be metaphorical. But society uses metaphor themes to discipline our bodies, for example by imposing clock and industrial time on the factory or office worker (chapter 2) or economic virtues which, by equating well-being or quality of life with wealth, discipline us to be frugal and hard-working. While these pathways through the model, and the labels of the corners, emphasise the social and bodily constraints on (body) thought, as is perhaps understandable in an ideological analysis, pathways in the opposite originating in psychology should not be underestimated. Individuals do express their thoughts in speech acts and thereby enter into dialogue with society, just as they make psychological decisions which result in physical actions. Subject positioning both allows action, dissent and resistance, while working within or against the constraints of ideology, language/metaphor and social institutions.

8.5 Envoi: a meditation on incarnation

My book ends on a poetical and theological note, an attempt, perhaps, to link two non-adjacent levels in a hierarchy, biology and theology. Whether one believes in God and Incarnation in a literal sense perhaps does not matter, for incarnation can have a symbolic and poetic meaning.

One meaning is that goodness or morality (truth) involves all parts of our lives and social practice, just as our bodies do. God becomes human. One of the main thrusts of Tawney's book *Religion and the Rise of Capitalism* is the notion that morality (God) has become increasingly remote from our social and economic lives, as religion has retreated and limited its scope. In 16th and 17th century England and Holland

> the theory of a hierarchy of values embracing all human interests and activities in a system of which the apex is religion, is replaced by the conception of separate and parallel compartments between which a due balance should be maintained, but which have no vital connection with each other (Tawney 1926/1938: 22).

The social philosophy of Christianity from medieval times into the reform era and even early 17th century held that, at least in theory, all economic activity should be related to a moral end. Economic appetites have their place in human life, but like other natural appetites, when they are "flattered and pampered and overfed, bring ruin to the soul and confusion to society" (p. 279). The economic philosophers we discussed earlier, by contrast, helped "to found a science of society upon the assumption that the appetite for economic gain is a constant and measurable force, to be accepted, like other natural forces, as an inevitable and self-evident *datum*" (p. 48).

Tawney deplores the fact that for the modern society of the 20th century "the attainment of material riches is the supreme object of human endeavour and the final criterion of human success". Religion, or Christianity, and through it human wisdom and well-being has thereby been marginalized and fatally undermined.

> Compromise is as impossible between the Church of Christ and the idolatry of wealth, which is the practical religion of capitalist societies, as it was between the Church and the State idolatry of the Roman Empire … a civilisation which has brought to the conquest of its material environment resources unknown in earlier ages, but which has not yet learned to master itself (p. 280).

Modern, post-Christian society has fallen for the temptations which Christ resisted: the economic and biological imperative to turn stones into bread, living by bread alone, like an animal; the exercise of unrestrained power over nature, the power to defy gravity by jumping off the temple roof and remaining unharmed; and then the unrestricted political power of ruling the whole world. The crucifixion, death and entombment of Christ is an acceptance of lack of power, lack of freedom, which paradoxically is the only guarantee of Godhead: the suffering servant washing his disciples' feet.

If a symbolic interpretation of incarnation sees it in terms of a morality that is intimately connected with our bodily practices, economic or otherwise, in society, a philosophical interpretation might see it in terms of the impossibility of truth without embodiment. This philosophical approach might, poetically at least, be a defence of the Lakoffian theory of the embodiment of thought through bodily and experientially-based metonymy and metaphor.

If we are to believe the experiential hypothesis, and Damasio who backs it up both by his theory and empirical evidence, our thinking and conceptualisation of the world is inextricably determined, we might even say limited, by our bodily experiences. It may not be fashionable to believe in absolute truth in this post-modern world, and this limitation would suggest that, even if such truth exists knowledge of it cannot be directly accessible to us, given our bodily limitations. However, I would like to explore the interface between the experientialist hypothesis and the theology of incarnation, touching on Hindu theology, but spending more time looking at Hegel's theology as analysed and developed by Hans Küng. Damasio would probably not be averse to this slant on the theory, for he says himself

> By connecting spiritual experiences to the neurobiology of feelings, my purpose is
> not to reduce the sublime to the mechanic and by so doing reduce its dignity. The
> purpose is to suggest that the sublimity of the spiritual is embodied in the sublim-
> ity of biology and that we can begin to understand the process in biological terms
> (Damasio 2003: 286).

Hinduism and Christianity both have strong traditions of incarnation – that God
can take human form. In Hinduism it is Vishnu who usually takes upon himself this
role. In both Hinduism and Christianity incarnation is something undertaken by God
in order to save the world.

> The restoration of the balance between good and evil is felt by Vishnu to be de-
> sirable, and he sends an incarnation of himself four times in Krita yuga, three in
> Treta yuga, two in Dwapara yuga and one in Kali yuga … A pattern develops in
> the myths … in which God enters the world in times of cosmic imbalance and
> manifests himself in visible form (Bassuk 1987: 16–17).

In the Ramayana myth Vishnu transforms himself into a human, Rama, to save the
world from the oppression of Ravana, the demon (p. 32). Jesus Christ, according to
Christian tradition, is sent into the world as a man to save humankind from the sin of
the first man, Adam.

The impulse for incarnation to bring about salvation is love for suffering humanity, and the incarnated one is the embodiment of love.

> At the core of the devotion to the God-man is the conviction that he is the em-
> bodiment of love, that he is the great Bhakta. His teaching is grounded in love,
> and it demonstrates God's unconditional love for man. As God graciously loves
> man, so man is to take counsel from this love and learn to love one another, and
> especially to love the God-man. Love is the essential lesson (p. 180).

Küng, quoting and paraphrasing Hegel, puts it in this rather mystical fashion:

> Love alone, which presupposes a fundamental equality and wills neither to domi-
> nate nor be dominated, can create true religion. For the gulf between subject and
> object can be closed neither by syntheses of theoretical reason which confront the
> subject as object, nor by practical reason whose subjectivity dissolves the object.
> Only in the love which unites God and man is neither God nor man a mere object,
> nor do man and God oppose each other as subject and object. On the contrary,
> in love the trans-objective unity of both is now experienced. "Religion is one with
> love. The beloved is not contrasted with us, he is one with our being. In him we
> see only ourselves, and yet again he is not identical with us. This is a wonder that
> we cannot grasp." (*N* 377) (Küng 1987: 117).

Despite some basic similarities the Hindu and Christian ideas of incarnation are
distinct. To start with, the nature of love differs. In Christianity God takes the initiative
in relationships with man.

> This is the image of the Divine shepherd going into the wilderness to seek a lost sheep, and this differs from the Hindu image of a flock of sheep needing guidance from the shepherd. Abba, the Christian God, loves to save; Baba, the Hindu Avatar, saves who love (Bassuk 1987: 191).

The consequence of this is a second difference: that the historicity of Jesus is important in a way in which historicity is not in Hinduism. For only by becoming a real human in an historical context can the Christian God claim to be going to the extreme point of seeking out the lost. Vishnu, by contrast, remains a mythic presence in nature. He represents the light, warmth, and energy of the sun.

> His navel is the place of birth and creation and the source of all existence. It is also the world's navel, the *axis mundi*. Being at the centre of the universe Vishnu can protect, preserve and sustain the forces of good. He is the waters, represented by the cosmic serpent, and he is the sky, symbolised by the garuda bird. He is a hierogamy, the divine mother and the heavenly father, the parents of all living creatures … In the Hindu religion the divine descent in the form of an Avatar is thought to come from the god Vishnu (pp. 21–22).

Partly as a corollary of these two differences, the point of incarnation seems to be different. A monist interpretation of Hinduism sees only one reality – that is spirit, and the material as an illusion. A dualist version sees matter as real but evolving towards the spiritual (p. 52). In either case the thrust in Hinduism seems to be away from the illusory world of matter towards a spiritual universe, and a consequent downplaying of historicity.

The Greek gods too were ahistorical and spiritual rather than flesh and blood, since they were distinguished by their immortality, incorruptibility (absence of decay) and divine paternity, as though they were disguised as humans. Against the background of this notion of godhood Jesus was not what you would expect a god to be. The early Greek interpreters of Jesus' message attempted to thrust a kind of dualism on him, to make him less human, as did John Wesley in 'Hark the Herald Angels Sing': "Veiled in flesh the Godhead see".

> The New Testament never explicitly states that Jesus has two natures. The idea … is a product of Greek philosophical thought based on categories of "substance" and "essence", and may well be an outgrowth of a two-fold description of Jesus, one as human and the other as divine (p. 178).

The Greek influence on early Christian doctrine can be seen in the way the nature of God was conceptualized: invisible, imperishable, untouchable, unbegotten, immutable, timeless, and impassible. Jesus Christ therefore had a double nature, in step with the dualism of Platonism: measurable/immeasurable, comprehensible/incomprehensible, circumscribed/uncircumscribed, finite/infinite (Küng 1987: 439).

Even the notion of the soul may have been a Greek idea, rather out of step with the teaching of the gospels. The bodily resurrection of Christ, rather than the survival of some spiritual presence, was obviously an important fact for the early Christians.

And Christ himself seems to have insisted that the distinction between soul and body was doubtful – when healing a crippled man he claims an equivalence in saying to him "your sins are forgiven" or "take up your bed and walk": the body and the soul are, if not one and the same, intimately connected.

In his interpretation of the Incarnation Hegel takes as his text the beginning of St. John's gospel: "The Word was made flesh and dwelt among us; and we beheld his glory, as of the only begotten of the Father, full of grace and truth" (p. 387). Here he rejects the dualism associated with Greek and Hindu ideas of incarnation, and also rejects the Kantian division between rationality and sensual experience (p. 89), in a way quite in tune with Damasio and Lakoff. Firstly, in order to be understood, God's truth has to be expressed in human form, which leads him to his first rejection of Kant "for love has an intense need of a face and loses heart before the 'physiognomically' inconceivable, before what is too 'pure' to be able to assume a shape or become flesh … But what if God always needs vehicles to be able to be 'real' for man?" (p. 88).

In fact, secondly, Hegel sees in the dialectic of grace, as manifest in the incarnation and death of Christ, the reconciliation of such Kantian antitheses. His theology is

> a philosophy which takes the unity of God and man seriously from the outset. Consequently we have here a philosophy which transcends the antithesis of intellect and feeling, reason and faith, philosophy and theology, rationalism and irrationalism, natural and positive religion, and heteronomy and autonomy. It is thus a philosophy at the very summit of its age, a philosophy which has irrevocably surpassed both enlightened rationalism, which would resolve everything historical in reason, and irrational romanticism, which would reduce the whole of religion to immediate feeling … (pp. 352–3).

In the case of the incarnation, life and death of Jesus, Hegel (according to Küng) sees many more specific antitheses dialectically resolved:

> God discloses his spirituality confined in the flesh, his vastness in limitation, his eternity in temporality, his omnipresence in being here, his immutability in growth, his infinity in privation, and his omniscience in silence. He reveals his omnipotence hidden in powerlessness, his simplicity in being poured out, his perfection in suffering, his righteousness in humiliation, indeed his holiness in the curse of sin, truth in condemnation, wisdom in foolishness, and life in death (p. 450).

The key idea in Hegel, and the one most important for us, is that God, the ultimate truth, only realises himself as God through incarnation and the experience of life and death, that he is somehow otherwise incomplete until he is made perfect through suffering. "While it is true that God displays his humanity and fellow humanity in humanity, he does not thereby reveal his non-divinity but rather the deepest divinity of his Godhead" (p. 450). Speaking of Christ's death Hegel says:

> This death is love itself, and in it we contemplate absolute love. It is the identity of the divine and human, that God is at home in the human and finite, and that this finite

is itself in this death a determination of God. Through this death God reconciled the world and eternally reconciles himself with himself (XIV: 166) (pp. 370–371).

The incarnation and loving death of God-Christ represents a revolutionary development from Judaism, from a Strict Father to a Nurturant Parent model of God (Lakoff, 1996: ch.14).

In insisting that Word can become Flesh, indeed, that without becoming flesh it is not truly word at all, Hegel's ideas on the incarnation would seem to be in line with Lakoff's experientialist philosophy. All our thought is embodied, so that all truth is embodied, and this is not a limitation, indeed it is a necessity, for without the flesh there is no idea or possibility of thought or understanding (Balkin 1998: 140). It would also seem to represent a kind of dialectical synthesis between objectivism and subjectivism, one that Lakoff saw in experientialism:

> A concretely thought philosophy of religion is, in the inter-relation of subjectivity and objectivity, a unifying, quintessentially divine-human philosophy: Just as God is also the finite, even so I am the infinite; God returns into himself in the ego as in that which cancels its own finitude, and it is only as this return that he is God. "*Without the world God is not God*" (XII: 150) (Küng 1987: 352–3).

If we take Hegel's philosophy seriously, or indeed Christianity seriously, then we have to recognize that it insists on universality and is against moral relativism (Lakoff 1996: 376). If the truth of the word comes in bodily form, even to the extent of death, it does so as a guarantee of its universal application to all cultures and all humans: so that being Jew or Greek, male or female, slave or free makes no distinction. The racially distinguished body of Linnaeus and other racial theory gives way to this universal body of the incarnation.

However, mystically, and paradoxically, God-Man becomes infinite by his finiteness, transcendent by his immanence. Simultaneously "I am what is and I am what is not". Unknowable even as knowledge incarnate. True to experience, but beyond experience. Such is the nature of metaphor or any model of reality.

Dionysius the Pseudo-Areopagite argued that to see God directly is to see nothing at all. As Feyerabend said: "God is emanations, you know? And they come down and become more and more material. And down, down at the last emanation, you can see a little trace of it and guess at it" (Feyerabend 1987: 309). Or in the words of the unknown author of the medieval *Cloud of Unknowing*:

> And the whiles that a soule is wonyng [dwelling] in this deedly [deadly] flesche, it schal evermore se and fele this combros [cumbrous] cloude of unknowyng bitwix him and God (chapter 28).

> For have a man never so moche [much] goostly [spiritual] understondyng in knowyng of alle maad [created] goostly thinges, yit [yet] may he never bi the werk of his understondyng com to the knowyng of an unmaad goostly thing, the whiche is nought bot God. Bot by the failyng it may; for whi [because] that thing that it failith in is nothyng elles bot only God. And therfore it was that Seynte

Denis seyde: "The most goodly knowyng of God is that, the whiche is knowyn bi unknowyng" (chapter 70).

This derknes and this cloude is, howsoever thou dost, bitwix thee and thi God, and letteth [prevents] thee that thou maist not see Him cleerly by light of understonding in thi reson, ne fele Him in swetnes of love in thin [your] affeccion. And therfore schap thee [prepare yourself] to bide in this derknes as longe as thou maist, evermore criing after Him that thou lovest; for yif [if] ever schalt thou fele Him or see Him, as it may be here, it behoveth [is necessary] alweis be in this cloude and in this derknes (chapter 3).

Than wil He sumtyme paraventure [perhaps] seend oute a beme of goostly [spiritual] light, peersyng [piercing] this cloude of unknowing that is bitwix thee and Hym, and schewe thee sum of His priveté [secrets], the whiche man may not, ne kan not, speke. Than schalt thou fele thine affeccion enflaumid with the fiire of His love, fer [far] more then I kan telle thee, or may, or wile [will], at this tyme. For of that werke that fallith to only God [belongs to God alone] dar I not take apon [upon] me to speke with my blabryng fleschely tonge (chapter 26).

Less poetically, Balkin has argued strongly that for CDA to be a valid enterprise it needs transcendental values in order to measure social practice against standards of truth and justice. Echoing the sense of the inadequacy of the immanent and the emotional longing for the unrealisable transcendent he defines a transcendent value as among other things:

> A value that can never be perfectly realised and against which all concrete articulations and exemplifications remain imperfect or incomplete…
> A value that appears to us as a demand or a longing. A transcendent value seems to call out to us to enact it in our culture and institutions. Our sense of justice seems to demand that we correct injustices when we recognise them; our value of truth seems to demand that we correct falsehood. (Balkin 1998: 144)

> The great irony here is that our ability to understand justice stems from our situatedness and our finitude. Our life experiences are the raw materials from which we make sense of the normative demands of life. Without them we cannot understand anything at all … This finitude, this historicity, this limitation, is what makes the transcendent appear to us as transcendent – beyond our grasp and full comprehension (pp. 158–9).

8.6 Summary and conclusion

The earlier chapters of this book, especially, 2, 3, and 5, have, I hope, shown how the metaphors we think with are realised non-linguistically in many aspects of contemporary life: building tall, levels of obesity, industrialisation, use of time, travelling fast, urbanisation, racial categorisation and exclusion, medical practice, sexual behaviour, militarisation, evaluation of quality by quantity, commodification of nature, treatment of animals, education and the concept of progress. Chapter 4 considered human identity in relation to the statement "Humans are animals", its status as metaphor or otherwise, and the differing possible grounds for classification or comparison. Chapter 7 showed how the conceptualisation of humans and nature constructed by the "literal" grammar of English was implicated in nature's exploitation and destruction and investigated grammatical metaphor and the "metaphor" of the Blackfoot language as means of mitigating or undermining these harmful conceptualisations. Chapters 6, 7 and 8 posed the question to what extent the metaphor themes driving this thought and behaviour are ideological constructs, dependent upon specific historical and cultural circumstances, and to what extent they are determined by universal bodily experiences. Chapter 6 gave convincing evidence that processes intimately associated with the body, such as emotion, or something like it, have a general tendency to depend upon the metonymies of experience as a basis for metaphorical development, though even here cultural factors have modified and differentiated the specific metaphorical conceptions in different languages. Chapter 8 gave exhaustive evidence of how many of the most important ideological metaphor themes, those which value wealth, competition, possessions, time, even if they had their origins within bodily experience, grew up and became dominant in a particular historical and cultural context. I even suggested that *The* Contemporary Theory of Metaphor might have had some of its ideological roots in this period.

We have seen the dangers of reductionism, especially of humans to animals, machines and commodities. Any categorisation and any metaphor reduces, by highlighting some features of experience at the expense of others. As Cameron reminds us, metaphor may have negative effects on thinking by providing a false sense of understanding and excluding alternative conceptualisation, or may structure the Target domain in ways which are too simple or too partial (Cameron 2003: 39). Metaphors, moreover, especially if one accepts the anthropic principle and uncertainty principle, have a tendency to form "regimes of truth" to create a (model of) reality – "thinking makes it so". We therefore need a variety of metaphors, just as we need a variety of species and languages to survive. Or, perhaps even more, we need a suspicion about all metaphors, all language and all knowledge, if we are to be open to the realities beyond it. If we forget that metaphors for humans (Gods/truth) are only metaphors we become guilty of a dangerous reductionism with fatal ideological implications. Might we attempt to clear our brains of the ideologies that work hand in hand with metaphor to tell us the totality of reality is knowable? To wash the brain with the merciful rain of the cloud of unknowing?

As the author of *The Cloud of Unknowing* might say: enough of my "blabbering *fleshly* tongue".

Bibliography

"A Tower to Reclaim the NY Skyline." *South China Morning Post* 20/12/2003: A1.

Acheson, D. 1987. *Present at the Creation: My Years in the State Department.* New York: Norton.

"Adversary System." *Wikipedia* http://en.wikipedia.org/wiki/Adversary system.

Ahrens, K., Liu, H-L., Lee, C-Y., Gong, S-P., Fang, S-Y., and Hsu, Y-Y. 2007. Functional MRI of conventional and anomalous metaphors in Mandarin Chinese, *Brain and Language,* 100(2): 163–171.

Alberts, J. and Decsy, G.J. 1990. "Terms of endearment." *Developmental Psychobiology* 23: 569–584.

An Urbanizing World: Global Report on Human Settlements 1996. UN Centre for Human Settlements (Habitat).

Ananthaswamy, A. 2003. "Has this chimp taught himself to talk?" *New Scientist* 14/1/2003: 12–13.

Anderson, C.A. 2001. "Heat and violence." *Current Directions in Psychological Science* 10: 33–38.

Anderson, L. 1999. *Genetic Engineering, Food and Our Environment.* Devon, England: Green Books.

Anderson, P. 1972. "More is Different." *Science* 177 (4047): 393–396.

Argyle, M. 1988. *Bodily Communication.* Madison Connecticut: International Universities Press.

Austin, J.L. 1962. *How to Do Things with Words.* Oxford: Clarendon Press.

Austin, J.L. 1979. *Philosophical Papers* (3rd edition). Oxford: Clarendon Press.

Baier, A. 1998. "David Hume." In *Routledge Encyclopedia of Philosophy, vol 4.* E. Craig (ed.), 543–562.

Balkin, J.M. 1998. *Cultural Software.* New Haven and London: Yale University Press.

Barcelona, A. (ed.). 2000a. *Metaphor and Metonymy at the Crossroads.* New York, Berlin: Mouton de Gruyter.

Barcelona, A. 2000b. "Introduction; the cognitive theory of metaphor and metonymy." In *Metaphor and Metonymy at the Crossroads,* A. Barcelona (ed.), 1–28. New York, Berlin: Mouton de Gruyter.

Barcelona, A. 2000c. "On the plausibility of claiming a metonymic motivation for conceptual metaphor." In *Metaphor and Metonymy at the Crossroads,* A. Barcelona (ed.), 31–58. New York, Berlin: Mouton de Gruyter.

Bassuk, D. E. 1987. *Incarnation in Hinduism and Christianity.* London: Macmillan.

Bateson, G. 1975. *Steps to an Ecology of Mind.* New York: Ballantine.

Baxter, R. 1678. *A Christian Directory.* London: Nevil Simmons.

Beck, U. 1992. *Risk Society: Towards a New Modernity,* Mark Ritter (trans.). London: Sage.

Bekar, C., and Lipsey, R.G. 2001. "Science, Institutions and the Industrial Revolution." retrieved from http://www.sfu.ca/~rlipsey/davis.

Berggren, D. 1962. "The use and abuse of metaphor." *Review of Metaphysics* 16. no.2: 237–258.

Black, M. 1962. *Models and Metaphors.* Ithaca New York: Cornell University Press.

Blokland, M., Braadbaart, O. and Schwartz, K. (eds.). 1999. *Private Business, Public Owners – Government Shareholdings in Water Enterprises*. Ministry of Housing, Spatial Planning and the Environment of the Netherlands.

Blumberg, M. 2002. *Body Heat*. Cambridge Mass.: Harvard University Press.

Bodde, D. 1953. "Harmony and conflict in Chinese philosophy." In *Studies in Chinese Thought*, Arthur F. Wright (ed.), 19–80. Chicago: American Anthropological Association.

Boderman, A., Freed, D.W. and Kinnucan, M.T. 1972. "Touch me, like me: testing an encounter group assumption." *Journal of Applied Behavioural Science* 8: 527–33.

Bohm, D. 1980. *Wholeness and the Implicate Order*. London: Routledge.

Bolinger, D. 1977. *Meaning and Form*. Harlow: Longman.

Bourdieu, P. 1990. *The Logic of Practice*. Cambridge UK: Polity Press.

Bourdieu, P. 1991. *Language and Symbolic Power*. John B Thompson (ed.), Gino Raymond and Matthew Adamson (trans.). Cambridge UK: Polity Press.

Bowler, P.J. 1990. *Charles Darwin: The Man and his Influence*. Oxford: Blackwell.

Boyd, R. and Richerson, P.J. 1985. *Culture and the Evolutionary Process*. Chicago: University of Chicago Press.

Brown, L. 1993. *State of the World*. The Worldwatch Institute/Norton: New York.

Brugman, C. 1990. "What is the invariance hypothesis?" *Cognitive Linguistics* 1–2: 257–266.

Buchsbaum, R. and Buchsbaum, M. 1957. *Basic Ecology*. Pittsburgh: Boxwood.

Burgoon, J. and Saine, T. 1978. *The Unspoken Dialogue*. Boston: Houghton Mifflin.

Bury, J.B. 1920. *The Idea of Progress: An Inquiry into its Origin and Growth*. Basingstoke: Macmillan.

Cameron, L. 2003. *Metaphor in Educational Discourse*. London: Continuum.

Capra, F. 1996. *The Web of Life*. London: HarperCollins.

Capra, F. n.d. "The immune system—our second brain." *Resurgence* 181. http://www. resurgence. org/resurgence/articles/capra.htm.

Causley, C. 1973. "Death of a Poet." In *Oxford Book of Twentieth Century English Verse*, Philip Larkin (ed.), 495. Oxford: Oxford University Press.

Chan, Kwok-bun. 2003. "The importance of sympathy." *South China Morning Post* 20/12/2003: A13.

Chang, J. 1991. *Wild Swans*. New York: Simon and Schuster.

Charteris-Black, J. 2005. *Politicians and Rhetoric: The Persuasive Power of Metaphor*. Basingstoke: Palgrave-Macmillan.

Chase-Dunn, C. and Gills, B. 2003. "Understanding waves of globalization and resistance in the capitalist world (-) system." Paper presented at the *Conference on Critical Globalization Studies*, University of California, Santa Barbara, May 2–4, 2003.

Chilton, P. 1996. *Security Metaphors: Cold War Discourse from Containment to Common House*. New York: Peter Lang.

Chun, L. 1997. *Bodily Metaphors in Mandarin*. Unpublished ms., Australian National University, Canberra.

Coghlan, A. and Cohen, P. 2002. "Of mice and men." *New Scientist* 7/12/2002: 12–13.

Cooper, M. 2002. "Life 2.0." *New Scientist* 8/6/2002: 30–32.

Crick, F. 1994. *The Astonishing Hypothesis*. New York: Scribner.

Crisp, P.G. 1993. "Western and Chinese eschatologies: challenging postmodernist theory." *Mosaic* 26/2: 1–20.

Critser, G. 2003. *Fat Land: How Americans Became the Fattest People in the World*. New York: Houghton Mifflin.

Cronon, W. 1991. *Nature's Metropolis: Chicago and the Great West*. New York: Norton.

Crowley, R. 1872. "The Way to Wealth." In *Select Works of Robert Crowley*, J. M. Cowper (ed.), 129–215. London: Trubner, Early English Text Society..

Crystal, D. 2000. *Language Death*. Cambridge: Cambridge University Press.

Damasio, A. 2003. *Looking For Spinoza*. London/NewYork: William Heinemann/Harcourt.

Darwin, C. 1872/1965. *The Expression of the Emotions in Man and Animals*. Chicago: Chicago University Press.

Darwin, C. 1859/1991. *The Origin of Species by means of Natural Selection.* New York: Prometheus Books.

Darwin, C. 1871/2004. *The Descent of Man*. Harmondsworth; Penguin.

Darwin, C. 1958. *Autobiography,* N. Barlow (ed.). London: Collins.

Davidse, K. 1992 "Transitivity/ergativity: the Janus-headed grammar of actions and events." In *Advances in Systemic Linguistics; recent theory and practice,* M. Davies and L. Ravelli (eds.), 105–166. London: Pinter.

Dawkins, R. 1990. *The Selfish Gene* (2nd edition). Oxford: Oxford University Press.

De Botton, A. 2004. *Status Anxiety.* London: Hamish Hamilton.

Dearden, R.F. 1984. "Balance and coherence: some curricular principles in recent reports." In *Theory and Practice in Education,* R.F.Dearden, 59–69. London: Routledge.

Degler, C. 1991. *In Search of Human Nature: The Decline and Revival of Darwinism in American Social Thought.* New York: Oxford University Press.

Deignan, A. 1995. *Collins Cobuild English Guides vol.7: Metaphor.* London: HarperCollins.

Dennett, D. 2003. "Free will, but not as we know it." *New Scientist* 24/05/2003: 40.

Derewianka, B. 1995. *Language Development in the Transition from Childhood to Adolescence: The Role of Grammatical Metaphor.* Unpublished thesis, Macquarie University, Sydney.

Dillner, L. 2003. "Aaarrgghhhh!" *The Guardian.* October 14, 2003.

Dirven, R. 1995. "The construal of cause: the case of prepositions." In *Language and the Cognitive Construal of the World,* J.R. Taylor, and R.E. MacLaury (eds.), 95–118. New York, Berlin: Mouton de Gruyter.

Dyson, F. 1988. *Infinite in All Directions.* New York: Harper and Row.

Eagleton, T. 1991. *Ideology: An Introduction.* London: Verso.

Edelman, M. 1971. *Politics as Symbolic Action: Mass Arousal and Quiescence.* Chicago: Markham.

Eggins, S., Wignell, P. and Martin, J.R. 1993. "The discourse of history: Distancing the recoverable past." In *Register Analysis: Theory and Practice,* M. Ghadessy (ed.), 75–109. London: Pinter.

Ekman, P. 2000. *Emotions Revealed.* London: Weidenfeld and Nicholson.

Elliott, D.E., Urban, J., Argo, C. and Weinstock, J.V. 2000. "Does the failure to acquire helminthic parasites predispose to IBD?." FASEBJ 14: 1848–1855.

Ellwood, W. 2003 "The great privatisation grab." *New Internationalist* 355 http://www. newint. org/issue355/keynote.htm.

Faden, R. 2002. "Spare parts for the rich." *New Scientist* 19/10/2002: 27.

Fairclough, N. 1992. *Critical Language Awareness.* Harlow: Longman.

Fairclough, N. 2001. *Language and Power* (2nd edition). Harlow: Longman.

Fairclough, N. 2003. *Analysing Discourse.* London: Routledge.

Fairclough, N. and Wodak, R. 1997. "Critical discourse analysis." In *Discourse as Social Interaction,* T. Van Dijk (ed.), 258–284. London: Sage.

Feyerabend, P. 1987. *Farewell to Reason.* London: Verso.

Fielding-Hall, H. 1920. *The Soul of a People.* London: Macmillan.

Findings Of Facts, Conclusion Of Law And Judgment in ROSE *and* INASIO ALAFONSO, *Plaintiffs, vs.* IOSUA *and* ITA SAREP *et al., Defendants.* CA No. 80–92 Trial: September 12, 1994, decided: September 20, 1995.

Fisher, J. D., Rytting, M. and Heslin, R. 1975. "Hands touching hands: affective and evaluative effects of an interpersonal touch." *Sociometry* 39: 416–29.

Foucault, M. 1972. *The Archaeology of Knowledge and the Discourse of Language,* A.M Sheridan Smith (trans.). New York: Pantheon Books.

Foucualt, M. 1977. *Discipline and Punish.* London: Tavistock Press.

Foucault, M. 1980. *Power/Knowledge.* Brighton: Harvester.

Fowler, R. 1991. *Language in the News.* London: Routledge.

Franz, D.G. 1991. *Blackfoot Grammar.* Toronto: University of Toronto Press.

"From Adversarial to Aspirational" http://www.partnership-at-work.com/ezine_plus/pawpub/story216.shtml, //www.unions21.org.uk/.

Fromm, E. 1983. *To Be or to Have.* New York: Bantam.

Fuller, L. 1971. "Mediation: Its forms and functions." *Southern California Law Review* 44: 305–39.

Gaarder, J. 1996. *Sophie's World.* New York: Berkley Books.

Geeraerts, D. and Grondelaers, S. 1995. "Cultural traditions and metaphorical patterns." In *Language and the Cognitive Construal of the World,* J.R. Taylor and R.E. MacLaury (eds.), 153–179. New York, Berlin: Mouton de Gruyter.

Geertz, C. 1973. *The Interpretation of Cultures.* New York: Basic Books.

Gibbs, R. 1999. "Researching metaphor." In *Researching and Applying Metaphor,* L. Cameron, and G. Low (eds.), 29-47. Cambridge: Cambridge University Press.

Gibbs, R. and O'Brien, J. 1990. "Idioms and mental imagery." *Cognition* 36: 35–68.

Givon, T. 1984. *Syntax: A Functional Typological Introduction.* Amsterdam, Philadelphia: Benjamins.

Givon, T. 1993. *English Grammar: A Function-based Introduction.* Amsterdam, Philadelphia: Benjamins.

Gleick, J. 1999. *Faster: the Acceleration of Almost Everything.* New York: Vintage Press.

Goatly, A. 1997. *The Language of Metaphors.* London: Routledge.

Goatly, A. 2000. *Critical Reading and Writing.* London: Routledge.

Goatly, A. 2002a. "The representation of nature on the BBC World Service." *Text* 22.1: 1–27.

Goatly, A. 2002b. "Conflicting metaphors in the Hong Kong SAR educational reform proposals." *Metaphor and Symbol* 17.4: 263–294.

Goatly, A. 2004."Corpus linguistics, systemic-functional grammar and literary meaning: A critical analysis of *Harry Potter and the Philosopher's Stone." Ilha do Desterro* 46: 115–154.

Godrej, D. 2002. "Patents/KEYNOTE." *New Internationalist* 349.

Golding, W. 1964. *The Spire.* London: Faber.

Goodman, N. 1968. *Languages of Art: An Approach to a Theory of Symbols.* Indianapolis: Bobbs-Merrill.

Govier, T. 1999. *The Philosophy of Argument.* Newark News.: Vale Press

Grady, J.E. 1997. *Foundations of Meaning: Primary Metaphors and Primary Scenes.* Unpublished Ph. D dissertation, University of California, Berkeley.

Grady, J.E. 1999. "A typology of motivation for conceptual metaphor: correlation vs. resemblance." In *Metaphor in Cognitive Linguistics,* R. Gibbs, and G. Steen (eds.), 79–100. Amsterdam: John Benjamins.

Graham-Rowe, D. 2002a. "Designed for life: an interview with Rodney Brooks." *New Scientist* 01/06/02: 46–49.

Graham-Rowe, D. 2002b. "High-flyers are scourge of the skies." *New Scientist* 19/10/2002: 5–6.

Gramsci, A.1971. *Selections from the Prison Notebooks of Antonio Gramsci*, Louis Marks (trans.). New York: International Publishers.

Grant, M. 1916/1970. *The Passing of the Great Race*. Manchester New Hampshire: Ayer Co. Publishers.

Gribbin, J. 1994. *In the Beginning: The Birth of the Living Universe*. Harmondsworth: Penguin.

Gurevich, A. 1985. *Categories of Medieval Culture*. London: Routledge.

Haakonssen, K. 1998. "Adam Smith." In *Routledge Encyclopedia of Philosophy*, Edward Craig (ed.), vol. 8: 815–822. London: Routledge.

Habgood, J. 2002. *The Concept of Nature*. London: Darton, Longman and Todd.

Haidt, J. 2003. "The moral emotions." In *Handbook of Affective Sciences*, R. J. Davidson, K. R. Scherer, H. Hill Goldsmith (eds.), 852–870. Oxford: Oxford University Press.

Hales, J. 1549/1893. *A Discourse of the Common Weal of this Realm of England*, E. Lamond, and W. Cunningham (eds.). Cambridge: Cambridge University Press.

Hall, E.T. 1966. *The Hidden Dimension*. New York: Doubleday.

Hall, S. 2001. "Foucault: Power, knowledge and discourse." In *Discourse Theory and Practice*, M. Wetherell, S. Taylor and S.J. Yates (eds.), 72–81. London: Sage.

Halliday, M.A.K. 1985. *An Introduction to Functional Grammar*. London: Arnold.

Halliday, M.A.K. 1988. "On the language of physical science." In *Registers of Written English: Situational Factors and Linguistic Features*. M. Ghadessy (ed.), 162–178. London: Pinter.

Halliday, M.A.K. and Martin, J.R. 1993. *Writing Science: Literacy and Discursive Power*. London: Falmer Press.

Haraway, D. 1990. "A manifesto for cyborgs: Science, technology and socialist feminism in the 1980s." In *Feminism/Postmodernism*, L.J. Nicolson (ed.), 190–233. London: Routledge.

Haraway, D. 1991. *Simians, Cyborgs and Women: The Reinvention of Nature*. London: Free Association.

Harré, R. 1979. *Social Being*. Oxford: Blackwell.

Harré, R. Clarke, D.D. and De Carlo, N. 1985. *Motives and Mechanisms*. London: Methuen.

Hartley, L.P. 1958. *The Go-Between*. Harmondsworth: Penguin.

Harvey, D. 1996. *Justice, Nature and the Geography of Difference*. Cambridge Mass.: Oxford.

Hayduk, L.A. 1983. "The permeability of personal space: where we stand now." *Psychological Bulletin* 94: 293–335.

Heidegger, M. 1971. *Poetry, Language, Thought*. New York: Harper and Row.

Heine, B. 1997. *Possession: Cognitive Sources, Forces, and Grammaticalization*. Cambridge: Cambridge University Press.

Herbert, R. 2002 "Review of Steven Wise's *Drawing the Line: Science and the case for Animal Rights*." New Scientist 7/9/2002: 54.

Herman, C.P. 1990. "Pessimistic rumination and electoral defeat: a shorter but wider view." *Psychological Inquiry* 1.1: 64–65.

Hinde, R.A. 1997. "War: some psychological causes and consequences." *Interdisciplinary Science Reviews* 22: 229–45.

Hiraga, M. 1991. "Metaphors Japanese women live by." *Working Papers on Language, Gender and Sexism* 1.1: 38–57. AILA Commission on Language and Gender.

Hobbes, Thomas. 1651/1983. *Leviathan*, C.B. Macpherson (ed.). Harmondsworth: Penguin.

Hobbes, Thomas. 1651/1997. *Leviathan*, R.E. Flathman and D. Johnston (eds.). New York, London: Norton Critical Editions.

Hodge, R. and Kress, G. 1993. *Language as Ideology* (2nd edition). London: Routledge.

Horgan, J. 1998. *The End of Science*. London: Abacus

Horizon: "The Big Chill" 2003, BBC.

http: // www.mentalhealth.com/book/p40-sad.html Retrieved July 16th 2003.

http://oak.cats.ohiou.edu/~ad361896/anne/cease.html.

http://www.fao.org/docrep/W8440e/W8440e26.htm.

http://www.rapecrisis.co.uk/statistics.htm 1991 Rape Crisis Federation of England and Wales, Kate Painter.

http://www2.ucsc.edu/rape-prevention/statistics.html UCSC Rape Prevention Education.

Human Population: Fundamentals of Growth and Change. 2001. Population Reference Bureau Report (June 2001), Population Reference Bureau.

Hume, D. 1740/1969. *A Treatise of Human Nature.* Harmondsworth: Penguin.

Hutton, C. 2000. "Cultural and conceptual relativism, universalism and the politics of linguistics." In *Language and Ideology vol. 1,* R. Dirven, B. Hawkins and E. Sandicioglu (eds.), 277–296. Amsterdam: Benjamins.

Hwang, D.H. 1989. *M. Butterfly.* Harmondsworth: Penguin.

Isačenko, A.V. 1974. "On 'have' and 'be' languages." In *Slavic Forum: Essays in Linguistics and Literature,* M.S. Flier (ed.). New York, Berlin: Mouton de Gruyter.

Isinolaw Research Center, November 2003.Retrieved from http:// www.isinolaw.com/index2. jsp?LangID=0

Jackendoff, R. 1983. *Semantics and Cognition.* Cambridge, Mass.: MIT Press.

Jacob, M.C. 1997. *Scientific Culture and the Making of the Industrial West.* Oxford: Oxford University Press.

Jacobson, N.P. 1988. *The Heart of Buddhist Philosophy.* Carbondale and Edwardsville: Southern Illinois University Press.

Jakel, O.1995. "The metaphorical concept of mind." In *Language and the Cognitive Construal of the World,* J.R. Taylor, and R.E. MacLaury (eds.),197–229. New York, Berlin: Mouton de Gruyter.

Jakobson, R. 1990. "Two aspects of language and two types of aphasic disorder." In *On Language,* L. Waugh and M. Monville-Buston (eds.), 115–33. Cambridge Mass.: Harvard University Press.

Johnson, M. 1987. *The Body in the Mind.* London: University of Chicago Press.

Jones, N. 2002. "Gene therapy gets the body to attack cancer." *New Scientist* 21/12/2002: 10.

Jones, P.E. 2000. "Cognitive linguistics and the Marxist approach to ideology." In *Language and Ideology vol. 1,* R. Dirven, B. Hawkins and E. Sandicioglu (eds.), 227–252. Amsterdam: Benjamins.

Josephson, P.R. 2002. *Industrialised Nature: Brute-force Technology and the Transformation of the Natural World.* London: Shearwater Books.

Judge, T.A. and Cable, D.M. 2004. "The effect of physical height on workplace success and income: preliminary test of a theoretical model." *Journal of Applied Psychology* 89.3: 428–441.

Kaufmann, S. 1997. *The Origins of Order: Self-Organisation and Selection in Evolution.* Griffin, Washington D.C.: University Press of America.

Kövecses, Z. 1986. *Metaphors of Anger, Pride and Love: A Lexical Approach to the Structure of Concepts.* Amsterdam: Benjamins.

Kövecses, Z. 1990. *Emotion Concepts.* New York: Springer-Verlag.

Kövecses, Z. 1991. "Happiness: a definitional effort." *Metaphor and Symbol* 6.1: 29–46.

Kövecses, Z. 1995. "Anger: its language, conceptualisation and physiology in the light of cross-cultural evidence." In *Language and the Cognitive Construal of the World,* J.R. Taylor, and R.E. MacLaury (eds.), 181–196. New York, Berlin: Mouton de Gruyter.

Kövecses, Z. 2000a. *Metaphor and Emotion*. Cambridge: Cambridge University Press.

Kövecses, Z. 2000b. "The scope of metaphor." In *Metaphor and Metonymy at the Crossroads*, A. Barcelona (ed.), 79–92. New York, Berlin: Mouton de Gruyter.

Kövecses, Z. 2002. *Metaphor: A Practical Introduction*. Oxford: Oxford University Press.

Kövecses, Z. 2005. *Metaphor in Culture: Universality and Variation*. Cambridge: Cambridge University Press.

Kövecses, Z. and Radden, G. 1998. "Metonymy: developing a cognitive linguistic view." *Cognitive Linguistics* 9–1: 37–77.

Kuhn, T. S. 1993. "Metaphor in Science." In *Metaphor and Thought*, A. Ortony (ed.), 533–542. Cambridge, UK: Cambridge University Press.

Küng, H. 1987. *The Incarnation of God: an Introduction to Hegel's Theological Thought as a Prolegomena to a Future Christology*, J.R. Stephenson (trans.). New York: Crossroad.

Laclau, E. and Mouffe, C. 1985. *Hegemony and Socialist Strategy*. London: Verso.

Lakoff, G. 1987. *Women, Fire and Dangerous Things*. Chicago: University of Chicago Press.

Lakoff, G. 1993. "The contemporary theory of metaphor." In *Metaphor and Thought*, A. Ortony (ed.), 202–252. Cambridge: Cambridge University Press.

Lakoff, G. 1995. "Metaphor, Morality and Politics." Institute for Cultural Democracy.

Lakoff, G. 1996. *Moral Politics: What Conservatives Know that Liberals Don't*. Chicago and London: University of Chicago Press.

Lakoff, G. 2001. "Metaphors of terror." http://www.press.uchicago.edu/ News/911lakoff.html.

Lakoff, G. and Johnson, M. 1980. *Metaphors We Live By*. Chicago: University of Chicago Press.

Lakoff, G. and Johnson, M. 1999. *Philosophy in the Flesh*. New York: Basic Books.

Lakoff, G. and Turner, M. 1989. *More than Cool Reason: A Field Guide to Poetic Metaphor* Chicago: University of Chicago Press.

Laland, K.N. and Brown, G.R. 2002. *Sense and Nonsense: Evolutionary Perspectives on Human Behaviour*. Oxford: Oxford University Press.

Landes, D. 1983. *Revolution in Time*. Cambridge Mass.: Harvard University Press.

Langacker, R. W. 1991. *Foundations of Cognitive grammar, vol. 2: Descriptive Applications*. Stanford: Stanford University Press.

Laud, W. 1847. "Sermon on the fast day." In *The Works of William Laud*, W. Scott (ed.), vol. I: 132–33. Oxford: Library of Anglo-Catholic Theology.

Lauer, R. H. 1973. "Temporality and social change; the case study of 19th century China and Japan." *Sociological Quarterly* 14 Autumn 1973: 451–464.

Lee, R. 2000. "Core-periphery model." *Dictionary of Human Geography 4th Edition*, R.J. Johnston, D. Gregory, G. Bratt, M. Watts (eds.), 115-117, London: Routledge.

Leech, G.N. 1983. *Principles of Pragmatics*. Harlow: Longman.

Lemke, J.L. 1990. *Talking Science: Language, Learning and Values*. Norwood NJ: Ablex.

Leroy Little Bear and Ryan Heavy Head. 2004. "A conceptual anatomy of the Blackfoot word." *Revision: A Journal of Consciousness and Transformation* 26.3: 31–38.

Ling, K. 2003. *Colour Collocations in English and Chinese Idioms*. Hong Kong: Unpublished Final Year Project, Lingnan University, Department of English.

Lorenz, K. 1974. *On Aggression*, Marjorie Kerr Wilson (trans.). San Diego, California: Harcourt Brace and Co. Harvest Books.

Lovejoy, A. O. 1960. *The Great Chain of Being: The Study of the History of an Idea*. New York: Harper.

Lovelock, J. 1986 "Gaia: the world as living organism." *New Scientist* 18/12/86: 25–8.

Lovelock, J. 1988. *The Ages of Gaia*. Oxford: OUP.

Lutz, C. A. 1988. *Unnatural Emotions*. Chicago: University of Chicago Press.

MacCormac, E. R. 1990. *A Cognitive Theory of Metaphor*. London: MIT Press.

Mack, D. 1975. "Metaphoring as speech act: some happiness conditions for implicit similes and simple metaphors." *Poetics* 4: 221–256.

MacRobbie, A. 1991. *Feminism and Youth Culture: From Jackie to Just Seventeen*. Basingstoke: Macmillan.

Malthus, T.R. 1992. (f.p. 1798, 1806, 1817). *An Essay on the Principle of Population*, Donald Winch (ed.). Cambridge: Cambridge University Press.

Malynes, G. de. 1622. *Consuetudo vel Lex Mercatoria*. London: John Evelyn.

Marks, J. 2002. *What it Means to be 98% Chimpanzee*. Berkeley, Los Angeles, London: University of California Press.

Marriott, E. 2003 "Men and porn." *The Guardian* Saturday November 8, 2003.

Martel, Yann, 2002. *Life of Pi*. Edinburgh: Canongate.

Martín Morillas, J. M. 1997. "The cultural cognitive model: a programmatic application." In *Cognitive Linguistics in the Study of the English Language and Literature*, A. Barcelona (ed.), 53–64, English Monograph issue of *Cuadernos de Filologia Inglesa* 6:2.

Martin, E. 1992. "The end of the body." *American Ethnologist* 19, 121–40.

Marx, K. 1967. *Capital: A Critique of Political Economy*, S. Moore and E. Aveling (trans.). New York: International.

Master List of metaphors http://cogsci.berkeley.edu/lakoff/.

Matsuki, K. 1995. "Metaphors of anger in Japanese." In *Language and the Cognitive Construal of the World*, J.R. Taylor, and R.E. MacLaury (eds.),137–151. New York, Berlin: Mouton de Gruyter.

May, M. 2003 "When jeep meets jump jet." *New Scientist* 14/6/2003: 42.

Mayr, E. 1988. *Toward a New Philosophy of Biology*. Cambridge Mass.: Harvard University Press.

McGee, T. 2001. "Urbanization takes on new dimensions in Asia's population giants." *New Internationalist*, October 2001.

Mehan, H. 1997. "The discourse of the illegal immigration debate." *Discourse and Society* 8.2: 249–70.

Mehrabian, A. 1968. "Inference of attitudes from the posture, orientation and distance of a communicator." *Journal of Consulting and Clinical Psychology* 32: 296–308.

Metalude www.ln.edu.hk/lle/cwd/project01/web/home.html
    or http: //www.ln.edu.hk/lle/cwd03/lnproject_chi/home.html.

Mey, J. 2006. "Metaphors and activity." *Essays on Metaphor in Language and Thought*, special edition of *D.E.L.T.A.* vol.22: 45–66.

Midgeley, M. 1998. "Review of *The Biotech Century* by Jeremy Rifkin." *New Scientist*, vol.160. 31/10/98: 56.

Mithen, S. "Thoroughly mobile minds." *New Scientist* 17/5/2003: 40–41.

Mo, T. 1986. *An Insular Possession*. London: Chatto and Windus.

Morgenthau, H.J. 1973. *Politics among Nations* (6th edition). New York: Knopf.

Morris, D. 1967. *The Naked Ape*. New York: Dell.

Morris, D. 1971. *Intimate Behaviour*. London: Cape.

Mossner, E.C. 1969 "Introduction." In *A Treatise of Human Nature*, D. Hume, 7–28. Harmondsworth: Penguin.

Muir, E. 1965. *Collected Poems*. New York: Oxford University Press.

Murphy, P. 2000. *Practical Guide to Evidence* (7th edition). London and Oxford: Blackstone Press.

Musolff, A. 2004. *Metaphor and Political Discourse*. Basingstoke: Palgrave-MacMillan

Needham, J. 1969. "Time and eastern man." In *The Grand Titration – Science and Society in East and West,* J. Needham, 218–298. London: Allen and Unwin.

Newton, I. 1687. *Philosophiæ Naturalis Principia Mathematica.* London: Royal Society.

Novak, R. "Rough justice." *New Scientist* 7/6/2003.

Noveck, Iran A., Bianco, M. and Castry, A. 2001. "The costs and benefits of metaphor." *Metaphor and Symbol* 16(1–2): 109–121.

Office for National Statistics; General Register Office for Scotland; Northern Ireland Statistics and Research Agency 2005.Retrieved from http://www.statistics.gov.uk /cci/nugget. asp?id=170 31/10/2005

O'Halloran, K. 2003. *Critical Discourse Analysis and Language Cognition.* Edinburgh: Edinburgh University Press.

Oreskes, N., Belitz, K. and Frechette, K.S. 1994. "Verification, validation and confirmation of numerical models in the Earth Sciences." *Science* February 4, 1994: 641–646.

Orr, R.A. 1992. Slavo-Celtica. *Canadian Slavonic Papers* 34.3: 245–68.

Pagan-Westphal, S. 2002. "Your money or your life." *New Scientist* 13/7/2002: 29–33.

Paprotte, W. and Dirven, R. (eds) 1985. *The Ubiquity of Metaphor.* Amsterdam: Benjamins.

Patenting life: special report, *The Guardian,* 15 November 2000, with research by GeneWatch UK.

Patterson, M.L. 1968. "Spatial factors in social interaction." *Human Relations* 21: 351–61.

Peat, D. 1996. *Blackfoot Physics: A Journey into the Native American Universe.* London: Fourth Estate.

Peirce, C.S. 1958. *Collected Papers of Charles Sanders Peirce.* Cambridge Mass.: Harvard University Press.

Philips, H. 2002. "Not just a pretty face." *New Scientist* 27/2/2002: 41–43.

Pinker, S. 2003. *The Blank Slate.* Harmondsworth: Allen Lane, Penguin.

Pires de Oliveira, R. 2000. "An interview with George Lakoff." In *Language and Ideology vol.1,* R. Dirven, B. Hawkins and E. Sandicioglu (eds.), 23–47. Amsterdam: Benjamins.

Plutchik, R. 1980. *Emotion: A Psychoevolutionary Synthesis.* New York: Harper and Row.

Pope, M. 1985. "Shakespeare's medical imagination." In *Shakespeare Survey I* vol. 38, S. Wells (ed.), 175–186. Cambridge: Cambridge University Press.

Popper, K.R. 1972. *Objective Knowledge: An Evolutionary Approach.* Oxford: Clarendon Press.

Prigogine, I. and Stengers, I. 1985. *Order out of Chaos.* London: Flamingo.

Pylyshyn, Z. 1993. "Metaphorical imprecision and the top-down research strategy." In *Metaphor and Thought* A. Ortony (ed.), 543–561. Cambridge, UK: Cambridge University Press.

Quinn, N. 1991. "The cultural basis of metaphor." In *Beyond Metaphor: The Theory of Tropes in Anthropology,* J.W. Fernandez (ed.), 56–93. Stanford, Calif.: Stanford University Press.

"Race to reverse declining birth rate." 2004. *South China Morning Post* 23/7/2004: A12.

Radden, G. 2000. "How metonymic are metaphors." In *Metaphor and Metonymy at the Crossroads,* A. Barcelona (ed.), 93–105. New York, Berlin: Mouton de Gruyter.

Randerson, J. 2002. "Cleanliness is next to godliness." *New Scientist* 01/06/02: 8

"Recent trends in military expenditure." 2003. Stockholm International Peace Research Institute. Retrieved July 25th 2003, http://www.sipri.org/contents/ milap/milex/mex trends.html.

Reddy, M.J. 1993. "The conduit metaphor: a case of frame conflict in our language about language." In *Metaphor and Thought,* A. Ortony (ed.), 164–202. Cambridge: Cambridge University Press.

Rickett, W. A.1956. *Kuan-Tzu: A Repository of Early Chinese Thought*. Hong Kong: Hong Kong University Press.

Ridley, M. 1997. *The Origins of Virtue*. Harmondsworth: Penguin.

Rifkin, J. 1987. *Time Wars*. New York: Touchstone/Simon and Schuster.

Rogers, J.A. 1972. "Darwinism and social Darwinism." *Journal of the History of Ideas* 33.2: 265–280.

Rosenfield, H. M. 1966. "Approval-seeking and approval inducing functions of verbal and non-verbal responses." *Journal of Personality and Social Psychology* 4: 597–605.

Ruggie, J. 1986. "Continuity and transformation in the world polity: Toward a neorealist synthesis." In *Neorealism and its Critics* R.O. Keohane (ed.), 131–157. New York: Columbia University Press.

Ryan, F. 2002. *Darwin's Blind Spot: Evolution beyond Natural Selection*. New York: Houghton Mifflin.

"Sale of human organs for profit reignites debate on ban." 2002. *South China Morning Post* 23/12/2002.

Sample, I. 2002. "Download your life into this computer." *New Scientist* 23/11/2002: 21.

Samuel, E. 2002. "Move over, darling." *New Scientist* 25/5/2002: 38.

Santa Ana, O. 1999. "Like an animal I was treated; Anti-immigrant metaphor in US public discourse." *Discourse and Society* 10.2: 191–224.

Schachter, S. 1971. *Emotion, Obesity and Crime*. New York: Academic Press.

Schank, R. and Abelson, R. 1979. *Scripts, Plans, Goals and Understanding*. Hillsdale NJ: Erlbaum.

Schumacher, E.F.1973/1999. *Small is Beautiful: Economics as if People Mattered*. Point Roberts WA and Vancouver: Hartley and Marks.

Searle, J.R. 1969. *Speech Acts*. Cambridge: Cambridge University Press.

Searle, J.R. 1995. *The Construction of Social Reality*. New York, London: Free Press.

Seligman, M.E.P. 2002. *Authentic Happiness*. New York, London: Free Press.

Shakespeare, T. 2002. "Birds, bees and laserbeams." *New Scientist* 16/11/2002: 23.

Sherburne, D.W. (ed.) 1981. *A Key to Whitehead's Process and Reality*. Chicago: University of Chicago Press.

Smith, A. 1776/1991. *Wealth of Nations*. Buffalo, New York: Prometheus Books.

Smith, S. 1975. *Collected Poems*. Harmondsworth: Penguin.

Sollas, W.J. 1911/1924. *Ancient Hunters and their Modern Representatives*. London: Macmillan.

Sonea, S. 1983. *A New Bacteriology*. Sudbury, Mass.: Jones and Bartlett.

Sontag, S. 1991. *Illness as Metaphor, AIDS and its Metaphors*. Harmondsworth: Penguin.

Sorell, T. 1998. "Thomas Hobbes." In *Routledge Encyclopedia of Philosophy vol. 4*, Edward Craig (ed.), 459–476. London: Routledge.

"Speed up/rush to nowhere." 2002. *New Internationalist* 343, March 2002.

Spencer, H. 1878. *The Study of Sociology*. New York: Appleton and Co.

Spengler, O. 1922. *The Decline of the West*. London: Allen and Unwin.

Stearns, P.N. 1994. *American Cool: Constructing a Twentieth-century Emotional Style*. New York: New York University Press.

Stewart, L. 1992. *The Rise of Public Science: Rhetoric, Technology and Natural Philosophy in Newtonian Britain, 1660-1750*. Cambridge: Cambridge University Press.

Stockwell, P. 2000. "Towards a Critical Cognitive Linguistics." In *Discourses of War and Conflict*, A. Combrink and I. Biermann (eds.), 510–28. Potchefstroom: Potchefstroom University Press.

Sulston, J. and Ferry, G. 2002. *The Common Thread*. London: Bantam Press.

Sutherland, W. 2003. "Tongues at risk." *New Scientist* 17/5/2003: 22.

Szalavitz, M. "Love is the drug." *New Scientist* 23/11/2002: 38–40.

Talmy, L. 1988. "Force dynamics in language and cognition." *Cognitive Science* 12: 49–100.

Tata, P. 2002. "Interview with Rajendra Singh." *New Scientist* 7/9/2002: 50.

Tawney, R.H. 1926/1938. *Religion and the Rise of Capitalism.* Harmondsworth: Penguin.

Taylor, J.R. and MacLaury, R.E. (eds.) 1995. *Language and the Cognitive Construal of the World.* Berlin, New York: Mouton de Gruyter.

Taylor, J.R. 1995. "Introduction: on construing the world." In *Language and the Cognitive Construal of the World* J.R. Taylor, and R.E. MacLaury (eds.), 1–22. Berlin, New York: Mouton de Gruyter.

Teng, S-Y. and Fairbank, J.K. 1967. *China's Response to the West.* New York: Atheneum.

Thatcher, M. 2002. *Statecraft: Strategies for a Changing World.* New York: HarperCollins.

"The word: isostatic rebound." No author. 2003. *New Scientist* 11/1/2003: 43.

Thomas, S. 2002. "Their hands on our genes." *New Scientist* 3/8/2002: 25.

Thompson, J. B. 1984. *Studies in the Theory of Ideology.* London: Polity Press.

Thompson, J. B. 1991. "Introduction." In *Language and Symbolic Power,* P. Bourdieu, J. B Thompson (ed.), Gino Raymond and Matthew Adamson (trans.), 1–34. Cambridge UK: Polity Press.

Thornhill, R. and Palmer, C.T. 2000. *A Natural History of Rape: Biological Bases of Sexual Coercion.* Cambridge, Mass.: MIT Press.

Thorpe, W.H. 1997. "The frontiers of biology: Does process thought help?." In *Mind in Nature,* John B. Cobb and David Ray Griffin (eds.), 1–11. Washington D.C.: University Press of America.

Tillyard, E.M.W. 1943. *The Elizabethan World Picture.* London: Chatto and Windus.

Toolan, M. 2002. *Critical Discourse Analysis.* London: Routledge.

Tressell, R. 1955/1991. *The Ragged-Trousered Philanthropists.* London: Paladin.

Trivers, R. 1971. "The evolution of reciprocal altruism." *Quarterly Review of Biology* 46: 35–57.

Trivers, R. 1972. "Parental investement and sexual selection." In *Sexual Selection and the Descent of Man, 1871–1971.* B. Campbell (ed.), 136–79. Chicago: Aldine.

Ungerer, F. 2000. "Muted metaphors and the activation of metonymies in advertising." In *Metaphor and Metonymy at the Crossroads,* A. Barcelona (ed.), 321–340. New York, Berlin: Mouton de Gruyter.

Van Dijk, T.A. 1998. *Ideology: a multidisciplinary approach.* London: Sage.

Varela, F. and Coutinho, A. 1991. "Immunoknowledge: The immune system as a learning process of somatic individuation." In *Doing Science* J. Brockman (ed.), 237–56. New York: Prentice-Hall.

Vendler, Z. 1968. *Adjectives and Nominalizations.* New York, Berlin: Mouton de Gruyter.

Warshaw, R. 1994. *I Never Called it Rape.* New York: Harper Perennial.

Watts, G. 2003. "Making peace with deadly bacteria." *New Scientist* 4/1/2003: 30.

Watts, J. 2003. "Hidden from the world, a village dies of Aids while China refuses to face a growing crisis." *The Guardian* Saturday October 25, 2003.

Weber, M. 1930/1992. *The Protestant Ethic and the Spirit of Capitalism,* trans. Talcott Parsons. London: Routledge.

Weinstock, J., Elliott, D., Summers, R. and Qadir, K. 1999. "Questions on research on potential helminthic therapy of inflammatory bowel disease." Unpublished paper, University of Iowa.

Westfall, R. S. "Newton, Sir Isaac." *Encyclopaedia Brittanica* Retrieved 21/2/2005 http://search.eb.com/eb/print?articleId=108764andfull Article=trueandtocId= 12255.

Whorf, B. J. 1956. *Language, Thought and Reality,* John B Carroll (ed.). Cambridge, Mass.: MIT Press.

"Why Should I be Concerned About Human Genetics?" Human Genetics Alert www.hgalert.org,.

Wierzbicka, A. 1999. *Emotions across Languages and Cultures: Diversity and Universals.* Cambridge: Cambridge University Press.

Wignell, P., Martin, J. R., and Eggins, S. 1993. "The discourse of geography: Ordering and explaining the experiential world." In *Writing Science: Literacy and Discursive power,* M. A. K. Halliday and J. R. Martin (eds.), 136–165. Pittsburgh, PA: University of Pittsburgh Press.

Wilkinson, P. R. 2002. *A Thesaurus of Traditional English Metaphors.* London: Routledge

Willis F.N. 1966. "Initial speaking distance as a function of the speakers' relationship." *Psychonomic Science* 5: 221–2.

Wilson, C. "Bank on it." *New Scientist* 10/8/2002: 35.

Wise, S. 2002. *Drawing the Line: Science and the case for Animal Rights.* New York: Perseus.

Wodak, R. and Meyer, M. (eds.) 2001. *Methods of Critical Discourse Analysis.* London: Sage.

WordsOnline http://www.collinswordbanks.co.uk/

World Urbanization Prospects: The 1999 Revision. 2000. Geneva: UN Population Division UNFPA.

Wrangham, R. and Peterson, D. 1996. *Demonic Males: Apes and the Origins of Human Violence.* Boston: Houghton Mifflin.

Wright, L. 1969. *Clockwork Man.* New York: Horizon Press.

Yergin, D., and Stanislaw, J. 1998. *Commanding Heights.* New York: Simon and Shuster.

Young, P.T. 1943. *Emotion in Man and Animal.* New York: Wiley.

Yu, Ning. 1995. "Metaphorical expressions of anger and happiness in English and Chinese." *Metaphor and Symbolic Activity* 10.2: 59–92.

Yu, Ning. 1998. *The Contemporary Theory of Metaphor: A Perspective from Chinese.* Amsterdam/ Philadelphia: Benjamins.

Main index

The page numbers in italics indicate where a term is defined or where the topic receives the most extensive or important treatment.

Name and author index

Index of languages

Index of metonymy themes (X AS Y), metaphor themes (X IS Y), metaphor equations (X = Y) and theme reversals*

In the series *Discourse Approaches to Politics, Society and Culture* the following titles have been published thus far or are scheduled for publication:

28 **DOLÓN, Rosana and Júlia TODOLÍ (eds.):** Analysing Identities in Discourse. 2008. xi, 204 pp.

27 **VERDOOLAEGE, Annelies:** Reconciliation Discourse. The case of the Truth and Reconciliation Commission. 2008. xiii, 238 pp.

26 **MILLAR, Sharon and John WILSON (eds.):** The Discourse of Europe. Talk and text in everyday life. 2007. viii, 200 pp.

25 **AZUELOS-ATIAS, Sol:** A Pragmatic Analysis of Legal Proofs of Criminal Intent. 2007. x, 180 pp.

24 **HODGES, Adam and Chad NILEP (eds.):** Discourse, War and Terrorism. 2007. x, 248 pp.

23 **GOATLY, Andrew:** Washing the Brain – Metaphor and Hidden Ideology. 2007. xvii, 431 pp.

22 **LE, Elisabeth:** The Spiral of 'Anti-Other Rhetoric'. Discourses of identity and the international media echo. 2006. xii, 280 pp.

21 **MYHILL, John:** Language, Religion and National Identity in Europe and the Middle East. A historical study. 2006. ix, 300 pp.

20 **OMONIYI, Tope and Joshua A. FISHMAN (eds.):** Explorations in the Sociology of Language and Religion. 2006. viii, 347 pp.

19 **HAUSENDORF, Heiko and Alfons BORA (eds.):** Analysing Citizenship Talk. Social positioning in political and legal decision-making processes. 2006. viii, 368 pp.

18 **LASSEN, Inger, Jeanne STRUNCK and Torben VESTERGAARD (eds.):** Mediating Ideology in Text and Image. Ten critical studies. 2006. xii, 254 pp.

17 **SAUSSURE, Louis de and Peter SCHULZ (eds.):** Manipulation and Ideologies in the Twentieth Century. Discourse, language, mind. 2005. xvi, 312 pp.

16 **ERREYGERS, Guido and Geert JACOBS (eds.):** Language, Communication and the Economy. 2005. viii, 239 pp.

15 **BLACKLEDGE, Adrian:** Discourse and Power in a Multilingual World. 2005. x, 252 pp.

14 **DIJK, Teun A. van:** Racism and Discourse in Spain and Latin America. 2005. xii, 198 pp.

13 **WODAK, Ruth and Paul CHILTON (eds.):** A New Agenda in (Critical) Discourse Analysis. Theory, methodology and interdisciplinarity. 2005. xviii, 320 pp.

12 **GRILLO, Eric (ed.):** Power Without Domination. Dialogism and the empowering property of communication. 2005. xviii, 247 pp.

11 **MUNTIGL, Peter:** Narrative Counselling. Social and linguistic processes of change. 2004. x, 347 pp.

10 **BAYLEY, Paul (ed.):** Cross-Cultural Perspectives on Parliamentary Discourse. 2004. vi, 385 pp.

9   **RICHARDSON, John E.:** (Mis)Representing Islam. The racism and rhetoric of British broadsheet newspapers. 2004. vi, 277 pp.

8   **MARTIN, J.R. and Ruth WODAK (eds.):** Re/reading the past. Critical and functional perspectives on time and value. 2003. vi, 277 pp.

7   **ENSINK, Titus and Christoph SAUER (eds.):** The Art of Commemoration. Fifty years after the Warsaw Uprising. 2003. xii, 246 pp.

6   **DUNNE, Michele Durocher:** Democracy in Contemporary Egyptian Political Discourse. 2003. xii, 179 pp.

5   **THIESMEYER, Lynn (ed.):** Discourse and Silencing. Representation and the language of displacement. 2003. x, 316 pp.

4   **CHILTON, Paul and Christina SCHÄFFNER (eds.):** Politics as Text and Talk. Analytic approaches to political discourse. 2002. x, 246 pp.

3   **CHNG, Huang Hoon:** Separate and Unequal. Judicial rhetoric and women's rights. 2002. viii, 157 pp.

2   **LITOSSELITI, Lia and Jane SUNDERLAND (eds.):** Gender Identity and Discourse Analysis. 2002. viii, 336 pp.

1   **GELBER, Katharine:** Speaking Back. The free speech versus hate speech debate. 2002. xiv, 177 pp.